**ALSO BY ALEC KLEIN**

*Stealing Time: Steve Case, Jerry Levin,
and the Collapse of AOL Time Warner*

**Fiction**

*Beast of Love*

# A Class Apart

*Prodigies, Pressure, and Passion Inside
One of America's Best High Schools*

## Alec Klein

Simon & Schuster
NEW YORK LONDON TORONTO SYDNEY

SIMON & SCHUSTER
1230 Avenue of the Americas
New York, NY 10020

First Simon & Schuster hardcover edition August 2007

SIMON & SCHUSTER and colophon are registered trademarks
of Simon & Schuster, Inc.

For information about special discounts for bulk purchases,
please contact Simon & Schuster Special Sales at 1-800-456-6798
or business@simonandschuster.com.

Designed by Paul Dippolito

Manufactured in the United States of America

1   3   5   7   9   10   8   6   4   2

Library of Congress Cataloging-in-Publication Data

Klein, Alec.
    A class apart : prodigies, pressure and passion inside
one of America's best high schools / by Alec Klein.
        p.   cm.
    Includes bibliographical references and index.
    1. Stuyvesant High School (New York, N.Y.)  2. Gifted
children—Education—New York (State)—New York.
I. Title.
LC3995.N5K54  2007
373.747'1—dc22                                    2007017058

ISBN-13: 978-0-7432-9944-2
ISBN-10:      0-7432-9944-2

*For Ryan Isabella*

*Gatsby believed in the green light, the orgiastic future that year by year recedes before us. It eluded us then, but that's no matter—tomorrow we will run faster, stretch out our arms farther. . . . And one fine morning—*

*So we beat on, boats against the current, borne back ceaselessly into the past.*

—F. SCOTT FITZGERALD, *THE GREAT GATSBY*

# Contents

### PART THREE: SENIORITIS
### LATE APRIL–LATE JUNE

# Prologue: Back to School

April 13, 2006, was like any other Thursday—except for this: I bought a pair of jeans riddled with shrapnel-sized holes. They call it the distressed look. But the only thing distressing about it was the price tag. Two rips by the zipper. One puncture of the left knee. Three gashes in the right shin. The backside shredded with four pockmarks. More than enough ventilation to produce an uncomfortable breeze. The jeans were brand-new but designed to look beat-up, as if I'd worn them in the most rugged of urban circumstances, like rappelling off the side of the Empire State Building. I could almost imagine the factory worker hunched over a worktable, whacking the jeans with a sturdy pickax to induce just the right number of fashionable holes. *So this is what it's come to*, I thought to myself, as I slipped on the torn jeans. *No. Check that. This is what* I've *come to. It's finally happened: I've become a teenager.*

Again.

Which is a strange thing for a middle-aged man like me who can barely remember puberty. When I graduated from Stuyvesant High School in 1985—was it that long ago?—I couldn't wait to get out, get on with the rest of my life, never thinking there was anything remarkable about this New York City school, never thinking I'd come back. But then, more than two decades later, I returned to high school. And the strangest thing of all, I stayed for a while.

In January of 2006, I took a leave of absence from the *Washington Post*, where I am a staff writer, to document the life and times of students and teachers at what is widely considered to be one of the best—and weirdest—high schools in America.

Where else is it cooler to be a nerd who aces a differential equations test than a jock who masters the touchdown jig? How many other high schools can boast that hundreds of seniors annually gain admission to Ivy League colleges? Or that their alumni include a handful of Nobel laureates, Oscar winners, and other luminaries of the arts, industry, and public service. In a glowing story about Stuyvesant, *Life* magazine once posed the question in its headline: "Is This the Best High School in America?"

And this is a *public* school.

Stuyvesant, on the eve of the hundredth anniversary of its first graduating class in 1908, remains a model of academic excellence—public or private—while educators and policy makers decry the state of education in America, including the nation's estimated 25 percent dropout rate, as U.S. students fall behind those of other nations in their mastery of such vital subjects as math and science. Which, by the way, happen to be Stuyvesant's great strengths.

Stuyvesant remains the alternate universe of high school, where students are proud to admit they pull caffeinated all-nighters to study, where they don't want to leave school at day's end. "We have to sweep them out of the building," says Assistant Principal Eric Grossman, the school's popular English department chairman. In a high school that feels more like a college, there are virtually no fistfights, mostly only tussles over grades, which students calculate to the second decimal place, and there are no official class rankings because, well, hundreds of students maintain a high grade-point average, so what's the point? While high school football is worshipped in places like Texas, the deities at this school near the southern tip of Manhattan are the science geeks and the math wonks, and if they don't win science and math championships, hell hath no fury like an overinvolved parent. To underscore the point: there is no football field, but the school has a dozen state-of-the-art science labs.

Thomas Jefferson might have called such a place an aristocracy of talent. Stuyvesant boosters call it a meritocracy. Any eighth- or ninth-grade student in New York City can take the test to gain entrance to Stuyvesant. Critics, however, say the test makes Stuyvesant nothing more than an exclusive club, where only about 3 percent of applicants gain admission, and they argue that acceptance is not a measure of academic skills but of financial resources for those parents who can afford to send their children to costly prep courses, tutors, and private academies, sometimes starting in elementary school, with the single aim of winning a seat at Stuyvesant.

Whichever is true, it's hard to argue against the powerful idea that Stuyvesant is a kind of educational lottery ticket—a free elite high school education for the brightest, or at least the best prepared.

Not that I appreciated the place. That is, until March of 2004, when the Stuyvesant High School Alumni Association invited me to speak on a panel about corporate scandals, the subject of my first book, *Stealing Time: Steve Case, Jerry Levin, and the Collapse of AOL Time Warner*. It was my first visit to the old stomping grounds since I escaped from adolescence relatively unscathed. Buried for years, that queasy feeling came back instantly: was I late to school again? That, and a sensation that what had seemed so grand as a teenager had been reduced in size now that I was an adult, even the romantic sweep of the staircase from the school lobby to the second floor, which no longer looked so grand or romantic. I couldn't remember a solitary thing I learned in high school classes, not even the Pythagorean theorem. But a dollop of reminiscence struck me: how, on the first day of freshman year, an upperclassman offered to sell me a pass for a pool that didn't exist. Of Ron Cancemi, a school counselor who believed in me when I didn't, rest his soul. Of the time I professed my love for a girl from a nearby high school by spray-painting in gigantic letters "I LOVE YOU" on the broken asphalt of her school courtyard. Her boyfriend wanted to kill me. Of Dr. Birdman, a Stuyvesant English teacher who handed back a creative writing assignment to me with high praise, including the subversive suggestion, "Why don't you become a writer!" (I recently found the paper on a sweltering summer day in a musty cardboard box deep in the bowels of my dusty garage.) It was just the tonic for a fifteen-year-old boy in need of an idea.

And then there was Frank McCourt, another of my high school English teachers before he became a literary phenomenon, who once burst out of the front doors of the school, his nose bloodied reputedly at the hands of a friend of a Stuyvesant math teacher. Mr. McCourt was tough on the reputed friends of math teachers, charitable with the students. He bestowed on me a grade of 98 on my report card (a faded copy of which I found in the same cardboard box).

Who knew at the time what a unique place this was? The Pulitzer Prize–winning McCourt wrote a brief but loving ode to his experience at the school in *Teacher Man*. The school has been stitched into the fabric of literature: "it was nerd, nerd, nerd," wrote Jonathan Lethem in his best-selling novel *The Fortress of Solitude*. But no one had ever taken an in-depth look at the school and what made it so different. And that visit to the old school got me thinking: what can be more important than our children and the future? Nearly nine out of ten students in the United States are educated in the public schools—more than 48 million students—and they affect everyone, whether you're a taxpayer, a student, a parent, a teacher, or an employer. Few things inspire more passion in people than the education of our children. Schools don't just determine what communities we live in. They tell us about ourselves, our values, whether in the strife of desegregation, one of my early subjects as an education reporter in the South, or in the debate over how to educate the gifted and talented, like the denizens at Stuyvesant. This bizarre high school, where the brainiacs prevail, nonetheless tells the universal story of high school. The question, though, was, how do I get to the heart of the matter? There seemed only one answer: return to high school.

It's a rare gift to go back without all the bad stuff that comes with high school: the unending battery of tests and homework, the looming Damocles sword of college applications, the confusion of peer pressure (do this) and parental pressure (don't do that), the pressure to succeed, to be all you can be, to fulfill your potential, yadayadaya. This time around, mercifully, I didn't have to take a drafting class to learn how to draw a straight line. But it wasn't until I returned to Stuyvesant as an adult that I saw with clarity how the school had given me the gift of opportunity. How, for one, I still write today because when I was fifteen, I was inspired by Shakespeare's *Othello* and wrote a school musical, a magical experience even though school administrators changed the title from *Dead in Bed* to the less risqué *Mystery Tonight*. It was only when I returned to Stuyvesant twenty-some years later that I saw clearly just how high school is a microcosm of our society, driven by our deeply held beliefs about competition and rugged individualism and the idea that the best will prevail, even if that notion is perhaps sometimes just an illusion. At Stuyvesant, I witnessed the drama of adolescence that I had forgotten about, that parents don't hear about: first loves, illicit drugs, sudden death. Broader questions about how we teach children played out below the surface: Is it better to separate gifted and talented students into their own school, like Stuyvesant? Or is this a debilitating case of elitism in public education? What makes Stuyvesant—the kids who pass the test, or the school that educates them? And how do students cope with academic integrity, sexual discovery, and the complex burdens of being smart?

This much is certain: Stuyvesant is to many the embodiment of the American Dream, a school founded more than a century ago as a manual training school for boys that has become a haven for immigrants and the children of immigrants who want a better life. Stuyvesant's roughly three thousand students—packed about thirty-four per class—represent a kaleidoscope of ethnicities. Today, with more than half the students of Asian background, the school represents virtually every nationality and socioeconomic level, offering a window into the ethnic politics that pervade not just schools but communities throughout the nation. The school also offers a window into the dark side of the American Dream—unyielding competition, massive pressure, chronic cheating, racial divisions—leaving no student untouched.

For this book, the challenge was focusing on a handful of people who represent the great breadth of talent inhabiting the school. They weren't hard to find, even if I stumbled into most of them: a ten-year-old prodigy who has the memory of a computer chip. A sixteen-year-old football captain who taught himself calculus. A seventeen-year-old heroin junkie whose gift is the beautiful poetry she scrawls on paper. A dedicated teacher who suffers from depression and isn't supposed to be teaching because he lacks a license. An assistant principal who regularly breaks the rules if it means helping the kids.

To his credit, the school principal, Stan Teitel, never told me whom to interview, nor did he ask for any control over the book; it was essential to have this freedom so that I could write a true and accurate account, however unflattering some of the passages might be. Throughout my time at the school, I was acutely aware that although I'm an alumnus, I was not there as an advocate. I was an outsider, a journalist, whose story would carry meaning only if it was fair and whole. Rarely do schools allow a writer such latitude over an extended period, if only because even in the best of places, things can and do go wrong. But I was given free rein to roam about the school, including an open letter tucked in my pocket from the principal asking his staff to extend to me "every courtesy" in case they were wondering what a thirty-nine-year-old man was doing wandering the hallways or attending class. I never needed to show that letter to the students. My real pass with them was simply that I had graduated from Stuyvesant. I *knew*.

Plus, I had gone to Brown University, a fact that I never thought carried much weight in my career as a writer but now finally paid off. It represented credibility in a school where many students and even more parents worship at the altar of the Ivy League.

There was little formality to the reporting process, although I did ask parents of students under the age of eighteen to sign a consent form allowing their children to be interviewed and photographed for this book. Other authors have employed fictional names in writing about teenagers and high school life, but despite the many delicacies involved, I never use pseudonyms in the book. The narrative is a faithful account of the time that I spent at the school, written in the present tense when the action occurred, with ages and other facts reflecting the time covered. Some parents asked for the right to review their children's quotes before the book's publication, fearing what their children might say; I refused in each case, explaining that such censorship would compromise the integrity of the journalism. One parent went so far as to ask me to sign a waiver before speaking to her. I didn't. What I did promise—to myself—was that I would practice compassionate journalism, which is to say that I would remember that I was in many cases interviewing children, not adults, and that as such, it was important to keep in mind the repercussions of what they said or did. When a student left what appeared to be a suicide note, my first duty was not to document it as a detached journalist but to rush to school to do something about it. Fortunately, the student was alive.

Little did I realize what I was getting myself into when the semester started. In the first week, I came to a swift conclusion: I had all the wrong accoutrements. I should have known as much from the undergraduate students to whom I teach journalism at Georgetown University. Out went the briefcase, in came the North Face backpack. When I began to renovate my wardrobe, my wife, Julie-Ann, became alarmed. "You're starting to morph into a teenager; suddenly you want new shoes. Before you never liked to shop. Now we go to J. Crew and you shop like a madman!" (She said this while lying in bed as I was at my nearby desk, firing e-mails back and forth with a high school freshman and a senior, just before midnight.) The next morning, when I showed her my new Stuyvesant photo ID, she worried that I was slipping into a midlife crisis and added, "No sports car!"

She needn't have worried. I wasn't entering midlife. I was reverting to teen life. I went back to New York City, living the life, experiencing that crazy high school ritual all over again, rushing to catch a crammed subway down to Chambers Street on a daily basis, along with the hordes of students. It didn't take me long to realize that students respond faster to e-mail than to phone calls, even though almost all of them have their own cell phones, that they respond even faster to IM (instant messaging, to those of you not in the know), and if you really want to know what's going on, check out their blogs. Within weeks, it became all too clear that high school has become decidedly tougher, more competitive, and increasingly professional, both the organization of the school and the students who learn to master it. A month and a half into the semester, I knew more kids than many of the kids, judging by the number of them I was high-fiving in the hallways on my way to my next class. Proof of my regression: more than twenty years after I left her precalculus class, my high school math teacher, Ms. Schimmel, who was still teaching math at Stuyvesant, mistook me for a student when I rushed past her on my way into school (late again).

Somewhere along the way, my point of view began to evolve, which is another way of saying I began to see things as a teenager, chief among them that everything is momentous—whether the question is where to go to lunch or where to go with the rest of your life; that even while everything is of great consequence, high school is made up of small moments, taken in incremental steps; that you're just trying to deal with loneliness and heartache and who you are; that some adults are inflexible; and that you have to endure the injustices of it all, though sometimes I wasn't quite sure what *it* was. Even peer pressure got to me. When an amiable freshman noted I had frequently worn a blue-checked button-down shirt, I proceeded to leave the shirt in the dresser for an extended vacation.

Never could I say I was immune from the harmless offhand comments of a fourteen-year-old. And never could I imagine what a chaotic and full-time job it was. I spent more than a year interviewing, researching, and writing this book, but I have focused the narrative on the spring semester—the most intense period for Stuyvesant students who were grappling with the school's great musical contest, not to mention college admissions, senioritis, prom, graduation, and all that other stuff that happens after the final bell rings. As Danny Jaye, Stuyvesant's beloved math chairman, likes to say, "The greatness of the school is what happens after three o'clock."

Every semester is packed with drama—it's the nature of high school—but I could never have anticipated that I was capturing a seminal moment in time, when great eras were coming to an end at Stuyvesant, when harrowing events would explode on the scene, and when new—and sometimes unwelcome—change was about to unfold. A semester that sped by so quickly at first descended into a grind by the latter stages. It's not easy being a kid today. Take it from an adult.

Near the end, I found myself asking students and teachers to sign my yearbook, even though it wasn't *my* yearbook (mine had become sealed shut by a suburban basement flood years ago).

"Enjoy being a kid again," scribbled senior Julie Gaynin in my yearbook before she headed off to Macalester College. "I hope you've had fun going back to high school. Don't feel embarrassed, lots of people need an extra year before graduating."

Wrote Harvard-bound Becky Cooper, "You've continuously asked me what it is exactly that drives me to work. Recently, I read a paper by

Faulkner that talked about why he writes. 'To appease the demons inside him' or something like that. Well, there aren't demons, but I would say I work for maybe the same reason you write. It's a long, sometimes painful process, but it's just something you have to do. (I think.) That's kind of what it's like for me. I work because I care and I care because I know nothing else."

Before moving on to Yale University, Stuyvesant Student Union President Kristen Ng wrote in my yearbook, "We're a diverse, and, dare I say, very odd bunch. Thanks for listening 2 us and deciding that diverse & odd is a good thing."

All along, I was aware of how foolish I probably looked, a veritable middle-aged man lugging around a yearbook meant for others. But I didn't care. That is the right of a veritable middle-aged man; I'm less afraid than teenagers to humiliate myself in public. I have had more practice in the art. Besides, the yearbook held a cherished place in my heart, for what it represented: the openness and innocence and the evanescence of youth. They tell the truth. They cry so easily. They thirst for knowledge, for connection, for beauty. They haven't become guarded, jaded adults yet. Thank goodness.

*Alec Klein*
*February 2007,*
*Washington, D.C.*

# PART ONE: DELANEY CARDS

*Early February–Early March*

CHAPTER ONE

# Romeo

IT'S 7:38 A.M., AND AN OLD MAN BOXES A PHANTOM on Grand Street, jabbing and slicing the crisp air with his withered fists, the first ambition of the day. The rest of the morning awakens in slow motion on this unforgiving stretch of asphalt on the Lower East Side, a hardscrabble neighborhood on the edge of Chinatown in Manhattan. The Grand Spa down the block isn't open yet. Nor is the next-door Liquor & Wines. Nor Chester Fried Chicken across the street. All that can be traced on this gray February morning is the wisp of breath billowing like wordless cartoon bubbles from anonymous pedestrians as they trudge to work, huddled against the coming snowstorm.

And then from out of a nondescript red brick high-rise, Romeo emerges. Like the old man, he looks ready to wage combat against the day. That's the message conveyed in his baggy black Sean John jacket and baggy black Sean John jeans and black scarf and black skullcap and black shoes. But it's just urban utilitarian fashion—black against the muted gray hues of the rising day—which does little to disguise his broad shoulders or his chiseled 195-pound frame or the ferocity that he brings to the football field as a bruising tight end and defensive end who also played running back last season because he's so good, the best on his team. Romeo can bench more than his own weight—225 pounds—no problem. Not that he needs to prove it. Jersey number ninety-eight commands respect, and the girls adore all six foot three inches of him—the swagger, the charm, the dreadlocks, the silver earring in the left ear, the dark brooding eyes, the ambiguous smile full of braces.

Romeo is an archetype of the high school idol, a popular, powerful captain of his football team, except for one thing—Romeo Alexander is also a sixteen-year-old math whiz.

He taught himself calculus by reading a tattered textbook. Then he got the top score on the advanced placement test and skipped a course in calculus to go straight into differential equations, the *really* hard kind of math. Girls flock to him for tutoring help, boys plead for help on homework.

Not your typical high school jock.

"I do a lot of math in my free time," he says without a hint of braggadocio. "After a while, it becomes a sport, fun."

If only the football team was as much fun. Last season, the team lost its first game sixty-four to zero, and it just got worse. The team stumbled to a one-and-eight record, its sole victory earned by default: the other team couldn't field enough players. Romeo's team was lucky to eke out the one victory. The school doesn't have its own football field. The team has to take a yellow school bus from Manhattan to Brooklyn to reach its so-called home field at another public school. The practice field is about a mile away, and it's not even a football field; it's a *soccer* field. Players say a mutiny forced the head coach to resign. "Almost nobody on the team liked him," a teammate was quoted in the school newspaper, the *Spectator*, which cited accusations of the coach's "extreme emotional outbursts." And to top it off, on a good day, only about ten Stuyvesant parents show up for a game.

"Nobody really cares," Romeo says. "It has its down moments."

A defensive tackle adds that it gets so bad that teammates don't like to brag about being on the team: "We don't really go around advertising it."

Perhaps the worst indignity, at least to Romeo, is the team name: the Peglegs. The moniker comes from the school's namesake, Peter Stuyvesant, the crotchety Dutch colonial governor of New Amsterdam, a man who hobbled around on one good leg, the other having been blown off by a cannon shot and replaced by a wooden leg. Such associations don't seem to inspire athletic greatness on the gridiron. Romeo would've preferred "the Flying Dutchmen." That suggests a certain grace—nay, supernatural abilities—which are sorely needed on the field.

But then again, this is Stuyvesant High School. And here, football doesn't matter. The brainiacs rule.

Romeo understands that, embraces it. Football drills under a baking sun don't match the pain of the academic workouts under a small pool of lamplight, the relentless nights when Romeo sits hunched over his small wooden desk, cloistered in his room, studying until two, three, four o'clock in the morning—unless he dozes off while studying. His mother, Catherine Wideman, sleeps fitfully, knowing her son is up late studying, the only evidence a sliver of illumination emanating from the slit at the bottom of his shut door.

"Do you know it's two o'clock in the morning?" she will ask, knocking on his door.

"When the lights are off, I can relax," she says.

Not Romeo. Recently, he printed eight-and-a-half by eleven-inch signs from his computer and taped them up in his room, lashing Orwellian words to inspire, drive, compel.

Over his desk: "Discipline."

Over his bed: "Work is fun."

On his door: "The world is yours."

Conquering the world begins when he climbs aboard the overcrowded M22 public bus as it careens toward Stuyvesant on this chilly morning. "I was always the type of person who said I have to work harder, suffer," he says matter-of-factly.

For Romeo, an average of four hours of sleep has yielded a grade-point average on the high end of 96 out of a 100—near perfection. "Some people calculate it to the last decimal," he says. Romeo, however, doesn't debase himself with such picayune detail. "The way I see it, it's high."

Now all he has to do is maintain that near perfection during this, his junior year, the most critical period in his high school career, the sweet spot for colleges examining the almighty academic transcript of grades.

At least, that's his goal. That, and acing the dreaded SAT, required by most colleges, the single exam that can wipe out all his academic success in one fell swoop if he doesn't get a high score. It's not a question of bombing on the SAT: there's no chance of that, it doesn't compute. But even a slight misstep—a mathematical miscalculation, a reading comprehension snafu—could lower his score ever so slightly, which would ruin Romeo's goal, achieving a perfect 2400, a rarity not even reached by most supersavants.

"Above twenty-three hundred is reasonable," he concedes.

That still leaves precious little margin for error. Which is why, tomorrow, he begins his SAT prep course at school, a grueling process involving forsaken Saturdays leading up to the test in June. Romeo, the product of a modest upbringing—the son of a struggling musician and a struggling freelance writer—is keenly aware of the five-hundred-dollar cost of the class, even though it pales in comparison to the expense of other private tutoring courses, totaling in the thousands, if not the tens of thousands, the built-in advantage of the wealthy and privileged.

For Romeo, this is only the beginning of the price of admission to the college of his dreams: Harvard University.

But now, sitting in the back of the bus on his way to school, peering through the smudged window as City Hall scrolls by, Harvard is a mirage, and the only sound he's hearing is the remembered voice of his father. Romeo calls it "the famous speech," the time when Romeo was fourteen and his divorced father, a former funk singer still known as Prinz Charles, who lives in Harlem, lectured him on the realities of life, urging his son to grab the American Dream—to go to school, get a job, be comfortable for the rest of his life. Father told son, *You've got to rise up and take the reins.*

His mother, a French former journalist, offered a different vision of the future, one in which Romeo would become a great scholar-athlete, much like her second husband, John Edgar Wideman, a Brown University professor and venerated author who became Romeo's stepfather about four years ago. Mr. Wideman was himself a celebrated student in his youth. At the age of twenty-one, he was the subject of a *Look* magazine article entitled "The Astonishing John Wideman," which hailed his many accomplishments, including a Rhodes Scholarship following his

Ivy League education at the University of Pennsylvania, where he was captain of the basketball team and elected to the prestigious Phi Beta Kappa honors society. It was at Romeo's age that Mr. Wideman's son, Jacob, stabbed to death another boy of sixteen, for which Jacob was sentenced to life in prison. Romeo doesn't talk about the tragedy, or the shadow of expectations that comes with an accomplished stepfather. Mother told son, *I just want you to be happy.*

And what does Romeo want?

"I want to help save the world."

He makes such a startling declaration with the same equanimity as a boy simply saying he is going to school, and both statements are to be believed. He doesn't know it yet, but today at school he will meet a seventy-eight-year-old New York University professor dying of cancer for whom Romeo will volunteer his services in unraveling the secrets of fusion. To Romeo, it will be an experiment for a prestigious national science contest, but if it's successful—more of a wild dream than a remote possibility—the project could provide energy to light entire cities, which would certainly fulfill his mission to achieve greatness. As a career choice, Romeo didn't have any say in the matter, not when the decision was made for him before birth. Or so he will soon write in his autobiography, an assignment for an upcoming English class:

> My dad wanted me to become a star, in the most general sense. One way to make that happen was by giving me a name that would catch people's attention, that would constantly put me under the spotlight. My father was a star himself—a musician—that's how he seduced my mother in France. My mother, along the same lines, wanted me to become a great intellectual genius. That, I believe, comes from her father, who would be very pleased if all his grandchildren went to prestigious universities. Thus, Romeo was planned out and defined before I was even born.

His father, speaking to his wife's pregnant belly, recited simple math while Romeo rested in the womb: one plus one, two plus two, four plus four. "I did it, and we got some pretty good results," Charles Alexander says. He continued to challenge his son after his birth, speaking to

Romeo not as a child but almost like an adult. "I didn't baby-talk him," he says. And always, the mantra was the same: "You can get this," his father would say, urging on his son. If his parents had any concern about Romeo as a child, it was that he was not aggressive. "Very passive," his father says. "Gandhi," that's what his mother called him. She always had great expectations for her only child. "I was on his case," she says, laughing shyly about the days when he was in elementary school and she was sometimes "screaming" at him to do his work, threatening to throw his video game out the window. She still prods him when his drive begins to flag. "I'm very ambitious for him," she says.

Another secret of his success: she started Romeo in martial arts when he was seven, demanding he never miss a class.

Romeo: "It taught me to get used to pain."

She says it taught something else: "Discipline."

"There is a life of the mind in this house that we value," adds Romeo's stepfather, referring to the way that he challenges Romeo to think, asking questions the teenager can't answer and talking at the dinner table about intellectually enriching issues like politics and history.

For Romeo, though, all that doesn't exactly explain how he got to this point, riding on this bus, going to this school, on the cusp of this future.

"I think a lot about that," he says, giving credit in part to good luck and what he calls "social Darwinism." But he isn't sure how to explain his accomplishments, except to say, "I always like to see it as my own doing, that I did it myself."

Football wasn't part of the plan. Until he was twelve, he didn't even like football. He watched the Super Bowl only for the ostentatious television commercials. But then his father taught him how to play a football video game, and it meant something deeper. "It was the first time I started hanging out with my dad," he says. It helped too that his father came from Boston, and the New England Patriots won their first Super Bowl. Success bred interest, and now his father tapes every one of his son's football games.

Math, though, was the way for Romeo to pave his way to stardom. In the eighth grade he joined the school math team. Then the summer after his freshman year at Stuyvesant, he borrowed a friend's textbook to teach himself calculus, which he viewed as an exalted form of math because students often don't learn it until college, if at all.

"I always thought calculus was one of the secrets of the world," he says.

Romeo was also smitten with a girl a grade above him who already was taking calculus. If he could learn calculus on his own, he figured he could skip the first-year course and catch up with the girl, sitting in the same class with her for second-year calculus. His friends teased him about the bookish, bespectacled girl. More brains than beauty, they said. But no matter.

With trepidation, Romeo ventured online to sign up for the advanced placement test and pushed the button to pay the eighty-dollar fee. Like a football player drilling himself to perfection, Romeo practiced calculus over spring break. The result: "The test was so easy." He earned a five, the top score. He also zipped through the school's department final with a grade of 98, and the Stuyvesant math chairman saw no reason to waste Romeo's time with first-year calculus. Romeo was in love—with math.

"When I met math and logic, it was like, 'Wow, this is how I'm going to understand the world,'" he says. "Maybe that's why I like math. I was searching for something."

But he quickly made another discovery: "In higher math," he says, "there are uncertainties."

So too with girls.

A month ago, he met a sophomore at a party. She asked him to dance. And now he has the first girlfriend of his life. Last night, his father gave him the birds and bees speech—"the advanced course," Romeo quips.

The girl chose him; he didn't choose her. That's what he tells himself. Otherwise, it wouldn't have happened. He wouldn't have allowed it. Girls, he thought, would be a distraction, take him from work. His friends, on the same grueling academic mission, preach the same ascetic gospel.

"We talk about dominating the world and power and how women bring you down—adolescent stuff," he says, aware of his own foolishness.

Just in case he needs a reminder, there's always a girl, Xevion Baptiste, a fellow junior, frequent lunch companion, and self-appointed conscience, to put Romeo in his place—or at least try.

"I'm always telling him to put down his book, and he won't listen to me," she says. "I'll call him at midnight and say, 'Talk to me.' He says, 'All right, I have two seconds.' He's brilliant. He just needs to lighten up a little."

It's a struggle. Romeo has conditioned himself to suppress his emotions, to be strong, to be heroic, driven by a need to win, succeed, achieve. He's reminded of Raskolnikov, the tormented figure who neglects human emotion in Dostoyevsky's *Crime and Punishment*, which he's reading for fun. (He also subscribes to the *Economist* for fun.) The internal conflict even imbues Romeo's own fiction: "You know as well as anyone else that the only way for there to be any productive progression in the history of humanity, science, and technology, you must be willing to make a few sacrifices of the mind and body," the main character tells himself in a science-fiction story that garnered Romeo a national writing award.

Suddenly, though, Romeo's been thrown off kilter. Maybe, he thinks, it's chemical. He just read an article in *National Geographic* about the physiological reactions of people in love. Their brains look like "someone who has a disorder," he says.

The only symptom Romeo detects in himself is some kind of stomach pain. But maybe it's just because it's all beginning—the morning, the semester, his life. It's 8:23 a.m., and Romeo is about to disembark from the bus and enter Stuyvesant High School, ready to wage combat against the day.

CHAPTER TWO

# The Gauntlet

AFTER ROMEO CLIMBS OFF THE RUMBLING BUS, HE shifts into automatic, taking morning steps choreographed by days of sheer repetition, from freshman to junior year, taking little notice of the immediate but unstated fact confronting him: that what he is fast approaching is an extraordinary place.

He begins by climbing a set of concrete stairs curving to the Tribeca Bridge. After he reaches the landing, for the next 250 feet, he is sealed in a 13-foot-wide passageway of glass above West Street, a hyperkinetic highway where drivers are hurtling in both directions. All the while, Romeo is oblivious to the enormity of the steel expanse he is crossing and the striving it implies—oblivious to the 5 tons of paint that it took to coat it, to the 250 tons suspended above Manhattan traffic, to its $10 million cost. What Romeo knows is, this pedestrian bridge is the only way students can enter and leave Stuyvesant High School—a span crossing an urban moat into a magical educational kingdom.

How else to explain the gleaming $150 million edifice that stands before him, one of the costliest high schools ever built?

At nearly twice its original price tag, the building replaced a dilapidated dwelling squatting unceremoniously across town on Fifteenth Street near First Avenue. The new building on the West Side opened to students on September 9, 1992, at 345 Chambers Street, where luxury housing was once intended, in the trendy milieu of Tribeca, haunt of well-appointed bistros, Robert De Niro, and New York hipsters with bank. Ensconced on the banks of the Hudson River, with spectacular views of the Statue of Liberty, the school sits near Wall Street on a land-fill packed with earth excavated when the World Trade Center was built. Now that site is Ground Zero, a crater four blocks away, an eerie, hollow reminder of the September 11, 2001, terrorist attacks that tem-porarily turned a traumatized Stuyvesant into an emergency shelter for rescue workers.

Bathed in early morning light, the school today sits majestically undisturbed, soaring from a base of limestone into a tan brick building ten stories high, twice the height of the usual New York City high school. Because it's wedged into a one-and-a-half-acre site, there was only one way to go: skyward.

The grandeur of the place is instantly conveyed from the first floor, a stately terrazzo entrance hall in black and gray accents, adorned with art deco lights and embellished with the following Latin phrase engraved in polished gray granite rising from a set of classic black columns:

## PRO SCIENTIA ATQUE SAPIENTIA

*For Knowledge and Wisdom.* A pair of gray marble staircases climb to the second floor, a subtle nod to the sweeping beaux arts staircase at the old school building. On the second level, one-legged Peter Stuyvesant sternly gazes down from an oil portrait that once hung in the paint-chipped school building across town. But just beyond the school's namesake is one feature disconnected from the past: a series of escala-tors that rise through the building's core—rise, that is, when they're not malfunctioning or a student hasn't hijacked an escalator key (black-market price: $1) and derailed students from scampering to their next class within the appointed four-minute break.

The real action takes place throughout the building in a series of sci-ence labs, robotics workshops, drafting rooms, and shops for metalworking, woodworking, plastics, ceramics, and photography. Classrooms come equipped with television monitors. Walls are lined with fiber optics. More than 450 computers populate the school. Students almost take for granted the world-class facilities—the wood-paneled theater with orchestra pit, balcony, and movable partitions; the dining hall (so named because it's not merely a cafeteria) that commands panoramic views of the Hudson River; the library with the sun-filtered southern exposure and the columned loggia.

It's true there are no playing fields—no football stadium, no baseball diamond, no tennis courts. But, hey, this is Stuyvesant, and as Mr. Teitel, the principal, says, "The superintendent [of New York City schools] is not going to call me if we don't have a winning basketball team . . . no one's going to call me if the football team has a three-and-five record." On the other hand, if Stuyvesant fails to win a slew of national math and science awards, he says with a knowing, if beleaguered, smile, "my phone will ring."

Besides, it's not as if the school ignores athletics altogether. Stuyvesant does have two full-size gyms and a seventy-five-foot-long swimming pool, standard for Public School Athletic League competition. And by the standards of public education, where some schools look more like prisons under lockdown, there's little like it.

"It's like going to school at Club Med," writes recent Stuyvesant graduate Ned Vizzini in his published autobiography, *Teen Angst? Naaah . . .*

The school designers are more humble about their work. "Its architecture will never live up to the institution itself," says Karen Cooper, a principal at Cooper, Robertson & Partners, one of the building's architects, "because obviously it's a rather formidable institution."

Actually, the feel of the place is anything but formidable. The students have made it their own, reducing the towering citadel of learning into a veritable homespun bulletin board, covering the building on a daily basis with taped-up flyers announcing extracurricular activities, such as "Pie a Teacher!!!" (The raffle ticket proceeds will help "build schools in villages in 3rd world countries!") Flyers are also the province of abject public apologies by a boyfriend, identified only as "pathetic loser," to a girlfriend for a forgotten special occasion: "If you made your girl feel special, help a stranger in making my girl feel like the one in a million billion gajillion girls that she is. . . ." And on some occasions, the makeshift flyers attempt to inspire:

> *Life has a higher end,*
> *than to be amused.*

—WILLIAM ELLERY CHANNING

In this free-flowing atmosphere, students sprawl out on hallway floors, camping out amid friends and the accoutrements of adolescence: iPods (playing the Beatles, cool again), North Face backpacks, cell phones with built-in cameras, and Sidekicks for instant messaging when spoken discourse just won't fly. And the language of the moment is a curious blend of slang where everything is "mad," if not "ill," or "sick," all of which are good things, while being "emo," or emotional, isn't cool, though "cool" isn't cool, but "hot" is, and the righteous "word" has made a strong comeback as a general affirmation and the perennial "whatever" suffices when nothing more need be said.

When language is too far removed from—or too close to—the idea being communicated, unspoken physicality still works, as in prevailing fashions, the gestalt of which seems to indicate that no effort was involved in the selection of clothes and accessories, that the ensemble was just thrown together, patterns butting heads with shapes, which, of course, is a complete lie, because it's all about coordination, cause and effect, especially among many of the girls. (The idea of fashion among the majority of boys is truly haphazard: a pair of jeans under an ill-fitting T-shirt.) Thick belts with massive buckles cinch around shirts so long that they serve as skirts. Frayed denim miniskirts cover a small amount of real estate over tights, thanks in part to teenage fashionista Lindsay Lohan, who helps give currency to the hip-hugging leggings and the dark nail polish painted on legions of like-minded girls. Owing to a teen icon of another generation, Jennifer Beals of *Flashdance* fame, sweatshirts torn at the neck and dripping off a shoulder are making a comeback. Of less determinate provenance, unless such purveyors as Urban Outfitters, Ecko, and Akademiks are to be blamed, are the frilly tops, the layer upon layer of cheap necklaces, the wisps of scarves, the cavalry of cowboy boots and those other throwbacks, Vans and Converse canvas white-tipped high-tops, particularly in shades of bright green.

But that could be any high school.

It could be argued that Stuyvesant is set apart from other schools by its more than two hundred clubs, ranging from the Bookworm to the N.A.R.F. (Neo-postmodern Artistic and Recreational Forum). Or by its thirty-some student publications, including *two* competing school newspapers and a third solely devoted to politics. Or by course offerings as diverse as the English department's existentialism and the biology department's vertebrate zoology.

But that's not it, not really.

"The *students* make Stuy what it is," says one who knows firsthand, Namita Biala, a senior off to Princeton University, echoing the sentiment of many students, teachers, and administrators.

Converging on the school from five boroughs, some traveling as long as two hours by subway, Stuyvesant students have compiled a stunning record of achievement. Laurels and trophies are regularly heaped on the math team—numbering about five hundred, or one in six students in the entire school—as well as the nationally recognized debate team and the official school newspaper, the *Spectator*, each claiming about two hundred members. Every year, Stuyvesant produces among the country's highest number of National Merit Scholars, whose distinction is based on students' performance on the Preliminary SAT/National Merit Scholarship Qualifying Test; in 2006, ninety-nine Stuyvesant students were finalists. By comparison, there is on average one finalist for about every two public high schools in America. Stuyvesant also consistently generates several semifinalists and finalists annually in the prestigious Intel Science Talent Search; the school has produced more than seven hundred semifinalists and over a hundred finalists since the contest's inception in the 1940s. And of the 2,800 advanced placement tests administered at the school yearly, usually more than 90 percent of the students earn at least a three out of five, school administrators say, a score that the College Board defines as meaning students are "qualified" to receive college credit or advanced placement. More than 70 percent achieve scores of four, considered "well qualified," or five, "extremely well qualified."

It's almost an afterthought that 97 percent of Stuyvesant students graduate within four years of the ninth grade, according to the New

York City Department of Education. But that's a notable achievement compared to only 75 percent nationally who graduate on time, U.S. Department of Education figures show.

Even more remarkable, Stuyvesant students' average SAT score is a 691 out of 800 in verbal and 725 in math, according to figures furnished by the school to the New York State Education Department. That places the average Stuyvesant student in about the 95th percentile nationally in both categories, according to statistics from the College Board, which administers the test. The average U.S. test scores are nowhere near—508 in verbal, 520 in math.

With such high SAT scores at Stuyvesant, it's not surprising that virtually all its graduates enroll in four-year colleges, school statistics show, compared to only 67 percent of high school graduates nationally who enroll in either two- or four-year colleges, according to the U.S. Department of Education. But what is stunning is that about one in four of Stuyvesant's graduating class of about eight hundred wins entrance to an Ivy League college, school administrators say. In some years, Harvard accepts more students from Stuyvesant—over twenty—than from any other public or private school. Many students view Ivies like Cornell University as a *safety* school. And Stuyvesant sends many students to several other popular destinations outside the Ivies, such as the Massachusetts Institute of Technology, Stanford University, and a number of other equally selective colleges.

Perhaps the truest measure of Stuyvesant's greatness is what its students do after they leave school. Four alumni have gone on to win the Nobel Prize: Joshua Lederberg, in 1958 for physiology or medicine, cited for "his discoveries concerning genetic recombination and the organization of the genetic material of bacteria"; Roald Hoffmann, in 1981 in chemistry, for theories "concerning the course of chemical reactions"; Robert W. Fogel, in 1993 in economics, for "having renewed research in economic history by applying economic theory and quantitative methods in order to explain economic and institutional change"; and Richard Axel, in 2004 in physiology or medicine, for "discoveries of odorant receptors and the organization of the olfactory system."

Few high schools can boast such an alumni lineup, which also includes Eric S. Lander, a leader of the Human Genome Project in the race to break the human genetic code, and Col. Ron Grabe, lead astronaut for the development of the International Space Station. He took a Stuyvesant pennant with him when the *Atlantis* space shuttle circled the globe in 1989. For a school traditionally strong in math and the sciences, Stuyvesant also has cultivated a wealth of artists and performers, such as Academy Award winners James Cagney and Tim Robbins, jazz musician Thelonious Monk, plus a number of Emmy and Grammy winners and even an international sex symbol, actress Lucy Liu.

Less heralded are the school's handful of Olympic medalists, members of Congress, federal judges, and industry titans, including Jeffrey Loria, owner of baseball's Florida Marlins, and Arthur Blank, cofounder of Home Depot, one of the largest retailers in the world. (See Appendix of Notable Alumni.)

Many who have gone on to achieve greatness share one trait: they first walked the halls of Stuyvesant as nerds.

The tradition continues today.

"I embrace being a dork," says Becky, a senior who scored a 790 in math, a perfect 800 in English, and a perfect 800 in the new writing category on the SAT, and carried a 97.79 average into this, the second semester of her last year.

As proof, Becky offers up the following joke: A neutron walks into a bar, and asks how much for beer.

The punch line: No charge.

Becky can get away with such a typical Stuyvesant joke because she's not only a nerd. She also happens to be a beautiful cheerleader whom many of the boys love. So she can be forgiven for going to Harvard.

Everybody's in on the joke, anyway, even late-night television comic Conan O'Brien, a high school dork in his day who also attended Harvard. As the commencement speaker at Stuyvesant's 2006 graduation, O'Brien paid tribute to the students by poking fun at them in the most appropriate way: "Today, Stuyvesant has a remarkably diverse and varied student body, ranging from math geeks to science nerds. Yes, you are a glorious, beautiful rainbow of brainiacs."

The laughter from the gallery was deafening—and knowing. The audience is all too aware that they derive from the same pool: a highly select group of students who passed the harrowing Specialized High Schools Admissions Test—otherwise known as the Stuy test. It's like the SAT, except that unlike the college admissions process, which also involves essays, teacher recommendations, and school transcripts, the Stuy test is basically an all-or-nothing affair. Make the test cutoff, and you're in Stuyvesant. If you come up short, no dice.

Stuyvesant is the most selective of the city's eight elite specialized public exam high schools. Of the estimated twenty-six thousand students who take the test annually, only those with the highest scores— about eight hundred students—gain entrance to Stuyvesant. (Students can be denied even if they reach the Stuyvesant cutoff, if they don't pick the school as their first choice.)

"It's harder to get into Stuy than to get into Harvard," says Wyndam Makowsky, the incoming editor in chief of the *Spectator*, the school newspaper. That's true at least on a statistical basis, since the high school accepts only about 3 percent of those who take the test, while Harvard admits about 9 percent of freshman applicants.

"You could theoretically buy your way into Harvard, but you can't buy your way into Stuyvesant," says Mr. Teitel, the principal.

The Stuy test is open to all New York City residents, although it's an open secret that some parents who live beyond the city limits will, to avoid expensive private schools or bad public ones, cheat on the residency requirement. For instance, they will have mail sent to a relative who lives in New York City to establish residency for the family and qualify their children for the test.

Such tactics hardly assure their children a seat at Stuyvesant.

The 150-minute multiple-choice test is divided into two grueling sections, verbal and math, each with its own twists and pitfalls.

The *Specialized High Schools Student Handbook* offers the following question as a verbal example of a logical reasoning question on the test:

There are five bookshelves on the wall. The bottom shelf is Shelf 1, the top shelf is Shelf 5. Each shelf is filled with books of one color.

1. The red books are above the green books.
2. The yellow books are below the blue books.

3. The orange books are between the red books and the yellow books.

4. The yellow books are on Shelf 2.

Which color books are on Shelf 1?

A. red
B. green
C. blue
D. orange
E. Cannot be determined from the information given.

(Answer: B)

The math questions are just as challenging. An example from the handbook:

What is the smallest positive odd integer that is not immediately adjacent to an integer power of 2?

A. 1
B. 3
C. 5
D. 11
E. There is no such number.

(Answer: D)

The competition for Stuyvesant's limited seats is so fierce that some students begin to prepare for the high school test several years in advance—when they are ten years old, or younger. Indeed, the demand to get into Stuyvesant is so great that a number of Asian academies designed to help students crack the test have sprung up throughout the borough of Queens, appealing to immigrants who see education—and Stuyvesant in particular—as the key to their families' future. Alexa Solimano, who is half Korean and half of mixed Irish and Italian descent, entered such an academy in the fifth grade, and she says, "I don't think I would've gotten into Stuyvesant without it."

Now a freshman, Alexa still attends the academy on Saturdays to get ahead, doing academy homework on top of her regular high school homework. While she is studying algebra and geometry at Stuyvesant this year, she's already digging into trigonometry and precalculus at the private academy to get a jump start on the next two years of math. She's also studying for the SAT, the first practice test for which she took in the sixth grade.

"College seems so far away," says the fourteen-year-old, "but I know it's not."

With such an attitude pervasive at Stuyvesant, what predominates are professional test-taking students who have accepted a culture of ambition, where pressure is a natural by-product. That pressure, though, is extreme and self-selective, like a rare strain of hyper-Darwinism, and it infects students in every grade.

Freshman Susan Levinson, at lunch, ponders, half kidding, the meaning of an algebra test she recently flubbed with a grade of 69, possibly the worst mark in her life: "I'm going to fail the class, which means I'm not going to get into college, which means I'm not going to get a job, then I'm going to live with my parents, then I'm not going to get a boyfriend, then I'm not going to have kids, I'll have nothing to live for, I'll do drugs and become a bum—because I failed a math test."

Sophomore Brittany DiSanto, at the school library, is pallid after her last class, in which she too thinks she just bombed her math test in algebra and trigonometry: "Everyone wants to have that good GPA." She says some students, though not she, smoke cigarettes "to relieve stress."

Junior Andrew Saviano, sitting in a third-floor hallway, shows no signs of fatigue even though he manages only about three to four hours of sleep a night. "I like to think of it as the mind doesn't get tired, the body does." Sometimes he works by the sole light of computer glare in the *Spectator* newspaper office so he won't get caught at school in the wee hours of the morning. He maintains a 97 average and nearly perfect SAT scores. He admits, however, "There's the stress, there's the not sleeping, there's the coffee and other stimulants," which, for him, means tea. He also admits there is a toll: "I do suffer from it. I don't grow." He has been five foot seven since the beginning of the school year. "I don't care about being tall," he says.

Senior Kristen Chambers, in a café outside school, ruminates about how she hates Stuyvesant. She tried to persuade her parents to let her transfer to a less stressful Catholic school in her Brooklyn neighborhood and can't wait to escape at graduation: "It's very competitive, it's not comforting to me, I'm always on edge."

Reminders of what's at stake are everywhere. An advertisement for the Kaplan test prep service in the school newspaper puts it in stark terms:

Higher score.
Brighter future.

Academic pressure is always in the air, a frequent topic of conversation in hallways, where the latest test is frequently followed by the refrain, "What'd you get? What'd you get?" Student publications bemoan students' obsession with tests, grades, and colleges. "In the midst of APs and college applications, many students have a hard time finding the meaning to it all," writes the opinions editor of the *Stuyvesant Standard* newspaper. "Classes are just taken for the grades, and those are only for the application to an Ivy League university." In another student publication, *Stuy Health*, a front-page article entitled "Stopping Stress at Stuyvesant" offers remedies that would be obvious to an otherwise normal student body, like having *friends*. The problem of pressure even comes up at a Parents' Association meeting, where students on a panel try to explain the Stuyvesant phenomenon. In a school of overachievers, "the pressure is crazy," one student says.

Teachers are acutely aware of the ponderous atmosphere weighing on students. Some are known to inflate students' grades, even unprompted. Others, like Michael Waxman, a popular social studies and foreign language teacher, can only wonder what the fuss is all about. He says that a student in his Hebrew class warned him at the beginning of the term that she "better get a ninety-six" in his class.

"Why?" he asked.

Apparently she was concerned about getting into college.

She was in the ninth grade.

As the semester wore on, she requested to see his grade book and demanded to know how he calculated her grade. During a Hebrew vocabulary test, she broke down crying, banged her desk, and rushed out of the room.

The problem? She couldn't remember a couple of answers.

Mr. Waxman gently tried to explain that it's okay not to be perfect, that she was allowed to get a couple of answers wrong. She wasn't convinced. Still upset, she proceeded to give him a negative rating on a popular Web site, www.ratemyteacher.com.

"The chutzpah," he says, resting his hand wearily against his forehead.

Chutzpah of another sort greeted Eleanor Archie, assistant principal for pupil services, from the moment she arrived at Stuyvesant in 1992 as a guidance counselor. Her first student barged into her office sobbing because of the grade she had just received in a math class: 97.

"I'm going, 'So where's the problem?'" Ms. Archie recalls.

The student had expected nothing less than perfection.

She too was a freshman.

"Then I realize, I'm in a population that's so stressful, everyone wants to get a hundred," Ms. Archie says.

"It is tempting, and easy, to become such a part of the system, to become so transformed by the work and the competition and the pressure that you lose yourself in them, so much so that, in the end, you yourself are responsible for sustaining them," Mr. Grossman, the English chairman, cautioned students in a graduation speech a couple of years ago. "It is dangerous too, because Stuyvesant's imperfections are the world's, it is a smaller city within a larger one."

But the pressure isn't coming only from students. "I have spoken to parents that will tell me, 'If my child doesn't get into an Ivy, I'm not paying for college,'" Ms. Archie says.

Irate, overbearing parents are a common phenomenon at Stuyvesant. One parent called Mr. Waxman, the Hebrew teacher, to ask, "Is there something wrong with my son?" There wasn't. The father then wanted an explanation for his son's grade. "Why did he only get a ninety-eight?" At the recent induction ceremony of the Stuyvesant National Hebrew Honor Society, one unscheduled feature was a parent who complained to Mr. Waxman that he moved too slowly in class for his daughter, after which the parent summarily left. And the mother of a student in his economics class wrote a note to Mr. Waxman, asking him to reschedule his upcoming test because her daughter had four other exams on the same day. As an incentive, the mother, who ran an Asian restaurant in Manhattan, offered to serve him sushi "free free free."

He declined.

"You can't make this stuff up," he marvels.

The school tries to counsel parents to ease up on their kids. At a School Tone Committee meeting, parents are given a handout entitled "Being a Stuyvesant Parent: What Your Kids Hope For."

Under the category "What You Shouldn't Be Doing," the flyer recommends against such common parental practices at Stuyvesant as

1. Demanding certain grades; instead ask that your child puts in his/her best effort;
2. Comparing your child's performance with other students or family members, or frequently asking how other students are doing;
3. Nagging underclassmen about college, portraying college as the be-all and end-all;
4. Deciding your goals for your child are synonymous with your child's goals for him/herself;
5. Pressuring kids to take more and harder classes. They should take classes in which they're interested, and should not take on too heavy a course load;
6. Worrying about college, numbers, rankings.

And under the heading "What Stuyvesant Students Consider the Greatest Sources of Stress," it ranks

1. Parents' expectations
2. College
3. Competition with other students
4. Workload

At times, the pressure gets so intense at Stuyvesant that Ms. Archie, the assistant principal, says some students "have a nervous breakdown" and are even "hospitalized, you know, because of the pressure."

Others resort to drugs, says Angel Colon, a school counselor. "Methamphetamine is becoming a big, big, big concern," he says. Some students are taking the illicit stimulant to help them stay awake to cram for tests, he says, but "eventually it really catches up with you." Some students say they have also resorted to using Adderall, a prescription drug intended to treat attention deficit disorder, to give them an academic edge.

It's hard to miss the bleary-eyed symptoms of students who've pulled all-nighters studying, if only fueled by Starbucks, conveniently located two blocks from school. The popular saying seems apropos: At Stuyvesant you can have only two of the following three—high grades, a social life, or sleep. Many forgo sleep. According to a recent survey by the *Spectator*, about 27 percent of Stuyvesant students say they use caffeine to stay awake during the day, while 60 percent say they get five to six hours of sleep a night, which is little more than half what is recommended for teenagers. And 75 percent say they sometimes or always sleep on a train, bus, or ferry, an indication that sleep-deprived students will doze whenever they can, even on the way to or from school.

Apparently, it's not nearly enough shut-eye.

*Stuy Health* reports that "students often complain about headaches, crankiness and feeling 'dead.'"

> *TAKE A CHANCE*
> *MAKE IT HAPPEN*
>
> —desktop graffiti, Stuyvesant High School

CHAPTER THREE

# The Wizard of Oz

DEAD OF NIGHT CLOAKS A MODEST TWO-STORY BRICK town house in a quiet Brooklyn neighborhood, until 4:34 a.m., when out of the front door bursts a bolt of lightning, a whirling dervish, an anarchist, a rebel, a ringleader, and a gale force all wrapped in black spandex leggings, a blue fleece thermal jacket, a floral skullcap, rimless glasses, blue and gray sneakers, and a Yale baseball hat.

Otherwise known as Mr. Jaye.

He looks like he's ready to run a marathon this early February morning. And that's what he's about to do, in a manner of speaking, when he arrives at school, where he runs amok until late into the evening, gleefully creating havoc, breaking rules, and inventing new ones in the name of helping students as the assistant principal and powerful and adored chairman of Stuyvesant's vaunted math department, the school's heart.

"When you work with kids," he says, "you better stay young, or they get the jump on you."

Mr. Jaye—grinning like he can't wait to get started—looks about twenty-four years old. He's fifty-four.

But it's dark, and now he's pushing the pedal in a black Honda

35

Accord along a deserted stretch of asphalt where, at this predawn hour, he says, "Only the drunks and me are on the road." Though the avenues have changed over the years, he's been on the same journey since 1972, when he started as a student teacher at Stuyvesant. But all that may be coming to a screeching end in a matter of months. After thirty-four years at Stuyvesant, Mr. Jaye believes this may be his final semester.

"I'm really torn about leaving because I love this institution," he says. "If I leave here, there's a hole they'll never fill."

Mr. Jaye doesn't want to leave. But he feels he may have no choice. For the past few years, he's expected his friend and boss, Mr. Teitel, to retire as principal. Each year, it hasn't happened, and it doesn't look like it's going to happen anytime soon. Mr. Teitel, himself fifty-seven years old, just received a bonus that would have counted toward his retirement, if he took it, but he didn't, even though there's no guarantee he'll get the bonus next year. Mr. Teitel has made no noise about walking away from the "blue chair," his coveted seat as principal of the nationally recognized school. Mr. Teitel's news—or lack thereof—has sent Mr. Jaye into a tailspin this morning, at the beginning of the semester. He's tired of waiting to become principal, the job he aspires to, which students and teachers alike assume is his one day for the taking.

"I've been prepared to be principal for three, four years," he says. "My time is now."

It's 4:52 a.m., and Mr. Jaye rumbles off the Brooklyn Bridge, thinking about what looms ahead: the possibility of the principal's job at another prestigious public high school, Bergen County Academies in New Jersey. The wheels have already been set in motion. Bergen officials have been wooing him, he's visited the school five times, and he's awaiting the results of the New Jersey principal licensing exam he recently took. The numbers make sense too: if he retires from Stuyvesant, he reckons he'd collect about $80,000 a year in his pension and bring in another $130,000 as principal—almost double what's he's bringing in now.

What's not to like?

Still, the thought of leaving Stuyvesant tugs at an unseen emotion as Mr. Jaye turns onto a darkened Chambers Street, barreling across West Street and parking in front of the school, not a soul in sight. That unsettling thought will have to wait. Time to move on. It's 4:58 a.m., and there are things to do.

Tucked in a corner of the school overlooking the Tribeca Bridge, room 402—the cramped math department office—is much like the man who barges into it this morning, jam-packed. There is lots of stuff: six computers, two printers, five tape dispensers, three staplers, seven dollar bills, four pairs of scissors, an ivory bust of bearded philosopher-mathematician-hero Pythagoras. A red message light flashes unanswered on the phone. Mr. Jaye's desk is peppered with papers, files, and tons of yellow stickies, reminders of pressing to-dos. On a cabinet, a certificate is posted: "Jennifer Michelle Jaye has been awarded admission to Yale University Class of 2007." She is his oldest daughter, a prototypical Stuyvesant graduate for whom the Ivies were preordained. On the bookshelves are the usual props of a math man—*Elementary Algebra, Trigonometry, Precalculus, Calculus,* along with *Never Give In: The Best of Winston Churchill's Speeches.* Dozens of math trophies of various shapes and sizes collect dust and rust on top of a file cabinet, like forgotten toys for children who have too many, next to a clunky computer, circa late 1980s. More prominent is a photo of Mr. Jaye—same Cheshire grin but younger, with a thin, wide mustache long since gone—standing next to a grown-up Tim Robbins, the Oscar-winning actor, on a visit to his old math teacher.

This is the fiefdom where Mr. Jaye gets things done—things that other administrators won't dare, that teachers can t fathom, and for which students praise him. Which is why they call him the Wizard of Oz. He puts it more carefully: "When you help kids you have to interpret rules favorably. Here's my motto: 'Make it happen.'"

Mr. Jaye has rarely seen an administrative roadblock he couldn't overcome, which is quite a feat in a complicated bureaucracy like the New York City schools, the largest public education system in the nation. If a student oversleeps and doesn't get to school on time for a math final, Mr. Jaye will arrange a makeup He lets students—like Romeo—skip a math course to get into a higher level without any red tape. And when a student has surpassed high school math altogether, Mr. Jaye will find the course that the student needs, even if it's a PhD class at NYU. What's more, he will get that student high school credit for the college class, no matter how loudly the high school guidance counselors howl in protest. "In this department," he crows, "there's nothing we can't do."

That statement—a double negative—is just the kind of math equation expected of an unreformed troublemaker who failed algebra in the ninth grade.


Born in the shadow of Stuyvesant, Daniel Jaye lived and learned to be a wise guy just a couple of blocks from the vaunted public school when it was on East Fifteenth Street. The middle-class son of a commercial real estate broker, he passed Stuyvesant every day on his way to take the Avenue A bus to his regular public school, Seward Park High. But never once did he wish he attended Stuyvesant, a forbidding place to him because it was then an all-boys' school where the boys looked miserable from the heavy workload. Danny liked to have fun, and school got in the way of fun.

School was such a breeze that Danny skipped the eighth grade, but all the classes he cut in the ninth grade finally caught up with him. He failed algebra with an abysmal 55, a grade he matched in French class. In his junior year, he did it again, attending about a third of his classes and failing math while achieving the dubious distinction of a perfect score on the statewide algebra and trigonometry final. Details are sketchy, but somehow, Danny negotiated a retroactive passing grade in the course.

"I was not actively engaged in the institution" is the way he puts it.

The same could be said of his subsequent experience at the City College of New York, where as an undergraduate he had no idea what he wanted to do—other than to avoid the Vietnam War. Despite his high school run-ins, numbers came easy to him, and he decided to major in math. But he minored in education for more practical considerations. Teaching, he says, "was a draft deferment. That's what it was about."

Until his senior year of college. Then by accident—or fate—it became about something else.

As part of a math methods course, his professor took him and his fellow college students to observe a classmate practice the craft, teaching a fifteen-minute lesson at a Bronx high school, a rough place where it was an achievement if the students merely showed up. On this day, the surprise was that the student teacher didn't show up. So Danny, as reckless as ever, volunteered to teach the class. Of all things, it was ninth-grade algebra, the subject he had himself failed.

But not on this day. Instead, he quickly scanned the Delaney book, a time-honored New York public school seating chart named after Edward C. Delaney, a Harvard-educated public school teacher. The attendance and grade book was filled with Delaney cards, tabs about the size of a business card containing the names of the thirty-some hardened students blankly staring at him at the front of the room.

Looking back at them, Danny began by asking how many students were interested in baseball, a question intended to elicit a popular response since the school was a stone's throw from Yankee Stadium.

About a third of the class raised hands.

Not bad.

Then he called on a boy in the last row, in the last seat—by name: Alan. Danny had strategically memorized the names of four students, one in each corner of the Delaney book. The classroom buzz was palpable. A little boy in the front row said, in an aside to a buddy, "Oh shit, he knows our names."

And Danny thought, *I got 'em.*

He pushed forward, asking how many students had heard of Joe DiMaggio, the great Yankee slugger.

Again, more hands.

What was he famous for?

A boy volunteered: a hitting streak.

Right. A hitting streak of consecutive games. Like consecutive numbers, or integers, the subject of today's lesson. And Danny was on his way. "I was intoxicated with the fact that the kids liked me," he recalls. "I was really enthralled this came so easy to me." So was his professor, who approached Danny at the end of the lesson and predicted, "You will be a great teacher."

His professor was right, but he couldn't have predicted this: Danny would coauthor with that professor, Alfred S. Posamentier, a book called *What Successful Math Teachers Do, Grades 6–12.*

———————

The book now sits on a shelf, a relic of the past lost in the din of teenage voices streaming into and out of Mr. Jaye's office at 8:35 a.m. Already, he's accomplished a lot, including taking his first morning bike jaunt of the semester on a path along the West Side Highway, from Stuyvesant to Harlem, with a colleague, Mike Zamansky, a Stuyvesant graduate who loved the school so much he's now its computer science coordinator. Mr. Jaye rode a Trek 6000 mountain bike spangled with two high beams and a flashing light on the front end, two flashing lights on the back side, and lights powering out of each end of the handlebar, a dazzling array of portable illumination that prompted his bike partner to say, "Danny's like a Christmas tree."

Now, though, Mr. Jaye is showered and garbed more appropriately for a math department chairman: black wing tips, black slacks, a massive ring of keys on his right hip, a blue collared shirt with "DJ" embroidered in white initials on the breast pocket, and a blue tie. In his pocket: five hundred dollars, just-in-case cash. And he's in the thick of it: he peeks from his doors at the line of students snaking out of the math department and yells to no one in particular, "Why does my line get bigger? I'm not giving anything away."

Well, he is.

Students know Mr. Jaye isn't just the math chairman. He's the fixer, the man you go to at the beginning of the semester to get your class schedule changed when you don't have the course you need or want, or when you have a class (or teacher) you want to get rid of. Word gets around.

"I hope I don't get in trouble for this," says a senior for whom Mr. Jaye just switched schedules with the stroke of a computer key.

He laughs it off with a math joke to distract her: "If your sister loves you and you love me, by the transitive property, she loves me."

The senior, still worrying about the schedule tinkering, isn't laughing. "It's, like, all done? It's perfect?"

"It's perfect," he assures her.

They high-five.

His next customer, a worried boy, asks, "Did my mom call?"

"No," he deadpans, "we don't talk to parents."

A teacher pokes her head in his office, looking for aspirin. His wife calls on his cell phone. He steps out into the hallway to rally the troops, "to spread my cheer throughout the building." He ducks into a secret elevator beyond an aqua green door marked, "Notice—Keep This Door Closed." He's corralled in the hallway by a student who wants to drop statistics, a killer course. He writes a note on the back of scrap paper and tells her to stop by his office.

"I love these kids," he says.

Adults are another matter.


At 11:45 a.m., Mr. Jaye is sitting at a long wooden table in a conference room adjoining the principal's office, and he's not happy. Nobody is. Sitting with him are the principal and the assistant principals of English and social studies, advisory members in a private gathering of the principal's inner circle—the "kitchen cabinet."

Today's burning issue: faculty uproar over a new school rule requiring them to flip over time cards to indicate their presence at school. Teachers don't want to do it. At Stuyvesant, where students are treated like adults, the adults complain that they feel as though they're being treated like children.

Mr. Jaye, sitting at the head of the table, as if he's already principal, takes charge, suggesting a compromise, that they require teachers to flip over time cards once, when they arrive, but not when they leave.

The idea seems to garner support.

Mr. Teitel, the principal, sitting to Mr. Jaye's side, suggests that they write a letter to the faculty, dictating out loud what he imagines to be the opening: "This has been a very upsetting week—"

At which, Mr. Grossman, the English chairman, interrupts, "Start with something positive."

Mr. Jaye adds, "Reflect on our successes."

Mr. Teitel piggybacks on the positives, deciding not to use the term "time cards." Sounds too . . . officious.

"Time check-in?" Mr. Grossman suggests.

"The truth is, I'm under direct order from the superintendent," Mr. Teitel says.

"Do this in the least intrusive way," Mr. Grossman offers.

Mr. Jaye's idea wins the day: one flip a day, whatever the time card is called.

"I can only lose my job once," muses Mr. Teitel, who, in his seventh year as principal and his twenty-third at Stuyvesant, looks like Abraham Lincoln after the Civil War—shaggy-bearded, emaciated, and incredibly tired.

The conversation devolves into group commiseration about new rules in the teachers' contract requiring them to do what many consider menial jobs, like monitoring the library. Mr. Teitel mentions that someone recommended that he bring in a conflict mediator to deal with a faction of angry English teachers. Someone received a dreaded "U"— "unsatisfactory"—teacher performance rating, which has roiled some on staff. Mr. Teitel says he couldn't eat after the last contentious faculty meeting.

On a wall across the room, a bank of head shots of the previous dozen principals of Stuyvesant—a select club of eleven men and one woman—gaze down on Mr. Teitel, as if sympathizing with his plight.

Then Mr. Jaye finally shows his cards, revealing what he really came here for, saying he wasn't consulted when one of his best teachers was assigned to patrol—*babysit*—the library during seventh and eighth periods instead of using those free periods to meet with students in math research, room 401.

Mr. Teitel knows better than to duke this out in front of everyone. At 12:28 p.m., he dismisses the cabinet, save Mr. Jaye, leaving the two of them like brothers ready to roll up their sleeves and kick dirt in each other's face, such is their mutual admiration. Mr. Teitel begins with the obvious salvo, explaining why he assigned the teacher in question to library duty: "He's a school aide."

The argument has the benefit of being true. The teacher is *not* a teacher, at least not officially. He's a school aide—not much higher in the school hierarchy than a custodial worker. Not that such labels stopped Mr. Jaye from assigning the school aide to teach a math research class to Stuyvesant freshmen and sophomores. Mr. Jaye hired the aide for his mathematical genius, ignoring minor details, such as his lack of a teacher's license because he hasn't been certified, which he can't be because he hasn't graduated from college, which he has flunked out of.

Mr. Jaye appealed to the college dean yesterday to get the aide reinstated, but so far, the college is unmoved, even though the teacher's aide recently won a Putnam Fellowship, making him one of the top five undergraduate mathematicians in North America.

"He's the smartest person in the building!" Mr. Jaye screams at the principal.

"Someone has to do it," Mr. Teitel says of the library duty.

"But the person who answers the phone can't do what [he] can do!"

"Stop," says Mr. Teitel, burying his head in his hands.

Mr. Jaye suggests installing security cameras in the library to catch vandals.

But Mr. Teitel moans, "We spent a fortune on the library. What do you want me to do? I need to supervise [students] in some way."

Now Mr. Jaye's worked himself into a lather. "We're not employing a genius and having him do security!" Then his anger dissolves into a well of tears in a set of deep brown eyes. "I'm not going to make him flip fucking burgers."

Mr. Teitel downshifts into a softer, conciliatory tone, saying how he respects Mr. Jaye more than anyone else, how they go back a long way. But he says, "The reality is, I've got to run a school." And here, emboldened, Mr. Teitel begins to build an argument about how he gets a set school budget from the city every year and how he can't foresee every eventuality, but then he falters, at first imperceptibly, and now he's agreeing what a terrible waste of talent it is to have a math genius police the library, and in the end, he says he'll try to get him out of there.

Mr. Teitel smiles wanly. "Okay," he says, "we'll find somebody."

It's all over. Mr. Teitel nods his head ruefully, sighs. Mr. Jaye rises to leave, renewed. Crisis averted. On his way out of the principal's office, practically skipping, he turns back and, with a lascivious grin, calls out to the secretaries, asking whether they want to join him in a "cuddle puddle."

*Cuddle puddle?*

CHAPTER FOUR

# Cuddle Puddle Muddle

BEHIND CLOSED DOORS FIVE DAYS LATER, MR. TEITEL is hunched uneasily, marooned in a maroon armchair in his office, speaking in urgent tones to a small gathering of lieutenants, as if hashing out military strategy in a hastily convened war council. And in a sense—just a week into the semester—he's already in a pitched battle.

Some teachers are still refusing to flip over their time cards. What's more, some are resisting the menial tasks of patrolling the various byways of the school, prompting an assistant principal to suggest a dire prospect: that the school may be forced to fire some teachers so it can free up money to hire aides who will perform the odious monitoring duties. But that's the least of Mr. Teitel's worries on this February day.

The bigger problem: parents are up in arms, deluging him with e-mails complaining about a just-released *New York* magazine cover story on Stuyvesant that dropped like an unexpected public relations bomb on his coffee table. The title: "Love and the Ambisexual, Heteroflexible Teen."

The cover photo features a high school principal's nightmare: a recumbent, bare-chested boy, à la Calvin Klein advertisements, right

45

arm bent at the elbow, his other embracing an impish girl with golden locks and a Mona Lisa expression of mischievous ennui.

The story delves into a Stuyvesant subculture involving a handful of students who heap themselves and their backpacks in a "cuddle puddle" on a second-floor hallway where "[t]here are girls petting girls and girls petting guys and guys petting guys." The author writes that it is "just one clique at Stuyvesant" but says the "cuddle puddle is emblematic of the changing landscape of high-school sexuality across the country," citing a recent survey showing that 11 percent of U.S. girls from fifteen to nineteen years old have had "same-sex encounters." Then the writer goes on to discuss the vague sexual boundaries of teenagers who call themselves "polysexual, ambisexual, pansexual, pansensual, polyfide, bi-curious, bi-queer, fluid, metroflexible, heteroflexible, heterosexual with lesbian tendencies . . ." Details ensue, such as an ice cube dropped down various pants.

How does Mr. Teitel, the principal, explain this away on a legal pad?

He reads aloud his scribbled attempt, a draft of a letter to one perturbed parent, acknowledging that sex, drugs, and alcohol do exist even at an august institution like Stuyvesant. But he adds that one of the great traditions of the school "is the almost college-like environment" of freedom. And he notes that "Stuyvesant has always been and will always continue to be a magnet for this kind of thing because of its 'elite' status."

But here, Mr. Teitel can't resist an aside to Mr. Grossman, the English chairman, who is sitting with him in commiseration. "They're teenagers!" Mr. Teitel says. "This is what happens!"

Mr. Grossman agrees and gives Mr. Teitel a good grade on his letter composition: "It's perfect."

Mr. Teitel isn't soothed. He buries his head in his hands, uttering, "God, I'm not going to get through these weeks."

It's remarkable that he's made it this far. If not for his weight, Mr. Teitel might be a retired cop today.


A Brooklyn boy, Stanley Teitel was the son of a New York police officer who grew up poor, selling apples on the streets, a searing memory that prompted the father to encourage the son to join the men in blue, stressing the steady paycheck and the early retirement, which he could take at age thirty-eight if he started at eighteen. Stan was willing. But there was one major sticking point: the teenager weighed 129 pounds—reed thin on a six foot one inch frame.

"I was tall enough," he says, "I just didn't weigh enough."

Stan was so underweight that he was pronounced 4-F—unfit for military service—which thrilled his mother because it kept him out of Vietnam. But that left Stan in a quandary about his future, the unfolding of which put a new wrinkle in the adage that those who can t, teach, or in his case, become the principal of one of the best high schools in America. He applied to dental school but didn't get in because of his mediocre college grades. He tried his hand briefly as a private investigator, but that didn't take either. He sold men's clothing. Then he took a flier on teaching. It was supposed to be a temporary gig. His high school alma mater needed a biology teacher to fill a vacancy until the end of a term, and young Stan had a knack for science going back to his childhood, when he idolized Albert Einstein and helped his dad fix carburetors for extra money. So he took the teaching job, which came as something of a surprise to the principal, who remembered young Stan as the former student whom he had suspended for five days. The former troublemaker won't say for what, for fear of encouraging naughtiness in his own students today. He says only, "I did something bad."

It wasn't bad enough to get him kicked out again. Teaching, he soon learned, shared some of the stability that his father had admired in the police force. And then there was this bonus about teaching: "I like summers off," Mr. Teitel says.

Today, though, is no vacation. The controversial cuddle puddle story spreads like a virus throughout the building, from the first-floor principal's office to the second-floor senior "bar," a lozenge-size block behind which a gaggle of girls is sitting cross-legged on the floor, gawking at the candid photos from the torn-out article as if they were contraband.

"That is so unnecessary," says Becky, the brainy cheerleader, glued to the page.

Fellow senior Nikki Bogopolskaya worries that she'll be mistaken for a sexually free girl named Nikki in the cuddle puddle. And the article mysteriously reminds another onlooker, senior Molly Ruben-Long, "I've come to the realization that I'm going to prom by myself." Though no one disputes the assertion, she quickly adds, "No, it's okay."

The angst levitates like a magic trick to room 640, where students in a journalism class debate the article's merits. Few are found.

"The journalism didn't seem morally correct, or ethically correct," says one editor of the *Spectator* school newspaper, criticizing how the *New York* magazine writer entered the school without the principal's authorization and used pseudonyms in the article. The author, Alex Morris, says later in an interview that she didn't realize she needed to obtain permission to enter the school. "I just walked in," says the twenty-seven-year-old author, noting that this was her first article as a freelance writer. She says she used pseudonyms to protect the students, especially those who had not told their parents about their sexuality. "One of our concerns was not 'outing' kids." She says she did not seek parental consent before interviewing the students, a general practice when writing about minors, but says the magazine did obtain parents' permission before publishing photographs of the students.

In class, the journalism students seem even more bothered by their perception that the story casts Stuyvesant as a sex-crazed school whose students struggle with ambiguous gender tendencies.

"We're not all like that," one girl says.

Another calls it cheap "entertainment."

A third says that her concerned mother asked whether she was a lesbian, eliciting nervous tittering in the classroom.

Alair, the sixteen-year-old *New York* cover girl, isn't here to air her own grievances about the article, but she has many. She says the story contains a good message about tolerance, but "it used sensationalism to cater to people's eyes." What's more, she says that she and her friends asked the *New York* magazine author not to use the term "cuddle puddle." Ms. Morris disputes that, saying, "They never asked me not to." Alair also takes exception to the way the students were characterized, saying, "It's not soft porn. We're just hanging out in the hallway."

Ms. Morris says, "I know some of them were upset," but she stresses, "That was never my intention." She acknowledges, though, that the article "is about teenagers and sex, you're not going to have a perfectly

Junior League article" and that the story lost "some of the more tender moments" during the editing process. "It's always a hard thing, being written about," she says.

Lately, Alair, the menthol chain-smoking junior, has taken to wearing sunglasses at school. Celebrity is not everything it's cracked up to be.

But the story has legs. The term "cuddle puddle" instantly enters the Stuyvesant lexicon, both student and teacher versions, becoming a derisive term of endearment. Overnight, the magazine cover shot becomes iconic, like a bad reproduction of Michelangelo's *Creation of Adam* in the Sistine Chapel. In a parody of the magazine photo of the two teenagers clutching each other, the Republican Club of Stuy tapes up flyers throughout the building, showing a shirtless boy draped in the American flag, a girl resting on top of him, grasping a doll of former President Ronald Reagan. Promoting its next meeting, the flyer touts "News and the Ambipolitical, Conservative Teen."

The *Spectator* takes a more serious tack, dissecting the *New York* article under the headline "Cuddle Puddle Muddle." A survey of students finds that most believe the school was misrepresented. Rounding out the general disapprobation, the *Spectator* also runs a student opinion piece, "Sex and Sensationalism at Stuy." None of which stops *New York* magazine from following up later with another salacious item about Stuyvesant. But then, perhaps this piece falls under the category of don't-shoot-the-messenger, as the article merely reports on a just-published book, *The Notebook Girls*, written by four girls during their recent years at Stuyvesant. It just happens to be chock-full of teenage talk about oral sex and lesbian lusts.

Fact is, talk of sex—or the engagement in it—isn't hard to find at Stuyvesant, or any other high school, for that matter. The topic, for instance, comes up casually during a meeting of the advisory School Tone Committee of parents, faculty, and students, one of whom talks about the distribution of condoms in school as if she were talking about handing out an item as ordinary as a lollipop. The topic of sex is just as breezy in the school library, where a sixteen-year-old honors student says that on an upcoming date, he plans to take his girlfriend to a shop that sells condoms to "check that out, then go out to eat." The junior also mentions that he recently ripped a condom while in use, and his parents simply told him to get his girlfriend a morning-after pill as an emergency contraceptive. His attitude: no big deal. "My dad knows," he says, "it's a natural thing when you're sixteen, you have a lot of sex."

Backing up that assertion is an article in the *Spectator* at the beginning of the semester. Ostensibly, the story is about the little-used Hudson staircase at the back of the school. But it's really about not how *little* it's used but *how* it's used. "The Hudson staircase is synonymous with sexual activity in the eyes of many students," the student reporter writes. School administrators acknowledge as much, saying in the *Spectator* that security guards patrol the stairwells to prevent unacceptable behavior. Nonetheless, a sophomore is quoted as saying the Hudson staircase is where students "go to have sex in," the details of which are left to the reader's imagination. Someone edited out of the story a graphic term for oral sex, according to a faculty member.

Someone else, meanwhile, manages to keep the cuddle puddle off the agenda at an after-school meeting of the School Leadership Team—known as the SLT—an advisory committee of students, teachers, and parents. But on this day in early February, when the *New York* magazine article reverberates throughout the school, Mr. Teitel, the principal, knows other trouble awaits at the SLT meeting. The first giveaway: as he enters room 615, it's claustrophobically hot from overactive radiators. "I can see the heat's up," he remarks, opening a window, which does nothing to cool off about twenty-five simmering parents and students—his "constituents," as he calls them.

The first order of business is another brewing controversy—the introduction of "kiosks," a euphemism to many frowning members of the committee for "lockdown." Stuyvesant, joining many other schools, is preparing to install computerized identification scanners, which would require students to use cards to swipe into and out of the building. No longer would teachers be required to keep a paper record of attendance; no longer would students simply flash a photo ID at a somnolent guard standing by the school entrance. Proponents, who seem to consist of school administrators and few others in the room, say the kiosks will automatically record students' attendance and enhance secu-

rity by keeping track of exactly who is in the school at any given time—
and who shouldn't be.

"It only takes one person to mess up a school," says an official of the
kiosk manufacturer, a featured speaker at the committee meeting.

Left unsaid are new facts of school life: the threat of terrorism, the
menace of a Columbine High School–type carnage.

Opponents, who seem to include almost everyone else in the room,
say that the scanners will only send a message of mistrust from the very
moment students enter the school. The devices, they fear, will also in-
vade students' privacy, collecting personal data that could be abused.
And at a cost of about sixty thousand dollars for the scanners, the opponents want to know, aren't there higher-priority expenses for a high
school like Stuyvesant, which boasts nearly no student violence and a 97
percent attendance rate?

"We don't need this," says impassioned committee member Marty
Davis, an involved parent of a senior. "We need more money for teachers. We need more money for space." The scanners, he says, will make
the school look less like an academic setting than "the subway system."

Nothing is resolved. The agenda item is tabled until the next meeting. But rumblings are already sounding elsewhere. The Student Union
government is planning to fight the installation of the scanners. Protest
marches—effective in past student clashes with the administration—
could erupt. The *Spectator* has weighed in as well, criticizing the school
administration in a student editorial that begins, "You may have heard
that Stuy is being put under lockdown." Andrew, the newspaper's managing editor, says the scanners threaten to extinguish the school's freedoms.

"It's kind of like prison," he says.

Despite the principal's attempt to maintain a collegial atmosphere
of student empowerment, many students and teachers believe a strict
law-and-order force is gaining momentum under the direction of Randi
Damesek, the effective assistant principal of organization.

There's a leaden mood about her that is more than the sum of her
parts, something about the way she prowls the halls cloaked in a dark
sweater over her shoulders. Believed to be forty-one years old, she would
be pretty if she didn't look so owlish—pale-faced, her raven hair pulled

back severely. Last semester, Ms. Damesek fired off a Grinch-like faculty memo, effectively banning food from class parties around Christmas, that became front-page fodder for the *Spectator*. Mr. Jaye, her equal as an assistant principal and her opposite in spirit, put the kibosh on her measure, as he likes to do, saying he intended to party it up with his students. Ms. Damesek promptly followed up at the beginning of this semester by ripping down a star-studded student banner on a second-floor wall. The infraction was unclear; the poster merely welcomed back seniors. With that swipe, Ms. Damesek again made the front page, which she trumped with a cameo appearance in a subsequent student editorial under the headline "Ms. Damesek, Talk to Us." For several years, she has refused to comment to the school newspaper, which complains that she is leaving students in the dark about such important issues as the pending installation of scanners. "We ask Damesek to consider talking to the *Spectator* in the interest of the Stuy community," the editorial implores, "for we are the body that serves to inform it."

Ms. Damesek's reply: deafening silence. (She also declined repeated requests to be interviewed for this book—the only teacher or administrator to do so. She later threatened, among other things, to sue this author and have the principal fired if she were cast in a bad light.)

It hasn't been an easy transition for Ms. Damesek since she arrived at Stuyvesant as an administrative intern about four years ago. Little could prepare her for the oddity that is Stuyvesant, not even her eleven years as a math teacher at Fiorello H. LaGuardia High School of Music & Art and Performing Arts, an acclaimed New York public school and the subject of the movie *Fame*. (LaGuardia has its own selective admissions based on auditions.) From the beginning, Stuyvesant students bristled at Ms. Damesek's restrictions on bake sales and hallway traffic even when such rules are the norm at other public schools.

Things have been particularly difficult for Ms. Damesek lately, according to school colleagues. Her father, a principal in the New York school system, passed away not long ago. By all accounts, clashes with Mr. Jaye only add to her tension. And even Mr. Teitel, admits that Ms. Damesek holds the unenviable position as the school's strict disciplinarian by default—because no one else, not even he, fills that role. "In every organization, someone has to be the heavy," he says. "In this one, she's it."

Mr. Grossman, the English chairman, says that Ms. Damesek has the best intentions even if students and teachers sometimes question them. For instance, he says, she will repeatedly remind students of a deadline, such as their payment for the advanced placement exams, but if they fail to hand in their checks on time, she won't budge. Ms. Damesek guards her privacy so well that few know that she will give students a few dollars when they need it or call students to get them out of bed in the morning, according to Mr. Grossman. "In her own way, she really loves the kids," he says. Mr. Teitel adds that she stretches the school budget as far as it will go, finding ways to save money. When students owed about seven thousand overdue school books, he says she came up with the idea to give them a couple of days of amnesty, but then take away their out-to-lunch privileges if they didn't return their textbooks. Within short order, students returned most of them. "This is a girl who works tirelessly for these kids," Mr. Teitel says. Arms akimbo, Ms. Damesek often stands outside her second-floor office, intently watching in silence over students, though they sometimes take the stance to mean something less than charitable.

If Ms. Damesek isn't forthcoming, one of the best chances for students to find out what the adults are up to is to attend a meeting of the School Leadership Team, which has moved on from the controversial scanners to a discussion of another perennial problem at Stuyvesant and other high schools: cheating.

Call it the ugly stepchild of excruciating competition in an excruciatingly competitive school. Some students will tap their desk, in a sort of Morse code, to transmit answers to nearby friends. Others will use M&M candies, each color representing letters A through D on multiple-choice tests, to convey to other students the right answer. Then there are the more primitive techniques, such as writing test answers on a leg or an arm or the brim of a hat, or on the back of a label of a bottle of water, one of the few objects allowed on students' desks during exams.

The problem is so institutionalized at Stuyvesant that it's parodied. A front-page article of *The Broken Escalator*, an underground student publication, once blared, "Students Cheat on Math Final, Sun Continues to Rise and Set." The story went on to say, "Much of the student body has responded with shock. 'I simply can't believe that at such a prestigious school, cheating goes on,' said a deaf, blind baby in an incubator."

Cheating makes it into more mainstream reading, including the School Leadership Team's handout, under the rubric "School Goal 6": "To improve ethical practices among the students, and the school tone, at Stuyvesant High School." The Academic Honesty Committee, which was "working to devise a policy on plagiarism and other forms of academic malfeasance," has been folded into another school-related organ, but the issue remains as intractable as ever. "I was told by students this was not a subject that could even be fixed," says a concerned mother at the meeting. "The problem is so big."

A school official agrees, blaming cheating on Stuyvesant's stressful environment. "It's more acute in a school that has higher academic standards," she says. A parent blames it on the awesome quantity of tests foisted on overwhelmed students. Another says it's the media's fault for glamorizing the rich and famous, some of whom got that way by compromising their integrity.

Students on a panel discussing "Life at Stuy" at a subsequent Parents' Association meeting explain that some of their peers justify cheating by saying there's too much pressure to achieve, too much emphasis on grades, and that the system is unfair to begin with: bad teachers give bad tests; tough teachers grade too toughly. Students also say they take many advanced placement classes because it looks good to prospective colleges, but the workload can be too much, prompting some to cheat.

"There's so much stress and so much work," says one student on the panel.

"Everyone wants to get the highest grade," says another.

The school culture fosters the idea of achieving "by any means necessary," says a third.

Whatever the cause, cheating is as difficult to stop as teen acne. It can be abated, but it will rear its ugly head again, even if students are threatened by the daunting prospect of having the incident placed in their permanent record. Usually, teachers handle the situation on their own. One says she designs a different test for each class so that students can't pass answers on to their friends who take the exam later in the day. Another teacher says he requires students to sign a document assuring their academic integrity. Matt Polazzo, a popular teacher of comparative government and the coordinator of student affairs, makes cheaters sign a contract vowing never to cheat again, then requires them to sing the contract aloud. None, he reports, has been caught cheating a second time. Other teachers have turned high-tech to ferret out classroom culprits. A service that's gaining traction at Stuyvesant and other public schools is www.turnitin.com, a Web site that detects plagiarism in student papers by comparing them against countless works found on the Internet and other databases.

But for every high-tech tool to prevent cheating, students find a way to foil it. One such method lies just a block from Stuyvesant, where hawkers pass out business cards offering to write students' research papers for sixteen dollars a page. Another advertises:

NO JOB IS TOO BIG; NO JOB IS TOO SMALL!
SAME DAY & NEXT DAY SERVICE IS AVAILABLE

Standardized tests can be gamed just as easily. A recent Stuyvesant graduate became the subject of a *New York Post* article entitled "Confessions of SAT Test Faker," in which he boasted how he became a test-taking gun for hire, armed with a fake ID and a student's social security number, helping high school students obtain the high scores they want on college entrance tests and other exams.

"The only complaint I've ever gotten was that I scored too high," he told the *Post*.

The intricacies of cheating are the subject of a class project documentary by junior Ada Ng, who wanders Stuyvesant's hallways interviewing students, using a Sony video camera resting on a tripod.

"Have you ever cheated before?" she asks a nervous girl on camera.

"Yes," the girl says, then quickly adds, "I don't recommend to do it all the time."

How do you cheat?

Glancing at another student's test from "the corner of my eye," the girl says.

Have you ever been caught?

No.

Have you helped others cheat?

Yes. Sometimes, the girl says, she will memorize the answers to questions on a test, then give those answers to friends who have the same class later in the day.

How do you feel about cheating as a way of getting by?

"It's not," says the girl, "the best method to use."

CHAPTER FIVE

# Jane's Addiction

THERE'S NO METHOD TO JANE'S MADNESS. IT'S ALL rage, and pain, and poetry, and love, and hate, and a childhood lost, and a father gone, and a search for something, a yearning for anything, or a hope for nothing, to simplify, to reduce, to forget everything in the unyielding vortex of a hit of heroin.

"My hobby is self-destruction," she says impassively.

A fight breaks out—something about how her mother is going to lock her in forever—before Jane takes off, instantaneously proving the point that forever doesn't even last a day, the day, incidentally, that she is supposed to take an advanced placement calculus test. For five days, seventeen-year-old Jane stays with a friend before returning home. By then, she has some explaining to do, not just to her mother, but to Stuyvesant, for her unexcused absences. So mother and daughter head down to the school in early February, first thing in the morning, first period. While her mother waits in the first-floor lobby by the school security guard, Jane marches into a nearby bathroom, brazenly leaves it unlocked, and injects herself with a shot of heroin.

The next day, Jane takes the makeup math test—and passes.

That day near the beginning of the new semester, Jane also decides to stop using heroin. For one, she says, "I ran out, I didn't have any money, I just got sick and tired." It helps too that waiting for her at the end of the day is a homemade detoxification concoction: the prescription painkiller OxyContin and a sleeping pill.

It doesn't take. The following day, Jane can't get out of bed, doesn't go to school, couldn't care less. It's noon. She's unconscious. Then suddenly, she's screaming and kicking and crying, and she's being rushed into an emergency room, fighting against the flow of methadone.

"I don't remember anything else," she says.

What follows is a blur, too—detox at the hospital, then home, then back in detox. And now here she is, back at school, barely hanging on to her senior year, oblivious to the scanner controversy, mildly amused by the cuddle puddle brouhaha. What sustains her is not the antidepressants, which she periodically pops, or the outpatient group therapy—rehab—which she considers a joke, but her will.

"Right now," she says, "I'm just trying to put back the pieces."

The pieces of Jane are so delicate and small—all five foot two inches and ninety pounds of her—she almost looks like fragile porcelain, too beautiful to break. And yet the feline ferocity in her eyes conveys the sense that the waiflike girl could tear you to shreds for looking at her the wrong way: with sympathy.

Such a ferocious effect could be owing to Jane's various contact lenses—purple, blue, green, hazel, gold, moonlight, or the gray of today. Or maybe it's the net effect of the incongruous purple baby's pacifier dangling below her form-fitting T-shirt, the long, golden-dyed talons of her dark hair, and her bare midriff. It could also be her earrings, which label her a "Rebel." Or her two arrests for carrying stilettos, which she calls "a nice accessory." Or her cell phone voice mail announcement, which tells you to "leave your message or fuck off."

The truth is, Jane isn't even sure how she came to this point. "I never saw it coming," she says.


Problems began just beyond Beijing, where Jane was born and raised in large part by her mother's grandparents. "I had a messed up childhood," she begins in Dickensian fashion. Her earliest memory, she says, is "pushing open a door, wondering why after you wake up, you're weak." Her father left Jane, an only child, in China when she was two so he could pursue a career in Europe as a painter. Her mother left a year later to join Jane's father. Over the next several years, Jane shuttled back and forth between China and Europe, living with a confusion of relatives, until her parents brought her to the United States in the sixth grade. Her father stayed for a couple of months, then left. Jane, meanwhile, barely spoke English, not even small conversation; she was limited to clipped, stultified sentences, as awkward as Eliza Doolittle uttering "How do you do?"

But Jane was gifted. Attending a Chinese academy in Queens to learn English, in just two years she achieved the highest score in her middle school on the Stuyvesant exam, gaining entrance to the elite school.

That, however, was all prologue to the pain of high school, where vicious rumors about her and a football player quickly made her an outcast, only motivating her to become even more of a pariah.

"I never even tried to fit in," she says, even though her mother always reminded her that the bird that stands out the most likely gets shot down first.

By her sophomore year, Jane stopped praying, became an atheist, and dated an Asian ghetto gangsta who dealt knives. The relationship did little to free her from an abiding sense of despair, the origins of which she could never locate. "It's like fighting an invisible enemy," she says, "but the enemy is yourself." The more that others at Stuyvesant pushed themselves academically, the less she tried. If they cared about grades, she wouldn't. The more the academic pressure mounted, the less she gave in to it. Rage consumed her, unspecified, unearthed. She hated her father in his absence. She screamed at her mother in her presence. She didn't learn of her parents' divorce, a secret for several years, until she was about thirteen. It was a lie—her parents' marriage, her place in it, role models, all of it. At the age of sixteen, Jane decided that it would be better to end it all. To be dead. Looking for ways to kill herself, she searched online, where she struck on the idea to overdose on heroin. Someone gave her a stash of the illicit drug, which she viewed as "sort of like your last meal before the prison execution." But it didn't work out that way. Instead, she says, "That's when I learned self-destruction is really fun."

Others at Stuyvesant have come to the same conclusion. While drugs plague high schools everywhere, the problem becomes especially striking when smart, successful students are caught in the act: Jane's classmates are generally otherwise well behaved. Violence of any kind is almost nonexistent at Stuyvesant, with zero "crimes against persons" reported in 2005. Suspensions are negligible as well, with fourteen reported in 2005, less than 10 percent of the average for a school its size. What few suspensions are doled out are usually for what Ms. Archie, the assistant principal, calls "silly things." Sometimes students will buy an escalator key on the black market and activate an escalator when it's supposed to be at a standstill.

"They think it's cool to turn it on," she says.

Some students also think it's cool to trade in illicit substances. Blared a *New York Post* headline a couple of years ago,

## EASY BUY AT STUY 'HIGH'
### TOP KIDS RUNNING AN OPEN DRUG MART

"The school, considered one of the best in the city and which has produced four Nobel laureates, has an outdoor black market where students brazenly exchange drugs, get high and sell illicit cigarettes in broad daylight," the article said. The *Post* writer went on to describe students exchanging what appeared to be LSD and marijuana and inhaling nitrous oxide a block from school on a long, mural-covered wall known simply as the Wall.

It's still called the Wall, or more specifically, the Stoner Wall. And Johnathan Khusid, incoming president of Arista, the Stuyvesant chapter of the National Honor Society, believes that the majority of students have tried pot. But he adds that academics temper drug use.

"If you have a calc test," he says, "you're not going to light a jay."

Many students view cigarettes as more evil than marijuana because tobacco "can give you cancer," he says, while the popular perception is that marijuana isn't a threat "aside from [causing] memory loss."

Demonstrating pot's popularity, one self-professed stoner says he arrived at Stuyvesant on a Monday with about twenty-seven dime bags of marijuana and by Wednesday, after brisk sales, he had one left. Business is expanding. "Acid, hallucinogens are big in this school," the sixteen-year-old says. One day, he says, he came to school with $6 and left with $231 after selling hits of acid at about seven bucks a pop.

Jane, for her part, is trying to abstain from drugs. Already, she says, "the amount of heroin I've done would kill a normal person," and the withdrawal is painful in a way she can't describe. Clarity, though, is beginning to pierce her general fog. "In a strange way," she says, "I've become the kid I always wanted to be. I always wanted to become the coolest kid, the rebel." But she blames no one but herself: "I chose my own path, I just didn't realize the repercussions."

What buoys her now is what's clutched in her pale, thin hand—a dog-eared copy of James Joyce's *A Portrait of the Artist as a Young Man*, a life raft of sorts and required reading in her "Great Books" class, which is taught by the one person in the building she respects, Mr. Grossman, the English chairman. Hers is a curious selection. Where Jane is all fire and fury, her English teacher is soft-spoken and understated. But she is not alone in her high opinion of Mr. Grossman. Many a schoolgirl finds him dreamy, his big blue eyes, his gravelly baritone voice, his gold earring in the left ear. At thirty-nine, he retains a youthfulness with which students can identify. They sense that he understands. That he's been there. That once he himself was a smart kid, a classic underachiever who was adrift in school and in love with music, despite an awful singing voice.

"I didn't want to be a teacher—it wasn't that I didn't want to be a teacher—I wanted to be a rock star," he says.

Teaching, strangely enough, grants him many of the same rewards that being a rock star would have: a stage on which he performs great acts before an adoring audience, an arena where creativity is rewarded, where ideas and art are exchanged, where he can feel his influence on others, like Jane.

They met in her freshman year, Jane and Mr. Grossman, before everything went haywire, when he was observing her class's discussion on Shakespeare's *Much Ado about Nothing*. Jane's hand shot up to volunteer a comment about how such comedies resolve in people pairing off romantically and how one of the characters was like a puppet master. Impressed, Mr. Grossman jotted a note, which he passed to her, saying that maybe Shakespeare was doing the same thing, pulling the play's strings. Mr. Grossman is pulling the strings now, allowing Jane to take his course even though it's supposed to be open only to upperclassmen with at least a 94 average in English, which she doesn't have, not nearly. But he still believes—wants to believe—in Jane. Rarely does he come across a student like Jane, who has what he calls that elusive "spark," a special intangible quality, a gift. So he is giving her one more chance. "I've got my fingers crossed," Mr. Grossman says.

Jane's gift is evident in her poetry:

> *I wish to bestow upon you God's most gracious gifts to me.*
> *no faith*
> *no comfort*
> *no response*
> *no escape*
> *no rescuer*
> *no hope*
> *no happiness*
> *no freedom*
> *no relief*
> *no air to breathe*
> *no will to live*
> *no means to die*
> *every intention of suicide*
> *no one who understands*
> *no conscience*
> *painful pleasure*
> *guilty secrets*
> *shameful truths*
> *disgusting habits*
> *grotesque interior*
> *decaying soul*

*banished father*
*dark thoughts penetrating every cell*
*poisoned blood screaming for*
*more poison*
*hungry veins*
*unsatiable appetite*
*disappointed disapproving dishonest*
*mother*
*and of course no one*
*but voyeurs*
*and most worst intentions*
*my loving curse*
*my cursed love*
*no peace*
*no rest*
*no sleep*
*eternal stupor*
*no way back*
*no lighted path*
*lost best friends*
*fake best friends*
*wasted affections*
*working in waste*
*basking in hate*
*waiting for revenge*
*or God*
*whom I*
*don't believe*
*no real words to express*
*anguished pain.*

The rage in her poetry isn't far from the surface never is. Fuming, Jane can't wait for the day she turns eighteen—just a few months from now—because then she can escape from her mother's supervision.

"The only thing she has over me, except love and shit like that, is that I'm underage," she says.

Jane can't wait to leave high school either. "I'm not sure Stuyvesant was a good thing or not," she says, thinking back on how her depression sank its teeth into her in freshman year and never let go.

"I represent the best and worst about Stuy," she says.

Jane doesn't have to say why. She's smart—fantastically smart—but the question is, will she graduate? She thinks she will, thanks to a surprisingly respectable 86 average, due largely to strong grades she earned before diving into drugs. Some of her teachers are less certain. College seems even more of a question mark. Jane, naturally, did well on the math and verbal sections of the SAT, with a combined score of 1470 out of 1600, but she has no extracurricular activities to speak of and even less of a will to go to college. A photographer recently approached her on the street. He took pictures of her. And now she's thinking of taking off a year before college to become a model.

"He said I was totally gifted," she says of the photographer.

Maybe Jane needs to hear that now, at the beginning of the semester, a time to begin again, when everything is new and possible. Yet she is less certain of herself, especially when it comes to her drug recovery.

"I don't think it's very sustainable," she says, and you can almost hear the echo of a clinician.

"I've gone through this before," she says, then parrots words thrown at her, how one day she will be "liberated from this addiction, blah, blah, blah." But Jane has a different take on her problems.

"I know me," she says. "I'm not optimistic."

CHAPTER SIX

# Open House

ROMEO, THE FOOTBALL CAPTAIN, EXUDES NOTHING BUT optimism as he stalks the escalators and hallways of Stuyvesant on the afternoon of February 16, week three of the semester. And why not? He practically owns the joint like an action hero in his own domain. Last Saturday, he took his first practice SAT, scoring in the 98th percentile. *Pow!* He just received his report card from last semester: a 97 average. *Bam!* This week—and it's not over yet—he's aced tests in biology, French, and math. *Whap!* He still had time to stay up late one night talking with his dad about "stuff," which translates into "girls." He's even allowed himself to hang out with friends after school—a novelty for him—chowing cheap Mexican food and making one-dollar bets on who will get the higher test scores in class.

He's already owed a buck.

And then there's next week. The pilgrimage to Harvard. He'll take the bus to Cambridge, Massachusetts, sit in on classes as a prospective student, and imagine himself there as a college freshman, his hope, his future.

But the present beckons. It's just an hour until Stuyvesant's "Open House," an orchestrated event for next year's incoming students and their parents, a chance for eighth and ninth graders to find out what's in store for them at the legendary pressure cooker of a high school. It's also an opportunity for Romeo to recruit football prospects, which is why he's patrolling the hallways after school, decked out in his royal blue and crimson football jersey—number ninety-eight—searching for the early arrivals.

"We need to get the younger guys," he says, always thinking of the future.

It wasn't so long ago that Romeo himself was recruited. Not for football, though. Stuyvesant was searching for something more important to it than athletes: diversity. Romeo was an ideal candidate. He is half black, half white. That makes him a rare commodity. Nearly thirty years ago, in 1979, 12.9 percent of Stuyvesant's students were black. By 1995, the numbers had dwindled: blacks made up only 4.8 percent of the school—even though nearly 40 percent of the city's public school students were then black.

"The racial demographics of the school have been a source of great embarrassment to educators in New York," says author Jonathan Kozol in *The Shame of the Nation*. Those educators included Ramon C. Cortines, New York City's schools chancellor at the time, who tried to address the troubling trend by launching a little-known program in 1995 called the Math and Science Institute. "As educators, we have a responsibility to ensure that every child has an opportunity to excel," Mr. Cortines said.

School administrators handpicked minority students with potential, like Romeo, for rigorous studies beginning in the summer after their sixth grade and continuing through the seventh and into the eighth grades. They were exposed to everything from algebra to great literature to chess until it came time for them to take the elite public high schools exam, the Stuy test. The idea was to avoid controversial quotas but to level the playing field for students who might not have the resources to hire tutors, attend private academies, or take special test prep courses. The rest was up to them.

"I see that as the beginning of my career," Romeo says.

Little compares to the constant pressure of a program of about sixteen months leading up to a high-stakes test for a boy of thirteen, which is why the pressure of getting into Harvard doesn't compare for a young man of sixteen today.

"I've been through worse," he says.

Romeo is reminded daily of those trials, especially when he eats breakfast, shoveling a tray of scrambled eggs and orange juice while sitting in Stuyvesant's dining hall, overlooking the glistening Hudson River beyond. This is where it happened. He studied for the Stuy test right here at Stuyvesant, a wondrous haven of panoramic views and shining escalators and sparkling students, all of which fueled the ambitions of a prepubescent boy.

"I loved this building," he says. "I knew this is where I wanted to be."

So did his mom.

She still smarts over the indignity of Romeo's rejection from UNIS, the private United Nations International School, when he was about five years old. He had lived with his grandparents in France from the ages of two to four, and when he returned to the United States, he spoke a mix of English and French that school officials took to mean that his verbal skills were not sufficiently developed.

"I wanted to prove them wrong," she says.

What's more, she wanted to prove that her multicultural, biracial child could succeed. "I wanted Romeo to be proof to the world that it can be achieved," she says.

It can and he was. But while he has succeeded, the program that helped prepare him for Stuyvesant hasn't. Black enrollment did inch up almost a percentage point to 5.5 percent by 1997, but it's been in decline since then.

Today, in a school system where more than 70 percent of the students are black or Hispanic, only 2.2 percent of Stuyvesant's students are black, a precipitous drop from 4.8 percent little more than a decade ago, while the number of Hispanics is down from 4.3 percent to 3 percent. White enrollment has dipped from 40 percent to about 39 percent of the school. Asians remain the majority-minority, growing from half of Stuyvesant to about 55 percent of the student body today.

All of which adds up to this: the Math and Science Institute didn't fulfill its mission. Instead the school system changed its name to the Specialized High Schools Institute and expanded its goal beyond preparing only black and Hispanic children for the test, as parents of white and Asian children clamored to gain the same advantage. The unintended result, though, was a decline in blacks and Hispanics at Stuyvesant.

"If you look at the program now, you see very few kids of color," says Ms. Archie, Stuyvesant's assistant principal of pupil services.

Other attempts to balance Stuyvesant's minority enrollment have fallen by the wayside, if not because of ineffectiveness then as a result of changing political winds. For several years, the Discovery program—as unheralded as the Math and Science Institute—allowed students who barely missed the Stuyvesant exam cutoff to get into the school if they took special summer classes and performed well. While the program didn't specifically target minorities, it had the same effect by qualifying what it termed "disadvantaged" students, whose families, among other things, relied on public assistance or were recent immigrants speaking a primary language other than English.

As many as twenty students a year gained admission to Stuyvesant even though they scored sometimes as much as fourteen points below the cutoff, school officials say. But as academic quotas have come under fire in recent years, the Discovery program has quietly taken a hiatus at Stuyvesant. Over the last two years, school officials say they have not accepted any students who failed to reach the exam cutoff. They say, however, they have not abolished the Discovery program.

The issue of diversity still percolates in full view at Stuyvesant. In a meeting of the advisory School Leadership Team at the beginning of the semester, students, teachers, and parents are given a handout that includes the explicit goal of a "more proactive outreach to minority student candidates, and new organizational resources necessary to increase enrollment of African American and Hispanic students." And in a subsequent page-one story, the *New York Times* reminds readers of the intractable problem at Stuyvesant and two other public exam high schools. Under the headline "In Elite Schools, a Dip in Blacks and Hispanics," the author writes, "City education officials said they were at a loss to explain the changes at the three high schools despite years of efforts to broaden the applicant pools."

Policy makers and others strain to identify the cause as well. Some say that private schools more aggressively recruit promising minority students, siphoning prospects from high schools like Stuyvesant. Others say schools and teachers in predominantly black and Hispanic neighborhoods sometimes fail to adequately prepare their students for the kind of math needed to pass the Stuy entrance test. And then there is the perennial problem of resources: white and Asian families have in many cases the financial wherewithal that others don't to pay for the costly tutoring needed to help their children win a seat. Ms. Archie, also the assistant principal in charge of admissions programs, remains perplexed by the problem.

"There's so much more that has to be done," she says.

The problem is not only that there are few blacks and Hispanics at Stuyvesant: that fact is also glaringly obvious. Students of different races and ethnicities segregate themselves in the school.

"Race is part of Stuy, no question, everyone has a label," says Mr. Polazzo, the coordinator of student affairs.

Predominantly white seniors stake out territory by the second-floor "senior bar," prime real estate near the school's bridge entrance, and underclassmen don't dare tread there unless invited. "We were told not to sit there because we'd be likely to get beaten up," writes a freshman in an opinion piece in the Stuyvesant Standard newspaper.

About ten feet away, Asian seniors have a lock on space along a wide hallway, and nary a non-Asian walks through. From there, status works in inverse relation to floor number: the higher the floor, the lower the caste. Asian juniors have territory by the gym on the third floor that is dubbed the "Asian atrium." Indians and Middle Eastern students—known here as "brown people"—occupy parts of the fourth floor. Blacks and Hispanics have a slice of land on the fifth floor by the dining hall—an area known as the "ghetto." Asian sophomores own the sixth-floor "Asian bar."

As for freshmen, they have such low status, regardless of race or ethnicity, they have to climb up to floors seven, eight, and nine for refuge. Apparently the highest floor, ten, is too toxic for anything but actual classes. White freshmen have lately carved out a niche near the second-floor staircase landing that looks more like a romper room where small bodies collide with high frequency.

The city's boroughs demarcate several other Stuyvesant cliques: Jews from Manhattan's Upper West Side, Russian immigrants from Brooklyn, and gangsta Asians from Queens. But there are no designations for the typical high school divisions—nerds or their opposites, the beautiful people—and that's hardly a saving grace. Virtually everyone's a nerd at Stuyvesant, even the beautiful people.

"At Stuyvesant, it's cool to have a higher average; at other schools it's nerdy," says freshman Samantha Whitmore, who is a nerd and a member of the beautiful people. "You can raise your hand a lot [in class], and people are not going to say you're a nerd." Even more, she says, "people disdain you if you have a low average."

The others who make up the rest of Stuyvesant's diaspora include people who go directly home from school, people who do drugs, people who do drugs but do well in school, people who play the fantasy Magic card game, the theater crowd, and now the recently anointed cuddle puddle, who are squeezed on the second floor between the white and Asian senior factions.

"The school is completely segregated," says junior Kieren James-Lubin, who is half black and half white like his friend Romeo. Then he quickly amends his statement, so stark are its implications. "Not completely, but mostly."

When an Eastern European girl tried to sit on the sixth-floor Asian bar, she says, she was summarily told to leave. A Korean girl who made friends with white students says she drew dirty looks from Asian friends, who called her a "twinkie"—yellow on the outside, white on the inside. An Indian freshman called an Asian boy a "chink"; the Asian boy responded by punching him in the eye, Ms. Archie says.

Students blame the problem on themselves.

"I think we self-segregate ourselves," says senior Liana-Marie Lien, the daughter of Vietnamese and Chinese immigrants, who settles in the second-floor Asian sector.

"At Stuy, it seems like more often than not, we stick to our own segregated cliques without a second thought," says an opinion piece in the *Spectator* newspaper. "We must strive to eliminate the sense of division."

Students do try. A talent show that celebrates the school's ethnic and racial melting pot invokes students to "Get your diversity on." A junior of Indian descent says she attempts to be color-blind: "I try not to define myself" through ethnicity. Her friends, however, do it for her, defining her as "the brown girl who hangs out with the Asians." And she says, "That's what I don't like about Stuyvesant. There are a lot of cliques." It's hard to avoid reminders. A flyer for an upcoming Black Students League meeting asks, "Have you ever been discriminated against b/c of your race?" Someone felt inspired to scrawl on it an emphatic answer: "Yeah!"

And yet, in a reflection of the contradictions and complexities of Stuyvesant, a tradition of tolerance persists. Being different is the norm. One out of five students is a first-generation American, and about a third are themselves immigrants, most commonly from distant points of the globe, including China, Russia, and Bangladesh. That explains why there is a Bengali Culture Club, not to mention the Chinese Students Association, the German Club, the Guyanese Culture Club, the Indian Culture Club, the Japanese Honor Society, the Romanian Club, the Filipino Club, the Greek Club, and the Korean Club.

The immigrant experience, where education is king, is infused in the Stuyvesant culture. So is the American Dream, which junior Katherine Kim can attest to. Her parents journeyed from Korea to the United States in the hopes of giving their children a better opportunity. "They came here for me," she says.

Her parents toil seven days a week running a Broadway deli, hoping for nothing less than Ivy League colleges for their two children. Her father, Katherine says, "wanted us to study; he didn't want us to taste the reality he was going through, the harsh reality." Katherine's brother made it, garnering a perfect SAT score and a scholarship to Columbia University. Now it's Katherine's turn.

"It's junior year—do or die," she says.

Six days a week, she attends a private Korean academy to get a leg up on the competition, taking classes in physics and precalculus. But it's not simply the coursework that sets the place apart. When Katherine enters the Kappa Community Center, a tidy little building hidden away from a main thoroughfare in Queens, it's as if she's been instantly transported back to an Asian sanctuary, led by tradition, respect, and a strict adherence to the rules.

At the threshold, Katherine removes her shoes and bows respectfully to the academy's revered principal. Inside, it is as quiet as a temple. Students shut doors with a light touch so as not to disturb others in deep academic contemplation. There is not an iota of desktop graffiti. Students clean up after themselves. A sheet of paper taped to a wall informs, "Excuses must be legitimate and true or consequences will follow." Outside the principal's office, a bank of thirty-two television monitors keeps track of every classroom, every student, every study hall. Classroom doors are adorned with gold labels of the names of famous American colleges to remind students of their goal: MIT. YALE. HARVARD. BROWN. UPENN. CORNELL. JOHNS HOPKINS. UC BERKELEY.

There should be another door: STUYVESANT. For many immigrant parents, that's why they first bring their children here. It's a collective mind-set, to get into the great American high school, the key to the great American college, which leads to the great American Dream, which is becoming a doctor or a lawyer or a professional of another ilk and taking care of the rest of the family. But first, parents clamor to get their children into this Asian academy, the demand for which is so great that despite its $300 to $400 monthly cost, it doesn't advertise. It doesn't need to. It is forced to turn away droves of applicants because it doesn't have enough space for them.

"They're all crazy about sending their kids to Stuyvesant," says the academy's principal, Michael Son, who is himself one of those parents. His oldest child is entering Stuyvesant next year.

If you get into that school, he says, the thinking goes, "You're on your way."

For other immigrants, like fifteen-year-old Daniel Alzugaray, the way to Stuyvesant is a solitary path. He started studying for the Stuy test a year before he even arrived on these shores.

Born in Cuba, the son of a Russian man and a Cuban woman, Daniel was living in Portugal with his mother and his American stepfather when they told him about Stuyvesant, the famous American school. So he went out and bought a study guide to prepare for the entrance exam. Just months after settling in the United States, he took the test and passed. But it still feels like a dream to Daniel, as it did when he first caught sight of the Hudson River from the windows of Stuyvesant.

"When I saw the view from the lunchroom, I said, 'How can it be?' It's surreal," Daniel says.

He still finds himself marveling at the sights. "I see the Empire State Building and say, 'Wow.'" Sometimes the freshman daydreams about the Internet service Google Earth and imagines how it shows the globe from the great distance of a satellite, then zooms in to Stuyvesant to where he sits, daydreaming in art class.

It might be a marvel that Daniel made the cutoff for Stuyvesant, given that he didn't even start speaking English until he was about ten, except that such circumstances are common at the school, where students are fluent in more than fifty-nine languages. The staccato of foreign speech that echoes through the hallways is part of the messy, discordant life of Stuyvesant, where students are anything but homogeneous. Different religions coexist, whether represented by the Seekers Christian Fellowship or a "Grand Shavuot Ice Cream Party" for the school's considerable Jewish population. Meanwhile, middle-class and upper-middle-class students regularly interact with poor kids, who make up nearly 17 percent of the student body, a figure based on the number eligible for free lunch.

And in one of the most visible signs of Stuyvesant's diversity, students openly express their sexual orientation. That includes members of the Gay Lesbian and Straight Spectrum. Once a year, droves of students commit to a "Day of Silence" to express their support for gender diversity. If you ask, they will hand you a slip of paper:

Please understand my reasons for not speaking today. I support lesbian, gay, bisexual, and transgender rights. People who are silent today believe that laws and attitudes should be inclusive of people of all sexual orientations and gender identities. The day of silence is to draw attention to those who have been silenced by hatred, oppression, and prejudice. Think about the voices you are not hearing. What can you do to end the silence?

Faculty don't interfere. Sometimes, actually, faculty get in the act. Such is the case with "Gay Day," an event in the first-floor lobby, where a teacher strums a guitar in solidarity with students. The affair has the staid feel of an ordinary PTA meeting, where chocolate-chip cookies are sold, except for a few telling details. A girl in a white satin robe presides over a twenty-five-cent marriage booth where same-sex kids kiss. For sale are T-shirts that read "Captain Fabulous!" and "LESBIONIC WOMAN." And a gaggle of cross-dressers enter in full regalia: high heels, purple spandex, gold chains. A teacher passing by mutters that such a spectacle would never fly in a more conservative place like Kansas: "Only in New York," she says.

Such an event wouldn't always play well at Stuyvesant, which may be why it occurs in June, near the end of the school year, not on this afternoon in mid February when hundreds of parents and incoming students are packing the auditorium for the school's Open House. Mr. Teitel, the principal, is standing at the podium in a conservative black suit, saying, "I've never seen any other school like it." He's talking about Stuyvesant's wealth of course offerings in math, science, and the humanities. But he could just as easily be talking about the school's wealth of diversity.

> *To be yourself is all that you can do*
> —desktop graffiti, Stuyvesant High School

# CHAPTER SEVEN

# Like a Polaroid

FOURTH PERIOD  ROOM 401. MATH RESEARCH CLASS.
The room contains all the telltale signs of a typical high school class:
boys in peach fuzz, straining to reach adulthood. Girls scribbling notes
not having anything to do with classwork. A poster of wild-haired Einstein, who's quoted saying, "The truth of a theory is in your mind, not in
your eyes." But off to the side, by the front of the class, listening intently
to the teacher discuss arcane math, is an anomaly that betrays the eyes:
a little boy topped off by bed-head vectors of blond fluff, not unlike the
messy mop Einstein reflects back. At four feet five inches and fifty-five
pounds, the little boy is dwarfed by many of his classmates. His feet
barely touch the floor from the perch of his swivel chair. Buried inside a
big blue parka to ward off the mid-February chill, he doesn't look anything like a surly teenager, and he's not. He's not even old enough to be
a member of next year's incoming freshman class. He's ten years old.
And if the principal is right that there's nothing like Stuyvesant, there's
certainly no one like Milo Beckman.

Named after a family friend's cat, Milo was born with a compulsion
to learn, process information, master knowledge. At the age of two,

while staying at a Florida hotel with his family, he would run from door to door, reciting four-digit room numbers. By two and a half, he was reading. When he was three, he would wind down at night in bed by reciting numbers in sequence: four, eight, twelve, sixteen . . . Or if that didn't work, then one plus one equals two, two plus two equals four . . . until he reached into the thousands, or into the ether of his dreams.

In preschool, Milo couldn't fathom why other children couldn't read and write as he did: "I remember feeling, 'Why aren't these kids writing normally? Why aren't they reading?'" All the other children would gather around Milo, like their teacher, as he read a story to them. By four, he wrote a novel, science fiction about an evil babysitter. Around then, friends encouraged his parents, struggling entrepreneurs who run the New York International Children's Film Festival, to test his intelligence. But the test failed: he hit the ceiling in every category. So he took another test designed for gifted children. The result: Milo was off the charts, somewhere between one in ten thousand and one in a million.

"It's not like there's something you can do to make it happen," says his mother, Emily Shapiro, who teaches a birthing class. "His memory is unlike anything I've witnessed before."

Adds Milo, "Dad said I have a memory like a Polaroid camera."

On his fourth birthday, Milo stared at a subway map and, from his mind's eye, wrote seventy pages about all the possible permutations of getting from Coney Island in the far reaches of Brooklyn to their home, then on Fulton Street in Lower Manhattan. "I couldn't get him to open any of his presents," his father says. His mother would take Milo on some of his elaborate subway routes, and the longer the trip, the better. Sometimes, when they reached their stop, they didn't even bother stepping off the platform; they'd just turn around, hop on another subway, and head home. It was about the journey, not the final destination.

Around that time, his parents were surprised to discover that Milo had created a spreadsheet of the solar system and written several chapters of a book he had never mentioned. So his parents decided it was time to hire a tutor. Neighbor Tim Novikoff, then an undergraduate student at NYU majoring in math, would come over, sit on the floor with Milo, and the two would talk math, practicing arithmetic without the aid of pen or paper, reciting such exercises as two times two equals four, two times four equals eight, two times eight equals sixteen.

"A four-year-old doing arithmetic in his head, that's nuts, that's crazy," Mr. Novikoff says. "He was born that way."

Milo would grasp concepts immediately and run with them. He knew how to compute area. He quickly learned prime factorization— that, for instance, twenty-four equals two times two times two times three, leaving Mr. Novikoff in awe.

"I'm thinking, on a selfish level, I can't believe I'm getting a chance to have this opportunity," he says. "It almost felt like an honor."

Sometimes it felt like a struggle. Milo's mind was so supple that he was easily distracted, his hyperactive brain wandering to random objects in his room while the tutor tried to lasso his charge's attention back to math. Eventually, Mr. Novikoff told Milo's parents that the little boy wasn't ready for a math tutor. A few years later, when Mr. Novikoff was in his first year teaching at Stuyvesant, he agreed to tutor Milo again. It was a matter of mercy. Then seven, Milo was distraught in his elementary school math class. It was too easy. He was bored. He broke down in fits.

"I used to drag him crying, to school . . . literally yanking his arm," his mother says.

Milo had already taught himself elementary school math, using a computer program to plow through multiplication, long division, fractions. Mr. Novikoff took him to the next level, teaching Milo high school math, including algebra, geometry, number theory. Finally, Mr. Novikoff felt that Milo was ready to take a math class at Stuyvesant. Maybe it was genius meeting good fortune. A neighbor becomes a math teacher, recommends Milo to Mr Jaye, a math chairman who has a congenital disregard for school rules and regulations and, thus, has no compunctions about allowing a ten-year-old prodigy to take classes at Stuyvesant without passing the entrance exam or being officially enrolled.

Milo started taking classes at Stuyvesant when he was eight. This year, his parents officially pulled him out of his fifth-grade class at P.S. 234 a couple of blocks from Stuyvesant. He was getting little out of it. Now he's homeschooled in English, history, and science, while he attends four classes at Stuyvesant, making him, in effect, a freshman without official portfolio. In addition to his math research class, Milo's taking a Stuyvesant course called math team and another in trigonometry. He's also in a class where students learn to build stereo speakers because Mr. Jaye simply thought it would be fun. But Milo can't get enough math. At home, Milo helps his older sister, Willa, with her seventh-grade math homework. "Only when she asks," he notes. She asks for help on problems like, if you know the radius of a bicycle wheel, what is its circumference? Milo practically frowns at the simplicity of the answer: multiply the radius by two, then multiply it by pi, which he recites to the twenty-fifth decimal place:

$$3.1415926535897932384626433$$

"It's a mixed blessing, and I think Milo knows that," his mother says of his gift. "It comes with pressure. It comes with feeling odd. It's not been easy and glamorous. . . . There was a period he hated when people called him a genius."

Milo adds, "It's sort of like name-calling." It's odd to see him nodding in agreement with his mother. He looks too young to comprehend the complexity of his situation. He looks like a fifth grader, small and cub-like and unformed, or not fully formed, not even close, and he sounds like a fifth grader, complete with the squeaky voice of a little boy, and yet what comes out are the elaborate words of an adult, the end product of a thought process too advanced for someone housed inside a ten-year-old's body.

"He didn't ask to be born with this brain, and he didn't necessarily want it," his mother says.

When she thought about asking a psychologist to evaluate Milo in the third grade, he responded in horror: "But, Mom, everyone will *know*."

"It was like a deep, dark secret," she says.

Only rarely does Milo betray his age. It reveals itself at the most unexpected of moments, when he pauses from, say, proving the Pythagorean theorem and chirps that if he does well in school, his father will reward him with a pizza party. Even when you are a child prodigy, prizes like that still matter.

They also almost reaffirm that Milo is just a regular fifth grader, except that he is all too aware that he's not. Mr. Novikoff, his former math tutor, was heartbroken when Milo once confided, *I wish I was normal.* Milo still wrestles with the separation from his fifth-grade friends. "It's sort of, I mean, I'd like to be with kids my age," he says. " . . . It's kind of weird because I'm not with them anymore." What's also strange, he says, is that he's attending a high school where students are nearly twice his age—and twice his size. "I'm kind of used to doing this when I'm talking to people," he says, demonstrating how he has to crane his neck, his big brown saucer eyes staring up at the fictional teenager standing before him, an imposing giant.

High school is tough enough for teenagers; for a ten-year-old, it's exponentially harder. Not that Milo grapples with the subject matter. Math is still a piece of cake. It's just that he's not used to getting an hour of math homework a night. His fifth-grade pals get about twenty minutes of homework altogether.

"It's intense, you could say."

Though he doesn't say it, high school is also lonely. It's not easy to find a teenager who wants to hang out with a ten-year-old. There is one, though—Daniel, the fifteen-year-old Cuban immigrant, who takes math research class with Milo. One day they went to get ice cream. Milo ordered chocolate-chip cookie dough, his favorite. At the counter, Daniel asked Milo how to spell the word for ten to the hundredth power, or the number one followed by a hundred zeros. Milo coolly replied, "*G-o-o-g-o-l*" not "*G-o-o-g-l-e*," the famous Internet search engine. Daniel was impressed. It was a trick question. "No one ever gets that," Daniel said. Milo brushed it off, saying, "That's my typical quiz question." Daniel upped the ante. What, he asked, is 36 times 36? The ten-year-old thought for a split second, then blurted it out: 1,296. How did he compute it so quickly in his head? Simple. His formula: $(30 + 6) \times (30 + 6)$, or $(30 + 6)^2$.

A friendship was born.


Milo has made another friend, his math research teacher, Jan Siwanowicz. They make an unlikely pair. At six foot three, Mr. Siwanowicz towers over Milo. A bedraggled, hulking figure with long, stringy blond locks and clunky tortoiseshell glasses hiding eyes red from sleepless nights, Mr. Siwanowicz has trouble remembering how old he is until he's reminded what year it is. He computes the math, then emits an output: he's twenty-nine years old.

But Mr. Siwanowicz used to be Milo.

Mr. Siwanowicz too was a math whiz. The son of an engineer and a statistician, he was born and raised in Warsaw, Poland, where as a child he read math books for amusement. In preschool, he counted not the traditional way—one, two, three—but in binary, using zeros and ones, like a computer program. After his family moved to the United States, he made it through several qualifying rounds in high school to represent Poland in the international mathematics Olympiads, winning bronze. Later he confirmed his extraordinary talent, becoming a winner in the prestigious William Lowell Putnam Mathematical Competition, effectively making him one of the top undergraduate mathematicians in North America. There was only one hiccup: he had already flunked out of one college and was well on his way to failing out of another.

"I stopped caring," he says.

While attending college in Poland, he stopped showing up to class. He stopped studying. He stopped eating. He doesn't know why. Alarmed, his parents brought him back to New York to convalesce and enrolled him at City College, where he proceeded to fail out again. In one course, he didn't attend any of the classes but aced the final, and still failed. In another, he was so incensed by the contents of a final exam, which he felt didn't reflect the coursework, that he handed it in blank. Just shy of gaining his undergraduate degree, his grade point average stands at a paltry 1.6.

Mr. Siwanowicz isn't supposed to be teaching. He doesn't have a license, which requires a college degree. He only has a high school diploma. He lives in a dusty room in his parents' apartment in Queens. He barely gets by on about $1,300 a month after taxes as a school aide at Stuyvesant, which is why he has to patrol the library, despite the efforts of Mr. Jaye, the math chairman, to release Mr. Siwanowicz from the lowly monitoring task. Mr. Jaye, ever the troublemaker, hired Mr. Siwanowicz to unofficially teach math research to freshmen and sophomores for one compelling reason: Mr. Jaye recognized Mr. Siwanowicz's math gifts in the same way he understands that ten-year-old Milo needs a place like Stuyvesant if he is to reach his potential. So a student who doesn't belong is being taught by a teacher who's not supposed to teach, and yet the two of them may be the most innately gifted people in the school.

Mr. Siwanowicz still struggles with bouts of depression. The episodes last about a week, then release him for a few weeks before ineluctably returning. He tries to cope by isolating himself in his cluttered room at his parents' home, listening to a relentless, orderly techno beat from Internet radio, which sounds to him like the reassuring rhythm of a march. The hard part comes after night falls, when he ponders the morning and the bright light of the day again.

"I know I'll wake up tomorrow and forget everything," he says, expressionless, a single tear streaking down his cheek.

Mr. Siwanowicz doesn't know if he'll finish college. He doesn't seem to care. He glazes at the mind-numbing thought of all the paperwork involved in being reinstated as an undergraduate student at City College. "I just don't have the mind to comprehend the bureaucracy," he says. And yet he wonders how he'll become a licensed math teacher, which is all that he wants, a calling he discovered when he was a high school senior and volunteered to teach a class. That moment, however, seems far away. He barely remembers the details of his own past. He seems almost embarrassed by the present.

"I'm not a role model," he says. "The last thing I want is the kids to grow up like me." But it's the kids who sustain him, "saving his life, giving him purpose," Mr. Jaye says. It gets Mr. Siwanowicz up in the morning, the urgency of getting to "the kiddies," as he affectionately calls them. In return, he imparts his sophisticated knowledge of math in gentle doses.

Mr. Novikoff, Milo's former tutor, once remarked how lucky Mr. Siwanowicz was for being so good at math, a strange compliment coming from someone who as a math teacher is skilled in the subject himself. Mr. Novikoff will never forget how his colleague responded. *Yes, I am lucky, but everything has its price,* Mr. Siwanowicz said. Mr. Novikoff just hopes Milo turns out well. He has every confidence that the little boy will find his way. Milo is motivated, he's well-adjusted, he's resilient. But like Mr. Siwanowicz, Milo suffers from bouts of insomnia, and if his teacher's experience is any guide, genius alone isn't enough to overcome life's intractable problems.

CHAPTER EIGHT

# Sing!

PROBLEMS ARE ESCALATING IN ROOM 339 AT 5 P.M. ON Friday, February 17, where a defiant girl is surrounded by a group of frustrated students. The girl, sitting cross-legged in a black swivel chair, won't budge. Neither will those circling her. The shades are nearly drawn, leaving a stark fluorescent sheen on the gathering. A window is cracked open, though it does little to let the tension escape.

"I would love to do something I'm proud of," says the girl, Xevion.

A boy shoots back that this isn't about doing earth-shattering work. Xevion frowns. That's not what she wanted to hear.

Then it comes out: Xevion, the best singer in the junior class, doesn't want to sing Aretha Franklin's classic, "Respect." It's about her own self-respect. Xevion doesn't only like to challenge her friend Romeo at lunch. She wants to challenge herself, and she thinks the famous R&B vocal is just too "cheesy." She'd rather perform something less obvious from the more contemporary R&B pop singer Deborah Cox. Xevion is thinking that the idea is to move people, and if you don't, what's the point? She isn't about to be intimidated by this group.

"When you're dealing with my mother," she says, "a room full of

83

teenagers won't scare you." Her mother, a Jamaican immigrant, always told her daughter to look people in the eye and speak her mind. Which she's doing now, assuring the juniors surrounding her that she will find the right song: "Give me until tonight."

Such is the plight of an idealistic diva and a school play in progress, which is what they are rehearsing after school on this icy February day. The stakes of putting on a play are high at Stuyvesant because this isn't an ordinary high school production. This is one of the biggest events of the year. Seniors, juniors, and a combined sophomore and freshman class engage in fierce competition against one another to stage the best musical. Several hundred students from every grade mobilize in a rare show of class unity to create virtually every aspect of each production, from intricate costumes to ornate sets to original scripts to a dizzying array of dance numbers ranging from hip-hop to Irish jigs. The only things the students don't create are the melodies, which are borrowed from famous songs, but even then, they invent new lyrics to fit their story line. The competition—three plays a night repeated over three days—is such a big deal that an exclamation point is a permanent appendage of its name: Sing! Every performance sells out—filling more than eight hundred seats a night—generating a whopping school profit of about $30,000. But for the students, the prize is something vastly more precious to them: class bragging rights.

For the adults, Sing! is little more than a distraction, especially on this Friday when Mr. Jaye has his own problems. For one, Mr. Siwanow-icz is still patrolling the library, despite Mr. Jaye's impassioned plea to the principal. For another, Mr. Jaye just emerged from a kitchen cabinet meeting, where he's still fuming about butting heads again with his nemesis, Ms. Damesek, the assistant principal of organization. She wants more faculty to patrol the hallways. He doesn't. "The perfect school for her would have no students," he says. Ms. Damesek's stance on school security especially galls Mr. Jaye because he recommended her for the job at Stuyvesant, and now all they do is argue. He's called her unmentionable names; she doesn't take the criticism lightly. So it goes.

Meanwhile, Mr. Jaye recently received word that he passed the principal's licensing exam, bringing him one step closer to taking the top job at the New Jersey high school—unless Mr. Teitel, Stuyvesant's principal, retires, a prospect with no hope, even though Mr. Jaye continues to harbor some.

"It's frustrating knowing you're ready to be the starting pitcher but you have to watch the World Series," he says.

Mr. Teitel has no intention of retiring, despite this Friday. As principal, he sees himself as the equivalent of a chief executive of a corporation with a budget of about $14 million, and right now, that budget is looking tight. He's preparing to hire counselors for the short-staffed guidance office, but that means he may have to let go of as many as a half-dozen teachers. It's the immutable law of any school budget: what it giveth in one area, it taketh away in another.

On top of that, Mr. Teitel is just beginning to realize that he underestimated student vitriol over the looming installation of scanners to record attendance. What's more, he's still grappling with the fallout from the cuddle puddle controversy, which seems to have the half-life of a nuclear meltdown, and it's gone all the way to the top of the food chain. He's already had a personal sit-down with New York City Schools Chancellor Joel I. Klein to discuss the controversial article. And before February's done, he'll find himself trying to placate worried parents on the School Tone Committee and at a Parents' Association meeting who want to know what in the cuddle puddle world is happening to their children.

At least, though, Mr. Teitel has resolved a couple of other controversies. Teachers have reluctantly agreed to take on the various monitoring duties stipulated in their new contract. Even better, they have agreed to flip over their time cards once a day, which leaves only the question of who will flip them back at the end of the day. Mr. Teitel has found an ideal candidate: himself. He is not above a little flipping. That, he can live with. But his job as principal is another matter. "It's hard," he says. "It'll be the nights that will force me to retire."

Mr. Grossman, the English chairman who helped the principal defuse the time card imbroglio, is preoccupied with a grave matter of his own: Jane. Until the senior recently returned to school, Mr. Grossman worried she would turn up dead. When she did turn up after a stint in drug rehab, he was shocked by how "scary skinny" she was. On her first day back in his English class, she raised her hand but didn t get called on. It wasn't his fault. The students are so advanced that he lets them call on one another. Her turn never came up. She felt slighted, as if her fellow students weren't willing to take her back. She cried a little. "It was just heartbreaking to me," he says. Mr. Grossman can't help but think that she's smart, that she's a great kid. He just doesn't know if she's going to make it in this class, let alone in life. For now, though, he is thankful for the little things. Jane is coming to class.

"I can feel the tension in my chest," he says.

Such concerns make Sing! seem almost trivial. And yet, the outcome of the musical competition weighs heavily on scores of students, especially seniors, because the way they see it, what hangs in the balance is history, or an attempt to avoid making it. The seniors never lose—well, almost never.

"If the seniors don't win," says Liz London, executive producer of their musical, "that would be horrifying."

According to school lore, when Sing! first replaced a popular student-faculty talent show in 1973, the seniors revolted by stumbling onstage drunk—or at least appearing so—as part of an over-the-top parody that offended the judges' sensibilities. Even with Paul Reiser, the future television star, as band director, the seniors couldn't avoid a last-place finish. The combined freshman and sophomore classes put on a good show, featuring a young Tim Robbins in the lead role, but he hadn't won an Oscar yet, and his thespian talents couldn't overcome a production that ran way too long. The contest came down to this: the juniors "sang well, their story was peppy, and so they won by a landslide," according to *Stuyvesant High School: The First 100 Years*, a project of faculty and alumni.

Seniors have never taken the competition lightly again. Since their debut debacle, they have dominated Sing!, except when struck by a peculiar affliction that they refer to in hushed tones: the six-year curse. About every six years, so goes the curse, the stars are misaligned, up is down, and the seniors lose in an ignominious Stuyvesant upset worse than ending up at their safety college. It's been seven years since they lost.

They're overdue.

Making matters more precarious, the performances have been moved up to late March from early April, bowing to Ms. Damesek, the assistant principal of organization, who makes the unpopular but wise decision to give students more time to focus on studying for the AP exams in May. The Student Union throws its own monkey wrench into Sing! by changing the scoring system this year. Each play will be rated on a scale from one to ten instead of one to three to give judges more latitude to express subtleties in their scoring. But the scoring changes could inject an element of uncertainty as well, foiling the predictability of the seniors' triumphant finish, which is just the way the upstart juniors want it.

"We're definitely going to win," crows eleventh grader Liam Ahern, who looks the part of confident codirector, which he is, ready-made in a red turtleneck, silver necklace, and dark-rimmed rectangular glasses.

Liam has reason to be confident. A few days have passed, and Xevion, the great junior vocalist, has relented and agreed to sing "Respect."

"I caved," she says, but then considers the upside. "It's a challenging song, and they promised if I did this song, we could do a different type of Sing!, more meaningful" next year when they're seniors. The prospect seems to buoy Xevion. She's given up her dream of becoming president of the United States. "He doesn't make enough money, and he's always under fire," she says. But perhaps hashing out vocal choices is good practice in the art of negotiation for a girl who now aspires to be a diplomat.

Confidence is at a lower ebb a couple of days later in the auditorium, where scant freshmen and sophomores are huddled in darkened front seats, trying to make sense of a script in which the main character, Pandora, gets fed up; organ transplants are plentiful; people live too long; Michael Jackson, John Lennon, and Napoleon intermingle in the underworld; and it's up to Hades, ruler of the netherworld by way of Greek mythology, another esoteric Stuyvesant specialty, to save the day.

Codirector Taylor Shung is wondering where everyone is. "We have some people absent, and it's frustrating," she says.

It doesn't help matters that a glass display in the nearby first-floor lobby lists the previous winners of Sing!, reminding her that soph/frosh, as they are known, has never come out on top. She isn't optimistic about their chances this year. But then again, she and her cadre of underclassmen have trafficked a secret copy of the juniors' script, which they think is weak. And in this topsy-turvy year, with all the rule changes, she believes that just about anything is possible.

CHAPTER NINE

# The Natural

OUTSIDE, IT'S SNOWING. INSIDE ROOM 231, DURING fifth period, it's the late nineteenth century, a topsy-turvy period in history when an acquisitive United States, ordained by "manifest destiny" and the "white man's burden" to bring civilization to the rest of world, is looking overseas to conquer new lands.

"Who wants to be Santa Claus?" the teacher asks.

A hand volunteers in the back. Who wants to play the part of the Cuban boy? Who wants to be the Filipino girl? Others pitch in. But a student interjects, saying he sees stereotypes in the class handout, a cartoon of children representing nations that are the objects of America's desire. In the drawing, the Cuban boy is depicted with Jheri curls. The Filipino girl is in tattered clothing. Santa Claus, a stand-in for the United States, is condescending, asking, "Have you children been good and behaving yourselves?"

"Do you see a modicum of racism?" the teacher asks.

Suddenly, even though dancing snowflakes beckon beyond the windowsill, she has riveted their attention. No longer are they talking about stultifying, antediluvian history that has no bearing on their teenage

89

lives. Now the conversation is about racism and stereotypes, pertinent issues in a class of thirty-two students, twenty-one of whom are Asian, many immigrants or first-generation Americans.

It's about here, now, Thursday, March 2, just over a month into the semester.

"What if God is black, or Asian?" wonders an Asian boy in the back.

It's not quite on point, but it doesn't matter; the teacher has them thinking, and she goes with it, grabbing the momentum, punctuating the air with small, chalk-smudged hands, exhorting her students to speak, as if she were a conductor, eliciting the right combination of notes from an orchestra.

"My, my, my, I couldn't have done that any better!" she enthuses at one student.

"The man, Chris!" she emotes at another.

"Give it to you, excellent!" she showers praise on a third.

Jennifer Lee is in her element, a diminutive teacher in perpetual motion who commands complete authority in this U.S. history class—except for one thing: she isn't their teacher. She isn't even being paid to stand before them. At twenty-six, she barely looks older than the students: a beautiful young woman with long, silky black hair framing a delicate, open face. Ms. Lee is herself a student, earning her master's degree at Teachers College, the vaunted program at Columbia University uptown. As part of her graduation requirements, she has to instruct a class as a student teacher, which is why she's here at Stuyvesant. She isn't just teaching. She's gaining classroom experience. But already, she's a natural. The strange thing is, she didn't intend any of this.

"I never saw myself as a future teacher," she says.

Nor did others, like attorney Jim Cocoros. But then, "You come to a point in life when you're completely miserable," he says. About seven years ago, he asked himself what he liked to do and the answer wasn't the law. It was math. Now thirty-three, he teaches precalculus at Stuyvesant, and notwithstanding his student loans from law school, this is where he's meant to be.

The same, however, cannot be said for all his colleagues.

While the students have to take a test to gain entrance to the school, the teachers don't. In fact, Stuyvesant draws from the same pool of teachers as any other school in the public school system. Some parents and teachers themselves say Stuyvesant has drawn a handful of weak teachers, blaming the teachers' contract, which for many years set aside vacancies for teachers with the most seniority. Teachers looking to transfer from one school to another could also bump a teacher with less seniority out of a position. The result, in some cases, was that older teachers who were looking to coast in their final years before retirement would transfer to Stuyvesant as a kind of final resting place—a vacation of sorts—where the common wisdom was that students would learn no matter what, in spite of bad teaching or even no teaching, say many parents, teachers, and school administrators.

"I'll be honest and tell you, the transfer system was a mixed bag," Mr. Teitel says. "Some people came and they were terrific and others came thinking this was going to be a three-year retirement before 'I decided it's time to retire.'"

When Mr. Polazzo, the government teacher and coordinator of student affairs, arrived at Stuyvesant six years ago, "teachers told me, a hundred percent of the students are smarter than seventy percent of the teachers." He adds, "Stuy can hide the flaws of some teachers."

Author Sol Stern, who graduated from Stuyvesant, as did his two sons, calls it "the school's dirty little secret" in his book *Breaking Free: Public School Lessons and the Imperative of School Choice.* "Incompetence was randomly distributed at the school," he writes.

The complaint is echoed nationally. "With a few notable exceptions, teaching is attracting fewer top college graduates than it once did," says the spring 2006 report of the Teaching Commission, a group that comprises leaders in government, business, and education, citing problems with inadequate teacher compensation and training programs.

In the mid-1990s, then Stuyvesant principal Jinx Cozzi Perullo complained that she had no say in filling as many as half the school's teacher vacancies in a given year because of the rules of so-called "seniority transfers." School administrators also complained about "integration transfers," another provision of the teachers' contract that gave black and Hispanic teachers preference in switching into schools, like Stuyvesant, lacking diversity. Their complaint wasn't about diversity but about the unintended consequences of the policy, that less qualified

minority teachers would supplant more qualified minority teachers.
"Integration transfers frequently displaced younger, dedicated minority
teachers at Stuyvesant who had been groomed by the principal but had
no seniority rights," Stern says.

Recent changes in the contract now empower the principal and
department heads to hire those they consider the most qualified. But
Mr. Jaye says, "We're still dealing with" vestiges of the old system. He
cites the example of a teacher who used the seniority transfer to obtain
his job at Stuyvesant and continues to be a problem this semester, giving
students tests that are too long and unfair. Mr. Jaye tries to work with
him, even though he knows there's little chance of improvement,
because the alternative—firing the teacher—is "a huge headache," he
says. It would require compiling massive documentation for the principal, fighting the teachers' union, and in the end, he says, he would end
up feeling that it was his own job on the line.

"It's like you're on trial," Mr. Jaye says.

Mr. Grossman, the English chairman, knows the feeling. Last year,
when he took the rare step of firing a teacher whom he determined to
be incompetent, a small faction of angry teachers took up the cause,
fighting to reverse the decision. The skirmishing has turned so nasty
behind the scenes this semester that a teacher who supports him
received an anonymous note smeared with what looked like feces.

"The most difficult part of my job is ensuring the quality of instruction," says Mr. Grossman, who was himself temporarily bumped out of a
teaching job early in his career at Stuyvesant by a teacher with more
seniority.

With a faculty of nearly two hundred, Stuyvesant boasts a battalion
of dedicated teachers who make an average salary of about $72,000, and
the best include the likes of rookie math teacher Oana Pascu, rising English teacher Jonathan Weil, and Robert Sandler, a tough but popular
social studies teacher. Many of the best found the profession by accident, like Mr. Grossman and Mr. Jaye. Their meandering path stands in
stark contrast to the beveled ambition of students whose compass was
set toward Stuyvesant from an early age. But maybe that's what makes
them such good teachers. The profession found them. So have the students, who know where to find the good teachers, as do their parents,

who frequently jockey behind the scenes to get their children into classes with the best teachers. They also know who the bad ones are, including one teacher who is known less for instruction than for surfing the Web for dates.

And then there is French teacher Marie Lorenzo, the longest-tenured instructor at Stuyvesant. Such was her beauty that students and teachers nicknamed her 'Legs Lorenzo." Today, decades after she started teaching here, Ms. Lorenzo is a stooped, bespectacled, gray-haired veteran who still teaches French. Though the right intentions are still there, to be sure, it is difficult to see any teaching happening on a recent day in her eighth-period class in room 505, where a volley of student voices drown each other out.

"Why are we talking all at once?" Ms. Lorenzo screams, to no avail.

She shuffles directly in front of a chattering girl in the front row and folds her arms, giving the student her best severe look. "One more word out of you, and you'll be failing this class," she seethes.

That takes care of that. But chattering continues to emanate from the back of the room, where freshman Sammy Sussman is boasting about how he received a 96 in Latin last year in middle school. His grade—or chatter—sends Ms. Lorenzo into a frenzy, which only worsens when another boy dispatches a paper airplane across the room, mysteriously prompting Ms. Lorenzo to send Sammy, not the airplane thrower, to the dean's office and order him to report to her after school.

"What did I do?" he asks.

No answer is forthcoming. Sammy mopes out of the class. Another paper airplane whizzes over Ms. Lorenzo's head. She is oblivious. A boy asks her about homework, which prompts her to yell at him, then she orders him to sit further back in class for no apparent reason. Outside the classroom moments later, Sammy is sitting on a bench, left hand on chin, rust bangs hanging low over moody blue eyes, in *The Thinker*'s position. He's come to the conclusion all on his own that his actions don't warrant a visit to the dean's office. He doesn't plan to meet Ms. Lorenzo at 3 p.m. either.

"She'll probably forget," he says, then adds, "This is my weirdest class."

But as soon as he hands down that verdict, Sammy seems to feel almost bad about it, as if it's his fault, all this weirdness. So he says he's learned some French already, like the word for "leave."

How do you say it in French?

Suddenly, he can't remember.

Sometimes it's hard for Ms. Lee, the student teacher, to remember things too. For her family, the past is marked by pain and disappointment, beginning when her father left Korea to find a better life in the United States.

"He was lured into this American Dream," she says.

But it didn't materialize. Barely able to speak English, he first worked in a deli, then as a stock clerk in a drugstore. When he made his big move, launching a Korean golf magazine, it failed. A second venture, making blouses, went down the tubes. Now he drives a yellow taxi in New York City.

The dream didn't die, though. It just took a different form, in his daughter. Ms. Lee would achieve academically. A poor grade would be met with the parental silent treatment until Ms. Lee internalized the ambition, making it her own. In the summer after sixth grade, she attended a private Korean academy, drilling in math and English for more than a year with the single aim of winning entrance to Stuyvesant. But a day before the test, her cherished aunt died of breast cancer, and Ms. Lee fell just short of making the cutoff for Stuyvesant. She did qualify for the Bronx High School of Science, a great school in its own right but considered a runner-up in the exam derby. It was a family disaster.

"We cried that day," she says.

In high school, Ms. Lee disappointed her parents again, achieving a respectable 89 grade point average, which wasn't high enough to win her acceptance into the college of her family's choice, Columbia. Her father's pronouncement still rings in memory. Father told daughter, "You failed one part of your life."

At Stony Brook University, Ms. Lee pushed herself to pass the next phase, gaining acceptance to the prestigious Phi Beta Kappa academic honors society. But when she applied to Columbia again, this time for a master's degree in political science, she fell short again. She wasn't dissuaded. Instead, she bided her time, living at home and tutoring Korean high school students, before applying to Columbia again. And again she was rejected. Still she remained unbowed. When she heard that she might have a better chance of getting into Columbia's Teachers College, she applied to that master's program, even though she had no intention of becoming a teacher. She simply thought it might be a springboard to a higher degree in political science. Finally, Columbia accepted her.

The day she found out, she stayed up until about two o'clock in the morning to greet her father returning from the taxi night shift. After she told him she had gained admission to Columbia, he gave her a high five. He had never done that before.

"I found an oasis," she says, on "a journey through the desert."

If Columbia's Teachers College wasn't part of the plan, neither was Stuyvesant. As a high school student, she had fallen short of its cutoff; as a student teacher, Stuyvesant just happened to be a practical place for Ms. Lee because of its relatively easy commute from Columbia. But once she arrived at the high school, she discovered an odd thing: joy. She loves teaching, and she loves Stuyvesant.

"I'm just having so much fun with this," she says. "Now that I'm here, I know why I'm here. Two years ago, I never would have imagined I'd be here." For the devoutly religious Ms. Lee, it was fate: "Was this an accident? I don't think so."

She doesn't know, however, whether she will remain at Stuyvesant. As a student teacher, she is, by definition, temporary. With graduation from Columbia looming just months away, Ms. Lee needs to find a permanent job, and she can picture herself teaching at only one place, Stuyvesant. But there are no openings. She is lost. That is, unless Mr. Jaye, the Wizard of Oz, can work his magic.

# PART TWO: DETENTION

*Early March–Mid April*

CHAPTER TEN

# Lost in *Gatsby*

"ALL THESE PEOPLE SEEM LOST," ROMEO MUSES.

The football captain is talking about the damaged characters in *The Great Gatsby*, required reading in English class, but his thoughts drift to a moment in time that has fossilized into a postcard of the mind. An indigo ocean. An idyllic seaside town in France. Arradon. Summertime. And centered within the frame is an eight-year-old boy named Romeo, who scampers down to a beach, where one of his teenage cousins is laughing with Romeo's mother about frivolous things like shoes. On his arrival, the two women rise to leave, as if not wanting to be bothered by his presence, which wounds the little boy, and a resolution instantly forms. "I promised myself I would never be a teenager like her," he says of his cousin. Instead, Romeo finds a role model in another cousin, an earnest teenager who harbors great academic ambitions. That summer in France, the two boys find a treasure map hidden inside the broken handle of a racquetball racquet. His cousin forgot that he had stowed the map there five years earlier. Curious, the two boys trace the clues to a tree under which they find the treasure—a smooth, round rock worth absolutely nothing but priceless to Romeo, who is transfixed by the idea that a place in time had been recaptured.

"My destiny started a long time ago," he says.

That destiny brings him to this day, eight years later, in early March, to this place: Stuyvesant, where teenagers like him are apt to be discussing the literary virtues of *The Great Gatsby* not only in class but in the dining hall over a slab of chicken, Spanish rice, and a helping of angst.

"I've been in a spell all week," Romeo is saying. "People say it's a history piece, but it relates to me." He sees Nick, the central character in Fitzgerald's classic novel, as a man tired of the artificiality of life until he meets Gatsby, a man of passion.

"Gatsby is incredibly idealistic," adds Romeo's lunchmate, Xevion, the great junior singer, putting aside her chicken lunch, what she refers to as her "mystery meat." Then Xevion, fresh from making a stand to sing a meaningful ballad in the school musical, finds a connection between Gatsby and herself. "I tend to be idealistic," she says.

Lately, Romeo has come to see himself as a "stoic romantic." It has something to do with an experience that he shares with another high school friend, Kieren, who also is half black, half white.

"We feel alienated from the world," Romeo says, his voice tinged with a vague sense of unease. "We claim we hate all of our peers."

Xevion, who is also black, pipes up, "Present company excepted, I hope."

Romeo lets the implied question linger unanswered as he finishes a thought. "At the same time, there's a yearning for passion, for love, but a reluctance to admit it," he says. Then he releases Xevion from suspense: "You're good."

She exhales audibly. "I feel better," she says.

*Gatsby* has Romeo thinking about his future too. So inspired is he by the novel that he's wondering if he should incorporate more literature in his college curriculum at Harvard. That he will be attending the famous American college in two years is accepted as fact, although he hasn't applied yet. Even Xevion, who'd be the first to downsize Romeo's ego as his self-appointed conscience, doesn't bother to dispute the notion because it seems so inevitable.

"I have my first year planned out, all the classes I want to take," he says of Harvard.

Romeo ticks off a course load of economics, advanced calculus, physics, and expository writing. Ivy League imaginings are hard to resist because he just returned from a tour of the Harvard campus, where he bumped into four other Stuyvesant students, who, like him, were casing out the university

Romeo likes the fit. His SAT prep class is humming along. So is his nascent project for the Intel science contest. Romeo was immediately taken with an NYU professor who gave a recent lecture in his Stuyvesant math research class, and now the two of them are about to start working together on Saturday mornings in an attempt to unravel the mysteries of magnetic fusion. Romeo shows off his new NYU photo ID, which identifies him as a "Visiting Scholar." He seems to like where he's heading with that moniker.

Romeo seems to like where the Peglegs are heading too. The football team starts lifting weights next week. Several players from last year's junior varsity team have moved up to varsity, and camaraderie is high. Romeo is feeling daring enough to allow himself to think of a football season with a winning record. "I'm excited," he says. "I'm surprised."

Xevion is less sure of herself. Later, during tenth period, she wanders into room 133, looking for an empty space to practice before her rehearsal for Sing! For Xevion, it wouldn't do to show up for rehearsal without being properly prepared. There are appearances to keep up, especially for one who has already sung at the hallowed Apollo Theater in Harlem. So she navigates around three seated students who are gossiping among themselves, apologizing for the intrusion, calling them "honey," even though they are contemporaries who don't comprehend such a term of endearment unless it comes from a parental figure. They pay her no mind until she abruptly breaks through the low drone of their conversation by belting out the first stanza of Shania Twain's "From This Moment On." They stop speaking. It can't be helped. It's the soprano voice. Fiercing and perfect. They look up. Xevion is strutting before the blackboard, as if this classroom were the Apollo and these were her fans, and in a way, it is and they are.

A music teacher barges in to pick up a Delaney book and just as quickly halts, listens, and dissolves into a beatific smile. Xevion's eyes are shut, her right hand modulating to the mellifluous sound of her voice, the ethereal feel of the music. When it ends, the students and teacher applaud.

"You're not in choir," says the teacher. "Why not?"

"That's a long story," Xevion says.

"It was an attitude problem, wasn't it?" says a student in the audience, one of her new fans.

"I don't have an *attitude*," she says with an attitude.

Xevion wouldn't be at Stuyvesant if she didn't have an attitude. When her middle school principal told her it was unlikely that she'd get in because she had only a few weeks to prepare for the entrance exam, Xevion took it as a challenge, studying from a textbook every night. "I just wanted to prove to her I could," she says. "I want to thank her. She did me a huge favor."

Her attitude, though, didn't do her any favors a year ago when she had a run-in with a choir teacher at Stuyvesant. Xevion had waited until the last minute to sign up for chorus class, which was not a good idea because the teacher was just heading out of the room and didn't have time to speak to her. When Xevion returned, the by-the-book teacher, known as something of a diva herself, wouldn't permit her to join the choir: it was too late. Xevion persisted. The teacher took doggedness as recalcitrance. Positions hardened. Xevion came back a third time, an assistant principal in tow, but it did no good. The teacher adamantly refused to let the best singer in her grade join the choir. Xevion shrugs it off now. She's singing, chorus class or not. "I feel sorry for her," she says of the teacher. And off to Sing! rehearsal Xevion goes.

If there's anyone who should be feeling sorry for himself, it's Mr. Siwanowicz, the brilliant school aide, who is on his hands and knees a day later, Friday, March 3, in room 406, the math storage room, pulling inky pages from the bowels of a Risograph CR1610 high-speed copier.

"What were they thinking?" he wonders aloud, and he could be talking about the offenders at school who broke the copy machine—or the dullards who gave him the task of fixing it.

Either way, Mr. Siwanowicz is agitated. The look is written in his pallid expression, in his eyes, which are fissured red under drooping lids. But it could be that he's simply fatigued. He's been playing online board games. He helped his parents repaint the living room. But he can't sleep, still. It's the depression and the debilitating inertia that grip him, at least when he contemplates resuming college so he can earn a degree so he can obtain a license to teach so he doesn't have to fix copiers anymore. He dismisses the thought with reverse logic. "College generally gets in the way of people's education," he grumbles. "College is not that necessary."

Mr. Siwanowicz fixates on the present, the math research class he unofficially teaches. He's encouraged by Daniel, the Cuban immigrant, who asks great questions. And Milo, the prodigy, who reminds Mr. Siwanowicz of himself when he was the same age, except that "Milo is a lot more social," he says. "I was more creepy." Mr. Siwanowicz is troubled by another student who is cutting his class, but he says, "There's nothing I can do." He fails to see the parallel to his own experience as a student who didn't show up to class. And he fails to see the perversity of being a brilliant mathematician, a Putnam fellow, who failed out of college.

"I don't see an irony," he says flatly, moments after fixing the copier.

Mr. Siwanowicz also can't fathom what he needs to do to get reinstated at City College. "I have absolutely no idea," he says. He blames it on his preoccupation with Stuyvesant. "I have way too much work," he says. Doing what? "I have copiers to fix, lightbulbs to replace," he says, deadpan.

He overlooks one other task: monitoring the library during two of his free periods. He's still doing that too.

Mr. Jaye hasn't given up on the fight to dislodge Mr. Siwanowicz from library duty so that the teacher's aide can do something more productive, like talk to kids about math. But at the moment—a period later—Mr. Jaye is sitting in his office, fuming about his other perennial problem: Ms. Damesek.

They've been at it again. In a meeting yesterday with the principal, Mr. Jaye had explained that he wanted to enlist parents as volunteers to proctor a prestigious international math contest, involving more than three hundred Stuyvesant students who had qualified for it. But Ms. Damesek, who is responsible for such matters, had refused, saying she didn't want to leave students in a room alone with a parent who could be a problem. At which point Mr. Jaye said, "I'm not asking for your *permission*, I'm *telling* you." Not backing down, Ms. Damesek said she didn't like the idea of kids hanging around after school unsupervised. To which Mr. Jaye retorted, "You don't like kids *in* school." Mr. Teitel, the principal, who had remained on the sidelines during the skirmish, couldn't help but laugh. Ms. Damesek didn't think it was funny. Nor was she amused this morning when she bumped into Mr. Jaye, who resumed the offensive when he suggested that she had been usurping Mr. Teitel in their last meeting. "I thought Stan was the principal," he said. "Was there something that happened I'm not aware of?"

That time, they refrained from exchanging further indelicacies.

Jane, the senior struggling with a drug addiction, has no such compunctions. By ninth period, she's in full battle mode, wearing a blue hooded jacket, blue jeans, and black sneakers, while her dark mane has been pulled back in a severe ponytail and her jewelry removed, the better to attack when the time comes. She's sitting in the sixth-floor library, waiting to finish a fistfight with a boy in the second-floor senior Asian territory.

They used to be friends. But after her latest bout with drugs, when she returned from detox, he told her he wouldn't put up with her anymore. "You pushed us away," he told her. "You chose drugs over us." Jane responded the only way she knew how: defiantly. "You owe me ten dollars," she told him. He looked back at her sadly. They moved into different groups, settling a safe distance apart on the floor until Jane couldn't help herself, started talking trash, marched up to him, and demanded, "Stand up and fight me." The large boy looked at the little girl and wouldn't move. She kicked him. She punched him. Finally, he said, "You pushed me away."

"Don't blame it on me!" she screamed at him. "Do you know what it means to be addicted?"

Jane lunged at him again, but another student held her at bay. The boy walked away.

Now, sitting in the library, Jane thinks of others who've abandoned her, fed up with her drug addiction—a best friend who ditched her, another good friend who wrote her off. "None of my friends had the capability of being there for me," she says, thinking of last semester when she was bedridden at home and no one called. A sense of discomfort casts a dark shadow over her thin, pale face. "When I say I don't have a conscience, maybe it's true," Jane says. "I'm a bad person."

The bell rings for tenth period. She has no intention of going to her next class, history; dismissing a lesson on the past, she instead grimly heads to the future, down the echoing stairwell to the second floor in the hopes of finding the boy.

"I'm not," she says, "afraid to die."

A day later, a bitterly cold Saturday, March 4, tension of another sort pervades the school, except now it emanates from room 735, where a group of students is wondering if they measure up. Dressed in ill-fitting grownup clothing—jackets and ties for boys, skirts and blouses for girls—students from various schools are participating in Model UN, a simulation of the United Nations where they play the role of ambassadors in the world of diplomacy. Ostensibly, they are discussing "Land Tenure Reform in Southern African Countries" and "Debt Reduction and Assessment Strategies." But the real discussion is occurring during the break in the hallway, where students visiting from other public schools are gawking at the magnificence of Stuyvesant's soaring structure.

"This is huge," says the Djibouti delegate, a sophomore at the David A. Stein Riverdale/Kingsbridge Academy, a neighborhood public school in the Bronx. He had studied a year for the entrance test, hoping to attend Stuyvesant. When he didn't get in, he was crushed. But now he's not so sure, given what he's hearing about the school's intensity. "The work at Stuyvesant is much harder, it's more competitive," he says. His classmate, a senior representing Malawi, is glad he didn't end up here. "Stuyvesant kids are pushed to do work," he says. "We have to take our education in our own hands."

School pride, of course, is in evidence among students at high schools across the nation—and for good reason. Many other schools, public and private, have established a national reputation, rivaling Stuyvesant in academic laurels and honors, such as Boston Latin School, a public school in Boston; Hunter College High School, a public school in New York City; the North Carolina School of Science and Mathematics, a public school in Durham; Phillips Academy, a private boarding school in Andover, Massachusetts; Phillips Exeter Academy, a private boarding school in Exeter, New Hampshire; Walnut Hills High School, a public school in Cincinnati; and Walt Whitman High School, a public school in Bethesda, Maryland.

There are many other great high schools, including those cited on *Newsweek*'s annual list, which is based on the number of advanced placement or international baccalaureate tests taken by all students in a school divided by the number of graduating seniors, a formula devised by education authority Jay Mathews, a *Washington Post* writer. While educators don't agree on how to accurately measure high school greatness, not surprisingly, many of the schools with the highest academic achievers share several traits with Stuyvesant. Many, for instance, are public schools that admit students based exclusively or in part on competitive exams, including Gretchen Whitney High School in Cerritos, California, where the stated mission is to get its students into the colleges that best suit them. Students there averaged an impressive 1344 on the old SAT, and the school is on a first-name basis with university admissions officers, while panels of school counselors and administrators interview every senior to find out where each wants to go to college. "We make no apologies about that," Whitney principal Patricia Hager says of the school mission. "There's no argument about whether you're going to go to college."

As at Stuyvesant, athletics remain on the sidelines at Whitney. Where there is no football field at Stuyvesant, there is no football *team* at Whitney. "We like to say we're undefeated," the principal quips. And in an atmosphere of freedom where academic achievement is expected, students feel good about themselves, a result that creates its own momentum, echoing another Stuyvesant strength. "You can't get them to go home," Ms. Hager says. "Our custodians leave at eleven [p.m.], and we still have kids floating around. This is their home."

The same can be said about students at New Trier High School, a top public school outside Chicago, where students averaged 1270 on the old

SAT. Long after the last bell, they can be found in the well-buffed hall-ways, pursuing their passion, whether it's working on displays for an AIDS awareness initiative or just hanging out with friends. Though the school doesn't impose an admissions test, it benefits from a different kind of selective process: you have to live in the neighborhood to attend the school, which sits on two campuses, and if you live in the neighbor-hood, there's a good chance you're well-off, a familiar phenomenon in other affluent suburbs across the nation.

With a strong local tax base, New Trier has the luxury of reducing teachers' workload so that more than 40 percent of them can serve part-time as "faculty advisers" to its more than four thousand students. Every morning, for twenty-five minutes, advisers meet with students in groups of about twenty-five, talking with them about their hopes, dreams, and fears. "We do an excellent job in the social and emotional connection of our kids," says Debra L. Stacey, principal of the main campus in Win-netka, Illinois. Advisers even make a "home visit" to talk to the students' parents during their sophomore year. "This is New Trier's attempt to make it a small school," says Jan Borja, principal of the freshman campus in Northfield, Illinois. School administrators acknowledge that the adviser system is expensive, but it's a tradition that dates back to 1928, and students love it. "It's so smart," says eighteen-year-old Cara Harsh-man, a senior off to the University of Wisconsin–Madison next year. "It's a support system. You all look out for each other."

At San Francisco's Lowell High School, a public school where admission is based in part on exams, students posted a solid 1236 aver-age SAT, benefiting from another support system: a cadre of parents intensely active in their children's education, much as Stuyvesant's par-ents are. In the wake of California's budget cuts, for instance, Lowell parents stepped in, raising funds to hire about a dozen teachers in such areas as the arts and counseling—a financial achievement in a school where about a third of the students are eligible for reduced-price lunch.

Parents are "critical not only to their kids' success but to the institu-tion," says Paul Cheng, the Lowell principal for sixteen years, until 2006.

Another top public school, Thomas Jefferson High School for Sci-ence and Technology in Fairfax County, Virginia, where admission is partly test-based, boasts a wealth of extracurricular activities much as Stuyvesant does. At T.J., as it's known, extracurricular activities are even built into the curriculum as part of an extended school day so that students can explore their interests, whether it's swing dance or math team. Students, whose average score well exceeded 1400 on the old SAT, can create their own extracurricular activities if they obtain administrators' approval. The result is that "the kids are there because they love to be there," says Principal Evan M. Glazer.

School pride is especially pronounced at Bronx Science, Stuyvesant's main competitor. The rivalry is a function of New York City's specialized high schools exam. After Stuyvesant, the toughest public high school to gain entrance to is Bronx Science. Students who barely miss the cutoff for Stuyvesant often end up at Bronx Science as their second choice. Lisa Ha knows this well. She attended a private Chinese academy, preparing a year for the test, goaded by her mother, a Chinese immigrant, whose goal was for her daughter to win a seat at Stuyvesant. "You have to be the best," she told her daughter. "You have to go to the best school." As an eighth grader, Lisa didn't care whether she made it into Stuyvesant as long as she earned a spot at one of the specialized schools. And she did, ending up at Bronx Science. Now a sophomore, Lisa is a top member of the school debate team, and whenever she beats Stuyvesant, which is often, she is sure to let her mother know.

"It's always good to point out, 'Oh, I beat Stuy.'"

The two schools compete in just about everything, not just debate, but also in the Intel science contest, admissions to the Ivy League, and even sports, like swimming, gymnastics, and soccer. The only thing that Lisa will concede is that Stuyvesant has a better-looking building than Bronx Science, an old, musty school. But she's quick to note that Bronx Science, whose students averaged a strong 1290 on the old SAT, has generated seven Nobel Prize winners, three more than Stuyvesant.

"We make do with what we have," Lisa says. "Imagine what we'd do if we had spent [$150 million] on our building. We might find the cure for cancer."

One of Lisa's debate teammates isn't convinced of Bronx Science's superiority. So Jerry Wang is transferring to Stuyvesant next year as a sophomore after reaching the cutoff on her second try on the entrance exam. But now that she's achieved her goal, Stuyvesant doesn't look so appealing.

For one, the freshman is filled with anxiety as she thinks of Stuyvesant's maze of ten floors and pictures herself getting lost, arriving late to math class. Friends whom she'll miss at Bronx Science have left graffiti on her locker, calling her a traitor for leaving their school for Stuyvesant. "Both of the high schools are, like, nerdy, but Stuy is, like, the nerdy-nerdy," she says. "We're, like, the nerdy-cool."

And then, there's the dreaded pool.

Jerry hasn't gone swimming since the fourth grade, which could present problems when she takes Stuyvesant's swim test. The prospect of failing gym weighs on her. So does the burden of work about to befall her. Stuyvesant recently notified her parents that it may behoove them to buy various math tomes so that Jerry can prepare for the placement test. The freshman couldn't believe it. As it is at Bronx Science, she had three tests last week, four this week, and she wakes up at 5 a.m. every morning just to keep up. "When do I have the time?" she appealed to her mother. Suddenly, the reality of Stuyvesant dawns on her. "The competition," she says, "is going to be so hard."


The reality of competition is just beginning to dawn on Stuyvesant freshmen and sophomores who are downstairs in the auditorium rehearsing for Sing! on this Saturday. The rehearsal is distinguished by one overriding feature: there is no rehearsing going on. Students are late, sick, out of town, or doing homework that will be eaten by the dog—anywhere but where they are supposed to be, which is here, less than three weeks before the curtain rises. Codirector Gui Bessa isn't getting much sleep. "It's so stressful," the sophomore says despondently. "We have to turn it on."

Boys trickle on stage to practice a hip-hop dance routine. It has nothing to do with the script's story line. But there is a rationale. "You put it in the plot because it looks awesome," says Alexa, the freshman coproducer.

At the time being, it looks less than awesome. Sammy, the freshman who drew his French teacher's ire for doing nothing, shows up late for the hip-hop routine. As a way of explaining, he wordlessly shrugs in his huge black parka, and it practically swallows him up. Hardly anyone notices. There are bigger issues with which to contend. The audio is so bad that singers can't be heard. Dialogue is indistinguishable. People are running on and off stage, out of sync, too early, or too late. Shell-shocked, Gui has wandered to a first-floor bench outside the auditorium, a quiet perch where he can slump in perfect misery. The codirector can't comprehend how they could be so bad. He doesn't know if there's enough time to turn the play around. He isn't convinced they will measure up to the juniors and seniors. "Terrible" is all he can say. "Nothing went right."

CHAPTER ELEVEN

# Great Expectations

NOTHING HAS GONE RIGHT LATELY FOR SOPHOMORE Mariya Goldman, who broods during fifth period on a thawing Monday, March 6, as she sits Indian-style on the second-floor landing, munching on a small bag of baked Lay's potato chips and digesting her failure to instigate a schoolwide rebellion. What had started as a promising petition drive to end homework during vacations has fizzled out quietly. In the span of a week, Mariya collected 117 signatures, which wasn't bad. But her coconspirator, another disgruntled student, gathered all of 5 names. Few cared. Worse, few thought the petition would work. Worst of all, some students welcome homework, even during vacations, because, after all, this is Stuyvesant. "It's sort of dead now," she says morosely, wearing gothic black, as if dressed to mourn the petition's passing.

Mariya looks drained. At fifteen years old, it's easy to fall into a tailspin for any number of reasons, including her dislike of being five foot eleven; she seems unaware that being a statuesque beauty will be an asset one day. She doesn't like boys staring at her—at her big brown eyes, her network of freckles—oblivious to the admiration that it implies. Not even the prospect of her upcoming two-month anniver-

111

sary—an eternity in high school—with her first love, a boy named Tom, can lift her spirits. "He's still my boyfriend," she says, as if the clock is about to run out.

Mariya refuses to emerge from her funk, struggling to let go of the homework ban, the inspiration for which was an English teacher who had the nerve to assign her humanities class what she calls a "really crazy project" over the recently ended midwinter recess. The homework: evaluate two translations of *Antigone*, the ancient Greek tragedy, and a poem based on it, in three essays.

"I hate Greek plays and stuff," Mariya says, grimacing at the recollection. "I really didn't want to do it. I wanted to come up with an excuse not to do it."

In the original version of the petition, she referred to teachers as "stupid" and "not understanding" and "evil monsters." Once she exorcized that from her system, she handed out a politer version, addressed to the principal and faculty:

> It has come to our attention that most teachers confuse the meaning of the term "vacation," or "time off," with "time off to do work." We would like to point out that a more accurate definition would be "time off to rest," and therefore insist that the multitude of projects, essays, and papers inevitably assigned during any such vacation are actually counterproductive to the purpose of such a period of time existing in the first place. Thus, in order for students to return to school rested and prepared to learn, as opposed to, say, on two and a half hours of sleep, we recommend that the following rules be put in effect immediately.

The proposed rules boiled down to this: no homework during vacation. Ending with a dour warning, the petition stated, "This rule should actually be followed all of the time, as opposed to certain other rules . . . that are sometimes followed."

Mariya, the undersigned, could have been addressing the petition to other taskmasters: her parents.

When Mariya recently came home with her report card, they were not pleased. For the last semester, she earned a grade point average of

94.86—practically straight As. That, however, was down from 95.29, a drop of less than half a percentage point—.43—from the previous marking period. Mariya could have made the argument that the difference was statistically insignificant, that a couple of mistakes on a single test could have ever so slightly skewed the report card results—a blip caused by poor sleep, a bad hair day, anything. More to the point, she could have argued that the marking period just ended doesn't count *because it doesn't*. Those grades are not factored into a student's overall grade point average they're simply an indicator of how a student is performing during the course of the semester before receiving final grades at the end of the term. But such arguments, no matter how reasonable, wouldn't have made any difference. The way that Mariya's parents viewed it, their daughter's grades slipped, which warranted a punishment right where it hurts: they took away her cell phone.

"It's sort of ridiculous that it'd be a big deal," Mariya says, grousing about how her parents 'expect me to get a full scholarship to a fancy Ivy League thing," which will lead to a fancy job so one day she can buy a fancy house. But Mariya is just venting. When she really thinks about it, she doesn't blame her parents for creating such great expectations for her. The family had less than a hundred dollars to their name when they left their home in Ukraine, arriving at Kennedy Airport little more than a decade ago in the aftermath of the collapse of the Soviet Union.

In Ukraine, her parents had sold leather necklaces, lacquer boxes, and other knickknacks at a street stand; in America, they thought life would be easier. It wasn't. Her mother became a maid, her father delivered pizzas. Now her father is an electrician while her mother is a clerical worker, and money is still tight. They sleep in the living room of their small Brooklyn apartment so that Mariya and her nine-year-old brother, Mark, can have their own bedrooms.

"I dream about *three* bedrooms," says her mother, Yelena Goldman, in clipped English.

In the dream, Mariya attends Columbia and grows up to work for a big company, with customers aplenty. Mariya would also have a daughter, whom Mrs. Goldman would secretly teach to speak Russian. And together, the family would move to a glorious house in Manhattan in a calm, quiet area, where Mariya's parents would live in the . . basement.

The *basement?* Mariya is appalled. Her mother isn't. "The basement is good enough," she says resolutely.

The basement of the future will have to wait. Mariya doesn't even know how she'll pay for college. She thinks she may have to join the military reserve to help defray the cost, but she worries about the possible price—being compelled to go to war. At the moment, though, there are more immediate concerns. The school bell is ringing, and Mariya has a chemistry test in two periods for which she has yet to study. She doesn't have to answer only to her parents. She faces the expectations of the parents of a classmate, another immigrant from the former Soviet Union, part of a growing demographic at Stuyvesant. Mariya is supposed to help fifteen-year-old Mariana Muravitsky, who is camped out on the second-floor landing with her, prepare for the same class. "If you don't help me study for the chemistry test," Mariana warns, "my mom is going to kill you."

As they rise to leave, Mariya mutters hopelessly, "It's a death threat."

Down the hall and around the corner, Milo, the ten-year-old prodigy, is leaving his speaker-building class in a decidedly better mood. There is something different about him this morning, though it is difficult to detect at first. He is still buried deep inside his big blue parka. His tuft of blond hair still diverges in Einstein-like fashion. But then there it is: the backpack. Red and blue and strapped to both narrow shoulders. Milo has ditched his old backpack, which he used to wheel around school by a handle, like a piece of carry-on luggage, such was the burden of his academic paraphernalia.

Milo says he threw out the old backpack because it had a hole in it. "It was kind of a drag to be dragging it," he says. Therein, he proves two things with one backpack: Milo is beginning to fit in at high school not just in his choice of luggage but also in his lingo.

But that's not all that accounts for the newfound levity in his step this morning. Milo has just made it to the semifinal round of a citywide high school math fair. Only a small number of Stuyvesant students who submitted papers gained entry to the contest, and only a handful of those who participated in the first round made it to the second, including Milo. In his paper, he invented a thesis on what he calls the "fair distribution of things," using seven different kinds of chocolates—Reese's, Hershey's, Butterfinger, and Baby Ruth among them—as examples.

"The judges are suckers for candy," he says.

What he created, he points out, is "not your normal math." Milo devised two formulas to determine what is fair in a scenario involving a number of "players." One formula he called "happiness":

Happiness = True, if the player's final portion is greater than, or equal to, 100 minus S over N, with N = to the number of players and S = to sympathy [a term "which I made up," Milo says].

The upshot is, "A lot of people have negative sympathies," he notes, apparently drawing from personal experience. That could include high school students who have no idea what it's like to be a little boy in their midst.

It's an overlooked luxury that at a school like Stuyvesant, administrators can find a place for a ten-year-old genius who isn't officially enrolled, while other public schools are not even sure whether they can find their students at all. It's a concern based on recent—and troubling—trends in education in America today.

Almost all Stuyvesant students graduate, compared to only about 70 percent of high school students across the nation, and that number has remained virtually unchanged since the 1970s, according to the Manhattan Institute for Policy Research.

In an April 2006 *Time* magazine cover story with the blunt headline, "Dropout Nation," the author writes, "the most astonishing statistic in the whole field of education" is that nearly one out of three public high school students will fail to graduate, and that the number is close to 50 percent for Latinos and blacks. "Virtually no community, small or large, rural or urban, has escaped the problem," the author says.

At about the same time, a 2006 study on behalf of the Bill & Melinda Gates Foundation calls the problem *The Silent Epidemic*. While the causes are endlessly debated, the researchers of this study isolated some of the problems, surveying nearly five hundred high school dropouts.

Most said they had passing grades and could have graduated, but 69 percent said they were "not motivated to work hard" and 66 percent said they would have "worked harder if more had been demanded of them." In addition, 71 percent of high school dropouts said they favored "better communication between parents and schools and more involvement from parents," which is exactly what Stuyvesant already experiences in spades.

The ramifications of dropping out of school are all too well known: students without a high school diploma risk falling into low-wage jobs or unemployment lines—unsavory prospects compounded by rising competition in a global marketplace where even cheap jobs are being exported. But if there's a crisis of competence in American education, it doesn't apply only to dropouts. Students are slipping in some of the most basic—and important—academic subjects in an increasingly complex, technological society, where many jobs over the next decade are expected to require more science, engineering, or technical training. For instance, in science, one of Stuyvesant's traditional strengths, 54 percent of twelfth graders nationally scored at or above the basic level in 2005, down 3 percentage points from a decade earlier, according to the U.S. Department of Education, which administered the test. Meanwhile, U.S. eighth graders score lower in science than those of seven other nations, four from Asia (including Hong Kong) and three from Europe, according to the closely followed Trends in International Mathematics and Science Study, an international education project.

"Our superiority was once the envy of the world," says *Time* on its February 2006 cover about America's decline in science achievement. "But we are slacking off just as other countries are getting stronger."

American students are faring little better in math, another key subject—and another Stuyvesant strong suit. U.S. eighth graders showed "no measurable change" in their math performance in recent years, according to the same international education project. Running in place, these American students have fallen behind their advancing counterparts in math in nine other countries, five from Asia (including Hong Kong) and four from Europe, including the tiny nation of Estonia.

Things don't improve when U.S. high school students reach the age of fifteen. Even then, they continue to post lower scores in math and science literacy than most of their peers from the Organisation for Economic Co-operation and Development member nations. That means America is lagging behind the bulk of the industrialized world. No longer does it seem that there are great expectations for today's U.S high school student.

What's happened to American education?

"No one really knows the answer," says Tom Loveless, director of the Brown Center on Education Policy and a senior fellow in governance studies at the Brookings Institution, a think tank in Washington, D.C. "I mean, I can speculate, but the serious, true answer is, people don't know."

Dr. Loveless reckons it's a "cultural thing," meaning that in the United States, many students—and parents—don't take academic achievement seriously while "in other countries, teenagers have a job, and that's going to school."

Other experts attribute the decline in American education to a variety of causes, including schools that are too big, teachers who don't have enough training, or parents who don't expect enough from their children. Mr. Teitel, Stuyvesant's principal, largely blames the decline in math and science achievement on the students themselves. "The problem we face now is that, you know, a lot of kids really don't want to go to the math and science field because it is, to some extent, more difficult than some of the other subject areas," he says. ". . . Kids don't want to take the tough subjects and struggle through them and parents don't want to see the kids struggle that hard." Which is why he won't diminish Stuyvesant's traditional emphasis on math, science, and technology, or MST, as he calls it. "I will not pull any punches to tell you that I am sure that many of my parents would not have any qualms about me just turning this into a school for gifted and talented, 'forget the MST part, pal. Just a school for gifted, pal, we could be very happy.' The reality is, I won't allow it." That's because he firmly believes such difficult subjects are needed.

Whatever the causes of the decline in American education, many policy makers and education leaders believe the long-term consequences may be great. "Unless we start figuring out far more effective ways to teach basic and high-level skills in our public schools, we will pay a serious price in economic competitiveness and social and political upheaval," says former chairman and chief executive of IBM Louis V. Gerstner Jr., chairman of the Teaching Commission, a group of leaders in government, business, and education, in its spring 2006 report. ". . . If we do not go far further, far faster, we will all soon be talking in the past tense about America's greatness."

The consequences of falling behind preoccupy a battalion of seniors after school on March 7 on the third floor, where they are rehearsing for Sing! with the grim determination of former juniors who nearly upset the seniors last year and aim to avoid such a dishonor now.

"Ready, from the top!" screams a stern choreographer leading a group of spandex-covered girls who are intently practicing a hip-hop dance step to Michael Jackson's "Smooth Criminal."

"I want to see energy and I want to see it good!" berates another fearsome senior, leading a group of grave girls nearby who are waving multicolored scarves in an intricate Indian dance step.

Observing off to the side is Liz Livingstone, the lighting director, marveling with a suggestion of trepidation at how quickly opening night is approaching. "Sing! is in two weeks, which is crazy," she says.

Upstairs in the fifth-floor dining hall, freshmen and sophomores are playing a Jackson 5 song, "ABC," though Alexa, the coproducer, doesn't like what she's hearing. The chorus needs to be louder, the band needs more practice. "It's not good," she says with a frown.

Hope, however, isn't lost. Based on the latest intelligence, word is that while the seniors are hungry after losing as juniors last year, this year's juniors are cocky and lazy, a notion reinforced today when the eleventh graders ended their rehearsal early. Some underclassmen sense a slight opening. "We might have a chance at beating the juniors because we're working hard," says freshman Erica Sands, a chorus member.

It's part of the life of Stuyvesant that after school on this day, as on almost every other, students are working hard throughout the building in a beehive of extracurricular activities. That includes the second floor, where a group of student boosters called Building Stuy Community is sitting in a semicircle discussing how to improve school life. The topic today: how to make the Stuyvesant Web site, www.stuy.edu, better.

Spurring them on is a comparison to rival Bronx Science which possesses a more robust Web site, including a student resource section. What Bronx Science has, Stuyvesant students believe it is their right to have, in this instance a Web site that offers useful information about, say, the guidance office. Can it be done?

The question puts the students' featured guest on the spot. Eddie Wong, assistant principal of technology services, squirms in his student desk-chair before he says, without making any promises, that he will see what he can do. "This is high school," he kids. "I'm not sure you want to make it, like, interesting."

It's no accident that at the same time students are working to improve the school community, some of those students' parents, deeply enmeshed in Stuyvesant life, are doing the identical thing four floors above at a meeting of the advisory School Leadership Team. As at last month's meeting, it's stifling hot in room 615, and a small rotating fan does little to move the stilled air or stir the parents, who remain calcified in their positions. Mr. Teitel is backed in a corner—this time literally sitting in a back corner chair—still trying to explain the imminent introduction of the controversial computerized identification scanners to mark students' attendance.

"I don't know how long it will take to work the bugs out," Mr. Teitel is saying.

"Will they magically appear?" questions Kristen, the Student Union president, one of the principal's favorite students despite her frequent—and open—challenges to his authority.

Mr. Teitel explains that the hardware is already here and just needs to be tested, which prompts a parent, concerned about privacy issues, to ask, "Have you decided what information you will collect?"

The principal assures him that the school will only track students' comings and goings, but that prompts another parent to note Stuyvesant's nearly perfect attendance record and question "why this is a priority."

The question goes unanswered.

> *5 minutes till bell*
>
> *4 minutes till bell*
>
> *3 minutes till bell*
>
> *2 minutes till bell*
>
> *1 minute till bell*
>
> *where is the bell?*
>
> —desktop graffiti, Stuyvesant High School

CHAPTER TWELVE

# The Real World

ON WEDNESDAY, MARCH 8, STUDENTS ARE DISCUSSING greatness in literature in the same room, 615, where last night parents grilled the principal on the merits of attendance scanners While topics have changed overnight, the room retains its basic character—the institutional white walls, the functional wooden chairs, the glaring fluorescent lighting, the dirty white tiles. A poster on the wall commands, BE PART OF THE EXPERIENCE. That seems to speak to the one incongruent element in this English class: Jane. She practically begs to be seen—witnessed—in her tight baby blue T-shirt, in her pink cotton-ball-like rolls on either side of her head, broadcasting like airplane warning lights, and the dozens of plastic multicolored bracelets—pinkyellowgreen—stacked along her left wrist, all the way up to her elbow, hiding the soft crease.

Jane's present. That's the amazing thing. She isn't punching anyone. She isn't screaming at someone. She's not shooting herself up. She's holding on to her book, Joyce's *A Portrait of the Artist as a Young Man*—her life raft. "Page fifty-six," calls out Mr. Grossman, the teacher, her father figure. "Stop there," he says. "Jot down what you notice." Students start calling on each other. Jane raises her pale, slender right fist, clutching a pen. Finally, a fellow student calls on her, and she says, "A person is defined by what he does." She is talking about Stephen, the novel's main character, not herself, and no one in the classroom says otherwise as Jane, fully reabsorbed in the culture of this classroom after her bout in detox, calls on another student, who passes the proverbial baton to another, and all is good. Words fly across the room as if this were a college seminar, substantial terms like "antipathy" and "intrinsic" and "crisis of conscience" and "ingrained" and "constrained." Mr. Grossman barely can get in a word—which makes it easier for him to resist the temptation to "chew the scenery," as he dubs it. When the bell rings at seven past eleven, not a single student rises to leave for the next class. It's a strange phenomenon: no one leaves—no one *wants* to leave—until Mr. Grossman dismisses them, hastening them out with the admonishment, "For tomorrow, up to [page] ninety-one."

He's all business, but within him is a profound sense of happiness at the depth of his students' insights when things in class go so incredibly right. But the joys of teaching are tempered by the immediate realities of his other duties as English chairman. A student comes to him to complain about a teacher in a different department who made inappropriate comments about religion, and when that student spoke up, the teacher made life difficult for her, which is not Mr. Grossman's problem, except that students know him to be fair, so they trust him. What they don't know is that this problematic instructor is aligned with other faculty members who are allied against Mr. Grossman for firing another teacher, which created a controversy that has just begun to die down.

With the school preparing to hire about six guidance counselors, Mr. Grossman is facing another controversy: some English teachers—he doesn't know how many yet—may lose their jobs in the cold calculation of public school personnel decisions. That number includes possibly some of his best, those he has spent the most time training and cultivating. It's an unintended consequence of a school system that eliminated seniority transfers but preserved a provision in which the last-hired teacher is the first fired. Such layoffs are based on length of service. "Fair?" He lets the word linger. "'Fair' is such a hard word," he says. There is no easy answer, not when the countervailing argument against keeping a qualified young teacher is the retention of a qualified veteran teacher. There is little consolation for Mr. Grossman in losing either kind.

"It's just a train barreling down," he says.

Barreling down too is the thought of what will happen to Jane. Even though she's showing up to class again, Mr. Grossman cringes at the possibility that she may succumb again to the nihilism of heroin. And yet lately she seems more coherent, not quite as frenzied. In a quiet moment of reflection, she says, "I get a sense we're not in the real world yet." She's aware that for all the strife of high school, it's make-believe in the sense that it doesn't quite count the way adulthood does, that mistakes are forgiven, expected, and that do-overs are permitted even if, in her case, she already has lived a life all too real. Her incipient clarity is helped, perhaps, by the Subutex tablets she pops to deal with the heroin withdrawal. Already, she can feel a difference. She can climb a set of stairs without asthmatic laboring. The grayness of her skin is dissipating. She's even being friendly with classmates. Jane's newfound felicity is amplified by the prospect of graduating in three months, which she believes will happen if she passes all her courses this term, and so far, she's doing fine, a few class cuts notwithstanding. Things have settled at home too, where she's stopped fighting with her mother. So she makes an allowance for herself, tempting the devil, occasionally smoking marijuana, convincing herself that it's not that bad, that it's just a taste, that it's harmless. Anyway, she's still writing, she still has her poetry:

> *aromatic amnesia is incessant*
> *oso redundant oso redundant*
> *one is too many and never enough always*
> *more*
> *constricted pupils—the instantaneous closed door,*
> *complete voluntary constricted movements*
> *of the heart*
> *sealed off heart secretes*
> *no tears to eyes,*
> *no need for blurred disguise*
> *the crossed broken line*
> *acuteness of a knife*

*charismatic adept lies*
*comes always*
*so easy*
*goes always*
*so hard*
*constricted*
*vision for reality*
*where the next line*
*breaks and what's the last word said*
*where the next step can only be intended and not*
*located*
*the uncertainty and inevitability*
*and this dichotomy persists*

Hiding the truth, Jane tells Mr. Grossman that she's keeping sober. He wants to believe her, but he knows. "I've seen this pattern before," he says. For the moment, though, he must attend to his duties as English chairman, withdrawing into his office in room 601. Waiting to speak to him is a senior who has a beef with the school administration. Its relationship with students is "horrendous," she says, citing the unwelcome arrival of the attendance scanners—due any day—which she believes is threatening the school's greatness.

"It's going to be more than monitoring attendance," she says, fearing a Big Brother scenario, where students' privacy is invaded. "If we were having attendance problems, that would be one thing," she says, "but it's unnecessary. It doesn't make sense."

That's why she and other student leaders are putting up a fight. As heads of Stuyvesant's Big Sibling program, an influential group in which upperclassmen counsel younger students, they are using their clout in writing a letter of protest to the New York City Department of Education. "Instead of being rewarded for our excellent performance and highly regarded reputation, our student rights are being infringed upon," they write. "We see the new ID Scanning System that Mr. Teitel plans to install as an unfair way for the administration to discipline the students." They go on to say that the principal didn't consult student leaders and others before presenting the scanners as a fait accompli and add, "This money would be much better spent on new textbooks, extracurricular activities, electives, additional college advisors, guidance counselors, etc."

The object of the students' scorn, Mr. Teitel, finds refuge in room 829, where he removes his principal's hat, forgetting for the moment the uncomfortable exigencies of attendance scanners and the rising tide of student ire to teach physics to a freshman class, a job that isn't required of a principal but one that he wants, needs. It gives him credibility among his faculty; it means he's still one of them. Then there's this unstated factor: Mr. Teitel is still in love with teaching.

Gone is his principal's mask of weariness; in its place is a broad smile from which booms a scratchy voice discussing the mysteries of current electricity, electron flow, and the way electrical energy is expended.

"What's that last word?" a student asks.

"*E-x-p-e-n-d-e-d,*" Mr. Teitel says.

Grasping a piece of chalk with a clear plastic glove like that of a surgeon, he inscribes a long, arcane equation on the blackboard, ending with a flourish. "I don't hear my applause," he says, to which the students clap obediently. This is where he belongs, a paper-thin teacher in command of his subject matter and his students, pacing back and forth in front of a blacktop experiment counter with shiny chrome faucets, his natural habitat.

Mr. Teitel proved his stick-to-itiveness when he started as a full-time science teacher in 1971 at William Howard Taft High School, a public school in the Bronx so tough that administrators had warned him not to walk out of the building alone at the end of the day because teachers were getting mugged. At first he told his ninth-grade students at Taft that he was a substitute teacher so they wouldn't really bother him, figuring he was temporary. But when he kept showing up, a student eventually raised a hand to ask, "Weren't you only going to stay for a week?"

Only later did Mr. Teitel find out that he had been hired because a student had hit the previous teacher on the head with a garbage can— and that teacher had promptly quit. An assistant principal had been making book, taking bets that Mr. Teitel wouldn't last a week. "I'm sure he was giving good odds," Mr. Teitel says.

He lasted a dozen years at Taft.

As a teacher at Stuyvesant, he didn't harbor notions of greatness, allowing himself only to dream of one day becoming assistant principal, which happened, to his surprise. But when Ms. Perullo, the principal, unexpectedly announced her retirement in the winter of 1999, Mr. Teitel went home to talk to his wife about applying for the top job. He took a practical tack, considering the long, hot summers he had worked as a teacher for extra income. "I said, 'Look, I've worked summer school many, many years, you know, for the money, and if I become principal, I will make enough money so that I won't have to work summer school anymore, and we'll still be financially better off than we were.'" His wife, herself a schoolteacher, agreed, not giving the prospect too much credence since his was a long-shot candidacy. Mr. Teitel was up against formidable rivals, including two other assistant principals. But then one of them was physically removed from the building in a pair of handcuffs.

An assistant principal of biology was accused of molesting a fifteen-year-old student, a charge to which he ultimately pleaded guilty. His punishment: three years' probation and retirement. After a newly initiated background check, Mr. Teitel was rewarded with the title of principal, and no one was more surprised than he. "I never envisioned this job," he says. "That's the truth."

His wife was not exactly pleased with his promotion. Shortly after he took over, the school system changed Mr. Teitel's job description, making the principal's position a twelve-month-a-year job.

The accidental principal hasn't had a summer off since 1984.

Ms. Lee, the accidental student teacher, can't remember the last day she's had off. Between teaching history and Korean and Sunday school and taking pedagogical classes for her master's degree at Columbia, the days and evenings begin to blur together, including this blustery Tuesday, March 14.

She is always on the go, and much of her life dangles from a thread around her neck in a small black computer memory stick that contains all of her lessons, homework assignments, and grades. Inside her backpack is Rick Warren's *The Purpose-Driven Life*. Today, she reads this passage: "You never understand some commands until you obey them." There is little else to adorn Ms. Lee. She obscures her quiet beauty in a functional outfit, a brown V-neck sweater, gray slacks, and brown shoes, adding no jewelry other than a pair of simple silver hoop earrings and a matching necklace, a minimalist look meant to avoid distracting students while she stands in front of them in class.

It's just one trick she quickly learned as a student teacher. Other lessons of the trade have come harder. Early on, a student challenged the question that Ms. Lee wrote on the chalkboard: "Was Abraham Lincoln really a great man?" Though Ms. Lee's mentor, a teacher of nearly thirty years at Stuyvesant, had used the same question, it provoked a different reaction coming from such a young, inexperienced teacher as Ms. Lee. "I don't think it's appropriate to question his greatness," the student scolded the teacher. Another student threw a paper ball at Ms. Lee while she was passing out a class assignment. "Every day," she says of those first trials, "I was challenged."

The experience reminds her of when she was a high school student at Bronx Science, not so long ago, when she and her classmates would look up arcane facts and then question their teacher about them. So Ms. Lee accepts the challenge now that it comes from Stuyvesant students. "I don't try to be something I'm not," she says.

Ms. Lee tries to have faith, something she learned in class not as a student but as a teacher. When a boy comes to class late, she doesn't lecture him; she calls on him but not in an intrusive way, asking him a question for which there is no wrong answer, his opinion, to give him confidence. When another boy fails to bring in his homework, she pulls him aside and gently asks not for all of it but only yesterday's. He complies by bringing in a stack of overdue homework assignments. He doesn't participate in class but does surprisingly well on an exam. "You never want to give up," she says. In a recent class, while a faculty visitor from Columbia was observing Ms. Lee's history class at Stuyvesant, the boy laid his head on his desk and fell asleep. She let him do it, knowing that she'd be criticized. "There are times you want to let it go," she says.

"I took it that he's a boy that needs a little time." That he comes to class every day is, she believes, a small victory. "I could be losing him entirely," she says. Such compassion isn't always the accepted norm of teaching, but it comes naturally to Ms. Lee, who is acutely aware of the pressures on her students, having once been one of them at Bronx Science, where the burdens of grades and college applications can be overwhelming too. "Sometimes," she says, "the best way to go is moderation." It's a philosophy that stands in stark contrast to the harsh dicta of success preached by her own parents, but perhaps that's the point. "Maybe that's why I take a different approach with my students," she says.

In return, students now shower her with an unusual degree of respect, especially those in her Korean class. As she passes her students in the crowded hallways of Stuyvesant, they will bow to her in the traditional Asian style, ignoring how the act clashes with the regular dyspeptic high school posture of studied uninterest. After school, she will be surprised to find her students by her side, walking with her on her way to the No. 2 or 3 subway on Chambers Street, speaking with her in Korean. She takes pride in their rediscovery of their Korean heritage, thinking about her own high school experience, when students jeered her Korean ancestry, calling her "FOB"—fresh off the boat—even though she was born in Queens. She tells her students that it's nothing to be ashamed of, that it's an advantage to be bilingual, that it would be foolish to renounce where they come from, even in what she calls a "white-centered society," including a school like Stuyvesant, where few of the teachers are Asian despite a majority-Asian student body. An Asian student who for the first time stumbled into her at school couldn't believe it, never thinking he'd come across an Asian teacher in the social studies department. "Wow, that's so cool," he marveled. Her response: "I want them to get that inspiration." She is an example—and a bridge to the school's many Korean parents, who have for years felt detached from the goings-on at Stuyvesant if only because of the language barrier. She translates school documents for them; she takes phone calls to explain issues to them; she meets them outside school to give them guidance.

"Right now, I'm having the time of my life," she says. "This semester is an unbelievable adventure." Already, the student teacher feels like a full-time staffer. "I play a more conspicuous role here. I'm not simply in the shadows."

But that may not last. There are still no teaching openings at Stuyvesant, and she worries, "If I go to a regular school, am I in for a rude awakening?" Here she says, "I was able to find this passion and joy." At another school, she fears, "it might not work."

A devout Christian, she prays for the opportunity to teach three periods of social studies and two periods of Korean at Stuyvesant when she graduates from Columbia and obtains her license as a social studies teacher in a matter of months. "I trust whatever path will be laid for me," she says.

She also trusts Mr. Jaye, who continues to work to find her a full-time job at Stuyvesant. But a day later, Wednesday, March 15, it seems that his own prayers are going unanswered. Sitting at his cluttered desk, he's absorbing the news that New Jersey denied his principal's license because he lacked one course in educational law and finance from his academic transcript. It's a technicality—he studied those issues in other classes—but it's slowing his courtship with Bergen County Academies.

Adding to his agita is another transcript snafu involving a student who has grades of 95 or above in all his classes except biology, in which he ended up with a lowly mark of 70. Mr. Jaye, ever the rabble-rouser, decided to investigate, even though the biology teacher did not fall under his purview as math chairman. What Mr. Jaye found confirmed his suspicions, that the teacher in question was a notoriously tough grader, to the point of being unfair, at least in the case of this otherwise straight-A student. Mr. Jaye took the matter to other administrators, asking whether they were aware of this biology teacher's aberrant grading policy, which could potentially damage the student's college prospects. Administrators were indeed aware. Mr. Jaye fumed, "You allow a teacher to grade outside the institutional standard? So I can give a hundred and five?" It was, to be sure, a rhetorical question, for there was no answer forthcoming.

But what's really galling Mr. Jaye today is the person he loves to hate: Ms. Damesek. In their latest dustup, Ms. Damesek told the principal that she didn't want Mr. Jaye attending the kitchen cabinet meetings, explaining that she thought it would be better if attendance were rotated among other school administrators. Mr. Jaye became livid, telling the principal, "You'll have to call security to get me out of the meeting." Still fulminating in his office hours later, Mr. Jaye relives the unpleasant episode with a neutral observer, Mr. Cocoros, the lawyer turned math teacher, who suggests that an appropriate solution would be to invite an advanced placement psychology class of students to mediate the kitchen cabinet meeting on the first floor. "Why do people downstairs make things so complicated?" Mr. Cocoros wants to know.

Again, a question with no answer.

In Mr. Jaye's outer office, Milo is sitting, head down, at a round wooden table, working out answers to questions for his homework in tomorrow's trigonometry class. He is also actively ignoring the three freshmen and one sophomore who are sitting at the table, talking about Milo as if he weren't present.

"Milo's, like, a junior," says one of the freshmen.

"He has the math mind of a junior," says another.

After a brief lull, Milo looks up and notes that the word *sophomore* actually means "clever fool," and it's unclear whether he just emitted a non sequitur or insulted those in attendance who might fall into that category. The boys around the table have no clue what Milo is talking about and begin laughing uncontrollably about nothing in particular.

Moments later, Milo clips his homework into his loose-leaf binder and removes himself to a quiet spot alone on the floor outside the math department. There Mr. Siwanowicz joins his kindred spirit. Without preface or pleasantries, Milo launches a math mind bender for Mr. Siwanowicz to solve on the spot: There are 13 pirates, 1 treasure chest, several locks and keys. For every lock, there can be more than 1 key. Every key fits only 1 lock. Any 6 pirates cannot open the treasure chest. Any 7 can. What is the least number of locks they need?

Within seconds, Mr. Siwanowicz computes an answer: 1,716. Milo douses the suspense by saying he doesn't know the answer; he just saw the question online. Suddenly, both man and boy look greatly fatigued, as if one is a reflection of the other, just at different points in the evolution of time.

Insomnia continues to afflict Mr. Siwanowicz. He can't fall asleep when he wants and he dozes at the most inopportune moments, like when he is standing in a subway car. "Several times," he says, "I nearly fell down."

If there's a silver lining, he says, his insomnia surmounts his depression. "I'm too tired to be sad."

He seems almost resigned to library duty during his free seventh and eighth periods, even though he'd rather be doing something more useful, like talking to students about math, which he views as his one unique talent. And he's come around to the idea that perhaps he should return to City College over the summer and finish his degree. But he's distracted from his own future by that of two troubled students in the math research class that he unofficially teaches. One is still failing to show up. The other shows up only sporadically. He wonders if he could be doing more. But he knows he won't reach every student. That is an unfortunate part of teaching, he admits, yet he says, 'I worry about them. They're developing habits which will impede them later."

Mr. Siwanowicz knows something about being impeded.


After school, Alexa is feeling impeded too. The freshman coproducer of Sing! is seething backstage about dirty tactics being employed by the enemy just a week before opening night. The juniors have allegedly appropriated the equipment that the freshmen and sophomores had intended to use to hold up their scenery. "It's a horrible thing to do," Alexa says. But she takes comfort in what the reputed act of thievery seems to imply, that soph/frosh is looking good enough to worry the upperclassmen. Maybe the juniors should be concerned. Later that evening, it is almost impossible to hear the voices of juniors trying to sing above the cacophony of amplified instruments during rehearsal. Hunched in orchestra seating, codirector Ben Alter has trouble removing the frown from his face. "It's pretty hectic," he says "but it'll come together." His codirector, Liam, is not his usual confident self either. "You never know," he says philosophically. "Sing! is like *Waiting for Godot.*" His mood isn't helped by Xevion, who is openly fretting. After worrying that "Respect" is an octave too high, and then deciding it isn't, she now hears that her biggest competitor, Molly, the senior, is planning to sing the classic Patti LaBelle hit disco song "Lady Marmalade," which Xevion is sure will bring down the house. What Xevion doesn't know, though, is that Molly is worried about Xevion's singing too. Such are their prodigious talents that their stentorian voices make them stand out like two giants in an open field of Lilliputians. But Molly also has this to contend with: she is not only the Big Fish, she is the seniors' last, great hope to graduate with a victory in the grand musical competition. "If we don't win," Molly says, her face flushing, "I don't know."

The following day over lunch, Xevion is still obsessing, telling Romeo that her rival is singing one of her favorite songs. "I'm worried about everything," she says. So is Romeo, who is competing with his own rival, just in a different arena: academics. Who, he wants to know, will get the higher SAT score?

One of his Stuyvesant friends just achieved near perfection on a practice exam—without studying. And Romeo, approaching the field of academia with the same fierce determination he shows on the football field, intends to practice his way to a better score. "I want to beat him," he says.

When it comes to football, Romeo's sheer effort is paying off. He is getting bigger and stronger, sweating in the cramped weight room, pushing himself with bench presses, military presses, squats, pull-ups, and Romanian dead lifts, which sound as painful as they are. Yet even as he builds mass and muscle, Romeo knows what he is up against, opposing players from regular public schools who could give a hoot about academics, who focus all of their energies on getting even stronger. He conjures up the immovable force at the line of scrimmage, fit linemen with big stocky legs.

"When they take their stance," he says, "they take up a lot of space."

Over a tray of roasted chicken, Xevion tries to make amends for a joke she made about Stuyvesant's woeful football team. "I'm sorry about the wisecrack," she says.

The well-intended apology touches a sore spot. "I don't remember anything you say," Romeo says in a knee-jerk reaction.

Xevion is wounded too, and Romeo immediately regrets it, saying that he generally remembers what she says, although that doesn't last because what he's recalling now is how he received only a 4.5 out of 5— a high score that wasn't high enough, by his standards—on his autobiographical essay assignment in English class. "I didn't push the narrative form as much as I could ve," he rues.

"Alexander, focus on what you did correctly," Xevion says; she calls Romeo by his last name when she's taking him to task. "You got a great score. Be happy."

Romeo tries to write off the less-than-perfect grade, saying he isn't worried about grades anymore. "I don't feel stress anymore,' he says, as if he is trying to convince himself.

Xevion notes how two nights ago Romeo went to sleep earlier than she did. "It's a miracle," she says.

"I didn't go to bed," he corrects her. "I read."

So much for easing up. The bell rings. In passing, as they head out of the dining hall, Romeo mentions that he recently broke up with his first girlfriend. The relationship, it turns out, wasn't so great. Maybe it wasn't love. Maybe it was a chemical reaction in the brain, as he had read about in that issue of *National Geographic*. Down the hall, he catches sight of a pretty blond sophomore, who flashes a big smile at him. Without a farewell, he pursues the girl, weaving through a jostling hallway of students, evading them like so many blockers on the football field. Watching him disappear, Xevion says absently, "I think he needs more of an emotional attachment.'

# CHAPTER THIRTEEN

# Protests and Demands

THAT THURSDAY NIGHT, MARCH 16, FATHER AND daughter are pursuing opposite ends of an intractable debate that has plagued them ever since she began contemplating attending Stuyvesant:

Is the school a good idea?

No, Mr. Davis maintains.

Yes, insists his daughter, Katie Johnston-Davis.

"My thing was to keep Katie out of a gifted and talented program," he says while frying flounder in a sizzling pan as the Beatles' "Drive My Car" plays in the background of his Upper West Side co-op.

"Oh, that worked well," says Katie with a heavy dose of sarcasm.

She is a seventeen-year-old senior at Stuyvesant.

Mr. Davis, the parent who made an impassioned plea against attendance scanners at the School Leadership Team meeting last month, never liked the idea of a public school that admitted only students who passed a test. A math teacher for pregnant students in the Bronx, Mr. Davis even turned down an opportunity to send Katie to a gifted and talented program in middle school, sending her instead to a more progressive, alternative public school. He doesn't believe in segregating students by academic ability. He believes that high-achieving students can learn from low-achieving students—and vice versa—and that school diversity is a good thing. "Everybody has something to offer," he says. Tests, he argues, "devaluate social worth, human worth," failing to take into consideration what he calls "multidimensional personalities" and "multiple intelligences."

Besides, he adds, "the test only tests for certain qualities."

Katie barely studied for the Stuyvesant entrance exam, but when she aced it anyway, her father told her it wasn't the kind of school he would choose for her.

Mr. Davis had graduated from Stuyvesant.

So, of course, Katie defied her father by choosing to attend his alma mater. And she loves it.

"I've gained so much from being around people who are so gifted," she says. Katie has thrived—a picture-perfect teenager, wholesomely pretty and well-adjusted even as she pushes herself as the captain of the girls' soccer team—the city champs last year—while maintaining a 93 grade point average.

"There's never been any pressure on her to get high grades," her father says. "That's her issue."

If anything, he tries to give her a break. At midnight on a Sunday, as she's hunkered down studying, he's apt to poke his head in her room to see if he can excuse her from school. "Katie, are you going to school tomorrow, or should I write a note?" he'll ask lovingly. At the same time, he says proudly, "I encouraged her to be all she could be," to which Katie rolls her bright blue eyes and says, "You're so cheesy." All that Mr. Davis will grudgingly admit is, "The Stuyvesant she goes to is better than the Stuyvesant I went to."

It's true, the school wasn't always a class apart, filled with brainiacs like Katie.

In the beginning, when Stuyvesant opened in 1904, it called itself a manual training school for boys. Educators named the school after Peter Stuyvesant, the son of a Dutch Reformed church minister who was a college dropout. Rising through the ranks of the Dutch West India

Company, he served as the commander of Curaçao, where a cannon-fire tussle with a Portuguese-run Caribbean island left his right leg severely damaged, requiring amputation below the knee. Thus the man's peg leg (and the football team's unseemly name).

Given a more prestigious appointment, the hobbled Stuyvesant arrived in New Amsterdam in 1647 as director-general of the unruly colony, commanding what later became Manhattan with a dictatorial style marked by unvarnished bigotry. He persecuted Quakers, Jews, and others, making him a curious selection for the namesake of a public high school filled with immigrants of various faiths more than two centuries later. But history's history, and back in Stuyvesant's day, the Lower East Side was a tremendous swamp until he purchased land there, building a chapel on what became known as Stuyvesant Town, site of the original high school.

A five-story beaux-arts-style limestone building, the original school cost what was then a princely sum—$1.5 million—a hundredth of the price of the new school built nearly a century later on the other side of town. In a ceremony to lay the cornerstone of the building at East Fifteenth Street, William H. Maxwell, then superintendent of the city's schools, boasted, "This school, so recently established, should become the greatest in the United States."

He couldn't have known then how those words would ring true one day.

At the time of Stuyvesant's founding, fewer than 7 percent of seventeen-year-old Americans graduated from high school, and there were just a handful of secondary schools in New York City. Most people with merely seven or eight years of schooling had little problem finding a job, whether as a farmer, a clerk, or an unskilled factory worker.

In the early 1900s, with the rise of the Industrial Age, when manufacturers were just beginning to mass-produce automobiles on the assembly line, high school enrollment was bulging and manual training was all the rage, especially popular among education reformers and business leaders who wanted to make school more practical, preparing students for the workforce and aiding the nation's budding commercialism, says Diane Ravitch, a research professor of education at NYU and noted education historian. "Now we are a nation of manufacturers and traders, and the army that we have to fear is not an army of any nation, equipped with guns, but a German army of skilled workmen with tools in their hands, directed by captains of industry educated in the match- less Prussian schools," said Thomas M. Balliet, NYU's dean of the School of Pedagogy, in an address at Stuyvesant in 1904. "No artificial protec- tion of our markets will avail to guard our industries permanently against the invasion of that army. Our only abiding protection must be found in the training of our own workmen and in the education of our industrial and commercial leaders."

Also at the turn of the century, millions of new immigrants from Eastern and Southern Europe poured into urban centers—and public schools—giving even more urgency to the growth of manual training schools catering to a clientele for whom English was a second language. When Stuyvesant opened, more than 70 percent of students in the New York City schools were children of foreign-born fathers.

"The island was just bursting at the seams with humanity," said Philip M. Scandura, a Stuyvesant teacher of the history of New York City.

The island of Manhattan also teemed with overcrowded tenements on the Lower East Side, a neighborhood carnival of street peddlers and lines of clothes hanging out to dry, not far from docks and harbors packed with exotic ships from all over the world. From these tenements, many poor immigrant boys walked to their local high school, Stuyvesant, where traditional academics, like English, history, and science, were cou- pled with practical courses in carpentry, pattern making, and forging. Among the lowest priorities was preparing students for college.

"Although the courses of study in the new school afford complete preparation for college, neither this school nor any other high school should be administered mainly in the interests of college preparatory work," said the school's first yearbook, the *Indicator* of 1905. ". . . The new high school is to be a preparatory school in a new and unusually broad sense, and will give unusual emphasis to the idea that schools pre- pare hundreds for life while preparing a few for college."

Instead, that first yearbook touted the benefits of manual training: "The city boy is confined at home, restricted on the street, and necessar- ily repressed in the ordinary school till he aches to do something with the motor cells of his brain and nerves acting through his growing muscles; hence more than half the disorder and mischief of troublesome boys. Manual training gives the boy an opportunity to do proper and serviceable things instead of creating a disturbance."

With rising enrollment, educators after 1920 restricted admission to Stuyvesant to those with high academic records in elementary school as the high school moved away from manual training to an increasing emphasis on math and science, according to New York City Landmarks Preservation Commission documents. When the nation descended into the Great Depression, parents kept their children in school longer so that more of the scant remaining jobs would go to the adults, but that created overcrowded conditions at schools like Stuyvesant. To limit enrollment, the school introduced an entrance exam in 1934. Students needed at least an eighth-grade average of 78 and one letter of recommendation to qualify for the test. The first entrance exams drew from questions written by an assistant to the principal and the chairman of the math department

Not until the social upheavals of the 1960s did activists begin to clamor against the idea of the test. Accusing Stuyvesant and the other specialized schools of being culturally biased against black and Hispanic students, activists demanded that such public exam schools in New York City be eliminated. They wanted to convert the exam schools into neighborhood schools open to any child in the community.

"It was a period of protests and demands," Dr. Ravitch says. "There was a great revolt against any form of elitism, privilege."

In response, Stuyvesant and the other two specialized schools—Bronx Science and Brooklyn Technical High School—then adopted the Discovery program, the affirmative action initiative to accept some minority students who barely missed the cutoff. That, however, did not allay criticism.

A few years later, some local educators joined activists in demanding the abolition of Stuyvesant and the other public exam schools, again charging that the test discriminated against black and Hispanic students. This time, the protesters gained more traction; the schools superintendent designated a commission to study the test, a move that alarmed supporters of the three specialized schools, especially those at Bronx

Science. Parents, alumni, and others mobilized quickly, garnering the political support of two little-known Bronx state lawmakers, who introduced a bill to preserve the admissions exam. The proposed legislation would ensure that a citywide standardized test would determine admissions, underscoring the notion that a meritocracy would prevail at these schools. As a compromise, lawmakers added the affirmative action Discovery program as a formal provision of the bill, even though it contradicted their promise to maintain a test-only admissions policy. Despite heated debate, lawmakers passed the Hecht-Calandra bill, named after the lawmakers.

Stuyvesant introduced the Math and Science Institute in 1995 to help disadvantaged students prepare for the test. But that did little to assuage critics as the proportion of black and Hispanic students continued to drop. The controversy flared up again in May 1997 when protesters barged into Stuyvesant, staging a demonstration in the school's lobby, accusing the school system of operating a "secret apartheid." The activists, known as the Association of Community Organizations for Reform Now, or ACORN, released a study charging that middle schools failed to adequately prepare many black and Hispanic students for the kind of material found on the admissions exam for Stuyvesant and the other specialized public schools.

"The current test for the specialized high schools must remain permanently suspect as the product of an institutional racism inappropriate to an educational system in a democracy," the report said.

In a statement, then schools chancellor Rudy Crew responded by saying it was "an unfortunate truth that African-American and Latino students traditionally have been underrepresented in the specialized high schools." He said he welcomed suggestions. The demonstrators called for the immediate suspension of the entrance exam. That suggestion went unheeded.

The debate continues to simmer.

Mr. Teitel, Stuyvesant's principal, is the first to come to the defense of his school—passionately. "There's a difference between a child who is gifted and talented and a child who simply works hard," he says, choosing his words carefully. "And we have lots of children in New York City who come to school every day and work hard, doing the right [thing] and are successful in their schools. . . . Those are good kids. But they're not gifted and talented kids, okay? Gifted and talented is a kid who sits in a math team class and has the insight to see where this problem's going. Gifted and talented is when I teach my physics class and I don't have to go through every single algebraic step. I can jump to here to there. I can go from step one to step four, and no one is going to raise their hand and go, 'How'd you do that?' They can be with me. That's gifted and talented."

Mr. Teitel is quick to point out that he doesn't include his own children among them. He is also quick to note that not only does Stuyvesant draw from the same pool of teachers as any other city school but that his school is like any other in another important respect: Stuyvesant receives the same funding as all the other schools in the system. It's based on enrollment, not achievement. "In fact, if anything," he asserts, "I'm getting underfunded" because Stuyvesant doesn't receive the additional federal money given to schools that serve underprivileged students. As a result, Stuyvesant administrators say, they frequently scramble to meet the special needs of gifted students, scraping funds together to cover extra costs of advanced math textbooks, for example, or new literary works not found on the school's shelves.

"Gifted children are the most underrepresented class in the United States," Mr. Jaye says.

He includes himself among them as a former student who went unchallenged and bored in a regular school. "I know what happens when you have a gifted student who isn't in a gifted program," he says. "It's child abuse." That's why he finds himself ensnared in an argument with a new administrator at City College, where he created a summer program for gifted high school students to earn college credits When the college administrator looked at the sea of faces in the auditorium, she saw only a handful of black students participating in the program. The administrator told him the program needed more diversity. Mr. Jaye said he wasn't "compromising on the quality." While Mr. Jaye agrees that the program hasn't "met its diversity target," he says admission is based on academic credentials. "We don't have to apologize for being elite," he says.

Such exclusivity isn't always an advantage for Stuyvesant students. For one, they are thrust in an environment where there is always someone better, which can be a rude awakening. "Where they came from, they may have been the star," says Ms. Archie, the assistant principal. " . . . And then they come here, and then they realize there are thirty-four kids [per class] that are stars."

Mr. Polazzo, coordinator of student affairs, goes as far as to say that, for the most selective colleges, "being at Stuy doesn't help you, in fact it probably hurts you." Students are vying for limited spots at the top colleges, he notes, and schools like Harvard will accept only so many students from Stuyvesant, no matter how gifted.

That's one reason Mariya, the Ukrainian immigrant, thinks she'd be better off at Edward R. Murrow High School, a public school that admits a mix of high- and low-achieving students not far from her home in Brooklyn. "With less pressure, I think I could do better there," says the Stuyvesant sophomore. It occurs to her too that she might "look better compared to some of the regular people." And there's the added benefit that her best friend, Natasha Borchakovskaia, another Ukrainian immigrant, is a junior at Murrow who likes the school. Unlike Stuyvesant, Natasha says, Murrow students have a social life, they have the freedom to make what they want of their education, grades are not as important, and while violence is an occasional problem—a stabbing took place Natasha's freshman year—somehow that seems more palatable to her than a school packed with nerds whose weapon of choice is a "pocket protector."

Still, there is a palpable sense among students that Stuyvesant is a privilege, whether it's a function of the rigorous admissions test, the $150 million building, or the students themselves. "Everyone here is brilliant," Xevion says. "We're like any other high school, except we have one thing in common. We are really bright. We have a lot of potential."

Many students at other city schools come to view their Stuyvesant peers differently as well. "Stuy kids, they are among the top," says junior Elaine Liu, herself a top student at Leon M. Goldstein High School for the Sciences, a well-respected public school in Brooklyn, where students are chosen based on a formula intended to ensure a balance of low and high achievers. Elaine had wanted to attend Stuyvesant, eyeing its wide range of advanced placement classes, some of which aren't offered at her school. "Another thing is reputation," she says. At Stuyvesant, "all they have is constant praise." By contrast, she says, 'if I tell people what school I go to, they go, like, 'What? Where is the school?'" Stuyvesant's fame has a tangible benefit, she says, discounting the theory that it's a disadvantage to be a star among many stars. Colleges, scouting prospective students, are apt to take kindly to Stuyvesant students. "They look at them [in] a better light than other kids," Elaine says. "They would choose Stuy kids over normal kids."

Even students who make it into the public exam schools wrestle with the privilege accorded them. "I guess it's not fair for those people who didn't get in," says Bronx Science sophomore Rosabella Magat, a Filipino immigrant. But if educators abolished the exam schools, she says, only students whose parents could afford private school would obtain the kind of specialized education that many colleges are seeking. "If it's not a competition of skill, then it'd be a competition of who can afford it, and I don't think that's fair," Rosabella says.

Yet gaining admission to public schools like Bronx Science and Stuyvesant is, to an extent, a competition of who can afford the costly private courses to prepare students for the exam, say many students and parents. Sixteen-year-old Francisco Bencosme makes that argument, saying he suffered the consequences because his parents—a security guard and an assistant in a doctor's office—couldn't afford such a prep course. He borrowed a friend's used Kaplan test prep book, studied for a week, and narrowly missed the Stuyvesant cutoff. Now a Bronx Science sophomore, Francisco still wonders what would have happened if he had the opportunity to take a prep course. "In the back of my head, I always think I could've gone to Stuyvesant if I did a little better on the test," he says. "I feel there's an economic advantage for parents who can afford these courses, whereas my parents couldn't." Francisco, though, is hard-pressed to come up with a better way to select students for elite public schools, if they are to be. Admission can't be determined by middle school grades, he says, because there is too much variation inherent in them. That, he reckons, leaves a uniform entrance test as perhaps the least of all evils.

"It's as fair as it can be," he says.

Educators and policy makers are equally confounded. Some say public exam schools send the wrong message to students about their self-worth if they fail to gain admission. Another concern is that removing gifted students from regular schools deprives those places of "the yeast that makes the whole school rise," Dr. Ravitch says. Still others challenge whether taxpayers should fund public exam schools when so many other students at the other end of the spectrum are in need of remedial education or are at risk of dropping out. How, they say, can you justify a school like Stuyvesant?

"It's elitist," says Thomas Toch, cofounder and codirector of Education Sector, a policy think tank in Washington, D.C. "Should you be spending public dollars in that way? It's a fundamental question." The answer, he says, "is a tough call because those schools are truly elitist in both the best and the worst sense of the word."

Katie, for her part, is at peace with her decision to attend Stuyvesant, despite her father's protests. The seventeen-year-old, though, is not without her own concerns about educational elitism. In less than two weeks, she will be hearing from the colleges to which she applied. She's a little nervous. One place she won't be hearing from: the Ivy League. Despite her high grade point average and SAT scores, she didn't apply to any of those colleges.

"I've crossed them off," she says.

Katie has always been unimpressed with the Stuyvesant frenzy over such brand-name schools, especially among students who from the beginning of freshman year are set on attending an Ivy League college before they know anything about the schools—let alone about themselves. "In the end," says Mr. Davis, a proud papa, beaming about his daughter's decision, "it's a badge of courage." Who needs Harvard when you have Haverford College? That is where Katie will eventually be heading—happily.

CHAPTER FOURTEEN

# Grief Virus

THEY ARE SO YOUNG, THEY KNOW SO LITTLE ABOUT themselves. But on the morning of March 17, they knew this much: Fourteen-year-old April Lao is a small but spirited freshman, a gifted piano player and talented swimmer on the Stuyvesant team who loves brownies and other sweet things. Sixteen-year-old sophomore Kevin Kwan, also a promising member of Stuyvesant's swim team, has a way of making you smile with that infectious laugh of his, and if he insults you, please don't take it personally; it probably only means that he likes you.

At about 5:30 a.m., April kisses and hugs her father, saying, "Goodbye, Daddy."

Then she and Kevin, members of the Flushing Flyers, a private swim team in Queens, head to a YMCA swim meet in Buffalo. Both swimmers' mothers and Kevin's and April's ten-year-old brothers accompany them. At about 7 a.m., Kevin's mother pulls over their minivan to check a flat tire, stopping in the right traffic lane instead of pulling onto the shoulder of the New York State Thruway. Just behind and around a slight bend, out of sight a tanker bears down in the same direction.

Another trucker, spotting the minivan stopped on the highway, desperately tries to radio the tanker to avoid it. "Get over!" the trucker screams into his CB radio. "Move over!" But the fifty-two-year-old tanker driver doesn't pick up the warning.

The trucker flashes his headlights to alert the tanker, but the driver remains unaware.

Kevin's mother climbs back in the minivan.

Barreling down the highway at sixty-five miles per hour, the tanker driver doesn't see the minivan until he is practically on top of it, and in the split second that he tries to swerve around it, his truck smashes into the back of the minivan, ripping off the car's roof and propelling the minivan about sixty feet down an embankment. In the sudden impact, Kevin is thrown from the demolished car. April lies nearby, bleeding, soundless.

Kevin dies there, as do his mother and his younger brother. A helicopter flies April to a nearby hospital, where hours later she cannot be saved. Her brother and mother survive.

"I have lost my beautiful daughter," April's father says. Kevin's father breaks down, inconsolable.

Police do not charge the distraught tanker driver, who is treated and released with a shoulder injury.

Word of the tragedy reaches school almost instantly. Students gather on the Tribeca Bridge outside the building and weep. Grief counselors arrive at Stuyvesant the following Monday. Students erect a garland-wreathed memorial at the second-floor entrance, spangled with helium balloons and photos of the dead children. Other impromptu memorials spring up throughout the building. R.I.P. APRIL AND KEVIN, announces one sign, showing two winged angels in flight. But the bereavement doesn't end. Instead, a grief virus spreads imperceptibly, a wrenching pall gripping even students like Namita, the senior, who never knew April or Kevin. Namita can't stop thinking about them, weeping quietly on a bench in the school lobby. On another bench, Alex Larsen, a freshman girl who did know April in biology class, also can't help but think of them.

"That could've been me," Alex says.

The fifteen-year-old sits, too stunned to show any emotion. "I couldn't imagine dying," she says sotto voce. "I have my agenda all planned out. I want to be a brain surgeon."

Alex also can't help thinking about her recent fight over a boy with another student, her best friend—ex-best friend. They haven't talked since. But April's and Kevin's deaths—the fragility of life—puts the squabble in a different light. What happened to April and Kevin gives a painful context and a blunt perspective to teenagers who, like Alex, feel that they're impervious, that they'll live forever, that every little thing counts. Now Alex is embarrassed about the fight with her good friend. "It wasn't even worth it," she says, and in that instant, she absolves her friend. "I forgive her," she says. Though Alex has trouble understanding the meaning of April's and Kevin's deaths, she finds certainty in thinking about her former best friend. One day, Alex knows, "we'll work things out."

The tragedy is hard for Mr. Teitel to fathom as well. In his nearly quarter century at Stuyvesant, the principal cannot recall a year when as many as two students died. For him, the only tragedy that compares occurred five years ago. No Stuyvesant student died then, but the entire school mourned.

Sitting at his desk on that morning, September 11, 2001, Mr. Teitel heard a blast, then noticed the lights flicker. "The whole building shook," he recalls. Looking out of his window, he could not believe the calamity he was witnessing only four blocks from Stuyvesant: the World Trade Center in a billowing haze of smoke and fire. In the chaos that ensued, FBI and Secret Service agents converged on the school. No one at Stuyvesant knew at first that terrorists had struck, and Mr. Teitel announced over the public address system that students were to remain in class. Then the first of the two towers came crashing down, sending reverberations throughout the school. Suddenly, it dawned on Mr. Teitel that the authorities did not know what was happening, and he ordered students to evacuate the building. Children in backpacks fled up the street, only turning back to witness debris and human remains descend like the mushroom cloud of an atomic bomb on Lower Manhattan.

"They saw this live, in living color," Mr. Teitel says, as if he still can't believe it.

Though no harm came to students that day, when Stuyvesant

reopened in October 2001, many students returned to school damaged, suffering from rashes, nosebleeds, and what many parents and others believed was a lingering case of post-traumatic stress disorder. The last class to witness the destruction of 9/11 graduated in 2005, with fewer laurels and prizes than usual for Stuyvesant, and an unsettling legacy remains for succeeding generations of students to ponder: a big gaping hole at the World Trade Center site.

With the pit full of cranes and hard hats and excavated dirt, time seems to have stood still since terrorists struck, leaving the site in a heap of construction delays and false starts blamed on political infighting and clashes about artistic visions over the new towers to rise again. It's enough of a morass to turn unspeakable tragedy into a distinctly American spectacle, one of the city's biggest tourist attractions, drawing a battalion of sightseeing buses and more than a million visitors a year.

But there's no way to recast the tragedy of two children lost in a car wreck. It is what it is.

"This was different," Mr. Teitel says.

At Stuyvesant, life sputters on. Five days after April's and Kevin's deaths, a sense of normalcy struggles to reemerge in Mr. Siwanowicz's fourth-period math research class. Several students straggle in late, as if it doesn't matter, the straggling or the lateness. "Stuff happens," Mr. Siwanowicz says, "but try to be on time in class." There's no venom in his voice. It's almost too perfunctory. The tardy students seem not to care. Nor does Mr. Siwanowicz. Maybe he's just too tired or too depressed or both. Mr. Jaye makes a cameo appearance in the room, attempting to inject more life into the class, exhorting the students to take this course seriously. "We really do want you to work," he says, and then he's gone. Taking his cue, Mr. Siwanowicz lumbers over to the whiteboard, a red marker in hand to make a point about Pascal's triangle, a mystery of math that seems to grab the attention of at least one student: Milo. Sitting in the first seat of the first row, the ten-year-old prodigy remains riveted by all things math at the same time that he continues to morph into something less childlike. He is wearing a horizontally striped sweater eerily reminiscent of that worn by the former prodigy, Mr. Siwanowicz. But Milo's jeans contain a feature lacking in his teacher's version—a well-placed hole in the right knee—which brings him a step closer to acceptable fashion in these teenage parts. Milo even wields a bottle of Poland Spring water, another standard Stuyvesant classroom accoutrement, except that he accidentally dumped most of it inside his backpack, soaking his papers in a soggy reminder that his transformation isn't complete.

"I can't teach how to ask questions," Mr. Siwanowicz is saying. "The key is to find one good question."

He's talking about how students need to ask questions to find a good math topic to research, but he might as well be asking questions about himself: Will he ever finish college? Will he ever obtain his teacher's license? Will he ever stop patrolling the library? But there are no answers to those questions, not on this day. It's his students' turn to ask questions. So Milo pairs with his Stuyvesant friend Daniel, the Cuban immigrant who went for ice cream with him that day not so long ago. Now the two boys huddle over a gray desk, searching for the right question.

Later, during seventh period, Mariya, the fifteen-year-old Ukrainian immigrant, is huddled over a gray desk of her own, listing to her left, head in hand, pondering the miseries of chemistry which are adding to the woes of her failed petition drive to eradicate that scourge, homework over vacation. On the blackboard resides a riddle: "How do you calculate ksp values?" The teacher asks Mariya's friend, Mariana, for the variable of a certain "A." Mariana answers, "Um," letting the utterance draw out until it dies of its own accord with no discernible answer. Evidently, Mariana's mother is going to kill Mariya, who was supposed to rescue Mariana from the last chemistry test.

Mariana failed spectacularly.

Mariya, though, faces perhaps a worse fate than the ire of Mariana's mother. If Mariya's parents punished her for a report card that dipped slightly below 95, she hasn't begun to imagine the repercussions of a disreputable 84 on her latest chemistry test. But it seems that Mariya cares less and less about grades, that the moorings of parental censure are loosening. It could be because Mariya recently celebrated—survived, is more like it—her two-month anniversary with her inscrutable first love, Tom. But more likely, it's because of April and Kevin, whose deaths linger in Mariya's consciousness, though she knew neither. She feels bleak about her own future, worrying about becoming one of those people who take a job just for the money. She feels overweight even though she isn't, not nearly. She feels nostalgic, if that's possible for a fifteen-year-old, for the old days when she and her best friend, Natasha, stood on the concrete handball courts of the park in their Brooklyn neighborhood, in a kind of Rockwellian portrait, innocent and pure, simply spinning round and round, going nowhere, not hoping for tomorrow to come because today is all they need.

But then, it seems that everyone in school wishes this day, Wednesday, March 22, had never arrived. Mr. Teitel even offered to postpone it. The principal consulted with the swim team to see whether he should move back tonight's opening performance of Sing! He also approached freshmen and sophomore leaders, since it was they who had lost their own in April and Kevin. All agreed: Sing! must go on.

On a practical level, it has to. By eighth period, only 8 of the 840 tickets remain for tonight's performance, even though it's merely a dress rehearsal known as "New Haven," named after the Broadway tradition of tuning up a musical in the Connecticut locale. Tickets for the real performances on Friday and Saturday nights are scalping for a hundred dollars a pop, five times face value. Already, the Student Union has spent six thousand dollars on Sing! T-shirts and sweatshirts, expecting to double that in profit. And a stockpile lies in wait: eight hundred bottles of water, cases of Mountain Dew, boxes of strawberry Pop-Tarts, Starburst, and Reese's—teenage booty.

Everything is in place, except the performers, the sets, the props, and just about everything else. "We're not as ready as we should be," says senior hip-hop dancer Olga Safronova in quiet understatement. She's referring to the mayhem on the second floor, where students are scrambling to finish making black and green toxic-mutant-fish dance costumes, airing them with a blow dryer on a clothesline. Sitting nearby, Allie Caccamo, a member of the Indian dance number, raises the ghost of the dreaded curse that every six years the seniors are fated to lose Sing! "Oh my God," says a fellow senior who is playing the animated character SpongeBob in the play. "That's not even funny." Even less funny is the condition of Molly, the seniors' star singer, who approaches with cheeks flushed red. The singer can't sing. She has lost her voice to strep throat, or tonsillitis, or a disease as yet undiagnosed, such as overwhelming anxiety, and she's about to leave school to see a doctor. The early prognosis from her grandfather, an otorhinolaryngologist, a term Molly can't define (an ear, nose, and throat specialist), is appropriately dire. He says she might burst a blood vessel in her throat if she sings. "I'm so sick, I don't know what to do," Molly says.

"If it makes you feel better, I'm worried about my song," says Xevion, the juniors' singer, who has wandered into enemy territory.

It's a rare act of sympathy between junior and senior—bitter rivals—on the eve of Sing! But Xevion rises above the intense competition, showing pathos for a fellow diva, confiding that she's nervous about her Aretha Franklin cover, that she forgot some of the alternative lyrics in a run-through yesterday. Molly returns the compassion, showing admiration for the junior class's stage handiwork. "I was really intimidated by your set," she says.

Outside, a group of freshmen and sophomores is heading up Chambers Street to buy sandwiches—and to try to resolve the jarring disconnect between tonight's celebratory performance and the searing memory of April and Kevin. One sophomore singer can't. She shudders at the thought of the soph/frosh musical. "Our Sing! is about death and wanting people to die," she says. "I don't want to have Sing! because I'm the one who has to go up there and say all those things."

Taylor, the freshman codirector, changed some of the lyrics because a boy in the choir, a good friend of Kevin, who had also been in the choir, would break down whenever the song mentioned death.

The lyric "It's not all that bad to die" became "It isn't that bad down here."

"We all want to stay alive" transformed into "We all want to see the world."

Alexa, the freshman coproducer, wrote the play's dedication to Kevin and April, whom she knew from attending the same private Asian academy. Alexa kept typing the dedication over and over. Each time, she says, "It didn't seem right." Sometimes, she understands, words cannot suffice.

At 5:41, the thirty-fourth annual Sing! opens to a darkened auditorium of parents, teachers, and students, who hold a moment of silence in memory of April and Kevin. It's an appropriate forum. Few things at school other than Sing! bring together so many disparate factions of Stuyvesant, students who would otherwise never interact, whether it's Katherine, the Korean immigrant who somehow has time to serve as an usher tonight, or Jane, the senior struggling with a drug addiction, whose presence in the audience is startling in its own right because it means she's not in rehab, or Milo, who's here with his mother to see what the fuss is all about.

Then, a spotlight on two boys in front of the curtain, strumming a guitar. And the heavy black curtains separate, distending the air of mourning until it dissolves, like speckles of dust in a shaft of light, into the mercy of forgetfulness, into the make-believe playground arrayed on stage: a swing set in green and yellow, a seesaw in orange and yellow, and a playhouse in red and yellow. Coltish boys and girls prance on stage, breaking out in a carefree dance and song drowned out by the static buzz and blare of balky speakers. But it doesn't matter. It's soph/frosh. It's messy. It's confusing. It's perfect.

One sophomore vocalist, playing the role of Pandora, climbs a makeshift throne, overcoming her misgivings about the deaths of April and Kevin to sing majestically. Sammy, the putative troublemaker from French class, amazes in a hip-hop dance. Another student, decked out all in black like a dominatrix, does a rousing imitation of Ms. Damesek, the assistant principal of organization, in the thinly disguised role of "Ms. Ramesak." "I'm going to crush your bones," she howls onstage to the delight of the audience. The real version, Ms. Damesek, isn't around to appreciate it. She's patrolling the lobby. "I've seen enough of it," she says later. When Pandora is foiled in the end, and the curtain closes, the audience erupts in applause, and even a grizzled math teacher, Richard Geller, a notoriously tough grader, sits in the audience in quiet approval.

"Pretty smooth," he says grudgingly.

Mr. Geller is even more impressed when the juniors take the stage next, storming a gloriously rendered pirate's ship, and it's instantly clear that rumors notwithstanding, the juniors are taking nothing for granted. Wyndam, editor of the school newspaper, inspires big laughs as a patch-eyed pirate. The girl Romeo likes in his advanced math class does a beautiful dance step in a red dress, looking bookish no longer.

And then there is Romeo's lunch companion, Xevian, who plays Captain Hook. When she sings her variation of Aretha Franklin's "Respect," the microphone stalls but it can't obfuscate the ethereal sound of her voice, which draws one of the biggest applauses of the evening. When the juniors bow off stage, one thing is clear: they have a legitimate chance to win.

The seniors seem to sense the challenge, opening the final musical of the night with a tentative version of the Bee Gees' "Stayin' Alive." They look so much bigger than the underclassmen, almost world-weary by comparison, and the difference in age is reflected in the dark underside of their comedic script about an alcoholic father with an unwanted child. For the only time tonight in any of the three plays, a boy on stage tells a girl, "I love you." Jokes abound about the imminent arrival of the school's attendance scanners and, of course, about Ms. Damesek. As a whip-wielding queen, Molly parodies the assistant principal of organization, screaming, "There will be no stopping my evil reign," drawing laughs from the gallery, but not from Ms. Damesek, who is now standing alone in black stiletto boots, mirthless, by the auditorium door. But there is something critically missing from the seniors' performance: Molly's voice. On doctor's orders, she is saving her lungs for Friday and Saturday nights, when it counts, when anonymous alumni judge the performances. But during tonight's New Haven performance, her voice is sorely missed.

When it's over, Mr. Geller, the math teacher, abruptly rises to leave without giving a thumbs-up to the seniors. Mr. Polazzo gives voice to the murmurs circulating in the audience after the show. It looks like soph/frosh is out of the running, in spite of its valiant effort but he says, "The juniors are going to give the seniors a run for their money." As for Ms. Damesek, she has no hard feelings, even if her image took a beating in two of the three Sing! plays. "Home, boys, home, go, go," she says softly, waving a group of students to the exit. "Be safe."


It's an invocation that finds an answer the next day, Thursday March 23, when Milo arrives in the safe embrace of the ice-skating rink at Chelsea Piers, just north of Stuyvesant along the Hudson River. Protecting his sandy blond head is a baby blue helmet. Surrounding him is the cocoon of high-pitched squeals belonging to dozens of tiny people. For once, no child in attendance is older than Milo, and it's comforting on this crisp, bright afternoon. Here pimply-faced teenagers are replaced by freckle-faced kindergartners to fifth graders. Here, where Milo's parents regularly send him to be around kids his age, no one judges him, and his genius is so ignored that an adult ties the white laces of Milo's black skates, same as for the rest of the kids. Milo lets him. And then he scampers onto the ice rink, promptly careening into a Bud Light advertising sign on the wall. He's okay. He's alone, teetering forward and backward, zooming precariously on the ice until he's joined by another ten-year-old boy, a friend from P.S. 234 before Milo left for high school. Together, the two little boys crash purposely into each other, on the ice and against the walls in a mindless physical activity, which is just what Milo needs. Happiness is conveyed in his easy smile: there's something freeing about roaming the smooth surface of the ice under soaring rafters.

"Here, he's a kid," says Gil Rubin, who oversees the mayhem as head of the after-school program, Gilsports for Kids.

The other kids know Milo is different but accept him here. During a break, Milo and his fifth-grade friend order pizza with extra cheese and join a table with second and third graders, where the level of conversation barely rises above the complexities of what a burp sounds like, backed up by impressive demonstrations. Milo, though, quickly grows fatigued. Dark circles ring his big brown eyes. Last night, he fell asleep at 10 p.m., woke up at 1 a.m., and couldn't wrestle himself into slumber until 3:30, before waking up again at 7 for school. He has no idea why. "I'm going to go dunk my head in the freezer," he says.

Rising, Milo marches over to an icebox stocked with Häagen-Dazs ice cream and burrows his head in it. Refreshed, he rejoins the group, where a third grader welcomes him back by calling Milo "Pre-K," as in "pre-kindergarten," as if that's the most heinous epithet the younger boy could muster. "Quite the opposite," Milo retorts. His fifth-grade friend comes to his side, predicting that Milo will be a great math or science teacher one day. "None of the kids would be able to outsmart him," his friend boasts. Milo remains silent on that point; he doesn't know what he wants to be when he grows up, and that's okay here.

The boys run back to the rink to collect trophies. All get one. There are no losers here at Gilsports for Kids. Not like at Stuyvesant, where everything, it seems, is at stake. Straddling both worlds, of teenagers and elementary school friends, Milo finds it impossible to choose one over the other. "That'll keep me up tonight," he sighs. Then he decides, "I choose Pluto."

In Queens the following day, mourners pay their final respects, bowing in Asian custom as they file by the polished wooden coffins of sixteen-year-old Kevin, his brother, and his mother. A woman feeds gold-leaf scrolls into a stove, where they vanish in lashes of fire. The Stuyvesant choir sings. Classmates leave notes to Kevin, words wished for but not spoken.

The same day, the long-awaited attendance scanners arrive at school, unannounced, for a trial run. Scanning is voluntary. There is no protest.

Sing! reaches a crescendo the next evening, Saturday, March 25, when the curtains close on the final performance and hundreds of students cram into the lobby, awaiting the judges' scores. The gathering quickly deteriorates into a mosh pit, like a punk rock concert, where boys are pumping fists and pounding drums, girls are bouncing on boys' shoulders, and students are literally climbing the walls, screaming rival chants.

"Senior Sing! has got to go! Hey-hey, ho-ho!"

"Junior Sing! has got to go! Hey-hey, ho-ho!"

Emotions are running so high, they are almost primal, full of fury. Students storm back into the auditorium, climbing on top of the seats while several boys, including Romeo, rip off their shirts, whirling them overhead. Mr. Teitel, the principal, tries to restore order, taking center stage, a bullhorn in hand. "Get off the furniture!" he shouts, but the order is drowned out by visceral chants of "Senior-senior Sing!" The principal looks on, speechless. Almost instantly, though, the room falls silent for the reading of the judges' scores.

Third place . . . soph/frosh.

Then second place . . . the juniors. And the auditorium explodes in a deafening roar: the seniors have won. Hundreds rush the stage, as if it's the game-winning home run in the World Series, hugging and pointing index fingers skyward.

The six-year curse is denied another year.

Later, it comes out that the juniors almost captured a victory Friday night, only to be overtaken by a big senior surge on Saturday, aided no doubt by Molly's vocal recovery. Later, it also comes out that several judges almost marred the final results by showing up at Sing! drunk. One inebriated judge, hoping to be bribed, was disqualified. Other soused judges, rooting for the soph/frosh underdogs, shamelessly heckled the upperclassmen.

By the following Tuesday, all four of the attendance scanners are up and running. Scanning is now compulsory. Weeks ago, several students had e-mailed one another, planning to stage a "slowdown," to take as much time as possible to swipe through the machines as a form of protest and thereby demonstrate the futility of the new system. But there seems little fight left in students now. Almost everyone scans efficiently, each in less than a second. Quietly, it appears they have begun to accept this new reality.

CHAPTER FIFTEEN

# Polazzo's Time

IN A CLUTTERED CUBBYHOLE OF AN OFFICE AT STUY-
vesant two days later, March 30, at least one individual remains who is
not willing to quietly accept the attendance scanners, a goateed rebel in
cargo khakis who is talking about the possibility of students staging a
march on City Hall and railing against the school system, even though
he is part of it: Mr. Polazzo. He teaches advanced placement comparative government, which puts him in a position to know a thing or two
about rebellions against an entrenched bureaucracy. At the age of thirty,
he knows even more about being a teenager.

"He's a kid—he's a big kid!" exclaims a junior who sounds more like
an exasperated mother talking about a wayward teenager, which in
some ways makes Mr. Polazzo the perfect coordinator of student affairs,
or in school lingo, the COSA. Teaching three classes instead of the regular five, he spends the rest of his days—and many of his evenings—
overseeing the student government, dances, plays, and elections, not to
mention the latest teenage cultural trends on MTV. No one at Stuyvesant cares about the kids more than Mr. Polazzo does. When he talks
about students, he is apt to use the pronoun "we," before he catches

157

himself. He's actually one of "them," the adults, although the grown-ups aren't always persuaded.

"I'm trying to convince the administration I can kick ass," he says.

Mr. Polazzo might start with a makeover of his Student Union office on the second floor, a magnet for students because it resembles their own natural habitat—a teenager's eclectic hangout—where they check e-mail, eat candy, toss rubber balls. A sign on the wall reads, "If you touch this air conditioner, hose, or plug, I will track you down and kill you. Love, M. Polazzo." On another wall hangs a row of clocks with one supposedly telling the time in Beijing and another in "Ricoville," named after a former addled student. There are also clocks telling the time in New York, Madagascar, and Bronx Science, as if the latter were in a different time zone, not just uptown. None of the clocks works, although one dubbed "Polazzo's Time" shows the second hand twitching, as if it wants to move forward but can't quite get beyond 8:44.

It's just as well. Mr. Polazzo has no intention of growing up to become an intransigent adult, especially at the moment when he is bemoaning the crackdown on student freedoms, namely, the introduction of attendance scanners.

"The kids are really upset about it," he says.

Not all of them, including Jonathan Edelman, a senior who enters the cramped office ready to challenge Mr. Polazzo. "What liberties did they take?" Jonathan asks, siding with the school administration. Underscoring that he's a contrarian, Jonathan is wearing a blue T-shirt that reads, "Nuke a godless communist gay baby seal for Christ."

Mr. Polazzo, settling into the role reversal, defends the students, saying that Jonathan has become "institutionalized," like a prisoner who's fallen in love with his cell bars. Mr. Polazzo also blames student "apathy," and for good measure, he thinks students like Jonathan are "overthinking things."

Jonathan isn't convinced. "What right is being taken away by the scanners?"

"It's an issue of trust," Mr. Polazzo says, but perhaps sensing he's losing the argument, he also questions the merit of spending a hundred thousand dollars (actually, sixty thousand) on scanners in a school with nearly perfect attendance. Furthermore, he wants to know, what effect will the scanners have on the school environment?

"It feels fairly innocuous to me." Jonathan shrugs.

Mr. Polazzo persists: "Why bring in something that creates a further division between students and the administration?"

But Jonathan likes the scanner system. "Maybe because it's new," he says.

It's no use. Jonathan is unmoved. Besides, Mr. Polazzo has his own personal battle to wage. Despite his immense popularity with the students—or because of it—he is in jeopardy of losing his beloved job as COSA, which would force him back into teaching full-time. The principal has indicated that he may appoint a new coordinator of student affairs at semester's end, making the argument that Mr. Polazzo is about to finish his fourth year in the position, and if four years is enough for a president's term, it's enough for a COSA, ignoring that he himself is in his seventh year as principal.

The thought of being stripped of the student coordinator job pains Mr. Polazzo, but he hides it well, maintaining a stoic front in solidarity with the students who have little idea—yet—that their greatest advocate is feeling the pressure. It's a strange predicament for a teacher who never intended to be a teacher. He had briefly contemplated becoming a lawyer but couldn't muster the energy to pursue it. He had tried his hand at writing, publishing book reviews and blurbs for a nonprofit. Then he figured he'd try teaching, thinking it was an interlude, never planning to follow in the footsteps of his father, who taught history at a Stuyvesant rival, Brooklyn Tech. But Mr. Polazzo realizes this now: he loves the students. And he intends to reapply for the job, even if his prospects look dim.

"It's all about the students," he says. "That's who I serve."

Prospects look dire upstairs in the dining hall, where Xevion is not eating what looks like turkey, instead poring over a prep book for the SAT, which is a mere two days away.

"I'm freaking out," she says.

Romeo isn't. Sitting with her, the football captain is casually study-ing for a differential equations quiz today before he changes the subject to resume a heated discussion between the two of them about the nature of love.

"I bet Xevion I would fall in love in the next few weeks," Romeo explains.

"I'm going to win this bet," Xevion says, already picturing collecting her winnings—Romeo taking her out to dinner and a movie. Fueling her confidence: Romeo isn't dating now.

"I'm hunting," he says defensively.

"He's playing," she corrects him, adding that he's nowhere close to falling in love. "Can't you tell? He's too relaxed."

Xevion can't say the same. Yesterday, her nerves were so frayed she almost screamed at her mother. Tomorrow, Friday, she plans to stay home from school to calm herself before taking the SAT on Saturday. Romeo plans a different pre-SAT ritual, catching up on sleep tomorrow. He'll also be reviewing vocabulary words and writing a few practice essays. One thing he won't bother reviewing: math, his specialty. But for the first time, Romeo is giving in slightly to the possibility of falling short of near perfection on the SAT. Lowering his expectations, he now expects to score at least a 2200 instead of a 2300 out of 2400, which is still stratos-pherically high. But he says he isn't sweating it.

"Romeo will take care of things," he says.

Xevion, rising from her chair in disbelief, says, "Did he just speak about himself in the *third* person?"

Romeo calmly explains, "I've built this machine." Today, on the last day of his SAT prep class, all he can do, he says, is "let this machine run." By disconnecting himself from the imminent college exam, Romeo doesn't need to say that he is compartmentalizing the pressure. Xevion gets it. But the machine's left knee is shaking under the table.

Other students are feeling the pressure today, and it's not just the SAT. College admissions—or rejection—letters are due to arrive in the mailboxes of seniors on the same day that the juniors take the SAT: April Fool's Day. This cruel joke of scheduling seems to be inducing a stomach virus that's quickly making its rounds at Stuyvesant, a queasy feeling compounded by another big worry on this Thursday: prom. Just as the frenzy of Sing! has subsided, the specter of prom has begun to emerge, more than two months before the Big Night. Reyna Ramirez, for one, doesn't have a date yet. The senior is trying to avoid her former boyfriend, who she knows is lying in wait to ask her to the prom. All the while, she wants to go with another boy whom she hardly knows. "It's all about the photo op," she says, worried that one day she'll look at her prom pictures and wonder why she went with him, whoever he is. Now *that's* pressure. "Somehow," she says, speaking generically about Stuyvesant students, "I think we look for things to stress ourselves about."

Senior Danielle Fernandes isn't stressing, not anymore. She just found out that she gained entrance to Cornell, Dartmouth, and Tufts, and to top it off, she found a prom date too. Her friend, senior Richard Lo, surprised her with a clutch of pink roses and tulips, nervously asking her to the big dance. Danielle didn't hesitate. Richard saved her from the machinations of Mr. Polazzo, who gave new meaning to his title as coordinator of student affairs when he scoured his Delaney book in search of a prom date for Danielle. "I wasn't going to go with random kids in his class," she says, smiling broadly.

Mr. Siwanowicz is animated on the last day of March, even displaying what appears to be the wisps of a smile. Surrounded by eight teenagers, playing board games after school, he is one of them again, a kid. Like Milo at the ice rink, or Mr. Polazzo in the Student Union office, Mr. Siwanowicz finds comfort in the easy banter of teenagers, partaking of Teddy Grahams passed around like so many energy fixes, forgetting for the moment the pressures of finishing college and obtaining his teacher's license. Here, in the back of the math research room, all that matters is who becomes the Great Dalmuti, a game of strategy recommended for anyone eight or older. The object of the game is to run out of cards as quickly as possible. For Mr. Siwanowicz, always engaged in the battle against depression, the object of the game is to keep his mind honed, an aim that he will mention in passing, as if not realizing that he's thinking aloud. But there's no chance that he will lose his edge, not this afternoon, when he's having fun, explaining that if you win the game, you get to choose where you sit, which tends to be the most comfortable chair at the head of the table, the winner naturally being called the Great Dalmuti. Those who don't fare as well are called greater or lesser peons, with the least of them relegated to an uncomfortable stool. Mr. Siwanowicz is positioned somewhere in the middle, neither winning nor losing greatly, which seems to be just where he wants to be. Until he becomes a lesser peon. Then in a mock constipated voice, he practically genuflects, telling a student in the role of the Great Dalmuti, "There will always be a place in the stable for you, my lord." The other kids, gathered around the table, giggle in unison, unaware how true it is that Mr. Siwanowicz has just been reduced to a lower station at Stuyvesant.

It's no laughing matter to Mr. Jaye, in the office next door. He's ranting about the bane of his school existence, Ms. Damesek. Without notifying him, she recently reassigned Mr. Siwanowicz. He's no longer monitoring the library during his free seventh and eighth periods; now he's monitoring the newly installed attendance scanners, which particularly stings Mr. Jaye, not just because Mr. Siwanowicz is a math genius who should be teaching math, but because Mr. Jaye had opposed the scanners. He can't believe that Ms. Damesek first tried to banish holiday food and now is trying to banish his talented school aide. "She stole Christmas, then she stole Jan!" Mr. Jaye bellows. And he can't believe that the principal is allowing Ms. Damesek to get away with the maneuver; it's obvious to Mr. Jaye that she's using Mr. Siwanowicz as a pawn in a proxy fight with him. "I'm not going to let Stan live!" he yells, producing a copy of a letter from a student to the principal, expressing similar outrage over Mr. Siwanowicz's scanner duties. "I will tell you it clearly: This is completely and utterly stupid," the student writes. ". . . You're wasting some of the best talent on one of the most pointless jobs out there."

Mr. Jaye is also mad at Mr. Wong, the assistant principal of technology services, who recently accused a teacher close to Mr. Jaye of removing a letter, without authorization, that Mr. Wong wrote and posted on the Stuyvesant Web site. Mr. Wong had written an oddly lighthearted letter in support of the attendance scanners. "We're looking to hire [monitors] who are approximately 400 lbs with 25 inch biceps and 60 inch chest," he wrote, adding a cautionary note in support of Mr. Teitel, the principal. "You should be aware that the school has a legal obligation to ensure the safety of all students and, therefore, you are not allowed out of the building during a free period. Although this seems unfair, we want to make sure that Mr. Teitel keeps his shirt (ugh!!)."

Mr. Jaye suspects that a student, not a teacher, removed the letter from the Web site. To settle the matter, he storms out of his office, heading downstairs to find and confront the alleged perpetrator—only she is nowhere to be found in school, leaving Mr. Jaye with nowhere to direct his considerable energies except at his own increasingly complicated situation. Suddenly he isn't up for one principal's job He's up for *two*. The new entry is Midwood High School, a good public school in Brooklyn, which has the added appeal of being the school where his younger daughter is enrolled. Earlier this week, he went for a job interview there, but not before he contacted officials at Bergen County Academies to let them know that he had resolved his New Jersey licensing issue and, more important, to see whether they were still interested in hiring him. They are.

Suddenly, he is facing the burden of possibly two great choices: heading a good public school in Brooklyn, where he can continue to build his pension fund in the New York City school system, or moving to New Jersey, where he can run another good public school, offsetting his city retirement benefits with a sizable salary. Either way, the math chairman knows his future is converging fast, and it doesn't look like Stuyvesant is in it. Next week, on the same day, he is meeting again with Brooklyn school officials, then heading to New Jersey to resume his courtship with the schools superintendent there. If—when—he leaves Stuyvesant, he vows to take Mr. Siwanowicz with him. Mr. Jaye knows that Mr. Siwanowicz is wounded by the indignity of his monitoring duties even though he accepts them in silence. There's no way Mr. Jaye will leave him at Stuyvesant, unprotected.

And yet the present tugs at Mr. Jaye. When he explained that he may be leaving Stuyvesant to Milo's mother, she broke down in tears, worried about what that may mean for her child. For the first time in his life, Milo recently woke up to the prospect of going to school by enthusiastically chirping, "Yay, it's Monday!" Gone is the dread of a school that doesn't challenge him. What will happen to Milo in Mr. Jaye's absence?

Will he be allowed to continue his education at Stuyvesant? How many other high school administrators would have welcomed a ten-year-old, no matter how gifted? Mr. Jaye himself worries about what his departure will mean. "I might be copping out 'cause what I should really do is stay [at Stuyvesant] to fix it," he says. It's not only about Milo. Mr. Jaye is helping Ms. Lee in her attempt to stay on at the school after she graduates from Columbia's Teachers College. But Mr. Jaye may not be able to see that through. Nor will he be able to fight the attendance scanners, which he considers the folly of the newfangled. "We have the technology to give every kid a CAT scan, but we don't do it!" he crows. Even more, he won't be at Stuyvesant to wage war against Ms. Damesek, who he worries will bully Mr. Teitel.

"Stan is so nice that he absorbs a lot of punches instead of just saying, 'This is the way it's going to be, you know, and deal with it,'" Mr. Jaye says.

And for all the tantalizing prospects of more money and more authority running schools elsewhere, when it comes down to it, Mr. Jaye doesn't want to leave his beloved Stuyvesant. But he doesn't feel that he has a choice because the principal isn't retiring, and Mr. Jaye believes that now is the time to seize his own opportunity to run a school. The decision, though, leaves him uneasy. "I feel like I'm deserting a sinking ship," Mr. Jaye says, "and the ship is sinking, trust me."

That Friday, a Buddhist monk presides over the funeral of fourteen-year-old April. Her father stands over her open coffin, touching her forehead, and the month of March comes to a merciful end.

> *I H8 supervised study*
>
> —desktop graffiti, Stuyvesant High School

# CHAPTER SIXTEEN

# Hell's Kitchen

ON THE FIRST OF APRIL, JANE IS PRESIDING OVER ROW upon row of white T-shirts and sparkly silver high heels and billowy dresses, the unwanted remnants of other people's lives, in a cavernous room under the harsh glare of fluorescent lighting. It's the unlikeliest of places to find Jane at nine on a Saturday morning: the used clothing section of the Salvation Army on Forty-sixth Street between Tenth and Eleventh avenues—Hell's Kitchen—a gritty neighborhood on the western edge of Manhattan known for its criminal element of yore and encroaching gentrification of today. But Jane isn't here by choice. She says she's here by court order, collecting plastic hangers, which constitutes community service for a public misconduct charge involving a fight that she doesn't want to talk about. Not that she's really here. She's withdrawn into a CD headset of grunge rock, courtesy of Kurt Cobain before he put a shotgun to his head and pulled the trigger.

Today is a gray contact lens day. Jane's eyes, though, are shrouded by the fog of marijuana, which she smoked before punching in for work. It's not enough. Later today, she plans to up the ante, plunging herself into the oblivion of angel dust. A recent drug test she took at rehab turned up a smorgasbord of cannabis, cocaine, and heroin. Jane says she's merely dabbling, that it's okay "as long as I don't get addicted." At the same time, she says bitterly, "I've been realizing that sobriety is a disappointment. Right now, there's no consolation. Tomorrow's going to suck too."

The other day wasn't so great either. In third-period gym, Jane argued with a girl who owed her money. The teacher kicked Jane out of class. Fifth period, a teacher caught Jane reading Toni Morrison's *Beloved*, her book from another class, Great Books, the only course she cares about. The teacher confiscated the novel. Jane promptly borrowed a library copy and, during sixth period, excused herself to the bathroom, where she broke a needle trying to shoot up. It was her last one. So seventh period, she skipped out of school to take the train to a nearby needle exchange just before it closed, grabbed three needles, and slipped into a restaurant bathroom, where she accidentally squirted out the last of her stash of heroin, lost forever.

"All my old stuff is coming back," she says. "I know drugs messed up my life, but guess what? I don't like my life." She says that all she has is the twin companionship of "depression and misery."

They, she says, are "my only muse," the fuel for her poetry:

> simple reduction
> if it really was that
> easy
> what the top and bottom have
> in common is deemed valueless
> simple compulsion
> if only it could be
> easy
> what I have is worthless
> that much we have in common
> so little
> mass and high
> density it's a blackhole
> I follow the scent of gravity and

*simply sink, the pull keeps my world together*
*and drags me under*
*a concurrent current joint by*
*my free falling willing.*
*I'm a blackhole*
*I turn*
*concrete to quicksand.*

What solace she finds in her poetry, she can't find elsewhere, certainly not in rehab. "No one can answer my questions," she says. The foremost question is, "What do you do when the problem is when you're sober?" Her own answer: she decided to stop taking her medication about a week ago. "I hate the idea of antidepressants, which is ironic," she says. "I just hate the idea of swallowing pills every day." She's also decided that she can't countenance her mother, who gives Jane cash but demands that her daughter save every receipt or package to prove that she didn't spend the money on drugs. Suffice it to say, their short-lived truce is over. Jane is thinking of finding a part-time job to raise money so she can move out when she turns eighteen in less than two months, setting her free from her mother for good.

Jane's almost free of Stuyvesant, saying she's on track to graduate in June despite her mounting absences from classes this semester. But even as the end nears, she still wonders about the beginning, whether attending this school was a good idea in the first place, given how she tumbled into drugs here. Past and present, though, fall by the wayside as she reconsiders the future, the possibility of attending college next year. Ever so briefly, Jane lowers her hardened exterior to admit that "dealing with the whole thing," life after Stuyvesant, leaves her "scared."

Mr. Grossman, her Great Books teacher, intervened about a week ago, persuading other teachers to retroactively raise some of her grades from last semester to improve her college prospects. It's not a common practice, he says, but "I just don't think she should be penalized for grades that she received while she's in the throes of a debilitating addiction, and it doesn't reflect the work that she's capable of doing, or the work that she's done."

He's also spoken to one of the college counselors, who told him it's not too late for Jane to apply for September admission to some universities. Mr. Grossman believes there is a place for her. He's told Jane about the grade changes, and he's urged her to stop by Stuyvesant's college office to figure out the next step. But then she responded by not showing up to his class, and he's concerned that he pushed the idea of college too hard. "I wonder if the prospect of being close to doing it just sent her back the other way," he says. "With her, I always worry."

As English chairman, Mr. Grossman has much to worry about these days. That includes the prodigious work that his teachers assign to overloaded students, a frequent topic of debate in his department. He poses the question, "What's a fair and productive amount of work and at what point does it become simply a stress that is crushing?" There isn't unanimity on the faculty, but he is of the opinion that the teachers, himself included, must take responsibility for sometimes placing too much pressure on the students, to "catch them when they fall," and he's not just talking about the Janes of the world. One of his hardworking students, perhaps striving beyond her reach, found herself wait-listed at every college to which she applied, prompting Mr. Grossman to write an extra recommendation for her. Parents have called Mr. Teitel, complaining of their children's being in similar predicaments, and he has been working to use Stuyvesant's good name in the hopes of tipping the balance in favor of such students in college purgatory.

In the meantime, Mr. Grossman is still trying to help some of his English teachers, who are dangling in their own purgatory. Now it looks as though as many as four may lose their jobs, displaced when the school completes its search for a handful of new guidance counselors. He can at least find consolation in one development: the controversy over his firing of an English teacher is finally beginning to subside. "It's quieted down a lot," he says. "The routine of school has reasserted itself."

On Monday, April 3, school administrators scramble to douse another controversy: the attendance scanners. Just when it seemed that students had acquiesced to the new devices, several begin agitating behind the scenes, threatening to disrupt the school if the administration doesn't broker a compromise. It turns out that students are resurrecting the idea of a march on City Hall and staging a slowdown while passing through the scanners, creating a perfect storm on the same day, tomorrow.

Mindful of the administration's embarrassment over the cuddle puddle controversy, the media-savvy students are planning to notify the press to ensure local coverage of their City Hall protest. They also are e-mailing just about everyone over the head of Mr Teitel, the principal, including his ultimate boss, the New York City schools chancellor. Apparently, Mr. Teitel gets the message just in time. This afternoon, less than twenty-four hours before the massive showdown, he invites student leaders to his office for a peace summit, and quickly, they reach a resolution. Students will be required to scan in only during their morning arrival; they will not have to scan out for lunch or at the end of the day. The administration also agrees to drop the one-dollar fee charged to students who lose their ID. Mr. Teitel can console himself that he gets to use scanners to take attendance, while the students exult in preserving their school freedoms.

"It seems like the bad atmosphere created by the scanners has been neutralized," says Nathan Buch, an official of the Student Union, on the renegade student Web site he operates, www.stuycom.net. In a flyer dispatched shortly after its powwow with the school administration, the Student Union writes, "All in all, the scanners do not seem anywhere close to a nightmare any longer."

Mariya, the fifteen-year-old Ukrainian immigrant has her own nightmare. As she wades through a sea of students passing through the second-floor entrance, she tries to camouflage a look of sorrow under the lid of her army green cap. What seemed an inevitability now shocks. It's over with her first love, Tom, just after their two-month anniversary. "I don't know why," she says, almost devoid of emotion. But on this afternoon, on April 5, as the glum sophomore heads out of school, tromping across the Tribeca Bridge, there's little time to contemplate the loss of love, or the gain of cynicism, the rite of passage to adulthood, because she's instantly assaulted by a burst of sunshine, then by two junior boys who cajole her into heading over to Burritoville, a fast-food joint, their after-school ritual of late.

There they grab a bunch of white paper plates and pile them high with tortilla chips and salsa, all of which is free, and that is the point. Their only cost is a single soda, $1.61 after taxes, which they constantly refill, also for free, rotating among Dr Pepper, Pepsi, and Mariya's favorite, Sierra Mist.

One boy places an index finger on his nose, and so does Mariya, leaving the other boy the odd man out, the loser who has to fetch the next refill. And in the act, and the ritual, Mariya loses herself, creating a memory of life at the moment that, looking back, will seem to have been nothing more complicated than teenagers sitting in a red vinyl booth, holding index fingers to their noses.

But then, one boy skips off to run track and the other heads to driver's ed, and it all comes rushing back to Mariya as she sits, remaining at the Formica table. It's not just Tom. It's Mom.

Mariya wonders how her parents will react to her latest grades. She knows computer science may be a problem. The classwork is packed with complicated computer commands involving lots of parentheses and memorizing. But if anything is going to drag down her grade point average, it's chemistry, which continues to befuddle her. A test next week may determine whether she finishes with a grade above or below 90 for the term, which in turn may determine whether she can surpass last semester's overall average of 94.86. And there's little chance her mother won't find out. The father of another student, who monitors his son's every academic step, works with Mariya's mother and keeps her informed of her daughter's progress, or lack thereof, in school. But Mariya just doesn't seem to care as much as she used to about grades, even though she knows that if her parents punished her when her average dipped slightly last semester, another minor drop would surely spell more trouble. "My mom will give me the I'm-so-disappointed speech," she says. Worse, Mariya reckons, her mother might punish her by making her play with her nine-year-old brother. Or worst: "Probably what will happen is, my mother won't let me hang out after school," Mariya says with the same dead voice that she used to announce the end of her first love.

---

After school on the following day, April 6, hundreds of students crowd into the auditorium in a school memorial for April and Kevin. One after another, friends step to the podium to express what words can't.

"I don't believe it, I don't believe it at all," says one student. "... When I think about it now, my heart aches with pain."

Another student quivers as she says she hasn't been able to keep track of time since their deaths. "I'm still stuck," she says. "... I feel sick and angry and most of all confused. .... I miss them. I miss them so much."

During a moment of personal reflection, the only sound is that of children quietly weeping.


A block away, the only sound is that of children laughing riotously in front of P.S. 234 on Friday, April 7, just as the rains of the day have given way to emerging spring buds. Finished with high school for the day, Milo reenters the red door of his former elementary school to work on the newspaper, the *234 Latte*, the umbilical cord to his otherwise departed fifth-grade life.

When Milo enters room 304, he is greeted by reminders of what drove him out: an education already surpassed. Above the blackboard reside the letters of the alphabet: *Aa Bb Cc Dd* . . . On the blackboard: "Factors of 100 . . . 1, 2, 4, 5, 10, 20, 25, 50, 100." A magnet pins a sheet of white paper to the board, touting "Writing with Interesting Language." Milo frowns as he begins reviewing an article that he wrote in the latest edition of the school paper. The topic: global warming, a serious concern of his. To his great consternation, the title, "What's With Winter," was changed to "What's With the Weather." It doesn't have quite the alliterative ring he had wanted. At least the editors didn't remove his reference to the Kyoto Global Warming Treaty, or his assessment of the worst-case scenario:

Global warming may eventually cause sudden severe changes in temperature either up or down; so severe that it might cause the next ice age. A bit less severe but still catastrophic is that global warming may make large parts of the world uninhabitable. This may

lead to food and beverage shortages. This in turn may lead to migra-
tions, which may lead into World War III.

A ponytailed girl musters the courage to sidle up to Milo, her face
just inches from his, to say, "I liked your article on"—and hesitates before
finding the right words—"global warming." Milo, deeply engrossed in
ferreting out the editing flaws of his story, completely ignores his fan.

Moments later, he heads down the hall to pose for yearbook photographs for an elementary school he no longer attends. Making funny
faces for the camera, including a raised brow, à la Clark Gable, he holds
against his red sweater a white plaque that reads "MILO Beckman 72."

"That's how old I am," he says, poking fun at the number representing the school's system of organizing students for the portraits.

Against a muslin-draped backdrop, Milo proceeds to trot out a series
of silly poses. Cross-eyed, *click*. Sleepy, *click*. His red shoes stacked on
top of his head, *click*. And for a moment, Milo is a fifth grader again. He
can put aside his struggles with sleep, forgetting that when he finally
succumbs to a restless slumber, he unconsciously rotates 180 degrees so
that his head is pointing north, like a compass drawn to an unseen beacon, when he awakes. He can also put aside his recent discomfort at
Stuyvesant when he received the lowest grade in his life: a 77 on a
trigonometry test. "Pretty horrible," he says. Milo is stunned by a new
reality. Even he has to study sometimes. But not now.

When he returns to the fifth-grade classroom, he joins a group of
other little boys at a table. One scrawls in pencil on loose-leaf paper,
"Have you got a pet that costs a lot of cash?" Another is writing in an
uneasy hand about a coyote found in Central Park. Milo, partaking in
the writing exercise, decides to describe a major discovery of an extinct
fish called the *Tiktaalik roseae*. "THE MISSING LINK," he entitles his
paper, explaining to the boy to his right, "They found these bones yesterday. It's a huge thing. It was in the *New York Times*." The boy, scratch-
ing his forehead, is not sure what to make of that. The boy, however, is
saved from his confusion when a little girl comes over to ask Milo for
the correct spelling of a term.

"*Fire trucks* is one word, right?"

"No," Milo says.

His mother, helping out in the class, arrives a moment later to recon-firm. "It's not one word?"

"No," Milo repeats patiently.

His mother shrugs as if to acknowledge that her ten-year-old son isn't to be disputed on such matters.

Milo responds by ripping up his unfinished paper on the *Tiktaalik roseae*, an act that he relishes, each tear causing delight, before he turns his attention to art. He draws a ball with lines spinning off it, creating a sense of motion on paper. Milo, however, doesn't move an inch as the class comes to an end. Instead, he finds consolation in the solitary confines of his imagination, continuing to draw his picture even as other children place chairs upside down on tables, and the entire room clears out, empty except for him.

> *Good Luck On Your Studying!*
>
> —desktop graffiti, Stuyvesant High School

CHAPTER SEVENTEEN

# The Contest

ON A DRIZZLING SATURDAY, APRIL 8, THE GYMNASIUM at Nyack High School in suburban New York lies empty before the big event, almost too quiet. The only sound is the hum of powerful beams of light projecting from the rafters, reflecting against the shiny wood floors below, moments before they are to be scuffed up in a rush of frenzied activity. On the wall, the scoreboard reads HOME OF THE INDIANS. And then the players begin to trickle in, carrying their gear: backpacks, tote bags, and . . . calculators. Unceremoniously, the star enters, a slouching Danny Zhu, last year's individual high scorer, a slight boy, remote and unsmiling, behind oval, black-rimmed glasses, decked out in blue jeans and a navy blue T-shirt, the front of which announces that he is a member of the vaunted New York City Math Team.

A Stuyvesant sophomore, Danny is here to defend his title as the best high school mathematician in the prestigious New York State Mathematics League annual contest, and his pose says it all: sitting in the first row, he holds up his head with his right hand; otherwise he might fall asleep. "I don't normally feel pressure about much," he says on another occasion. His dark hair stands up in different directions, as if

175

it were static electrified when he woke up and he didn't bother to do anything about it. Perhaps the fifteen-year-old didn't get enough sleep. Minutes before the contest starts, he rests his head on his desk, as 409 of the best teenage mathematicians in New York State, mostly seniors, about thirty from Stuyvesant, take their seats. It's an incongruous sight, an army of pencil-wielding math assassins assembling in rows of little school desks arrayed across an echoing gym, not a bouncing ball in sight. And yet there is an athletic dimension to the spectacle as the students take on the personalities of rival baseball clubs, twenty-seven teams dressed in T-shirt uniforms of green, yellow, and other shades of allegiance.

On the sidelines, Mr. Teitel is wearing a baby blue Stuyvesant jersey—the Yankees pinstripe of high school math. He loosens the neck as if he is about to join the field of battle, carefree about today's outcome.

"I already have too many trophies in my office," he boasts.

It's true. But it's also true that this is a big event in the life of Stuyvesant competition. The Peglegs may stumble on the football field, but the young masters of math—the "mathletes," as they are known— bring greater glory to the school in its sport of choice, the bloodless, silent warfare of mathematics.

"This is football in Texas," says Mr. Jaye, here for the kickoff.

Danny removes his glasses and yawns. Math contests have become old hat for the academic sharpshooter. He entered his first math competition, sponsored by a Chinese newspaper in Queens, when he was a second grader, and finished in first place, getting every question right, even though he was the smallest child there. Other contests quickly followed. Like a gunslinger, Danny would show up, the outsider, at competitions sponsored by private Asian academies that he did not attend, and he'd win, taking home their trophies and their fifty-dollar checks.

One Chinese parent, desperate to learn the secret of Danny's success, did not ask permission when she photocopied the problem-solving examples that she found in his book bag. Other Chinese parents clamored to find out what Asian academy Danny attended to become such an incredible math machine, so fast, so efficient. But his parents didn't send him anywhere. He was a homegrown product.

Displaying curiosity and a long attention span at an early age, he learned the basics of math at the knee of his mother, a math teacher, and his father, a computer programmer, both from China. When he was four, Danny learned the meaning of positive and negative numbers from the example of cars rushing back and forth along the highway during a family trip to Washington, D.C. Before the third grade, Danny's mother introduced him to algebra, and at the age of nine, he took the statewide high school algebra test, finishing in a mere hour—two hours early—and easily posting a score of 94.

"That was the beginning of his acceleration," says his mother, Jie Zhang, now an administrator in the city school system.

In the fourth grade, Danny took tenth-grade geometry, earning a 100 on the statewide exam. The next year, he studied trigonometry and biology. In the sixth grade, precalculus and physics. As a seventh grader, he posted an amazing 1440 on the SAT, including a perfect math score.

Danny can't explain his academic wizardry, but what he loves about math is reminiscent of the pleasure that Romeo finds in it—that it has a specific formula, a right and a wrong, unlike people, who, Danny says, are "more fuzzy."

By the time he arrived at Stuyvesant as a freshman, Danny had little to learn from high school math. "He came in almost done," Mr. Jaye says. Last year, Danny took calculus. This semester, he's taking a graduate-level class at NYU in linear algebra, even though he has never taken the required undergraduate course leading up to it. And for the first time in his life, Danny finds himself struggling in math.

But not today. At 11:19 a.m., head down, feet tucked under chair, he begins the statewide contest of elimination, a test of skill, pressure, and speed involving math up to and including precalculus. Danny and his peers have exactly ten minutes to answer the first two questions, one of which asks them to "compute the sum of all the positive integer factors of 2006." Five minutes later, he scratches the back of his head. At 11:28, a contest organizer announces, "One minute." Then, "Fifteen seconds." Finally, "Stop." Proctors collect the answer sheets. When the organizer announces the solution to the first question, he asks those who answered correctly to raise their hands. Danny does so, as do scores of other students. When the organizer announces the answer to the second question, Danny raises his hand again.

Perfect, so far.

Proctors hand out a slip of paper for questions three and four. Ten minutes later, he raises his hand again. He's four for four. The questions become increasingly difficult, and when the organizer announces the answers to questions five and six, an immediate buzz races around the gym as one student screams out a euphoric, "Yes!" Danny simply raises his left hand, still alive. Six for six. He is now one of fewer than twenty remaining who have answered all questions correctly.

Questions seven and eight will determine who wins or faces off in a tiebreaker. With eight minutes left on the clock, Danny waggles his head side to side, as if to loosen his brain. Three minutes later, he shakes out a stiff right arm. Then time's up. Danny raises his head, weaving his fingers together before him, at eye level, like a mandarin in quiet repose. Other students murmur about the test, awaiting the answers. Question seven: Danny raises his left hand. Question eight: up goes the hand. Danny, the defending champ, is back in the final round—one of six students left.

"In its own sick way, it's exciting," Mr. Jaye says.

Danny and the other finalists retire to the auditorium, which is packed like opening night at the opera with hundreds of students, teachers, and parents, and take seats in the front row for the tiebreaker. They have five minutes to solve the following problem:

Compute the number of ordered pairs of positive integers $(m, n)$ that solve

$$2m + 6n = 2006$$

and for which $m + n$ is a multiple of 13.

Danny tilts his head toward the green ceiling. He mouths words. He frowns. He stops writing. Then drops his head—something registers—and he nods, furiously beginning to scribble. Stops. Raises his head again. One minute to go. He seems confused. Fifteen seconds. Just before time expires, he hands in his answer. Adults confer at the front of the auditorium until one breaks off to shake Danny's hand. It's not the expected outcome. Not entirely. Danny answered correctly—but so did one other student, not from rival Bronx Science or Hunter or Brooklyn Tech but from Benjamin N. Cardozo High School, a neighborhood school in Queens that also selectively admits some students into specialized programs. There will be another tiebreaker. Whoever answers the question first within five minutes will be crowned champion. The two boys shake hands before the resumption of hostilities.

Go.

Danny glances at the question, then dashes off an answer in a single minute, and in the second after he submits it, he buries his head in his hands, immediately realizing he botched it. The other boy, noting Danny's blunder, calmly continues to work on the problem, knowing he can take the full five minutes to reach the right answer. Danny betrays a rare human emotion, banging a fist into his thigh. The other boy submits his answer. It should be over, but it isn't. Neither answered correctly. A third tiebreaker falls by the wayside with the same result. Danny actually chuckles. They move to a fourth tiebreaker, and this time, Danny instantly grasps the dimensions of the problem, racing to an answer. His head pops up; he's ready to hand in his paper. But he takes one last look, then, with two hands, he reaches out to submit his answer, like an offering to the math deities, while the other boy continues to work the problem.

The adults confer, and then the organizer announces finally, "We have a first-place winner."

Danny.

He is utterly expressionless. He lowers his head, appearing to work on another math problem, though there are none left. The two-time winner of the statewide math contest wins a sweatshirt and a $150 check. When asked how he feels, he distills his reaction into a one-word computation: "Tired."

It happens with little notice on the following day that Danny's fellow prodigy, ten-year-old Milo, wins a medal in the citywide high school math fair, along with several other students, including his friend, Daniel, the Cuban immigrant.

That night, Mr. Teitel receives a call that Stuyvesant biology teacher Susan Biering—known to her students for her fun classes and her free associations that bump into memories like her first kiss—has passed away after a bout with emphysema.

When Ms. Biering, an inveterate cigarette smoker, took ill in February, Mr. Teitel always thought she would return to school, but he says, "She just never gave up smoking even when she became sick. She used to stand in front of the building and smoke. This was a *biology* teacher, so the rest of us used to look at her and go, 'How do you not understand what's going on here?'" And yet, Mr. Teitel does understand. He himself began smoking when he was thirteen and continued—at one point smoking two packs a day of Marlboro—until he was thirty-one, and he learned that his wife was pregnant. Then, after consulting with his doctor, he promptly gave up the habit. But he knows, more than a quarter century later, "If somebody developed a cigarette tomorrow in which there was a guarantee that there would be no adverse effect to my health"—and here he snaps his fingers—"I'd be in the store tomorrow morning. I loved it."

Ms. Biering is buried on Tuesday, April 11, at Mount Ararat Cemetery just east of New York City.

On the same day, miles from the mourning, Ms. Lee is in a state of sorrow sitting in room 365 at Columbia's Teachers College. Today, she isn't a student teacher at Stuyvesant with limited prospects of staying on as a full-time faculty member; rather, she is a graduate student in a course about alternative models for a social studies curriculum. Stuyvesant seems a distant place as the student who would teach is shunted into an old-fashioned wooden school chair attached to a small, arm-length writing surface. Surrounding Ms. Lee are rickety, exposed radiators painted the same off-white color as the cracked walls, which complement worn wooden floors and the musty scent of age wafting to the high ceilings. Now the class is discussing the assigned reading, *Putting the Actors Back on Stage: Oral History in the Secondary School Classroom*, by Margaret Smith Crocco. Now they're talking about incorporating oral history— and family history—in a classroom exercise in social studies. Now Ms. Lee is paired with a late-arriving student. They ask each other why they want to be teachers.

"It was by chance I stumbled upon this career, but I found the right career," she begins.

"What is your inspiration?" the other student asks.

But before Ms. Lee can explain it all—the disappointments of a father, the demands of a mother—she runs out of time as the teacher resumes the lecture.

Ms. Lee feels like she is running out of time at Stuyvesant. With little more than two months left in the semester, there are still no openings in the social studies department. It's another curious feature of the system that teachers need not give early notice to the principal if they intend to retire, meaning that Ms. Lee may be forced to wait until the last minute to learn if there's an opening. While she waits, Mr. Jaye continues to plot. In his latest scheme he suggested that she create an independent study curriculum in Korean, then persuade one of the city colleges to sponsor it, so that she can be licensed as a Korean-language teacher. But it's a gamble—a big gamble. She'd be accumulating more school debt, and there's no guarantee that Stuyvesant would hire her anyway. In a recent meeting with Mr. Teitel, the principal assumed the paternal role, telling her, "I won't let you do this."

In a testament to her effectiveness as a teacher, parents of Korean students have offered to pay to send Ms. Lee to Los Angeles to take a Korean proficiency exam that could bolster her chances of staying on at Stuyvesant. But she doesn't feel right about accepting the largesse, especially when it may come to naught.

"I need to ask myself how badly I want to stay at Stuyvesant," she says.

The alternative—teaching students in a regular urban public high school—is difficult for her to accept. "Could I be challenging them in a way that's impossible for them?" At a regular school, she worries that history lessons may be reduced to the simplest terms. She worries that it would be difficult to ask nuanced questions about say, the Holocaust, such as, "Were the Americans liberators, or were they collaborators?" That, she says, you can't do in many urban schools.

"They're going to say, 'What? What was the Holocaust?' I mean, you have to teach them the basics."

But her younger sister, an undergraduate student at Barnard College, challenges that assumption, arguing that it is precisely these kids—the regular students—who need the better teachers, who need someone like Ms. Lee. "You never know," her sister says. "You can change these kids' lives. They need inspiration."

Ms. Lee isn't prepared to cede that point. She holds on dearly to those Stuyvesant students whom she has come to adore. Her Korean students expect to take her class next year. A history student asked whether she would write a college recommendation next year. The common denominator: next year. A place for her to be. "If it weren't for them," she says, "I wouldn't be able to test my limits." Besides, she doesn't think that with her tiny frame—a mere ninety pounds—she could hold her own in some of the notoriously tough urban schools, a fear that her sister would concede.

"She knows deep down I wouldn't be able to survive in a place like that," Ms. Lee says.

Yet that knowledge doesn't comfort her. She is troubled, confused, unsure. "This is the worst state I have been in," she says. Today she takes a ten-minute stroll through a career fair at Columbia without bringing her résumé. "That's how disinterested I am in regard to other schools," she says. All she can do, she says, is pray, letting go of her attempt to control life: "I'm going to surrender."

Romeo is surrendering as well. He's giving up on his bet with Xevion that he would fall in love in a matter of weeks. Under a crush of upcoming tests, he simply doesn't have the time for matters of the heart. He needs to postpone them until he can shoehorn them into his frenetic schedule.

"In the middle of all this schoolwork," he says, "I can't fall in love until June."

Xevion isn't at lunch in the dining room on April 12 to gloat over her victory. And perhaps that's for the best. Romeo has his hands full with a history test today, three advanced placement exams in about two weeks, followed by three SAT II tests in June, the same month he faces a series of statewide subject exams. Adding to his load is an even weightier subject lately: his mother. "My mom gets on my back," he says. She's particularly concerned about his performance in French, her native tongue. Last semester, Romeo posted a 95 in French, but this term, he slipped on one test, earning a 78, bracketed between two high grades, endangering his overall grade point average because he didn't know one grammatical rule. And now, Romeo's mother is assigning him homework on top of his homework: French articles to read and transcribe to improve his comprehension. The problem is, it was eleven o'clock the other night, and Romeo was studying history when she insisted that he do his French dictation. He said no. She persisted. He relented but made several mistakes because he wasn't paying close attention. She stormed off, slamming a door behind her and refusing to talk to her son until the next day. Romeo forgives her.

"I mean a lot to her," he acknowledges.

Even at sixteen, Romeo has the wisdom to understand where she is coming from: that his mother once was a rebel in her French family, that she defied her demanding father by wandering off to America, where, he notes, she "married a black musician." And now, Romeo surmises, "it would make her feel more worthy if she felt like she produced a son who is productive."

That's another way of saying, "She wants me to go to Harvard." In another setting, when she imagines her son at the historic American college, her eyes lift to the heavens, and she says reverentially, "There's this myth . . ."

But now, seated alone with his chicken-patty lunch, Romeo says, "I've always felt isolated," though it's unclear whether it's because he imposes so many expectations on himself, or because he's black and white, not quite at home in either world. But from his freshman year, he has erected what he calls a "coping mechanism," an ideology of himself as invincible. His role model is Odysseus. Romeo pledges he will not fail. He will not go out. He will not rest. Sometimes, though, reality intrudes. Because sometimes, he says, "I feel like I'm burning out."

Like now.

Yesterday, after weight lifting at football practice, Romeo arrived home to study but dozed off. When he awoke, he made another run at his schoolwork but ended up listening to Internet radio, a desultory mix of Prince, Jimi Hendrix, Devo, Duran Duran, and David Bowie. It was as if he needed a rest from his mind, from the words of exhortation that remain on his walls, beckoning, "The world is yours." Those words, he says, have "lost [their] effect." Next week is a welcome spring break. It's also a crucial moment in time when Romeo will find out how he fared on the SAT and whether the world he wants—that his mother wants too—is still within his grasp.

# PART THREE: SENIORITIS

*Late April–Late June*

> *BLAH BLAH*
>
> *BLAH BLAH*
>
> *BLAH BLAH*
>
> —desktop graffiti, Stuyvesant High School

# CHAPTER EIGHTEEN

# Zero Tolerance

A RATTY BROWN COUCH, OF INDETERMINATE HYGIENE, resides in the outer chamber of the Student Union, site of untold numbers of despondent, confused, enamored, foolish, frolicking, studious, slumbering, dreamy teenagers. But today, Wednesday, April 26, the ratty brown couch is serving as a psychiatrist's ratty brown couch, where two of the sanest teachers in the school are commiserating about the end of spring break and probing the inner psyche of an academic asylum that they are beginning to suspect is going, quite simply, batty.

At one end sits Mr. Grossman, right ankle over left knee, hugging a pillow, bemoaning the school's selection of committee members who are drawn from the faculty to hire guidance counselors, key personnel who will help steer students to their college of choice the ultimate Stuyvesant coda. "I think it's important to point out how corrupt the process is," he says. By corrupt, he really means *daft*, noting that the selection committee includes no English teachers, himself included, even though guidance counselors' jobs are largely to write secondary school reports for seniors applying to college, essays that give a litany of students' unique talents but, in the wrong hands, can start to sound to admissions officers like blah, blah, blah.

The whole thing seems particularly daft to Kristen, the Student Union president, a representative on the selection committee. On another occasion, she had noted that a school administrator crossed out a specific word from the panel's written description of the kind of educational consultant who will assist in training the hired guidance counselors in writing college reports. The deleted word: "qualified."

"Only in school would you have such incompetence," agrees Mr. Polazzo, sitting at the other end of the couch, arms folded against his chest. Mr. Polazzo then wonders about an even more inscrutable issue: whether he can save his own job. Other faculty members are now angling to find a replacement for Mr. Polazzo as coordinator of student affairs while student leaders have met privately with Mr. Teitel to express their support for Mr. Polazzo.

"It's all a war of shadows," Mr. Polazzo says.

But the real target of Mr. Polazzo's and Mr. Grossman's discontent today lurks beyond the school in the form of New York City mayor Michael R. Bloomberg.

The mayor introduced a major new policy on the first day of spring break, when no one was around to protest it, like a stealth rider to a bill in Congress. With no warning, police will bring mobile metal detectors—akin to those used to screen airline passengers—to random middle and high schools as a way to ferret out dangerous weapons.

"This will be a systemwide deterrent," the mayor said at a news conference outside an empty Abraham Lincoln High School, one of the most dangerous public schools in Brooklyn. "Our reasons for doing this couldn't be clearer or more compelling: we have zero tolerance for weapons of any kind in city schools."

About 20 percent of the city's high schools already are equipped with metal detectors, but the mayor said he wanted to assure the safety of the remaining 80 percent. The number of illegal weapons confiscated in city schools this year has increased by 5 percent to 307, including 20 guns. But the mayor was quick to cite general gains in school safety. Since the 2003–2004 school year, violent crime has dropped by 27 percent.

That decline reflects the broader national trend. The rate of violent crime in public and private schools across the country has dropped by about 50 percent since 1992, according to the most recent joint study of the Justice and Education departments. There were about 740,000 violent crimes in schools in 2003, with an estimated 150,000 reports of rape, sexual assault, robbery, or aggravated assault. Students reported feeling less fear in school and getting involved in fewer school fights.

As the National Education Association observed, students are more likely to be victims of violent crimes outside school. "In fact," the education association said, "this study shows that school is still the safest place for kids—more so than any place they go all day, including their homes."

Stuyvesant is among the safest havens of all. The school reported zero "crimes against persons" and only three property crimes in 2005, the most recent year for which data are available. Which explains why Mr. Polazzo is sitting on the ratty brown couch, dumbfounded. "We don't have a security problem," he says. "We are the showpiece school." Adds an equally perplexed Mr. Grossman, "They all know we are different." And yet the school did not elude the mayor's new city-wide metal detector edict. In a follow-up letter to parents, Mr. Teitel dutifully wrote that the detectors, when and if they arrive at Stuyvesant, "will identify not only weapons but other objects that are never permitted in our building and will help us to keep everyone safe in our school."

Those other forbidden objects, he noted, "include blades, knives, other sharp metal instruments"—and then he lowered the boom—"cell phones, beepers, iPods, MP3 players, etc."

*Cell phones?*

*Beepers?*

*iPods?*

Those are merely among the most common items found on a typical Stuyvesant student, second only to that other teenage accessory, insecurity. Suddenly, the students' challenge of the *attendance* scanners seems like a hollow victory. Even Mr. Teitel had attempted to forestall the introduction of security metal detectors at the school after the September 11, 2001, terrorist attacks, when some parents began clamoring for them. "I resisted," he recalls, "saying I did not feel that that would be an educationally sound thing for our school. . . . It will only give [students] the feeling that this is not a school anymore." Now Mr. Teitel pales at the thought of the metal detectors randomly finding their way to Stuyvesant and the herculean logistics of confiscating somewhere in the vicinity of three thousand cell phones, a student's lifeline to parents who, at Stuyvesant, use wireless devices as a kind of radar to track in real time the whereabouts of their children.

"My parents, of course, are going nuts," Mr. Teitel says.

Already, he is conceding a major loss should the metal detectors arrive: an entire school day, wiped out. "Here's what's going to happen," he says. "I went out and bought three thousand zip-lock freezer bags, and should these scanners show up, I will hand out the bags, tell the children to put their cell phones and their iPods in the bags." Then, later in the day, students would line up—in the line from hell—to gather their belongings.

Already, students are posting signs of rebellion around the school building:

THEY WILL
TAKE YOUR
CELLPHONE AND iPOD.
WILL YOU
SIT BACK
AND LET THEM?
IF THE METAL DETECTORS ARE INSTALLED,
DON'T GO TO CLASS THAT DAY,
PROTEST!

Battling signs with signs, a formal warning is soon posted on the first-floor entrance:

ALL STUDENTS AND VISITORS ENTERING THIS BUILD-ING MAY BE REQUIRED TO SUBMIT TO A METAL DETEC-TOR SCAN AND A PERSONAL SEARCH, IF NECESSARY, TO ENSURE THAT WEAPONS ARE NOT BROUGHT INTO THIS BUILDING. BAGS AND PARCELS MAY ALSO BE

SEARCHED BY MEANS OF METAL DETECTING DEVICES,
BY HAND OR OTHERWISE.

Miffed students abound, including Nathan, the senior who runs the
renegade stuycom.net Web site. He doesn't understand the security
threat that cell phones and music players pose. "You're going to stab
someone with an antenna?" he wonders. "I don't really see someone getting hurt with an MP3 player." Adds Molly, the senior singer, "Of all the
schools to be checking, why would they check ours?"

It's a question almost as mystical in nature as the existential wander-
ings of Mr. Polazzo, who is now preoccupied with thoughts on the meaning of life and death and love and desire and his dog, Norton, may he rest
in peace, none of which has anything to do with the arrival of metal
detectors, or with his possible demise as coordinator of student affairs,
but all of which perhaps serve as a close proxy for that which he can't
fathom. "It's the questing that really, I think, ultimately is the essence of
living and life," he says, ruminating aloud before a small gathering of students in his cramped second-floor Student Union office. "I mean, even
though it's great to reach the end point and making the discovery, I
mean, it's like Alexander the Great, you know. They say that when he
completed his conquest of Persia, he wept, and the general said, 'Why are
you weeping?' And he said, 'There's nothing left to conquer.'"

Mr. Polazzo is just warming up.

"I think you should let your desire flourish, but you have to be careful because if you ever get your desire—I mean, the Buddhist philosophy is that death is death," he says. ". . . It may well be true that desire is
a bottomless vessel, but it's a beautiful vessel, you know? That's what
keeps us going, keeps us moving. Like there was an interesting NPR special about this guy who had this condition where something happened
to his body and he stopped producing testosterone, and I thought it was
going to be interesting because he was going to talk about, like, the
bizarre side effects, which would have been kind of neat, but instead it
turned into this weird discourse. Apparently women have testosterone
too, less than men, but it's what makes you desire. Testosterone is the
chemical synthesis of desire, and he said, like, when he stopped manufacturing testosterone, he stopped wanting to do anything. He would

just, like, sit there in his room. He didn't know he had this condition until a while later, but he would just sit there, like stare. He didn't know what was going on, what was wrong with him. He didn't want to do anything at all. And I think that's, like, what desire is, it's kind of like testosterone in that sense. It drives you forward, and you know, yes, it's . . . all consuming. But it's what gets you out of bed in the morning, you know what I mean?"

He doesn't wait for an answer from his audience of pupils.

"I mean, I bought a lottery ticket the other day," he continues. "I knew there was no chance I was going to win, but there was a need to buy the idea that I might possibly win. Too much of that, and you're gambling. But you know, a little bit is okay. . . . I'd like to believe in an afterlife. I mean, look, I can't prove it. I was in a philosophy of religion class in college, and we spent all day arguing about God and this and that, but one thing I took out of the class. I don't think you can either prove or disprove God's existence. It's a matter of faith, and faith is a very personal thing. I mean, like being religious is like being in love. When you fall in love, you have this deep emotional attachment to somebody, and it might be right and it might be wrong, you know, like it might be somebody who's going to be bad, wrong for you, but your friends aren't going to be able to talk you out of it, but neither will you be able to talk your friends into feeling that same way. I guess religion is a little different because with religion, you really can inspire that fervor among people if you do it well enough, but I don't know, I think it's a very personal thing."

The students, as if sitting in a fascinating college lecture, remain rapt in attention.

"For me, I just don't see it," he says, ". . . although I do have a very bizarre, like, ontological philosophy that makes me feel better about it. Okay, so here it is, this is how I feel better about oblivion. It's kind of crazy but bear with me for a second. What I was thinking about is the nature of time and existence, and if you think about time—and I'm sure there are, like, physicists, quantum physicists who'd, like, slap me in the face for all of this, but just my layman's knowledge, if you think about it, if you think about time as the fourth dimension, right, it's something we move through, it's something that impacts us, yet we lack the ability to step outside of it and perceive it. Think for a second about a being that's flat, that cannot perceive depth, right, it, like, lives on the surface of this piece of paper. Now that being might interact with something that has depth, but he or she or it would never be able to really understand what they were dealing with. The best analogy is, imagine that you are treading water in a swimming pool and your eyes are at water level but all you can see is that waterline, nothing above it, nothing below it, and now let's say a three-dimensional object intersects that. Let's say someone drops this Snapple bottle into the water." He gestures at a bottle on his desk. "Well, what would you see? You would see a line that stays the same shape and then it would get smaller and smaller and then bigger and then it would disappear. So after the event had occurred, you could say, 'Oh, maybe a Snapple bottle passed through,' or something shaped like this, but at the time of the event, you had no idea. For all you knew, right over here it was going to start zigging and zagging; you didn't know until it was done. In that way, depth affects a flat creature the way that time affects us. An event occurs. As it's occurring, we don't know exactly what's going to happen, but when the event is over, we can say, 'Oh, that event occurred.' So now the interesting thing is, as the event is occurring, it seems to us that anything possibly could happen, you know, like this plane could crash, that basketball could go in or could go out, but after it was done, that was it. To me, each event is like the Snapple bottle. It's already fully formed. It's just that we are passing through time."

Total silence.

"I have no basis to believe any of this stuff," he adds. ". . . I mean, the most likely thing is probably just that you die. . . . But to me, anything is better than this bleak idea of oblivion, even though if you were oblivious, you wouldn't know . . . but still, I like existence."

Here he laughs.

"I hope I'm wrong," he says. "I hope that, like, after I die, I'm surrounded in a field of loved ones, and my dog. I'd love to see my dog."


Upstairs, in room 401, Mr. Siwanowicz is feeling breezy, and it's not only the caress of spring wafting through the crack of a window. There's an aura about him. The depressed, sleep-deprived school aide is neither depressed nor sleep-deprived.

There's something indescribably leavened about his mood, such that the lumbering figure is almost sprightly in his response to a small boy who approaches him during his lunch break, asking for help on a math problem from a class taught by another teacher.

"I don't understand anything," the boy confesses. "Could you write it out?"

Mr. Siwanowicz obliges, instantly comprehending the mathematical hieroglyphics even though the problem fills an entire pencil-written page of the boy's loose-leaf binder. With a red pen, Mr. Siwanowicz fills the back side of a sheet of paper with another series of computations— something to do with $x^2 - 3x + 2$—to which the boy nods wordlessly, peering over Mr. Siwanowicz's hulking shoulder.

"Do you get it?" the unofficial teacher asks.

"Yes, I'm good," the boy responds, and he disappears without so much as a thank-you. Not that it would've made a difference. Mr. Siwanowicz is not to be shaken, not today, not even as he races down-stairs to man the second-floor landing by the Tribeca Bridge entrance, standing behind a single red rope, linked on either end by a silver metal-lic stand, the kind used at movie theaters to cordon off ticket buyers. Nothing is being bought here, except a new attendance scanning system to which he is attached as a monitor, observing the comings and goings of students.

"Why are you so late?" he berates a group of students lollygagging back from lunch. "Where were you? Connecticut?"

The students ignore him. Mr. Siwanowicz doesn't care. He's kidding anyway. Suddenly, it doesn't matter anymore, not the indignity of mon-itoring duties, not the inability to get a college degree, not the lack of a teacher's license. Heck, bring on the broken photocopiers! There's no rebellion in Mr. Siwanowicz's peaceful posture. He could not care less— all because of one new, solitary fact.

He has a girlfriend.

To recall the last time he had such a companion, he squeezes his eyes shut in deep concentration, thinking back until he computes the math: *five* years ago. Perhaps it was a mathematical probability that it would eventually happen, the intersection of two people at a board game center in midtown, a hole-in-the-wall place Mr. Siwanowicz frequents late into the evenings. And perhaps it was an inevitability too that he would encounter someone who could match wits with him, was faster than him, could beat him, even at what he calls "full capacity," which is precisely what she did in a game of pattern matching and recognition when they first met.

"She kicked my butt," he says. "I was impressed."

Mr. Siwanowicz was a goner. They started e-mailing each other. She is a PhD who teaches music history at NYU, which turns out to be a good match for a college dropout who teaches math at Stuyvesant. They met. They took a stroll that became a journey across practically the whole city, ending up at Penn Station.

Kate. Dear Kate.

She's meeting him after tenth period today, a lifetime from now as Mr. Siwanowicz lurches back to room 401 to grade papers. A ponytailed girl approaches him there, almost on tiptoes, trembling.

"I have a question," says the nervous junior. "It's not about math." She pulls up a chair and whispers confidentially, as if she's about to confess to a major felony. "I want to take calculus," she says, already thinking of her course load next year, "but will I survive?"

Mr. Siwanowicz, showing tender mercies, assures her that she can handle calculus, that in some ways it's easier than precalculus.

"I just don't want to die," the girl says.

"You won't die," he volleys.

"I've been wanting to take calculus all my life," she says, still not convinced.

"Once you get past the first month, it gets easier," he insists.

The girl takes a deep breath and rises to leave, girding herself for the rigors of calculus. She turns back one last time, for one last reassurance. "So I won't have a nervous breakdown, right?"

The bell rings before he can commit. Instead, Mr. Siwanowicz offers a wordless wave of his left hand, a gesture of carefree hope, and that does the trick as the girl, nervous no more, recedes into the crowded hallway.

> *MCDONALDS RULES*
>
> —desktop graffiti, Stuyvesant High School

# CHAPTER NINETEEN

# College Night

ROMEO ISN'T QUITE READY TO FACE THE CROWDS. Which is why he's perched alone atop the Wall a block from school on the evening of April 27, draped in his Sean John black jeans and Sean John black jacket, less than an hour from the official onset of his future, an annual rite of passage at Stuyvesant when more than 150 colleges converge on the school, setting up recruiting booths throughout the building in what devolves into a frenzied courtship over higher education.

They call it "College Night."

But Romeo isn't thinking of what is to come when he enters the school. He's thinking of what has already transpired, long before his time, how John F. Kennedy won the Navy and Marine Corps Medal for his courage in World War II and how his elder brother, Joe, immediately signed up for a dangerous military mission in an attempt to outshine John—only to perish when his plane, packed with explosives, accidentally exploded shortly after takeoff.

"Competition," Romeo says, "can kill you."

There is time to ponder other pitfalls. Like today's math test. He made a careless mistake that may have cost him five points, and he begins to scold himself, as if he's internalized what a parent might say in such a circumstance, telling himself that he can't afford to make such slipups in the real world and how he doesn't know what he'll do if the troubling trend "keeps up."

Then again, Romeo, always driving, always pushing, is rarely satisfied with his own performance. The other day, he logged onto the computer to find out how he did on the SAT. He left the score up on the monitor for his mother to see for herself: 2200. A hundred points below his goal—but stellar nonetheless. To Romeo's surprise, he scored slightly higher in reading, 750, and writing, 730, than he did in his favored subject of math, 720. His mother was thrilled. He was moderately pleased. "Realistically, it's good," he says. "My id and ego are satisfied, my superego isn't." He can't help but think of two other juniors who achieved nearly perfect scores, identical 2340s. It stings until he ponders the vagaries of chance and circumstance, the accidents of birth, where they were raised, and the infinitesimal difference those early years of academic training may have made, a slight advantage, no matter how hard he strives to catch up.

But here's the thing: with his SAT scores and outstanding grades, Harvard is well within his grasp.

Romeo already has a plan for tonight. "I'll do the whole tour of the Ivies," he says. Princeton, Brown, Columbia. A guidance counselor suggested he visit the University of Chicago as well. "It's like dating," he says. "You try to get their attention. Then once they like you, they try to get your attention."

Senior Deke Hill has been through the courtship already. He won the hand of Cornell, but he's not ready to commit because he's still trying to grab the attention of Harvard, which wait-listed him.

That's why he's standing outside school. His mother called a Harvard admissions officer, who suggested that Deke stop by at Stuyvesant's College Night. He dressed for the occasion in a brown leather jacket, black jeans, a pink polo shirt, and a simple gold hoop earring in his left ear, an accessory that he says his mother thought would tell Harvard, "This is not your average Stuyvesant student."

The seventeen-year-old has managed to distinguish himself but not in the way he meant. While Deke maintained a 94.8 overall average through last semester, he has been struck by an early bout of a debilitating high school disease known as senioritis. Last term, he slacked off, at least by his standards, barely pulling a 90 average, which he thinks ruined any chance he had of early admission to Harvard. This semester, the slackening has worsened. Deke is particularly worried about his class in differential equations. "Every time I come out of that class," he says, he asks himself, " 'What just happened?' "

What's happening so far is that he's in jeopardy of landing a low grade. "If they see one grade of eighty, that can be a killer" he says.

But it gets worse. "The gym grade is not going to be good," Deke admits. "At the moment, I'm in danger of failing, which would not be the best thing." The problem is that gym is his first class of the day, which happens to be third period, not exactly the crack of dawn, but early enough that he's made a habit of arriving late. None of which he intends to share with Harvard tonight.

"The key," Deke says, "is to make an impression'

At 6:59, a minute before his date with Harvard, he wades in.

They're all here. All the great and good colleges, from Adelphi University to Yale University, filling classrooms with expectant herds of juniors—as well as an inordinate number of freshmen and sophomores planning ahead—and their parents, many of whom have brought pen and pad for obsessive note taking of the relevant particulars, any shred of intelligence to get a leg up on the competition: Is a college looking for anything in particular other than a high SAT score and a robust grade point average? A gifted flutist? A record of charity work? An expertise in the classics? And just how important are teacher recommendations? Is financial aid a factor in admissions? And how many advanced placement credits can be racked up? Yet it goes the other way too, with the colleges not just fielding questions but showing off their best features: small classes, leafy campuses, notable professors. So packed is the school tonight—a potluck soup of students and parents bubbling throughout the building—that there is hardly room to fit everyone in. Fifty-four colleges are squeezed together in the dining hall alone. "Throughout the night, the number of people in rooms 739 (Harvard), 735 (Yale) and

327 (Princeton) grew considerably past the fire-hazard limitation," writes a student in a follow-up opinion piece in the *Spectator*.

A boy who evidently doesn't want to be here is garbed in a T-shirt that announces, COLLEGE IS OVERRATED. On arrival, a mother is instantly mapping strategy, circling in red pen the colleges she wants to visit—not necessarily those her child prefers—which include the usual suspects: Yale, Princeton, Stanford. Another parent flips on his cell phone, communicating like a member of a SWAT team with his child, who is located elsewhere in the building. "Which school do you want to start with?" the father asks urgently. "You want to start with Brown?"

The mania is par for the course at Stuyvesant, despite the spiraling cost of a college education. The average tuition and fee charges at four-year private colleges, the target of most Stuyvesant students, amount to $22,218 in 2006–07, up 5.9 percent over the previous year. It gets worse when room and board charges are thrown in. Then the average total cost is a whopping $30,367. The expense is even higher for many of the elite private universities. But as the College Board notes, college can pay off down the road. The gap in earning widens over time between those who graduate from college and those who don't. In 2005, women between the ages of twenty-five and thirty-four with a bachelor's degree earned 70 percent more than those with only a high school diploma; for men, the gap was nearly as wide at 63 percent. Not surprisingly, enrollment in degree-granting institutions is increasing rapidly in the United States. Between 1984 and 1994, enrollment rose by 17 percent, and it jumped 21 percent from 1994 to 2004, when more than 17 million students crowded into the nation's burgeoning colleges and universities.

At Stuyvesant, the Gold Rush remains the attainment of the Ivy League, that select handful of northeastern colleges, where about a quarter of the Stuyvesant senior class will end up. This fact may help explain why room 511 is virtually empty tonight. In one corner is the University of Aberdeen, all the way from Scotland. In another corner is Babson College, a fine institution in Wellesley, Massachusetts, not far from Harvard, represented by a hip twenty-four-year-old recruiter with a small gold stud lodged in her left nostril. On her green tablecloth, a neat stack of Babson pamphlets sits virtually untouched. "You know you're about to make one of the most important decisions of your life," the school says in its literature. "You want the best education you can get. You want a career that will take you wherever you want to go. You're proud of your achievements and you want a new challenge." Then in bigger letters: "You know what," followed by "IT'S POSSIBLE. AT BABSON." The pamphlet seems to speak directly to the typical Stuyvesant student, but it's not what draws three stragglers, finally, to the display table. One boy comes right out with it, saying he has no intention of applying to Babson. He and his buddies simply want the green pens. That's what Babson is giving away. Taken aback, the recruiter hesitates, and the boy amends his rejection of Babson, saying that he may want to teach economics there one day. It's unlikely. But it's a start. The pens go. The recruiter knows it's a small price to pay if it might help ever so slightly raise her small school's profile.

"We'd love to get students from here," the recruiter says. "It's a great school."

Two floors above and a million miles away, Harvard isn't giving away anything except the legend of its weighty reputation before a rapt crowd of more than forty students, nearly half sophomores, and their parents—all that this biology demonstration classroom can hold. The blackboard isn't just erased clean, it's *sponged* clean, a meticulous measure stating what is unstated, that this is a special gathering. In front of the blackboard, behind a lab counter, is the equally meticulous Harvard recruiter, a well-preserved middle-aged woman with a carefully coiffed blond bob and a massive, glittering rock the size of an eyeball on her ring finger. She takes notice of a parent carrying a bag with MIT's logo.

"MIT's outdone us—they've given away *bags*?" she cries playfully in falsetto.

The recruiter recovers quickly, beginning by saying that Harvard is the oldest college in the nation, founded in 1636, a fact that is causing a fury of scribbling from a stable of parents in the classroom stadium seating. She notes that Harvard offers more than 3,500 classes from which students can choose. She dispels what she calls myths, that Harvard is "inaccessible, snobby, students don't have any fun." And she mentions that Harvard did go to the Rose Bowl—in 1928—which draws stiff guffaws from the gallery. Just as students are here to sell themselves, Harvard is making a pitch, which it states in a glossy handout: "The pursuit of excellence has long been a hallmark of Harvard."

"We know Stuyvesant is a great school," the recruiter says, mentioning the "long, long history" of association between the great college and the great high school, which results in the admission of many students every year to Harvard. "We're not worried about the level of preparation you're going to experience here," she says, adding that Harvard isn't only looking at applicants' grades and test scores. "We're looking at you as a whole person," she says.

Sitting in the front row, Romeo has stopped taking notes to absorb what the recruiter is saying, as if trying to unlock the secrets of the Rosetta stone. But there's little wisdom to glean from the presentation other than the implicit message that Harvard is really special. When the thirteen-minute presentation ends, Romeo rises and makes his way over to one of the admissions officers in attendance, saying he'd like to speak with the Harvard football coach. It's a perfunctory exchange, one of countless tonight, but necessary, and Romeo seems to know it as soon as he steps out. "It was nothing new," he says, as he heads next door to another packed encounter with an Ivy, Brown.

Deke, the senior, leaves Harvard unimpressed as well. In the few minutes he spoke with the Harvard recruiter, he had the distinct impression that she was maintaining a "fake smile" the whole time that he tried to make his case to be admitted from the waiting list. Deke's not convinced she was moved by the idea that he put forward, that he could take a year off before attending college. He even offered to send his upcoming grades, a risky tactic given the state of his academic affairs. She simply told him to send the grades if he wants. So Deke shrugs.

"It's a very murky process," he says.

It's okay, though, because Deke is thinking of the magic of spring washing over his final days at Stuyvesant and the riverside park behind the school where he and his friends hang out. Now the idea of waiting to hear from Harvard doesn't seem so onerous after all.

"It can be worse," he says, reminded of the Langston Hughes poem "A Dream Deferred."

"What happens to a dream deferred?" he asks. "Answer: It gets wait-listed in April." While Deke makes light of the situation, his brow darkens ever so minutely as he begins to resign himself to the inevitable. Harvard isn't going to happen. It's not over but it's over. He will have to settle for the consolation prize of merely another prestigious Ivy League school. Look out, Cornell, here he comes.

> *I've run out of plans, same as you*
>
> —desktop graffiti, Stuyvesant High School

# CHAPTER TWENTY

# Peter Pan Tilts

MILO, THE LITTLE MAN-CHILD, ENTERS HIS EMPTY bedroom after school on an overcast Tuesday, May 2, and his visage darkens at the wreck before him. "It's not usually like this," says the embarrassed ten-year-old. His room, which he shares with his three-year-old brother, Romy, is too tidy. "It's *never* clean," he says, explaining that it's his mother's fault since she had the *nerve* to straighten things up before a couple came over for one of her birthing classes. But he gets over the infraction, moving to his desk, over which is taped a picture he drew of George W. Bush. The president has a set of fierce horns, red beady eyes, and a pierced earring. In a bubble of dialogue, Milo, the political cartoonist, has Bush saying, "More bombs." A pile of books lies on the little sophisticate's desk, including *To Kill a Mockingbird* and *A Short History of Nearly Everything*. On the nearby windowsill stands a gathering of trophies, profits of the prodigy, including his first-place finish in the "3rd Annual Youth Chess Tournament." Milo trounced a bunch of kids in Central Park. They never had a chance. He knows the Sicilian defense. He toys with the English opening. He pummels adult wannabes. Years ago, he beat his older sister, Willa, taunting her that he would checkmate her in four moves as he proceeded to checkmate her in four moves. She hasn't played him since. Then there's the gold medal from the math fair. And that trophy from Gilsports for Kids, the award given to all the children. It's a hint of his life outside high school, a segue along his baby blue walls to a series of shelves displaying the remnants of a childhood, artifacts like the board games Othello and Operation and Mouse Trap. *Peter Pan* tilts on a shelf. But the tale of a little boy who wouldn't grow up gives way to the ruminations of a little boy who can't help but grow up, so unbridled is his vast intellect.

"I always have trouble sleeping," he says.

The scenario is always the same. He flips. He rolls over. Eventually, his eyes flutter shut. And still Milo can't explain the insomnia. He's running out of ideas. Things are actually good at Stuyvesant—better. Sure, he misses his elementary school friends, but trigonometry is going well, although the class still requires an hour of homework a night. He's even made a second friend in high school, another smart boy in his math research class, which is captivating his attention as he prepares a research paper on the predictability of the climate. "It's not really about the weather," he says. "It's about chaos."

Plus, he loves his teacher, Mr. Siwanowicz. "We think alike," Milo says, though he can't explain how. But more than anything, deep into this semester, he has reached a new plateau in his career at Stuyvesant, an elusive step that also is difficult to define, and there's nothing tangible to point to, other than when he says, almost surprised himself, "I sort of feel like a freshman."

Emboldened, the unofficial freshman wanders over to the door of his sister's room, where a sticker hints at the grave risk involved in disturbing the girl who lies beyond it: WHAT PART OF NO DON'T YOU UNDERSTAND. But when Willa emerges, she's in a charitable mood. "Milo knows everything," says the seventh grader. She notes, however, that she has more common sense, recalling when he was seven and "putting on his pants backwards." When she adds, "*Smart* is something he has going for him," the remark seems laden with an undertone of resentment as dark as a Slavic novel. It turns out that, even though Willa is incredibly bright, a whiz in school who doesn't have to work hard to maintain a 95 average, being two years older than a prodigy has its pitfalls. Willa isn't shy about explaining why: if they take the Stuyvesant entrance exam at the same time this year, they'd end up in the same grade next year. "I won't go to Stuyvesant because he'll be there," she says, referring to the boy the top of whose head doesn't yet reach the bottom of her chin. "We'd be in the same year, and he'd probably take some classes ahead of me."

By now, Milo has retreated behind the half-closed door of his parents' adjoining bedroom.

"There's the whole sibling competition," Willa says.

Milo peeks out from behind the door. "How would we be competing?"

If an answer is forthcoming, it's lost in the tumult that ensues as Milo launches a sneak attack, whacking his sister with a stuffed elephant, and she orders him to get away. And just like that, the natural balance of things has been restored, the younger brother yielding to the older sister.


The following morning, things begin to fall into place for Mr. Jaye. He's offered the principal's job at Brooklyn's Midwood High School. And he promptly rejects it. That's because he's on the cusp of taking the job at Bergen County Academies, the New Jersey school he really wants. They've come to terms on a salary of $130,000, which doesn't include the pension he'll earn when he retires from the New York City school system. There's only one sticking point—his title. The school already has a principal. For now, he doesn't know what title he'd hold. Mr Jaye can live with that because he knows this: he has taken less money in the hopes that he can bring Mr. Siwanowicz with him to Bergen County.

"I negotiated—are you ready for this?—a thirty-three-thousand-dollar increase in his salary," Mr. Jaye says, proud of his wheeling and dealing on behalf of Mr. Siwanowicz. As an added bonus, if the deal goes through, the school aide won't be manning attendance scanners; for that matter, the school aide wouldn't be a school aide. At the New Jersey school, Mr. Siwanowicz would be a technology staff developer who'd also help teach the math team. With the new job all but a certainty, Mr. Jaye urges Mr. Siwanowicz to think about moving out of his parents' apartment, maybe move in with his new girlfriend, who lives uptown, where it would be easier for Mr. Siwanowicz to commute to Bergen County.

"It's time to grow up," Mr. Jaye tells him. "It's time to get a real job, make real money, take the next step up in terms of responsibility."

"I'm ready, let's go," Mr. Siwanowicz says.

Mr. Jaye is already figuring out how Mr. Siwanowicz can finish his college degree, if not at City College, then at Fairleigh Dickinson University in New Jersey. "I don't care if he does it through a correspondence school," he says.

Oddly enough, Mr. Jaye can indirectly thank Ms. Damesek for all this good fortune; after all, he blames her for foisting the scanning duties on Mr. Siwanowicz. "It got me so soured on the way things are run here that I can't take living in a place where someone like Jan would be asked to scan," Mr. Jaye says.

When the math chairman informs the principal of his impending departure, Mr. Teitel doesn't try to persuade him to stay at Stuyvesant. The principal knows that Mr. Jaye aspires to be a principal himself. Mr. Teitel simply wishes him good luck. "It'll be a big loss for us, a tremendous loss," he says. Though they argue like brothers, they are close like brothers too. Mr. Teitel says he will miss Mr. Jaye, who says the same. And Mr. Jaye means it because, in light of his new job, he comes to see something different about the principal, that while he always criticized Mr. Teitel for being too nice, for giving his people too much latitude, Mr. Jaye now understands that the principal also gave him the freedom to grow, even while allowing Ms. Damesek to grow too. "His inability to control her might also be a willingness to allow people to be themselves," Mr. Jaye says. Forgiveness comes with knowing that his time at Stuyvesant is almost up. Which prompts him to think of all the people he has come to know here, making him the unofficial mayor of Stuyvesant.

"I walk in this building, I know everyone," he says, "from the guy who sweeps the cafeteria to the cops on the street to every kid, every parent, every merchant, every person who has anything to do with the school. . . . It's real tough." He thinks about what he must leave behind, the math department he built, the teachers he hired, a family to him. Mr.

Jaye almost thought of staying at Stuyvesant. But then his wife gave him a nudge. "When I was waffling, I said, 'Why don't I just stay at Stuy?' And she said, 'No, go to Bergen, the money's too good.'"

Mr. Jaye always thought that he would retire from Stuyvesant, hoping for a plaque erected in his honor. But the school bestows such an honor only on teachers who have passed away. "It's probably not going to happen," he says. ". . . I'm not dead." He's just tempted enough to "buy my own plaque." After thirty-four years at Stuyvesant, he reasons, "if you walk out under your own power, or [are] carried out [in] an ambulance, what is the difference?"

But Mr. Jaye is getting ahead of himself. He hasn't signed a contract with Bergen County yet. His departure from Stuyvesant is to remain a closely held secret until then. It will be hard to keep to himself the knowledge that his time is quickly running out. When the phone rings, Mr. Jaye picks it up and, after a beat, says into the receiver, "No, I'm not here. This is an apparition, but a goddamn good-looking one." The apparition, decked out in a conservative blue button-down shirt, dark slacks, and a navy tie, then adds, "I'm totally naked."


That afternoon, Mariya, the fifteen-year-old Ukrainian immigrant, is a bundle of unarticulated emotions as she comes home, near the end of the subway line in a working-class Russian section of Brooklyn not far from Midwood, the high school Mr. Jaye just rejected. Hers is a nondescript tenement where graffiti has migrated to the edges of the red-brick exterior. The elevator is the old-fashioned kind; when it arrives, she has to open the door to enter it, and it's impossible not to be assaulted by the stench of Clorox swabbed on the elevator floor. Her bedroom assaults the senses too, beginning with the door, on which there is an excerpt from Dante's *Inferno*: "Through me the way into the suffering city, Through me the way to the eternal pain, Through me the way that runs among the lost. Justice urged on my high artificer; My maker was divine authority, The highest wisdom, and the primal love. Before me nothing but eternal things were made, And I endure eternally. Abandon every hope, ye who enter here."

It's not a commentary on her state of mind, notwithstanding the failed petition drive to eradicate homework over vacation, despite the end of her first love, regardless of the parental pressure she faces. The excerpt is just, as she says, "really cool." As is the sign on the inside of the door, which announces, MEAN PEOPLE SUCK. This, after all, is the natural habitat of a high school sophomore. Which is why there's a poster of her favorite band, Disturbed. On her computer thumps the techno-rock beat of Celldweller. By her bed rest chunky textbooks, including the dreaded *Chemistry: Connections to Our Changing World*. And then it all comes rushing back: school. Things are getting worse. Not that her mother has an inkling. Mariya has evaded detection through a new technique.

"I haven't been telling her my grades lately because they've been eighty-seven-ish," she says. "When it's ninety or above, I'll tell her about it."

That means the indelicate issue of grades won't be coming up over dinner tonight. Instead, over Ukrainian borscht at the small kitchen table, talk turns to the more digestible topic of Mariya's transformation into a great student years ago, while the present tense gets a merciful bye.

Mrs. Goldman, marveling at her daughter as if she were an unexpected gift, can't think of anything that she did to help her daughter academically. "Nothing, nothing special," she says in her staccato Eastern European accent.

Mariya corrects her. "My mother always helped me with my homework," she says.

Mrs. Goldman corrects her in turn, saying that her English was so limited that she could do little to help her daughter after the first grade, when Mrs. Goldman could no longer understand the books that Mariya was reading in school. "Then," her mother says, "she started to know more than me."

Neither she nor Mariya spoke much English when they arrived in the United States in 1995. But what language couldn't convey, a parent's love did. From Mariya's earliest days, her mother impressed upon her the importance of education and how Mrs. Goldman had herself been a good student in school, a potent combination that left a deep impression on young Mariya. "I wanted to be like my mom," she says.

At parent-teacher conferences, Mrs. Goldman always showed up, even though she invariably heard the same refrain, that her daughter was a wonderful student, which actually was why Mrs. Goldman came. She just wanted to hear that, and who could have blamed her? "I thought she is smart girl, but I am mother," she says, dismissing her own bias.

Mariya discounted her own talent too. A few years ago, when she was passing by Stuyvesant, she pointed it out to her mother who had no idea what the place signified, until Mariya explained "This is a school for very smart kids," she told her. "I can't even dream about this school." Mariya didn't bother studying for the entrance exam—what was the use?—which made her acceptance all the more shocking.

"I was happy and proud," Mrs. Goldman says with restraint. Then she quietly rises from the kitchen table and gently kisses the top of her daughter's head, where all that magnificent intelligence resides.

Still, Mrs. Goldman is perplexed by her daughter's academic success. She wonders if it has to do with the magic potion of mixing parents of widely different ages, as she is sixteen years younger than her husband. But she doesn't wonder about all those times when she pushed Mariya to work harder. That pressure goes unstated even while it persists. Mariya lets it go too, at least for tonight.

"If I can be similar to her and her parenting," Mariya says, "that would be really cool."

The next day, Thursday, May 4, the new issue of the *Spectator* hits the stands by the second-floor entrance. On the front page blares the headline: "COSA Up for Reappointment." The plight of Mr. Polazzo, the beloved coordinator of student affairs, has finally come to light for all the students to see, and the news doesn't bode well for the school administration. In an accompanying editorial, the newspaper says, "It is our duty as the student body to join this fight to protect Polazzo in his time of need. As a student advocate in the face of the administration, Polazzo has been an ally of the student body and has always fought for its best interests. Now it is time for us all to return the favor."

Meanwhile, around the corner from the hustle and bustle of the newspaper stand, somber students are gathering to protect the memory of two of their own. They are selling blue plastic bracelets at two dollars apiece to raise funds for a memorial to Kevin and April. The bracelets carry a simple message, that they haven't been forgotten, that the day of the crash is remembered: "April & Kevin 03-17-06."

CHAPTER TWENTY-ONE

# Neutral Ground

MR. SIWANOWICZ SEEMS TO FLOAT ABOVE THE BUSTLE of Chambers Street as he makes his way to the subway station after school on the evening of Thursday, May 4, oblivious to the glare of traffic, ignoring the congestion of humanity, disregarding his own screeching depression, which isn't screeching today. Not even remotely. Across the street from Stuyvesant, he takes note of the block where the day before Tom Cruise had made a cameo appearance at a gala premiere of his latest blockbuster, *Mission Impossible III*. A crush of adoring fans swarmed the movie star, a spectacle at which Mr. Siwanowicz scoffs "I wouldn't trade places with him," he says. "I have a better job." And it's about to get better yet. When he joins Mr. Jaye at Bergen County Academies next year—and it's all but a certainty—Mr. Siwanowicz expects he'll be doing what he loves, teaching math, without the distractions of monitoring attendance scanners or fixing photocopiers. Still, he says, "I'll miss the kids" at Stuyvesant. And still, he has trouble sleeping. While Milo rotates 180 degrees in his sleep, Mr. Siwanowicz rises, walks a few steps to his alarm clock, and turns it off without waking up without remembering a thing. But why let it get him down? It's springtime, and as he

213

notes, "Sunlight chemically produces stuff that makes us feel better. That's why people move to Florida."

Mr. Siwanowicz has no intentions of moving south; he is thinking of moving uptown into an apartment with his girlfriend, Kate. "I don't know what the future holds," he says, "but it's going great." His parents think so too. They met Kate and instantly adored her, and now it's on his "to-do list" to meet her parents. His parents also think it'd be a good idea if he moved out of his room in their apartment and found his own place. He's almost thirty years old; it's time. "It's the natural order of things," he says.

On the No. 1 train heading uptown, Mr. Siwanowicz can't help but muse about Kate, admiring her natural abilities, her keen mind, which, while lacking the knowledge of such minutiae as multivariable calculus that packs his brain, nonetheless still implicitly understands math, a close kin to her expertise in music, another language of symbols that in the right sequence produces a specific and beautiful outcome.

So he better be ready.

At precisely 6:30 p.m., Mr. Siwanowicz arrives at the entrance of Neutral Ground on Twenty-sixth Street, where, he explains, "People beat the crap out of each other." Relishing the challenge, he takes the elevator to the fourth floor and enters a large, musty room that could pass for a poker parlor, except for the dearth of cigar smoke, the substitute for which is the waft of nuked popcorn and the whiff of fantasy, of hobbits and dungeons and dragons and abnormally muscular superheroes. The rattle of dice pierces the stale air as he wends his way over scuffed wood floors, under exposed red-painted piping, past a fire-escape door left open and massive windows painted shut and covered with steel bars. People are hunched in red vinyl chairs busted open with the innards of yellow fluff oozing out; the place is a repository for boys in backward baseball caps, bearded men in yarmulkes, ghetto gangstas in skullcaps, blacks, Asians, Hispanics, and one pregnant woman.

For one dollar, the price of admission, they do here what they could just as easily do at home: play board games. But Neutral Ground isn't just a place to play games. It's a community, a subculture of smart people—a Web designer, a Columbia University fellow, a 401(k) pension consultant, a brilliant school aide—who are looking for a fix of intellectual stimulation in the form of a game.

And then there's Kate, a revelation, playing against type. She's not just a brainiac, she's a beautiful brainiac, out of the Michelle Pfeiffer mold, petite, doe-eyed, a startling contrast to the hulking, bedraggled figure of Mr. Siwanowicz. Kate lights up as soon as she sees him approach, pausing from the throes of a board game, the Cities & Knights of Catan, which she's playing with three others. But her greeting is a blip on the screen. She resumes her game as he takes a seat at the table in front of her and plunges into a card game called Jambo. He can't see what she's doing. Maybe that's the way he wants it. Maybe it's so perfect, watching her would be too scary. Or maybe, even with his back to her, he doesn't need to see because he knows she's here with him and that's enough.


Nothing is ever enough, not two nights later, a warm Saturday evening, when Jane plunges into a frenzied crowd milling about at Union Square along Fourteenth Street. She's pumped. She's jazzed. She's power walking. Dragging behind her is an angular twenty-year-old named Mike whom she met a couple of days ago. They strike an odd contrast, she in fashionable sandals, jeans, and a pink halter top, he in a gangsta's getup, a New York Yankees cap and jersey of a baseball team he doesn't follow, his baggy jeans drooping far below his waist, a puddle at his ankles. On his sloped back is a black backpack, although he's not in school anymore. He did a month or so of community college, like a prison sentence, before he became gainfully employed selling what he calls "blue haze," potent marijuana. It turns out shoplifting didn't pay. Jane isn't listening. She's pounding pavement until she submerges into Sahara East, a hookah bar on First Avenue, where they pile into the back, under a dark red tent, to a corner table pockmarked with burn holes in the tablecloth. As soon as she sits, Jane begins to reach into her white Coach handbag and almost as immediately, Mike says, "Just save it. You told me not to let you."

Reminded of her own admonition, Jane complies, letting go of whatever she was about to remove, instead pulling out of the little handbag an unexpected accessory, a novel, *The Feast of Love*, like a rabbit out of a magician's hat. Required reading in her Great Books class. A life raft. Her English teacher, Mr. Grossman, would be proud.

Except that he's scared.

One day she's in class, the next she's not. When she returned to class on a recent day, she casually apologized by saying, "I'm sorry I wasn't around. I was kind of on suicide watch." It's a feeling she can't shake and can't explain. She can only respond to it, alternately smoking marijuana and watching endless episodes of mindless Japanese anime online, gaining ten pounds, then losing ten pounds in a span of two weeks. Mr. Grossman responded as a teacher would: with a lesson. He gave her the example of a farmer who every day feeds a chicken, so that the chicken comes to associate the farmer with food, a logical assumption until the farmer, one day, picks up the chicken and twists its neck, killing it. The farmer had only been fattening the chicken for slaughter. The chicken couldn't have known this; it had only a limited experience on which to base its assumptions, just as Jane, at the tender age of seventeen, has limited experience about life, about things not getting better, about things getting worse. Jane liked the parable, especially the way he worked in a chicken, as if Mr. Grossman were sending a subtle message that she was herself a chicken, threatening to opt out of life, which was indeed part of the point.

"The world's a much happier place for me with a little freak like you in it, so don't be selfish," he told her, making her laugh, which was the point too.

The point now, though, is to choose a hookah flavor to inhale, and Jane selects the Tony Montana flavor, which is apropos given that it's named after a movie character with a major drug addiction. It's perhaps the only thing that makes sense, as her mind is a disjointed caravan, ricocheting from one thought to another about how "anarchy rules" and "democracy is one step closer to anarchy."

Her new friend, Mike, plays it safe and remains silent until Jane says, "I don't think it's possible to live life without breaking the law."

Now he gets it. "That's true," he says.

Jane has a particular vantage point because she was recently arrested. The last time she checked in at rehab, she again tested dirty—registering marijuana, cocaine, and heroin in her system—prompting a search of her bag, which turned up two dime bags of marijuana. Police arrived, handcuffed her, and took her down to the precinct, where she was placed in a small holding cell along with several other women, one charged with shoplifting, another with child neglect From about 6 p.m. to 2 a.m., Jane lost herself in the role of nursemaid, consoling the women for their misfortune. Then police officers took her to central booking, where she was shoved into another cell, which held little more than a toilet seat. She was robbed in her sleep. Awake, her mind kept churning in an endless loop, telling her, "This is my limit. This is my limit. This is my limit." When she was finally released—facing another sentence of community service—she began to think it was time to change. She began thinking about the future. About graduation. About prom. About a boy whom she barely knew who asked her to go as his date. And she began thinking more seriously about applying to college for next fall. She screamed, "Hell, no," when her estranged father recently called, asking to see her either for her eighteenth birthday later this month or for graduation in June, but still, Jane seemed to be in a better mood. Until now.

"I mean, what do you think the point of life is?" she asks in the darkened hookah bar.

"Be happy, be successful, help out your family," says Mike, her companion for the evening.

"How do you define success?" she wants to know.

"I don't need to be rich," he says, "but I want shelter."

She's unimpressed. "That's pretty basic."

He doesn't know how to respond to that. So Jane picks up the thread of conversation, gives it a different stitch. "Do you know that addiction can be genetic?" she asks.

"Alcoholism runs in my family," says Mike, who has a stomachache from drinking today.

"Everybody's addicted to something—food, television, even religion," Jane says. "I mean, we all need something to define us." She thinks of her past. "I used to be so against drinking and drugs. Why are there so many ironies in life?"

Another question Mike can't answer. Instead, his eyes flit about as he checks his cell phone repeatedly, finally saying he needs to get home before his mother does. That's their cue. They charge out of the hookah bar to catch the L train to head to his house, but just before Jane ducks into the subway station, she's caught by a final, stray thought. "I think life is so much better if you don't believe in God," she says. "We're personally responsible for what happens in our lives. There's no fate."

On Wednesday, May 10, Mr. Polazzo is wondering about his own fate, appealing to a higher power: the principal.

Even though his prospects remain dim, Mr. Polazzo has just reapplied as the coordinator of student affairs, submitting an application enumerating his accomplishments over the past four years.

"I kind of took credit for what the kids did," he confesses from his usual perch in the Student Union office, "but it happened on my watch."

"Like when the president takes credit for job creation?" queries one of the SU regulars, Nathan, the renegade Web master, who's off to Princeton next year.

It's a regular Stuyvesant occurrence: a future Ivy Leaguer keeping a teacher in check. Though, in truth, Mr. Polazzo didn't really take all the credit. "Ever since I arrived at Stuyvesant in November 2000, I have been consistently amazed at the brilliance, dedication, and excellence of the student body," he wrote in his application for the job. And each time he listed an accomplishment, he diminished his own role as student coordinator by naming the students who deserved credit, whether it was automating the sale and distribution of Sing! tickets or organizing a massive school blood drive.

"This is the worst job in the building," Nathan says.

Mr. Polazzo has at least one thing going for him: no one else has applied to be coordinator of student affairs, despite the behind-the-scenes efforts of some school administrators to prop up a rival candidate, and the deadline expires in two days. He would disavow his regular cracked-pepper-turkey-on-a-roll lunch forever for the chance to be reappointed, but he readily agrees that the job stinks. "Whenever a student does something wrong, I'm the first person they come to," he says of *them*, the adults. As exhibit A, Mr. Polazzo refers to what he calls the "chaperone's dilemma." At a dance, which he oversees, what do you do if a student is caught imbibing alcohol? Option one, he says, is to let the kid go. Option two is to call the parents, "but that kind of ruins the kid's life," he notes. Or option three, if the student is already drunk, call an ambulance "in loco parentis," he says. He doesn't particularly relish any of the options, though he's been forced to resort to option three, visiting a hospital, at least eight times.

Just then, Mr. Teitel barges into Mr. Polazzo's office, a rare sighting in this student hangout. It seems almost too good to be true. Has the principal already made a decision about the job?

"Did I win the lottery?" Mr. Polazzo asks.

Mr. Teitel leans in, excited. Then he breaks the news: a television news show wants to do a live shot at Stuyvesant, hoping to enlist more than eight hundred students to create a Guinness-record human wave. Mr. Polazzo hasn't won the lottery. He has won the task of getting the word out to students. The news segment will be heralding the upcoming flick *Poseidon*. It was too good to be true.

It may be too good to be true, but on Friday, May 12, it appears that Ms. Lee, the student teacher, may have found a permanent job. Not at Stuyvesant, however. She just returned from an interview at Syosset High School, a regular public school on Long Island. It all happened so quickly. Her mentor, Stuyvesant history teacher Warren Donin, had been offered the chance to apply for the job at Syosset, but he wasn't interested, so he suggested that she try. She didn't want to. She still wanted Stuyvesant. Besides, Syosset didn't want to hire a student teacher; the school wanted a veteran. But Mr. Donin kept pestering Ms. Lee, telling her there were no openings at Stuyvesant, that this was a chance for her to land at another good school with a full-time job and *benefits*. Then Ms. Lee learned that the Syosset teacher who had tried to recruit Mr. Donin was the daughter of Ms. Lee's mother's calligraphy teacher, and the coincidence seemed like a good omen.

Finally, Ms. Lee relented, though not enthusiastically. "What's the worst that can happen?" she asked herself.

The worst that could happen was that she could apply to Syosset and find out that she liked it, which is exactly what happened. She met with the head of the social studies department and instantly hit it off with him. The interview was supposed to be merely a courtesy. But the department head especially liked how she responded to a tough interview question: What do you do if a student is failing? Her answer: Think A-Rod. She was watching the Yankees on television the other night, she explained. Alex Rodriguez, the slugger, was mired in a slump when he crushed a mighty home run, and with one sweet stroke of the bat, he was back on track. Similarly, Ms. Lee told the Syosset administrator, she wants her students to know that they can always come back if they are failing. "I want them to be perceived by me as all potential A-plus students," she explained. The Syosset administrator, not expecting a baseball analogy from the diminutive Asian woman, was impressed.

Ms. Lee had hit a home run.

The job, though, isn't a lock. Far from it. Next week, she will return for round two of the interview process, when she meets with a six-teacher committee and conducts a demonstration history lesson in front of a live classroom. If she makes it through those hoops, she still faces interviews with the school principal and other officials.

"Everything will be decided in the next two weeks," she says.

It may be scary to contemplate, but for the first time, Ms. Lee has come to understand that she has no choice, that it's time to move on. "I was so focused, if it's not Stuy, it's nowhere," she says, echoing her high school experience when she fell short of Stuyvesant, settling for Bronx Science. Now, she realizes, "There are other schools out there." And perhaps she is willing to believe there is life outside Stuyvesant. "Maybe," she says, "I won't hate teaching at another place."

> *I love you*
> *I always have*
>
> —desktop graffiti, Stuyvesant High School

CHAPTER TWENTY-TWO

# Love Notes

OUTSIDE, ON A QUIET PATCH OF MIDTOWN PAVEMENT, there is no sign of the pulsating, primal, hip-grinding bedlam that is about to bust out here on the evening of Saturday, May 13. In fact, there is no sign at all. T New York, a chic nightclub, sits incognito an anonymous front of maroon stucco walls, its identity betrayed only by three stone-faced, burly bouncers standing sentry by a strip of felt rope cordoning off the entrance. But the momentary tranquility is disrupted at four minutes to six when Mr. Polazzo, the coordinator of student affairs, blows in, wielding a weapon of mass deterrence.

"Hopefully, we'll keep it clean," he tells the proprietor "I have a Breathalyzer."

It's the calm before the soph/frosh semiformal.

It's been a harried few days for Mr. Polazzo. He found out just the other day that at least two rival teachers are now vying for the student coordinator job—unexpected candidates who've emerged at the last minute, just as his reappointment seemed assured. Then a girl who goes around school posing as a boy named "Max" was playing Hacky Sack when she fell, hit her head, and suffered a seizure, forcing Mr.

Polazzo to take the student on his umpteenth trip to a hospital emergency room.

And now, tonight.

A gaggle of girls begins to clatter inside, teetering on high heels, looking as uncomfortable as circus performers wobbling on precarious stilts. A battalion of boys tramples in, hair spiked toward the ceiling like shards of stalagmites in a cave. What follows is a kaleidoscope of white T-shirts and powerful cologne and purses and flip-flops and denim miniskirts over dark leggings and ankle bracelets. The freshmen and sophomores look either ten years old or twenty-five, depending on the angle of the lighting.

In they go, all of them, a crush of bodies piling into a tiled room, through a darkened hall, and out into an empty chamber, where they come to a halt at the edge of the dance floor, as if avoiding an invisible force field. The only dancing is that of the flashing lights glinting off the walls, a lonely Morse code of blue, green, and red. Two girls probe the perimeter, and two other girls join in, but the dancing fizzles out like the last pop of popcorn in the pan. It's too early. It's not too early, though, for Mr. Polazzo to worry and strategize, as he hits upon the idea to foil would-be imbibers by checking students' water bottles because such containers are commonly used to disguise alcoholic contents. Then, suddenly, like a herd of buffalo stampeding an open plain, about thirty girls storm the dance floor, because they're teenagers and there's comfort in numbers, and all hell breaks loose: random screams, the emergence of the first hip-grinding couple, and by 6:39 p.m., there's a critical mass on the dance floor as stereo speakers shake the ground, blasting out the lyrics, "Don't cha wish your girlfriend was hot like me," and it's degrees hotter and the air is thick, and manufactured smoke begins to spew out, and now more than three hundred boys and girls madly bounce off each other while bolder dancers climb on raised cube platforms, the better for unobstructed exhibitionism, gyrating wildly, hair flying, minds evidently blank.

Thus have they descended into a primitive state, an unleashing of anarchy, and *Lord of the Flies* comes to mind. But for this: on closer inspection, the faces retain the innocence of youth. The eyes cast uncertain glances, as if asking, *Do I look stupid? Am I dancing in rhythm? Am I cool?* On the balcony, a smattering of shy observers watches the frenzied spectacle below, outcasts in high school, loners here too. When the DJ flips on a slow song, dancers howl in protest, with most retreating to the sidelines, waiting to dance to a song less intimate. Still out there is a boy kissing a girl, and it's just that, a gentle, little peck. With practiced casualness, boys and girls lean against the wooden edge of the bar, ordering nothing harder than a Shirley Temple with a cherry on top.

But Mr. Polazzo, the mother hen, knows better. A bouncer caught a chaperone slipping a drink to a student. The chaperone insisted the student grabbed the drink out of his hand. The video camera says otherwise. The chaperone won't be chaperoning next year. It could've been worse.

"Last year, a lot of my chaperones got drunk," Mr. Polazzo says.

When it's dark, and it's a Saturday night, and there's a room packed with fourteen- and fifteen-year-olds dancing their heads off, drama inevitably follows. A girl weeps in the hallway near the men's bathroom. A brave boy makes a doomed dance request of a girl who responds by pinching her nose, a hand signal, like a third base coach calling a steal sign, which prompts another girl to slide to her rescue, to save the girl from the fate of a dance with a boy that can never, ever happen. Another boy observes on the sidelines, holding up a look of disdain because he doesn't intend to ask a girl to dance. "You can usually judge the situation if they mind," he notes sagely. How? "Experience," he says, and a period can almost be heard at the end of the one-word sentence.

It's a strange phenomenon but absolutely true here: girls mature faster than boys, and not just intellectually. Even in the dancing shadows and the flashing lights, many of the boys simply look younger—an awkward assemblage of skin and bones, a mass of puzzle pieces that don't quite fit together yet—than many of the girls who are the same age. But the girls show uncanny forbearance.

"I can't wait until the freshmen boys grow," giggles Taylor, herself a freshman.

By 9:01, they are growing up faster. On the dance floor, the grinding becomes a little more unstructured, sweatier, soupier. Girls are pounding the floor in bare feet in a kind of tribal drumbeat. Boys are knocking into each other with more force, threatening violence. Upstairs becomes a tangle of bodies in various wrestling poses that, in the light of day and direct supervision, would elicit appalled parental disapproval. But before a major infraction occurs, at precisely 10 p.m., the music snaps off, and just like that, the mood shuts off like a light switch. Boys and girls blink in the rising lights, becoming themselves. Mr. Polazzo, relieved, takes the mike to announce the dance is over. He's booed. It's time for them to go home, children once again.

Back at Stuyvesant, another transmutation has occurred, and an ineffable quality permeates the air. The hallways are emptier, almost bereft, as students are drawn, like sun worshippers, to the magnetic pull of the riverside park behind school to bathe in the warmth of springtime. In the crevices of school, the Hudson staircase among them, an unusual number of boys and girls nestle in embraces, discovering first loves. Students continue to trudge to class but, for many, their thoughts have fled to the not-so-distant future, to the end of the semester, just weeks away, to the end of school, to the beginning of summer, and, for seniors, to the beginning of college next year.

"Ultimately, what it's about is starting the process of disengaging, you know, and saying good-bye," says Mr. Grossman, the English chairman, who, with a hint of sadness, sees the same cycle play out every year. ". . . It's a mood and an energy rather than a specific set of activities and behaviors."

There is, however, a name for it: senioritis.

Wikipedia, the online encyclopedia popular with students, defines the dreaded affliction as

The decreased motivation towards studies displayed by students who are nearing the end of their high school or college careers. It is typically said to include slowness, procrastination, apathy regarding school work, and a tendency towards truancy.

At Stuyvesant, senioritis is defined by a cautionary note taped to the wall outside the second-floor guidance office:

Seniors—Read it and Weep Or—Try Going to Class . . .

What follows are letters to two seniors saddled with senioritis whose names have been whited out so as not to embarrass them. From Virginia Tech: "Dear [blank] . . . Because we are concerned about your desire to succeed here, the committee is considering withdrawing your offer of admission. . . ." And from the University of Delaware: "We were therefore surprised to see such a marked decline in your grades during your senior year."

Around the corner, signs of another kind herald on Friday, May 19, the definitive arrival of senioritis. Hundreds of love notes cover the entire gray tiled wall—about thirty feet long and ten feet high—bridging the white senior bar and the Asian senior bar like a rainbow of long-held truths. Here, in the twilight of their final year of high school, boys and girls have placed their names on the wall in a remarkable display of honesty—a frankness born of the imminent parting of ways—confessing their love and affection for those who never knew. They call them "Senior Crush Lists."

School lore has it that Peter Stuyvesant, the ornery Dutch commander, instigated the tradition by tacking up a list of people he wanted to kill, followed by a list of women he found attractive. No doubt wildly apocryphal, the legend finds more authenticity in the recent version of the story, which pegs the crush lists to about a decade ago when students faced insurmountable problems finding dates for the prom.

Whatever the origins, the annual tradition has become so entrenched that even in this arena, students engage in heated competition, going to great lengths to outdo one another with the most creative, over-the-top crush lists. This year, that includes a heart-shaped list that, when flipped open to reveal the names of the loved ones, automatically plays the love ballads of Barry White. Leave it to Stuyvesant's tech wonders. Or to one of the more literary types, whose crush list includes the author Robert Penn Warren because she loves his classic novel *All the King's Men*.

This, though, is serious business as clusters of students slowly shuffle along, examining love notes. The confessions even draw out teachers, like Mr. Polazzo, who's made it onto a handful of crush lists. "There's no accounting for taste," he kids.

But the truth is, many of the students do adore the coordinator of student affairs. Which is why, here at the wall, they are gathering to launch "Operation SPJ"—Saving Polazzo's Job. "It's a cause I whole-heartedly support," says Jonathan, the senior who had backed the attendance scanners, despite Mr. Polazzo's opposition to them. Jonathan overlooks their disagreement, worrying what will happen if Mr. Polazzo is replaced. So after school today, several student leaders from the Student Union, the Big Sibling program, the Arista honors society, and the *Spectator* are meeting with Mr. Teitel in a rare demonstration of student unity to register their support for Mr. Polazzo. The principal has no idea what he's in for.

Jane has no idea what she just missed. The troubled senior walks into the auditorium about five minutes too late. A friend, senior Elisa Lee, has just finished performing a monologue for her "Women's Voices" class to which she had invited Jane. The assignment called for Elisa to find a woman's story that has been silenced in some way. She chose Jane's story of drug addiction, wearing pink baggy UFO pants and a pacifier necklace in her subject's honor. The monologue, entitled "Once Is Too Much, A Thousand Never Enough," borrowed from snatches of Jane's own disjointed words, which Elisa recorded earlier in an interview but read like a haiku to the inexorable pull of narcotics:

> *Going to detox was mah own decision*
> *Cuz*
> *I was just sick of*
> *Just all the things I had to do*
> *I was sick of*
> *Having*
> *Like*
> *Waking up in the morning*
> *And needing something or*
> *Being sick when I don't have it*
> *And I was sick just thinking about it*
> *So I decided to stop*
> *And well*
> *I didn't really have a choice*

*Because*
*By that time it was just time for me to stop.*

But Jane hasn't stopped. She's resumed. She's consumed. And what she's been waiting for has finally happened, a way to escape from her mother, their fights, the distrust. Jane just celebrated a birthday. She's eighteen. She's an adult, legally. No one can tell her what to do anymore. No one can stop her. Not even she herself.

CHAPTER TWENTY-THREE

# The Players

NO ONE CAN STOP ROMEO. THE JUNIOR IS THE TALLEST, strongest, fittest player on the field, with an upper torso cut in the shape of a heroic V, as he glides effortlessly across the green expanse toward an imaginary goal. Football is still months away. But practice is in full swing on the afternoon of May 24 on the rooftop of Pier 40, about a mile from Stuyvesant, which looms like a glistening mirage in the distance. It's peaceful, the sound of Manhattan traffic muffled by the three flights separating the Astroturf from the concrete sidewalk below. Only the high rises, like mountain peaks, come into view up here, including the Mount Everest of the Empire State Building, making it possible to forget the crush of pedestrians at ground level.

It's almost too beautiful a day for boys to be practicing the art of bone-crushing tackles. A chalky blue sky stretches to infinity above, almost pastel in hue and dappled with little white clouds as if rendered by an Impressionist painter, so perfect is the vista. One imperfection, though, mars the landscape. The football field is not a football field. It's a soccer field. But it's not even that either. It's a *miniature* soccer field. A nearby aluminum bench serves as a kind of open-air locker with sneak-

ers and backpacks strewn about haphazardly. A sign at the field's
entrance warns NO DOGS ALLOWED ON LAWNS. It's a stark reminder
that despite the massive expense of Stuyvesant's building, the school
was constructed for brains, not brawn.

Romeo climbs into a harness. Two boys on either side of him pull
down on straps, trying to hold him down. But it's no use. When he coils
and jumps, his powerful legs propel him skyward, threatening to uproot
the two boys and take them with him. "Explode up!" exhorts the new
head coach, Brian Sacks. "Good! Fifteen seconds!" When the boys move
to the next drill, one doughy player collapses in the middle of the field,
unable to crawl any further. He tries to pick himself up but crumbles
again until Romeo and the others gather around, urging him on, clap-
ping politely, as only civilized Stuyvesant students are wont to do, as the
wheezing boy musters just enough energy to grasp and claw his way, on
all fours, to the finish line.

"Team's looking great," the coach pronounces after practice ends. But
the prognosis becomes grimmer as Romeo and the other boys walk back
to school, aching and dirty and pessimistic. One player bemoans the lack
of fans. Another says he mistook Mr. Teitel, the principal, for the team
mascot, thinking the bearded man was the peg-legged Peter Stuyvesant.
Their first game in September is against a regular public school that
crushed them last year sixty-four to zero. "They're bigger, blacker,
stronger, and faster," says a Stuyvesant running back who is Asian.

Romeo says nothing. He's used to black kids on opposing teams
coming up to him, picking him out as one of *them*, asking him how it
feels, being a solitary figure in a sea of white and Asian faces framed in
the Pegleg helmets. And yet Romeo is one of the Stuyvesant regulars
too—a brainiac—and as the boys slump back to school together in the
twilight of the day, talk turns to ways of using their biggest muscle—
their minds—to come up with better schemes to beat physically superior opponents. The coach has already made one significant adjustment,
shifting Romeo from tight end and defensive end to running back and
receiver so that his best player will be in a better position to score more
touchdowns. Romeo has made an adjustment of his own, switching to
jersey number thirty-seven, reflecting his new role on the team. Mean-

while, he recently met a Harvard football coach, who asked to see more of Romeo's football tapes. His father had sent them. His PR man. His dad. Romeo had stayed with him recently, up in Harlem. It had been the first time in a month or so, and Romeo realized he needed to make the trip more often. His father in Harlem gave him something that his mother on the Lower East Side couldn't. Romeo felt that his mother worried too much. When he did the same, his father quickly told him to stop, as if he couldn't stand the sight of insecurity, weakness of any kind, in his son. It was always that way with the two of them. Once, Romeo had complained that he couldn't draw well, and his father shot back, "That's the attitude I hate," ordering his son to teach himself, to *will* himself to become good at it. Romeo complied, buying a bunch of books on the craft, including *Drawing for Dummies*. Now his dad may be leaving. He's been offered a full-time teaching job at the prestigious Berklee College of Music in Boston, his hometown. His father doesn't want to leave. He already teaches at NYU and the Institute of Audio Research. But it's not that. It's that he, like his son, wants to make it big, and there's nowhere to make it bigger as a musician than in New York. Romeo sees the parallel and yet can't help but feel their differences, son to father. His father is always telling him about the importance of selling his personality. He's always talking to him about presentation and style, but Romeo looks at himself as too serious, not funny enough. His father is always saying that Romeo is trying to break away from his past, from his blackness. "He likes to see it as a reverence for the struggle of our ancestors," Romeo says. The reverence is there. The son doesn't forget. But for Romeo, there's more to his striving, although it's so complicated that sometimes he says he feels he's "losing a sense of identity." The feeling came to a head recently when he flubbed a test—at least by his standards—with an 82 in math. When he arrived home he remedied the situation by taping up on his wall an old album cover of his dad's band, Prinz Charles & the City Beat Band. Under the title "I'LL BE THERE FOR YOU," a photo of his father stares back at Romeo, a picture of a confident, dashing man with a dare-me look and a pair of large sunglasses resting on his forehead. Romeo also taped up a postcard of the idyllic seaside town of Arradon in France, home of his mother's family.

Little sailboats dot the indigo, picturesque waters along the coast. And between his father's photo and his mother's hometown, there's just enough room on the wall for a mirror where Romeo can contemplate where he fits in.

Mr. Polazzo, the embattled coordinator of student affairs, is hunched in his usual perch in the Student Union, chomping on his usual cracked-pepper-turkey sandwich, but on this Thursday, May 25, he finds himself contemplating an unusual problem: is a free hug okay? It isn't a metaphysical question. It's a campaign question. A senior running for class president wants to post a flyer offering the affectionate freebie. And Jamie Paul, cochair of the student elections, waits patiently for an answer.

"That's up to you," Mr. Polazzo decides.

Jamie decides it's okay. It's not like the candidate is offering a hug in return for a vote. But, she wants to know, is it also okay for candidates to play music from their boom boxes to draw attention? That's okay too, Mr. Polazzo determines. Just about everything is okay with the easygoing Mr. Polazzo but his own fate as coordinator of student affairs, which continues to dangle uncertainly. For the moment, however, he tables his own worries as he wades into these student elections, a remote facsimile of democracy in action. What isn't okay is "profanity, defamation, sex, or drugs" in campaign literature, according to the official rules and regulations of the Stuyvesant Board of Elections. What also isn't okay is for students to make signs except those that are eight and a half by eleven inches in size. The school doesn't want candidates with deep pockets, or too much time on their hands, to start employing billboards, neon, and other outsized campaign paraphernalia, which would be a distinct possibility in a school as hypercompetitive as Stuyvesant.

"It's to level out the playing field," Jamie explains.

But it's almost impossible to level the playing field, at least in a school where racial politics predominate. With an electorate that's more than 50 percent Asian, candidates of the same background typically prevail in student elections. "The Asians are the silent majority," Mr. Polazzo says.

One factor can upset the equation: if several Asian candidates run for the same office, they can effectively split the vote, which is not uncommon in the primaries, the first round, before the candidates with the highest vote totals go head-to-head in the general elections. Therefore, the white vote, a bloc consisting of about 40 percent of the student body, can't be ignored, especially since candidates for president and vice president of the Student Union are required to run as a joint ticket. That's why the conventional wisdom is that an "Asian-white pair" is a winning combination, says Harvard-bound senior Amanda Wallace, a Student Union regular who is black. The proof is in last year's election: the Student Union president is Asian, the vice president, white. Race is "definitely a factor but an unstated factor," Mr. Polazzo says. Sophomore Marta Bralic, who is running for Student Union vice president on an all-white ticket, is well aware of how past precedent doesn't bode well for her and her running mate. "We're two white kids," she says. "These are disadvantages."

Nonetheless, Mr. Polazzo is going against the grain in handicapping the players in this year's election. He reckons the front-runner is the all-white ticket of Marta, the Student Union special events director, and would-be president Michael Zaytsev, the Student Union chief financial officer, because of their vast experience in school government. But not to be overlooked is the pairing of a presidential candidate who is a white junior and Student Union chief of staff and his vice presidential hopeful, the sophomore president, who is half Thai and half Filipino. And then there's the dark horse candidacy of a white junior and cheerleading captain for president and her running mate, the sophomore vice president, who is half Asian. Each ticket offers a slew of reforms concerning hot-button topics like the need for more school dances and better food at the school convenience store. An even more common refrain among the candidates is the idea of recapturing students' rights against an encroaching school administration. Or as Mike and Marta note nostalgically in their campaign pamphlet, "IN THE PAST . . . Students were allowed many freedoms and Stuy was generally a good place to be. Students had many rights and fun and happiness had not been forbidden yet. However, the administration has been slowly but surely taking away rights that every student should be able to enjoy."

Cited as an example was students' former right to laugh. An accompanying stick-figure drawing in the campaign literature shows an individual, unshaven and unsmiling, locked behind bars.

Just as grim is the way the students reflect the grown-ups in their general apathy about elections. Not even a third of the school votes. "In a true democracy, voting is a right," intones a *Spectator* editorial. "Yet our student body does not seem to value it." Others find evident value in the process. Veteran filmmakers Caroline Suh and Erika Frankel have just arrived at Stuyvesant to chronicle the race for Student Union president and vice president in a documentary called *The Ticket*. In written handouts to students, they describe Stuyvesant as "arguably the best public high school in the city (if not the country)," saying they intend to explore "how democracy works—specifically, how young adults engage in the democratic process" and how the student elections serve "as a sort of microcosm of a national election." Among Stuyvesant's famous alumni, they hope to interview Dick Morris, the noted Bill Clinton campaign strategist. According to school legend, and his own accounts, the political adviser cut his teeth as a behind-the-scenes operative during high school campaigns in the sixties.

So far this year, electioneering is decidedly genteel. Indeed, it's difficult to detect an election in the offing at all, except for a smattering of posters that have begun to elbow their way onto crowded school bulletin boards, one of the most provocative of which proclaims, "The struggle endures, 'til proletarian rule." But it's early. There's still time for the fireworks of perfectly illegitimate campaign skulduggery and voter fraud.


It's early, but it's there, lurking somewhere in Mariya's expression of world-weariness, beneath the gothic layers of leather and studs, apart from the parental pressure, eons away from failed petition drives. There. Right there. A restrained smile, not even a complete smile, it's so ephemeral that it vanishes in the lunchtime shadows of Cafe Amore's, a block from school. Mariya nibbles on a slice of pizza, almost unaware of what she's eating. Because it's happened: Mariya met a boy in school. His name is Jarek Lupinski. They kissed. And just like that, because she's a sophomore in high school, and he's a junior, and things can be as sublimely simple as that, she's his first real girlfriend, and he's her first true love on this Friday, May 26. Which is why Mariya didn't even try to hide her latest report card from her mother. Mariya knew she had slacked off in English. She was well aware that she hadn't done all her homework. She was fully cognizant of the consequences of not studying hard for a variety of tests. But she says, "I sort of stopped caring as much." Her mother didn't stop caring, not even close. When she absorbed the shock of her daughter's grades, "she blew up," Mariya says. "She told me I was throwing my life away." She told Mariya that no college would want her. She stormed off, then returned twenty minutes later and started yelling at Mariya again before doling out a new edict: Mariya is not allowed to hang out after school for the rest of the school year. She is to come home immediately. This was the sentence Mariya received for coming home with a grade point average of 93.5.

The grades don't count toward Mariya's overall average. They're a kind of midterm indicator of her progress before the real grades are meted out at semester's end. But that, to her mother, is just an insignificant detail in the big picture, which is that her daughter's average dropped just over a point from 94.86 last term.

"It's a *point*, and it's not even the final grade," Mariya rails.

A point, though, takes on larger meaning in the context of a struggling family that uprooted its life in Ukraine in the hopes of grasping a piece of the American Dream—a dream made vivid by Mariya's dazzling academic potential. "To me, if I don't do as well, it's not as big of a deal to myself," she says. "To my mother, it's a different story." As for the future, Mariya says, "That's so far off. I still feel like a kid."

The future, however, continues to tug at her. Already several colleges, noticing the same potential in Mariya, particularly her high score on the Preliminary SAT (for which she didn't study), have come beckoning, sending the sophomore flattering notes, two years before she is to apply to college, like football recruiters getting an early jump on a brawny young high school prospect.

"Dear Mariya, Mount Holyoke is a remarkable place—and one of the nation's top liberal arts colleges," begins an e-mail from the dean of admissions. ". . . I'd love to meet you, have our tour guides show you our stunning campus, and talk about how Mount Holyoke can help you achieve your goals."

From Marist College: "Dear Mariya, I am writing you today to invite you to become a part of a new, exclusive web-based program designed for a select group of high school students like yourself."

And another: "Dear Mariya, Welcome to Oxford College of Emory University! . . . Take a look at Emory's academic majors, and browse its Career Center website anytime. Maybe Oxford College will be your next step to a successful future!"

The letters keep coming. "Every week, I throw out a stack that tall," she says, spreading her hands about a foot apart.

Mariya can't think about college yet; she can barely think beyond tomorrow, her sweet-sixteen birthday. It's hard to keep up. She feels the innate contradiction of being a teenager, for whom things can't move fast enough while things are happening too fast. She doesn't hang out with her two friends at Burritoville anymore. She's drifted away from Mariana, her good friend from chemistry class. High school friendships are like amoebas, having no definite form. And then there's the constant of Jarek, her new beau, a strapping, blond junior who tells her he's the last living heir of the last Polish knight, and chivalry isn't dead. Her mother blames him, and the player before him, Tom, for distracting Mariya from her academic mission. But Mariya sees it differently. "It's not anyone's fault," she says. Actually, Jarek's had a good influence, at least in one respect. Mariya wakes up thirty minutes earlier than usual, at 5:50 a.m., just so she can meet Jarek, who lives two stops away on the local Q train, on the way to school. "It's really nice," she says, "because no matter what goes wrong, I have this to fall back on." It's true, though, that he's not exactly a stellar student and that he's persuaded her to cut school after lunch today. "He wouldn't let me go to class," she says, as if she has no choice in the matter. Mariya worries about missing gym class. She frets about being caught. She doesn't know what she and Jarek will do today. There's no plan, no pressure, no expectations. Maybe they'll board a train to Hoboken and sit on a park bench and do nothing but hold hands. That, all of sudden, sounds gloriously unproductive.

CHAPTER TWENTY-FOUR

# The Human Element

IT'S 8:58 A.M. ON A LAZY SATURDAY, MAY 27, AND while his classmates are fast asleep, Romeo is already cutting a wide swath over the gray, empty pavement of Grand Street, a ghost town at this hour on the Lower East Side, his mind racing over a series of plans, pressures, and expectations A glimpse: Romeo at Harvard He's envisioning the day when he's in Cambridge, Massachusetts, out to dinner with his father, who will be in the neighborhood because he's taking that job teaching music in Boston after all. But almost as quickly as that pleasing thought materializes, it collides with the reality that Romeo's behind in his work on his Intel science project, which is why he's heading to NYU now. He's meeting his adviser, a professor who's dying of prostate cancer but who, in his final days, is attempting, with Romeo, to discover a novel model to unlock the power of nuclear fusion. "Nobody's listening to him," Romeo grumbles, turning right on Lafayette Street, sounding like an old man himself. Romeo could have ignored the seventy-eight-year-old professor too, coasting this semester by taking ceramics or a class in video production. But he didn't. He felt an obligation—there's always an obligation, a responsibility—to tackle

237

an imposing Intel project. It's part of a pact he struck with his ambitious friends, dating back to their freshman year together at Stuyvesant. "We told ourselves we are the next generation," says the striving junior.

Romeo didn't want to take the easy road. He kept telling himself happiness didn't matter. He disdained students in school who lived only for the present. "I started to forget the human element," he says, turning right on Greene Street. Even now, he can't help but scold himself for making a few sloppy errors on a recent math test. "The mistakes I'm making are stupid, on the level of typos," he says, now sounding like a parent. And by his reckoning, little mistakes are just as unforgivable as big mistakes because if he's building a bridge, a slight miscalculation in its construction can lead to its eventual collapse. Never mind that he's nearly perfect, still maintaining a 96 grade point average, on a righteous path to Harvard.

Romeo makes a left on Houston Street, thinking he needs to practice the piano more, reminding himself that he has to rehearse for a salsa dance show next week. But then the noise of thoughts halts when Romeo is confronted by the impatient, stooped, sagging figure of Paul Garabedian in the lobby of NYU's Courant Institute of Mathematical Sciences. It's as if the aged professor, defying his chemotherapy treatment, couldn't wait for Romeo to arrive, so he took the elevator from his office down to the lobby, the quicker to get started with his sixteen-year-old charge.

"Of course, I have to bear down on him because he has a lot of obligations," Dr. Garabedian says, as if Romeo isn't present.

But then the professor seems to become aware, asking Romeo what time he went to sleep last night. Romeo says midnight. The professor chuckles, saying Romeo must've been on a poor date to arrive home so early in the evening. Though they have been working together on these quiet Saturdays for about three months, only now does the curmudgeonly mathematician think to ask Romeo a serious question about his future.

"What are your plans?"

Without hesitation, Romeo says, "Applying early to Harvard."

The professor and the student could hardly be more unlike, one so near the end he can almost see it, the other so close to the beginning that the future seems like an infinite highway; one so frail it looks as though a gentle breeze could knock him over, the other so powerful in his jersey number thirty-seven that he looks as if he could plow right through the professor's office walls. And yet, they share uncommon traits. Like Romeo, Dr. Garabedian as a boy taught himself calculus simply by reading a book. He too aspired to Harvard receiving his PhD there in mathematics. And both of his daughters graduated from Stuyvesant. But neither mentor nor acolyte seems terribly interested in finding the common bond the human element. There are mysteries of fusion to unravel, and who cares about cancer or chemo? "The point is to keep working on the project," the professor says. He doesn't say it, but it seems that this project with Romeo helps to sustain the professor, to wrap him in what he calls a "cocoon" of work. For Romeo, there's a benefit left unsaid as well in the study of fusion. These Saturdays bring him one step closer to that unceasing goal of his, to save the world.

Milo has just dashed off an article on fusion, writing it not with any visions of rescuing the world but simply to fill a page of his elementary school newspaper, the *234 Latte*. It's the least he can do since he dropped out of the fifth grade, leaving his little friends behind for the challenge of high school. He won't be donning a cap and gown at the upcoming fifth-grade graduation ceremony, though he plans to sit in the audience, like a proud parent, watching the giddy kids on stage. "I'm going to go there, but I'm not going through it because I'm not officially in the fifth grade," he says cynically, all facts, no sentiment. And yet something seems to be bothering him on this balmy, hazy Sunday, May 28. Milo's waiting on an undulating dock near Stuyvesant for a water taxi to take him on a leisurely excursion to the New Jersey side of the Hudson. But he's not all there. Whatever preoccupies him, he's keeping it hidden under the lid of his strawberry-colored baseball hat, which is pushed down low and tight on his forehead, as if that'll preserve the secrets contained therein. All that he gives away is on the front of the cap, a green patch with white lettering:

MILE
0

It's a riddle wrapped in a math equation: MILE − E + O = MILO. An inside joke, except he's not laughing. He's thinking of the other day when his mom packed a bologna sandwich for him, and he ate it in the park with his old fifth-grade pals. He saw them the next day when he joined them on a field trip, where they played kickball and nobody won or lost, an ambiguous result that he says "was really stupid." He's not sure what he likes about hanging out with other ten-year-olds. Suddenly he is acting his age: monosyllabic, nearly mute. He can't decide which he likes better, his fifth grade or Stuyvesant; he shrugs and waves his arms in surrender. He doesn't know why, but he's beginning to sleep more restfully, even if he still wakes up with his head pointing north. Milo knows this, though: in his trigonometry class, there's still a lot of homework, but he's scoring well on the tests with grades of 85, 90, and 92, and he plans to take the statewide high school math exam at year's end because, he says, "How could math not be fun?" Milo knows this too: he plans to take the Stuyvesant entrance exam in the fall so that he can officially enroll next year. He doesn't seem worried about the test, unlike his older sister, who's changed her mind and decided to apply too, as long as she doesn't have to compare scores with Milo.

And then, there he is, on the New Jersey shore. The whole trip—boarding the water taxi, navigating the Hudson, and debarking—practically happened in his absence. But now that he's here, he remembers. "I noticed something that's really weird," he begins, becoming present in the moment, freed from the confines of the other side of the river, where it all takes place, high school, math, restless nights, all of it. But now Manhattan might as well be on the other side of the planet.

"I read everything I see, and it gets stored in the back of my head," he says as if he's confessing a terrible truth, like seeing monsters in his closets.

On the back of his home keys, Milo can't help but notice the words "Corbin Russwin." It's impossible to forget the slogan of Lay's potato chips: "Betcha can't eat just one." Heading out of his speaker-building class on the second floor, he'll pass a classroom where a string spins in the vortex of a blowing fan. He'll then pass a poster in the hallway, black against red letters: "RU?" He doesn't know what it means. It just sticks. Just as it stuck when he was five years old, sitting in the back of a Volvo, reading license plates. He doesn't remember where the family was heading. But he can't shake the license plates from memory. One of them: ACE 1092. "It's just weird," he says. Then he clams up. It's time to catch a water taxi back to the other side.


On Tuesday, May 30, there is no sign of Jane in school. The eighteen-year-old senior has returned to the other side, the vortex, the oblivion, the needle. Mr. Grossman knows without knowing. He notices her absence in his Great Books class today. It's impossible to miss the absence of a supernova even in a room full of superstars. After class, he wanders across the street to the Pan Latin Café, a quiet refuge that isn't so quiet today. An infant is wailing uncontrollably at a nearby table, but Mr. Grossman doesn't take notice. He too is feeling inconsolable. He's now certain to lose two of his teachers to budget cuts, possibly three. And then there's the loss of Jane.

"I have all these great, successful students, all of whom I love and adore and respect and admire, and Jane takes up so much of my mental energy because she's so lost and I'm so scared for her," he says.

A recent memory almost makes him laugh in sadness. Jane had missed a few days of school. When she returned, she paraphrased Oscar Wilde, telling Mr. Grossman that her excuse was merely, "I can resist everything but temptation," and he immediately understood what she was trying to convey to him. "She basically said, 'This is who I am. These are the choices I've made. I'm miserable when I'm using. I'm miserable when I'm not. It's a whole lot easier to be using, and I know what this means.'"

Mr. Grossman doesn't know that Jane has been carrying around his current required reading—*The Feast of Love*—to the forbidding places she frequents, but he knows what she has told him. "If it weren't for your class, I would've stopped coming to school ages ago." But now that slender lifeline has snapped too. Their last conversation frightens him. "She seemed to be divesting herself of those kind of moorings," he says. "She doesn't care about graduating. She doesn't care about going to college. In other discussions, she's at least been ambivalent, acknowledged there was probably some good in doing those things, and she seemed to be committed to a course of action."

No more. It makes him feel helpless, leaving him grasping for a way to find Jane's salvation until he reaches the point of absurdity. "There are those people who you can hire, like, to kidnap someone in jeopardy and, like, tie them to a chair in a room in the Midwest for nine months, and, like, for a whole lot of reasons, I can't really do that, although that's really what I want to do," he says, unconsciously mimicking the fragmented sentence pattern of the teenager. "You know, guidance knows about her. Her mother knows about her." And still, he worries, one day she'll turn up dead.

Already, she's left her mark, not just on him but on her classmates in Great Books, who constantly quote the words raging from Jane about literature and life. "I can't tell you how many papers I've read that allude to something she said in class," Mr. Grossman says. ". . . She's really real, and when she has things to say, there's no veneer of, like, 'I just want to hear myself talk.' . . . People are responding to her because there's something at stake in every comment. . . . When she participates, there's genuinely something on the line. She's trying to work something essential for her survival out."

He tries not to fathom the unspeakable ways in which she supports an expensive drug habit. "Just thinking about what her life outside of school is gives me such shivers," he says, recalling a recent conversation when she confided to him that she felt compromised, that it was too late for her.

"Look, I'm just bad," she told him.

"Of course you're not bad," he said. "You're smart and you're interesting and you're literate."

"I didn't say I don't have good qualities," she said.

Even now, he marvels at the girl's undeniable spunk. "How can you not adore that?" he wonders. He knows he'll never see her kind again. From her freshman year, Jane recognized something in Mr. Grossman, he in her, and it galvanized student and teacher in a bond that not even the hammer of heroin could break in the intervening time. "That's my heartbreak for the year," he says.


Ms. Lee, the student teacher, is feeling her own heartbreak. She's running a marathon but can never reach the finish line. It's all work, no reward. And she's beginning to question her faith. "I haven't been relying and seeking God as much as I had," she says after another exhausting day at Stuyvesant. "I know I have to get out of this. It's like a slump. I have to snap out of it." It's hard, though. Just when it seemed like the teaching job at Syosset was a lock, it's slipping away.

After her promising first interview at the Long Island high school, Ms. Lee had returned to Syosset for round two, where she sat at an imposing conference table, facing a committee of six teachers, who grilled her with such intensity that she barely had time to answer one question before they aimed another one. None were softballs.

What was the last book you read?

*"The Juggler—"*

Where do you see yourself in five years?

"I see students coming back and thanking me for the great influence and impact that I had made—"

What course do you want to teach in the social studies department here?

"It would be one where I could contribute as an Asian American—"

Round three: Ms. Lee returned to Syosset a couple of days later to teach social studies—a "demo" lesson—having no idea that she was being given one of the most disruptive classes in the school. Administrators wanted to see how the petite, young teacher could handle what they politely refer to as a classroom management problem. What unfolded in the class shocked them: utter silence.

Ms. Lee had made a crucial strategic decision, placing name tags in front of each student so that she could call on them by name. There was no hiding. They were known. And accountable. Before the students could recover to lob a grenade of mischief at Ms. Lee, she stunned them with a battery of provocative statements about the Cold War, her prepared lesson of the day.

The McCarthy era was the Salem witch trials revisited. Agree or disagree?

*What?*

They didn't expect this. Where was the regurgitation of historical fact? What happened to the litany of notable dates to dutifully record?

The Truman Doctrine and the Marshall Plan were excuses to expand American imperialism. Debate.

*Huh?*

That wasn't a high school question. This was something more. Ms. Lee was implicitly demanding a sophisticated level of thought, higher reasoning, something akin to an answer from a *college* student.

The high school students got it. They began to make connections. It wasn't just a history lesson anymore. McCarthyism was about the here and now and the question of privacy in the war against terrorism today. When class ended, several students walked up to Ms. Lee and thanked her.

Later that day, the school called her, asking her to return the next day for an interview with the principal. Round four. Things couldn't have looked any better—until Ms. Lee gave the wrong answer. During the interview, she told the principal how she would foster the kind of relationship where students would trust her as a confidante, which she would use as a lure to engage them in class. Fair enough. But, the principal asked, how far are you willing to go to be a student's confidante? What, he burrowed ahead, would you do if a student confides that she's pregnant?

Oh no.

Ms. Lee hadn't foreseen that. She couldn't imagine it. She wasn't prepared to answer. But she did, saying she would keep the student's trust until the end, holding the girl's pregnancy confidential. It wasn't the answer the principal was looking for. The right answer, he explained, is that if a student's general welfare is in danger or compromised—and that includes a pregnancy—the teacher must report it.

"I thought I blew it right there," Ms. Lee says.

But things only got worse when she returned to meet the school system's deputy superintendent. Round five: would you, he asked, be interested in teaching middle school? It seemed like a throwaway query, a casual thought tossed out there. But in fact, it was a targeted question. The middle school had a potential opening. But to Ms. Lee, the question was horrific. She had wanted nothing more than to teach at Stuyvesant. She had done everything in her power to make that happen. But she had been forced to give up that hope. She had then doggedly worked her way to this moment to teach at another high school. And now they wanted her to teach *middle school?*

No.

She let it be known that she wasn't interested, politely saying middle school wouldn't present a teaching challenge for her, that the classroom material would be less extensive. Whether the school official didn't comprehend what she was saying or simply chose to ignore it was unclear, but he responded by telling her to give him a call if she wanted to come in to do another demo lesson for the middle school job.

She hasn't called.

The school hasn't called her either.

It's been more than a week.

The silence is suffocating.

Now all that Ms. Lee can think about are the dwindling odds at Syosset. Two teaching positions. Two hundred applications. One out of a hundred. She'd have a better chance at the roulette table. And yet, she's made an all-or-nothing bet on the Long Island high school. She has no other options. Stuyvesant is effectively out. She's pursued no other schools. When the semester ends, she'll be out of a job—a student teaching job, at that. "I should not have all my eggs in one basket," she says, "but I do."

It's like a form of paralysis. Ms. Lee just started taking her summer courses to finish her master's degree at Columbia, but she completely forgot about the existence of one of her classes, missing a major assignment. In the history class she teaches at Stuyvesant, she's so behind that she hasn't returned to students their grades on an exam that they took about a month ago. And a strange feeling has come over her: indifference. "Maybe it's because I feel there's not one thing I'm looking forward to," she says. "I don't know." What she does know is "I can't breathe right now."

> *The ghost of you is all that I have left*
>
> —desktop graffiti, Stuyvesant High School

CHAPTER TWENTY-FIVE

# The Last Dance

IT'S A STRANGE FEELING: IT'S JUNE 8, LESS THAN A week before the last day of classes, and yet it already feels like the semester is over, summer's come and gone and the school's fast forwarded into a new year. Maybe it has to do with its being a vacation day on a Thursday, and the building's crawling with students who look young enough to be next year's incoming ninth and tenth graders. Which is what they are. In an otherwise empty building, scores of students who passed the Stuy test are milling about—smaller, shorter, and higher-pitched than the usual crowd—with some dressed for the occasion in appropriate Stuyvesant attire announcing their lofty aspirations in Harvard T-shirts.

They call this day "Camp Stuy."

It's a chance for next year's fresh batch of students to have a look-see at what's in store for them come next September. It's also a chance for them to audition for band or chorus, or to take placement tests in math and foreign languages. And it's a chance for overprotective parents to be reduced to an emotional meltdown when they practically refuse to leave the school after dropping off their children at Stuyvesant for the

247

one-day visit. "They're attached by crazy glue," says Harvey Blumm, Stuyvesant's empathic parent coordinator. It's even more nerve-racking for many incoming students because today they have to take the dreaded swim test. "It's always traumatic for them," Mr. Blumm says. "They don't want to show their bodies."

That includes two thirteen-year-old girls who are standing in line, holding hands in solidarity, as they wait to dive into the pool. "I'm a good swimmer, but I'm not a good bathing suit wearer," says one of the girls. "So we're all nervous about it."

Michael, the eleventh grader who's running for Student Union president, tries to distract jittery swimmers. A Big Sibling volunteer, he's playing a child's singing game with a group of eighth graders who are sitting Indian style in a circle on the floor of the school lobby, waiting their turn for the swim test. But even for an old Stuyvesant hand like Michael, the gathering of next year's incoming class is a little strange. "Some of them are really small," he says in wonder.

One of the smaller ones stands in line on the second floor, unaware that she is treading in the senior Asian bar—forbidden territory on any other day—as she moves to sit for a photo ID. The thirteen-year-old is told to smile. She does so stiffly, clutching both sides of the metal chair as if holding on for dear life on a roller coaster in a swan dive. For the eighth grader, who took a private prep course for two grueling years to prepare for the entrance exam, there's no way to describe the feeling now that she's here—now that she's one of them. But then she blurts out, "Excited, nervous."

Upstairs in his office, Mr. Jaye is anything but. The firebrand is almost subdued, a sight as rare as Halley's comet. He's supposed to be overseeing the math placement test for incoming students, but his team is in place, and the machinery is operating on automatic, so he can preoccupy himself with the perusal of an e-mail from a parent congratulating him on his new job at Bergen County Academies. Borrowing from Mark Twain, Mr. Jaye fires back in an e-mail, "Rumors of my death are greatly exaggerated." The job still isn't quite his.

School officials have requested his academic transcripts. They've taken his fingerprints. They've even concocted a title for him, the nebulous "director of academy programs." The school board hasn't voted to make it official yet. Mr. Jaye, though, isn't one to wait. Now he's composing another e-mail, this one to Bergen school officials, negotiating on behalf of a gifted math teacher from Brooklyn whom he'd like to recruit to the New Jersey school that he himself doesn't work for yet. "I want to get her a decent salary package," he says resolutely. He's trying to do the same for Mr. Siwanowicz. That's not a done deal, either. "I'm working on that too," he says. But Mr. Jaye's wheeling and dealing are interrupted when his brother, Gary, also a math teacher at Stuyvesant, pokes his head in to ask a question about where to store some things for his brother. Mr. Jaye, still engrossed in his negotiations, absently tells him to have Mr. Siwanowicz "lock them up in the sex closet."

"In the sex closet?" his brother asks casually.

"Yes," Mr. Jaye says flatly.

They could be talking about the weather, so neutral is their tone, and yet, the sex closet is called the sex closet because it's a secret place to which not even the school custodians have a key. Only Mr. Jaye and Mr. Siwanowicz possess that level of security clearance. The most tantalizing thing in there is Mr. Jaye's bike. But the off-the-cuff remark is a reminder that this domain—the math department—belongs to Mr. Jaye in a personal, private way, if only for a short while longer.

"The fourth floor is my floor," he still insists.

Perhaps the most telling sign that it won't be for long is the number of yellow stickies populating the surface of his desk: two. That's all that's left. He's down to two last remaining to-dos, little slips of square yellow paper that can be peeled away all too quickly. Mr. Jaye doesn't even seem to have much reserve of anger left for Ms. Damesek, the assistant principal of organization. "I've spent a little too much time fighting with people," he says. After thirty-four years at Stuyvesant, he's finally beginning to think it may be the right time to let go. "I've gotten stale here," he says. ". . . All I do is come in and fight Randi." And even the fighting has lost its luster. After vying for the top job at Stuyvesant—the principal's blue chair—the position doesn't seem worth it anymore. Not financially, anyway, given the better deal he's negotiated with Bergen. But it's more than that. "You know what?" he says. "I'll sit in another chair."

---

Mr. Polazzo is in his familiar pose in the Student Union office, gobbling his cracked-pepper-turkey sandwich, but on this Friday, June 9, it looks like his days in this chair are numbered.

Operation SPJ—Saving Polazzo's Job—did not have the intended effect.

It started off well enough. Several student leaders met with Mr. Teitel, urging the principal to reappoint Mr. Polazzo as the coordinator of student affairs, questioning the experience of the other two candidates, neither of whom has worked with students to the extent that Mr. Polazzo has. The *Spectator* newspaper ran a page-one story above the fold with the banner headline: "Student Leaders Oppose New COSA Applicants." In a subsequent editorial, the newspaper wrote, "If it ain't broke, don't fix it. Matthew Polazzo, the current coordinator of student affairs (COSA), has succeeded in championing student rights and is respected by the entire student body. Despite this, the administration has chosen to consider other candidates for a position that does not need to be replaced." And the junior class president posted news of the students' meeting with the principal on his Web site, www.stuy07.org, including their criticism that the teachers vying for Mr. Polazzo's job aren't as qualified. But the uprising backfired, enraging and embarrassing Mr. Polazzo's two rivals and prompting Mr. Teitel to rush to their defense by taking the unusual step of ordering the editors of the school newspaper to insert a letter he dashed off at the last minute to address the burgeoning controversy. Such was the urgency that Andrew, the managing editor, says he was pulled out of his classroom to stuff issues of the newspaper with the principal's letter.

"I am sorry if the fact that I asked to hear students' concerns about the candidates played some part, however inadvertent, in creating an environment in which students felt that it was valid to criticize faculty publicly," the principal wrote in his June 9 letter. "While Stuyvesant is not a democracy, it should reflect the values of a democratic society, and I believe that the free and open exchange of ideas is vital to the healthy functioning of the community. I understand, too, that some conflict is inevitable."

Now in full retreat, the junior class president offered an abject mea culpa on his Web site for reporting news of the meeting in which students criticized Mr. Polazzo's rivals. "I formally and sincerely apologize to any people that may have been offended, including the applicants for COSA," he wrote. "Please let it be known that I did not mean to slander or disparage, nor attempt to influence anyone, but simply inform my fellow juniors as I usually do." The junior class president tried to clarify, like a product disclaimer, that Mr. Polazzo had nothing to do with any of the "aforesaid." But the growing perception, at least among some administrators, was that the coordinator of student affairs had orchestrated the student rebellion to save his job because—come on—how many students would really go out of their way for any adult, let alone a high school teacher?

Now all that Mr. Polazzo can do is wait in the bunker of the Student Union for the principal to decide his fate.

"Is not Mr. Teitel going to make a decision?" asks an impatient Kristen, the Student Union president.

"Maybe you can ask him," Mr. Polazzo says delicately.

Kristen, who makes a habit of challenging the principal, bolts out of the Student Union office determined to do just that.

Another senior, Alex Schleider, stays behind to offer moral support, saying that if the principal selects one of the other candidates, the Student Union "would fall apart."

"The SU would cease to exist," Mr. Polazzo agrees placidly.

"Maybe that's what they want," Alex speculates.

"What can I do?" Mr. Polazzo wonders.

The only thing he can do is change the subject. So Mr. Polazzo turns his attention to the other campaign—for student government—which is well under way and just as uncertain as his own campaign to save his job. Mike and Marta, the favorites despite their all-white pairing, lost in an upset in the primary. "It was pretty shocking," Mr. Polazzo says. But he reckons that "racial politics" played a role in a school where a white-Asian pairing presents a more effective demographic one-two punch. Indeed, the white junior who made it through to the general election as a presidential candidate did have an Asian vice presidential candidate on her ticket, as did the other slate, which also made it to the general election. But before Mr. Polazzo can proffer his latest election prognostication, Kristen, the lame-duck Student

Union president, barges back into his office to report on her just-ended tête-à-tête with the principal.

"He's a very weird man," Kristen begins, then recounts the conversation: She asked to know the choice for coordinator of student affairs before she graduates in two weeks. Mr. Teitel told her that he didn't want to lie to her. So don't, she retorted. Then the principal promised to make a decision by the end of June—after which he steered the conversation to the prom, which is tomorrow night, saying how Kristen will always remember it and how he doesn't expect students today to listen to music from the 1950s. At this point in the tale, Mr. Polazzo can't resist interjecting, "He's big into 'Hey Ya!'" The students instantly get the joke. It's funny to picture Mr. Teitel, a straitlaced man of nearly sixty, crooning to the hip-hop single from OutKast.

It's hard to imagine, but four intense, grinding, insane, mordant, ridiculous, laughable, sublime, pressurized years of high school culminate here, on Saturday, June 10, at the historic Waldorf-Astoria, one of the world's grand hotels, the luxurious Park Avenue site of Stuyvesant's prom.

"It's so gorgeous, oh my God," marvels senior Siyu "Daisy" Duan, entering the first-floor reception, gazing wide-eyed at the vaulted gilded ceiling, the massive stone pillars, the antique clock peaked with a gold replica of the Statue of Liberty. But Daisy could just as well be gawking at herself and her fellow seniors, boys looking dashing, like James Bond in tuxedos, girls done up like movie stars in flowing gowns of every hue, from midnight blue to blood red. In the muted lighting, playing tricks on the eye, they all look like grown-ups. Perhaps tonight they are.

Upstairs, in the three-tiered Grand Ball Room, Senior Class Adviser James Lonardo, a faculty member, is keeping close watch over final preparations as tuxedoed waiters lay down flatware on numbered tables. Mr. Lonardo missed his own prom but he's been to sixteen since coming to Stuyvesant. He knows the drill. There will be 662 kids tonight. "There'll be a lot of energy out there," he says knowingly, if apprehensively.

Momentum builds in the next-door East Foyer, where small clusters of students begin to coalesce, like cloud formations, nibbling on vegetable dip and small conversation. NYU-bound Nameeta Kamath sits stiffly at a corner table with friends, as if she doesn't want to upset her beautiful raven updo. And for good reason. It took three hours to assemble it at the salon this morning. "My mom forbid me from moving," she says, apparently still heeding the edict. "She refused to let me pick up even a single thing." After spending most of the day confined to her room, Nameeta escaped in a white Lincoln Town Car with her friends, the first limo ride of her life. A glorious thirty-five minutes, too short. No New York traffic.

Of all the days.

Mr. Teitel cleans up well in a white tuxedo as he stands at the threshold of the Grand Ball Room, trying in vain to make sense of the throbbing drumbeat pounding from the giant stereo speakers. Amid a kaleidoscope of flashing lights, seniors begin to hit the parquet dance floor, gyrating in a synchronized coolness that is as mysterious and baroque to the principal as a distant African tribal ritual.

"I don't understand this music at all," he says, grimacing.

For Mr. Teitel, though, the rest of the evening is old hat. Seniors may laugh. Seniors may cry. Seniors may make out. But one thing is for sure. This year, seniors will not streak naked across the ballroom. One boy did that several years ago, eluding capture because Mr. Teitel was seated at a table on the ballroom's first level, where it was impossible for the principal to track the boy's movements as he melted anonymously into the crowd of seniors. Not a chance now. Mr. Teitel has moved his table to the center of the second-level balcony, the kind of spot where kings might hold court at a fancy shindig like this, but which for the principal only serves to give him a bird's-eye view of potential mischief below on the dance floor.

"I'm here to supervise," he says resolutely.

If Mr. Teitel takes joy in the prom, it stems from the secret knowledge that he carries—the seniors think they know it all—that at 11:30 p.m., waiters will roll out an elaborate ice cream bar. Or maybe the principal is just looking forward to the ice cream himself.

Deke, for his part, isn't sure what to look forward to. The senior, who is going to Cornell after falling short of Harvard, looks as debonair in evening attire as Cary Grant. But he appears afflicted with a general malaise as he sits with his girlfriend on a quiet bench in the foyer just beyond the growing madness of the ballroom. The prom feels to him like his tenth-year high school reunion, only ten years earlier. People are friendlier than they are in school, even if you don't know them. Boys and girls have already taken a smoke break on the curb outside the Waldorf, shedding the artifice of hats and high heels in a moment of unvarnished friendship built over four long years of shared experience. "It's the end of high school," Deke says, chalking the feeling up to sentimentality. "So we're letting it all go anyway." Deke, though, isn't quite ready to let go. He vows to report to gym first thing Monday morning, lest he fail that class and jeopardize his future at Cornell.

"I will," he promises, "be in gym on time."

It's 9:33 p.m., and on the dance floor, boys start to lose their tuxedo straitjackets, while girls escape their stiletto prisons, the better to collide against each other like go-carts at an amusement park, unpracticed, wildly free. In the hallway, friends hug as if they haven't seen each other in ages, like long-lost relatives reuniting at the airport.

"Remember, this is only the beginning!" the DJ bellows.

For Katie, the senior who spurned the Ivies in favor of Haverford, it certainly doesn't seem like high school's over. As she stands at the perimeter of the darkened dance floor, at the edge of an endless ocean, taking it all in—the romantic melody of Barry White and the beauty of the sparkling people and the glorious place—she can't help but be transported back to the stark reality of Stuyvesant and next week's math test. "I don't know that it's hit me, that it's the end yet," she says wistfully. "When I'm on the dance floor, it's another dance."

Not for Jane. The senior, abdicating to her addiction, never showed.

Andrew, the managing editor of the school paper, did. The date of a senior, Andrew came prepared for the prom, not with the typical paraphernalia, a flask of whiskey, but with a heavy dose of facts. "I brought my history textbook," says the junior, upholding the Stuyvesant tradition of books before bacchanalia. He has an advanced placement exam in U.S. history on Monday, and between now and then, he plans to squeeze in a little studying while staying up as part of an extended prom party. "If I have less sleep," he says, "I function better the next day." He calls the phenomenon "hyperdrive."

By 12:37 a.m., the evening is winding down. A strange quietude overcomes the ballroom, giving it a mood of fin de siecle. The dance floor thins out. Bodies slump languidly at linen tables where the ruins of ice cream sundaes topple, reminiscent of the remnants of a lost civilization. At 1:04 a.m., the lights come up, and the magic dissipates, as for Cinderella after midnight, in the bright glare of smudged mascara, torn stockings, and the irresolute look of teenagers on their way into the night and into the rest of their lives. Mr. Teitel leans over the balcony railing, alone, scanning these final snapshots of another senior class on their way out the door. This year, to his great relief, there are no naked streakers.

On Monday, June 12, students make their way to the ballot box in what turns into a landslide victory in the election for the proverbial oval office of the Student Union. The white-Asian pairing prevails again. But the real drama unfolds in the election for senior class president, usually an afterthought. The election board discovers that fifty-five forged votes were stuffed in the ballot box. It turns out, someone had photocopied an authentic ballot and stamped on it BOE APPROVED, the board of election's imprimatur. But the fake contained a slight flaw in the first *P* in APPROVED. And if that wasn't a dead giveaway, the forged ballots were stuck together like a stack of pancakes. Fifty-two of the fake ballots cast votes for a candidate who lost by a wide margin. The other three forged ballots went for the winning candidate, who didn't need them to carry the day. The election skulduggery remains an unguarded secret lost in the vapor trail of the recently departed prom. Classes are almost over. A stretch of finals is about to begin. Mr. Polazzo, the coordinator of student affairs, shrugs off the forgeries "The way I see it," he says, "it's like a hacker attack. We improve our defenses." Besides, the real scandal circulating through school is that in the wee hours of an after-prom party, an inebriated student had the audacity to vomit in the sink at the home of a friend's relative, a movie star of an earlier generation, Kathleen Turner.

> *Forever My Skool*
>
> —desktop graffiti, Stuyvesant High School

CHAPTER TWENTY-SIX

# The Final Days

MONDAY, JUNE 12, THE SECOND-TO-LAST DAY OF classes, is almost over as the clock nears the end of tenth period in room 840, sophomore English, where Mariya sits by the teacher's desk, her right hand holding up her forehead in a pose of complete catatonia or undiluted concentration, such is her perfect equipoise. When the bell rings, Mariya heaves her blue backpack over her shoulders and approaches the teacher, girding herself for the devastating news about to befall her, that she earned a mere 90 on her last test. "I'm scared because my mother's going to freak out,' she says, heading out the door, where the excuse is already forming. "I'll tell her the story that goes along with it," she says, "that everyone else did bad, et cetera." But Mariya's heart isn't in the excuse. She isn't selling it with verve. She doesn't really care. What she really cares about is four floors down, faithfully waiting for her by her locker, Jarek.

At six foot five, he towers over Mariya, looking like he just outgrew Jack-and-the-Beanstalk style, the long denim shorts he's wearing. The front of his black T-shirt announces, CAME OVER. Most of his wardrobe, he says, is either black or blue, matching Mariya's getup gothic for gothic, including her own black T-shirt today, which portrays an abstract devil's skull.

Ah, young love.

They head down the escalator, which isn't working, as usual, while holding hands. Jarek wants to walk to nearby Chinatown. Mariya doesn't. So they resolve their differences the only way mature teenagers can: in a game of rock, paper, scissors. Jarek wins. Chinatown, it is. At the onset, Jarek bemoans the loss of his beloved Poland in the World Cup. It must be a terrible blow because Mariya, now all of sixteen, cups his broad face in her hands and gently kisses his cheek. "Don't worry," she coos. They've been dating for a month and six days but have the easy playfulness of lovers who've known each other for years. Already, they have their favorite places, like the little hole in the wall in Chinatown where Jarek likes to buy Mariya steaming hot sixty-cent pork buns. That's where they're heading now. Along the way, as they move up Worth Street, the conversation turns to their differences. "She studies too much," Jarek says. "I study too little."

Mariya, though, protests, as if studying is a badge of dishonor. "I don't study at all," she says. "I don't remember the last time I did my homework." Then she immediately corrects herself. "Actually, last night," she says sheepishly, "I did my homework."

A left on Mulberry Street, and they're now in another world, where ancient Asian women hunch on stools on the sidewalk amid a series of fishmongers speaking in foreign tongues. Jarek and Mariya plunge into a little shop and order their pork buns, then make their way to a nearby park, where a couple of weeks ago they cut class and lay out on a bench during a downpour.

"I kind of feel like it's over," Jarek says of school, even though he still faces a few statewide exams.

"You've felt like it's over for a *month*," Mariya says.

"Sun's shining," Jarek says, offering a sunny smile by way of explanation.

The sun's been shining on Jarek since he began dating Mariya, which coincidentally started at about the same time that he felt school had effectively ended. Recently, when he met Mr. Jaye, the ubiquitous math chairman asked Jarek what was new. Mr. Jaye intended the question to elicit an answer that he could incorporate in a college report on Jarek's behalf, but the student could think of only one thing noteworthy in his life.

"Well," Jarek said, "I got a new girlfriend."

Mr. Jaye wasn't impressed. "I don't think colleges are interested in your sex life," he responded.

To Jarek and Mariya, school seems a fast-receding fact, about to be replaced by the coming summer, when he'll be traveling to a small village in Poland to train to be a camp counselor, while Mariya will be off to the Poconos resort area in search of a part-time job. He promises to e-mail her once a day and, being an old-fashioned romantic, to send a handwritten letter once a week too. She can't wait for the handwritten notes. It's so quaint in a twentieth-century way—and so authentic. But there is still time to enjoy before the note writing. They are holding hands as they rise, heading for the subway station. They haven't let go since leaving school nearly an hour ago. Making their way to the end of the platform, they hop on the local Q train. He can't take his eyes off her. "What?" she wants to know, blushing. "Don't look at me like that." But he says, unabashed, "I'm just looking." She lets him. It can't be helped. This is what happens. When the train jolts to a stop at Avenue J in Brooklyn, they step off together, walking against the gust of the train suddenly barreling away, the last bell at Stuyvesant long forgotten; they're still holding hands.

The last bell of the last period of the last day of class rings at 3:35 on Tuesday, June 13, signaling the end of an impossibly long semester, now a montage sequence of brutal nights of studying, a conveyor belt of tests, homework, expectations, pressure, and performance, and yet all that Romeo can muster the energy to do in this final moment is to rise from his desk chair and approach his notoriously tough history teacher. "Thank you a lot, Mr. Sandler," Romeo says. "I learned a lot."

Romeo reaches out to shake his hand, an offering that seems to catch the teacher off guard, so unusual is the little gesture of appreciation. The ambitious junior doesn't have to curry favor. His grade will be astronomically high. That, they both know. "There's not many kids like him,"

Mr. Sandler says, when Romeo isn't around to hear the compliment. At the moment, though, Mr. Sandler doesn't let on. Stoically, he recovers in time to shake Romeo's hand, the teacher's admiration left unsaid. Romeo heads out of room 339, maintaining his grim game face.

"I'm still in work mode," he explains.

The only thing that stops Romeo is the frenzied sound of hip-hop booming by the white senior bar, where, as if by spontaneous combustion, several girls are breaking out in a wild celebration of the semester's end, dancing, hugging, banging lockers, taking digital pictures. A circle of students forms around the revelers, while Romeo looks on, mesmerized but apart from the moment. He doesn't stay for long, moving toward the second-floor bridge exit when he's intercepted by Xevion, his lunchtime companion, his conscience. They lock arms around each other's shoulders and share a quick greeting; it seems like it's been ages since they last spoke, but it doesn't last. Romeo peels off, as if in a hurry to catch a cab, though he doesn't have anywhere particular to go. It could just be that he's tired. Last night, he managed only four hours of sleep, and with two statewide tests, in biology and U.S. history, and one final, in differential equations, on the immediate horizon, he knows there are more sleepless nights to come.

"I just tell myself I've done it before, I can do it again," he says.

For now, though, Romeo follows the strong undertow of students surging toward the riverside park behind school. When he arrives at the edge of the expansive lawn, he approaches no one, choosing instead to pick up his cell phone—school contraband if discovered. He calls his father in Harlem, his PR man who sends football tapes to Harvard recruiters, the voice in Romeo's head, telling him that there's no *can't*, only *how*, who wants his son to pay tribute to his black forefathers, the man whom Romeo feels he hardly sees anymore. Before long, his father will be moving to Boston. Romeo hopes to be heading up there soon too. Harvard. It's almost Father's Day. Romeo already bought him a teddy bear. He'll be buying him cologne too. The phone rings. No answer.

That leaves Romeo to contemplate the scene unfolding before him, boys and girls recklessly thumping a soccer ball, fecklessly flinging a Frisbee, carefree, unbound. "I should be more of a kid," he observes ruefully, as if it's too late for him. "I feel like I'm too serious." He spots a lanky blond boy on the playing field. They used to be the best of friends in eighth grade. They used to play chess. And now. That boy is a Hacky Sack–playing ladies' man. Romeo chose a different path. Which is okay. Romeo isn't big on best friends at the moment. Fiends are fine, he notes, "as long as it's at a distance." And that distance is growing now that he's on the cusp of becoming, finally, a senior. "There's going to be no one to look up to," he says. "It's going to be strange." Students will be looking up to him. But then, they already do that. So do the adults. Romeo is the future, and he feels the burden of that responsibility. Which is why he's still pursuing his Intel science project at NYU. He isn't succeeding just for himself, his mother, or his father. There's a great, big world needing rescuing out there, and he calculates it doesn't need another writer, even if he's a gifted writer, and that's why he says his calling lies elsewhere. "There are too many humanities people. We need more scientists. I feel like I'd be betraying it if I leave it alone."

The phone rings. On the other end of the line come the familiar sound of a father's reminder, a scolding. Romeo, the dutiful son, listens, promises not to do something, then mumbles, "Love you, bye." It's time now. Romeo lies down alone in the grass in this park behind this school on this glorious afternoon, under a pastel blue sky and a receding sun, and closes his eyes, if only for the briefest of moments, to rest.

Rest is the last thing on Milo's mind as he steps out of his apartment building on a gusty Thursday, June 15, heading for the last time this year to Stuyvesant, armed with a power bar, a calculator, three sharpened pencils, and a ruler—weapons of math destruction contained in a black backpack that reads PS 234 TRIBECA, now just a relic of his former fifth-grade life. The little man-child is on his way to take a statewide math final in algebra, geometry, and trigonometry intended for students who are generally older by about 50 percent, mathematically speaking. "There's nothing hard about the test," he notes. "You just have to focus."

Milo isn't sweating that today's test is weighted as *two* tests toward his final grade in his trig class. He's already done the math. Worst-case scenario, he bogeys the test with an 80, which would be, like, a total disgrace, not to mention a major improbability. But even with that unbearable eventuality, Milo calculates he'd still finish with a respectable 90 in the high school class. The grade, though, doesn't really mean anything. It doesn't count toward a real report card. It's just a number. Less than that. It's a game. Milo doesn't compile a high school transcript yet. He's not officially enrolled. Heck, he's years from puberty. But the grade is a symbolic representation of achievement, of a semester of homework, of hard work. Even more, if he aces the test, he figures it may represent something more tangible. "I hope my Dad gives me a pizza party," he says.

For Milo, it all happened so fast, the withdrawal from fifth grade, the homeschooling, the last semester at Stuyvesant. It's hard to believe the term is over. He's pretty sure he learned a lot about math. He thinks he may have grown an inch, topping out at about four and a half feet. But what he learned about high school, he says, "I don't know." There's little time to contemplate that conundrum now. The future is fast approaching, including this summer, when he plans to read about an eighteenth-century mathematical hero in *Euler: The Master of Us All*. Milo already has next semester mapped out at Stuyvesant, a course load probably including honors precalculus, math team, math research, advanced placement computer science, history, and a double period of chemistry.

Piece of cake. By then, he'll be the ripe old age of eleven.

But now, Milo's ten, and he has a pizza party to win. He enters Stuyvesant, where the escalator transports him to the fourth floor and a scene of anxious teenagers cramming last-minute for the test. Milo swiftly cuts through the crowd, like a child in a forest of towering redwoods, making his way to the front, where the hall proctor, a chiseled gym teacher wise to the ways of crowd control, stands at the mouth of the corridor, blocking the way until it's time. Marveling at the restive group, the gym teacher finally puts the students out of their misery, giving the word, a simple "Okay." With that, the test takers are unleashed, flooding into classrooms, scrambling to take position for the statewide math exam. Milo, a Zen master in the art of test taking, saunters into room 431 and calmly slips into a seat, front row center, where he removes his three pencils and calculator and neatly lines them up on his desk. The test starts promptly at 12:30 p.m. They have until 4 p.m.

to finish. The earliest they can leave is 2:30. At precisely 2:31, Milo moves to leave, making him the first to finish. He was done at 2:05 but bided his time, munching on his energy bar. Somehow, you get the feeling that if Milo can solve the riddles of algebra, geometry, and trigonometry with such ease, it's just a matter of time before the ten-year-old figures out this whole high school thing too. After all, it's just the beginning for Milo. On his way out of the exam, the little boy whispers, "It was really easy."

On Monday, June 26, seniors gather around the gushing fountain of the grand courtyard of Lincoln Center, site of world-class ballet, the genius of Mozart, and, in just a few moments, the end of the beginning of their lives.

It's the only place that the city would crown the jewel of its school system, the best digs in Manhattan, an epic monument to civilization, like the Roman Colosseum. And yet the mood is strangely subdued as seniors wait for their big moment, idling awkwardly, posing stiffly for pictures, and reluctantly embracing friends under a gray sky threatening a downpour. It's as if the end of high school is unfathomable. The tests are over, the all-nighters finished, the race to college done. Now what? A tuxedoed man finally offers purpose, waving them inside Lincoln Center's Avery Fisher Hall. "Let's go, graduates."

What lies beyond is almost an archetype, so familiar is the commencement tableau: A high school music teacher swings his arms like a metronome, conducting a student orchestra that is something less than an oiled machine, behind which hangs a banner in blue with red lettering: STUYVESANT HIGH SCHOOL. The principal, garbed in a black robe like a priest, takes the podium. "Ladies and gentlemen, good morning and welcome," Mr. Teitel begins. "Please rise and allow me to introduce you to Stuyvesant's spectacular class of 2006." Cheers erupt from the cavernous hall—except nothing follows. There is no class of 2006, spectacular or otherwise. Parents crane their necks, camcorders rolling, orchestra booming bombastically, all waiting for the star attraction, the graduates, to march down the aisles, but they are nowhere to be seen. Mr. Teitel nods his head with a rueful smile—this feels more like a high-school production than *La Traviata* at Lincoln Center—and gestures to his wristwatch, which has no effect. The principal stands alone on one of the world's great stages, performing nothing so much as a sheepish stance for about three full minutes before thousands of onlookers. He punctuates the performance snafu with histrionics more suitable for the theater of the absurd: a shrug, palms up. But then it happens: seniors begin to pour down the right aisle, then the left, an army draped in blue satin gowns, a processional that, from the balconies above, appears as identical square hats filling row after row of the orchestra seats to Verdi's "Triumphal March" from *Aida*.

Back on track, the principal reads from a set of notes, barely looking up, though a similar script echoes in high school graduation ceremonies in gymnasiums and auditoriums throughout the land. "Once again, as often in our history, the hope for mankind lies in our youth," Mr. Teitel intones, like Moses handing down the tablets to the masses, adding, "We at Stuyvesant are confident that you have been prepared to meet the challenge of keeping the United States ahead of the pack."

Apparently, Conan O'Brien didn't get the memo. The late-night television comic takes the podium as the keynote speaker—again, only the best for a gold-plated graduation—dismissing all semblance of gravity. "Just last year," he says, "I was offered fifty thousand dollars to speak at a graduation, but I said, 'You go to hell, Bronx Science.'" It's a smart opening strategy, launching right into a joke at the expense of Stuyvesant's rival to win over the partisan crowd, which roars in approval. "Then they said sixty thousand, and I took it, but I never showed up." Another roar. "Those guys are idiots." Referring to his own alma mater, Harvard, he informs the Stuyvesant students, "I'm a pompous, self-important jackass," and he's now completely won them over. Recalling his graduation from Brookline High, a public school outside Boston, he says, "Just like you, I sat in a large auditorium, daydreaming about experiences yet to come—college, my first job, puberty." Another eruption from the crowd. His father "put his hand on my shoulder, looked me right in the eye, and said, 'I'm not your father.' Then he wrapped me in his strong Samoan arms and said, 'Don't ever call me.'" It's a perfect salve for four painful, harrowing years of high school: the forgetfulness of laughter. The comedian is just loosening up.

"Your school is named after Peter Stuyvesant, head of the Dutch West Indian trading company, which explains, by the way, why your teachers are still paid in grain and salt." Now he's won over the adults too. "In 1950," he continues with his history lesson, "students at Stuyvesant tried to build a particle accelerator. By way of comparison, that's the same year my public high school discovered fire." By now, the students are doubled over. "In 1969," he moves on, "girls were admitted to Stuyvesant for the first time. This started a new trend among the boys called showering."

More jokes ensue, increasingly sophomoric, which is just the way the students want it, until Conan O'Brien has them just where he wants them—circling back to an unexpected moment of seriousness so he can impart a bit of advice from the heart. "I did a lot of things in high school not because I enjoyed them but because I thought they'd look good on an application, if you know what I'm talking about." They do. But on a lark in college, he wrote a piece for the *Harvard Lampoon*, the school's humor magazine, and he found joy. "I honestly didn't care where it took me, or what it paid." When he graduated from Harvard, he says, "I told my parents, thanks for the amazing Ivy League education now I want to be a comedian." The laughter resumes. "Later, in the emergency room, after they woke up, they said they were fine with my decision, and I was on my way." And then the final punch line: "Don't get me wrong. I've worked extremely hard at being an ass, and yes, I make some sweet, sweet coin."

It might have been enough to end graduation right there, letting the seniors float off on a heliumlike high. But reality intrudes, and the ceremony is immediately grounded by a jarring pivot, when the schools chancellor takes center stage and presents symbolic diplomas to the relatives of April and Kevin, the two students who perished in the car accident. Around this time, the principal conveys more somber news, whispering on stage to Mr. Polazzo that he will not be reappointed coordinator of student affairs. True to his word, Mr. Teitel made a decision before the end of June, but he picked a time to deliver it when those who cared the most, the seniors at graduation, would care the least. The moment passes as anonymously as a shot fired in the dark, and the only one who feels its penetration is the target, Mr. Polazzo, who can do nothing but wince. "I lose all my superpowers," he says. Not that the decision was easy on Mr. Teitel. The principal has lost about ten pounds in the past two weeks, unable to sleep or eat as his mind constantly turns over the pressing issues in front of him, whether it's the fate of the coordinator of student affairs, budget cuts, or staff evaluations. "I sleep when I'm absolutely tired," he says at another time in the quiet of his office, "but as soon as I'm not, I wake up because there's too many things on my mind, you know, that I'm constantly thinking about." At least he hasn't had to deal with the cell phone ban. The school system has yet to install the metal detectors, sparing him that headache. Still, the prospect of retirement tugs at him. It's not long off. About five years ago, Mr. Teitel sat for a head shot photo, preparing for the day when his picture would be framed, perhaps in haste, along with the other dozen principals who came before him. In that snapshot, he possessed a full head of brown hair. Now it's streaked gray.

On this day, though, the strain doesn't show. One by one, seniors soberly step on stage to shake hands with the principal and accept their diplomas in this final rite of high school passage. There they go: Jamie and Olga and Barbara and Elizabeth and Reyna and Amanda and Namita and Deke and Becky and Daisy and Nathan and Sophia and Naomi and Molly and Jonathan and Erica and Rachel and Kristen and Elisa and all the rest. One name isn't called. Jane. She isn't here. She didn't graduate. The recovering drug addict didn't recover.


The following day, Ms. Lee, the student teacher, shuffles down the stairs after class at Columbia, a step closer to her own graduation, a step further away from Stuyvesant, the school already becoming a fond memory growing ever more distant. On her last day teaching there, several of her students lingered by her desk to present going-away gifts to her—a scented candle, a bag of chocolate truffles, a collection of unspoken admiration. When she returned to Stuyvesant one last time, the end came almost imperceptibly in the quotidian task of submitting grades in her history and Korean classes. The building was empty, except for a residue of teachers loitering in the fourth-floor faculty lounge. Ms. Lee said her good-byes. That was all. She had nothing to do. She had nothing to take, no belongings, not even a desk to call her own. But that's okay. Ms. Lee got the call.

The Syosset superintendent asked Ms. Lee to come in. The meeting took less time than the wait outside her office before the meeting, all of about five minutes. The superintendent asked how Ms. Lee was doing, how her classes were going at Columbia. And then she asked if Ms. Lee wanted to teach history at Syosset High School. The moment, so long in coming, so hard to come by, so dearly coveted, seemed surreal. Ms. Lee may have said thank you but can't be sure. All she is certain of is that, afterward, she picked up her cell phone right away and called her father.

"I got the job," she said, still seeking approval from the man who once told her she had failed part of her life when she was rejected by the Ivy League. She will have to wait for her father's approval yet. He was thrilled about her new job but gave all credit to God, not to his daughter. How else could he explain that such a good school as Syosset would hire a mere student teacher when there were so many more qualified candidates? Nor was Ms. Lee's mother's reaction terribly satisfying as she noted that being a high school teacher wasn't enough. Her daughter, she said, should now aspire to something greater, to become a *college professor*. It turns out, Ms. Lee isn't entirely satisfied herself. "I am entering a realm where I can be acknowledged and I can be part of that greater vision of an American Dream," she says. "But I can't say I've achieved it yet, not quite yet." Her parents have taught her well, perhaps all too well.

Mr. Jaye isn't satisfied either. That's because it's Thursday, June 29, and the fourth floor of Stuyvesant no longer belongs to him. The math chairman isn't the math chairman anymore, a fact underscored by the number of yellow stickies left on his desk: none. A multitude of cardboard boxes covers his office and spills out into the hallway, which is deathly still, bereft of the clamor of shrill student voices gone until next semester. How do you pack thirty-four years of history?

Quietly. A fan blows hot air from an open window, rustling the last remaining papers on his desk, accompanied by the muffled sound of a radio on low. Mr. Jaye rifles through folders, tosses out some detritus, files other stuff in cabinets in what feels like a pantomime act because it can't possibly be happening, because it doesn't seem right, what with Mr. Jaye not in a crisp button-down and tie but in a casual, flaming red shirt, opened two buttons at the collar, exposing a thick gold chain. And yet it's happening. It's happened. He still hasn't signed a contract with the New Jersey school, but it's all but a certainty. Yesterday he went for a physical and, more to the point, Mr. Teitel announced at a staff meeting that Mr. Jaye was retiring, making it official. And yet, it didn't feel right. After making the cursory announcement, the principal moved on, making Mr. Jaye feel as if his retirement were little more than a signpost noted and passed on the highway to other end-of-semester matters. "I never got a chance to stand up and thank all the people I worked with," Mr. Jaye says. "And you know what? I'm an interesting character in this building in that there's a lot of people who hate me, and they should, and there's a lot of people who love me, and they should." Earlier today, though, Mr. Jaye got in a last word, interjecting at the principal's kitchen cabinet meeting, fighting to make sure his replacement as math chairman is assured a seat at these private gatherings. The assistant principal for social studies rose to thank Mr. Jaye for always finding creative ways to solve any problem, which was a polite way of applauding him for being a productive troublemaker. That meant a lot to Mr. Jaye.

Now, surrounded by a cascade of lifted memories, like overturned rocks, he picks up a random slip of paper on his desk. Ah, yes. A student's math exam. Mr. Jaye immediately recalls the details. The girl had mis-bubbled her score sheet, giving answers to the wrong questions. When she received a low score, her incensed mother, a prominent New York journalist, called Mr. Jaye, threatening to use her considerable clout unless they regraded her child's test to accurately reflect her performance. Mr. Jaye didn't begrudge her. Here was a mother fighting for her child. It's what *he* does. "When you have kids, you've got to advocate for your kid," he says. But he wasn't sure what to do. That is, until he took the problem to another administrator, who simply told him to regrade the test; after all, it wasn't that the girl didn't know the answers to the test. She had just lost her way on the bubble sheet. With that, Mr. Jaye tosses the once-controversial exam into the classroom paper recycling bin.

"This is such a weird place," he says.

Mr. Jaye resumes packing, stacking boxes on a trolley. Inside them: Billy Joel's *The Nylon Curtain* CD; a pair of suede work gloves; *Higher Arithmetic*, an 1848 book preserved in a plastic sandwich bag. And he begins to free-associate, his mind leaping from his oldest daughter's visit today to his tutoring business, which helps to pay for her education at Yale, to the scolding from a wealthy New Yorker who once told him he should be ashamed of himself for letting his family down by forgoing what would have come naturally to him—a lucrative career on Wall Street—given his uncanny penchant for numbers and negotiations. Why, the wealthy woman asked, do you teach? "Because," he said, "I love it, and I'm good at it."

But now Mr. Jaye is worried. Not about himself but about Mr. Siwanowicz, who's joining him at the school in New Jersey next semester. Mr. Siwanowicz recently fell into a deep funk when he lost out on an application for an apartment that he intended to rent with his girlfriend. The problem: he doesn't have a credit card. Mr. Jaye told him to get one. Mr. Siwanowicz refused on principle, much as he had refused to take a college exam, saying he would not borrow from anyone. Mr. Jaye explained that he didn't need a credit card to borrow money; he needed it to obtain a rental. "You have to enter society." Mr. Jaye tried to reason with him. What else can he do?

Mr. Zamansky, the computer science coordinator, crops by They won't be taking early-morning bike rides up to Harlem anymore. Mr. Zamansky refrains from saying that. Perhaps it's too sentimental. Instead, he looks in wonder at the packing in progress, taking note of the clutch of Stuyvesant math trophies collecting dust on top of a set of cabinets.

"You going to take all your trophies?" he asks.

Mr. Jaye wasn't planning to. "Yeah," he says.

Mr. Jaye ties a box closed. "It's amazing," he says. "I can't believe I'm doing this."

A custodial worker enters his office to empty a garbage bin. She can't believe Mr. Jaye is doing this, either. "You'll be back," she says, embracing him. "You'll miss us."

Moments later, Mr. Grossman pays a visit. Mr. Jaye continues to pack, removing tacks from a cabinet behind his desk. There isn't much to say that hasn't already been said. Mr. Grossman doesn't mention Jane, his heartbreak. He doesn't mention that she had recently left three voice mail messages for him at his office, that she said she hadn't meant to call him but proceeded to recite some of her writings into the recording. He doesn't mention that in her final voice mail, she read from a suicide note, and how he tried to call her but didn't get through, or how he saw her later in school, wearing a kimono and crying to him that she was scared, or how he told her to come back the next day to help him with some paperwork, but she didn't.

What Mr. Grossman says is "I see you're hard at work clearing your office."

Mr. Jaye doesn't mention his own heartbreak, that he's leaving behind a school he never wanted to leave. He doesn't mention how he worries about the department he built, the people whom he hired. He doesn't mention that he has no idea how he's going to pack thirty-four years of his life.

What Mr. Jaye says is this, that even with his departure, the end of an era at Stuyvesant, there's at least one thing about this school he will never worry about. "The kids," he says, "will remain great."

# Epilogue: Back to the Future

Gone is the North Face backpack. Taking its place is the battered leather briefcase, which sat in a closet, awaiting my return to the *Washington Post* after studying that oddest of cultures, high school life in that strangest of places, Stuyvesant High School. Lugging the briefcase to the office, leaning against the wind of a wintry day, I refuse to carry it by the handles. Not cool. Instead, I sling the briefcase strap over my shoulder, an unspoken nod to the cavalier attitude of the teenage world from which I have just emerged. Instantly, I think of a fourteen-year-old freshman who would have approved of the subtle gesture. *Mad*, she might have said with a goofy but golden smile that would have broken my heart. The stone-faced adults take no notice of my minor rebellion. Why should they? I look like one of them. No more clumpy, black combat boots, just civilized lace-up cordovan shoes. And dry-cleaned tailored slacks have replaced those trusty pockmarked jeans, which I've retired to a lower drawer of the dresser, the Florida of my wardrobe, brought out only on the occasional day off when it doesn't matter.

There's a stab of regret. My days back in high school more than two decades after my own graduation from Stuyvesant were a kind of Indian summer, a kaleidoscope of yearnings, aspirations, and hopes that recede in the ramble of time. So I pay the bills. I rake the leaves. And I miss the kids, the whole messy lot of them at Stuyvesant. How they didn't show up when we had an appointment. How I learned their class bell schedules so I knew where to intercept them in the hallway. How they wanted to make the world a better place, no matter how corny that sounds, because it was true and sincere and right.

They are gone, remnants in my mind, but Stuyvesant remains stubbornly immutable. The place is a fierce anachronism whose ideal dates back to a Jeffersonian notion. The founding father believed in the idea of making education available to every citizen as a way to ward off tyranny, but he also believed in fostering an aristocracy of talent. The great irony is that when Stuyvesant was founded a century ago, it wasn't intended to be a selective public school, merely a manual training school for boys, a reflection of the emerging industrialization then. As Mr. Mathews, the education expert, says of the introduction of the entrance exam, "Educators decided you could create an absolutely magic atmosphere if you bring together all the best kids."

That, however, isn't the prevailing sentiment today. Now, he says, "It goes against the mainstream movement that you should not segregate the great brains." Dr. Loveless, another education authority, describes the Stuyvesant mission bluntly: "It's politically incorrect and it's completely fallen out of favor."

The argument against schools like Stuyvesant is the same argument that civic activists have made in decades past, that it's an elitist institution, a leading objection being that such public exam schools deprive regular schools and regular students of a milieu in which academically driven students can serve as a spark to raise the collective performance of an entire school.

"The greatest force in American high schools is peer pressure," Mr. Mathews says. "If you don't have peers who are very academically oriented, if you cut back on that, you have fewer peers who admire these kids, and it reduces the amount of academic interest in the school. . . . Then it affects all the other students in the school."

Which brings educators and policy makers to today's overarching problem: "Based on students' performance, American education is generally flat, where it has been for the last thirty, thirty-five years in terms of [student] test results, graduation rates," says Chester E. Finn Jr., president of the Washington, D.C.–based Thomas B. Fordham Foundation, which supports research in education reform.

The debate in education circles has turned to the paucity of academic improvement, particularly among students in secondary schools. "Only one in three high school freshmen graduate on time with the academic preparation necessary to succeed in college," writes Craig D. Jerald in *A Report on the High School Reform Movement* for Education Sector, an education think tank in Washington, D.C. He notes that "today's 17-year-olds score no higher in reading and math than did teenagers in the early 1970s."

Says Mr. Toch, Education Sector's cofounder and codirector, "At the high school level, we haven't done much."

Educators and policy makers ascribe a dizzying array of causes to the intransigent problem: that teachers don't expect enough of students. That schools create a disruptive learning environment. That parents don't take their children's education seriously enough. That schools are too big and impersonal and bureaucratic. That schools are too small and balkanized and disorganized. That education standards are higher in Asia and Europe. That teachers are better trained in foreign nations. That we watch too much television. That we don't read enough. That we are a profligate, decadent, id-obsessed, Internet-surfing, consumer-driven, sports-crazed society.

This much they can agree on: there is no agreement.

In recent years, with good reason, educators and policy makers have paid particular attention to disadvantaged students who need the most help and resources, introducing such initiatives as the No Child Left Behind Act, which stresses, among other things, measuring progress through testing and standards, and charter schools, which operate independently of traditional school systems. Policy makers and education reformers have offered up other solutions, such as school vouchers, as a way to give students more choice about which school they can attend. Also on the rise are magnet schools that build around a theme, like the sciences or arts, but shy away from selective admissions policies like those at Stuyvesant. And lately, foundations have been pouring money into developing smaller schools. But often overlooked are gifted and talented students.

"They are the forgotten group today," says Dr. Ravitch, the noted education historian.

The sense among many educators and policy makers is that students at schools like Stuyvesant will succeed no matter what, that they are the exception to the rule, a thin layer at the top academic echelon whose experience doesn't apply to the rest of the student population in the United States. Mr. Teitel, Stuyvesant's principal, argues otherwise. The school isn't just the test, he asserts. What makes Stuyvesant great isn't merely its selective admissions policy. Mr. Teitel talks about the importance of maintaining a truly "rigorous curriculum," not just giving lip service to the idea, a policy which he says other schools could heed. "Some schools, what they've done, they've taken a one-year course and in order to get the kids through it, they've stretched it to either a year and a half or two years," he says. "Well, then, it's really not that rigorous. When you say 'rigor,' it means if a course is supposed to be taught in one year, it's taught in one year, that's it. You don't get any extras, folks, put it in there."

Implicit in what Mr. Teitel advocates is a powerful idea that can find a place at other schools: high expectations. They flourish at Stuyvesant. Teachers expect nothing but the best from their students. It's ingrained in the culture. High expectations, Stuyvesant hands like to say, create their own momentum. The school tells the students that they are the best, and then they work hard to make it so. Students at Stuyvesant push each other academically, sometimes to a fault. Indeed, the pressure is enormous, and some students—and parents—take it too far, becoming obsessed with grades to the extent that cheating is widespread, health sacrificed. Other students, recoiling from the pressure, defy school altogether, sometimes finding solace in drugs. But Stuyvesant veterans say there's no motivating force so effective as students who feel good about themselves. A school like Stuyvesant, to be sure, has the luxury of creating such lofty aspirations for its driven students. But for other schools, the attempt to raise expectations would cost nothing.

Stuyvesant benefits from another powerful idea: freedom. Students study on the hallway floors. They hang around school until late in the evening, practicing dances, rehearsing instruments, playing chess, building robots, strumming to their iPods. It's their home, and they are encouraged to make it so. It becomes something more than a forbidding citadel of learning. It becomes a place of exploration, a refuge. Again, at a school like Stuyvesant, creating such a freewheeling atmosphere is easier than for most, especially at a time when mounting concerns about safety and terrorism are making metal detectors a permanent feature at schools everywhere, including Stuyvesant. But for other schools, the attempt to foster a sense of freedom would cost nothing.

At Stuyvesant, there is one other great force, largely unseen but perhaps wielding the greatest influence: parents. They drive cabs. They run delis seven days a week. They are, for the most part, of modest means. And yet, they have spent years equipping their children with a wealth of experience—piano lessons, math camp, computer tutorials—so that by the time they arrive at Stuyvesant as freshmen, they are already ahead of the game. And the parents don't stop there. They get involved. They join various after-school committees. They bake cookies to raise school funds. They e-mail teachers. Their presence is always felt if not always seen, sometimes to an extreme, but they ensure the best for their children. Again, at a school like Stuyvesant, parental involvement is almost a given. But for other schools, the attempt to involve parents more would cost nothing.

The payoff is priceless. Today's Stuyvesant students, like generations before them, will make great breakthroughs in medicine. They will solve mysteries of science. They will travel in space. They will enact laws in the chambers of Congress, build new industries, create lasting literature. You can't see the future, though, at least not by walking the empty halls on a lonely summer day when school is out.

I miss Milo, the ten-year-old unofficial freshman. I miss playing chess with him. He beat me once. I miss playing foosball with him. He beat me every time. He did pretty well in school too, finishing the Stuyvesant term with a 95 in honors trigonometry, a 99 in math research, and a 100 in his speaker-building class for an even 98 overall grade point average. Not bad for a kid who isn't even enrolled in high school yet. (He also received credit for math team class.) As for that statewide math exam, Milo didn't just finish it before any of the other students in the class: he earned a 91. Meanwhile, he and his older sister, Willa, recently took the Stuy test. Reports Milo in an e-mail, "We both thought that it was easy." And they both got in.

I miss Mariya, the sophomore immigrant from Ukraine. I miss lunchtime, sitting on the Wall, talking with Mariya about life and parents and the miseries of chemistry, a class in which, incidentally, she ended up with a final grade of 88. She matched that in her other tough class, computer science, but fared better otherwise with a 92 in Japanese, a 94 in math, a 96 in both English and history, and a 99 in Spanish, finishing the term with a 93.29 average. More than respectable. But her overall average fell from 94.86 the previous semester. "My mom was pretty mad but calmed down when I swore to do better next year," Mariya says. She can comfort herself with this thought: Jarek is still the last living heir of the last Polish knight, and chivalry isn't dead.

I miss Romeo, the junior football captain. I miss our long talks about aspiring to greatness, about the challenges of being biracial, about the question of love and its possibilities. For Romeo, it's all possible. He completed the term with a 95 in biology, a 96 in French, a 97 in both English and differential equations, a 98 in both gym and U.S. history, a 99 in math research, and a 100 in precalculus. That's a cool 97.5 average. And the football team finished the season five and five—an amazing accomplishment for a motley crew of brainiacs. But Romeo didn't win the Intel science contest. It's okay, though. His partner on the project, the aged professor, marches on as of this writing. So does Romeo. On Friday, December 15, 2006, he received one particular e-mail from a certain university: "In making each admission decision, the Committee keeps in mind that the excellence of Harvard College depends most of all on the talent and promise of the people assembled here, particularly our students. In voting to offer you admission, the Committee has demonstrated its firm belief that you can make important contributions during your college years and beyond." Harvard decided early to admit Romeo. So he'll be joining his father in moving to Massachusetts after all. Romeo, though, won't be joining his conscience, Xevion. "As for prom," she writes in an e-mail, "I'll be going with my boyfriend—

and sorry, it's not who you're probably hoping." Romeo is taking his first real girlfriend, Jenny, whom he's been dating for months. Love, after all, is possible.

I miss Jane, the senior struggling with a demon of a crack addiction. She essentially stopped speaking to me after one evening late in the semester when she called my cell phone while I was waiting to board a plane. In a frenzied, nearly incoherent state, she asked to borrow a hundred dollars to pay her drug dealer. I said no. She hung up on me. I tried calling her back. I wanted to explain why, that as a journalist writing about her and the school, I couldn't give her money because it could have potentially cast doubt on the veracity of her story. That as an adult, I couldn't in good conscience lend her money, knowing that it was going to be used for illicit drugs. That as someone who cared, I couldn't give her money that would have contributed to her destructive path. But I never got to tell her any of that. I couldn't get through. When I tried to talk to her in school, she skulked away. When I e-mailed her, she didn't respond. When I called, she didn't return my messages, except once, when she left a happy yet scrambled message for me the din of loud music and partying in the background. It was difficult to hear what she was saying in the recording. She sounded euphoric. She sounded surrounded by friends. Perhaps it was a sign of change. After the term ended, Jane began attending night school in Maryland to finish her high school diploma. She's even planning to apply to college.

I miss the adults too. Mr. Polazzo is a mere mortal again, shorn of his duties as coordinator of student affairs, even though no one may have been better suited for the job. So dearly did he love the students that he seemed a student himself. But maybe that was the problem. Mr. Teitel had trouble finding a replacement. He said he sought out one candidate, who declined the offer. He then offered the position to another teacher who didn't apply for the job. That teacher agreed but had second thoughts and tried to resign before assuming the job. His resignation wasn't accepted. Two teachers now share the student coordinator duties. So goes high school politics. Mr. Polazzo, meanwhile, holds court from his classroom, where he continues to delight students as a government teacher. For her part, Ms. Lee, the gifted student teacher, is now a full-time teacher at Syosset High, dazzling students there just as she did at Stuyvesant. Mr. Siwanowicz is now substitute-teaching and training teachers to use technology at Bergen County, along with his protector and advocate, Mr. Jaye, who's now director of academy programs there, causing his usual trouble and loving every minute of it. Meanwhile, Ms. Damesek, the assistant principal of organization, remains at Stuyvesant. Some notice a change in her. "She's even got a posse of students who she's adopted and who hang out in her office all the time now," Mr. Grossman, the English chairman, says in an e-mail. "And even though it doesn't often show, she is very sensitive."

It's a funny thing. Stuyvesant, like all high schools, possesses a short, merciless memory. Every year, a senior class departs, and with it goes four years of shared history. It's as if what came before doesn't exist anymore as another class enters, and the cycle begins anew. "It's like you've never been there before," says a wistful senior, Emily Hoffman, on the last day of school before heading off to Yale. "It's the nature of the school. It's a student factory. Everything seemed so monumental. All the drama seemed so important, and no one's going to remember it."

There is only what lies ahead.

# Appendix: Notable Alumni

**Leo Roon, 1908**

Chemist; chief, chemical division, Squibb & Sons; chairman, board of trustees, Columbia College of Pharmacy

**Lewis Mumford, 1912**

Urban planner; architecture and social critic; author; awarded U.S. Medal of Freedom; made Knight Commander of the British Empire

**Charles W. Taussig, 1914 June**

Industrialist; member of FDR's New Deal brain trust

**Jack Kriendler, 1917 January**

Restaurateur; founder and owner of "21" Club

**Ray Arcel, 1917**

Inducted into International Boxing Hall of Fame; trained twenty world boxing champions including Larry Holmes

**James Cagney, 1917 or 1918**

Won Academy Award, best actor; awarded American Film Institute's Life Achievement Award; founding member of Screen Actors Guild; named "14th greatest movie star of all time" by *Entertainment Weekly*

**Ted Husing, 1919**

Sportscaster; largely responsible for play-by-play broadcasting

**Marcus Kogel, MD, 1921 June**

Founding dean, Albert Einstein College of Medicine

**Peter Sammartino, PhD, 1921**

Chancellor, Fairleigh Dickinson University; member, President's Commission on Higher Education

**Irving Saypol, 1923 January**

Attorney and judge; prosecutor in espionage case against Julius and Ethel Rosenberg and Morton Sobell

**Sidney Sugarman, 1922**

U.S. District Court judge

**Herbert Zelenko, 1922**

U.S. congressman

**Norman C. Armitage (Cohn), PhD, 1923 June**

Fencer; member of six U.S. Olympic teams; won Olympic bronze medal

**Lt. General Garrison H. Davidson, 1923**

Coach, Army football team; superintendent, U.S. Military Academy; commanding general, U.S. Seventh Army and First Army; U.S. military representative to the United Nations

**Herbert Tenzer, 1923 June**

U.S. congressman; philanthropist

**Frank Hussey, believed to have graduated in 1924**

Won Olympic gold medal, 400-meter relay—record-setting

**Joseph Mankiewicz, 1924**

Won four Academy Awards for writing and directing

**Sheldon Leonard, 1925**

Won Emmy Awards for producing and directing; film and TV actor, director, and producer

**John R. Ragazzini, 1927 June**

Dean of engineering and science, New York University; participated in Manhattan Project during World War II

**Robert Alda, 1930**

Actor and entertainer; father of Alan Alda

**Gustave J. Dammin, MD, 1930**

Professor of pathology, Harvard Medical School; awarded Legion of Merit for research on dysentery in India and Burma; part of team that performed first kidney transplant; conducted important research on Lyme disease; the tick *Ixodes dammini* named after him

**Edward V. Kolman, 1931 January**

NFL player, Chicago Bears, and coach, New York Giants

**Irving V. Glick, MD, 1933 January**

Orthopedist and sports medicine pioneer; inducted into International Tennis Hall of Fame

**Bernard Meltzer, 1934 June**

Radio show host; chairman, Philadelphia Planning Commission

**Thomas Macioce, 1935 June**

Chief executive officer, Allied Stores; member of the board of trustees, Columbia University

**Thelonious Monk, 1935 (did not graduate)**

Jazz musician

**Albert "Albie" Axelrod, 1938 June**

Fencing great; member of five U.S. Olympic teams; Won Olympic bronze medal

**Charles W. Dryden, 1938**

Commanded the first group of Tuskegee Airmen to engage in aerial combat against Germany; author, *A-Train: Memoirs of a Tuskegee Airman*

**Eugene Garfield, 1938**

Founder and chairman emeritus, Thompson Scientific

**John L. Tatta, 1938**

President of Cablevision

**Benjamin Rosenthal, 1940 June**

U.S. congressman

**Joshua Lederberg, PhD, 1941 January**

Awarded Nobel Prize for medicine (1958); awarded National Medal of Science (1989); president, Rockefeller University

**Marshall Rosenbluth, PhD, 1942 June (year he graduated)**

Nuclear scientist; worked on hydrogen bomb project

**Jan Merlin, 1942**

Won Emmy Award for writing

**Art Baer, 1943 June**

Won Emmy Award for writing

**Rolf W. Landauer, PhD, 1943**

Pioneer in computer theory

**Samuel P. Huntington, PhD, 1943 June**

Political theorist

**Robert W. Fogel, PhD, 1944 June**

Awarded Nobel Prize in economics (1993)

**Howard Cane (Cohen), 1944 January**

Actor; played Major Hochstetter on *Hogan's Heroes*

**William Greaves, 1944 January**
Won Emmy Award for executive producing

**Mace Neufeld, 1945 June**
Film and TV producer

**Otto Eckstein, PhD, 1946**
Economist; member, Council of Economic Advisers; economic consultant to President Lyndon Johnson

**Albert Shanker, 1946 June**
President of the American Federation of Teachers; awarded Presidential Medal of Freedom

**David Margolis, 1947**
Chairman and chief executive officer, Coltec Industries; board member of NYU Stern School of Business

**Hans Mark, PhD, 1947**
Chancellor, University of Texas

**Ben Gazzara, 1948 (did not graduate)**
Actor; Won Emmy Award for acting

**Sidney I. Lirtzman, PhD, 1948**
President, Baruch College

**Sherwood M. Schwarz, 1948**
Owner, Toronto Argonauts football team

**Elias Stein, 1949 January**
Awarded Wolf Prize in mathematics (1999)

**Paul J. Cohen, 1950**
Mathematician; awarded Fields Medal (1966)

**Kenneth H. Keller, PhD, 1952**
President, University of Minnesota

**Robert Moses, 1952**
Civil rights leader; codirector of the Council of Federated Organizations during the Mississippi Freedom Summer in 1964; awarded MacArthur Foundation "genius" grant

**Alvin Poussaint, MD, 1952 June**
Consultant to Bill Cosby television programs; associate dean of Harvard Medical School

**Frank Conroy, 1953**
Author, *Body and Soul* and *Stop-Time*

**David Durk, 1953**
New York police officer; worked with Frank Serpico to reform police department

**Neil Grabois, 1953**
President, Colgate University

**Alan Heim, 1954**
Won Academy Award and Emmy Award for film editing

**Bernard Nussbaum, 1954**
Special counsel to President Bill Clinton

**Joe Paletta, 1954**
Fencer; member, U.S. Olympic team

**Herbert J. Stern, 1954**
U.S. District Court judge

**Roald Hoffman, PhD, 1955**
Awarded Nobel Prize in chemistry (1981)

**Edmar Mednis, 1955**
Chess grandmaster; first player to beat Bobby Fischer in a U.S. Chess Championship tournament

**Saul Katz, 1956**
President, New York Mets

**Jeffrey Loria, 1957**
Florida Marlins owner

**Peter Biskind, 1958**
Author, *Easy Riders, Raging Bulls*

**Richard Ben-Veniste, 1960**
Task force leader for Watergate prosecutions; member of 9/11 Commission

**Arthur Blank, 1960**
Founder of Home Depot; Atlanta Falcons owner

**Harvey Pitt, 1961**
President of the SEC

**Bobby Colomby, 1962**
Musician and producer; drummer, Blood, Sweat & Tears

**Col. Ron Grabe, 1962**
Lead astronaut for development of the International Space Station

**Michael Silverstein, PhD, 1962**
Professor of anthropology, linguistics, and psychology, University of Chicago; awarded MacArthur Foundation "genius" grant

**Richard Axel, 1963**
Awarded Nobel Prize in physiology/medicine (2004)

**Ron Silver, 1963**
Actor, director, producer

**Dick Morris, 1964**
Political consultant

**Robert Siegel, 1964**
Host, National Public Radio's *All Things Considered*

**Charles Scott, 1964 (did not graduate; left after spring 1963)**
Won Olympic gold medal, basketball; NBA guard

**Jerrold Nadler, 1965**
U.S. Congressman

**Walter Becker, 1967**
Half of the band Steely Dan; won three Grammys in 2000; inducted into Rock and Roll Hall of Fame (2001)

**Chris Albrecht, 1969**
Chairman and chief executive officer, HBO

**Martin Brest, 1969**
Director, *Scent of a Woman*, won Golden Globe for Best Picture; directed *Meet Joe Black*, *Midnight Run*, and *Beverly Hills Cop*

**Joseph A. Grundfest, 1969**
Professor, Stanford Law School; SEC commissioner and presidential economic adviser

**Denny Chin, 1971**
U.S. District Court judge

**Paul Levitz, 1973**
President, DC Comics and *Mad* magazine

**Paul Reiser, 1973**
Television actor, *Mad About You*

**Eric S. Lander, PhD, 1974**
Leader, Human Genome Project; Rhodes Scholar

**Tim Robbins, 1976**
Won Academy Award, best supporting actor

**Brian Greene, 1980**

Rhodes Scholar; best-selling author, *The Elegant Universe*

**Helen Reale, 1980 (née Kochlitzer)**

Professional beach volleyball player

**Noam Elkies, PhD, 1982**

Youngest full-tenured professor at Harvard at the age of 27; won Math Olympiad gold medal

**Kate Schellenbach, 1983**

Drummer, Beastie Boys

**Lucy Liu, 1986**

Actor

**Gary Shteyngart, 1991**

Author, *The Russian Debutante's Handbook*

Source: *Stuyvesant High School: The First 100 Years*; Stuyvesant High School Alumni Association; other historical resources.

# Notes

## Prologue

2  *How many other high schools:* Stan Teitel, interview with author.
2  Life *magazine once posed* 'Is This the Best High School in America?" *Life,* October 1994.
2  *on the eve of:* Stuyvesant High School, *Indicator,* 1908 yearbook. p. 10.
2  *the nation's estimated 25 percent dropout rate:* U.S. Department of Education, 2006 report.
2  *"We have to sweep them":* Eric Grossman, interview with author.
2  *there are no official class rankings:* Susan E. Meyer, *Stuyvesant High School: The First 100 Years* (New York: The Campaign for Stuyvesant/Alumni[ae] & Friends Endowment Fund Inc., 2005), p. 37.
3  *aristocracy of talent:* Thomas Jefferson, *Autobiography* (1821), reprinted with preface by Philip S. Foner, ed., *Basic Writings of Thomas Jefferson* (Garden City, NY: Halcyon House 1950), p. 430.
3  *Any eighth- or ninth-grade student:* New York City Department of Education, *The Specialized High Schools Student Handbook,* p. 4.
3  *about 3 percent:* Stuyvesant High School.
4  *loving ode:* Frank McCourt, *Teacher Man* (New York: Scribner, 2005), pp. 183–257.
4  *"it was nerd, nerd, nerd":* Jonathan Lethem, *The Fortress of Solitude* (New York: Vintage Books, 2004), p. 218.
4  *Nearly nine out of ten students:* Nancy Kober, *A Public Education Primer* (Washington, DC: Center on Education Policy, 2006), p. 5.
5  *a century ago:* Meyer, p. 10.
5  *three thousand students:* New York City Department of Education, 2004–2005 Annual School Report, p. 1.

5   *more than half:* Ibid., p. 2.

8   *"The greatness of the school":* Danny Jaye, interview with author.

8   *"Enjoy being a kid again":* Julie Gaynin, yearbook note to author.

8   *"You've continuously asked":* Becky Cooper, yearbook note to author.

9   *"We're a diverse":* Kristen Ng, yearbook note to author.

## PART 1: DELANEY CARDS

### 1. Romeo

13   *It's 7:38 a.m.:* Author observations.

14   *"I do a lot of math":* Romeo Alexander, interview with author.

14   *"Almost nobody on the team":* "Coach Burnett Gets Sacked," *Spectator,* March 9, 2006.

14   *"Nobody really cares":* Romeo Alexander, interview with author.

14   *"We don't really":* Stuyvesant defensive tackle, interview with author.

14   *The moniker comes from:* Russell Shorto, *The Island at the Center of the World* (New York: Doubleday, 2004), p. 147.

15   *His mother, Catherine:* Catherine Wideman, interview with author.

15   *"I was always":* Romeo Alexander, interview with author.

16   *At the age of:* "The Astonishing John Wideman," *Look,* May 21, 1963.

17   *It was at Romeo's age:* "Writer's Son Given Life Term in Death of New York Youth," *New York Times,* October 16, 1988.

17   *"My dad wanted me":* Romeo Alexander, unpublished autobiography, Stuyvesant High School English class assignment, printed with permission.

17   *His father, speaking to:* Charles Alexander, interview with author.

18   *"I was on his case":* Catherine Wideman, interview with author.

18   *"There is a life of the mind":* John Edgar Wideman, interview with author.

18   *"I think a lot about that":* Romeo Alexander, interview with author.

20   *"I'm always telling him":* Xevion Baptiste, interview with author.

20   *"You know as well":* Romeo Alexander, story, Stuyvesant High School English class, printed with permission.

20   *"someone who has a disorder":* Romeo Alexander, interview with author.

20   *It's 8:23 a.m.:* Author observations.

### 2. The Gauntlet

21   *250 feet:* Meyer, p. 182.

21   *$10 million:* "Feds Probe School Span Pacts," *Newsday,* February 5, 1993.

21   *$150 million edifice:* "Building Flaws Tarnish Stuyvesant's Showcase," *New York Times,* January 28, 1993.

22   *September 9, 1992:* "Finally, a Façade to Fit Stuyvesant," *New York Times,* September 8, 1992.

22   *on a landfill packed:* Meyer, p. 175.

22   *emergency shelter:* "Stuy Reinvented," *Spectator*, Special Stuyvesant Edition, Fall 2001.

22   *twice the height:* "On the Hudson, Launching Minds Instead of Ships," *New York Times*, June 6, 1993.

22   For Knowledge and Wisdom: Stuyvesant High School Alumni Association, www.shsaa.org.

22   *four-minute break.* www.stuy.edu.

23   *450 computers:* Ibid.

23   *"The superintendent":* Stan Teitel, interview with author.

23   *"It's like going to":* Ned Vizzini, *Teen Angst? Naaah* . . . (Minneapolis, MN: Free Spirit Publishing, 2000), pp. 36–37.

23   *"Its architecture":* Karen Cooper, interview with author.

23   *"Pie a Teacher!!!":* School fund-raising flyer.

23   *"pathetic loser":* Student flyer.

24   *"Life has a higher end":* School flyer.

25   *more than two hundred clubs:* Stuyvesant High School, *Comprehensive Educational Plan 2006–2007,* p. 6.

25   *Bookworm:* Stuyvesant High School, *Indicator*, 2006 yearbook, pp. 209–10.

25   *thirty-some student publications:* Stuyvesant High School, *Comprehensive Educational Plan 2006–2007,* p. 6.

25   *existentialism:* Stuyvesant High School.

25   *"The* students *make":* Namita Biala, interview with author.

25   *about five hundred:* Danny Jaye, interview with author.

25   *two hundred members:* Stuyvesant High School students and faculty, interviews with author.

25   *Stuyvesant produces among:* Stuyvesant High School, *Comprehensive Educational Plan 2006–2007,* p. 6.

25   *on the Preliminary:* http://www.nationalmerit.org.

25   *ninety-nine Stuyvesant students:* 2006 Stuyvesant commencement program.

25   *By comparison:* http://www.nationalmerit.org and "The Hundred Best High Schools in America," *Newsweek*, May 16, 2005.

25   *more than seven hundred:* Meyer, p. 58.

25   *2,800 advanced placement:* Stan Teitel, interview with author.

25   *"qualified" to receive:* The College Board, www.collegeboard.com.

25   *97 percent:* New York City Department of Education, 2004–2005 Annual School Report, p. 9.

26   *only 75 percent:* U.S. Department of Education, 2006 report.

26   *average SAT score is a 691:* Stuyvesant High School, *Comprehensive Educational Plan 2006–2007,* p. 10.

26   *95th percentile:* The College Board, www.collegeboard.com.

26   *average U.S. test scores:* The College Board, press release, August 30, 2005.

26   *enroll in four-year colleges:* Stuyvesant High School, *Comprehensive Educational Plan 2006–2007,* p. 10.

26  *only 67 percent:* U.S. Department of Education, 2006 report.

26  *one in four:* Stan Teitel, interview with author.

26  *Harvard accepts more:* "Putting Dreams to the Test: A Special Report; Elite High School Is a Grueling Exam Away," *New York Times*, April 2, 1998.

26  *to win the Nobel Prize:* http://nobelprize.org.

27  *Eric S. Lander:* "Eric Lander: Unraveling the Threads of Life," *Time*, April 26, 2004.

27  *lead astronaut:* Orbital Sciences Corp, www.orbital.com.

27  *Stuyvesant pennant:* "New York's Stuyvesant High School, a Young Achiever's Dream," *Los Angeles Times*, December 30, 1990.

27  *For a school:* Stuyvesant High School Alumni Association; Meyer, pp. 200–18.

27  *"I embrace being":* Becky Cooper, interview with author.

27  *"Today, Stuyvesant has":* Conan O'Brien, commencement speech, Stuyvesant High School, 2006.

28  *twenty-six thousand:* Stan Teitel, interview with author.

28  *9 percent:* America's Best Colleges 2007, http://www.usnews.com.

28  *"You could theoretically":* Stan Teitel, interview with author.

28  *150-minute:* New York City Department of Education, *2005–2006 Specialized High Schools Student Handbook*, p. 10.

28  *"There are five bookshelves":* Ibid., p. 17.

29  *"What is the smallest positive":* Ibid., p. 23.

29  *"I don't think":* Alexa Solimano, interview with author.

30  *"I'm going to fail":* Susan Levinson, interview with author.

30  *"Everyone wants to":* Brittany DiSanto, interview with author.

30  *"I like to think":* Andrew Saviano, interview with author.

31  *"It's very competitive":* Kristen Chambers, interview with author.

31  *"Higher score":* advertisement, *Spectator*, June 9, 2006.

31  *"Classes are just taken":* "Religion at Stuy?" *Stuyvesant Standard*, May 24, 2006.

31  *"Stopping Stress":* "Stopping Stress at Stuyvesant," *Stuy Health*, 2006.

31  *"the pressure is crazy":* Student panel member, Parents' Association meeting.

31  *He says that:* Michael Waxman, interview with author.

32  *Her first student:* Eleanor Archie, interview with author.

32  *"It is tempting":* Eric Grossman, graduation speech transcript, 2004.

32  *"I have spoken":* Eleanor Archie, interview with author.

32  *One parent called:* Michael Waxman, interview with author.

33  *"free free free":* Copy of parent letter to teacher, January 9, 2006.

33  *"You can't make":* Michael Waxman, interview with author.

33  *"Being a Stuyvesant Parent":* School Tone Committee meeting handout.

33  *"have a nervous breakdown":* Eleanor Archie, interview with author.

34  *"Methamphetamine is becoming":* Angel Colon, interview with author.

34  *Adderall, a prescription drug:* Stuyvesant students, interviews with author.

34   *According to a recent survey:* "A Survey on Sleep Habits of Students," *Spectator*, January 19, 2006.
34   *recommended for teenagers:* "Adolescent Sleep Needs and Patterns," National Sleep Foundation, 2000.
34   *"students often complain":* "Lack of Sleep," *Stuy Health*, 2006.

## 3. The Wizard of Oz

35   *Dead of night:* Author observations.
35   *"When you work":* Danny Jaye, interview with author
36   *It's 4:52:* Author observations.
36   *looms ahead:* Danny Jaye, interview with author.
37   *Tucked in a corner:* Author observations.
37   *He puts it more:* Danny Jaye, interview with author.
37   *largest public education system:* "Bucking School Reform, a Leader Gets Results," *New York Times*, December 4, 2006.
37   *If a student:* Danny Jaye, interview with author.
39   *Edward C. Delaney:* "The Cards That Put Students in Their Place," *New York Times*, September 14, 2003.
39   *The attendance and grade:* Danny Jaye, interview with author.
40   *The book now sits:* Author observations.
40   *"Danny's like a":* Mike Zamansky, interview with author.
40   *garbed more appropriately:* Author observations.
41   *Mr. Jaye is sitting:* Ibid.
42   *lack of a teacher's license:* New York State Education Department, www.highered.nysed.gov.
43   *Putnam Fellowship:* Mathematical Association of America, math.scu.edu.
43   *"He's the smartest":* Author observations.

## 4. Cuddle Puddle Muddle

45   *Behind closed doors:* Author observations.
45   *"Love and the Ambisexual":* *New York*, February 6, 2006.
46   *He reads aloud:* Author observations.
46   *A Brooklyn boy:* Stan Teitel, interview with author.
47   *spreads like a virus:* Author observations.
48   *room 640, where:* Ibid.
48   *The author, Alex:* Alex Morris, interview with author.
48   *In class, the journalism:* Author observations.
48   *"it used sensationalism":* Alair, interview with author.
48   *Ms. Morris disputes:* Alex Morris, interview with author.
48   *"It's not soft porn":* Alair, interview with author.
48   *"I know some of them":* Alex Morris, interview with author.

49 *story has legs:* Author observations.

49 *serious tack, dissecting:* "Cuddle Puddle Muddle," *Spectator*, February 16, 2006.

49 *None of which stops:* "Sex, Drugs, and Enticing Jew-Fros," *New York*, April 10, 2006.

49 *chock-full of teenage:* Julia Baskin, Lindsey Newman, Sophie Pollitt-Cohen, and Courtney Toombs, *The Notebook Girls* (New York: Warner Books, 2006).

49 *The topic, for instance:* Author observations.

50 *"check that out":* Honors student, interview with author.

50 *"The Hudson staircase is":* "The Hudson Staircase," *Spectator*, February 2, 2006.

50 *Someone edited out:* Faculty member, interview with author.

50 *as he enters room 615:* Author observations.

51 *97 percent attendance:* Stuyvesant High School, *Comprehensive Educational Plan 2006–2007*, p. 8.

51 *"We don't need":* Author observations.

51 *The Student Union government:* Student Union representatives, interviews with author.

51 *weighed in as well:* "Why Make Us Beg?" *Spectator*, January 19, 2006.

51 *"kind of like prison":* Andrew Saviano, interview with author.

51 *believe a strict:* Students and teachers, interviews with author.

51 *Believed to be forty-one:* public records, Lexis-Nexis database.

52 *Grinch-like:* "Party Policy Challenged," *Spectator*, December 22, 2005.

52 *ripping down a star-studded:* "Not So Welcome: Second Term Senior Signs Removed," *Spectator*, February 2, 2006.

52 *subsequent student editorial:* "Ms. Damesek, Talk to Us," *Spectator*, February 16, 2006.

52 *It hasn't been an easy:* "Stuyvesant Sprouts Six New Heads," *Spectator* Online, http://www.stuyspectator.com, September 10, 2002. See also Clara Hemphill with Pamela Wheaton and Jacqueline Wayans, *New York City's Best Public High Schools* (New York: Teachers College, Columbia University, 2003), p. 92.

52 *From the beginning:* "Students and Assistant Principal Must Work to Mend the Fences," *Spectator* Online, http://www.stuyspectator.com, May 15, 2003.

52 *Her father:* Eric Grossman and Stan Teitel, interviews with author.

52 *clashes with Mr. Jaye:* Eric Grossman and other school faculty, interviews with author.

52 *And even Mr. Teitel:* Stan Teitel, interview with author.

53 *the best intentions:* Eric Grossman, interview with author.

53 *guards her privacy:* Ibid.

53 *Mr. Teitel adds:* Stan Teitel, interview with author.

53 *Arms akimbo:* Author observations and interviews with students.

53    *a discussion of:* Author observations.
53    *Some students will try:* Stuyvesant students and faculty, interviews with author.
53    *A front-page article:* "Students Cheat on Math Final, Sun Continues to Rise and Set," *The Broken Elevator,* June 2003.
54    *mainstream reading:* School Leadership Team committee meeting handout.
54    *"I was told":* Author observations.
54    *"It's more acute":* Ibid.
54    *at a subsequent:* Student panel members, Parents' Association meeting.
54    *Usually, teachers:* Stuyvesant teachers, interviews with author.
55    *sing the contract:* Matt Polazzo, interview with author.
55    *A service that's gaining:* "The Twists and Turns of Turnitin," *Spectator,* February 16, 2006; "High Tech War against Plagiarism Is Coming to New York Schools," *New York Sun,* March 2, 2006.
55    *hawkers pass out:* business card advertisements.
55    *A recent Stuyvesant graduate:* "Confessions of SAT Test Faker," *New York Post,* May 14, 2006.
55    *The intricacies of cheating:* Author observations.

## 5. Jane's Addiction

57    *"My hobby is":* Jane, a Stuyvesant senior, interview with author.
60    *Violence of any:* New York City Department of Education, 2004–2005 Annual School Report, p. 2.
60    *Suspensions are:* Ibid.
60    *"silly things":* Eleanor Archie, interview with author.
60    *a couple of years:* "Easy Buy at Stuy 'High': Top Kids Running an Open Drug Mart," *New York Post,* December 12, 2004.
60    *"If you have a calc":* Johnathan Krasid, interview with author.
60    *Demonstrating pot's:* Sixteen-year-old Stuyvesant student, interview with author.
61    *"the amount of":* Jane, interview with author.
61    *"I didn't want":* Eric Grossman, interview with author.
61    *They met in:* Jane, interview with author.
62    *calls that elusive:* Eric Grossman, interview with author.
62    *"I wish to bestow":* Jane's unpublished poetry, printed with permission.
63    *"The only thing":* Jane, interview with author.

## 6. Open House

65    *stalks the escalators:* Author observations.
65    *Last Saturday:* Romeo Alexander, interview with author.
66    *Nearly thirty years:* "Cortines Has Plan to Coach Minorities into Top Schools," *New York Times,* March 18, 1995.

66  *even though nearly:* "More Minority Students Enter Elite Schools," *New York Times*, May 8, 1997.

66  *"The racial demographics":* Jonathan Kozol, *The Shame of the Nation* (New York: Crown Publishers, 2005), p. 140.

66  *"As educators":* "Cortines Has Plan to Coach Minorities Into Top Schools."

66  *"I see that":* Romeo Alexander, interview with author.

67  *"I wanted to prove":* Catherine Wideman, interview with author.

67  *5.5 percent by 1997:* "More Minority Students Enter Elite Schools," *New York Times*, May 8, 1997.

67  *more than 70 percent:* Kozol, p. 140.

67  *only 2.2 percent:* "In Elite Schools, a Dip in Blacks and Hispanics," *New York Times*, August 18, 2006.

67  *down from 4.3 percent:* "Cortines Has Plan to Coach Minorities into Top Schools."

67  *to 3 percent:* New York City Department of Education, 2004–2005 Annual School Report, p. 2.

67  *dipped from 40 percent:* "Cortines Has Plan to Coach Minorities into Top Schools."

67  *to about 39 percent:* New York City Department of Education, 2004–2005 Annual School Report, p. 2.

67  *half of Stuyvesant:* "Cortines Has Plan to Coach Minorities into Top Schools."

67  *about 55 percent:* New York City Department of Education, 2004–2005 Annual School Report, p. 2.

67  *Specialized High Schools Institute:* Eleanor Archie, interview with author.

68  *"disadvantaged" students:* New York City Department of Education, *The Specialized High Schools Student Handbook*, p. 14.

68  *As many as:* Eleanor Archie, interview with author.

68  *"more proactive outreach":* School Leadership Team committee meeting handout.

68  *the author writes:* "In Elite Schools, a Dip in Blacks and Hispanics."

68  *Policy makers and others:* Policy makers, educators, and others, interviews with author.

69  *"There's so much more":* Eleanor Archie, interview with author.

69  *glaringly obvious:* Author observations.

69  *"Race is part of":* Matt Polazzo, interview with author.

69  *Predominantly white seniors:* Stuyvesant students, author interviews, and author observations.

69  *"We were told":* "Outcast by Design," *Stuyvesant Standard*, May 24, 2006.

69  *About ten feet away:* Stuyvesant students, author interviews, and author observations.

70  *"it's cool":* Samantha Whitmore, interview with author.

70  *The others who:* Stuyvesant students, author interviews, and author observations.

70   *"The school is"*: Kieren James-Lubin, interview with author.

70   *When an Eastern:* Stuyvesant student, interview with author.

70   *A Korean girl:* Stuyvesant student, interview with author.

70   *An Indian freshman:* Eleanor Archie, interview with author.

70   *"I think we self-segregate"*: Liana-Marie Lien, interview with author.

70   *"At Stuy, it seems"*: "Diversity Week," *Spectator*, March 9, 2006.

71   *"Get your diversity on"*: School flyer.

71   *"I try not to"*: Stuyvesant junior, interview with author.

71   *"Have you ever"*: Black Students League flyer.

71   *One out of five:* Stuyvesant High School, *The Case for Stuyvesant High School*, 2003. See also "Seeking the American Dream," *Spectator*, May 24, 2006.

71   *That explains why:* Stuyvesant students, interviews with author, and Stuyvesant High School, *Indicator*, 2005.

71   *"They came here"*: Katherine Kim, interview with author.

72   *At the threshold:* Author observations.

72   *"They're all crazy"*: Michael Son, interview with author.

73   *"When I saw the view"*: Daniel Alzugaray, interview with author.

73   *fifty-nine languages:* " 'Do You Speak Stuyvesantian?' " *Spectator*, April 12, 2006.

73   *The staccato:* Stuyvesant students, interviews with author, and author observations.

73   *17 percent:* New York City Department of Education, 2004–2005 Annual School Report, p. 2.

73   *visible signs:* Author observations.

73   *"Please understand my"*: Student handout.

74   *an event in:* Author observations.

74   *"Only in New York"*: Stuyvesant teacher, interview with author.

74   *packing the auditorium:* Author observations.

74   *"I've never seen"*: Stan Teitel, Stuyvesant Open House address.

## 7. Like a Polaroid

75   *the telltale signs:* Author observations.

75   *Named after a:* Milo Beckman and Emily Shapiro, interviews with author.

76   *"I remember feeling"*: Milo Beckman, interview with author.

76   *"It's not like"*: Emily Shapiro, interview with author.

76   *"Dad said I"*: Milo Beckman, interview with author.

76   *"I couldn't get"*: Eric Beckman, interview with author.

77   *"A four-year-old"*: Tim Novikoff, interview with author.

77   *"I used to drag"*: Emily Shapiro, interview with author.

77   *the next level:* Tim Novikoff, interview with author.

77   *started taking classes:* Milo Beckman and Emily Shapiro, interviews with author.

78   *"Only when she"*: Milo Beckman, interview with author.

78   *"It's a mixed"*: Emily Shapiro, interview with author.

78   *"like name-calling"*: Milo Beckman, interview with author.

78   *"He didn't ask"*: Emily Shapiro, interview with author.

79   *was heartbroken when*: Tim Novikoff, interview with author.

79   *"with kids my age"*: Milo Beckman, interview with author.

80   *"I stopped caring"*: Jan Siwanowicz, interview with author.

80   *which requires a*: New York State Education Department, www.highered. nysed.gov.

80   *He only has*: Jan Siwanowicz, interview with author.

81   *"saving his life"*: Danny Jaye, interview with author.

81   *once remarked*: Tim Novikoff, interview with author.

## 8. Sing!

83   *Problems are escalating*: Author observations.

83   *"When you're dealing"*: Xevion Baptiste, interview with author.

84   *biggest events*: Stuyvesant High School faculty and students, interviews with author.

84   *generating a whopping*: Matt Polazzo, interview with author.

84   *"The perfect school"*: Danny Jaye, interview with author.

85   *with a budget of*: Stan Teitel, interview with author.

85   *"scary skinny"*: Eric Grossman, interview with author.

86   *"If the seniors"*: Liz London, interview with author.

86   *According to school*: Meyer, p. 87.

86   *Seniors have never taken*: Stuyvesant students, interviews with author.

87   *"We're definitely"*: Liam Ahern, interview with author.

87   *"I caved"*: Xevion Baptiste, interview with author.

87   *Confidence is at*: Stuyvesant students, interviews with author, and author observations.

87   *"We have some"*: Taylor Shung, interview with author.

## 9. The Natural

89   *Outside, it's*: Author observations.

90   *"I never saw"*: Jennifer Lee, interview with author.

90   *"You come to a point"*: Jim Cocoros, interview with author.

91   *Some parents and*: Stuyvesant parents and teachers, interviews with author.

91   *Teachers looking to*: Sol Stern, *Breaking Free: Public School Lessons and the Imperative of School Choice* (San Francisco: Encounter Books, 2003), p. 68.

91   *"I'll be honest"*: Stan Teitel, interview with author.

91   *"teachers told me"*: Matt Polazzo, interview with author.

91   *"dirty little secret"*: Stern, p. 68.

91  *"Incompetence was"*: Ibid., p. 81.

91  *"With a few notable"*. The Teaching Commission, *Teaching at Risk: Progress & Potholes*, Spring 2006, p. 16.

91  *In the mid-1990s:* Stern, p. 77.

92  *"Integration transfers frequently"*: Ibid., p. 74.

92  *Recent changes in:* "The UFT Agreement," *New York Sun*, October 4, 2005. See also "Bloomy & UFT: It's a Deal! 15% Pay Hike, Longer Hours for Teachers," *New York Daily News*, October 4, 2005; "Guide to UFT Contract Changes," New York City Board of Education memo, November 29, 2006.

92  *"We're still dealing"*: Danny Jaye, interview with author.

92  *"The most difficult"*: Eric Grossman, interview with author.

92  *about $72,000:* Stan Teitel, interview with author.

92  *the best include:* Stuyvesant students and faculty, interviews with author.

93  *longest-tenured:* Stan Teitel interview with author.

93  *"Why are we"*: Author observations.

93  *"She'll probably forget"*: Sammy Sussman, interview with author.

94  *"He was lured"*: Jennifer Lee, interview with author.

## PART 2: DETENTION

### 10. Lost in Gatsby

99  *"All these people"*: Romeo Alexander, interview with author.

100  *"Gatsby is incredibly"*: Author observations.

101  *"I have my"*: Romeo Alexander, interview with author.

101  *she wanders into:* Author observations.

102  *"I just wanted:* Xevion Baptiste, interview with author.

102  *on his hands:* Author observations.

102  *"What were they"*: Jan Siwanowicz, interview with author.

103  *In a meeting:* Danny Jaye, interview with author.

104  *full battle mode:* Author observations.

104  *But after her latest:* Jane, interview with author.

105  *A day later:* Author observations.

105  *"This is huge"*: David A. Stein Riverdale/Kingsbridge Academy sophomore, interview with author.

105  *"Stuyvesant kids are"*: David A. Stein Riverdale/Kingsbridge Academy senior, interview with author.

105  *Many other schools:* School officials, educators, and others, interviews with author.

106  *annual list:* "2006 America's Best High Schools: The Top 100 and the 'Public Elites,'" *Newsweek*, May 8, 2006. p. 54.

106  *impressive 1344:* Gretchen Whitney High School, School Accountability Report Card Reported for School Year 2002–2003, p. 13.

106  *"We make no"*: Patricia Hager, interview with author.

106  *averaged 1270:* New Trier High School New Trier High School 2006–2007 Profile, pamphlet, p. 2.

107  *Long after the last:* Author observations.

107  *With a strong:* New Trier High School teachers, and administrators, interviews with author.

107  *"We do an excellent":* Debra L. Stacey, interview with author.

107  *"This is New Trier's":* Jan Borja, interview with author.

107  *"It's so smart":* Cara Harshman, interview with author.

107  *solid 1236 average:* Lowell High School 2002–2003 Profile, fact sheet, p. 2.

107  *"critical not only":* Paul Cheng, interview with author.

108  *score well exceeded:* http://www.prepreview.com.

108  *"the kids are there":* Evan M. Glazer, interview with author.

108  *She attended a:* Lisa Ha, interview with author.

108  *a strong 1290:* Hemphill, p. 119.

108  *seven Nobel Prize:* http://bxscience.edu.

108  *"We make do":* Lisa Ha, interview with author.

109  *For one, the freshman:* Jerry Wang, interview with author.

109  *overriding feature:* Author observations.

109  *"It's so stressful":* Gui Bessa, interview with author.

109  *"You put it":* Alexa Solimano, interview with author.

110  *"Terrible":* Gui Bessa, interview with author.


## 11. Great Expectations

111  *who broods:* Author observations.

111  *"It's sort of dead":* Mariya Goldman, interview with author.

112  *"It has come to":* Copy of Mariya's petition.

113  *"It's sort of ridiculous":* Mariya Goldman, interview with author.

113  *"I dream about":* Yelena Goldman, interview with author.

114  *part of a growing:* Stuyvesant High School faculty members, interviews with author.

114  *"If you don't help":* Author observations.

114  *Down the hall:* Ibid.

114  *"It was kind of a drag":* Milo Beckman, interview with author.

115  *only about 70 percent:* "Public High School Graduation and College-Readiness Rates: 1991–2002," Manhattan Institute for Policy Research, February 2005.

115  *In an April:* "Dropout Nation," *Time,* April 17, 2006.

115  *At about the same:* *The Silent Epidemic: Perspectives on High School Dropouts,* Bill & Melinda Gates Foundation, March 2006.

116  *or technical training:* U.S. Department of Education, 2006 fact sheet.

116  *For instance, in science:* U.S. Department of Education, 2006 report.

116  *U.S. eighth graders:* Trends in International Mathematics and Science study, 2003.

116  *"Our superiority was":* "Is America Flunking Science?" *Time,* February 13, 2006.

116  *"no measurable":* Trends in International Mathematics and Science study, 2003.

116  *Things don't improve:* U.S. Department of Education, 2006 report.

117  *"No one really":* Tom Loveless, interview with author.

117  *Other experts:* Educators, policy makers, and others, interviews with author.

117  *"The problem we":* Stan Teitel, interview with author.

117  *"Unless we start":* The Teaching Commission, p. 11.

118  *on the third floor:* Author observations.

118  *"Sing! is in":* Liz Livingstone, interview with author.

118  *"It's not good":* Alexa Solimano, interview with author.

118  *"We might have":* Erica Sands, interview with author.

119  *The question puts:* Author observations.

119  *It's no accident:* Ibid.

## 12. The Real World

121  *students are discussing:* Author observations.

122  *He's all business:* Eric Grossman, interview with author.

122  *in which the last-hired:* The United Federation of Teachers contract.

122  *"Fair?":* Eric Grossman, interview with author.

123  *"I get a sense":* Jane, interview with author.

123  *"aromatic amnesia":* Jane's unpublished poetry, printed with permission.

124  *"I've seen this":* Eric Grossman, interview with author.

124  *Its relationship with:* Stuyvesant senior, interview with author.

124  *"Instead of being":* Copy of students' letter to the New York City Department of Education.

125  *The object of the:* Author observations.

125  *Mr. Teitel proved his:* Stan Teitel, interview with author.

126  *pair of handcuffs:* Ibid.

126  *assistant principal of biology:* "Two Teachers at Stuyvesant Suspended after Accusations by Students of Misconduct," *New York Times,* September 23, 1999.

126  *After a newly initiated:* Stan Teitel, interview with author.

126  *always on the go:* Jennifer Lee, interview with author.

129  *Sitting at his cluttered:* Danny Jaye, interview with author.

130  *"Why do people":* Author observations.

130  *at a round:* Ibid.

131  *"Several times":* Jan Siwanowicz, interview with author.

131   *"It's a horrible"*: Alexa Solimano, interview with author.

131   *"It's pretty hectic"*: Ben Alter, interview with author.

131   *"You never know"*: Liam Ahern, interview with author.

132   *"If we don't win"*: Molly Ruben-Long, interview with author.

132   *"I'm worried about"*: Author observations.

133   *"I think he needs"*: Xevion Baptiste, interview with author.


### 13. Protests and Demands

135   *Thursday night:* Author observations.

135   *"My thing was"*: Marty Davis, interview with author.

135   *"Oh, that worked"*: Author observations.

136   *"Everybody has"*: Marty Davis, interview with author.

136   *"I've gained so"*: Katie Johnston-Davis, interview with author.

136   *"There's never been"*: Marty Davis, interview with author.

136   *"You're so cheesy"*: Author observations.

136   *"The Stuyvesant she"*: Marty Davis, interview with author.

136   *In the beginning:* Landmarks Preservation Commission records, May 20, 1997, p. 1. See also http://www.stuy.edu; Stuyvesant High School, *Indicator*, 1905 yearbook, pp. 11–19.

136   *Peter Stuyvesant:* Henry H. Kessler and Eugene Rachlis, *Peter Stuyvesant and His New York* (New York: Random House, 1959), p. 37.

136   *college dropout:* Shorto, p. 149.

137   *a tremendous swamp:* Philip M. Scandura, interview with author.

137   *A five-story:* Landmarks Preservation Commission records, May 20, 1997.

137   *In a ceremony:* Meyer, p. 10.

137   *fewer than 7 percent:* Education Week staff, *Lessons of a Century: A Nation's Schools Come of Age* (Bethesda, MD: Editorial Projects in Education, 2000), p. 12.

137   *Most people with:* Diane Ravitch, interview with author.

137   *"Now we are a nation"*: Stuyvesant High School, *Indicator*, 1905 yearbook, p. 12.

138   *more than 70:* Diane Ravitch, *Left Back: A Century of Battles over School Reform* (New York: Touchstone, 2000), p. 56.

138   *"The island was just"*: Philip M. Scandura, interview with author.

138   *Manhattan also teemed:* Ibid. See also Jacob A. Riis, *How the Other Half Lives* (New York: Charles Scribner's Sons, 1890; repr., New York: Penguin Books, 1997); Luc Sante, *Low Life: Lures and Snares of Old New York* (New York: Farrar, Straus and Giroux, 1991).

138   *where traditional academics:* Stuyvesant High School, *Indicator*, 1905 yearbook, p. 18.

138   *"The city boy"*: Ibid., p. 17.

139   *With rising enrollment:* Landmarks Preservation Commission records, May 20, 1997, p. 5.

139   *exam in 1934:* Meyer, pp. 25–26.

139   *The first entrance: Stuyvesant High School Parent Handbook* (New York: Stuyvesant Parents' Association), p. 28.

139   *Not until the:* Meyer, p. 27.

139   *"It was a period":* Diane Ravitch, interview with author.

139   *In response, Stuyvesant:* 'How Gotham's Elite High Schools Escaped the Leveller's Ax," *City Journal,* Spring 1999.

140   *As a compromise:* Abstract, *New York Times,* May 20, 1971.

140   *The controversy flared:* Meyer, p. 27. See also "HS Admission Biased—Study Sez Many Denied Key Prep Course," *New York Daily News,* May 8, 1997.

140   *The activists, known:* "Secret Apartheid II," Association of Community Organizations for Reform Now, 1997.

140   *In a statement:* "HS Admission Biased—Study Sez Many Denied Key Prep Course."

140   *"There's a difference":* Stan Teitel, interview with author.

141   *"Gifted children":* Danny Jaye, interview with author.

142   *"Where they came":* Eleanor Archie, interview with author

142   *"being at Stuy":* Matt Polazzo, interview with author.

142   *"With less pressure":* Mariya Goldman, interview with author.

142   *Unlike Stuyvesant:* Natasha Borchakovskaia, interview with author.

142   *"Everyone here is":* Xevion Baptiste, interview with author

142   *"Stuy kids":* Elaine Liu, interview with author.

143   *"I guess it's not":* Rosabella Mazat, interview with author.

143   *"In the back":* Francisco Bencosme, interview with author.

144   *"the yeast that":* Diane Ravitch, interview with author.

144   *"It's elitist":* Thomas Toch, interview with author.

144   *"I've crossed them":* Katie Johnston-Davis, interview with author.

144   *"In the end":* Marty Davis, interview with author.

## 14. Grief Virus

145   *gifted piano:* "Thruway Horror—Tanker Crash Kills 4 in QNS. Kids' 'Y' Van," *New York Post,* March 18, 2006.

145   *"Good-bye, Daddy":* "Van in Twist of Fate; Thruway Trucker Missed CB Alarm for Swim Moms' Vehicle," *New York Post,* March 19, 2006.

145   *At about 7 a.m.:* "Thruway Tragedy Kills 4, 3 Kids & Woman Die in Crash on Way to YMCA Meet," *New York Daily News,* March 18, 2006.

146   *"Get over!":* "His Warning Came Too Late," *New York Daily News,* March 19, 2006.

146   *about sixty feet:* "Thruway Tragedy Kills 4, 3 Kids & Woman Die in Crash on Way to YMCA Meet."

146  *In the sudden:* "A Dad's Agonizing News; Father Tells Injured Son His Sister Was Killed in Crash That Also Left 3 Others Dead and His Mom Hospitalized," *Newsday*, March 19, 2006.

146  *Kevin dies there:* "His Warning Came Too Late."

146  *"I have lost":* "Thruway Tragedy Kills 4, 3 Kids & Woman Die in Crash on Way to YMCA Meet."

146  *Police do not:* "His Warning Came Too Late"; "Thruway Tragedy Kills 4, 3 Kids & Woman Die in Crash on Way to YMCA Meet."

146  *Word of the tragedy:* Stuyvesant students, interviews with author, and author observations. See also "Two Stuy Students Killed in Tragic Car Accident," *Spectator*, March 29, 2006; "Students Cope with Loss," *Spectator*, March 29, 2006.

146  *Namita can't stop:* Namita Biala, interview with author.

146  *"That could've been":* Alex Larson, interview with author.

147  *the principal cannot:* Stan Teitel, interview with author.

147  *In the chaos:* "An Administration in Crisis," *Spectator*, Special Stuyvesant Edition, Fall 2001.

147  *"They saw this":* Stan Teitel, interview with author.

148  *many students returned:* "Anxieties over Toxins Rise at Ground Zero," *USA Today*, February 7, 2002.

148  *The last class:* "Dread of the Class, 9-11 Casts Shadow on Seniors at Elite Stuyvesant High School Then Now," *New York Daily News*, March 7, 2005.

148  *a big gaping:* Author observations. See also "Attack Location Remains an Open Wound," *Weekend Australian*, September 9, 2006; "The Long and Winding Road to Rebuilding Ground Zero," *Agence France-Presse*, September 3, 2006.

148  *American spectacle:* "Discord Delays Ground Zero Rebirth; After Half a Decade, the Site Remains Largely a Hole in the Ground," *USA Today*, September 6, 2006.

148  *"This was different":* Stan Teitel, interview with author.

148  *Several students straggle:* Author observations.

149  *during seventh period:* Ibid.

150  *The principal consulted:* Stan Teitel, interview with author.

150  *By eighth period:* Matt Polazzo, interview with author.

150  *"We're not as ready":* Olga Safronova, interview with author.

150  *mayhem on the:* Author observations.

151  *"Our Sing! is about":* Sophomore singer, interview with author.

151  *changed some of the:* Taylor Shung, interview with author.

151  *"It didn't seem":* Alexa Solimano, interview with author.

151  *At 5:41, the thirty-fourth:* Author observations.

152  *"Pretty smooth":* Richard Geller, interview with author.

152  *juniors take the stage:* Author observations.

153   *"The juniors are going"*: Matt Polazzo, interview with author.

153   *no hard feelings:* Author observations.

153   *Chelsea Piers:* Author observations.

154   *"Here, he's a kid"*: Gil Rubin, interview with author.

154   *During a break, Milo:* Author observations.

155   *"That'll keep me"*: Milo Beckman, interview with author.

155   *In Queens the following day:* "Family's Goodbye for Crash Victims Is Rooted in Ritual," *New York Times*, March 25, 2006.

155   *attendance scanners arrive:* "Long-Anticipated ID Scanners Installed," *Spectator*, March 29, 2006.

155   *Sing! reaches a crescendo:* Author observations.

156   *Later, it comes out:* "Sing! Scores," *Spectator*, March 29, 2006.

156   *at Sing! drunk:* "Sing! Judges Inebriated," *Spectator*, March 29, 2006.

156   *By the following:* Students, interviews with author, and author observations.

## 15. Polazzo's Time

157   *In a cluttered cubbyhole:* Author observations.

157   *"He's a kid"*: a Stuyvesant junior, interview with author.

158   *"I'm trying to convince"*: Matt Polazzo, interview with author.

158   *Student Union office:* Author observations.

158   *"The kids are really"*: Matt Polazzo, interview with author

158   *Not all of them:* Author observations.

159   *The principal has indicated.* Stan Teitel, interview with author.

159   *The thought of being:* Matt Polazzo, interview with author.

159   *"I'm freaking"*: Xevion Baptiste, interview with author.

160   *"I bet Xevion"*: Romeo Alexander, interview with author.

160   *"I'm going to win"*: Author observations.

160   *"He's playing"*: Xevion Baptiste, interview with author.

160   *Romeo plans a:* Romeo Alexander, interview with author.

160   *Xevion, rising from:* Xevion Baptiste, interview with author.

160   *Romeo calmly explains:* Romeo Alexander, interview with author.

161   *"It's all about"*: Reyna Ramirez, interview with author.

161   *"I wasn't going"*: Danielle Fernandes, interview with author

161   *is animated:* Author observations.

162   *He's ranting about:* Danny Jaye, interview with author.

162   *producing a copy:* Copy of student letter to principal.

162   *"We're looking to"*: Copy of Eddie Wong letter.

163   *Mr. Jaye suspects:* Danny Jaye, interview with author and author observations.

163   *Milo's mother:* Emily Shapiro, interview with author.

164   *"copping out"*: Danny Jaye, interview with author.

164  *a Buddhist monk:* "Teenager Killed in Thruway Accident Is Buried," *Associated Press*, March 31, 2006. See also "Last Teary Farewell to Swim Team Teen, 'A 15-Year-Old Shouldn't Be Burying Her Friends,'" *New York Daily News*, April 1, 2006.

## 16. Hell's Kitchen

165  *On the first:* Author observations.
165  *But Jane isn't:* Jane, interview with author.
166  *"simple reduction":* Jane's unpublished poetry, printed with permission.
167  *"No one can":* Jane, interview with author.
167  *intervened about a:* Eric Grossman, interview with author.
168  *Parents have called:* Stan Teitel, interview with author.
168  *In the meantime:* Eric Grossman, interview with author.
168  *begin agitating:* Students, interview with author. See also http://www.stuy-com.net.
169  *gets the message:* Ibid.; Stan Teitel, interview with author; also "Scanners Here to Stay," *Spectator*, April 12, 2006.
169  *"It seems like":* Nathan Buch, http://www.stuycom.net.
169  *"All in all":* "What's Up with Those Scanners?," *S.U. Newsletter!*, April 11, 2006.
169  *own nightmare:* Mariya Goldman, interview with author.
170  *There they grab:* Author observations.
170  *Mariya wonders:* Mariya Goldman, interview with author.
171  *After school:* Author observations.
171  *A block away:* Ibid.
171  *great consternation:* Milo Beckman, interview with author.
171  *"Global warming may":* "What's With the Weather?," *234 Latte*, issue 3.
172  *A ponytailed girl:* Author observations.
172  *"That's how old":* Milo Beckman, interview with author.
172  *Against a muslin-draped:* Author observations.
172  *unconsciously rotates:* Milo Beckman, interview with author.
172  *When he returns:* Author observations.

## 17. The Contest

175  *On a drizzling:* Author observations.
175  *"I don't normally":* Danny Zhu, interview with author.
176  *Minutes before:* Author observations.
176  *"I already have":* Stan Teitel, interview with author.
176  *"This is football":* Danny Jaye, interview with author.
176  *He entered his:* Jie Zhang, interview with author.
177  *Danny can't explain:* Danny Zhu, interview with author.

177    *"He came in"*: Danny Jaye, interview with author.

177    *11:19 a.m.*: Author observations.

178    *"In its own"*: Danny Jaye, interview with author.

178    *retire to the*: Author observations.

179    *"Tired"*: Danny Zhu, interview with author.

179    *It happens with*: Milo Beckman, interview with author.

179    *That night*: Stan Teitel, interview with author. See also "Susan Biering, Biology Teacher, Passes Away," *Spectator*, April 12, 2006.

180    *Ms. Biering is buried*: "Susan Biering, Biology Teacher, Passes Away."

180    *state of sorrow*: Author observations.

181    *Ms. Lee feels*: Jennifer Lee, interview with author.

182    *is surrendering*: Romeo Alexander, interview with author.

183    *her eyes lift*: Catherine Wideman, interview with author.

183    *"I've always felt"*: Romeo Alexander, interview with author.

## PART 3: SENIORITIS

### 18. Zero Tolerance

187    *At one end*: Author observations.

188    *particularly daft*: Kristen Ng, interview with author.

188    *"Only in school"*: Matt Polazzo, interview with author.

188    *while student leaders*: Students, interviews with author. See also "COSA Up for Reappointment," *Spectator*, May 4, 2006.

188    *"It's all a war"*: Matt Polazzo, interview with author.

188    *The mayor introduced*: New York City government, press release, April 13, 2006. See also "Students to Get No Warning Before Searches," *New York Times*, April 14, 2006.

188    *About 20 percent*: "Students to Get No Warning Before Searches."

188    *illegal weapons*: New York City government, press release, April 13, 2006.

188    *violent crime has dropped*: Ibid.

189    *The rate of violent*: U.S. Department of Justice, press release, November 20, 2005.

189    *students are more likely*: National Education Association, www.nea.org.

189    *The school reported*: New York City Department of Education, 2004–2005 Annual School Report, p. 2.

189    *"We don't have"*: Matt Polazzo, interview with author.

189    *"They all know"*: Eric Grossman, interview with author.

189    *In a follow-up letter*: Copy of principal's letter to parents.

189    *"I resisted"*: Stan Teitel, interview with author.

190    *students are posting*: Student flyer.

190    *a formal warning*: School notice.

191    *"You're going to stab"*: Nathan Buch, interview with author.

191    *"Of all the schools"*: Molly Ruben-Long, interview with author.

191   *"It's the questing":* Author observations.

193   *Upstairs, in room 401:* Ibid.

194   *To recall the last:* Jan Siwanowicz, interview with author.

195   *almost on tiptoes:* Author observations.

## 19. College Night

197   *perched alone atop:* Author observations.

197   *John F. Kennedy:* Edward Klein, *The Kennedy Curse* (New York: St. Martin's Press, 2003), p. 148.

197   *"Competition":* Romeo Alexander, interview with author.

198   *Senior Deke Hill:* Author observations.

198   *"This is not your":* Deke Hill, interview with author.

199   *They're all here:* Author observations.

199   *"Throughout the night":* "College Acceptance, The Other Way Around," *Spectator,* May 4, 2006.

200   *A boy who:* Author observations.

200   *The average tuition:* The College Board, press release, October 24, 2006.

200   *Between 1984 and 1994:* National Center for Education Statistics.

200   *about a quarter:* Stan Teitel, Interview with author.

200   *room 511 is virtually:* Author observations.

200   *"You know you're":* Babson College pamphlet.

201   *"We'd love to get":* Babson College recruiter, interview with author.

201   *Harvard isn't giving:* Author observations.

202   *"The pursuit of excellence":* Harvard College pamphlet.

202   *"We know Stuyvesant":* Author observations.

202   *"It was nothing":* Romeo Alexander, interview with author.

202   *Deke, the senior, leaves:* Deke Hill, interview with author.

## 20. Peter Pan Tilts

205   *the little man-child:* Author observations.

205   *"It's not usually":* Milo Beckman, interview with author.

205   *his desk, over which:* Author observations.

206   *"I always have trouble":* Milo Beckman, interview with author.

206   *wanders over to:* Author observations.

206   *"Milo knows everything":* Willa Beckman, interview with author.

207   *By now, Milo:* Author observations.

207   *The following morning:* Danny Jaye, interview with author.

208   *The principal knows:* Stan Teitel, interview with author.

208   *"His inability to control":* Danny Jaye, interview with author.

209   *When the phone rings:* Author observations.

209   *That afternoon, Mariya:* Ibid.

210   *"really cool":* Mariya Goldman, interview with author.
210   *As is the sign:* Author observations.
210   *"I haven't been telling":* Mariya Goldman, interview with author.
210   *marveling at her daughter:* Yelena Goldman, interview with author.
210   *"My mother always":* Mariya Goldman, interview with author.
210   *Mrs. Goldman corrects:* Yelena Goldman, interview with author.
210   *"I wanted to be like":* Mariya Goldman, interview with author
211   *At parent-teacher conferences:* Yelena Goldman, interview with author.
211   *discounted her own:* Mariya Goldman, interview with author.
211   *"I was happy":* Yelena Goldman, interview with author.
211   *"If I can be similar":* Mariya Goldman, interview with author.
211   *The next day, Thursday:* "COSA Up for Reappointment," *Spectator* May 4, 2006.
211   *accompanying editorial.* "A Fight for the Crusader," *Spectator,* May 4, 2006.
211   *around the corner:* Author observations.


## 21. Neutral Ground

213   *seems to float:* Author observations.
213   *"I wouldn't trade":* Jan Siwanowicz, interview with author.
215   *a warm Saturday:* Author observations.
215   *He did a month:* Mike, interview with author.
215   *pounding pavement:* Author observations.
216   *he's scared:* Eric Grossman, interview with author.
216   *she can't shake:* Jane, interview with author.
216   *with a lesson:* Eric Grossman, interview with author.
216   *Tony Montana flavor:* Author observations.
216   *particular vantage point:* Jane, interview with author.
217   *Until now:* Author observations.
218   *"I think life is so":* Jane, interview with author.
218   *his own fate:* Author observations.
218   *"I kind of took":* Matt Polazzo, interview with author.
218   *"Like when the":* Author observations.
218   *"Ever since I arrived":* Copy of Matt Polazzo's application.
218   *"This is the worst":* Author observations.
218   *"Whenever a student":* Matt Polazzo, interview with author
219   *Teitel barges:* Author observations.
219   *Friday, May 12:* Jennifer Lee, interview with author.


## 22. Love Notes

221   *on a quiet patch:* Author observations.
221   *harried few days:* Matt Polazzo, interview with author.
222   *A gaggle of girls:* Author observations.

222   *primitive state:* Author observations.
223   *the mother hen:* Matt Polazzo, interview with author.
223   *When it's dark:* Author observations.
223   *"I can't wait until":* Taylor Shung, interview with author.
223   *growing up faster:* Author observations.
224   *another transmutation:* Ibid.
224   *"Ultimately, what it's":* Eric Grossman, interview with author.
224   *the dreaded affliction:* http://en.wikipedia.org.
224   *a cautionary note:* Stuyvesant and college postings.
225   *Around the corner:* Author observations.
225   *School lore has it:* Students and teachers, author interviews.
225   *over-the-top crush:* Author observations.
225   *"There's no accounting":* Matt Polazzo, interview with author.
225   *here at the wall:* Author observations.
226   *"It's a cause":* Jonathan Edelman, interview with author.
226   *after school today:* Students, interviews with author. See also "Student Leaders Oppose New COSA Applicants," *Spectator*, May 24, 2006.
226   *just finished performing:* Elisa Lee, interview with author.
226   *pull of narcotics:* Elisa Lee's unpublished monologue, printed with permission.
227   *But Jane hasn't stopped:* Jane, interview with author.

### 23. The Players

229   *No one can stop:* Author observations.
230   *climbs into a harness:* Author observations.
230   *"They're bigger, blacker":* Stuyvesant running back, interview with author.
230   *Romeo says nothing:* Author observations.
230   *He's used to:* Romeo Alexander, interview with author.
231   *"He likes to see":* Ibid.
232   *hunched in his:* Author observations.
232   *"profanity, defamation":* Stuyvesant High School Board of Elections, *Official Rules and Regulations for the Spring 2006 Student Union Elections.*
232   *"It's to level":* Jamie Paul, interview with author.
232   *"The Asians are":* Matt Polazzo, interview with author.
233   *"Asian-white pair":* Amanda Wallace, interview with author.
233   *"definitely a factor":* Matt Polazzo, interview with author.
233   *"We're two white kids":* Marta Bralic, interview with author.
233   *going against the grain:* Matt Polazzo, interview with author.
233   *half Thai and half Filipino:* Student e-mail to author.
233   *who is half Asian:* Ibid.
233   *"IN THE PAST":* Campaign pamphlet.
234   *Not even a third:* "The Ideal Democracy," *Spectator*, May 24, 2006.

234 *"arguably the best"*: Suh Films, letter to Stuyvesant students and parents, May 1, 2006.

234 *his own accounts*: Dick Morris, *Behind the Oval Office: Winning the Presidency in the Nineties* (New York: Random House, 1997), p. 44.

234 *"struggle endures"*: Campaign poster.

234 *world-weariness*: Author observations.

234 *Mariya met a boy*: Mariya Goldman, interview with author.

235 *"Dear Mariya, Mount Holyoke"*: Mount Holyoke College e-mail.

236 *From Marist College*: Marist College e-mail.

236 *And another*: Oxford College of Emory University e-mail.

236 *"Every week, I throw"*: Mariya Goldman, interview with author.

## 24. The Human Element

237 *It's 8:58 a.m.*: Author observations.

237 *his mind racing*: Romec Alexander, interview with author.

238 *"Of course, I have to"*: Paul Garabedian, interview with author.

238 *seems to become aware*: Author observations.

239 *"The point is to keep"*: Paul Garabedian, interview with author.

239 *"I'm going to go"*: Milo Beckman, interview with author.

239 *undulating dock*: Author observations.

240 *"was really stupid"*: Milo Beckman, interview with author.

241 *On Tuesday*: Author observations.

241 *"I have all these"*: Eric Grossman, interview with author.

242 *her own heartbreak*: Jennifer Lee, interview with author.

## 25. The Last Dance

247 *It's a strange*: Author observations.

248 *"They're attached by"*: Harvey Blumm, interview with author.

248 *That includes two*: Author observations.

248 *"Some of them"*: Michael Zaytsev, interview with author.

248 *One of the smaller*: Author observations.

248 *Upstairs in his office*: Ibid.

248 *School officials have*: Danny Jaye, interview with author.

249 *pokes his head*: Author observations.

249 *"The fourth floor"*: Danny Jaye, interview with author.

249 *most telling sign*: Author observations.

249 *"I've spent a little"*: Danny Jaye, interview with author.

250 *familiar pose*: Author observations.

250 *It started off*: Stuyvesant student leaders, interviews with author. See also "Stuyvesant Leaders Oppose New COSA Applicants."

250 *In a subsequent*: "A Mishandled Controversy," *Spectator*, June 9, 2006.

250 *prompting Mr. Teitel:* Andrew Saviano, interview with author.
250 *"I am sorry":* Stan Teitel, letter to Stuyvesant community, June 9, 2006.
251 *"I formally and":* Junior class president, letter.
251 *growing perception:* School administrators, interviews with author.
251 *decide his fate:* Author observations.
251 *"It was pretty":* Matt Polazzo, interview with author.
252 *barges back into:* Author observations.
252 *"It's so gorgeous":* Siyu "Daisy" Duan, interview with author.
252 *Upstairs, in the:* Author observations.
252 *"There'll be a lot":* James Lonardo, interview with author.
252 *Momentum builds:* Author observations.
253 *"My mom forbid":* Nameeta Kamath, interview with author.
253 *cleans up well:* Author observations.
253 *"I don't understand":* Stan Teitel, interview with author.
253 *Deke, for his:* Deke Hill, interview with author.
254 *It's 9:33 p.m.:* Author observations.
254 *"I don't know":* Katie Johnston-Davis, interview with author.
254 *Not for Jane:* Author observations.
254 *"I brought my":* Andrew Saviano, interview with author.
255 *By 12:37 a.m.:* Author observations.
255 *The election board:* Matt Polazzo, interview with author.

## 26. The Final Days

257 *Monday, June 12:* Author observations.
257 *"I'm scared because":* Mariya Goldman, interview with author.
257 *At six foot five:* Author observations.
258 *"She studies too":* Jarek Lupinski, interview with author.
258 *"I don't study":* Mariya Goldman, interview with author.
258 *A left on:* Author observations.
258 *when he met:* Jarek Lupinski, interview with author.
259 *Mariya will be:* Mariya Goldman, interview with author.
259 *holding hands as they rise:* Author observations.
259 *The last bell:* Ibid.
259 *"There's not many":* Robert Sandler, interview with author.
260 *At the moment:* Author observations.
260 *"I'm still in":* Romeo Alexander, interview with author.
260 *frenzied sound of:* Author observations.
260 *"I just tell":* Romeo Alexander, interview with author.
260 *strong undertow of:* Author observations.
260 *"I should be":* Romeo Alexander, interview with author.
261 *The phone rings:* Author observations.

261  *steps out of:* Ibid.

261  *"There's nothing hard":* Milo Beckman, interview with author.

262  *He enters Stuyvesant:* Author observations.

263  *"It was really easy":* Milo Beckman, interview with author.

263  *On Monday, June 26:* Author observations.

265  *Around this time:* Matt Polazzo, interview with author.

266  *Not that the decision:* Stan Teitel, interview with author.

266  *One by one:* Author observations.

266  *The following day:* Ibid.

266  *On her last day:* Jennifer Lee, interview with author.

267  *Mr. Jaye isn't:* Author observations.

268  *Yesterday he went:* Danny Jaye, interview with author.

269  *drops by:* Author observations.

270  *doesn't mention Jane:* Eric Grossman, interview with author.

270  *What Mr. Grossman:* Author observations.

270  *his own heartbreak:* Danny Jaye, interview with author.

270  *What Mr. Jaye says:* Author observations.


## Epilogue

272  *Jeffersonian notion:* Jefferson, p. 430.

272  *"Educators decided":* Jay Mathews, interview with author.

272  *"It's politically incorrect":* Tom Loveless, interview with author.

272  *"The greatest force":* Jay Mathews, interview with author.

272  *"Based on students'":* Chester E. Finn Jr., interview with author.

273  *"Only one in three":* "A Report on the High School Reform Movement," Education Sector, March 2006.

273  *"At the high school":* Thomas Toch, interview with author.

273  *a dizzying array:* Educators and policy makers, interviews with author.

274  *"They are the forgotten":* Diane Ravitch, interview with author.

274  *The sense among:* Educators and policy makers, interviews with author.

274  *argues otherwise:* Stan Teitel, interview with author.

274  *They flourish:* Stuyvesant administrators, parents, and students, interviews with author.

275  *I miss Milo:* Milo Beckman and Emily Shapiro, interviews with author.

276  *I miss Mariya:* Mariya Goldman, interview with author

276  *I miss Romeo:* Romeo Alexander, interview with author.

276  *"In making each":* Copy of Harvard College letter to Romeo Alexander, December 15, 2006.

276  *joining his conscience:* Xevion Baptiste e-mail to author.

277  *After the term ended:* Stuyvesant teacher, interview with author.

277  *trouble finding a replacement:* Stan Teitel, interview with author.

277 *That teacher agreed:* Copy of resignation letter to Stan Teitel and interviews with school faculty.

277 *For her part:* Jennifer Lee, interview with author.

278 *director of academy programs:* Danny Jaye, interview with author.

278 *"She's even got":* Eric Grossman e-mail to author.

278 *"It's like you've":* Emily Hoffman, interview with author.

# Selected Bibliography

Arak, Jonathan. *Cracking the New York City Specialized High Schools Admissions Test*. New York: Random House, 2003.

Baskin, Julia, Lindsey Newman, Sophie Pollitt-Cohen, and Courtney Toombs. *The Notebook Girls*. New York: Warner Books, 2006.

Bissinger, H. G. *Friday Night Lights: A Town, a Team, and a Dream*. Cambridge, MA: Da Capo Press, 2004.

Boynton, Robert S. *The New New Journalism: Conversations with America's Best Nonfiction Writers on Their Craft*. New York: Vintage Books, 2005.

Bridgeland, John M., John J. Dilulio Jr., and Karen Burke Morison. *The Silent Epidemic: Perspectives of High School Dropouts*. Bill & Melinda Gates Foundation, March 2006.

Cagney, James. *Cagney by Cagney*. Garden City, NY: Doubleday, 1976.

Dostoyevsky, Fyodor. *Crime and Punishment*. Trans. David McDuff. London: Penguin Books, 1991.

*Education Week* staff. *Lessons of a Century: A Nation's Schools Come of Age*. Bethesda, MD: Editorial Projects in Education, 2000.

Fitzgerald, F. Scott. *The Great Gatsby*. New York: Scribner, 1925.

Freedman, Samuel G. *Small Victories: The Real World of a Teacher, Her Students, and Their High School*. New York: Harper Perennial, 1990.

Golden, Daniel. *The Price of Admission: How America's Ruling Class Buys Its Way into Elite Colleges—and Who Gets Left Outside the Gates*. New York: Crown Publishers, 2006.

Hemphill, Clara, with Pamela Wheaton and Jacqueline Wayans. *New York City's Best Public High Schools.* New York: Teachers College, Columbia University, 2003.

Humes, Edward. *School of Dreams: Making the Grade at a Top American High School.* New York: A Harvest Book, 2003.

Jefferson, Thomas. *Thomas Jefferson: Autobiography.* 1821. In *Basic Writings of Thomas Jefferson,* edited by Philip S. Foner. Garden City, NY: Halcyon House, 1950.

Jerald, Craig D. *Measured Progress: A Report on the High School Reform Movement.* Washington, DC: Education Sector, 2006.

Kessler, Henry H., and Eugene Rachlis. *Peter Stuyvesant and His New York.* New York: Random House, 1959.

Klein, Edward. *The Kennedy Curse.* New York: St. Martin's Press, 2003.

Kober, Nancy. *A Public Education Primer.* Washington, DC: Center on Education Policy, 2006.

Kouwenhoven, John A. *The Columbia Historical Portrait of New York.* New York: Icon Editions, Harper & Row, 1972.

Kozol, Jonathan. *The Shame of the Nation: The Restoration of Apartheid Schooling in America.* New York: Crown Publishers, 2005.

Landmarks Preservation Commission. Archival records, Designation list 20, LP-1958. May 20, 1997.

Lethem, Jonathan. *The Fortress of Solitude.* New York: Vintage Books, 2004.

Maran, Meredith. *Class Dismissed: A Year in the Life of an American High School, a Glimpse into the Heart of a Nation.* New York: St. Martin's Griffin, 2000.

McCabe, John. *Cagney.* New York: Alfred A. Knopf, 1997.

McCourt, Frank. *Teacher Man.* New York: Scribner, 2005.

Meyer, Susan E. *Stuyvesant High School: The First 100 Years.* New York: Campaign for Stuyvesant/Alumni(ae) & Friends Endowment Fund, 2005.

Miller, Donald L. *Lewis Mumford: A Life.* New York: Weidenfeld & Nicolson, 1989.

Morris, Dick. *Behind the Oval Office: Winning the Presidency in the Nineties.* New York: Random House, 1997.

Mumford, Lewis. *Sketches from Life.* New York: Dial Press, 1982.

———. *My Works and Days: A Personal Chronicle.* New York: Harcourt Brace Jovanovich, 1979.

New York City Board of Education. *Stuyvesant High School Course Guide.*
2002–2003.

New York City Department of Education. *The Specialized High Schools Student Handbook.* 2005–2006.

———. 2004–2005 Annual School Report. 2006.

Ravitch, Diane. *The Great School Wars: A History of the New York City Public Schools.* Baltimore Johns Hopkins University Press, 2000.

———. *Left Back: A Century of Battles over School Reform.* New York: Touchstone, 2000.

Riis, Jacob A. *How the Other Half Lives: Studies among the Tenements of New York.* New York: Charles Scribner's Sons, 1890. Repr., New York: Penguin Books, 1997.

Robbins, Alexandra. *The Overachievers: The Secret Lives of Driven Kids.* New York: Hyperion, 2006.

Sante, Luc. *Low Life: Lures and Snares of Old New York.* New York: Farrar, Straus and Giroux, 1991.

Shorto, Russell. *The Island at the Center of the World.* New York: Doubleday, 2004.

Sittenfeld, Curtis. *Prep.* New York: Random House, 2005.

Stern, Sol. *Breaking Free: Public School Lessons and the Imperative of School Choice.* San Francisco: Encounter Books, 2003.

Stuyvesant High School. *The Case for Stuyvesant High School.* 2003.

———. *Indicator.* 1905 yearbook.

———. *Indicator.* 1908 yearbook.

———. *Indicator.* 1985 yearbook.

———. *Indicator.* 2005 yearbook.

———. *Indicator.* 2006 yearbook.

———. *The Spectator,* Special Stuyvesant Edition. Fall 2001.

Teaching Commission. *Teaching at Risk: Progress & Potholes.* New York: The Teaching Commission, Spring 2006.

Vizzini, Ned. *Teen Angst? Naaah. . . .* Minneapolis, MN: Free Spirit Publishing, 2000.

# Acknowledgments

Thank you, Stuyvesant High School. Once upon a time, you gave me my first kiss. You gave me my first heartbreak. You gave me the inspiration to write. And you welcomed me back, as if I'd never left more than twenty years later, so that I could take one last test to write this book. Now I want to give back. I am donating a portion of my royalties from this book to Stuyvesant, designating the money for the school newspaper, the *Spectator*, which helped give me my start in journalism way back when. I will also donate copies of this book for school fund-raising purposes. It's the least I can do. I received a free high school education at Stuyvesant—twice.

I want to thank Stan Teitel, Stuyvesant's principal, a good and kind man who had the wisdom and foresight to give students and teachers—and this writer—the freedom to grow and learn.

I want to thank Romeo Alexander, for his dreams of greatness and sense of great responsibility; Milo Beckman, for his sublime ability to retain the purity of his childhood even while he surpasses adults in intellect; Mariya Goldman, for choosing love over grades; Jane, for trying to overcome her addiction and recognizing the beauty in poetry; Danny Jaye, for being an expert troublemaker in the name of helping students; Jennifer Lee, for her uncommon grace under great expectations; Matt

Polazzo, for being an overgrown kid because that's what the kids needed; and Jan Siwanowicz, for finding daily sustenance in the undiluted world of teenagers.

For sharing their lives, hopes, and fears, I want to thank all of the other Stuyvesant students, an incredible array of talent, including Liam Ahern; Karim Ahmed; Alair; Ben Alter; Daniel Alzugaray; Atrish Bagchi; Xevion Baptiste; Lucy Baranyuk; Eleonora Bershadskaya; Gui Bessa; Namita Biala; Nikki Bogopolskaya; Guergana Borissova; Marta Bralic; Nathan Buch; Allie Caccamo; Kristen Chambers; Lauren Chan; Vanessa Charubhumi; Abraham Chien; Yun-ke Chin-Lee; Becky Cooper; Brittany DiSanto; Siyu "Daisy" Duan; Jonathan Edelman; Cat Emil; Rachel Ensign; Danielle Fernandes; Zach Frankel; Hannah Freiman; Julie Gaynin; Lauren Gonzalez; Emma Gorin; Deke Hill; Emily Hoffman; Lingji Hon; Jackie Hsieh; Kieren James-Lubin; Katie Johnston-Davis; Talia Kagan; Nameeta Kamath; Tina Khiani; Johnathan Khusid; Katherine Kim; Samantha Krug; Fadi Laham; Alex Larsen; Elisa Lee; Stacey Lee; Eileen LeGuillou; Susan Levinson; Amy Li; Sandy Liang; Liana-Marie Lien; Liz Livingstone; Richard Lo; Liz London; Jarek Lupinski; Yasha Magarik; Wyndam Makowsky; Eli Mlyn; Mariana Muravitsky; Ada Ng; Kristen Ng; Jamie Paul; Reyna Ramirez; Molly Ruben-Long; Anna Rubin; Olga Safronova; Erica Sands; Maria Santos; Stella Savarimuthu; Andrew Saviano; Alex Schleider; Alix Schneider; Taylor Shung; Paul Silverman; Alexa Solimano; Suman Som; Naomi Sosner; Sammy Sussman; John Taylor; Dylan Tramontin; Rukshan Uddin; Amanda Wallace; Anna Weissman; Samantha Whitmore; Barbara Yang; Michael Zaytsev; and Danny Zhu.

For making this a better book, I am also grateful to the quiet heroes of Stuyvesant—a remarkable collection of teachers, administrators, and staff—as well as Stuyvesant friends and family members, educational and other authorities, and students, teachers, and administrators from other schools, including Charles Alexander; Eleanor Archie; Christopher Asch; Eric Beckman; Willa Beckman; Francisco Bencosme; Laura Blair Bertani; Roz Bierig; Harvey Blumm; Vito Bonsignore; Natasha Borchakovskaia; Jan Borja; Paul Cheng; Robert Y. R. Chung; Jim Cocoros; Angel Colon; Karen Cooper; Michael Cooper; Randi Damesek; Marty Davis; Warren Donin; Lynne Evans; Maryann Ferrara; Chester E. Finn Jr.; Donna

Fiscina; Paul Flaig; Katherine Fletcher; Erika Frankel; Paul Garabedian; Richard Geller; Evan M. Glazer; Yelena Goldman; Eric Grossman; Lisa Ha; Patricia Hager; Holly Hall; Cara Harshman; Ashvin Jaishankar; Gary Jaye; Barbara Johnston; Susan Kalish; Wendy Keyes; Elaine Liu; James Lonardo; Marie Lorenzo; Tom Loveless; Rosabella Magat; Melissa McDermott; Kelly McMahon; Susan E. Meyer; Emily Moore; Alex Morris; Philip Mott; Tim Novikoff; Oana Pascu; Mary Patchel; Bonnie Pizzarelli; Diane Ravitch; Gil Rubin; Brian Sacks; Dero Saclarides; Robert Sandler; Philip M. Scandura; Joy Schimmel; Emily Shapiro; Julie Sheinman; Lisa Shuman; Michael Son; Debra L. Stacey; Caroline Suh; Jennifer Suri; Annie Thoms; Thomas Toch; Jerry Wang; Michael Waxman; Jonathan Weil; Raymond Wheeler; Catherine and John Edgar Wideman; Bruce Winokur; Eddie Wong; Mike Zamansky; and Jie Zhang.

For their support from beginning to end, a special thanks goes to the Stuyvesant High School Alumni Association, including Henry Grossberg, Sari Halper Dickson, and Tara Regist-Tomlinson.

I am thankful to my gifted research assistants for all of their contributions to the book: Ellen Herman, a Georgetown University undergraduate; Jean Hwang, an English master's degree student, also at Georgetown; and Danielle Ulman, who is earning a master's degree in journalism from the University of Maryland.

To my former Georgetown University students, I appreciate all the advice during my time last year at Stuyvesant. Thank you, Lizette Baghdadi; Nicholas Barnicle; Brittany Bassett; Michael Birrer; Katherine Boyle; Geoffrey Greene; Catherine Kelley; Amy Koizim; Elizabeth Lee; Margaret Lenahan; Christina Livadiotis; Kurt McLeod; Regina Moore; Matthew Nemeth; Alison Noelker; Jessica Rettig; Leila Sidawy; and Christine Strait. I would also like to thank my Georgetown students from last semester, who always reminded me of the compassion needed in a project like this, including Jessica Bachman; John Burke; Esha Chhabra; Luann Dallojacono; Erin Delmore; Ben Fierberg; Chantal Grinderslev; David Loebsack; Kate Moody; Claudia Nairn; Meghan Orie; Michael Schlembach; Rebecca Sinderbrand; Mary Katherine Stump; and Jane Yu.

Esther Newberg is simply the best literary agent in the business. Thank you, Esther, for truly understanding an author's passion.

Bob Bender, my editor at Simon & Schuster, is a writer's dream. Thank you, Bob, for bringing great wisdom, a gentle but clear vision, and perfect understanding to the project. Thanks also to Peg Haller, Amber L. Husbands, Johanna Li, David Rosenthal, and Brian Ulicky. I want to acknowledge the Smith Richardson Foundation for its generous support and Mark Steinmeyer in particular for helping to identify several important issues of education and public policy relevant to this project. Thanks also to the Education Writers Association, especially Lisa Walker, and the Reporters Committee for Freedom of the Press for their assistance.

At the *Washington Post*, the best of all newspapers, I want to thank the leadership of Phil Bennett, Len Downie, Jill Dutt, Don Graham, Sandy Sugawara, and Greg Schneider for supporting me in the pursuit of this project. Thanks also to Alice Crites, Eric Lieberman, Jay Mathews, Larry Roberts, and Griff Witte for their keen insights. And to Andrea Caumont and Henry Wyko for helping to point me in the right direction.

Thanks also to Dan Golden of the *Wall Street Journal*, Cindy Hanson, and Doris and Sorin Iarovici for their sage suggestions to improve the manuscript. And to Barbara Feinman Todd of Georgetown University for her wise counsel throughout. Additional thanks to Kathy Temple, also of Georgetown, American University's Rose Ann Robertson, and Penny Bender Fuchs and Steve Crane, both of the University of Maryland, for their help.

I will always cherish my old Stuyvesant friends who made high school a magical time, so much so that I wanted to return to the place more than two decades later: Sorin and Laura and James and James and Jeff and Jeff and Stephen and Bram and Jessica and David and David and Sam and Lenny and Jason and all the rest of the motley crew. Thanks also to my old Stuyvesant teachers, whom I never got to thank, especially Dr. Bindman and Mr. McCourt for encouraging me to get into this cockamamie business of writing. And to Ron Cancemi, not just a school counselor but a true friend even now in memory.

Special gratitude goes to my family for their unconditional support, especially my sister Kathy Goodnough, a great roommate and sounding board during my time in New York while I was researching Stuyvesant into the small hours of the morning. Also to my father, Edward Klein, for teaching me the eternal lessons of good and right journalism. To my mother, Emiko Goodnough, sister Karen Hirsch, and brother-in-law, Steven Hirsch, for listening to my rants as I tried to swim through a sea of information and find my way to the heart of the story. And to Delores Barrett, Bob Goodnough, and the rest of the extended family. Thanks also to the wonderful Chicago clan for their unwavering support: Eileen Graziano; Frida and Jim Graziano; Alexis, Mia, Nicholas, Paul, and Julie Graziano; J. P. Graziano; and Ann-Marie, Joe, J. P. and Reilly Hayes.

The greatest thanks of all belongs to my wife, Julie-Ann, and to my daughter, Ryan Isabella, in whose names and for whom I do everything.

# About the Author

Alec Klein is an award-winning journalist and author. His first book, *Stealing Time: Steve Case, Jerry Levin, and the Collapse of AOL Time Warner*, was an acclaimed national best seller that was translated into Japanese and Chinese, excerpted in Great Britain, and hailed by the *New York Times* as "vivid and harrowing" and a "compelling parable of greed and power and hubris."

For nearly twenty years, Klein has worked as a newspaper reporter, starting at the *Virginian-Pilot* covering education before moving on to the *Baltimore Sun*, the *Wall Street Journal*, and the *Washington Post*, where for the past seven years he has been a staff writer. Klein's investigations have led to significant reforms, congressional hearings, federal law, millions in government fines, and criminal convictions. He has won numerous national journalism awards.

Klein, a frequent guest speaker on various writing, media, education, and business issues, teaches journalism at Georgetown University and conducts workshops throughout the country on investigative reporting.

Klein is also a playwright, novelist, and Phi Beta Kappa graduate of Brown University. Born in Sleepy Hollow, New York, and raised in New York City, he is the son of an American journalist and a Japanese artist. He lives in Washington, D.C., with his wife, Julie-Ann, and their daughter, Ryan Isabella.

# THE
# POISON
# SQUAD

# THE
# POISON
# SQUAD

*One Chemist's Single-Minded*

*Crusade for Food Safety*

*at the Turn of the*

*Twentieth Century*

———— ◆ ————

# DEBORAH BLUM

PENGUIN PRESS ✦ NEW YORK ✦ 2018

PENGUIN PRESS
An imprint of Penguin Random House LLC
375 Hudson Street
New York, New York 10014
penguin.com

Illustration credits appear on page 320.

ISBN 9781594205149 (hardcover)
ISBN 9780525560289 (ebook)

Printed in the United States of America
1   3   5   7   9   10   8   6   4   2

DESIGNED BY AMANDA DEWEY

*To Peter, who makes all things possible*

# CONTENTS

———◦———

## "I WONDER WHAT'S IN IT"

We sit at a table delightfully spread
And teeming with good things to eat.
And daintily finger the cream-tinted bread,
Just needing to make it complete
A film of the butter so yellow and sweet,
Well suited to make every minute
A dream of delight. And yet while we eat
We cannot help asking, "What's in it?"
Oh, maybe this bread contains alum or chalk
Or sawdust chopped up very fine
Or gypsum in powder about which they talk,
Terra alba just out of the mine.
And our faith in the butter is apt to be weak,
For we haven't a good place to pin it
Annato's so yellow and beef fat so sleek
Oh, I wish I could know what is in it.
The pepper perhaps contains cocoanut shells,
And the mustard is cottonseed meal;
And the coffee, in sooth, of baked chicory smells,
And the terrapin tastes like roast veal.
The wine which you drink never heard of a grape,
But of tannin and coal tar is made;
And you could not be certain, except for their shape,
That the eggs by a chicken were laid.
And the salad which bears such an innocent look
And whispers of fields that are green
Is covered with germs, each armed with a hook
To grapple with liver and spleen.
The banquet how fine, don't begin it
Till you think of the past and the future and sigh,
"How I wonder, I wonder, what's in it."

HARVEY WASHINGTON WILEY, 1899

# CAST OF CHARACTERS

This account of Harvey Wiley's life and his battle for the enactment and enforcement of the United States' first national law regulating food, drink, and drugs includes many people whose lives or careers intersected with or influenced Wiley's. Among them were all U.S. presidents from Chester A. Arthur to Calvin Coolidge.

Others included:

*Jane Addams*: The Chicago activist and reformer, cofounder of the nation's first settlement house, also cofounded the National Consumers League.

*Nelson Aldrich*: This powerful and wealthy U.S. senator, a Rhode Island Republican so influential in government that the press nicknamed him "General Manager of the Nation," was a friend to many major corporations and strongly opposed the idea of regulating food and drink for safety.

*Russell A. Alger*: As secretary of war, he somewhat reluctantly ordered investigations into the food that had been supplied to army troops during the Spanish-American War.

*Robert M. Allen*: The chief food chemist for the state of Kentucky was an outspoken advocate of pure-food legislation and a valuable Wiley ally.

*Carl L. Alsberg*: Succeeding Wiley as chief of the USDA Bureau of Chemistry, he continued to pursue many of his predecessor's key cases, including lawsuits against the Coca-Cola Company and the producers of saccharin.

*Thomas Antisell*: This early USDA chief chemist investigated food adulteration during the 1860s and found it a problem but acknowledged that there was no mechanism for regulation.

*J. Ogden Armour*: The heir to founder Philip Armour's Armour and Company meatpacking in Chicago; he, like his father, opposed food safety regulations. The company was the basis for Upton Sinclair's fictional "Anderson" food-processing company in his bestselling novel *The Jungle*.

*Ray Stannard Baker*: A muckraking *McClure's* journalist, he advised his friend Upton Sinclair on proposed revisions to *The Jungle*.

*Jesse Park Battershall*: Author of a leading book, *Food Adulteration and Its Detection*, the nineteenth-century chemist blasted processors, bemoaned the lack of regulation, and described home purity tests that could be used by anxious family cooks.

*Albert Beveridge*: A progressive Republican senator from Indiana, he played a role in pushing pure-food legislation, especially the Meat Inspection Law of 1906.

*Willard Bigelow*: The lead chemist for the Hygienic Table Trials, also known as the Poison Squad, he was a dedicated ally of Wiley's and a dedicated chemist, once described as a "man of blue blazes and sulfurous smokes."

*Charles J. Bonaparte*: The U.S. attorney general under Theodore Roosevelt issued a key ruling agreeing with Wiley on whiskey-labeling requirements.

*George Rothwell Brown*: A *Washington Post* reporter, he made the Poison Squad experiments famous but also wrote fake news stories about them.

*Joseph Gurney Cannon*: The powerful and corrupt Speaker of the House opposed regulation and battled with Wiley over proposed pure-food legislation.

*Russell Chittenden*: As a Yale physiologist, he warned against some additives but on the Remsen Board, established after passage of the 1906 law, he was often a pro-industry defender of preservatives.

*Norman J. Coleman*: As commissioner of agriculture in Grover Cleveland's first term, he was a Wiley ally who initiated investigations into food purity.

*Peter Collier*: Wiley's predecessor as chief chemist clashed with the agriculture commissioner. Angry at being replaced, he orchestrated attacks on Wiley in an attempt to get his job back.

*C. A. Crampton*: A chemist on Wiley's staff, he authored a report that found potentially dangerous doses of salicylic acid in alcoholic beverages.

*Chauncey Depew*: A reporter's tale of corruption by this senator from New York, a wealthy former railroad lawyer and a friend of Theodore Roosevelt, caused the president to lash out at the "muckraking" press.

*Grenville Dodge*: A Civil War veteran and businessman, he headed the Dodge Commission investigation into allegations of adulterated army rations during the Spanish-American War.

*Henry Irving Dodge*: The writer worked with Willard Bigelow on "The Truth About Food Adulteration," a high-profile series for *Woman's Home Companion* magazine.

*Frank Nelson Doubleday*: The publishing firm founder somewhat reluctantly agreed, at his partner's urgings, to publish Upton Sinclair's novel *The Jungle*.

*Herbert Henry Dow*: The founder of Dow Chemical Company opposed pure-food legislation and complained that Wiley ran a "disinformation campaign" against chemical additives to food.

*Frederick L. Dunlap*: An ambitious, politically minded academic, he was appointed "associate chemist" as the agriculture secretary sought to undermine Wiley's authority.

*Finley Peter Dunne*: The humor columnist, through his fictional character Mr. Dooley, poked fun at President Roosevelt's combative habits—including the president's reaction to grisly details in *The Jungle*.

*Charles P. Eagan*: Army commissary general during the Spanish-American War, he became enraged at accusations that he fed "embalmed beef" to troops.

*Mark Hanna*: A businessman, political operative, and U.S. senator, he became a close ally and adviser to President McKinley.

*Henry J. Heinz*: The food processor and founder of H.J. Heinz Company advocated for pure food and decent working conditions, developed a preservative-free commercial ketchup recipe, and actively promoted his products as the safest in the country.

*Albert Heller*: A Chicago manufacturer, he vigorously defended food preservatives, especially his product Freezine, which used formaldehyde to slow decomposition of meat and milk.

*William P. Hepburn*: An Iowa congressman, he led efforts in the House to pass a pure-food law and cosponsored the Hepburn-McCumber bill, which preceded the 1906 law.

*Weldon Heyburn*: The U.S. senator from Idaho chaired the Committee on Manufactures from 1903 to 1913. Although not usually a reformer, he pushed food and drug legislation largely because of his dislike of false advertising by drugmakers.

*August Wilhelm von Hofmann*: A leading German chemist of the 1800s, his research laid groundwork for the development of coal-tar dyes, which became the leading coloring agents used in food and drink.

*Harry L. Hollingworth*: A Columbia University psychologist, he did precise measurements of caffeine's effects on human subjects and testified as an expert witness for Coca-Cola in a 1911 trial

*Warwick Hough*: A lawyer and lobbyist for the National Wholesale Liquor Distributors Association and for Monsanto, he fought fiercely against regulation of his clients.

*Burton Howard*: The chief of the Chemistry Bureau's Microchemical Laboratory coauthored a study on home detection of food adulteration.

*John Hurty*: The Indiana state health officer crusaded against preservatives in milk and for public-health laws, successfully persuading the state to pass food safety regulations ahead of the federal government. Like Wiley, he had been on the faculty at Purdue University.

*Lyman Kebler*: The USDA chemist specializing in pharmaceuticals exposed many patent medicines as worthless and/or harmful. He worked particularly hard to identify the unlabeled use of stimulants in American soft drinks.

*Anna "Nan" Kelton*: See Anna Wiley.

*Josephine Kelton*: She disapproved when the much-older Wiley courted her daughter but eventually became his mother-in-law.

*Edwin F. Ladd*: The outspoken North Dakota food chemist successfully campaigned for a state food safety law and went on to fight for food purity on a national scale, becoming a leading critic of corporate politics at the U.S. Department of Agriculture. He was elected to the U.S. Senate in 1920.

*Alice Lakey*: A progressive activist from New Jersey, this Wiley ally became the influential head of the Pure Food Committee of the National Consumers League.

*George Loring*: The commissioner of agriculture under President Arthur, he hired Harvey Wiley as the department's chief chemist.

*Isaac Marcosson*: An editor at Doubleday, Page & Company with a strong interest in marketing campaigns, he enthusiastically urged publication of Upton Sinclair's *The Jungle*.

*John Marshall*: A professor of chemistry at the University of Pennsylvania and a nationally known toxicologist, he tested the effects of borax (with which he dosed himself), a popular early-twentieth-century food preservative, and the stimulant caffeine.

*William Mason*: The reformist U.S. senator from Illinois convened, in 1899, an extensive series of hearings investigating the contamination of the nation's food supply and introduced legislation, ultimately successfully, to regulate for that problem.

*George P. McCabe*: The Agriculture Department's industry-friendly solicitor worked against Wiley's most aggressive attempts to enforce the pure-food law.

*Porter J. McCumber*: A U.S. senator from North Dakota, he sponsored pure-food legislation and scheduled hearings on the issue of adulteration.

*Hippolyte Mège-Mouriès*: A chemist, he entered a contest to invent a butter substitute and came up with what he called *oléomargarine*, made from beef fat.

*Nelson Miles*: The army's commanding general called for an investigation into the quality of the food supplied to his troops in the Spanish-American War, accusing the military of feeding his men "embalmed beef."

*Julius Sterling Morton*: The secretary of agriculture during the second Cleveland administration was an obsessive budget cutter who suppressed Wiley's work in food safety and refused congressional money to support food safety research.

*Sebastian Mueller*: An executive of the H.J. Heinz Company, he defied his peers in the food-processing industry both by developing preservative-free products and advocating for pure-food legislation.

*John Mullaly*: The American journalist authored a mid-nineteenth-century book about the sickening practices employed by the dairy industry in New York City, from watering down milk to the use of toxic additives.

*Henry Needham:* A muckraking journalist and an activist, he publicly criticized Theodore Roosevelt's agriculture secretary as too close to industry, supported Wiley in his departmental battles, and helped form a pro-consumer activist group called the People's Lobby.

*Charles P. Neill:* President Roosevelt sent Neill, his commissioner of labor, to investigate the meatpacking industry in Chicago after *The Jungle* was published.

*Algernon Paddock:* A U.S. senator from Nebraska, he sponsored a proposed food-regulation law in 1891. It failed but presaged the 1906 law.

*Walter Hines Page:* A partner in Doubleday, Page & Company, he advocated the publication of the shocking novel *The Jungle* and helped publicize it.

*S. S. Perry:* As the initial chef for Wiley's Hygienic Table Trials, he ran a meticulous kitchen but was talkative and tended to let secrets slip.

*David Graham Phillips:* The reformist journalist, author of a book on government corruption titled *The Treason of the Senate*, and critic of what he saw as a watered-down food law infuriated President Theodore Roosevelt.

*Paul Pierce:* An advocate of moderation and pure food and a Wiley ally, he was a writer, editor, and publisher of *What to Eat*, later *National Food Magazine*, based in Chicago.

*John F. Queeny:* The founder of Monsanto Chemical Company made saccharin and the crystalline form of caffeine used in soft drinks. He steadfastly opposed regulation of industry products.

*Ira Remsen:* A codiscoverer of saccharin, the Johns Hopkins University chemist headed a high-priced consulting panel formed to review and often countermand Wiley's findings.

*James B. Reynolds:* Roosevelt sent Reynolds, an activist and a settlement house manager, along with Charles P. Neill to investigate Chicago meatpackers.

*Clifford Richardson*: A chemist on Wiley's staff, Richardson investigated the rampant adulteration of spices. His findings revealed revolting practices, including the use of ground shells, dirt, and rock dust.

*Elihu Root*: As U.S. secretary of war, he helped modernize the American military after the Spanish-American War. He also backed importation of Cuban sugar in the war's aftermath. As secretary of state, he tempered some of Roosevelt's more explosive tendencies.

*Jeremiah Rusk*: As secretary of agriculture in the Benjamin Harrison administration, he greatly expanded investigations of food adulteration, which he considered one of his farmer-friendly policies.

*James Shepard*: The South Dakota food commissioner investigated nitrates in flour, backed Wiley's pure-food cause, and opposed Agriculture Secretary James Wilson.

*James S. Sherman*: His canning company used saccharin as a sweetener. As a New York congressman, he opposed requiring that labels list ingredients.

*Upton Sinclair*: An avowed socialist, he wrote *The Jungle* to expose brutal work conditions, but its lurid descriptions of meatpacking practices shocked readers far more.

*Lincoln Steffens*: The muckraking journalist advised Upton Sinclair on proposed revisions to *The Jungle* and later scolded Roosevelt over an antipress speech that accused reporters of being doom-and-gloom muckrakers.

*Mark Sullivan*: An investigative journalist and author, Sullivan wrote about drug fraud for national magazines and also about Wiley's public campaign to win support for the pure-food bill. He included that work in his best-selling history of the United States, titled *Our Times*.

*Louis Swift*: The heir to the Swift & Company meatpacking firm, he rebutted all evidence of shoddy production and defended his business as "conducted in a proper and sanitary manner" during the scandal generated by publication of *The Jungle*.

*Alonzo E. Taylor*: A physiological chemist at the University of Pennsylvania, Taylor was a member of the Remsen Board, which reviewed Wiley's decisions.

*Edmund Haynes Taylor Jr.*: Known by the Kentucky honorific "Colonel," he was a distiller of aged bourbon and namesake of the Old Taylor brand, who fought the idea that blended whiskeys were of equal quality to his own products.

*James W. Wadsworth*: A New York Republican, he chaired the House Committee on Agriculture and preferentially called upon industry witnesses at a hearing on a meat-inspection amendment following publication of *The Jungle*.

*Alex Wedderburn*: In the 1890s, Wiley hired this activist-writer to produce consumer-friendly information about Chemistry Bureau findings for the public, especially concerning issues of food safety.

*Anna "Nan" Kelton Wiley*: A librarian at the Agriculture Department and later the Library of Congress, she married Harvey Wiley in 1910. She was known in her own right as a suffragette and longtime advocate of public health and social justice issues in general.

*James Wilson*: A former Iowa farmer and the secretary of agriculture through the McKinley, Roosevelt, and Taft administrations, Wilson was at first a supporter of Harvey Wiley, but later clashes over the pure-food law enforcement led him to become increasingly hostile.

*John H. Young*: A Northwestern University chemist specializing in pharmacology, he was a member of the Remsen Board, which served as a foil to Wiley.

# INTRODUCTION

We tend these days to cast a romantic glow over the foods of our forefathers. In such rosy light, we may imagine grandparents or great-grandparents thriving happily—and solely—on farm-fresh produce and pasture-raised livestock. We may even believe that they ate and drank in a world untouched by the chemically enhanced and deceptive food manufacturing practices of today.

In this we would be wrong.

By the mid-nineteenth century, in fact, many foods and drinks sold in the United States had earned a reputation as often untrustworthy and occasionally downright dangerous.

Milk offers a stunning case in point. Dairymen, especially those serving crowded American cities in the nineteenth century, learned that there were profits to be made by skimming and watering down their product. The standard recipe was a pint of lukewarm water to every quart of milk—after the cream had been skimmed off. To improve the bluish look of the remaining liquid, milk producers learned to add whitening agents such as plaster of paris or chalk. Sometimes they added a dollop of molasses to give the liquid a more golden, creamy color. To mimic the expected layer of cream on top, they might also add a final squirt of something yellowish, occasionally pureed calf brains.

"Where are the police?" demanded New York journalist John Mullaly as he detailed such practices and worse in his 1853 book, *The Milk Trade in New York and Vicinity*. Mullaly's evidence included reports from frustrated physicians stating that thousands of children were killed in New York City every year by dirty (bacteria-laden) and deliberately tainted milk. His demands for prosecution were partly theater. Despite his and others' outraged demands for change, no laws existed to make such adulterations illegal. Still Mullaly continued to ask, when would enough be enough?

Fakery and adulteration ran rampant in other American products as well. "Honey" often proved to be thickened, colored corn syrup, and "vanilla" extract a mixture of alcohol and brown food coloring. "Strawberry" jam could be sweetened paste made from mashed apple peelings laced with grass seeds and dyed red. "Coffee" might be largely sawdust, or wheat, beans, beets, peas, and dandelion seeds, scorched black and ground to resemble the genuine article. Containers of "pepper," "cinnamon," or "nutmeg" were frequently laced with a cheaper filler material such as pulverized coconut shells, charred rope, or occasionally floor sweepings. "Flour" routinely contained crushed stone or gypsum as a cheap extender. Ground insects could be mixed into brown sugar, often without detection—their use linked to an unpleasant condition known as "grocer's itch."

By the end of the nineteenth century, the sweeping industrial revolution—and the rise of industrial chemistry—had also brought a host of new chemical additives and synthetic compounds into the food supply. Still unchecked by government regulation, basic safety testing, or even labeling requirements, food and drink manufacturers embraced the new materials with enthusiasm, mixing them into goods destined for the grocery store at sometimes lethal levels.

The most popular preservative for milk—a product prone to rot in an era that lacked effective refrigeration—was formaldehyde, its use adapted from the newest embalming practices of undertakers. Processors employed formaldehyde solutions—sold under innocuous names such as Preservaline—to restore decaying meats as well. Other popular preservatives included salicylic acid, a pharmaceutical compound, and borax, a mineral-based material best known as a cleaning product.

Food manufacturers also adopted new synthetic dyes, derived from coal by-products, to improve the color of their less appealing products. They found inexpensive synthetic compounds that they could secretly substitute into food and drink—saccharin to replace sugar; acetic acid instead of lemon juice; lab-created alcohols, dyed and flavored, to mimic aged whiskeys and fine wines. As progressive Wisconsin senator Robert M. La Follette described such practices in 1886: "Ingenuity, striking hands with cunning trickery, compounds a substance to counterfeit an article of food. It is made to look like something it is not; to taste and smell like something it is not; to sell something it is not, and so do deceive the purchaser."

No wonder, then, that when alarmed citizens began pushing for federal help in checking such fraud and fakery, they did so under the banner of purity. They saw themselves as "pure food" crusaders, fighting to clean up not only a contaminated supply chain but also a system that was dirty to its roots and protected by politicians friendly to industry. As Mullaly had done decades earlier, the new crusaders—scientists and journalists, state health officials and leaders of women's groups—loudly deplored their national government's willingness to allow such corrupt practices to continue.

The leaders of the pure-food movement united behind the idea that regulatory oversight was the only realistic answer. They'd seen many times that the country's food processors and manufacturers felt little or no responsibility to protect the food supply, especially if it meant reducing profits. Formaldehyde, for instance, had been directly linked to deaths—notably of children drinking what came to be called embalmed milk—without any move by producers to discontinue the preservative's use. The preservative's usefulness in salvaging bad milk—otherwise unsalable—was too valuable to lose.

American corporations had successfully and repeatedly blocked efforts to pass even modest food safety legislation. This especially galled consumer safety advocates because governments in Europe *were* enacting protective measures; some foods and drinks sold freely in the United States were now banned abroad. Unlike their American counterparts, European beer and wine makers were blocked from using risky preservatives in their beverages (although they could put them in products destined for U.S. sales).

At the first National Pure Food and Drug Congress, held in Washington, DC, in 1898, delegates noted that American food fraud had continued to flourish since La Follette's speech on the floor of the Senate some thirteen years earlier. How long would the country go without some policy or plan to deal with industrial food? No one knew. But surely, one delegate suggested hopefully, "this great country [must eventually] take its proper place among civilized nations and protect its citizens."

Many of the several hundred pure-food advocates at the congress saw their best chance for progress in what might have seemed an unlikely source of heroics: a small chemistry unit in the U.S. Department of Agriculture and its chief scientist, a middle-aged Indiana native who'd trained in chemistry at Harvard University.

But that was, in reality, a savvy choice.

Decades before the federal government had even considered anything resembling a food and drug administration, the Department of Agriculture (created in 1862 by President Abraham Lincoln) was tasked with analyzing the composition of American food and drink. It was the only agency to do so and that work was mostly in response to unhappy farmers who saw manufactured food undercutting their market. An 1870s complaint from a Minnesota agricultural association asked the division to investigate the "misapplication of science to deodorize rotten eggs, revive rancid butter, and dye pithy peas" green again.

But it wasn't until the Agriculture Department named Harvey Washington Wiley chief chemist in 1883—recruiting him from a job at Purdue University—that the agency began methodically investigating food and drink fraud. Although best known as an expert in sugar chemistry, Wiley had studied food fakery while still in Indiana and had warned then that "counterfeit" products could be considered a threat to public health. Upon arrival at the Agriculture Department, he promptly initiated a series of investigations of products ranging from butter to spices to wine and beer, building a detailed and sometimes horrifying portrait of the country's food supply. Those reports would lead him, in the early twentieth century, to test some of the most suspect chemical additives on human volunteers, a series of experiments dubbed the "Poison Squad" studies by the nation's newspapers.

His food and drink investigations—and the detailed criticism they contained—both infuriated manufacturers and alarmed Wiley's business-minded supervisors. But he refused, under pressure, to stop the studies. And as the pure-food advocates noted with admiration, Wiley stuck by his research—and his researchers—even when they reached conclusions that embarrassed powerful corporate and political interests.

Even worse, in the view of those interests, he publicized the findings. He steadfastly sought to inform not just government officials and lawmakers but also the public at large—including pure-food activists—about what his investigations revealed. The years of research findings, he told a congressional committee, had convinced him that polite resignation was unacceptable.

And Wiley tended to stand out anyway. He was a tall man, dark haired and dark eyed, imposing in stature, humorously charming in private, by turns ministerial and theatrical in public. He would become the best-known face of the national battle for food safety regulation at the turn of the twentieth century, building an alliance of consumer advocates and rallying them, in the face of repeated setbacks, to stay in the fight. He was America's first great food safety chemist, but his greatest contribution to the cause—even more than the scientific work he conducted and supervised, even more than his considerable ability to dramatize the cause—was "the inspired generalship he offered," wrote public-health historian Oscar Anderson Jr. Wiley, he added, "was the one leader who consistently saw the big picture," the long-term goal of strong consumer protection.

Wiley also had his imperfections. The son of a lay preacher, he tended to claim the moral high ground largely for his alliance alone. Faced with hostility, he became more rigid in his stance, often refusing to compromise even on small details. He quarreled over pictures on labels as firmly as he quarreled over toxic compounds in baked goods. His refusal to make nice, even when nitpicking, strained his alliances and, some felt, limited his effectiveness. He knew that too.

He failed, Wiley himself believed, to achieve the kind of fearlessly tough regulatory protections he wanted for his country. He could not forget or forgive the times that he'd stood up alone in—and sometimes lost—the fight against corporate interference in the law. His own criticisms of his grand achievement—the passage and enforcement of the landmark 1906 Pure Food and Drug Act—may well have undercut our perceptions of his accomplishments and caused us to undervalue his contributions.

But in that too we would be wrong.

Yes, we are still fighting for pure food. But let us recognize that we've come a wonderfully long way from the unregulated food, drink, and drug horrors of the nineteenth century. And in an era when business interests rail—as they did in Wiley's time—about government overreach and the need to eliminate regulations, we should remember how much Wiley's work laid the foundation that allows us to stand up to that. He changed the way we regulate, and he was essential in changing the way we think about food, health, and consumer protection.

It may not always serve us to cast a rosy glow over the past—or even over its heroes. But we should take care not to forget those early lessons on protecting our country—and ourselves. And as we look back to that first fierce battle for federal consumer protection, we would do well to remember what an intensely personal fight it often was. There's a remarkable and revealing story—one that illuminates where we stand today—behind the simple fact that what we now call the "pure food and drug law" was once known, coast to coast, as "Dr. Wiley's Law."

# PART I

*One*

# A CHEMICAL WILDERNESS

## 1844–1887

———— ● ————

*We sit at a table delightfully spread*
*And teeming with good things to eat.*

The sixth of seven children, Harvey Washington Wiley was born on April 16, 1844, in a log cabin on a small farm in Kent, Indiana, about a hundred miles northeast of the farm where Abraham Lincoln had grown up a few decades earlier.

The humble timber dwelling was an icon of authenticity for nineteenth-century Americans, particularly because Lincoln (born in adjacent Kentucky), as well as presidents such as Andrew Jackson and Zachary Taylor, had made their log-cabin beginnings a keystone of their respective political images. In later years Wiley liked to joke about his similarly modest origins. "I am not possessed with a common prejudice that a man must be born in a log cabin to attain greatness in the United States," he said.

But like those political luminaries, Wiley grew up working the land. By age six he was driving the family cows back to the barn for milking each day. At ten he was behind a plow. His father, Preston, was one of the first Indiana farmers to grow sorghum cane, and with curious son Harvey helping, the boy learned to boil down juice pressed from the grassy grain crop into a sweet syrup. That transformation helped spur his interest in food processing and in other types of sugars, one of the inspirations for his later career.

Preston Wiley had little schooling but valued learning, another strong influence on his second-youngest child. The father, who was a lay minister as well as a farmer, had even taught himself Greek. A fierce opponent of slavery—he made a point of gathering his children around for evening readings of the powerful abolitionist novel *Uncle Tom's Cabin*—farmer Wiley also believed in acting upon one's principles. Only three miles from the Ohio River, the family farm became Indiana's southernmost stop on the Underground Railroad. Escaped slaves from Kentucky, once they'd made it across the water, knew to seek out Preston Wiley. Under cover of darkness, he would escort them safely to the next stop, eight miles northward.

Harvey Wiley was preparing for college when the Civil War broke out, and his parents, despite their antislavery stance, were determined that he continue with it. He enrolled at nearby Hanover College in 1863 but a year later decided he could no longer sit out the war. After joining the 137th Indiana Infantry, he was deployed to Tennessee and Alabama, where he guarded Union-held railroad lines and spent his spare hours studying anatomy, reciting daily from a textbook to a fellow soldier. It was only a few months later that he and many of his fellows fell ill in a plague of measles sweeping through the camp. He was still ailing when his regiment returned to Indianapolis that September. He received a discharge, went home to recuperate, and then returned to Hanover, where he earned a bachelor's and then a master of arts degree in 1867. But he had by then, influenced by his army days, determined to become a physician. In his graduation address, he spoke of his then-chosen profession with typical over-the-top exuberance. The medical man, Wiley declaimed, "can not climb to Heaven and pull down immortality," but he can help achieve a longer life "full of health and happiness and hope."

To earn money for medical school, Wiley first taught Latin and Greek at a small Christian school in Indianapolis. He spent the following summer apprenticed to a country physician in Kentucky, then enrolled in Indiana Medical College, where he earned an MD, graduating in 1871. By that time, though, he'd learned that although he admired the work of medical practitioners, he did not enjoy caring for sick people. He accepted an offer to teach chemistry in the Indianapolis public high schools and there began to appreciate the insights offered by that branch of science or, as he came to see it, the "nobility and magnitude" of chemistry. Realizing he had a passion for the rapidly advancing field, he went back to school yet again, this time to study chemistry at Harvard University, which—as was typical at the time—awarded him a bachelor of science degree after only a few months of study. In 1874 he accepted a position at Indiana's newly opened Purdue University as its first (and only) chemistry professor.

"I find so many things that I do not know as I pursue my studies," he wrote in his diary during that first year at Purdue, as he struggled to assemble a working laboratory. "My own profession is still a wilderness." During the following years, though, Wiley developed a reputation as the state's go-to scientist for analyzing virtually anything—from water quality to rocks to soil samples—and especially foodstuffs. This was accelerated by a working sabbatical in 1878 in the newly united German Empire, considered the global leader in chemical research. He studied at one of the empire's pioneering food-quality laboratories and attended lectures by world-renowned scientist August Wilhelm von Hofmann, who had been the first director of the Royal College of Chemistry in London. Von Hofmann was a pioneering industry chemist. Famed for his 1866 discovery of formaldehyde, he would later do work leading to the development of industrial dyes that the food industry embraced in the late nineteenth century. When Wiley returned to Purdue, he brought back specialized instruments for analyzing food chemistry, acquired in Germany and paid for with his own savings when the university refused to do so.

European governments—especially those of Germany and Great Britain—had been far quicker than the U.S. government to recognize and to address problems of food adulteration. In 1820 a pioneering book by chemist Fredrick Accum, titled *A Treatise on Adulterations of Food, and Culinary Poisons,* had aroused widespread public outrage when it was published in London. Accum minced no words: "Our pickles are made green by copper; our vinegar rendered sharp by sulphuric acid; our cream composed of rice powder or arrowroot in bad milk; our comfits mixed of sugar, starch and clay, and coloured with preparations of copper and lead; our catsup often formed of the dregs of distilled vinegar with a decoction of the outer green husk of walnuts, and seasoned with all-spice," he wrote.

As Accum noted, the poisonous practices of his time dated back many years. Long before the nineteenth century's new industrial dyes, merchants and processors used various colorful substances to make their wares look more enticing. Confectioners often turned to poisonous metallic elements and compounds. Green came from arsenic or copper, yellow from lead chromate, cheerful rose and pink tones from red lead. In 1830 an editorial in *The Lancet,* the British medical journal, complained that "millions of children are thus daily dosed" with lethal substances. But the practices continued, largely due to business pressures on would-be government regulators.

By midcentury, though, casualties were starting to mount in Britain. In 1847 three English children fell seriously ill after eating birthday cake decorated with arsenic-tinted green leaves. Five years later, two London brothers died after eating a cake whose frosting contained both arsenic and copper. In an 1854 report, London physician Arthur Hassall tracked forty cases of child poisoning caused by penny candies.

Three years later, twenty-one people in Bradford, Yorkshire, died after consuming candy accidentally laced with deadly arsenic trioxide—"accidentally" because the confectioner meant to mix in plaster of paris instead. Although he had noticed his workers falling ill while mixing up the stuff, the business owner had put the candy on sale anyway. He was arrested and jailed, as was the pharmacist who'd mistakenly sold him the poison in place of plaster. But they could not be convicted of any crime. Britain had no law against making unsafe—or even lethal—food products.

Fury over the Bradford incident spurred the passage in 1860 of Britain's Act for Preventing Adulteration in Food and Drink. Business interests managed to limit the fine for poisoning food to a mere £5, but at least it was a precedent.

Although not yet nearly loud enough to prod Congress, there were voices of outrage in America too, where journalists like John Mullaly railed against "milk-poison" and George Thorndike Angell, a Massachusetts lawyer and philanthropist better known for his work against cruelty to animals, loudly derided dishonest food producers. In an 1879 speech to the American Social Science Public Health Association, Angell recited a disgusting list of commercially sold foods that included diseased and parasite-ridden meat and processed animal fat passed off as butter and cheese.

"They poison and cheat the consumer; affect, and in many cases destroy, the health not only of the rich but of the poor," Angell charged, blasting dishonest food producers as little better than "the pirates who plunder our ships on the ocean or the highway men who rob and murder on the land." For good measure, he mailed the text of his speech to newspapers nationwide—and to the dismay of food processors, it received prominent display. The *American Grocer*, a trade publication, dismissed him as sensationalist and "doing a disservice to consumers." But the *Grocer* acknowledged that some problems were real, especially the too-often poisonous nature of milk and colored candy, and the reputation harm done by fraudsters. That year, in response to Angell's concerns, Virginia congressman Richard Lee T. Beale introduced legislation that would have banned interstate commerce in chemically altered foods. A report to the Committee on Manufactures warned: "Not only are substances of less value commingled with those of greater, but such as are injurious to health, and we have no doubt often destructive of life, are freely used in manufacturing and preparing for consuming the necessaries and luxuries of life." The bill was referred out of committee, where it promptly died through lack of further action. But an uneasy awareness of a troubled food supply was starting to grow.

In 1881 the Indiana State Board of Health asked Wiley to examine the purity of commercially sold sweet substances, particularly honey and maple syrup. At Purdue, Wiley had been studying potential new crops and methods for making sweeteners. Inspired by his father's venture into sorghum, he had even worked out an improved process for getting syrup from its woody stalks. After his studies in Germany, Wiley possessed the right training and tools to conduct the study, and through presentations at the American Association for the Advancement of Science he'd gained a reputation as one of the country's leading sugar chemists. The investigation requested by the state—and the political fallout—would serve to plunge him further into his life's work. It was, as he later remembered, "my first participation in the fray."

A report from the National Academy of Sciences had already warned that jars labeled "honey" were often tinted corn syrup, with a scrap of honeycomb tossed in to complete the deception. Corn syrup—not the much later "high-fructose" version—was a nineteenth-century innovation. Russian chemist Gottlieb Kirchhoff had in 1812 devised an inexpensive process for turning cornstarch into the sugar glucose. He combined the starch with diluted hydrochloric acid and heated the mixture under pressure. The process proved hugely profitable in the corn-rich United States. By 1881 almost two dozen factories were operating in the Midwest, turning

25,000 bushels of corn a day into sugary products. "The manufacture of sirup and sugar from corn-starch is an industry which in this country is scarcely a dozen years old and yet is one of no inconsiderable magnitude," Wiley wrote in his report.

In much of the English-speaking world, "corn" could mean any kind of grain crop—barley or wheat, for example. But in English-speaking North America it had long meant maize, a staple of indigenous people in the Western Hemisphere for thousands of years. When Europeans arrived, they called it Indian corn and began growing it for themselves. By the mid-1800s corn had become a primary crop of farmlands from Pennsylvania to Nebraska, from Minnesota to Missouri and beyond—and engendered a whole new array of manufactured food products.

"Corn, the new American king," Wiley wrote, "now supplies us with bread, meat, and sugar, which we need, as well as with the whiskey we could do without." He estimated that corn-derived glucose had about two-thirds the sweetening power of cane sugar; it was also far cheaper, produced for less than half the cost.

Those who made and sold the sweetener often labeled it either "corn sugar" or "corn syrup." This was after European practice. Germany had "potato sugar," for example, and France produced a "grape sugar." But Wiley, always a stickler for accuracy (a trait that would over the years irritate more plainspoken colleagues, including President Roosevelt), thought the corn-based product should be called glucose or glucose syrup. This, he emphasized, both was the technically accurate term and also clearly differentiated it from traditional sugars made from cane or beet. (In the twenty-first century, amid a diabetes epidemic, many think of "glucose" in terms of human blood sugar levels. But the sugar product derived from cornstarch—or from wheat, potatoes, and other starches—does bear the same molecular signature.)

In Wiley's day such scientific precision could seem essential to maintaining a sense of order in research. Chemists of the midnineteenth century had only begun to tease out the nature of molecular bonds. In the late 1850s the German chemist Friedrich August Kekulé put forth the first theory of how atoms come together to form a molecule. Chemistry superstar Von Hofmann, then at the University of Berlin, made the first stick-and-ball models of molecules in the 1860s. In Germany, Wiley had learned to respect such precision, a point illustrated by the instruments he'd brought home with him. One of his favorites was called a polariscope (or polarimeter). At Purdue he used it to tell the difference between types of sugars by passing polarized light through sweetened substances and measuring the angle at which the light rotated. "Glucose presents several anomalies when examined with polarized light," Wiley explained, compared with the true sugars.

He was not shocked when his tests showed that a full 90 percent of his syrup samples were fakes. Shop owners had told him that these new syrups were so sweet and inexpensive that they had almost "driven all others out of the market." Testing of honey samples also turned up rampant fakery. He somewhat mockingly referred to the counterfeit product as "entirely free of bee mediation," noting that even the bit of honeycomb that producers stuck in the jar was phony, made from paraffin. In his report, Wiley found no fault with corn syrup per se—it was, after all, a natural sweetener—but he thought that a food or ingredient ought to be called what it was. To fill a bottle with "glucose" and label it as more-expensive maple syrup was to deceive the consumer. In addition to finding corn syrup masquerading as other sugars, the study turned up impurities left by the manufacturing process. There was copper from mixing tubs and some chemical remnants of charred animal bones (used as a charcoal filter), and in some samples he detected sulfuric acid.

Wiley's report, published both in the state record and in *Popular Science* in the summer of 1881, gratified those in the real maple syrup business, but it annoyed corn growers, corn-syrup manufacturers, and the bottlers of the mislabeled products—which, put together, made a far larger and more influential interest group than that consisting of maple tree tappers. Wiley, as he would for the rest of his career, had begun making powerful enemies.

Surprisingly, the group that seemed most bothered by his report was beekeepers. Instead of thanking him for exposing what the chemist called "the injury done to the honey industry" by the corn-based fakes, that industry's trade journals denounced him and the study, referring to it as "Wiley's Lie." The honey producers worried about damage to their reputations. But it became obvious as well that there were "beekeepers" who had not, of late, been bothering to keep bees.

Wiley, characteristically, doubled down. He wrote a more in-depth report for the Indiana Board of Health, stressing the importance of truthful labeling. The second report included instructions for how to detect adulterations, and it strongly recommended that Indiana set purity standards for sugar products produced and sold in the state. "The dangers of adulteration are underrated," he wrote, "when it is for a moment supposed that any counterfeit food can be tolerated without depraving the public taste, and impairing the public safeguards of human life."

Despite the political pushback, he closed with a firm call for action. It was high time, he wrote, that "the demand for honest food should be heard in terms making no denial." He wasn't afraid, as he would say throughout his career, to stand up for what he thought right. After all, he'd been raised that way.

Like Harvey Wiley, Peter Collier, chief chemist of the Department of Agriculture, was fascinated by the science of sugars and the plants from which they could be produced. Even more enthusiastic about sorghum cane than Wiley was, the Yale-educated Collier saw it as a crop of the future. He envisioned glowing copper-and-green sorghum fields across the country, a potential source of sugar as bountiful as corn or even sugarcane.

His boss, the pragmatic George Loring, did not share Collier's vision. Commissioner Loring (titled "commissioner" because the USDA was not yet a cabinet-level department) was a former Massachusetts physician with a special interest in treating the often-crippling diseases of farm animals. The sorghum disagreement between Collier and Loring might have stayed a matter of internal discussion except for one problem. Whenever Collier felt aggrieved, he had a habit of complaining about the commissioner to the Washington press. Exasperated by newspaper stories in which his chief chemist suggested that he was an idiot, Loring in 1882 sought and received permission from President Chester A. Arthur to replace Collier with a more amiable scientist. Later that year, at a December meeting of Mississippi sugarcane growers, Loring heard a speech by Harvey Wiley, who had been invited to present an overview of sugar-producing crops. It was, thought Loring, a balanced presentation. It was objective. Unlike Collier, who had become increasingly fanatic about the dreamy future of sorghum, Wiley gave each crop its due. The Purdue scientist impressed the commissioner as the reasonable man he was looking for.

Two months later, Loring offered Wiley the chief chemist job. The timing was perfect. Wiley had been feeling increasingly stifled and unappreciated at Purdue. Conservative members of the university's board of trustees hadn't cared for the negative attention his state honey and syrup study had drawn, especially from the influential corn industry. One trustee had declared publicly that scientific progress was "the devil's tool." The board even publicly disapproved of Wiley's personal life, including his regular baseball games with the college students and the high-wheel bicycle that he rode to campus daily, dressed in knee breeches. Trustees had called him into a meeting to upbraid him for making a spectacle of himself, even comparing him to a circus monkey. Wiley, as he wrote in his diary, would have taken insult if he hadn't found the scolding so amusing. Yet he admitted frustration. He had just that year been considered, but passed over, for the post of university president. For the thirty-nine-year-old bachelor, Loring's offer seemed a lifeline out of a job that increasingly felt like a trap.

But he had not anticipated that the ever-combative Collier would turn his attention from Loring to him. Furious at the loss of his job and status, Collier promptly engineered a series of attacks on his designated successor. His well-placed allies wrote to farm trade journals, denigrating the Indiana sugar studies and suggesting that their author was an inferior scientist. Collier also persuaded the senators from his home state of Vermont to visit President Arthur, demanding that Wiley be denied the position. The aggressive campaign only irritated the president and it did not win Collier his job back. But it was successful in embarrassing Wiley.

"These were the first public attacks on me and they cut to the quick," Wiley later wrote. "I felt hurt to be the victim of such insinuations and misstatements." He wrote to the same publications, attempting to defend and justify his work. Collier's faction, in turn, accused him of bragging. The best way to respond to such attacks, he would gradually come to believe, "is to go about one's business and let enemies do their worst." He began packing up for the move to Washington, DC.

In 1883, the Agriculture Department's sprawling campus was situated between the Smithsonian Institution's redbrick castle and the almost-completed Washington Monument. The grounds boasted experimental gardens, greenhouses, conservatories, and a grand, modern main building, built in the 1870s, with a stylish mansard roof. The tiny Division of Chemistry, however, was tucked into what Wiley called a "damp, illy-ventilated, and wholly unsuitable" basement.

One of the first acts of the new chief chemist was to ban smoking. Not only was the laboratory air stale already but a stray spark, he feared, would have turned the place into a bonfire.

For his living quarters, Wiley rented a bedroom from a Washington family, with whom he would happily stay for the next twenty years. Treated as a well-liked family member he frequently spent evenings helping the children with their homework. Social by nature, he accepted an invitation to join the prestigious Cosmos Club, a men-only, intellectually inclined organization whose members included Alexander Graham Bell and Mark Twain. He also joined the more casual Six O'Clock Club, which by contrast did admit women and boasted American Red Cross founder Clara Barton on its executive committee.

New to the charged political climate of Washington, Wiley scored an early coup in 1885, when Grover Cleveland became president. A dedicated Republican, Wiley knew that his job security could well depend on Democrat Cleveland's choice to replace Loring as commissioner of agriculture. The chemist started a letter-writing campaign to influential friends, urging the appointment of Norman J. Coleman, a Missouri Democrat and a longtime publisher of farm trade journals, who approved of Wiley's research. The campaign worked, and Wiley was blessed with a grateful and supportive new boss.

Coleman, who would help create a national network of agricultural experiment stations, also believed that it was a public servant's duty to champion the public interest. In fact, he wanted the chief chemist to be more aggressive in tackling food safety issues—something Wiley too had been advocating. Coleman even had a suggestion for some timely official investigations. He recommended that the Chemistry Division report on the quality and healthfulness of commercially sold milk. The scientists, he proposed, also should investigate dairy products such as butter and evaluate the new and highly suspect industry of butter substitutes.

The problems of the dairy industry had continued to fester

basically unchecked. Mullaly had written in 1853 about the practice wherein distillers housed dairy cows in stinking urban warehouses where each animal was tethered immobile and fed on the spent mash, or "swill," from the fermentation process used in making whiskey, an arrangement that enriched the owners but was linked to a host of public health problems.

In the 1850s *Frank Leslie's Illustrated Newspaper* had exposed these fly-ridden, maggot-infested milk factories, where the animals stood in their own waste, subsisting on the warm swill, which still contained residual sugar and alcohol but little nutrition. Over the cow's short, miserable life, its teeth tended to rot out before the animal stopped giving milk and was sent to slaughter—or dropped dead in the stall. Pediatricians linked swill milk to a list of childhood symptoms of ill health. "I have every year grown more suspicious of distillery milk," one doctor wrote, "whenever I have seen a child presenting a sickly appearance, loose flabby flesh, weak joints, capricious appetite, frequent retchings and occasional vomitage, irregular bowels with tendency to diarrhea and fetid breath."

The notoriously corrupt Tammany Hall government of New York City resisted reform, but finally, in 1862, passed a city ordinance outlawing swill milk, to little effect. Difficult to enforce even in the city, the new law did nothing to help manage poor dairy practices beyond its boundaries. More than two decades later a study published in the *Journal of the American Chemical Society* looked at swill milk still being produced just across the Hudson River in New Jersey and found "so numerous a proportion of liquefying colonies [of bacteria] that further counting was discontinued." A subsequent report in Indiana by that state's board of health added that a random sampling of milk found "sticks, hairs, insects, blood, pus and filth."

Under Wiley the Agriculture Department's first detailed examination of food products, *Foods and Food Adulterants* (technical Bulletin no. 13), was published in three parts in 1887. It revealed, as expected, that little had improved with regard to how milk was produced and what it contained. Wiley's investigating chemists had found a routinely thinned product, dirty and whitened with chalk. It wasn't just bacteria swimming in the milk. At least one of the samples that Wiley's crew tested had worms wriggling in the bottom of the bottle. The Division of Chemistry's findings about other dairy products were more eye opening. Much of the "butter" that the scientists found on the market had nothing to do with dairy products at all except for the fictitious name on the product.

The ability of producers to so mislead resulted from the work of several French chemists, including one of the nineteenth century's greatest, Michel Eugène Chevreul. He drew from the Greek word *margarites*, meaning pearl, and added the Latin for olive, *oleum*, to coin the term *oléomargarine*, which is what he called a glossy, whitish, semisolid that two colleagues had derived from olive oil. In 1869 inventor Hippolyte Mège-Mouriès appropriated Chevreul's terminology and applied it to a butter substitute he made from beef tallow and finely ground animal stomachs. The latter was the basis of a host of butter substitutes embraced by American food processors, which began manufacturing an inventive range of such products in 1876.

Eager to expand a new market, U.S. innovators competed to improve oleomargarine, seeking patents for variations such as "suine" (from suet) and "lardine" (made from pork fat). The industry especially took off after the powerful meatpacking interests realized the potential for profit from the by-products of slaughterhouses and canneries. Barely had the idea of oleomargarine reached the fast-growing Chicago stockyards when some processors decided that if they added just a dab of actual milk to the product, they might cast off its meaty association. Trying for a more appealing name, meatpackers like the Armour brothers and Gustavus Swift borrowed another term for margarine that was in use in Britain, one that at least sounded dairy based: "butterine." Other manufacturers didn't even bother with that terminology; they simply called their oleomargarine "butter."

In his 1883 book *Life on the Mississippi*, Mark Twain recounted overheard comments made by an oleomargarine salesman from Ohio. "You can't tell it from butter," the salesman said. "By George, an EXPERT can't. . . . You are going to see the day, pretty soon, when you can't find an ounce of butter to bless yourself with, in any hotel in the Mississippi and Ohio Valleys, outside of the biggest cities. Why, we are turning out oleomargarine NOW by the thousands of tons. And we can sell it so dirt-cheap that the whole country has GOT to take it—can't get around it, you see. Butter don't stand any show. . . . Butter's had its DAY."

The dairy industry, not surprisingly, disagreed. And furiously. Dairy organizations petitioned members of Congress, demanding action and protection from such deceptive practices. The resulting hearings in both the U.S. Senate and the House of Representatives in 1885 reflected that bitterness, taking up the issue of whether margarine should even be allowed for sale in the United States.

"We face a new situation in history. Ingenuity, striking hands with cunning trickery, compounds a substance to counterfeit an article of food," charged U.S. senator Robert La Follette. A Wisconsin Republican, La Follette was firmly in the corner of that state's numerous dairymen. They objected especially to the practice of coloring oleomargarine to make it look like butter. La Follette conveniently overlooked the fact that butter itself, when produced in the winter from cows fed on hay rather than pasture grass, turns out more white than yellow—and that in addition to diluting and adulterating milk, some dairies routinely added golden coloring to their pale butter. The new, nondairy spreads were nothing better than "counterfeit butter," the senator charged. Congressman William Grout, Republican of Vermont, went further, dubbing the products "bastard butter." Without regulation, who knew what might be in the stuff? Grout called it "the mystery of mysteries."

Patent applications for margarine listed such ingredients as nitric acid, sulfate of lime, and even sugar of lead. Congressman Charles O'Ferral, a Virginia Democrat, decried the inclusion of bromo-chloralum, a disinfectant also used to treat smallpox. O'Ferral charged that the disinfectant's purpose in margarine was "to destroy the smell and prevent detection of the putrid mass" of ground-up sheep, cow, and pig stomachs used in many recipes. Lawmakers wanted to know if other leftover bits of dead animals were finding their way into the recipes. "You do not think that you could make good oleomargarine out of a dead cat or dog?" asked Senator James K. Jones, a Democrat from Arkansas, questioning an industry representative. "It has reached the point in the history of the country where the city scavenger butters your bread," declared Congressman David B. Henderson, an Iowa Republican. Witness L. W. Morton protested. "An ounce of stale fat put into a ton of good fresh fat will spoil the whole," Morton testified, pointing out that it was common knowledge that butter also went bad.

The hearings led to the Butter Act of 1886, which passed with support from both parties and was signed by President Cleveland. But thanks to intervention from the meatpackers, the law was less than hard-hitting, imposing a tax of merely two cents a pound on margarine, leaving the imitation still cheaper to produce than the real thing. The law did define butter as "made exclusively from milk or cream" (with the possible addition of salt or dye), meaning that products like butterine had to be labeled "oleomargarine." False labelers could be fined up to $1,000—assuming they could be caught.

Members of Wiley's staff had been witnesses at the hearings, but their findings in the new Bulletin 13 series weren't issued until the next year, 1887, which made the report an anticlimax of sorts. The studies by the agriculture chemists clearly established, however, that at least a third of what was sold commercially as farm-fresh butter was oleomargarine. The bulletin also noted that thirty-seven American factories were producing more than three million pounds of oleomargarine from animal fats every month. The quality varied widely and there was at least a possibility that some animal parasites could survive the manufacturing process and be present in the spread that consumers purchased. "It is undoubtedly true that a great deal of artificial butter has been thrown on the market that is carelessly made," Wiley wrote.

Still, the Agriculture Department did not offer a blanket condemnation. The division chemists found that if animal-fat oleomargarine was made with care, the product was in many ways comparable to butter, with "nearly the same chemical composition in digestibility. There may be a slight balance in favor of butter but for healthy persons this difference can hardly be of any considerable consequence."

The primary health concerns, the investigation found, derived from dyes used to improve the look of butter and margarine. Traditional butter dyes had been vegetable products: annatto (from the fruit of a South American tree), turmeric, saffron, marigold, and even carrot juice—all benign if pure. But suppliers were adulterating the dyes. Annatto, the most popular, often had brick dust, chalk, and traces of red ocher mixed into it. Processors were also using industrial dyes such as chromate of lead, already notorious for instances of lead poisoning from eating yellow candy. Similar problems occurred in cheese, where manufacturers used red lead to enrich color. In all food products, the report warned, "the use of mineral coloring like chromate of lead is highly reprehensible."

The Division of Chemistry included in the report descriptions of several methods for testing products. With the use of a microscope and a little knowledge of what to look for, it was easy to tell if a spread was butter or margarine. At the molecular level, butter displayed long, delicate, needlelike crystalline structures. Melted, it appeared as shorter needles gathered in bundles. Beef fat crystals, by contrast, appeared as spiky, needle-studded globes, like a "sea urchin or hedgehog." Oleomargarine was a messy tumble of crystalline clumps resembling flattened cauliflowers. Complete with photos, these were handy instructions for anyone with access to a microscope but of little use to the average consumer in 1887.

That same year a New York chemist, Jesse Park Battershall, published a book called *Food Adulteration and Its Detection*, which offered easier home tests. Some, such as one to detect adulterations in tea, could be conducted in any home kitchen. Battershall recommended simply putting the "tea" into a cylinder containing cold water, capping it, and shaking it hard. Ingredients other than tea would form either a scum on the top or a sludge on the bottom. "In this way, Prussian blue (cyanide, used as dye), indigo (another dye), soapstone, gypsum, sand, and turmeric can be separated," Battershall explained. And, he added, housewives should not be too surprised to find them there.

Against the backdrop of rising public concern, and with Commissioner Coleman's support, Wiley resolved to continue raising awareness about impurities and fakery in American food products. The 1887 issues of Bulletin 13 examined three broad areas of food and beverage manufacture, dairy being only the first. The second subject had gotten far less attention—certainly nothing like congressional hearings, let alone a regulatory law—but it concerned products even more rife with fakery. "Could only a portion of the unfortunate dislike for oleomargarine be directed toward the spices?" Wiley wrote in an official letter to his boss.

*Two*

# CHEATED, FOOLED,
# AND BAMBOOZLED

## 1887–1896

═══●═══

*And daintily finger the cream-tinted bread,*
*Just needing to make it complete*

At the U.S. Customs Service laboratory in New York City, where he was a supervisor, colleagues described chemist Jesse Park Battershall as a rather shy, meticulously cautious scientist. Yet Battershall's 1887 book on food adulteration seethed with outrage over virtually every product that American grocers sold. His list included milk and butter, of course, as well as cheese, coffee, chocolate and cocoa, bread, and "baker's chemicals" (baking powders and sodas), and an appalling amount of candy laced with poisonous metallic dyes. He had tested 198 samples of candy and found that a full 115 were tainted by the use of dangerous dyes, mostly arsenic and lead chromate. Forty-one out of forty-eight samples of yellow and orange-colored candy, in fact, contained lead. He had warned of cyanide, indigo, soapstone, gypsum, sand, and turmeric in teas, but he'd also found that the leaves themselves represented a variety of cheats. In standard black and green teas, Battershall found mixtures of backyard leaves from rosebushes, wisteria vines, and trees, including beech, hawthorn, willow, elm, and poplar.

But even this paled, according to the Chemistry Division's report on spices and condiments, to the fakery involved in these products. This was not entirely a surprise. Ground, flaked, or powdered food products had long been known as easy to cut with something else or be replaced entirely by some other, cheaper powder. Ancient Roman documents tell of first-century BCE merchants selling mustard seed and ground juniper berries as pepper. In thirteenth-century England, there were tradespeople called garblers (from an old Arabic word for sieve), hired to inspect imported spices and sift out grain and grit. Predictably, some garblers, those in the employ of unscrupulous importers or merchants, did just the opposite, mixing ground twigs and sand into the spices themselves. Eventually the very word "garble" came to mean mixing things up incorrectly.

By the late nineteenth century, some countries—notably Great Britain—had laws regulating spices. Clifford Richardson, the scientist whom Wiley assigned to take the lead on the USDA spice study, noted in the bulletin that the Dominion of Canada, then still part of the British Empire, did a much better job monitoring foodstuffs than the United States did. But even so, a recent Canadian marketplace survey had found widespread and rather astonishing levels of fakery.

Richardson, writing in the bulletin, tallied up the damage: Commercially sold dry mustard registered at 100 percent adulteration, allspice at 92.5 percent, cloves 83.3 percent, and ginger 55.5 percent. The Canadian analysis also provided some specifics. For instance, scientists there had found a mixture of ground wheat chaff colored with red clay, with a little inexpensive cayenne pepper thrown in, masquerading as ground ginger. When Richardson examined American-sold "ginger," he discovered burned shells, cracker dust, ground seed husks, and dyes. He also noted that some states— Massachusetts, New York, New Jersey, and Michigan—did require spices to be tested for authenticity and purity and that the results had been appalling. In 1882 Massachusetts regulators had found 100 percent adulteration of ground "cloves," which seemed to be mostly burned seashells. The same year, the state's black "pepper" samples turned up as largely charcoal and sawdust.

When Wiley's team did its own ground pepper analysis, the chemists found it difficult to list or even figure out everything that was in the mixtures: sawdust, cereal crumbs, gypsum, potato scraps, hemp seed, and "to an astonishing extent" powdered olive stones, walnut shells, almond shells, "mineral matter," sand, soil, and more. The chemists mockingly called the spice "pepperette." A new, inexpensive product labeled "pepper dust" they found to be literal dust, apparently common floor sweepings.

"Pepper is more in demand than any other spice and is in consequence more adulterated," explained Richardson. Consumers were too trusting and didn't examine the spices they bought. With his naked eye, he'd been able to pick out crumbled crackers and charcoal in a black pepper sample. He could also pick out the crumbles of brick dust in so-called cayenne pepper. Using a microscope, he detected sawdust in the spice mixes, distinguishing the larger tree cells from the finer cellular structure of a peppercorn.

Some manufacturers took a one-size-fits-all approach to fakery. One New York firm—a purveyor of pepper, mustard, cloves, cinnamon, cassia, allspice, nutmeg, ginger, and mace—had purchased five thousand pounds of coconut shells a year for grinding and adding to every spice on that list.

Other cheats made "mustard" by mixing water with coarsely ground flour or crumbled gypsum, a mineral commonly used to make plaster. To give the resulting sludge a mustardlike tint, Martin's yellow (more technically 2,4-Dinitro-1-naphthol yellow), a coal-tar dye containing benzene (and related to naphthalene, a primary ingredient in moth balls), was added. The chemists had discovered this by adding alcohol to the "mustard" powder, separating out the dye, and analyzing its formula.

Richardson predicted that if manufacturers realized how easily this fakery could be detected, they would find another, perhaps even more harmful, chemical to substitute. With bureaucratic understatement, he noted that spices offered "large scope for inventive genius."

With Wiley's collaboration, he wrote an overtly political call to action in his conclusion to the report. It would be difficult to prevent the rise of such "manufactured" food, he said, "without some governmental action." Crooked spice processors undercut the prices of their honest competitors, leaving no economic incentive for pure products. "When proper legislation has found a place on the statute-books," the report continued, "the manufacturers will find themselves in a position where, without detriment to themselves, they can all unite in giving up the practice." Wiley underlined the point in the letter to Coleman that served as the preface to the spice report: "The necessity for some means for the suppression of the present universal sophistication of spices and condiments seems urgent." Richardson was so disgusted by his findings that he asked to be transferred to another line of research and spent the next years analyzing seeds and grasses.

The third and final Bulletin 13 report of 1887 was devoted to "Fermented Alcoholic Beverages, Malt Liquors, Wine, and Cider." That particular investigation was prompted at least in part by a growing concern about salicylic acid, a preservative that wine bottlers increasingly used—and in increasing amounts—to lengthen the shelf life of their products.

Found in plants such as meadowsweet, wintergreen, and most commonly the bark of willow trees, this natural substance had been used as a pain reliever dating back to ancient Egypt. The Greek physician Hippocrates praised it in the fifth century BCE and Native American healers knew it well. But the name "salicylic acid" or "salicin" was coined after early-nineteenth-century scientists learned to extract the pure compound from the white willow, *Salix alba*, in the early nineteenth century. They also discovered a side effect. When ingested in high doses, pure salicylic acid caused gastric bleeding.

A few decades later, in Germany, pioneering organic chemist Hermann Kolbe and lab partner Rudolf Schmitt developed an economical method for synthesizing large quantities of salicylic acid in a laboratory. They used sodium carbonate as a base for creating needle-shaped crystals that could be replicated time and time again and then ground into a fine powder. Laboratory workers learned to avoid getting a whiff of the crystalline dust, which produced almost instant irritation of the mucous membranes in the nose and set off a sneezing fit. Seeking to establish a safe dose, Kolbe used himself as a test subject, ingesting one-half to one gram daily over several days with no apparent ill effect. His conclusion was that the compound was basically safe if administered in cautious doses.

Other researchers disagreed. French chemists successfully raised safety concerns earlier, in 1881 persuading their government to ban its use as a preservative in wine. Germany also banned salicylic acid in both wine and beer made for domestic use. The Germans, however, did permit breweries to use the chemical in beers made for export to the United States. After all, American authorities had shown no interest in regulating its use. "In this country but little attention seems to have been given to the use of salicylic acid as a preservative," the Chemistry Division's report noted, somewhat sadly, in its conclusion.

The Division of Chemistry staff worried that the compound's use in alcoholic beverages could add up to a harmful dose, especially for a person who consumed several drinks a day. Authored by C. A. Crampton, one of Wiley's staffers, the fermented beverages report noted that American wines contained, on average, almost 2 grams of salicylic acid per bottle. Beers averaged 1.2 grams. But some measured higher. One case of wine contained a full therapeutic dose—3.9 grams—in every bottle tested. Not every vintner used it, but the Chemistry Division had tested seventy American wines—from Riesling to zinfandel, from New York to California—and found that more than one-fourth contained salicylic acid. The same was true for the beers and ales tested. And as a report by New York's Department of Public Health pointed out, the preservative was increasingly found not just in alcoholic beverages but in a wide range of other grocery products, upping the odds of consumers getting a stiff dose every day.

Cyrus Edson, author of the New York report, wrote to Wiley's division, requesting that the federal government take a protective stand against salicylic acid. Edson cited evidence that in addition to causing gastrointestinal bleeding, the compound could damage other organs, including the kidneys, possibly permanently. "This report closes with the recommendation that the addition of salicylic acid, even in small amounts, be absolutely prohibited by law," he wrote. "I would respectfully recommend that some action be taken by this department toward this injurious substance."

He found a receptive audience in Wiley, who was starting to worry that continual exposure to low doses of industrial chemicals—yet to be tested for safety—might indeed be a health issue. Although the chief chemist believed that "a healthy stomach can, from time to time, receive with impunity food containing small qualities of preservatives," he grew increasingly uneasy about the effects of repeating such a dose over and over. In people suffering from ill health, the elderly, the very young, and invalids with "weak or diseased stomachs," he warned that the effects of such constant dosage might be much worse. At least, he argued, there should be a requirement of accurate information on labels, which should, at a minimum, "give the name of the preservative and the quantity employed."

But Wiley also wondered what good it would do to list the ingredients in a food product if no one knew whether those ingredients were safe and in what doses. He began thinking about how he could test to see how much of such additives a person could consume safely. Would it be possible to conduct trials, not just of salicylic acid but other preservatives too, on human subjects?

In 1888 Grover Cleveland lost his bid for reelection. Before he left office, he signed a bill elevating the Agriculture Department to cabinet status. Norman Coleman became the country's first secretary of agriculture, but only for his last month in office, before making way for President Benjamin Harrison's pick, Governor Jeremiah Rusk of Wisconsin.

Like Wiley, Rusk had grown up on a midwestern farm. And like Wiley, the new secretary saw the rise in manufactured, adulterated foods as an evil that needed to be addressed. Rusk, a genial man nicknamed "Uncle Jerry" by the agency staffers, was determined to build up the department as a support system for farmers. Over his few years in the office, the USDA grew rapidly, adding staff to the Chemistry Division and field stations for research around the country. And Rusk tripled the budget for the continuing Bulletin 13 reports, from $5,000 to $15,000 yearly.

After Crampton's report on fermented beverages had rounded out the 1887 edition, Wiley published a study of lard and lard adulterants and, with the additional money from the new Republican administration, scheduled investigations into baking powders; sugar, molasses, honey, and syrup; tea, coffee, and cocoa; and canned vegetables.

The lard study again highlighted the routine nature of adulteration—and the routine false advertising that came with it. Packages of lard—labeled as the best pure hog fat—often contained cheaper fats, mostly waste products from beef manufacturing or cottonseed oil, or both. As he had earlier with oleomargarine, Wiley noted that these particular adulterations were poorly understood in terms of health effects. There was no scientific data to show that pig fat was healthier than cottonseed oil or the other way around. But packages marked "pure lard" that contained no lard lacked such ambiguity. They could be considered only another example of deceptive labeling. He also noted that the Division of Chemistry was finding unlabeled cottonseed oil in a slew of other products, especially in "olive" oils. Almost 200 million pounds of cottonseed oil were now produced in the United States and manufacturers of purportedly higher-end oil and fat products had seized upon this cheaper but "innocuous" raw material. "To do this is a fraud upon the consumer," Wiley wrote in his summary, once again recommending that the ingredients actually be listed on the packaging.

Increasingly frustrated that only a tiny readership—fellow scientists, bureaucrats, lobbyists, and legislative staffers—ever saw his technical reports, Wiley decided to try for a broader audience. In 1890 he hired Alex Wedderburn, a journalist and pure-food advocate, to write easy-to-read copy for the public—in effect, press releases or consumer brochures. And although he thought Wedderburn's first such report contained a little too much advocacy—it blasted the "utter recklessness and hard-heartedness" of food adulterers and condemned their "unlawful and dishonest methods"—he supported its publication, merely advising the writer to tone it down next time.

Not that he and his chemistry staff weren't busy supplying Wedderburn with additional ammunition. The division's 1892 investigation into coffee, teas, and cocoa, for instance, stood out for the level of inventive fraud it uncovered. Tea, as Battershall had already noted, was routinely adulterated, so much so that some manufacturers didn't bother to disguise it. The federal chemists made a point of analyzing a product proudly labeled as "Lie Tea": "This substance, as its name implied, was an imitation of tea, usually containing fragments or dust of the genuine leaves, foreign leaves, and mineral matters, held together by means of a starch solution." As for cocoa, "there is probably no more misleading or abused term in the English language." Cocoa powders contained everything from clay to sand to iron oxides (the latter used as a coloring agent). "Finely powdered tin is sometimes added to give the chocolate a metallic luster," the report added.

Coffee, long America's hot beverage of choice, had frequently been cut with all manner of adulterants ranging from tree bark, sawdust, and ground beets and acorns to relatively flavorful substitutions such as chicory root and the bitter seeds of the blue lupine flower. During the Civil War, Union troops had enjoyed the advantage of coffee that was made—at least in large part—from actual coffee beans while their Confederate counterparts made do with brews of charred wheat, corn, peas, and beans. But that was the ground product. A consumer with access to whole coffee beans and a grinder had, it was assumed, the assurance that the resulting brew was genuine.

By 1892 Wiley's staff had determined that about 87 percent of all ground coffee samples tested were adulterated. "One sample contained no coffee at all." But they'd also found that processors had devised a way to make coffee-free "beans" by pressing a mixture of flour, molasses, and occasionally dirt and sawdust into molds. The chemists discovered that the average scoop of coffee beans in Washington, DC, contained "as high as 25 percent of these artificial bodies." "Dear Sir," began one letter from a distributor to a grocer. "I send you by mail this sample of 'imitation coffee.' This is a manufactured bean and composed of flour; you can easily mix 15 percent of this substitute in with genuine coffee." A flyer from another supplier offered "coffee pellets" consisting of three-fourths filler, 15 percent coffee, and 10 percent chicory. "This makes a very desirable cup of coffee." The flyer further assured grocers it could be sold at full price and was undetectable to consumers.

Producers had also taken to coloring light-colored, inexpensive coffee beans and passing them off as costlier Java beans, recognizable by their glossy, dark appearance. The Division of Chemistry found coffee-coloring agents included charcoal, drop black (a powder made with charred bone), and finely powdered iron. They also turned up traces of more dangerous dyes, such as Scheele's green (arsenic), Prussian blue (cyanide), and chrome yellow (lead). The fake beans were usually polished to an enticing shine using glycerin, palm oil, or even Vaseline (a petroleum-based jelly patented by the British-born chemist Robert Chesebrough in 1872). "Consumers, and especially the poor, are being grossly deceived," the bulletin report concluded. "Very little pure ground coffee is sold, and even the whole coffee does not escape sophistication."

And in case any reader missed the point: "Stringent laws are certainly needed to suppress these frauds."

Lawmakers had taken only small notice of any of the Chemistry Division's food and drink bulletins. Back in 1888, Virginia congressman William H. F. "Rooney" Lee, the son of Confederate general Robert E. Lee, had introduced a bill requiring detailed labeling of products. That legislation failed, but a more powerful advocate had introduced another bill in the upper house in 1891. "The devil has got hold of the food supply in this country," declared sponsor Algernon Paddock of Nebraska, chairman of the Agriculture and Forestry Committee. Industry lobbyists and other opponents of regulation saw signs that Senator Paddock's bill was gaining support. In response, they gathered thousands of signatures on petitions aimed at blocking it. Grocers and factory owners, the National Farmers' Alliance, and the National Colored Farmers' Alliance were among the petitioners. The strongest opposition came from the southern states and their legislators, who, even decades after the Civil War, remained suspicious of any action that might further consolidate federal power. Senators from Tennessee and Georgia railed against the anticipated intrusion, suggesting that the USDA wanted to send spies and informers into the countryside to conduct unwarranted searches of homes and businesses.

Paddock responded by citing the food fraud studies from the Agriculture Department reports. He insisted that Wiley's Chemistry Division was "as nearly nonpartisan in its work as such an institution can be under our system." This was not about states' rights but about responsibility. If the federal government didn't accept its responsibility to keep the food supply honest, American citizens eventually would hold it accountable. The United States was the only Western country that lacked a national law regulating food safety, he pointed out. "Take heed when people demand bread that you continue not to give them a stone," he said, referring to flour that Wiley and his team had discovered to be cut with gypsum and rock dust. Paddock managed to wear down his opponents in the Senate, which did, rather grudgingly, pass his bill. But industry lobbyists blocked a parallel proposal from even getting a hearing on the floor of the House, effectively halting the legislation.

Wiley had advised Paddock on the food safety act at the senator's request. After the measure's failure, he pondered what he saw as a curious lack of support for reform from the public at large. In a paper titled "The Adulteration of Food," Wiley invoked the famously cynical showman P. T. Barnum, writing, "To be cheated, fooled, bamboozled, cajoled, deceived, pettifogged, demagogued, hypnotized, manicured and chiropodized are privileges dear to us all."

He sent the paper to Paddock, who agreed but encouraged him to soldier on anyway. The senator predicted that eventually consumers would come to appreciate that they could not protect themselves against systemic cheating without regulatory help. "Angry waves of popular discontent," he said, would eventually lead to change.

"A cold northeast wind and sleet makes nature look as I feel after yesterday's vote," Wiley wrote in his diary on the morning after Election Day 1892. Former president Grover Cleveland had won his old job back, meaning the well-liked secretary of agriculture Rusk was on his way out. Tired of the uncertainties of politics, Wiley considered leaving his government post. "I have thought for some time of giving it up to go into private business." But he still had such a long list of food safety investigations planned; he decided to stay and hope for the best. That hope would not last long.

The new secretary was Julius Sterling Morton of Nebraska. Like

President Cleveland, he belonged to the conservative wing of his party, often disparagingly referred to as the "Bourbon" Democrats, a reference both to bourbon whiskey and to the Bourbon dynasty in France. Like the French Bourbons in that country's bloody revolution, conservative Democrats had been swept from power with the Civil War. But the Bourbon kings returned to power in 1814 and the Bourbon Democrats had regained legislative power after Reconstruction. Morton, who had been governor of the Nebraska Territory before it became a state in 1867, was a wealthy businessman, a former newspaper editor, and a fierce believer in small government. He came to the USDA determined to make it leaner and more efficient, in keeping with the austerity policies of Cleveland's second term. Under the openhanded benevolence of Harrison appointee Rusk, Morton complained, the Agriculture Department had been "well on the way to becoming a national feed bag."

Morton was in office for a month before he called Wiley into his office to renew the chief chemist's contract and to inform him of plans for a stripped-down Division of Chemistry. The secretary wanted department chemists to concentrate only on science that could directly benefit farmers. He favored research into bettering soils, making more effective fertilizers and pesticides, and developing superior species of grains, hay, and other crops. Eliminating what he judged to be unnecessary services, Morton ordered sorghum and sugar research halted, the scientists doing that work dismissed, and USDA research stations sold off to private interests. He cut the budget for food-purity research by two-thirds. "Is there any necessity for . . . inspectors of food or seekers after adulterants in food?" he wrote in a memo to Wiley. "Would the public interest suffer if these gentlemen cease to draw salaries for what they are alleged to be doing at this time?" In 1893 Congress appropriated another $15,000, requested under Rusk, for Wiley's investigations of food adulteration, but Morton slashed that back to $5,000 and warned the chemist that he had plans to eliminate the studies entirely.

One part of Bulletin 13, an examination of canned vegetables, was still under way, and that, Morton told Wiley, would be the last. The secretary also ordered that Wiley stop sharing his division's findings with the public and recommended that Wiley get rid of the public science writer position held by Alexander Wedderburn. The Agriculture Department's mission did not include educating the public, he insisted.

To say that Wiley disagreed would be an understatement. Morton's demands led to months of exchanges with his chief chemist, during which Wiley fought to keep Wedderburn on the payroll until he could finish one last consumer piece. "It will afford me great gratification if you will show me wherein Mr. Wedderburn, during his connection with the department, has broadened the farmer's market or increased the demand or price of his products," Morton wrote to Wiley. The more people were informed about adulteration, the more they would demand untainted food, Wiley replied. "Such a consummation would be of great benefit to agriculture by relieving the farmer who sells pure foods from competition with the adulterated articles."

Morton then peppered Wiley with questions about Wedderburn's fitness to be part of the Chemistry Department. He asked how many analyses Wedderburn had done. What substances did he analyze? What chemistry school did he go to? How much experience as an analytical chemist did he have? "To your first question," Wiley replied, "None. To your second, none." The man was a talented writer with a gift for explaining science. In other words, Wedderburn was not a graduate of a chemical school and "has never had any experience as a chemist, never professed to be a chemist, and has no reputation as a chemist." Morton wrote back, "So tell me what peculiar fitness and adaptation you found in Mr. Wedderburn for the work of investigating food adulterations."

"I have endeavored in two previous communications to set plainly before you the character of Mr. Wedderburn's work," Wiley wrote, before asking if Morton was willing to throw away the paid hours that Wedderburn had already devoted to the document he was working on. The appeal to frugality worked. Morton agreed to pay the writer one final month's salary so that he could finish the promised document.

But as the secretary had feared, the result was another searing indictment of food manufacturing practices, focused on the increasing use of chemical preservatives and coal tar–derived coloring agents, which Wedderburn described as "poisonous adulterations that have, in many cases, not only impaired the health of the consumer but frequently caused death." Morton was appalled by what he saw as an attack on American business. Again, in the interest of thrift, he didn't kill the report. But he ordered a limited printing of fewer than five hundred copies and told his staff not to publicize it in any way.

Wedderburn, no longer a department employee, was free to defy Morton's order. He mailed copies of his work to farm journals and agricultural publications. This prompted a gratifying response from at least one reader, a farmer, who wrote, "The sentiment and truths contained therein can but meet the indorsement and approval of every honest man throughout our land. If there was ever a time in our history when it became the duty of the farming and laboring class of our people to organize and act in concert for the protection of their families against adulterated and poisoned food, that time is now."

Morton might have sacked Wiley too, but the chief chemist had achieved immense stature in his field, which reflected well on the department. Wiley was, at that point, president of the chemistry section of the American Association of the Advancement of Science, president of the Chemical Society of Washington, and president of the Association of Official Agricultural Chemists, which he had helped found. "President of all the chemical societies in the United States" was his new ambition, Wiley joked. The positions were certainly more gratifying, at the moment, than the position of chief chemist at the Agriculture Department.

He'd learned that the jobs of his staff members researching food adulteration were also under threat. He wrote to Morton that the services of these chemists, who earned an average of a mere $600 per year, after all, "could not be dispensed with without detriment to the public service." Morton's response was that perhaps it would make more sense to cut clerical staff. Wiley fended off that too, pointing out that the support employees, even more modestly compensated, allowed the chemists more time to do their valuable work: "The secretary can rest assured that in their retention there will be no waste of public funds."

Wearing of Wiley's apparently unlimited capacity for pushback, Morton decided the best strategy was to keep his prickly chief chemist busy. "You are hereby directed to proceed to Chicago for duty in connection with the food and cereal exhibit of the Columbian Exposition of 1893," he instructed. Wiley's job would be to promote American agriculture and the public image of the department. He added, "Your traveling expenses to and from Chicago will be paid from the fund appropriated for the investigation of the adulteration of foods."

Wiley wasn't happy about the funding but also appreciated the break from battle—and the chance to be part of the dazzle of the Chicago exposition. Six hundred miles removed from Julius Morton, he was free to conduct a series of public presentations, talks that he delivered personally, focusing on the sad state of the American food supply and his division's work in the detection of fake spices, adulterated cheese, tainted milk, and more. The exhibit he helped organize included a full-scale model of a food chemistry laboratory, live demonstrations of analyses of everything from bread to beer, and a public lecture series on modern chemistry. When it was Wiley's turn to speak, he emphasized his belief that chemistry was a science that had enormous power to improve and be part of people's lives—and that scientists themselves should share their work with others: "The chemist is a social being, and there is a life outside of the laboratory as beautiful and useful as the life within. The highest culture is not found in books, but in men. And thus to widen his horizon and broaden his views the chemist must leave his desk and seek the acquaintance of his fellows."

In the last week of the exposition, Wiley received a note from a woman he'd met after one of the talks: Helen Louise Thompson, an editor at the popular food magazine *Table Talk* ("devoted to the interests of progressive housewives"). Leaving the great fair had been like "saying goodbye to a fairyland I never expect to see again," she wrote. But she also wanted him to know that she was taking with her, back to the real world, a new conviction that food additives were a dangerous problem, one her readers needed to know about. She asked Wiley for copies of all the old Bulletin 13 publications, and any that might still be upcoming as well, and to write for her magazine, proposing that he do "six or seven papers for the coming year on food adulterations, of the kind to be of interest to the housekeeper who does not know chicory from coffee and who really prefers cottonseed to olive oil."

With Algernon Paddock's prediction that Congress would take up food safety regulation only when American consumers cared enough to force action in mind, Wiley accepted. He did not consult Secretary Morton, who, it was becoming clear, regarded Wiley as an enemy. Morton's most recent cost-cutting move had been to reduce the division's budget for test tubes and beakers. During the process of shutting down the sugar research field stations, Morton had deliberately sought evidence that he could use to discipline his chief chemist. After one report from the field, the secretary charged that Wiley had illegally spent twenty-four cents of department funds on shipping whiskey back home while inspecting research operations in Kansas. The accusation turned out to be as false as it was vindictive "I was the manager of that company and I am very positive that no bill was ever paid for liquors, or anything else for that matter," wrote an executive at the Parkinson Sugar Company in Fort Scott, Kansas, to Morton. "To those acquainted with Dr. Wiley and his habits, the insinuation that he had liquors shipped here for his own or anybody's private use is absurd." Morton withdrew the charge without apology.

But Wiley recognized that he had to step lightly. In the year after the Columbian Exposition, the Chemistry Division's work focused almost entirely on crop research. Typical was an 1894 bulletin on the chemical composition of the cassava plant. Wiley's public speaking schedule reflected the same approach; at the Brooklyn Institute of Arts and Sciences he discussed "The Relation of Chemistry to Agriculture." Still, occasionally he could push through a small adulteration study.

In the summer of 1894, on his way to help shutter a sugar station in California, he begged a little department money to investigate wine production, especially the use of preservatives. "These are matters which relate particularly to the wholesomeness of a wine and the purity of a food product." Morton agreed to let him have a maximum of $150, which of course proved too little. Wiley spent $250 and Morton made him pay the overrun out of his own pocket.

In 1896 the secretary began requiring that he personally approve every purchase in the department. A request to restock the funnels used in experiments took two months to win his go-ahead, and only after Wiley agreed to sign a document stating "I certify that the following named articles are needed for use in the Division of Chemistry and that the public interest demands their earliest delivery." Wiley tried to economize by skimping on office supplies, but Morton complained that the chief chemist's letters, typed using a nearly spent

typewriter ribbon, were too hard to read. "The letters are all returned to you with the request that they be prepared anew."

In private, Wiley complained that Morton ran the department
with "repression, persecution, and sham reform." Even members of
Congress had noticed. In February, Congressman Chester Long of
Kansas, chairman of the House Committee on Agriculture, wrote to
Wiley directly to tell him that the secretary had once again slashed
the Chemistry Division's budget. "It is difficult usually to do anything under such circumstances but the House at present is not disposed to follow the suggestions of the Secretary of Agriculture,"
Long wrote. He hoped, sincerely, that the department's admired
chief chemist would not give up.

# Three

# THE BEEF COURT

## 1896–1899

———◦———

*A film of the butter so yellow and sweet,*
*Well suited to make every minute*
*A dream of delight.*

W iley, as he confided in his diary, was depressed. Some of that was purely personal. His mother, Lucinda, died shortly after Morton took office in 1893. "I was plunged at once out of my long boyhood," Wiley wrote gloomily. Two years later his father, Preston, died as well, leaving him feeling further adrift and alone—an aging bachelor, renting a room in another family's house. His job now was the central focus of his life. And that too seemed to be foundering.

The election of William McKinley in 1896 brightened his outlook. McKinley was not a reformer but he was at least not a Democrat. With a Republican back in the White House wanting his own team, the chief chemist felt confident that Morton would be replaced. And when Wiley received his first-ever invitation to an inaugural ball, he allowed himself to hope it was a signal of resurgence, not just for him but also for the status of the Chemistry Division.

The early signs for that were good. McKinley appointed a former congressman, James Wilson, as the USDA's next secretary. A sixty-two-year-old professor of agriculture from Iowa State University, Wilson still farmed, growing feed corn in Iowa's Tama County, which had earned him the nickname "Tama Jim." The new secretary told Wiley immediately that his job was secure and within six months had restored full funding to the Division of Chemistry, encouraging him to begin planning new food-adulteration studies.

Perhaps it was under the influence of such a wave of renewed optimism that the chief chemist, at the age of fifty-three, took an unexpected and uncharacteristic step. He fell in love at first sight with a twenty-one-year-old USDA librarian. "I saw a young woman with a book in her hand, apparently looking for the proper place to deposit it. I was immediately struck by her appearance," he confided to a friend. She was slight, fine featured, with light brown hair and dark blue eyes. He noticed with admiration her direct, intelligent gaze. As he liked to tell the story, Wiley grabbed the arm of Edward Cutter, the library manager, and demanded to know the woman's name. The manager identified her as Anna Kelton.

"Cutter," Wiley said, "I'm going to marry that girl."

"Perhaps it would be well for you to meet the young lady before proposing matrimony," Cutter replied. Wiley greeted Anna Kelton politely, as befitted a senior official in the department, but he resolutely began plotting a courtship.

Anna "Nan" Kelton, a graduate of George Washington University, was more intent on a career. Her protective mother, Josephine, recently widowed, was even more intent in that desire. Born in Oakland, California, Anna had come with her family to Washington in 1893, when her father, Colonel John C. Kelton, was appointed governor of the Soldiers Home, a military retirement facility in the northwest quadrant of the capital. He had died of an infection just a year after taking the post, leaving his widow determined to see that her children thrived in their own right.

Wiley knew the odds were against him, but he began by politely asking Cutter if he could borrow Miss Kelton for some stenography work. From there, she gradually came to take over many of the chemistry chief's secretarial needs. Also gradually, she allowed him to escort her to the occasional play or concert. But when he called at her home, Josephine deliberately made him feel unwelcome, and he found himself again balanced between hope and discouragement.

As McKinley's presidential term began, Congress once again reluctantly considered the quality of the nation's food and beverages. The legislative attention was focused, though, on a particular beverage—and, as newspapers cheerfully pointed out, one that enjoyed legislative favor. That would be whiskey, and the rule under consideration was one setting "bonded" standards for the spirit.

The term dated to an 1868 law, which had granted distillers a delay between the time when they produced their product and when they had to pay a federal tax on it. This "bonded period" had originally been set at a year but over time was increased. It provided a financial incentive for letting spirits sit in barrels before being bottled for sale, and it resulted in aged whiskey—amber colored and more complex and mellow in taste. A distiller could charge considerably more for a well-aged bottle of spirits than for liquor straight from the still. High-end makers began to campaign for federal regulation that would do more than give them a tax-free grace period but that would also protect their profitable reputations for making the good stuff. Edmund Haynes Taylor Jr.—who bore the Kentucky honorific "colonel" and was the namesake of Old Taylor brand bourbon—was among the distillers who sought rules to distinguish products like his from, as he put it, "carelessly made whiskeys whose aim is quantity and whose objective is mere chaffering for cheapness."

Those chafferers, as Taylor called them, sometimes sold their lesser products with phony labels proclaiming them to be Taylor's brand or Jasper "Jack" Daniel's famed Old No. 7. The fakes were often made using rectified alcohol, also called neutral spirits. These were a concentrated form of ethyl alcohol, usually produced on an industrial scale by repeatedly distilling the liquid to purify it and increase its strength. To simulate whiskey, the product was diluted with water and tinted brown—often with tobacco extracts, tincture of iodine, burned sugar, or prune juice.

In 1897, after decades of complaints over the widespread adulteration and fakery of alcoholic spirits, Congress passed the Bottled-in-Bond Act, which attempted to encourage basic quality standards. The act stated that each bottle of spirits could be marked with a green "bonded" seal from the government if it was aged for at least four years in a supervised federal warehouse. Bonded whiskey was also labeled for proof (a measurement set in the United States as twice the percentage of alcohol) and the location of the specific distillery.

Makers of blended whiskeys, meanwhile, were also trying to fend off counterfeiters and set quality standards. Blended whiskeys are, as the name indicates, made from a mixture of distilled spirits. They usually contain a high-quality aged product, derived from a single distillation, to establish flavor, together with other, lesser whiskeys added for economy. Sometimes, in lower-quality blends, there are also neutral spirits added to the mix, along with dyes to enhance color.

Although they could not qualify for the bonded designation at their best, blends could be high-quality products sold at premium prices—prime targets for the counterfeit-label scam. In the nineteenth century, Canada's Hiram Walker Company, producer of Canadian Club blended whiskey, reacted to fakery in the U.S. market by hiring detectives to hunt cheats. The company took out newspaper advertisements listing the perpetrators or had the names listed on billboard posters proclaiming "A Swindle, These People Sell Bogus

Liquors." Yet inexpensive blended whiskeys were too often no better than the counterfeits. For that reason, producers of blended whiskeys were sometimes lumped together under the somewhat derogatory label "rectifiers." Wiley—who of an evening often enjoyed a glass of fine, aged bourbon—had little regard for anything called a blend and tended to dismiss any alternatives to straight whiskey as belonging to a catalog of fakes, admittedly of varying quality.

After the Bottled-in-Bond Act, Colonel Taylor and his friends began publishing advertisements touting bonded whiskey as the only "real" whiskey. Producers of blends—both good and bad—protested, to little effect at the time. But their sense of a real injustice did not end, and neither did their determination to fight for a change. The rectifiers, and their quest for equality, would lead to years of wrangling over what could rightly be called whiskey, plaguing Wiley, Wilson, and a series of presidents in the years ahead.

McKinley himself showed no interest in the topic—or in food or drink quality in general. He had other far more pressing issues, including a politically charged decision to go to war with Spain over Cuban independence in 1898. Although the conflict was brief—lasting only from April to August of that year—the aftershocks were profound. The United States became something of an imperial power, gaining former Spanish colonial possessions, including Puerto Rico, Guam, and the Philippines. And although the war was brief, it showcased so many examples of outdated and inept management of the U.S. military that McKinley was forced to replace the secretary of war, John Hay.

To the president's dismay, among the most stubborn scandals regarding mismanagement was one involving the quality of food fed to the troops. The story—which made newspaper headlines coast to coast—involved the shoddy state of the beef fed to American soldiers during the conflict. Testimony at the resulting hearings before the War Department would range from Wiley as an expert witness on food safety to then–New York governor Theodore Roosevelt as an aggrieved former soldier.

The "embalmed beef" scandal arose soon after the war's end in August. Major General Nelson Miles, commanding general of the army, called for an investigation of food that had been supplied to soldiers in Cuba. He'd asked all the commanders stationed in the Caribbean to write evaluations of the canned beef delivered to their regiments. Miles, citing reports of a chemical smell wafting from the product, called it "embalmed beef," a term that caught on in the nation's newspapers. The press reported that Miles had received descriptions of cans swarming with maggots and cans supposedly containing a mix of meat and charred rope. The *Chicago Tribune*— a paper particularly interested in the business of the meatpacking industry—quoted soldiers who said that often when the cans were opened they "had to retire to a distance to prevent being overcome" by the stench.

As Miles was airing his complaints, the War Department (roughly analogous to today's Department of the Army) began a general inquiry into the overall conduct of the war. At the direction of President McKinley, secretary of war Russell A. Alger appointed a long-retired Civil War officer, Major General Grenville Dodge, to lead an investigative panel that became known as the Dodge Commission. A wealthy businessman and former congressman, Dodge transported the commission aboard his own private railroad car to interview witnesses around the country. He also held numerous hearings in Washington, DC, where Miles was called to testify that December.

Miles cited a letter from one army doctor, which claimed that much of the canned beef shipped from the United States was "apparently preserved by injected chemicals to aid deficient refrigeration." The canned meat smelled like formaldehyde when opened, the doctor said, and when cooked tasted of chemical preservatives. Another officer described the canned meat as having an "unnatural. mawk-ish, sickening" odor. It was a national disgrace, Miles said, to serve chemically tainted meat with "no life or nourishment in it" to men who had put their lives at risk for their country.

Miles's angry remarks prompted an even angrier response from Brigadier General Charles P. Eagan, commissary general of subsistence, when he testified before the commission the following month. "He lies in his throat, he lies in his heart, he lies in every hair on his head and every pore in his body," said Eagan about Miles. "I wish to force the lie back in his throat, covered with the contents of a camp latrine."

In February 1899, the Dodge Commission issued a voluminous document titled "Report of the Commission Appointed by the President to Investigate the Conduct of the War Department During the War with Spain." It reflected none of the anger expressed by Eagan and Miles. Rather it contained cautious recommendations regarding army medical practices, supplies, troop movements, and more. And it did not reach a conclusion about the bad-smelling beef. The only officer punished in the wake of the hearings was Eagan, not for procuring distasteful meat or shipping it to the troops but for the grave offense of insulting his senior officer in public. Found guilty, Eagan, already in his late fifties, was relieved of duty until he reached the mandatory retirement age of sixty-four.

The Dodge hearings satisfied neither Miles nor the public, who remained furious that America's fighting men had been fed bad rations. Newspapers tracking the story accused the army of covering up its own substandard practices; private citizens telegraphed the White House in outrage. Under pressure, an increasingly irate President McKinley ordered the War Department to hold another inquiry on the specific question of the quality of the beef that had been supplied to U.S. troops. The *Chicago Tribune* immediately christened this second tribunal the "Beef Court." It convened in March 1899.

In anticipation, the president had summoned Secretary Wilson to the White House to ask for help with chemical analysis from Harvey Wiley's crew. "I called on Secretary Alger to request that he send me samples of the canned beef that were furnished to the soldiers last summer," Wilson wrote to Wiley, "for the purpose of determining whether any deleterious substances have been added to them in the course of preparation to more perfectly preserve them."

Wiley and his chemists had already begun to draw a precise and unappetizing portrait of all American canned beef—not just military rations. Every can they opened contained a soupy mix of meat scraps and fat. The fat was standard in canned meat production because manufacturers used it to fill spaces between the scraps. Before a can was sealed, hot fat or a boiled-bone gelatin was poured in to "fill all the interstices not occupied by pieces of meat." Finding a thick paste of gelatinous fat embedded with shreds and chunks of meat wasn't unexpected and, in fact, the chemists noted, the solid mass probably prevented some bacterial spoilage.

Wiley drew test samples from military supplies and from cans available in stores from three of the nation's biggest packinghouses, Libby, McNeil & Libby, Armour, and Cudahy, all residents of Chicago's Union Stockyards. All three had grown bigger since the oleomargarine study in the 1880s. The yards now processed close to twenty million animals a year. "Packingtown," as the locals called it, had become even more notorious for its pervasive dirt, gore, and offal.

This was a community of immigrant labor—Irish, German, Polish, Russian, anyone in desperate need of a job. The workers manned "the killing floors" for ten-hour shifts, earning perhaps ten cents an hour. Women could be hired for half that; they were employed mostly to pack the meat into boxes or cans. Children were cheaper yet; a six-year-old boy could be paid to run messages around a factory for a mere penny an hour. As the industry emphasized, Americans liked their meat inexpensive. Fresh beef could be found in the grocery store for twelve cents a pound. The average housewife could pick up three cans of corned beef for a quarter. When the War Department's Commissary Division had wanted an even better deal, the packers had found it easy to comply. Libby, McNeill & Libby alone had unloaded seven million pounds of canned meat into the military supply depots, as the army's investigating panel would note.

The Beef Court convened in the new State, War, and Navy Building on Washington's Pennsylvania Avenue. The hearing chamber was crammed with journalists, annoying both War Department officials and the meatpackers, who were angry over being portrayed publicly as poisoners of American soldiers. Roosevelt, then the thirty-nine-year-old governor of New York, appeared as a star witness early in the proceedings. At the beginning of the war, he had famously left his post as assistant secretary of the navy to form the First U.S. Volunteer Cavalry Regiment, popularly known as the Rough Riders. Bearing the rank of colonel, Roosevelt had been hailed as one of the heroes of the brief conflict, and his testimony was front-page news.

"I first knew there was trouble with the beef while we were lying off the quay in Tampa Bay," he said. "I noticed a man named Ash—I think he was from Kentucky—preparing to throw away his portion of canned roast beef. I asked him why he was throwing it away. He said, 'I can't eat it.' I told him that he was a baby and that he did not go to war to eat fancy menus and that if he was not satisfied with the rations he had better go home. He ate the meat and vomited." The governor said he had then examined the rations. "When the cans were opened, the top was nothing more than a layer of slime. It was disagreeable looking and nasty. The beef was stringy and coarse and seemed to be nothing more than a bundle of fibers."

Roosevelt stressed that the issue was that good men had been served poorly by their country, sent into war with provisions that were "uneatable, unpalatable, unwholesome . . . utterly unsafe and utterly unfit." He added that his men, unable to eat what was supplied, were half starved much of the time in Cuba. Roosevelt said he had personally quit eating the army meat rations, subsisting on beans and rice while awaiting food packages sent by his family. "I would rather have eaten my hat," he said.

Newspapers reported that Roosevelt was flushed and ill tempered by the time he finished testifying. Stamping out of the hearing room, trailed by a crowd of fascinated journalists, he turned to a friend and snapped, "It was a disgrace to our country." He was followed on the stand by dozens of equally embittered former soldiers. One after another, they described a slimy product with a chemical tang and, often, visible rot. Army cooks cited the thick greenish deposit they routinely scraped out of roast beef cans. There was also a lengthy discussion of the so-called fresh beef shipped down from the yards. One soldier marveled over a heavily preserved side of beef that, he claimed, hung in the sun for hours in a state of eerie stasis, showing no sign of decomposition. A medical officer testified that much of the beef "had an odor similar to that of a dead human body after being injected with formaldehyde, and it tasted when first cooked like decomposed boric acid." A funeral home director who had served as a soldier in Cuba also mentioned the familiar aroma of embalming chemicals. More than that, he said, the cans of beef were crowded with crystals that looked eerily like the ones that formed in corpses when he injected preservatives. "It did not look like roast beef," a corporal testified.

Eventually, expert witness Harvey Wiley came quietly to the stand. At least a few of the reporters in attendance leaned forward. The chemistry chief was in no way as famous as Governor Roosevelt, but he enjoyed a certain reputation for the trouble he had caused producers of dirty coffee and acid-laced wines. At a recent party, a food trade journal editor had refused to shake Wiley's hand, explaining that he felt no need to be civil to "the man who is doing all he can to destroy American business."

Wiley testified calmly that his staff had found traces of "all of the preservatives ordinarily employed in meat products" in the army supplies. These included "boric acid, salicylic acid, sulfites and sulfurous acid," all of them common and all considered relatively safe, although Wiley, if he had been pressed, would have admitted that he lacked data about how safe they might be and in what doses. The cans sold to the War Department had not been adulterated with the latest industrial chemicals, certainly not synthesized formaldehyde, he said. Instead, the packers had relied mostly on far cheaper sodium chloride—plain old table salt—in combination with potassium nitrate, also relatively inexpensive. Widely known as saltpeter, the latter substance was also an ingredient in gunpowder. Salts had been used this way since the Middle Ages and undoubtedly much earlier. Potassium nitrate, usually mined from guano deposits, was used not only to stop decay but also to treat disease. Eighteenth-century physicians had dosed patients with it to treat everything from asthma to arthritis. In the tiny amounts found in the cans, the compound shouldn't pose any particular risk, Wiley said.

The canned beef had been garden-variety cheap meat—stringy, gristly, poorly handled, and too quick to decompose. And rather than using preservatives too heavily, the cost-conscious meatpackers hadn't used enough salts to prevent decomposition when the cans were exposed to the Cuban heat. This lack had accounted for much of the rot and discoloration found in many cans when they were opened. Wiley speculated that eventually, the very appearance of the stuff "might produce a feeling of nausea or distaste in the person eating it." But he also gave credence to the reports of widespread illnesses blamed on the meat. Many were probably ptomaine poisoning, the general term for bacterial contamination, he said. He testified that the army should have put in place "a supervising agent to check for decay or signs of failed sterilization."

A member of his team, food chemist Willard Bigelow, also testified, reinforcing Wiley's points and adding details. Bigelow—slight, bespectacled and bearded, meticulously tidy, and intense by nature—was known as a tireless and stubborn investigator. For this analysis, he'd visited meatpacking operations not only in Chicago but also in Kansas City and Omaha. He'd run chemical analyses and taste-tested every sample. If the cans had been loaded with industrial preservatives, Bigelow testified, "the taste would be so bitter that it would soon be detected." He made it clear that he'd not enjoyed tasting meat that he judged to be from "the poorest cattle"—possibly diseased. It was terrible-quality beef, he said, but contrary to widespread rumor, it was indeed beef. He'd found no evidence that the soldiers had been dished up diced horse meat.

Perhaps the most condemnatory conclusion that the USDA chemists had reached was that the canned meat that had so disgusted soldiers in Cuba was almost exactly what U.S. consumers were finding on grocery shelves. In response, representatives from the meatpacking firms accepted none of this; they firmly defended their products. Libby issued a statement pointing out that it had been in business for twenty-five years and knew a lot more about meat and its quality than the average soldier: "We sold millions of pounds of canned meat to the government for use in the war and no cans have ever been returned to us as bad," which was true, as the War Department had destroyed the bad meat. The company suggested the real problem was lousy cooks: "All meats require pepper and salt and as the soldiers did not have any seasoning, it is likely the canned meat tasted flat to them. That may have had some effect on them." A spokesman for Augustus Swift's company declared that the packinghouse had not used embalming compounds in meat sold to the military—or to anyone else. It would be, he said, bad business.

The Beef Court concluded by issuing findings that expressed dissatisfaction with almost everyone involved, including General Miles, for raising such a fuss. The judicial panel noted that it was difficult to assess just how substandard the food had been because much of the spoiled or tainted meat was "burned or buried" rather than served to the men. The presiding officers also pointed out that the destruction of food would have left the military kitchens undersupplied if not for the fact that "the entire army was so reduced by sickness and debilitation, due to climatic influences," that many of the men hadn't been eating anyway.

There was nothing in the investigation, the panel continued, to suggest that tainted meat was the major cause of illness. The evil effects of bad water and tropical fevers were found to be the major cause: "The court finds it impossible to conclude that either the canned beef or the refrigerated beef appeared to an appreciable extent as causes of intestinal disease." Taking a cue from Wiley and Bigelow, the ruling found that supplies sent to Cuba had been no "better or worse than any other," although they were probably not suitably packaged to withstand tropical heat and perhaps were inadequately spiced or prepared in the field.

Soldiers who had served in Cuba remained unconvinced. Spanish-American War veterans insisted ever after that the meat had stunk of formaldehyde. One of them was the poet Carl Sandburg, who said years later that he could not forget the stink of the army meat. "It was embalmed," he said, "every suck of nourishment gone from it though having nevertheless a putridity of odor more pungent than ever reaches the nostrils from a properly embalmed cadaver."

The army also sought the Chemistry Division's help in investigating the death of nineteen-year-old Private Ross Gibbons of Peoria, Illinois, who had collapsed in convulsions after dining on a can of corned beef at a Tennessee training camp. A day later he died. Chemical analysis showed that the contents of the can had been saturated with the neurotoxic metal lead, which had apparently seeped out of the container itself. Lead was also found in his body.

Metal poisoning from canned goods didn't surprise Wiley. His laboratory had flagged the problem years earlier. The coffee investigation had noted that "relatively large" amounts of tin were seeping into canned foods. And in the part of Bulletin 13 investigating

canned vegetables, which was printed—and promptly shelved—just
before Julius Morton had shut down the food investigations, lead
poisoning had been highlighted as a primary concern.

Lead solder was then the preferred method for sealing the seams
of tin cans. But while European countries regulated lead levels in
solder, the United States had set no standards, not even for food containers. The Chemistry Division had found that some of the solders
used in tin cans were 50 percent lead. Further, the "tin" used to
make cans was an unregulated alloy of whatever metals the manufacturer had handy. "In this country there is no restriction whatever
in regard to character of the tin employed and as a result of this the
tin of some of the cans has been found to contain as high as 12 percent of lead." The analysis also found other toxic metals including
zinc and copper. Even glass containers used for canning could be
contaminated. Jars were capped with lead tops and sealed with rubber pads or rings that contained sulfate of lead. Testing of jar-canned
goods had found that the food inside sometimes contained higher
lead levels than those found in the tin cans. As the study, overseen by
the tireless Willard Bigelow, concluded: "The general result of the
examination of the canned goods exposed for sale in this country
leads to the rather unpleasant conclusion that the consumers thereof
are exposed to . . . poisoning from copper, zinc, tin and lead."

Those earlier findings had been suppressed, but under Secretary
Wilson, Wiley was again free to publicize his laboratory's food safety
findings. And after the beef court, he realized that his cause was finally in the public eye. Editors were eager to feature his writing,
which appeared frequently in publications that ranged from somber
scientific journals to the liberal, reform-minded *Arena* to popular
*Munsey's* magazine, with its circulation of more than 700,000 readers. In a *Munsey's* article, Wiley detailed his division's survey of
bread and cake "flour" sold in the United States, which they had
found to be liberally laced with ground white clay and powdered
white rocks called "barites." Some flour, labeled as made from

wheat, was really cheaper corn flour, whitened with sulfuric acid. Manufacturers made the acid-treated corn product, labeled "flour-ine," and the ground clay product, called "mineraline," specifically for sale to flour companies. In his article, Wiley quoted from a marketing bulletin that read, "Gentlemen: We invite your attention to our mineraline, which is without a doubt the greatest existing discovery. There is no flourmill man who can afford not to use it for several reasons. Your flour will be much whiter and nicer. And you will realize a profit of between $400 to $1600 per carload of shipped flour barrels."

Almost as soon as the beef court had concluded, there were new, tragic reports of not just "embalmed beef" but also "embalmed milk" causing sickness and death in places like Ohio, Nebraska, and Indiana. In June 1899 the city of Cincinnati warned citizens of "an epidemic of stomach trouble, due practically entirely to embalmed beef." More than one thousand people had fallen ill in a single week after eating beef. The Cincinnati health department had first suspected salicylic acid. As Willard Bigelow had noted in the embalmed beef hearings, this compound was increasingly popular with commercial butchers, who had discovered it could freshen the look of graying beef, setting off a chemical reaction that made old meat look newly pink for a good twelve hours. That time frame, Bigelow had said, was just long enough to move the meat out of the store and into the home kitchen.

Cincinnati's public health chemist, to his surprise, did not find salicylic acid in the samples tested. Instead he discovered two new brand-name preservatives, both of which confirmed widespread public suspicion and finally justified the use of the term "embalmed beef." One was Freezine, a sulfur-rich mixture containing a small percentage of formaldehyde. Freezine's promotional literature boasted: "Meat can be exposed for sale, returned to ice, more of the preparation applied, and still look good to the eye." The other, Preservaline, contained formaldehyde as its main active ingredient.

Cincinnati officials recommended that citizens play it safe and avoid beef altogether.

That same month, the city of Omaha reported an "embalmed milk" crisis that had led directly to the deaths of an alarming number of children. The Nebraska health department warned "all families, as far as possible, to cease the use of milk and cream furnished by local dairies." The problem again was Preservaline. The dairy industry had also discovered that formaldehyde was a useful food additive. Not only did it slow the souring of milk, but its oddly sweet taste could also mask the somewhat acrid tang of milk that had already gone bad. "It is noticeable," announced the city's public health officer, "that more infants have died in Omaha this spring than ever before." And spring, he continued, was usually "a time when the general health conditions should have been good." Following the uptick in child deaths, the department had surveyed physicians and found that almost all the recent infant deaths were related to preservatives in milk.

Hardly had the Omaha milk scandal died down when another flared in Indiana. Dairies near Indianapolis apparently weren't bothering with commercially prepared formulas like Preservaline. They were simply pouring straight formaldehyde into rotting milk. Then they sold it on the cheap to poor families and to budget-strapped facilities like orphanages. The practice had been linked to the deaths of more than two dozen children in Indianapolis orphanages.

The Indiana state health officer, Dr. John Hurty, a former professor of pharmacy at Purdue University and an old friend of Harvey Wiley, had also earned a reputation as a tireless crusader. His work for causes ranging from smallpox vaccination to pasteurization of milk would eventually lead to his election as president of the American Public Health Association. In the aftermath of the orphanage deaths, Hurty explained to journalists that the toxic compounds had proven an economic boon to dairymen, who used to have to throw out milk when it went bad. "Two drops of a forty percent solution of formaldehyde will preserve a pint of milk for several days," Hurty said. There were no safety tests available, but businessmen had gambled that the amount put into food and drink was too low to cause harm. It turned out some dairymen were adding extra drops of formaldehyde solution on the principle that it would even better preserve their product.

Hurty's department advised that even an "infinitesimal amount" of formaldehyde could be dangerous, especially to infants. "Such being the fact, it should not be used for preserving foods," he insisted. When a newspaper reporter sympathetic to the dairy industry asked him why he was making such a big deal about it, Hurty snapped back: "Well, it's embalming fluid that you are adding to the milk. I guess it's all right if you want to embalm the baby." After his press conference, the *Indianapolis News* published a cartoon showing a large glass bottle labeled "Milk" with a monster coiling from the bottle's open mouth. The creature was an evil-eyed scaly thing with jagged teeth and sharp claws. A baby in a diaper stood looking up at the monster, holding only a rattle to defend itself. "It looks like a tough battle for the little fellow" read the caption.

Hurty had been trying for years to get the Indiana legislature to pass a food safety law, arguing that it was essential due to the lack of federal action. With more victims every day—the embalmed milk epidemic would eventually kill an estimated four hundred children in the state—and a corresponding rise in public outrage, the state passed its Pure Food Law in 1898. Hurty promptly banned all use of formaldehyde in milk. He also launched a campaign to clean up dairy practices in general. Many dairies were still notoriously unsanitary, and milk routinely contained dangerous colonies of disease-causing bacteria, among other impurities. Commercially sold milk that Hurty's department had recently analyzed contained horsehair worms, flakes of moss, and traces of manure. Further, the chief health officer could "state confidently that this milk has been adulterated with stagnant water."

He strongly recommended adoption of the flash-heat process for killing microorganisms and preventing spoilage in beverages, a method developed in the 1860s by French scientist Louis Pasteur. Pasteurization had proven a success in the wine and beer industries in Europe and had more recently begun being used by European dairies to kill bacteria in their product. It was time, Hurty said, for the United States to catch up.

*Four*

# WHAT'S IN IT?

## 1899–1901

———————●———————

*And yet while we eat*
*We cannot help asking, "What's in it?"*


In 1899 U.S. senator William Mason of Illinois asked for and received permission from Secretary Wilson for Wiley to serve as scientific adviser for a new series of hearings on the country's tainted food and drink supply. Mason, a Republican from Chicago described by newspapers as "a champion of liberty," had a reputation as a progressive legislator and a reform-minded opponent of machine politics.

The Mason hearings began that very spring, with meetings scheduled not only for Washington but also for New York and Chicago. They would continue for nearly a year, encompassing fifty different sessions and almost two hundred witnesses. The Chemistry Division would be nearly overwhelmed by the need to analyze hundreds of additional samples of food and drink. State public health officials lined up to testify, from Indiana's Hurty, caught up in his state's milk scandal, to the chief chemist from Connecticut, whose laboratory had discovered that spice processors in that state were burning old rope and using the ash as filler in ground spices such as ginger. Businessmen also testified, the honest ones decrying unfair competition from fraudsters. Representatives from the cream of tartar industry warned that baking powders were tainted with aluminum. Representatives from the dairy industry testified that makers of oleomargarine (by which they meant meatpackers) were still consistently mislabeling their product as butter.

Without federal help, dairy states had little recourse; the state of New Hampshire had tried requiring that all margarine be dyed pink, but the U.S. Supreme Court had struck down that legislation in 1890, declaring it an illegal tax. Dairymen complained at the Mason hearings that margarine makers were nothing but cheats and liars. The meatpackers, in turn, accused the dairy industry of being stuck in the primitive past. Anyone, they insisted, could tell the difference between old-fashioned, often rancid butter and ever-fresh oleomargarine, which was "a product of the advanced age."

At Mason's request, the Chemistry Division's Willard Bigelow had looked again at dishonesty in the wine industry, finding the usual preservatives, such as salicylic acid, swirling through many bottles. He'd also found many bottles that were labeled as wine but were merely factory-produced ethanol colored with coal-tar dyes and flavored with fruit peels. One wine dealer, when visited by Bigelow posing as a shop owner, had asked "what distinguished label" his visitor desired. He'd taken Bigelow's list and then, while the chemist watched, filled everything from the same cask, simply pasting labels on the different bottles to identify them as claret, Burgundy, or Bordeaux.

For almost every food product, the Chemistry Division could point to a trick involved in its manufacture. Doctors continued to worry over continued reports of "grocer's itch," a side effect of the deceptive practice of grinding up insects and passing the result off as brown sugar. Sometimes live lice survived the process. Beer, which most consumers imagined to be derived from malted barley and hops, was often made from a cheaper ferment of rice or even corn grits. So-called aged whiskey often was still routinely rectified alcohol, diluted and colored brown. As Wiley had found twenty years earlier at Purdue, corn syrup was widely used as the basis for fake versions of honey and maple syrup.

Many manufacturers argued that they had to fake products to stay competitive. Detroit canner Walter Williams, of Williams Brothers, described the making of his Highland Strawberry Preserves. The jam was, he said, 45 percent sugar, 35 percent corn syrup, 15 percent apple juice made from discarded apple skins, some scraps of apple skin and cores, and usually one or two pieces of strawberry. The strawberries cost him, he added. Many comparably priced preserves were just glucose, apple juice, red dye, and timothy seed added to simulate strawberry seeds. "If we could sell pure goods, I would be pleased," Williams insisted. "I believe they should be labeled, showing their ingredients and showing the quality of the goods." But as there was no law setting such standards and as he had to compete with less scrupulous canners, there was no way for him to stay in business unless he cut costs to match.

Wiley testified that about 5 percent of all foods were routinely adulterated, with the number being much higher—up to 90 percent— in categories such as coffee, spices, and "food products made for selling to the poor." This proved to be a little too sedate a summary for some of the tabloid journals; reporters exaggerated his testimony, stating that Wiley believed 90 percent of *all* food and beverage products to be adulterated. The careless reporting dismayed Wiley, his boss Wilson, and even the president—especially after alarmed American trade representatives wrote from Europe that grocers there were talking about boycotting U.S. food entirely. Wilson had to send clarifications and copies of Wiley's actual testimony to the State Department in order to reassure importers of American food and drink.

In other testimony, Wiley concentrated on preservatives and dyes. For example, he cited the practice of improving the color of canned peas by spiking them with copper sulfate and zinc salts. In small doses, these metals might pose little risk, he said, but no one really knew what those safe doses were. As he had earlier, he also warned of a possible cumulative dose: Who could ensure that a steady diet of the stuff, over months or even years, wouldn't lead to heavy metal poisoning? Another witness, chemical physiologist Russell Chittenden of Yale University, echoed that point even more strongly, warning that most people eating canned vegetables would eventually be harmed by repeated exposure to metals. He urged that copper, in particular, be banned as an additive from American food products as soon as possible.

Wiley again emphasized that the biggest worry was for vulnerable populations: young children, people with chronic health problems, and the elderly. Those with a healthy stomach, as he put it, were unlikely to be harmed by an occasional exposure to copper or zinc. The problem was that no one was sure who would be harmed: "Many people they do hurt and the least possible amount upsets the digestion."

Unlike Chittenden, Wiley did not urge an immediate ban. Rather, Wiley told the assembled senators that such regulations needed to be grounded in good science. He urged that the government invest in studying the health effects of such additives. If risks were clearly and methodically identified, then those compounds should be removed from all food and drink. And, somewhat wearily, he once again recommended that manufacturers be required to tell consumers, on labels, what was being mixed into their products. "Were it as harmless as distilled water," he said, "there would be no excuse of its addition to food without notification to the consumer."

State food chemists also expressed dismay over the new additives. A. S. Mitchell, food chemist for the state of Wisconsin, brought to the hearings samples of three of the most popular new preservatives: Rosaline Berliner, Freezine, and Preservaline, the formaldehyde-rich culprit in the Indiana milk poisonings. He pointed out that none of them had been safety-tested; that all of them had been found in samples of commercially sold ice cream, cottage cheese, beef, chicken, pork, and shellfish; and, finally, that none of those foodstuffs bore a label listing ingredients.

With the Rosaline Berliner, Mitchell highlighted what he saw as the alarming increase in the use of its active ingredient—sodium borate, or borax. A naturally occurring mineral salt, it had been used in various forms of manufacturing for centuries. The name came from the old Arabic word *būraq* (بورق), which meant white. First discovered in the dry lake beds of Tibet, the powder, which easily dissolved in water and could be used to enhance enamel glazing, had been traded along the Silk Road as early as the eighth century CE. But its modern use had been driven by discovery of vast deposits of borax in California and by the aggressive marketing of the Pacific Coast Borax Company. A Wisconsin-born miner named Francis Marion Smith, with a natural flair for marketing his product, had founded the company. Smith, known to consumers as the "Borax King," had purchased the rights to a rich vein of borax in the Mojave region, known as the "Twenty Mule Team Mine" for the long wagon trains used to haul out the mineral deposits. On the advice of his manager, he developed a cleaning formula promoted as "Twenty Mule Team Borax" for its powerful action and then went on to market his product for that and many other uses, including as a handy preservative.

Borax was already known at that point as both a cheap and versatile preservative. It slowed fungal growth and it appeared to inhibit bacteria as well. Long before Smith's industrious marketing, food manufacturers had been gradually taking up its use. Meat producers had started using it in the mid-1870s, after British importers had complained that American bacon and ham tasted too salty. The dairy industry had followed by using borax as a butter preservative, again avoiding a salty taste. During the Mason hearings, one dairy spokesman suggested that the British had, in fact, come to prefer the slightly metallic taste of borax in butter. The meatpackers used borax to preserve everything from canned meat to oleomargarine. In a rare moment of agreement, they joined with dairy representatives in attacking complaints like Mitchell's, pointing out that refrigeration options were extremely limited when sending products overseas. One could do only so much by packing with ice; it served no one to sell slimy meat and rancid butter abroad. The meatpackers also moved to quell the suggestion that borax might not be a healthy additive. They hired toxicologist Walter Haines, from the University of Chicago, to assure the Senate that borax was safe. Haines didn't exactly stick to script. He said that he'd seen no convincing evidence that borax was harming people but refused unambiguous endorsement. For the moment, Haines explained, illnesses caused by decaying foods, the dreaded "ptomaines," seemed to him to be a far worse option.

Such scientific caution failed to satisfy preservative makers, whose position was made clear by Albert Heller of Chicago, manufacturer of the formaldehyde-infused Freezine. Yes, Heller said, Freezine was now used in everything from cream puffs to canned corned beef. But American consumers were lucky to find it there. By preventing decay, it reduced the number of illnesses caused by the ptomaines. For all he knew, it reduced other terrible diseases like cholera as well. The American public should embrace chemical preservatives, he argued, and smart consumers already did. "I wish to say that every one of us eats embalmed meat and we know it and we like it," Heller said.

I n the early spring of 1900, after reviewing the hearing testimony, Senator Mason delivered a fiery speech on the Senate floor. "This is the only civilized country in the world that does not protect the consumer of food products against the adulterations of manufacturers," he charged. The country's food was full of aluminum, "sulfuric acid, copper salts, zinc and other poisonous substances." And if it wasn't contaminated with toxic substances, it was faked, disguised, or otherwise adulterated. He'd had enough and he hoped the American people and his fellow legislators felt the same, Mason said. He was proud to introduce legislation that would require safety testing of additives and substitutes and prohibit those found dangerous. Further, his pure-food bill would require accurate labeling of all ingredients. If it passed, companies that failed to comply, he added, would be fined or even taken to court. He was proud to announce that comparable legislation was being introduced in the House.

The whole parade of food and drink manufacturers—dairy, meat, eggs, flour, baking soda, beer, wine, whiskey—not to mention the chemical companies, immediately lined up against the legislation. Despite his strong language in support of the Senate bill, Mason warned Wiley privately to expect its failure. The sponsor of the House version of the bill, Congressman Marriott Brosius from Pennsylvania, was equally pessimistic. His assessment, as he also told Wiley, was that the most positive result was likely to be simply keeping the issue "before the public eye."

Within weeks, both bills were shut down in committee by legislators friendly to the different manufacturing interests. It was frustrating, Wiley wrote to Mason, because he did think public support was turning their way. He'd collected dozens of newspaper clippings about the Mason hearings and every single one of them had applauded the action of the committee.

Many people also had written directly to Wiley requesting copies of committee testimony, issues of Bulletin 13, and even a tongue-in-cheek piece of doggerel that Wiley had written for a Pure Food Congress and impulsively decided to read aloud as part of his testimony. The verses, also published in New York's *Pharmaceutical Era Weekly*, concluded pointedly:

> The banquet how fine, don't begin it
> Till you think of the past and the future and sigh,
> "How I wonder, I wonder, what's in it."

That same spring of 1900, in late May, Wiley proposed marriage to Anna Kelton. Her written answer—though not an immediate refusal—was less welcoming than he'd hoped it would be. "What worries me most of all is that I am not happier," she wrote to him. "I had always pictured to myself that love would be consuming and overwhelming in its joy and I am on the verge of tears. What is the matter with me do you think?" She was painfully aware of the great age difference, of her mother's staunch disapproval, and most of all of her own ambition to be independent and self-sustaining. "Browning's line about 'the best is yet to be' comes into my mind but still this hobgoblin thought keeps popping up and it is that I am sacrificing my ideals, however childish they may be."

Late that month, she called it off. "I am only full of reproaches for myself and for my weakness and lack of womanliness in not knowing my own mind and for letting you even this week harbor any hope of my sharing your future life," she wrote. "But oh please believe it is that same honesty in me that before you admired which now makes me tell you this before it is too late." She said she lacked that "sacred, sweet, overpowering feeling" that should accompany real love. "And so goodbye," she concluded. "Goodbye with respect and the sincerest regards, I am always yours, Anna."

Wiley couldn't bring himself to accept that as a final answer. A brief separation was pending—he'd been appointed to represent the Agriculture Department that summer in Paris, at the Exposition Universelle de 1900, and to organize an exhibit there showcasing the excellence of American wines and beers. With some difficulty, he persuaded her to wait until he returned from France, suggesting she take some time to think things over before definitively telling him no. They held on to that fragile truce until he sailed in mid-July. But he was still shipboard in the middle of the Atlantic when Anna Kelton requested and received a transfer from the Agriculture Department to the Library of Congress. "When I left for Paris I had a perfect understanding with her but I had not been here long before I received a very sensible letter from her saying that she had concluded that our agreement had better be terminated," he wrote to a friend. "At the same time I gathered from what she wrote that she had been influenced in this by her family." They thought, he knew, that it was wrong for a man of his age to court a woman in her twenties. But "I have yet to learn that loving a pretty girl in a proper way and being loved by her in return has anything blameworthy in it."

To Anna he wrote a tender good-bye letter. "You say, 'Why don't you make me love you?' Love, dear heart, does not come by making nor does it go by unmaking. . . . I want you to know, dear heart, how much zest you have brought into my life." She did not reply. But still he could not bring himself to remove her photo from the inside cover of his pocket watch.

Secretary Wilson wrote to Wiley in Paris to celebrate the good reception that he and his exhibit on alcoholic beverages had received, "which pleases me very much." Wilson also added a note of reassurance regarding job stability. The next presidential election was coming up in November. "The campaign has not yet opened up but the indications are quite good regarding Mr. McKinley's re-election."

McKinley had been forced to select a new running mate, as his popular vice president, Garret Hobart, had died in November of 1898. After much political wrangling, the party had chosen the progressive New York governor Theodore Roosevelt to take his place. McKinley's closest advisers were unenthusiastic: Roosevelt had not backed McKinley's nomination in 1894 and Roosevelt had an un-McKinley-like reputation as a reformer. But that turned out to be a major campaign advantage.

The Democrats had once again named William Jennings Bryan, who had lost to McKinley four years earlier, as their candidate. As the campaign began, Bryan fiercely attacked McKinley as a corporate insider, a president beholden to banks and railroads. As he was close to those industries, McKinley decided to keep a low profile. The president gave only one speech during the campaign. The energetic Roosevelt, by contrast, gave more than 673 speeches, in 567 cities and towns, in 24 states. On November 3, Election Day, McKinley and Roosevelt won by a wide margin. Wilson's job was secure for another four years and—as the secretary had predicted—so were both his chief chemist's job and his food safety crusade.

In 1901, shortly after McKinley's inauguration, Anheuser-Busch of St. Louis and Pabst Brewing Company of Milwaukee wrote to Wiley asking for analyses of their new "temperance beverages." These bottled malt brews, with little alcohol content, were a relatively new take on the concept of "small beer," which had been around in one form or another at least since medieval times, when it was often served to children. The big American brewers, producers of higher-alcohol beers and ales, began making temperance beverages to sell to nondrinkers and former drinkers and to curry favor from increasingly prominent anti-alcohol activists.

The Woman's Christian Temperance Union had been organized in the early 1870s with the stated goal of "achieving a sober and pure world." It was far from the first American temperance organization, but along with the Anti-Saloon League, organized in 1893, the WCTU had become one of the most strident and effective forces opposed to alcohol consumption. With its slogan, "Agitate. Educate. Legislate," the WCTU linked this cause to another growing social movement, that of women's suffrage. Frances Willard, WCTU leader, saw suffrage as a key to power. She argued that if women had the vote, they could better protect their communities from drunkenness and other vices. By 1901 the organization boasted more than 150,000 members nationwide. Its activism—and growing popularity—was making American brewers and other alcohol producers increasingly nervous.

So the brewing companies had double hopes for their temperance beverages: new markets plus the alleviation of hostilities. Wisconsin-based Pabst had two years earlier gotten the Chemistry Division to analyze its Malt Mead, seeking a stamp of approval to help market it. The lab had confirmed that the drink contained less than 2 percent alcohol. Now the company wanted Wiley's support for another new low-alcohol beverage called Nutria. Pabst intended to sell it in Indian Territory (in the eastern half of what is now Oklahoma), where tribes including the Cherokee and Muscogee had been resettled after they were forced from ancestral lands in the Southeast. Pabst's complaint was that the Department of Indian Affairs, which prohibited the sale of any alcoholic beverages in Indian Territory, had analyzed Nutria and declared it an intoxicating drink. It was shoddy chemistry, the company complained. Could Wiley's more able crew set things right? The Chemistry Division's analysis confirmed Pabst's position and Nutria went on sale in Indian Territory.

Anheuser-Busch, meanwhile, had created a drink called American Hop Ale, essentially a beer-flavored soft drink, and wanted Wiley and Bigelow to analyze it so that the company could use the official Chemistry Division findings as part of its marketing campaign. The chemists complied, and Wiley wrote to the company to inform it that the division had detected traces of alcohol in the product. This, the brewery responded, was merely a preservative. "This is our secret," a reply from Anheuser-Busch explained, but surely it didn't alter the basic nature of the beverage? "Could not a small percentage of alcohol be added to the soft stuff to make it keep?" It could, the Chemistry Division allowed, and shortly later the company launched a new near-beer campaign.

In May 1901 the Pan-American Exposition in Buffalo opened. This latest world's fair, with its dazzle of electric lighting powered by nearby Niagara Falls, sprawled across 350 acres and celebrated the new century under the slogan "Commercial well-being and good understanding among the American Republics." As part of the U.S. government's contribution, the Agriculture Department presented exhibits featuring innovations ranging from new crops to modern farm machinery. Wiley's scientific division, now renamed the Bureau of Chemistry, participated with three displays, two of which—one highlighting the sugar beet industry, the other celebrating experimental use of plant products in road building—fit the fair's theme and a third, organized by Willard Bigelow, on "Pure and Adulterated Foods," that defiantly did not.

Bigelow's exhibit was made eye-catching by some brightly dyed flags, which were labeled as exemplifying the coal-tar agents used to color food and drink. It also featured a display of faked products, ranging from vinegar to whiskey, highlighting a newly developed technique of adding soap to rectified alcohol to simulate the way aged bourbons would bead and cling on glass. But perhaps the most pointed section dealt with the rising tide of new industrial preservatives. On these shelves were not only food samples but also glass jars and beakers containing preservatives extracted from everyday foods. The exhibit divided preservatives into "undoubtedly injurious, such as formaldehyde, salicylic acid, and sulfites" and possibly injurious, such as borax and benzoic acid.

"It is claimed by those interested in their use that the amount of preservatives added to foods is so small as to be unimportant." But in this time of no food safety regulation, "small" was left entirely to the discretion of the manufacturer. Some foods were basically soaked in the new compounds. Or as Bigelow put it: "The amount added sometimes greatly exceeds that which is believed to be necessary by those who favor the use of chemical preservatives."

The popular exposition ran for seven months and attracted eight million visitors, including President McKinley, who arrived in early September to make a speech against American isolationism. On the afternoon of September 6, he stood at the head of a receiving line in the exposition's grand Temple of Music, cheerfully shaking hands with enthusiastic citizens. Reporter John D. Wells of the *Buffalo Morning News*, assigned to cover the event, stood taking notes, carefully describing each encounter. He would later recount that when one smiling young man got up to the president, he raised his right hand, which held a pistol wrapped in a handkerchief. Leon Czolgosz fired the pistol twice. The first bullet grazed McKinley's chest. The second ripped through his stomach and sent him stumbling backward. The assassin was jumped by both police and attendees and transported to the local jail; the gravely injured president was rushed by ambulance to the local hospital.

Still, doctors reassured Vice President Roosevelt and cabinet members who had rushed to Buffalo to be by McKinley's side that the wounds were not fatal. The president was expected to recover. Roosevelt departed for a working vacation in Vermont, where he was scheduled to address the state's Fish and Game League. But the local Buffalo doctors, refusing to use newfangled X-ray machines, had not successfully removed all the debris left by the fragmenting bullet or fully sterilized the internal injuries. The wounds became infected, gangrene set in, and on September 14, nine days after the shooting, McKinley died.

Roosevelt rushed back—cobbling together a trip by horse, car, and train—to take the oath of office. He received a less-than-enthusiastic welcome from reform-wary leaders of his party. "I told William McKinley it was a mistake to nominate that wild man at Philadelphia," said Senator Mark Hanna of Ohio. "Now look, that damned cowboy is president of the United States."

Czolgosz, a former steelworker and a self-proclaimed anarchist, was rapidly charged, tried, and convicted. He received the death sentence, at the unanimous recommendation of the jury, and died in the electric chair at Auburn (New York) Prison on October 29, just forty-five days after the shooting.

I n the weeks after McKinley's death, Roosevelt sought at first to
reassure the country: "In this hour of deep and terrible bereavement, I wish to state that I shall continue unbroken the policy of
President McKinley for the peace, prosperity, and the honor of the
country."

But the new president was biding his time. In February 1902,
Roosevelt's administration filed an antitrust suit against a giant holding company created by a consortium that included such Gilded Age
titans as J. P. Morgan, Cornelius Vanderbilt, and the Rockefellers.
The *Wall Street Journal* angrily called it the greatest shock to the
stock market since McKinley's assassination. By contrast, Harvey
Wiley was pleased to see the president show his more volatile, reformist side and hoped to see pure food and drink become one of Roosevelt's causes. Unfortunately Wiley had stumbled already, and
stumbled badly, in the opinion of the new chief executive.

Since his adventure in Cuba, Roosevelt had become a booster of
the newly independent island country. With the support of Elihu
Root, the secretary of war, the president proposed an agreement that
would, among other things, foster economic growth by reducing the
American tariff on Cuban-grown sugar. In January 1902 the House
Committee on Ways and Means began hearings on the issue. Wiley,
long considered an expert on the growing and processing of sugars,
was called to testify.

Wiley feared that if the tariff on Cuban sugar was lowered, powerful American companies would see an opportunity for easy profit,
buy up the imports, and resell them to American consumers at higher
prices. The losers, he suspected, would be American farmers, undercut by the Cuban competition. He didn't want to say all of this,
however, in a public hearing. He knew it wouldn't sit well with Roosevelt, but he wasn't willing to testify contrary to what he believed.
So Wiley asked Secretary Wilson to get the congressional summons

withdrawn. "'If I go up there I shall tell what I believe to be the truth and thus get in trouble,'" wrote Wiley, quoting himself in his conversation with the secretary.

Unfortunately for Wiley and his future relations with Roosevelt, Wilson shared the chemist's reservations about Cuban sugar and wanted those doubts to be aired in testimony before Congress. Wilson also knew he'd damage his own standing with the president if he delivered the testimony himself. As a member of the cabinet, he said, he dared not say what he thought. Wiley could. The chief chemist agreed, reluctantly, to be a witness and, characteristically, he spoke his mind. "I consider it a very unwise piece of legislation and one which will damage, to a very serious extent, our domestic sugar industry," Wiley testified. "Do you contemplate remaining in the Agricultural Department?" a legislator asked as other committee members burst out laughing.

The president was not amused. He summoned Wilson to demand that the chemist be fired on the spot. Wilson, realizing the extent of the damage he'd done to his subordinate, told the president that the chemist had been following departmental orders. It would be wrong to fire Wiley for doing what he was told, said the secretary. Grudgingly, Roosevelt agreed. He sent Wilson back with a message for the chief chemist: "I will let you off this time but don't do it again." Later that year, Roosevelt successfully negotiated a treaty that included a 20 percent tariff reduction on Cuban sugar. "I ran afoul of his good will in the first months of his administration," Wiley later wrote ruefully. "I fear that this man with whom I had many contacts after he became president never had a very good opinion of me."

*Five*

# ONLY THE BRAVE

## 1901–1903

———◉———

*Oh, maybe this bread contains alum or chalk*
*Or sawdust chopped up very fine*
*Or gypsum in powder about which they talk,*
*Terra alba just out of the mine*

B y 1901 the Bureau of Chemistry had identified 152 "new" patent preservatives on the U.S. market. Although the term "new," the government scientists found, was often merely an advertising ploy rather than a sign of innovation. Many of these products were simply remixes of old standbys like formaldehyde or copper sulfate. The main difference was that the formulas contained these compounds in greater quantities than their predecessors—and, as a result, promised astonishing shelf life. As one advertising circular put it, a good preservative was "guaranteed to keep meat, fish, poultry, etc. for *any* length of time without ice." The idea of indestructible food products fascinated many in an era when kitchens were equipped with, at best, an icebox to delay spoilage.

The American chemical industry was quick to recognize a

lucrative market in such food- and drinking-enhancing products. In addition to preservatives, companies developed synthetic compounds to make food production cheaper. The sweetener saccharin, discovered in 1879 at Johns Hopkins University, cost far less than sugar and quickly replaced it as a cost-saving alternative. Flavoring agents such as laboratory-brewed citric acid or peppermint extracts could now be used in drinks and other products instead of fresh lemon juice or mint—again saving costs, and again crowding the farmer out of the supply chain.

The pioneering industrial chemist Charles Pfizer, who had founded his New York pharmaceutical company in 1849, now also produced borax, boric acid, cream of tartar, and citric acid for use in food and drink. Chicago's Joseph Baur, whose Liquid Carbonic Company produced the pressurized gas used in the fizzing drinks of soda fountains, had become so interested in artificial sweeteners that in 1901 he had invested in a new business in St. Louis, the Monsanto Chemical Company, to produce saccharin in large quantities. Saccharin production had also launched the Heyden Chemical Works of New York City in 1900, although that company also branched into the preservative market, producing salicylic acid, formaldehyde, and sodium benzoate for use in food and drinks. The food and drink market also attracted Herbert Henry Dow, founder at age thirty-one of the Dow Chemical Company in Midlands, Michigan. Dow had been a chemistry student at the Case Institute of Technology (eventually merged into Case Western Reserve University) in Cleveland, Ohio, and in 1897 with financial backing from both friends and former professors, he'd launched his own company, Dow Chemical. The company's first venture was based on a new process Dow had invented for extracting the element bromine from brine for antiseptic use. But within a few years, Dow also made magnesium for incendiary flares, phenol for explosives, and agricultural pesticides—and was becoming a major producer of food preservatives such as sodium benzoate.

The bureau's scientists learned much of what they knew about food additives from state-employed chemists in independent-minded, agriculture-rich places like Kentucky, Wisconsin, and North Dakota, where farmers were all too aware that industry was under-cutting the fresh-food market with increasing use of artificial ingredients. Prominent examples included Indiana's outspoken John Hurty and the even more combative Edwin Ladd, analytical chemist at the North Dakota Agricultural College in Fargo. Ladd's analysis of food and drink sold in the state had led him to believe that big corporations basically regarded North Dakota as "a dumping ground for chemically-enhanced waste food products." In 1901 he launched a statewide campaign for a pure-food law, bombarding North Dakota legislators and citizens with a catalog of dismaying data.

"More than 90 percent of local meat markets in the state were using chemical preservatives and in nearly every butcher shop could be found a bottle of Freezine, Preservaline, or Iceine," he reported. "In the dried beef, in the smoked meats, in the canned bacon, in the canned chipped beef, boracic acid or borates (products of the borax industry) are a common ingredient." In almost every food product Ladd analyzed he found unlabeled industrial compounds that had never been tested for safety, although some were known toxins. "Ninety per cent of the so-called French peas we have taken up in North Dakota were found to contain copper salts." Baked goods were often loaded with "alum," a salt of aluminum and potassium, used as a preservative, in baking powders, and to whiten bread.

Ladd was particularly critical of what bottlers were passing off as "catsup" or "ketchup." (The spellings were already interchangeable.) It was often unrelated to the well-known tomato product. The cheapest of these sauces were frequently made from unwanted pumpkin skins and rinds, stewed, dyed red, and spiced up with vinegar and a little cayenne or paprika. Or ketchup was a soup of "waste products from canners—pulp, skins, ripe tomatoes, green tomatoes, starch paste, coal-tar colors, and chemical preservatives, usually benzoate of soda or salicylic acid." The North Dakota food chemistry analysis, which Ladd would issue in full the following year, revealed that 100 percent of ketchups were rich in coal-tar dyes, preservatives, and waste products. He also found similar problems in a range of other products, reporting "one hundred percent adulteration" of jams and jellies, 88 percent adulteration of canned corn, and 50 percent of canned peas. And the list went on.

Ladd sent newspapers around the state details of every adulteration finding that he'd uncovered. In response, the National Biscuit Company (later renamed Nabisco) had its legal department engage in an expensive long-distance phone call, suggesting that he tone it down. Ladd, as the local papers gleefully reported, responded by losing his temper. His secretary reported hearing his shouting: "By God, no Eastern lawyer is going to tell me what we can eat out here in North Dakota!"

Ladd's friend and colleague South Dakota food chemist James Shepard, meanwhile, had launched a similar campaign for a food safety law. To showcase the problem for state residents, Shepard created and publicized a daily meal plan to illustrate the seep of industrial chemistry into the average dinner. His menu, Shepard announced, was such that "any family in the United States might possibly use":

### BREAKFAST

*Sausage*: coal-tar dye and borax

*Bread*: alum

*Butter*: coal-tar dye

*Canned cherries*: coal-tar dye and salicylic acid

*Pancakes*: alum

*Syrup*: sodium sulphite [then the spelling of sulfite]

THIS GIVES EIGHT DOSES OF CHEMICALS AND DYES FOR BREAKFAST.

### DINNER

*Tomato soup*: coal-tar dye and benzoic acid

*Cabbage and corned beef*: saltpeter

*Canned scallops*: sulfuric acid and formaldehyde

*Canned peas*: salicylic acid

*Catsup*: coal-tar dye and benzoic acid

*Vinegar*: coal-tar dye

*Bread and butter*: alum and coal-tar dye

*Mince pie*: boracic acid

*Pickles*: coppers, sodium sulphite, and salicylic acid

*Lemon ice cream*: methyl alcohol

THIS GIVES SIXTEEN DOSES FOR DINNER.

### SUPPER

*Bread and butter*: alum and coal-tar dye

*Canned beef*: borax

*Canned peaches*: sodium sulfite, coal-tar dye, and salicylic acid

*Pickles*: copper, sodium sulfite, and formaldehyde

*Catsup*: coal-tar dye and benzoic acid

*Lemon cake*: alum

*Baked pork and beans*: formaldehyde

*Vinegar*: coal-tar dye

*Currant jelly*: coal-tar dye and salicylic acid

*Cheese*: coal-tar dye

THIS GIVES SIXTEEN DOSES FOR SUPPER.

"According to this menu," Shepard announced to his state's newspapers, "the unconscious and unwilling patient gets forty doses of chemicals and colors per day."

But the additives were so little studied that even concerned scientists like Shepard and Ladd could only guess at what risk they might pose. There were some animal studies on these new food additives, but they were limited at best. One standard approach involved making a solution of residues from food and drink products and injecting that solution into rabbits. If the rabbits didn't die within minutes, food manufacturers would declare the material to be nonpoisonous and safe for human beings.

Wiley had long worried about this lack of guidance, lack of dosage limits, lack of basic information. If Americans consumed multiple doses of untested compounds in every meal with no assurance of their safety, he thought, then government officials like himself were failing them. The only way to fix that, he'd decided, was to devise some real public health experiments. And the most direct way to get the information would be by using human volunteers. So that same year, 1901, he asked Congress to fund a study that he described as "hygienic table trials." His plan was to sit people down at "hygienic" tables—by which he meant a clean and carefully controlled setting—and feed them precisely measured meals. Half of the diners would eat fresh, additive-free dishes. The others would receive specific doses of a chemical preservative with each meal. The diners were not to know who was consuming what. Wiley and staff would monitor the health effects, if any, from these diets.

He proposed that his human guinea pigs be tough male specimens, "young, robust fellows, with maximum resistance to deleterious effects of adulterated foods." If such individuals were sickened, he reasoned, then this would be much more of a warning flag than if the test subjects were already considered fragile. "If they should show signs of injury after they were fed such substances for a period of time, the deduction would naturally follow that children and older persons, more susceptible than they, would be greater sufferers from similar causes." The hygienic table trials, he explained in his proposal to Congress, would address "whether such preservatives should ever be used or not, and if so, what preservatives and in what quantities?" He added that the experiments could also address questions about other additives, such as food dyes. He had no idea what these experiments might find, he emphasized. But he could make a good case for giving them a try. And after all, the lawmakers were eating and drinking these unknown compounds too.

In March, Congress authorized a grant of $5,000 (about $150,000 in today's dollars) to, as the legislation put it, "enable the Secretary of Agriculture to investigate the character of food preservatives, coloring matters and other substances added to foods, to determine their relation to digestion and health, and to establish the principles which should guide their use."

The sum was only a third of what Wiley had requested, but it was a start. Now he just had to figure out how to launch the country's first food-toxicity trials involving human subjects. He had no equipment. No supplies, food or otherwise. Nor did he have any test subjects nor any assurance that anyone would sign up to be poisoned.

He needed a kitchen, a dining room, and a cook. For economy's sake, and with Wilson's permission, he decided to build his experimental restaurant in the basement at the Department of Agriculture. The resulting dining room was sparely furnished with two round tables of dark stained oak covered with white tablecloths. Six stiff ladder-back chairs gathered around each table. The china was plain white, the walls painted white and unadorned. Shelving, neatly divided into small cubbies, lined one wall and contained everything from pepper grinders to measuring tools, including a sturdy brass scale for weighing out the food.

The adjoining kitchen was furnished with cooking necessities and no more. But the area was scrupulously clean and reasonably pleasant. "Cheerful surroundings, good company, and in general an agreeable environment, tend to promote the favorable progress of digestion," he wrote. "A reversal of the conditions of the environment have exactly the opposite effect."

He wanted the meals to be wholesome, tasty, and dished out on a precise schedule: breakfast at 8:00 a.m., luncheon at noon, dinner at 5:30 p.m., "these being the customary meal-times" for civil service employees. He wanted strictly fresh ingredients with no trace of preservatives. He'd budgeted for roast beef, beefsteak, veal, pork, chicken, turkey, fish, oysters, and an array of fruits and vegetables. Cream and milk were allowed, but these had to be pasteurized to avoid both bacterial infections and unmonitored chemical preservatives. Some canned soups, fruits, and vegetables were also allowed, but only in specially ordered, preservative-free batches from selected manufacturers. "The greatest pains were taken to secure absolute freedom from antiseptics in the whole of the food consumed."

The Bureau of Chemistry recruited volunteers by posting an advertisement, circulated to government employees, promising three free meals daily in exchange for participation in the study. As the *Washington Post* put it, the U.S. government was about to "open, for the first time in history, a scientific boarding house under the direction of Prof. Wiley." To the professor's relief, volunteers applied in abundance. Young men, earning perhaps a few hundred a year, struggling to make ends meet in the nation's capital, saw a chance to stretch their budgets. Wiley, who had lived poor himself, understood that: "They are clerks, working for small salaries, and the item of free board will be a big one to them," he said.

The Chemistry Bureau also received a deluge of applications from fascinated citizens around the country: "Dear Sir," wrote one applicant. "I read in the paper of your experiments on diet. I have a stomach that can stand anything. I have a stomach that will surprise you. . . . What do you think of it? My stomach can hold anything."

Two of Wiley's chemist friends in Ohio wrote in jest to apply for positions. He wrote an amused reply, but one that probably gave them more insight into his perspective than he was willing to allow in public: "You will begin with a diet of borax garnished with salicylic acid—with a dash of alum on the side. You will then have a course in chromatics—beginning with the beautiful yellow of oleomargarine and including the green of the French canned peas. . . . Please report for duty about September 10th. Blanks for wills and coroner's certificates must be furnished by the guests." But in actual practice, he and his staff, including the ever-reliable Bigelow, decided to limit applicants to the presumably upright people who had passed the civil service exam, "so they came to us with a good character."

For the first round of experimental meals, he lined up twelve young clerks, mostly from the Agriculture Department. He'd wanted to use more but could not afford it. Still, as far as he knew, this was the largest group ever yet used in a human health experiment of this kind. The trial design was straightforward. Each compound would be studied during a six-week period, and the test subjects would be divided during that time into two different seating arrangements. For the first two weeks, those sitting at table 1 would receive untainted food and those at table 2 would be dosed with a given preservative. The scientists would track the health differences, if any, between the two groups.

They would then switch so that table 1 received the preservative and table 2 was allowed two weeks of recovery. Then back again for a final round of comparison. Critics would later point out, with jus-tification, that two weeks wasn't sufficient time to measure an effect; that it would have been better to have maintained his control group and test group throughout. Wiley conceded that point. The hygienic table trials weren't perfect, he admitted, but they had potential to increase understanding of health effects from these mostly untested compounds. Another reason he'd kept the test periods short was to minimize any harm to his young volunteers, who'd been required to sign a liability waiver. "Did you explain that this was a dangerous process?" a congressman would ask later, during a hearing following publication of the first findings. Wiley replied that the volunteers were told about the planned procedure (although he wouldn't guar-antee they understood all the implications).

The department would not have done the work, he emphasized, if he'd believed at the start that chemical compounds deliberately mixed into American food posed an immediate deadly risk. He'd gone in hoping the materials were safe, and his worst-case guess before the trials started was "that there might be some disturbance to their systems." ("So," the congressman would say, "you thought that there was nothing; but you took a release because there was danger of losing life, in a sense." That, Wiley agreed, was correct.) Test subjects could consume only what was dished out in Wiley's test kitchen. They had to refuse any other snacks or drinks: "Each individual subject pledged himself to abstain entirely from food and drink not prepared by the scientists in charge of the dining room."

As the details of the project became known, newspaper reporters covered the deprivations with a mixture of amusement and horror: "Should they become hungry between meals, they must wait until the official dinner bell rings. If they grow thirsty during working hours, they may watch the water cooler with longing eyes but nothing more. . . . They cannot even drink a friendly glass of beer."

The volunteers had to record everything they ate and drank, noting the precise amounts of every portion. They had to record their weight, temperature, and pulse rate before every meal. Twice a week they had to be examined by doctors from the Public Health and Marine Hospital Service. They had to behave in an upright way, to "pursue their ordinary vocations without any excesses and to take their ordinary hours of sleep." They also had to agree to collect their urine and feces—"every particle of their excreta," in Wiley's words—and bring it to the chemistry laboratory for analysis. In retrospect, it seems astonishing that anyone volunteered and that none of the test subjects backed out before the experiment even began.

Wiley chose the preservative borax as the first additive to test. It was one of the most widely used food preservatives. Further, the few studies conducted thus far on borax suggested that it was relatively, but not completely, benign. Here was a chance to explore the questions raised about its consumption without, he thought, putting his volunteers at too much risk.

A study published the previous year in which mice were fed varying amounts of borax and boric acid had concluded that in small doses the compounds "have no influence upon the general health of the animals." Another test with baby pigs had reached a similar conclusion. If the dose was ratcheted up, though, the compound appeared to pose some problems. There was some evidence of a disruption in metabolism; there was the occasional animal that suffered digestive upsets, nausea, and vomiting. There were also some warning signals arising from a few human studies, but those tests were idiosyncratic at best.

One of them involved a scientist mixing boric acid into his own milk for a couple weeks; he'd felt fine, he said. Another experiment, done in London, had involved dosing three young children with borax and boric acid for several months. Those results were both reassuring and a little puzzling.

Unlike Wiley, who had carefully explained his choice of sturdy test subjects, the British researchers were vague about the selection process. They had chosen a two-year-old boy, a five-year-old boy, and a four-year-old girl who "was delicate, being convalescent from pneumonia," leading to some suspicion that they'd merely selected a few children whose parents were agreeable. They had found that borax could cause some temporary nausea and diarrhea but concluded that, in the big picture, "neither boric acid nor borax in any way affected the health and well-being" of the test subjects. That is to say, the three children appeared to be okay at the end of the experiment.

Meanwhile, John Marshall, a professor of chemistry and toxicology at the University of Pennsylvania, had also dosed himself with borax, and he'd reported some severe diarrhea ("the food escapes without assimilation") and nausea. But Marshall was interested in acute toxicity and had given himself a hefty dose after being called as a witness in the trial of a butcher accused of using the preservative to restore slightly rotten meat. So, while his self-experiment suggested that a stiff dose of borax produced unpleasant symptoms, it did not predict that most Americans, receiving a daily low-level exposure while consuming products ranging from meat to milk, would become so ill.

Wiley knew his study plan was by no means perfect either. But he also believed that its design was better than anything else out there. He had a larger study group of subjects, all of comparable age and health. He would be dividing them into two groups for purposes of comparison, a far cry from one man sipping milk or the use of three random children. His tests would continue for longer and look at a greater range of doses. He still thought that he wouldn't find anything much. But if borax did pose a risk, he also thought he'd have a better chance of finding that out than any work done so far.

He struggled with the best way to deliver the borax. In the British studies, the vehicle had been milk. As the authors of the experiment with children had pointed out, this made sense because "milk forms such a large proportion of their diet." Wiley decided to try butter instead; buttered bread and rolls were a staple of the American meal and he hoped they'd be consumed with enthusiasm. He wasn't worried about the taste putting off his diners. "It is pointed out that an important point of distinction between modern preservatives and the long-established ones—salt, sugar, vinegar, and wood-smoke—is that in the small amounts used they are almost without taste and odor, and their presence in a food product would not be noticed by the consumer unless specifically proclaimed."

In November 1902, just over six months after Wiley received his grant, the dining room opened its doors for the first round of tests. In its honor, a squad member propped up a sign at the entrance to the little dining room. Like the room itself, there was nothing fancy about it, just seven black-stenciled words on a white-painted board. They read: ONLY THE BRAVE DARE EAT THE FARE.

The first snag in Wiley's tidy plan came early. His volunteers soon realized—possibly through the study's garrulous chef, S. S.

Perry—that the borax had been secreted in the butter. They quit putting butter on their bread. Wiley then quietly resorted to the British approach, serving borax-dosed glasses of milk. The diners figured that out too. "Those who thought the preservative was concealed in the butter were disposed to find the butter unpalatable and the same was true with those who thought it might be in the milk or the coffee." After a few more attempts to sneak the preservative onto the table, he decided on a straightforward approach. The table settings for the first group now included a dish of borax capsules, and either he or Bigelow or one of the other chemists stood by, monitoring to make sure that the squad members took the requisite amount. He did not take the borax capsules himself. But that didn't stop him from being referred to in the *Washington Post* as "Old Borax."

Wiley's plan had been to conduct a quietly managed study and then report the results in discreet scientific fashion. It was with some dismay that he realized his experiment had attracted the amused attention of an ambitious young reporter for the *Washington Post*, George Rothwell Brown. The son of a Washington physician, Brown, twenty-three, had started a neighborhood newspaper in the basement of his family's Capitol Hill home when he was still in high school. He'd already put in a few years reporting for the *Washington Times* when, in 1902, the *Post* hired him away. While reporting on Congress, Brown came across a dry description of Wiley's proposal while looking over the federal budget. The journalist scented a good story and hurried over to talk to Wiley and his staff.

Brown found them less helpful than he had hoped. Although he often sought to engage the public in his campaign for pure foods, Wiley feared in this case that too much showy attention might bias the study and rob it of scientific dignity. He also worried that things would go wrong and that he wouldn't be able to manage the resulting bad news.

So Wiley warned his employees against granting interviews. "I can't say anything about anything," one chemist told Brown about the experiment. Wiley also warned that volunteers would be dropped from the program if they were caught talking with journalists. Brown countered by hanging around outside the Chemistry Bureau building and following volunteers down the street. Wiley caught him several times chatting cordially with Chef Perry through a basement window.

Brown's first story was headlined DR. WILEY AND HIS BOARDERS. The *Post* published it in early November. "The kitchen at the bureau of chemistry has been painted and put in excellent condition, and the chef is ready for business." Wiley apparently didn't approve of the breezy, cheerful tone, as Brown made evident in his next story: "The authorities are apprehensive that unless the public can be brought to look upon the experiments as an enterprise undertaken by scientific men and carried out in sober earnest, with a view to deciding a question of vast import to the country at large, the results of their self-sacrificing labors and patient investigation will be partially if not entirely lost. Any suspicion or belief in the public mind that there is a humorous or insincere element or phase connected with the experiments deserving of scoffing or ridicule would be deplorable in its effect."

But Brown and his editors shared a concern that the *Post*'s readers were never going to warm up to a story about "hygienic table trials." They needed more human interest and a catchier description. He spent long hours hunting down the identities of the first group of volunteers, who were "braving the perils of a course on food preservatives." The standout among them was B. J. Teasdale, whom Brown described as "a famous Yale sprinter and a former captain in a high school cadet regiment." Teasdale had set a record in the one-hundred-yard dash. The others, none as distinguished, were "the fat boarder," "the thin boarder," the Irishman whom Brown called "the only one of the Emerald Isle's sons among the twelve subjects," and volunteers whom he identified geographically as being from Mississippi, New York, and Pennsylvania. But collectively they were a band of brothers. And, to give them credit, Brown believed that it took some courage to venture into the chemical unknown. With that in mind, he found a better name for the study. He would simply call it the "Poison Squad."

That didn't stop him from seeing that the idea of borax in food offered limitless opportunities for entertainment. As the study continued into December, he imagined, for readers of the newspaper, what that year's Christmas dinner menu might look like:

Apple Sauce.
Borax.
Soup.
Borax. Turkey. Borax.
Borax.
Canned String Beans.
Sweet Potatoes. White Potatoes.
Turnips.
Borax.
Chipped Beef. Cream Gravy.
Cranberry Sauce. Celery. Pickles.
Rice Pudding.
Milk. Bread and Butter. Tea. Coffee.
A Little Borax.

Wiley was known in the department for having a lively sense of humor; Secretary Wilson himself publicly admired it. So he could live with being called Old Borax in his city's newspaper. He could even laugh about it. He could also see the humor in the supposed holiday menu. He'd drafted a joke menu himself, although that he managed to keep a secret.

That December he'd been asked by the American Association for the Advancement of Science to help organize holiday social events for the organization's friends and for respected scientists and politicians and—as the note to Wiley read—to stand as a "representative of the best people in Washington." He'd responded with invitations to a "poison dinner" of his own, inscribed with skulls and crossbones, undertaker advertisements, and pictures of skeletons labeled "after." The invitations featured a menu of preservatives, additives, and adulterations woven into a tongue-in-cheek play on fine French dining:

*MENU DU SOUPER EMPOISONNE*

*Le 13 Decembre 1902*

*Huitres queu de coq—sauce Formaldehyde (Xeres adroitment falsifie)*

*Hors d'oeuvres varies a l'aude benzoique (Sauternes a l'aide sulfereuz)*

*Howards a la Nouvelle Dills aux ptomaines*

*Callies (perdeux) a pain brulee sauce borate de soude*

*Salade coucobre a l'huile de coton*

*Fromage aux falsifications diverses*

*Café artificial*

*Liqueurs de tête mort*

*Tabac—a former*

*Matin—Bromo-selzer a volante*

*Invitation du Monsieur le Docteur Wiley d'assister*

*a un coupfer a la Roland B. Molineux*

Molineux was one of the country's more notorous cyanide murderers. A member of an aristocratic New York family—and the grandson of a decorated Civil War general—he'd been convicted in 1900 of killing two people he disliked by mailing them gifts spiked with poison.

Wiley was indeed grateful that Brown hadn't gotten his hands on a copy of that menu. But as the dismayed scientists at the Chemistry Bureau came to realize, if Brown couldn't find an element of interest in that week's work, the lively-minded journalist just made it up. For example, there was the story accusing the Chemistry Bureau of nearly starving the squad members: "F.B. Linton, who weighs out the food when Dr. Wiley is otherwise engaged, will bite a bean in half" rather than give the diners too much food. Another *Post* article reported that after only a few weeks on the borax diet, half the boarders were losing weight and the cook was so depressed that in his distraction he'd burned a turkey dinner. Another said that one of the volunteers was putting on weight and another was losing it, baffling the scientists: "Dr. Wiley is in despair." Brown reported that the volunteers also were messing with the study, relating the tale of a test subject who "in the spirit of mischief" dropped quinine into another boarder's coffee. The victim of the joke, wrote Brown, went home "prepared to die in the interests of science."

Brown's most fanciful masterpiece appeared more than six months into the Poison Squad work, in the summer of 1903. Headlined BOARDERS TURN PINK, it claimed that the steady diet of borax had wrought a marked and permanent change in the skin color of all members of the Poison Squad: "The change in the complexion of the chemical scholars has not been of an alarming character. On the contrary, each of the young men undergoing the course of treatment has blossomed out with a bright-pink complexion that would make a society bride sick with envy." The excited agricultural chemists, he added, were in the process of drafting a pamphlet about their revolutionary discovery. To Wiley's annoyance, Brown's widely distributed story—promising skin as rosy as "the inside of a strawberry"—resulted in a small deluge of letters to the Agriculture Department from women seeking the new secret to youthful skin.

By that time, the once sedate hygienic table trials had found their place in popular culture. Entertainer Lew Dockstader was performing "Song of the Poison Squad," written by S. W. Gillilan, in his minstrel shows.

*O we're the merriest herd of hulks*
*That ever the world has seen;*
*We don't shy off from your*
*Rough on Rats or even from Paris green*
*We're on the hunt for a toxic dope*
*That's certain to kill, sans fail*
*But 'tis a tricky, elusive thing and*
*Knows we are on its trail;*
*For all the things that could kill*
*We've downed in many a gruesome wad,*
*And still we're gaining a pound a day,*
*For we are the Pizen Squad.*

Rough on Rats was an arsenic-based rodent poison. Paris green, formed from copper, acetate, and arsenic, was used in pest control and as a coloring agent. Neither Wiley nor Secretary Wilson was pleased—neither by the notion that they were deliberately poisoning their volunteers nor that the Chemistry Bureau's research was now featured in musical satire.

The secretary and the chief chemist both complained repeatedly to the *Post* over the months that Brown's articles were making the department a laughingstock. They got little satisfaction. But after the BOARDERS TURN PINK story, the paper's editors had to acknowledge that their reporter had invented the whole thing. What the editors didn't catch—not then, anyway—was that Brown had missed the most important, if not the most entertaining, aspect of the Poison Squad story. By the summer of 1903, Wiley was looking at results that suggested steady ingestion of borax was not nearly as benign as had been assumed.

# Six

# LESSONS IN FOOD POISONING

## 1903—1904

*And our faith in the butter is apt to be weak,*
*For we haven't a good place to pin it*
*Annato's so yellow and beef fat so sleek*
*Oh, I wish I could know what is in it.*

In 1903 Fannie Farmer was the most famous cookbook author in the United States. She had become a household name after publishing *The Boston Cooking-School Cook Book* seven years earlier. In it she had included more than recipes, written about more than preparation, presentation, and flavor. She'd also discussed food chemistry and principles of nutrition as she understood them.

"Food," the book began simply, "is anything that nourishes the body." She proceeded to explain that "thirteen elements enter into the composition of the body: oxygen, 62½ percent; carbon, 21½ percent; hydrogen, 10 percent; nitrogen, 3 percent; calcium, phosphorus, potassium, sulphur, chlorine, sodium, magnesium, iron, and fluorine the remaining 3 percent." While other chemical elements were found in food, she noted, "as their uses are unknown, [they] will not be considered." Farmer's editor at Little, Brown and Company of Boston had wondered whether women needed such chemical information. Cookbooks, replied Farmer, were an essential form of education for American women, most of whom were afforded little if any opportunity to attend college.

Little, Brown eventually agreed to print the book, but only if the author herself paid for the first print run. Within a year, Farmer's 1896 opus had been reprinted three times; within a decade it had sold close to 400,000 copies (and by the midtwentieth century that number would top two million). Little, Brown's hesitation worked to Farmer's advantage. She had agreed to pay for publishing the book only if she retained control of the rights. By her death in 1914, thanks to her cookbook sales, she held stock in businesses that ranged from railroad companies to chocolate factories.

In 1903 she was already financially secure. At forty-six, she could write as she chose. She chose to write a book that she would consider the most important of her career: *Food and Cookery for the Sick and Convalescent.* The idea had arisen directly out of her own struggles for good health. Born in 1857, the youngest daughter of a Boston printer, she'd suffered a collapse at the age of sixteen. Doctors diagnosed the cause as a "paralytic stroke," although later experts would wonder if the girl had suffered a polio infection. For several years Fannie was unable to walk. Her mother nursed her; her father carried her from bed to chair. She was in her twenties before she began to hobble around the house; thirty before she was independent enough to enroll as a student at the Boston Cooking School.

There, in addition to cooking techniques, students learned about germ theory—the understanding that microbes cause illness, still a cutting-edge idea in the nineteenth century—and how to apply hygienic principles. They studied the chemistry of food and read the latest research into the principles of nutrition. Within three years she was assisting the principal, and by the time she wrote her famous first cookbook, she had become the head of the cooking school.

Farmer may have been the most influential author so far to warn of impurities in the food supply. Her devoted audience—composed largely of mothers and homemakers—was particularly receptive to the warning. An entire section of *Food and Cookery for the Sick and Convalescent* was focused on the "unappetizing and unhealthful pollution" of commercially sold milk. This supposedly "pure" food, she wrote, was still filthy, still too often thinned with water, full of chalk, food dyes, and harmful microorganisms. She joined other Americans advocating for pasteurization, the pathogen-killing heat process widely used in Europe. "The pathogenic germs in milk are often causes of typhoid fever, diphtheria, scarlet fever, tuberculosis, and cholera," she warned. Some American dairies, especially in the larger cities, had begun employing the process, but it made their products more expensive. Most dairymen continued to prefer far cheaper chemical preservations. Farmer wanted to alert her devoted readers of the dangers of "borax, boracic acid, salicylic acid, benzoic acid, potassium chromate, and carbonate of soda."

Earlier cookbook authors had also warned of the risks of food fakery; nineteenth-century recipes had routinely included asides about fraudulent spices or sham coffees. But *Food and Cookery for the Sick and Convalescent* gained extra attention because of its famous author and because it was published in 1904, a year in which public awareness of food problems was increasing, partly due to press coverage of Wiley's experiments. That May the *New York Times* announced that the first group of Chemistry Bureau volunteers had officially retired from the job of "eating poisons under the direction of the Agricultural Department" and been allowed to resume their normal lives. "The ill effects of eating drugs used in preserving articles of diet are said to be visible on all members of the squad, and one or two of them appear to be on the verge of breaking down," the *Times* noted.

Wiley had turned in his borax report, nearly five hundred pages, to Secretary Wilson for review. The department had "declined to give out figures" without Wilson's approval. But the *Times* anticipated the conclusion. Its subhead read PROFESSOR WILEY HELD THE MICROSCOPE WHILE THE VOLUNTEERS WRIGGLED. The experiments, the story explained, were designed to help solve the "poison mysteries" related to eating canned and preserved foods. How much "poison"—as the paper repeatedly called borax—did the squad members consume? "It is known that each of the martyrs to science ate several ounces of poison—about the same amount fed to soldiers in Cuba in the unpleasantness with Spain." (The newspaper gave no source for this dubious comparison.) Did the study prove that preservatives were indeed poisonous? "The result shows that many preservatives are deadly, causing pronounced inflammation of the digestive tract."

In June the Department of Agriculture released its official report on the borax experiment. Wilson had hesitated to make the results public, but sensationalistic press coverage had rendered such reluctance futile. At best, the report had the potential to temper the tone of what had been written elsewhere about the trials. Titled *Influence of Food Preservatives and Artificial Colors on Digestion and Health. I. Boric Acid and Borax*, it did not throw around the word "poison." It did not suggest that volunteers were tottering toward death or had turned pink. It did state that a steady diet of borax was shown to harm the human system.

Wiley had put his volunteers through five rounds of differing dose tests. In all cases the squad members spent time eating borax-laced meals alternating with time dining preservative free. Every squad member, he said, had been tested at the start of every toxicity phase and retested after the recovery period. Whenever they were eating a "clean" diet, all men had been in solid good health. During the dosage period, all had not been so well. Only half of the test subjects had endured to the end of the fifth series of borax testing. The other half dropped out due to illness.

"The experience of the previous series having shown that the administration of increasing doses of borax produced feelings of distress in both the stomach and head," the scientists attempted to alleviate the problems by decreasing the dose in the final test series. Throughout, the high dose was three grams and the low dose was a "minute" half gram. But by the fifth round, Wiley suspected the illnesses were due to a cumulative effect: "If continued for a long time in quantities not exceeding a half gram per day, they [borax-laced capsules] cause occasional periods of loss of appetite, bad feeling, fullness in the head and distress in the stomach. If given in larger and increasing doses, these symptoms are more rapidly developed and accentuated with a slight clouding of the mental processes. When increased to three grams a day the doses sometimes cause nausea and vomiting."

Most people would never—knowingly, at least—consume three grams of borax a day, but because the product was in such a range of food products, it was possible that an enthusiastic eater might risk such a level. But the chemists had concluded that a higher, more acutely toxic dose wasn't the real issue. The issue—as Wiley himself had long worried—was chronic daily exposure with cumulative effects: "On the whole, the results show that ½ gram per day is too much for the normal man to receive regularly."

Wiley and his chemists had tested a range of foods preserved with these compounds, notably butter and meat. They calculated that a person who ate buttered bread with each meal could consume a half gram of borax and/or boric acid each day, just from the butter. More if they ate meat. Not only that, but the average consumer also would be taking in "salicylic acid, saccharin, sulfurous acid and sulfites, together with the whole list of the remaining preservatives."

Wiley speculated that the borax, and probably those others, adversely affected the kidneys, if not other organs, thus leading to "disturbances of appetite, of digestions and of health." His first Poison Squad experiment admittedly was too small and too short to yield the definitive evidence he'd have liked to find. "On the other hand, the logical conclusion which seems to follow from the data at our disposal is that the use of boric acid and equivalent amounts of borax should be restricted," especially since in many cases the food could be preserved by safer means.

He repeated his argument that consumers had a right to know what manufacturers were mixing into their food. "As a matter of public information, and especially for protection of the young, the debilitated, and the sick . . . each article of food should be plainly labeled and branded in regard to the character and quantity of the preservative employed."

By the time the report was released, the next group of volunteers was consuming salicylic acid instead of borax, and they were exhibiting worse symptoms, already showing signs of nausea and dizziness.

As songs were performed, cookbook authors worried, and the studies continued, public awareness grew and pressure built. Congress once again weighed the idea of basic protective rules, not only for food and drink but also for the unrestricted, anything-goes patent remedies and other so-called medications in the United States. Two legislators from agricultural states—Congressman William P. Hepburn of Iowa and Senator Porter J. McCumber of North Dakota—spearheaded the efforts in their respective houses. Both scheduled committee hearings on the issue and both, not surprisingly, invited Wiley as the government's leading expert on chemical additives to food and drink to testify. Wiley, keenly aware of the power of the food-processing industry to stymie legislation, proceeded with caution. He stressed the need for accurate labeling first. "The real evil of food adulteration is deception of the consumer," he said.

The American Medical Association also sent representatives to support the proposed Hepburn-McCumber legislation. So did the National Association of State Dairy and Food Departments. Wisconsin, Indiana, Texas, Louisiana, California, New Jersey, Tennessee, Vermont, Kansas, New Hampshire, West Virginia, Delaware,

Maine, New York, Illinois, Pennsylvania, and Kentucky had all
crafted food legislation to try to protect their citizens. But these were
a patchwork of different rules and standards. The health officers in
all those states were united in thinking that this wasn't enough; there
ought to be nationally consistent rules for food safety.

Kentucky's chief food chemist, Robert M. Allen, assured the Senate Committee on Manufactures, which McCumber chaired, that a
national law was widely desired. Even manufacturers thought uniform federal rules would work to their benefit, he insisted. But although Allen's public persona was one of cheerful optimism, in
private he was far less sure of the outcome. He wrote to Wiley that
the meatpacking industry was aggressively fighting the legislation;
Allen had also heard that the railroads, which held a big stake in the
packing industry, were quietly working against the legislation.

Meanwhile, the processed-food industry had formed a new organization, the National Food Manufacturers Association, which was
seeking a "proper" law, one that would sidestep both Wiley and his
recommendations. The association offered high fees to scientists
willing to testify at the hearings that preservatives were chemically
harmless and that because the compounds prevented decay, they also
prevented countless Americans from contracting ptomaine poisoning. The association included some three hundred members, ranging
from importers of tea and coffee to fish packers and mustard purveyors to the meatpackers. And it was joined in opposing the Heyburn-
McCumber legislation by the dairy industry, with its growing
dependence on formaldehyde to salvage sour milk; the baking industry, which worried about limits on aluminum in products such as
baking powder; the bleached flour industry; and the industrial chemical industry, with its growing investment in preservatives and aniline dyes. Whiskey blenders and rectifiers also stood in opposition to
label requirements, which would have forced them to list synthetic
ethanol as a key ingredient.

As Warwick Hough, the chief lobbyist for the National

Wholesale Liquor Distributors Association, once again wrote to remind Wiley, barrel-aged whiskey also contained toxic compounds. It was unfair to keep "natural poisons" off the label while forcing manufacturers who might use dyes or other materials to list them on the label. Hough urged that whiskey be removed from the legislation entirely—surely those issues could be dealt with separately. And the rectifiers were both wealthy and powerful enough that many of the bill's supporters warned Wiley that including whiskey in the regulations could doom the legislation.

Wiley feared that if whiskey was exempted, producers of other substances might lobby for exemptions too. He also worried that without the inclusion of alcoholic beverages, the bill might lose the support of the also-powerful temperance movement. Despite those fears, Wiley did eventually opt for pragmatism and recommended that the requirement for labeling the chemical constituents of whiskeys be removed from the bill. But Hepburn and McCumber overruled him on that point; they also were wary of exemptions that might weaken the bill. Exasperated, the liquor wholesalers' group urged its members to work against the legislation. Hough, ignoring Wiley's efforts on his behalf, publicly accused the chief chemist of being in league with the straight-whiskey industry, increasing the bitter relations between the two men. But Hough insisted that his message was cautionary. Wiley's known and friendly ties to the straight-whiskey industry gave the appearance of bias, Hough said, and "will seriously impair your usefulness as an officer of the government in a position which calls for the exercise of utmost impartiality."

The decision to add nostrums and over-the-counter patent medicines to the bill brought out new but equally bitter opponents. The issue of drug fakery had never been Wiley's primary cause; his focus had always been on food and drink. But as public indignation over pharmaceutical fraud had grown, the Bureau of Chemistry decided to add deceptively advertised tonics and cure-alls to the products it examined. Wiley hired a talented chemist named Lyman Kebler, a former pharmaceutical company researcher with an obsession for precise measurements, to lead the bureau's investigations into snake-oil promises. It didn't take Kebler long to find that many "medicines" were little more than flavored drinking alcohol. One of the country's most popular "women's remedies," Lydia E. Pinkham's Vegetable Compound, turned out to be 20.6 percent ethanol. The digestive tonic Baker's Stomach Bitters measured at 42.6 percent ethanol, or about 85 proof.

The Proprietary Association, an alliance representing manufacturers of such popular nostrums and "cures," struck back by calling the studies an attack on personal freedom. Its officers warned publicly that if their products became subject to regulation, government control of people's lives would know no limits. "If the Federal Government should regulate the Interstate traffic in drugs on the basis of their therapeutic value, why not regulate traffic in theology by excluding from transportation all theological books which Dr. Wiley and his assistants, upon the examination, should find to be 'misleading in any particular,'" read a communication from the association.

Both the House and Senate versions of the bill died in committee that spring. Hepburn and McCumber promised Wiley that they would reintroduce their legislation again later that year. Hepburn had written directly to Roosevelt, asking him to include a favorable reference to the proposed food and drug act in a congressional address, but the president had declined. It was an election year and he was picking his battles, Roosevelt explained. "It will take more than my recommendation to get the law passed," he added. "I understand there is some very stubborn opposition" to even the idea of a pure-food and drug act.

Wiley, looking at another round of failed legislation, now accepted that his longtime strategy of working with legislators and scientific experts was not enough. If the regulations he dreamed of were to stand a chance, he needed new allies. He already had friends in the increasingly politics-savvy community of women activists; now he further sought their help. Through the consciousness raising of

Fannie Farmer and cookbook authors like her, with their warnings that commercial foods could not be trusted, women were helping to shape the nation's opinion about the problem of food adulteration. And women-led organizations were recognized as growing agents of change, as in the case of the Woman's Christian Temperance Union.

That group had in recent years broadened its focus from opposing alcoholic beverages and promoting women's suffrage to other issues—including the movement for food and drug regulation. The organization's leaders had come to that cause by way of studies like those from the Chemistry Bureau, showing that alcohol-rich patent "medicines" contributed to the problem of drunkenness. The WCTU had also decided to tackle the problem of intoxicating substances in "tonics" and soft drinks, including the popular and famously stimulating drink Coca-Cola. WCTU had been prominent among women's groups that had pressured the beverage company to drastically reduce the amount of cocaine in its formula around 1902.

Wiley started supplying the organization's leaders with copies of Kebler's reports on patent remedies. He also began courting favor with other women's groups, volunteering to give talks—as his secretary noted, dressing up for these with respectful formality, including a top hat—and scheduling friendly meetings with their leaders. His persistence, some said his obsession, on the issue of food and drug regulation kept earning him opponents. But he was also forging new partnerships, and the drive and determination of the women's organizations gave him a fresh source of hope.

Although log cabin born and farm raised, he'd grown up with the understanding that women were strong, capable, smart, and worthy of respect. His parents had sent all three of his sisters to college, a rarity in the midnineteenth century. In his Hanover College days, he had once given an address heralding the unfettered woman of the future: "She will claim all the avenues of usefulness be opened to her, that she no longer be compelled to depend upon the bounty of a father or a friend, to marry without love or choice, to keep a crowded school which kills or wash her sister's dishes which degrades." As chief chemist, he occasionally startled his colleagues with such views. In a talk to chemists visiting from Europe, he said, "Man's highest ambition in this country is to strive to be the equal of woman."

At other times he sounded more dismissive, arguing like a privileged man of his time, echoing the sentiments of his companions. In an essay for the *Annals of the American Academy of Political and Social Science*, he wrote: "I know she is not intended by nature, taste, or by education, as a rule to follow the pursuits which are reserved for men." But he then proceeded to point out that women had intelligence, energy, and the ability to drive public opinion. Nothing was gained, Wiley went on, by excluding women "from a participation, in an organized way, in the great problems which look to the uplifting of man."

At a meeting of the Cranston, New Jersey, Village Improvement Association, where he'd been invited to speak, Wiley met the event's organizer, Alice Lakey, who would become one of his staunchest allies. Born in 1856, Lakey had once dreamed of being a concert singer, but she was sidetracked by ill health. Illness also plagued her parents. She helped look after them and, after her mother died in 1896, continued to keep house for her ailing father. Seeking to understand and alleviate both their health problems, she, rather like Fannie Farmer, developed a deep interest in nutrition. At least partly through careful devotion to a healthy diet, Lakey succeeded in becoming much stronger and, as a result, had become a dedicated advocate for nutrition, a balanced diet, and pure, untainted food and drink.

She'd joined the village association as a member of its Domestic Science Division and became association president, the post she held when Wiley came to speak. The two crusaders struck up an instant bond. Under Lakey's leadership, the Cranston Village Improvement Association petitioned Congress to pass food and drug legislation and she persuaded the New Jersey Federation of Women's Clubs to do the same. She then began a push for more support at the national level, contacting the National Consumers League and encouraging its more famous leaders to speak out on the issue.

Started in 1899 by influential social reformers Josephine Lowell and Jane Addams, the league primarily focused on helping the working poor. Addams—whose tireless work to help the disadvantaged would be honored in 1931 with a Nobel Peace Prize—had become nationally known for pioneering programs to bring education to America's low-income communities. She was the cofounder of one of the country's best-known settlement houses in Chicago, Hull House, which offered a range of classes and recreational activities for immigrant workers and also did detailed studies on the results. Addams recognized that shoddy food especially undermined the health of the poor. It took little urging from Lakey for Addams to begin to speak publicly in favor of pure-food legislation. Even the "most conservative woman," even the most traditional housewife, Addams emphasized at a national women's club convention, had a stake in the fight. It was shameful that she could not keep a "clean and wholesome" house, or feed her children safely, or buy "untainted meat" for the family dinner due to the troubled state of the American food supply.

Lakey also joined the pure-food committee of another national organization, the General Federation of Women's Clubs. Founded in 1890 by New York journalist Jane Cunningham Croly, a pioneer of American feminism, the federation linked volunteer women's clubs across the country. Like the WCTU, the federation had become interested in food and drug safety regulations some years earlier: Members had written pamphlets on "The Chemistry of Food" and invited speakers including Fannie Farmer to discuss preservatives and other issues in food science. They'd also backed state food regulations across the country. The federation members, Wiley wrote, were "the most efficient organizations now existing" in terms of political activity and good works.

"I think women's clubs of this country have done great work in whatever they have undertaken to the betterment of the condition of society," he wrote to one club president. "There is something wonderful in the power which organized effort can develop and the women of this country, through organized effort, in my opinion can secure any good thing which they demand."

Lakey urged Wiley to take a further lesson from the cookbook writers. There was a reason that domestic science was so popular among women frustrated by the lack of educational opportunities. The Chemistry Bureau's publications contained a wealth of scientific information. Why not, she asked, put that to practical use in the country's kitchens? Not only would it be helpful, but also it would serve to remind women that the simple act of assembling a meal could, far too often, put their families at risk. Her idea was to publish a guide to simple tests that home cooks might use to identify adulterated products.

There had been precedents for that in the private sector. In 1861 the Boston physician Thomas A. Hoskins had published a book called *What We Eat: An Account of the Most Common Adulterations of Food and Drink with Simple Tests by Which Many of Them May Be Detected*. "For the purpose of adding something to the means of self-protection," Hoskins explained, "I have endeavored to furnish simple directions, by which many of the more dangerous frauds in foods may be detected."

Battershall's 1887 book on food adulteration had also included many such home tests, and more recently the magazine *What to Eat* had published an article titled "How to Detect Food Adulterations," by John Peterson, food commissioner of Utah. It included several pages of instructions for testing milk, cream, ice cream, coffee, spices, sugar, salt, baking soda, cream of tartar, and extracts of lemon and vanilla. For example, Peterson advised adding a few drops of tincture of iodine to a sample of ice cream to find out if it was genuine or made from skim milk thickened with cornstarch. "A deep blue color is instantly developed if corn starch or flour is present," he wrote. He suggested introducing a little vinegar to test a sample of milk. The resultant curds should be white. If they turned "a distinct orange color," it meant the liquid had been colored with an aniline coal-tar dye. If the curds were brownish, it meant the vegetable dye annatto was present.

The test for formaldehyde and its ilk was simpler yet: "Keep the milk or cream in a warm place for forty-eight hours. If the sample is still sweet at the expiration of this time, a preservative is strongly indicated."

Because so much had already been published on the topic, Wiley wasn't sure there was a need for an official USDA report, but he admitted that the bureau's chemists could do a better job of sharing their expertise with the public. He had his staff prepare a new publication: Bulletin 100, *Some Forms of Food Adulteration and Simple Methods for Their Detection*. More than sixty pages long, it was coauthored by Willard Bigelow, now head of the bureau's food division, and Burton Howard, chief of its microchemical laboratory.

"Sir," wrote Wiley to Secretary Wilson, "I have the honor to submit for your approval a manuscript on food adulteration and simple methods for the detection of some of the more prevalent forms. This bulletin has been prepared to meet the numerous demands for non-technical information. . . . It is believed that it will be of service both to housekeepers and to dealers."

The bulletin's diplomatic introduction took pains not to accuse food processors of deliberate malice. "It is not in their interests to shorten the lives of their customers nor to impair their appetites," it noted. "We must assume they honestly believe the products they employ to be wholesome. Therefore, in judging the wholesomeness of preservatives and other products added in the preparation of foods, the subject must be treated in a conservative manner and no criminal or even dishonest motives attributed to those who disagree with us on the subject."

Among the easiest tests that the bulletin recommended was simply looking at the product. A cook could easily detect copper sulfate: "We sometimes find upon our market, pickles of a bright green hue which is not suggestive of any natural food." The same remained true for so-called fancy French peas. The report noted that of thirty-seven cans of peas examined by the bureau, thirty-five were loaded with copper sulfate.

More than half of bulletin 100 consisted of tables and charts detailing the continued problems of food adulteration in the United States. Twelve of thirteen samples of sausage had been found to contain borax. Ten of nineteen additional samples were packed with more cornstarch than meat. Coffee continued to be only partly coffee. Spices continued to be adulterated with ground coconut shells, Indian corn, almond shells, olive pits, and sawdust. Fraud was not just pervasive; it was standard practice.

Bigelow and Howard recommended that the curious cook invest in a strong magnifying glass, a small glass funnel (perhaps three inches in diameter), some filter paper, and some golden-brown "turmeric paper," heavily embedded with that spice and known to be useful in specific tests.

They also recommended that the household cook buy a few reagents, including grain alcohol, chloroform, potassium permanganate, tincture of iodine, and hydrochloric acid. These could all easily be purchased at a local pharmacy and were also useful in testing food and drink. The authors also issued a strong warning: "CAUTION: The corrosive nature of hydrochloric acid must not be forgotten. It must not be allowed to touch the skin, clothes or any metal."

Once equipped, and dressed protectively, the home cook could follow instructions to detect fakes and chemical additives in her groceries. As a typical example, the federal scientists offered this way to check for the preservative borax in meat: Macerate a tablespoon of chopped meat with hot water, press it through a bag, and then put two or three tablespoons into a sauce dish. Drip in fifteen to twenty drops of hydrochloric acid per tablespoon. Pour the liquid through the filter-paper-lined funnel. Then dip a piece of turmeric paper into the filtered liquid and dry the wet paper near a stove or lamp. "If boric acid or borax were used for preserving the sample, the turmeric paper should turn a bright cherry red."

The chemists provided several other kitchen-table experiments, but they also admitted that for some tests a laboratory was needed. "Although spices are very frequently adulterated, there are few methods that may be used by one who has not had chemical training and who is not skilled in the use of a compound microscope for the detection of the adulterants employed."

On April 30, 1904, the bustling city of St. Louis opened the gates to yet another spectacular world's fair, an exposition designed to outdo those hosted earlier by Chicago and Buffalo. Food, in its many incarnations, held a starring role. The daily *World's Fair Bulletin* announced that some of the "swellest" restaurants in the country could be found along the midway—known as the Pike—or integrated into exhibits. The fair boasted 125 eateries, ranging from the upscale, serving fifteen-course meals, to crowded snack stands. A simulated coal mine included a restaurant staffed by waiters dressed as miners. At a farm exhibit, visitors could look over a flock of chickens and pick out the specific bird they wanted roasted for their dinner.

In the midst of this cornucopia, Wiley's growing contingent of pure-food enthusiasts staged their own counter-display. They had been inspired partly by the Chemistry Bureau's modest presentation at the Pan-American Exposition, with its samples of adulterated products. This time they wanted something bigger, more dramatic, a showy staging that would garner national attention. They had spent more than a year planning a pure-food exhibit designed to shock fairgoers with its display of adulterations and dangers.

As well as the Kentucky food chemist Allen, representing the

National Association of State Dairy and Food Departments, and the tireless Alice Lakey, the organizers of the exhibit included the Chicago-based writer and editor Paul Pierce. Slender, meticulously groomed, fastidious in his habits, Pierce had for years campaigned against overeating and obesity. He considered far too many Americans—especially of the era's upper classes—to be "over-fed gluttons." Yet his interests in food and nutrition were wide-ranging and eclectic, as reflected in his magazine *What to Eat.* In its first issue, printed in August 1896, Pierce had promised that "no food or practice will be slighted" and it featured topics ranging from nine-course party menus to a discussion of the pure-food movement's battle against adulterations. "There is no more doubt that plain food is conducive to good health, than there is that pure air is good for respiratory organs," Pierce wrote in his opening essay.

In the years since he'd launched the magazine, Pierce had grown more adamant in his opposition to adulteration and fakery. The pages of *What to Eat* were increasingly packed with horror stories about chemically poisoned groceries, bitter commentary on the government's failure to protect its citizens from predatory manufacturers, and practical tips for surviving the current era of high-risk food. Like Wiley, he had become convinced that the nation's activist women, through their closely knit associations, would be key in winning the fight for regulation. "Now let the food adulterer quail, for we have the women on our side" read one of his editorials. "With a million women in our ranks fighting for such a cause, we will fear no foe that man and the might of millions in money can muster."

Wiley had successfully negotiated for an astonishingly large display space within the fair's Agriculture Palace, a pavilion surrounded by brilliant gardens that spread across twenty acres. Within that complex, the pure-food exhibit would cover two full acres. As rumors spread about their plans, Allen discovered that some unhappy food processors and manufacturers had considered seeking an injunction against the exhibit but had dropped the idea, deciding that the resulting furor would only "increase public interest" in the display.

To create the exhibit, Pierce wrote to food commissioners around the country, asking them to provide examples of adulterated, over-dyed, heavily preserved, or otherwise problematic food and drinks. As the boxes and cartons began piling up, it rapidly became obvious that two acres would hardly do justice to the problem.

The organizers decided to exhibit only two thousand different brands representing tainted food and drink sold in the United States. North Dakota sent canned meats: "While potted chicken and potted turkey are common products, I have never yet found a can in the State which really contained in determinable quantity either chicken or turkey," noted North Dakota food chemist Edwin Ladd. Minnesota and South Dakota sent sheets of silk and wool, each five feet square, brilliantly colored with coal-tar dyes extracted from strawberry syrups, ketchup, jams and jellies, and red wine. Michigan sent samples of a lemon extract in which the manufacturer had used cheap but deadly wood alcohol as the base. Illinois provided more faked extracts, such as "vanilla" made only of alcohol and brown food coloring, and a display of bottles carefully curved and carved to hide the fact that they held less than the advertised amount. Kansas offered up lemon drops colored yellow by poisonous lead chromate and chocolate faked by using burned sienna, a pigment made from oxides of iron and manganese.

Participating states provided forty brands of ketchup, labeled as a tomato product, that were mostly stewed pumpkin rind dyed red, and some fifty brands of baking powder that were largely well-ground chalk enhanced by aluminum compounds. To the fury of food industry executives, the fair's head of publicity, Mark Bennett, sent out a news release titled "Lessons in Food Poisoning," which noted: "If you want to have your faith in mankind rather rudely shaken, take the time to look about in the exhibit of the State Food Commissioners in the south end of the Palace of Agriculture."

For those who hadn't been following the issue, Bennett offered a guide to some of the continuing problems. "Maple syrup" was still likely to be mostly corn-derived glucose dyed brown; "cider vinegar" was found to be lab-made acetic acid colored with a little burned sugar; "lard" was mostly tallow (rendered mutton fat); "butter" still often turned out to be deliberately mislabeled oleomargarine; spices like "cayenne" were mostly ground nut shells; and, according to Bennett's release, "jellies and jams are any old thing," dyed any old color with coal-tar dyes. "Down a long list we might go, telling the secrets of those who are putting dollars into their pockets by putting poisons into our foods." Pierce happily reprinted Bennett's news release in his magazine.

Almost twenty million people—including President Roosevelt, who scheduled an elaborate and patriotically themed banquet—attended the fair. Roosevelt, in the midst of an election campaign to remain in office, did not mention the pure-food exhibit in his St. Louis remarks. But another attendee, the New York–based investigative journalist Mark Sullivan, made a point of doing so. Sullivan described the pure-food exhibit admiringly as "one of the most effective bits of propaganda ever achieved, for pure food or for any other purpose."

The fair also was home, in late September 1904, to the eighth meeting of the International Pure Food Congress. Secretary Wilson declined to attend but sent personal regrets and, naturally, his chief chemist. Harvey Wiley gave three speeches, one on his inspection work, one on adulteration—"The real evil of food adulteration is the deception of the consumer"—and the last on his preservative research. Regarding the latter, he put a strong emphasis on the groups most at risk. The work with borax and his current study of salicylic acid demonstrated, he said, that while exposure to such compounds was obviously survivable by healthy young men, they posed a greater risk to children, the elderly, the ill, the "least resistant."

As part of the Poison Squad tests, his staff was still evaluating the effects of salicylic acid ingestion on the bureau's volunteer diners, so Wiley held his fire on the topic of that preservative, but he urged strong protective action against the use of borax in food products. "It should not, I believe, be put in foods of any kind, except when they are plainly marked, and even not then except in special cases and for special purposes." Later that year in a speech at City College of New York, he clarified what he meant by "special purposes," emphasizing that they would be quite limited and specific. "It is true that there may be occasions where chemical antiseptics are necessary. It is far better to have food preserved with chemical antiseptics than to have no food at all. If I were going, for instance, to the North Pole—which I hope I never do—or any other long journey where access to foods would be cut off, it might be safer to use chemical preservatives in the foods which were taken along than to trust other sources."

In 1904 Wiley was taking a far tougher line on chemical additives than he had even a few years earlier. And he was further alarming his opponents within the food industry. They had reason to be alarmed, judging from the mood at September's Pure Food Congress. In his talk opening the congress, delegate James W. Bailey of Oregon hailed the unprecedented number of participants and the intensity of their advocacy.

"There are times in life when one is awed by the greatness of the occasion," said Bailey, who was the newly elected president of the National Association of State Dairy and Food Departments. "Such is my feeling today when I arise to address this, the greatest meeting ever held in the interests of pure food." The cause, he declared, had finally come of age. "Like every new idea, the pure food movement was at first thought to be merely a fad and hailed as a farce." But now the activists were getting through to the public. People were listening, and the St. Louis exhibit would, he predicted, surely change minds and spur reform. "I doubt if some of the sins of our manufacturers will be shown up more plainly on the day of judgment than they are at this exhibit." Bailey went on to predict that safe and healthy food would soon be seen as "one of the dire necessities of the land and coexistent with our welfare and happiness."

Makers of distilled spirits clashed again at the Pure Food Congress, and Wiley once again was drawn into the fight. As his friends and fellow social club members well knew, he favored good, aged bourbon—to drink and on principle. At the gathering, as in other public testimony, he continued to champion the traditional process of fermenting mash and barrel aging, citing the rich natural chemistry that produced a complex, satisfying taste that rectified whiskey could never match. He continued—despite warnings from Warwick Hough—to praise it also as a healthier drink than the lab-made and blended alternatives. As Wiley noted, aged whiskey required no dyes; it simply darkened as it aged. Barrel aging for at least four years also modified or eliminated most of the impurities, he claimed, and the old-fashioned way of making whiskey gave it certain characteristics of "health, purity, and flavor" that the artificial version could never attain.

Hough was also in attendance at the St. Louis fair, and he made it clear that he did not agree and did not appreciate the straight whiskey friendly corner of the food exhibit. Both in person and in correspondence, he once again urged Wiley to reconsider his arguments.

"I agree with you that false labeling is a deception which should be prohibited," Hough wrote to Wiley after the congress. "To brand a Bourbon whiskey as a Rye whiskey, or to assert that a whiskey is not a blend when in fact it is a blend, or to say that whiskey is ten years old, when in fact it is only five years old. But it is an equal deception for you or any of the distillers interested in the bottled in bond goods to attempt to create the impression upon the public, that the stamp on bottled in bond goods guarantees either the quality or the purity of the whiskey." The rectifiers, he said, were not finished with this fight. And the combative exhibits at the St. Louis fair had only stiffened that resolve.

# Seven

# THE YELLOW CHEMIST
## 1904–1906

———●———

*The pepper perhaps contains cocoanut shells,*
*And the mustard is cottonseed meal;*
*And the coffee, in sooth, of baked chicory smells*

I n early November 1904, just as Theodore Roosevelt won election to the presidency in his own right, the writer Upton Sinclair traveled by train from the East Coast to Chicago, where he moved into a bare-bones settlement house, intent on researching his next novel.

The previous July, butchers had gone on a wage strike at packinghouses in nine cities, from Omaha to New York. The two-month strike failed because meatpacking firms, using a strategy developed by Chicago's famously ruthless Armour family, hired unskilled, nonunion replacements who could be paid less than the union butchers.

Sinclair, a twenty-eight-year-old son of a New York shoe salesman, was instantly sympathetic. He had barely paid for his own education at City College by writing jokes, dime novels, and magazine articles. Upon graduation in 1897, the aspiring novelist and freelance journalist had joined the worker-friendly socialist cause, partly inspired by his own struggles to make a living. He had written up a passionately pro-strike article and sent it, unsolicited, to the Kansas-based socialist newspaper, *Appeal to Reason*. In the same package Sinclair included a copy of his recent Civil War novel, *Manassas*, which had been a critical, if not commercial, success. The combination prompted the paper's editor, Julius Wayland, to make him an offer. He would print Sinclair's essay on the butchers' strike, and he would pay the writer $500 for a serialized novel telling the story of the valiant workers of Chicago's stockyards. Sinclair quickly accepted. He then persuaded his editor at Macmillan Publishing to give him another $500 contract to turn the serialized novel into a print book.

Flush with a grubstake of $1,000 (about $30,000 today), Sinclair spent seven weeks in Chicago's yards, living in a settlement house operated by a friend of Jane Addams's, often dressing in the grubby clothing of a worker to blend in. He observed and interviewed, gathering notes and sketches before returning to the East Coast, where with his wife and son he moved into a New Jersey farmhouse and settled down to write the most influential book of his prolific career.

The novel's main character was a Lithuanian immigrant, carrying that familiar dream of building a good life in America. "I will take care of us," he tells his wife. "I will work harder." In the end, the hardworking laborer is nearly destroyed by working conditions at the fictional "Anderson" meat-processing company. He eventually loses his health, family, and friends in the meatpacking industry but in Sinclair's conclusion finds some hope, at least, by embracing the brotherhood of socialism.

In February 1905 *Appeal to Reason* began serializing Sinclair's novel. By pure coincidence, the publication occurred just as other tales of troubled food production were unfolding in Congress, where advocates of pure-food legislation again sought to advance their cause. Both McCumber and Hepburn were still determined supporters of the proposed food and drug law, although Hepburn, as chair of the House Committee on Interstate and Foreign Commerce, was now mostly working with Roosevelt on railroad legislation. And a new senator from Idaho, Weldon Heyburn, had replaced McCumber as chairman of the Committee on Manufactures.

Heyburn, fifty-one, was a Republican but not in the least a Roosevelt progressive. He was an attorney who had made a living representing bankers and timber barons in his home state. During his time in the Senate, he would oppose the president on issues ranging from creation of new national forests to child labor laws. But like McCumber, he represented a frontier state—Idaho had become the forty-third state in 1890—where consumers believed, as did their counterparts in North Dakota, that their grocery stores were being treated as dumping grounds for cheap, adulterated food ginned up in the East. He also represented one of only four states in the country that had so far granted women the vote (the others were Wyoming, Utah, and Washington). Before the 1902 election, which saw Heyburn come into office, Idaho club women had met with every one of the state's political candidates to say that they would vote in a bloc against any who failed to support pure-food legislation.

Heyburn rose to the challenge. He found himself genuinely appalled by false claims made for mislabeled, largely useless products— especially those sold by the patent medicine industry. "I am in favor of stopping the advertisements of these nostrums in every paper in the country," he said. When industry representatives chastised him for supporting the proposed legislation, he replied, "The object of this bill is not to protect the dealer. It is to protect the persons who consume the articles."

The confrontational Heyburn tended to make enemies, among them Washington journalists. His press coverage was so often critical that he had fired back by describing reporters allowed into government buildings as mere guests of the state who "had no right to make disparaging remarks about senators." He had also antagonized many of his fellow lawmakers, who often, even publicly, described him as arrogant and humorless. Still, many Capitol colleagues succumbed to the force of his determination.

By January 1905 Heyburn had a food and drug bill called up before the full Senate. Two weary veterans of the fight, McCumber and Wiley attempted to temper his expectations, suggesting strategic concessions, such as to the whiskey rectifiers. Heyburn, as was typical, refused to compromise.

Food-processing industries had hardened their opposition to reform. The National Food Manufacturers Association lobbied for Heyburn to sponsor a different Senate bill, one that permitted the use of preservatives, excluded reports from the Bureau of Chemistry, and transferred regulatory authority over food and drink from the Agriculture Department to the business-friendly Department of Commerce and Labor.

Meanwhile, the blended-whiskey interests had been outraged to learn that the straight-whiskey men had secretly given financial support to the pure-food exhibit in St. Louis. Colonel Taylor himself had delivered a $3,000 check to the Kentucky food commissioner, Robert Allen, along with several cases of good bourbon to be displayed as examples of the "right" kind of whiskey. Allen had not shared that information with the other exhibit organizers, which in turn created outrage among his allies as well as the rectifiers. Paul Pierce wrote for *What to Eat* several angry pieces on the corrupting influence of Taylor and his like, but rectifiers weren't mollified.

In a story headlined LABELING RUINOUS TO LIQUOR TRADE, published in the *New York Journal of Commerce*, a major liquor distributor declared that if rectified whiskey was fully labeled as to dyes, additives, and synthetic alcohol, it would do untold damage to businessmen and government income derived from its sale. Taxes, the distributor predicted, would "suffer to an extent never dreamed of heretofore." The rectifiers' chief lobbyist, the obstreperous Hough, notified every member of Congress that his members flatly insisted on removing *any* whiskey-labeling requirements from the legislation.

Hough further sent out a circular urging all blenders, rectifiers, and distributors to stand together against such "hostile measures" before Congress. From the baking powder producers to the patent medicine industry to the meatpackers, manufacturers joined to fight any sign of food, drink, or drug regulation.

William Randolph Hearst, publisher of the *New York Evening Journal*, wrote: "There is a bill in the Senate of the United States called the Pure Food Bill. Its purpose is to prevent food adulteration, the swindling and poisoning of the public. Nobody in the Senate says a word against this bill; nobody dares go on record, of course, in behalf of adulteration. Yet it is certain that the bill will not be passed." The business of Congress was to take care of businessmen, Hearst wrote, and even some of the country's most "respectable" businessmen reaped huge profits by producing, misrepresenting, and selling adulterated, diluted, and downright faked food and drink. "Who is that shabby looking, patched-up individual trying to get on the floor of the House?" mused the editors of *Life* magazine. "O, that's old Pure Food Bill. When he first came around here he looked pretty good, but now he has been knocked around and changed so much that his friends don't know him at all. In a minute you'll see him thrown out bodily again."

As predicted, the proposed legislation collapsed in both houses within just a couple of months. "What now?" wrote the chairman of the Federation of Women's Clubs pure-food committee to Wiley. "Does this mean the [final] defeat of the Pure Food Bill or shall we keep on with our petitions and letters?" Wiley could almost imagine himself as the living incarnation of that shabby, patched-up bill described by *Life*. His advocacy for the legislation had increasingly made him a public target. An editorial in the *California Fruit Grower*, titled "Chemistry on the Rampage," had demanded, "Let somebody muzzle the yellow chemist who would destroy our appetite with Borgian tales," and the trade journal *Grocery World*, which represented the wholesalers, had chimed in: "The greater part of Dr. Wiley's time seems to be taken up in the delivering of sensational lectures on food frauds and the writing of articles on such subjects" as poisoned foods. "Dr. Wiley seems to thirst deeply for notoriety. He is happiest when looking complacently into the horror-stricken eyes of women he has just scared half to death." The journal's editors had even recommended that Wilson officially reprimand Wiley. The secretary had not done so, but he had once again called his chief chemist into his office to recommend discretion.

Wiley—somewhat to the secretary's frustration—instead returned to the lecture trail with renewed vigor. "I believe in chemistry and its application to the welfare of humanity," he told students at Cornell University. "But at the same time I can't help noticing how it is abused." He put the whole force of his personality behind the arguments, observed the muckraking progressive journalist Mark Sullivan: "On the platform the forcefulness and originality of his utterances gained from the impressiveness of his appearance: his large head capping the pedestal of broad shoulders, his salient nose shaped like the bow of an ice-breaker, and his piercing eyes compelled attention." It was a "great battle," Wiley would later write, and any battle, he thought, needed a general, someone who could coordinate the different factions into an effective army. At this moment he seemed to be the natural, perhaps the only, choice for that role. He urged the federated women's clubs to renew their activities, to protest the stalled legislation to every senator, every congressman, and every newspaper. His friends in the WCTU needed little urging to do the same. The National Association of State Dairy and Food Departments returned to the issue with increased urgency. Pushing past Allen's ties to the whiskey-distilling industry, the association joined Wiley in this new offensive push. It created a traveling exhibit, smaller but more graphic than the one at the St. Louis fair, a "chamber of horrors" that could be used to provide tangible illustration of adulterated food and drink at lectures. The state commissioners were nearing desperation. If the legislation failed yet again, their cause might die. They feared that they'd reached the critical moment, that if they didn't succeed now there might not be another chance for food and drug reform, or perhaps for any kind of consumer protection law, in their lifetimes.

The serialized version of Sinclair's novel, which he titled *The Jungle*, had a limited socialist readership, but he was counting on his editor at Macmillan to grow that audience. He mailed the installments to the publishing firm and, chapter by chapter, his editor became more dismayed. The book described diseased cattle arriving by railroad in Chicago to be butchered and sold to American housewives. "It was a nasty job killing these," Sinclair wrote, "for when you plunged your knife into them they would burst and splash foul smelly stuff into your face." Sinclair also evoked the embarrassing food scandals of the Spanish-American War: "It was stuff such as this that made the 'embalmed beef' that killed several times as many United States soldiers as all the bullets of the Spaniards; only the army beef, besides, was not fresh canned, it was old stuff that had been lying around for years in cellars."

Pickled beef had to be bathed in acid; the men working that line had their fingers eaten away by repeated exposure. Tuberculosis germs thrived in the moist, stinking air of the processing plants and spread from animal to animal, worker to worker. In the rendering rooms, there were open vats of acid set into the floor, to help break down the carcasses. Workers occasionally fell in, and "when they were fished out, there was never enough of them left to be worth exhibiting." Sometimes, Sinclair wrote, an exhausted worker, staying after hours to earn a little more, would slip into a vat and "be overlooked for days till all but the bones of them had gone out into the world as Anderson's [his thin disguise for Armour's] Pure Leaf Lard."

His editor sent chapters out for review by well-connected friends and advisers. Equally dismayed, they wrote back to insist that the descriptions couldn't be true. In late summer a new chapter recounted the ways that meat in a state of decay, even when fuzzed over with mold, could be cleaned, "dosed with borax and glycerin and dumped into hoppers and made over again for home consumption." It related that the packers routinely put out poisoned bread to keep the rat population down, and "then the rats, bread and meat would go into the hoppers together."

It was too much. His editor declared that the book was "gloom and horror unrelieved." Macmillan asked Sinclair to remove objectionable passages. Sinclair took the recommendations to some of his fellow writers, among them reformist journalists Lincoln Steffens and Ray Stannard Baker. Both those journalists had made names for themselves writing for the muckraking magazine *McClure's* with articles centered on government and corporation corruption. Both encouraged Sinclair to reject the cuts that Macmillan wanted and to keep his novel rich in the blood-spattered details of the Chicago stockyards. Steffens did warn him, though, that he should expect continued resistance and revulsion. Sometimes, the veteran journalist noted gloomily, "it is useless to tell things that are incredible, even though they may be true." Baker, whose exposés of the railroad industry had led to Roosevelt's obsession with reforming it, thought Sinclair should have written a nonfiction book instead of a novel, but he counseled his friend not to back down.

Sinclair determined that "I had to tell the truth and let people make of it what they would." In September 1905 Macmillan canceled his contract, generously offering that he keep the $500 advance. Disappointed, Sinclair shopped *The Jungle* around to other publishers but found no takers. He arranged to publish a "sustainers edition," essentially self-publishing. Issued under the Jungle Publishing Company imprint, it was offered to subscribers of the *Appeal*, and sold surprisingly well—netting him almost $4,000—but, to his disappointment, failed to gain any real national attention.

Meanwhile, other writers continued to drive interest in the subject of the country's appalling food supply. The illustrated monthly *Everybody's Magazine* published an investigation into the National Packing Company, a trust established by Armour, Swift, and Morris. Its author, investigative journalist Charles Edward Russell, then published a book, in that fall of 1905, called *The Greatest Trust in the World,* devoted to the further evils of the meatpacking industry. Its angry dissection of price-fixing, inhumane working conditions, and corrupt practices at the Chicago stockyards would help Upton Sinclair sharpen many of the demoralizing descriptions in subsequent editions of *The Jungle.* Crusading women's magazines also took aim at the toxic nature of processed food. In the spring of 1905, the *Woman's Home Companion,* a monthly magazine founded in 1873 and with a circulation approaching two million, published a three-part series titled "The Truth About Food Adulteration," written by Henry Irving Dodge. The journalist had worked in collaboration with none other than Willard Bigelow, chief of the Division of Foods at the Bureau of Chemistry. "The series is therefore a thoroughly authoritative account of this most dangerous and growing practice," read the magazine's promotional copy.

Bigelow described for Dodge some of the clever ways that American businessmen legally deceived consumers. He cited a popular product, Old Reliable Coffee, which was described on its elaborately scrolled label as "a compound of delicious drinking coffee, guaranteed to please those who like a full-bodied cup of coffee." There was not, Bigelow said, one grain of coffee inside the can. But the use of the word "compound" allowed the manufacturer to make coffee claims under both state and federal law. Bigelow encouraged Dodge to examine food samples through a microscope, revealing to the journalist the ground pumice stone in baking powder, the pulverized olive pits in spices, demonstrating the difference between a rectilinear crystal of lard and a bush-shaped crystal of beef fat. None of these fakes, Dodge wrote admiringly, escaped the department's chemistry analyst, whom he further described as a "man of blue blazes and sulfurous smokes."

Part 2 of the series was titled "How the Baby Pays the Tax: The Food Poisoner Reaches the Height of His Crime When He Attacks the Baby, upon Whose Well-Being the Fate of the Nation Depends." The story was illustrated by a drawing of a child dining at one end of a well-stocked table and a skeleton watching him from the other. The words "Glucose, Sulphate of Copper, Boracic Acid, Aniline Dyes, Benzoic Acid, Formaldehyde" were embroidered along the edge of the tablecloth. "The man who poisons food for gain builds a palace of bones upon a graveyard" was the opening sentence of Dodge's next salvo.

The focus was milk, still widely adulterated and either filthy with bacteria or poisoned with formaldehyde. Dodge cited a plethora of anecdotes to support this conclusion, from Brooklyn to Chicago, where authorities had been recently forced to condemn almost five hundred vats of milk in a single week. A doctor in New Jersey had recently blamed an uptick in child deaths on continued used of formaldehyde in milk, and another in New York had noted that unpasteurized supplies had contributed to yet another outbreak of typhoid. In the year 1904, Dodge noted, more than twenty thousand children under the age of two had died in New York City and that milk was considered a major contributor to those fatalities. "The cry 'Poisoned Milk'" rings through the land, he wrote, as it had over decades of government inaction and corruption.

Dodge had learned from a friend in the U.S. Senate that manufacturers were prepared to spend more than $250,000 to defeat any regulations and had already made major contributions to the campaigns of senators considered friendly to the cause. No wonder the proposed food legislation was going nowhere, he wrote: "The Senate does not indulge in bawling opposition to the bill. Oh no, its weapons are much more effective and more deadly. It lets the bill die." The

American government, he concluded, would rather protect wealthy business interests than protect the American people.

Also in 1905, Pierce's magazine, *What to Eat*, published a four-part series titled "The Slaughter of Americans." In his opening editor's note, Pierce wrote: "In view of the widespread adulteration of foods in America, that is adding so greatly to the death roll and causing more sickness and misery than all the other sources combined, *What to Eat* has decided to publish a series of carefully compiled articles revealing to Americans the actual condition of the food we eat today." The series provided a detailed list of the reasons that Pierce and his food-reform allies were so frustrated and angry. In one article Pierce assured his readers that butter now contained enough coal-tar dye to kill a cat. Another article in the series said that more than 400,000 infants were killed by unwholesome food and formaldehyde-tainted milk every year in the United States. A restless urgency crackled through Pierce's series and through the writings, speeches, and letters, both private and public, of all of Wiley's growing army of food-reform allies. They were fed up with foot-dragging federal lawmakers.

U pton Sinclair refused to give up on his novel. He kept shopping *The Jungle* to established publishing firms.

He suffered more rejections from publishers wary of potential lawsuits but got a meeting with Isaac Marcosson, who worked for the publishing house Doubleday, Page & Company. As a newspaper writer in Louisville, Kentucky, Marcosson had written a positive review of Sinclair's 1903 novel, *The Journal of Arthur Stirling*. He welcomed the author into his office and listened to Sinclair's promise that the hefty bundle of pages he carried was "something sensational." Marcosson lugged the manuscript home and became engrossed, staying up all night reading it. In the morning he presented it enthusiastically to his boss, Walter Hines Page.

Both Page and his partner, Frank Nelson Doubleday, needed persuading. Page shared much of Marcosson's enthusiasm but agreed with more dubious Doubleday that the story's revolting details might be too much for readers to stomach. Page cautioned their young employee that if they did contract for Sinclair's book, it would be with the understanding that Marcosson would be responsible for "launching and exploiting" *The Jungle*. The publishers also insisted on sending a copy of the manuscript to the *Chicago Tribune* for an opinion on whether the book's grisly descriptions had any basis in reality. *Tribune* editors responded with a two-dozen-page rebuttal of the packinghouse descriptions. Alarmed, Page and Doubleday called Sinclair to their offices. But Sinclair promptly began picking apart the *Tribune*'s critique.

For instance, the paper had denied that the tuberculosis bacterium could survive on walls or floors of the packing rooms. Sinclair pointed out that the germ could indeed survive on those surfaces and could transfer to anything that touched them. He'd brought medical studies to prove it, as well as other evidence to back up his story. He further noted that the paper's owners were obviously friendly with the meatpackers and sided with them. In fact, it would turn out that the newspaper's management had not assigned a reporter to study Sinclair's claims but instead passed the task on to a publicist who worked for the meatpackers.

The *Tribune*'s fervent denial of the story made Page, also a former reporter, suspicious. As well as a book publisher, he was editor of the business magazine *World's Work*. His journalist's instincts told him something wasn't right about the *Tribune* report. It smelled like a whitewash. He decided on an independent investigation. The publishing company sent Marcosson and the company's lawyer on an expedition to Chicago. Both men returned disgusted and horrified by what they'd seen. They'd also secured multiple sources willing to provide public statements about the odious conditions in the yards. Page became convinced and he persuaded his partner Double-day to agree. Page also decided that when *The Jungle* went on sale, he would buttress it by publishing factual reporting on the horrors of the yards in *World's Work*. Sinclair signed his book contract with the publishing firm on January 6, 1906.

R obert Allen recovered, for the most part, from the scandal re-garding his cozy deal with bourbon distillers during the pure-food exhibition in St. Louis. Allies in the movement forgave him, perhaps in recognition that he had accepted the whiskey men's $3,000 not for personal gain but to finance the exhibit. Again sup-ported by the well-connected bourbon barons, he secured a meeting with President Roosevelt in the summer of 1905, and several promi-nent food reform advocates agreed to attend. Wiley wasn't among them. The chief chemist asked for and received from Wilson an as-surance that the Agriculture Department officially supported the meeting. But he believed that there was more power in a delegation of private citizens, especially when the president already knew Wi-ley's position all too well. The delegation included Alice Lakey, food commissioners from Ohio and Connecticut, a representative of the retail grocers' association, and a representative from the H.J. Heinz Company of Pittsburgh, which was now very successfully marketing a preservative-free ketchup made from actual tomatoes. They pre-sented their case to Roosevelt but, as Allen related with some disap-pointment afterward, the president remained noncommittal.

Then later that year, in November, Roosevelt invited the delega-tion back to the White House, revealing that he had taken the trouble to talk over their issue with a range of experts, from Wiley to Ira Remsen of Johns Hopkins University, codiscoverer of the sweetener saccharin. The president had even discussed the matter with his per-sonal physician. The result was, the president said, that he had decided at last to support the beleaguered food and drug law in his end-of-the-year message to Congress. He told the group that he had little expectation that his advocacy would change anything—opposition to food and regulation remained both stubborn and powerful—but on December 5 Roosevelt formally announced that he was backing the legislation: "I recommend that a law be enacted to regulate interstate commerce in misbranded and adulterated foods, drinks and drugs. Such a law would protect the legitimate manufacturer and commerce and would tend to secure the health and welfare of the consuming public." The speech made it clear that the president had been following Wiley's research and its conclusions: "Traffic in foodstuffs which have been debased or adulterated so as to injure health and deceive the public should be forbidden."

Senator Heyburn promptly brought the bill back to the manufacturing committee, hoping to move it quickly to a vote by the full chamber. But the president had accurately assessed the hostility gathered against the legislation. It appeared, in fact, that Roosevelt's intervention had stirred up even stronger resistance. The Republican leader of the Senate, Nelson Aldrich of Rhode Island, had made his fortune as a wholesale grocer with strong ties to the food manufacturing industry. He now took to the floor to attack the bill as an affront to individual liberty: "Are we to take up the question as to what a man shall eat and what a man shall drink and put him under severe penalties if he is eating or drinking something different from what the chemists of the Agricultural Department think desirable?" Angrily, McCumber replied: "On the contrary, it is the purpose of the bill that a man may determine for himself what he will eat and what he will not eat. It is the purpose of the bill that he may go into the market and when he pays for what he asks for that he shall get it and not get some poisonous substance in lieu of that."

Aldrich stood unmoved. He flatly refused to bring the bill forward for a full Senate vote. Roosevelt tried to suggest, in a private meeting, that Aldrich should let the bill go forward. It would look better publicly and, after all, Aldrich didn't have to vote for it. The senator would not budge.

But in early February 1906, the Rhode Island senator was forced into an unhappy meeting with a powerful backer of the bill, the director of the American Medical Association's legislative council. The AMA was less interested in food safety than in the problem of snake-oil medicines, but the two issues were bonded together in the law. The organization wanted those patent cures regulated and was prepared, Aldrich was informed, to rally all 135,000 physicians in the country, including all of those located in the senator's home state, to get the bill passed. The doctors would, if need be, contact every patient, county by county. The AMA had a reputation for avoiding partisan politics, but its board had decided to take this legislation on as a personal cause. And according to Charles Reed, the AMA legislative council director, the senator from Rhode Island could take this as a personal warning. Shortly after that meeting, Aldrich called a more junior senator into his office—Albert Beveridge of Indiana—and told him to carry a message to Heyburn: It was now good timing for Heyburn to bring his bill up for a vote again.

Beveridge later told journalist Mark Sullivan that he had suspected that his errand was just for show. He thought that any Senate vote in favor of the bill would prove futile. The legislation was clearly destined to die in the House, where leadership was just as firmly opposed. But the Indianan obediently went to Heyburn's office. As he also recounted to Sullivan, "Heyburn said he could not believe it and said he was tired of being made a fool of by asking useless consideration [for the bill] which he had asked so many times before." Beveridge ventured the opinion that the game seemed, for the minute, to be going Heyburn's way and that he might as well take advantage of it. That afternoon Heyburn requested a vote on his bill. On February 26 the food and drug bill passed 63–4, with Aldrich abstaining. The bill then went to the House and, as predicted, Sullivan wrote, "There it slept."

Back at the Bureau of Chemistry—which Wiley had taken to calling "America's test kitchen"—the toxicity testing of preservatives continued to tell an alarming story. Bigelow remained lead chemist for the trials and Wiley himself had assumed a more hands-on role. He no longer had the help of physicians from the Marine Hospital Service, who had found the twice-weekly examinations of Poison Squad volunteers too time-consuming. So Wiley was conducting the physicals himself. As with borax in the previous trial, in the second round of tests on salicylic acid, doses were administered either in capsules or tablets. Wiley publicly acknowledged that industry-backed scientists had criticized this in the borax study, arguing that it failed to represent normal intake of the preservative, which was usually premixed into food. Yet he dismissed the criticism. "It is hardly necessary to call attention to the futility of such an objection," he added. "A preservative administered in this way at the time of the meals, as was always the case, is rapidly mixed with the contents of the stomach during the process of digestion, and could not in any way exert any injurious effect by reason of the form of its administration."

Another repeated criticism was that Wiley and his staff did not constantly monitor the men's activities and could not be sure they didn't cheat on their prescribed diets. These were working government employees who came to the test kitchen only for meals and checkups. This was a real limitation. "The attempt has been made to control, as far as possible, all conditions of the experimental work," he said, but "the difficulties attending the task are so enormous that it is not possible that complete success should be secured." Still, he thought, the chemistry crew had done enough checks, interviews, questionnaires, and follow-ups to be sure that their volunteers were not ill, taking medications, or experiencing other unusual exposures.

Again they tested the suspect preservative at varying dosages, ranging from about two hundred milligrams to a full two grams daily. Wiley again believed that although the higher dose, not unexpectedly, produced more severe effects, the real issue was the subtler risk of daily chronic exposure at low doses and an apparent cumulative effect. "Like other ordinary preservatives, it is not one that can be classified as a poison in the usual sense of the word." Salicylic acid's long history in folk medicine, as well as its use as a prescribed pharmaceutical, tended to reassure consumers that it was benign. Wiley agreed that salicylic acid was "often beneficial when prescribed by a competent physician." It was also a base for synthesizing the milder acetylsalicylic acid, an active ingredient in aspirin, with which it was sometimes confused. But, just as Wiley's lab had reported in its 1887 study of alcoholic beverages, its use as a preservative raised the risk of a cumulative overdose. When salicylic acid was mixed into either drink or food and consumed day after day, meal after meal, it became far more of a hazard than a health aid. During the months of the salicylic acid tests, the scientists had recorded chronic stomach pain, nausea, appetite loss, and weight loss in their squad members. Bigelow's written conclusion was that taken chronically, even in small quantities, salicylic acid "exerts a depressing and harmful influence upon the digestion and health and general metabolic activities of the body." The chemists again pointed out that the use of such compounds could be reduced if manufacturers would merely process foods in clean conditions.

Wiley sent Wilson an early copy of the report. It reinforced the secretary's concern that his bureau chief had become more crusader than objective chemist. The end of the salicylic acid report, in fact, came awfully close to sounding like a Paul Pierce diatribe: "The addition of salicylic acids and salicylates to foods is therefore a process which is reprehensible in every respect and leads to injury to the consumer, which though in many cases not easily measured, must finally be productive of great harm." This was not the same prudent, methodical Harvey Wiley who had spoken so judiciously about the preservative issue during the embalmed-beef hearings. Wilson had long supported Wiley's activities, but his growing stridency was starting to alienate the chief chemist from his politically cautious boss.

As Doubleday, Page prepared to publish *The Jungle* in early 1906, Marcosson told Sinclair that the firm wanted major revisions. The serialized version of the novel, the last chapter of which had appeared in *Appeal to Reason* the previous November, featured too much overwrought, preachy philosophy, including its many references to exploitive employers preying on hapless workers. Doubleday, Page wanted to excise Sinclair's overt comparisons of worker life to an existence in a wild forest with "the strong devouring the weak"—the source of his title. At such a late date, after his struggles to find a publisher, he gave in. The publisher cut thirty thousand words and ordered an initial print run of twenty thousand copies. Publication was set for February 26, which was, again by pure coincidence, the day the Senate passed Heyburn's food and drug bill.

Marcosson speculated that the book would either be "a sensational success or a magnificent failure." To help get the word out, Sinclair sent an early copy to his muckraking journalist friend Baker at *McClure's*. Marcosson sent copies to the wire services Associated Press and United Press with a note urging them to quote at will. And he sent extra copies to newspapers and magazines in every major American city. The publishing company also sent a copy to President Roosevelt, autographed by Sinclair, of course.

# Eight

# THE JUNGLE

## 1906

———◉———

*And the terrapin tastes like roast veal.*
*The wine which you drink never heard of a grape,*
*But of tannin and coal tar is made.*

With the legislation seeming permanently stalled in Congress, Harvey Wiley had taken to writing protest letters to newspapers and magazines, complaining about their advertising of fake remedies and fraudulent foods. Their practices weren't illegal, he acknowledged, but they were dismayingly dishonest.

To the *Washington Star* he wrote in early 1906: "I have read with regret in your issue of Monday, [January] 29th of the probably fatal illness of Buck Ewing, the celebrated catcher." Ewing, a former star player and manager for the New York Giants, had been diagnosed with Bright's disease, an inflammation of blood vessels in the kidneys, dreaded as bringing on a rapid and painful death.

But Wiley noted that the *Star* was apparently prepared to offer a solution to such a devastating diagnosis, as illustrated by "your issue of Sunday, the 28th instant, of Dr. Kilmer's Swamp Root. This remedy, which I always keep near me," he added sarcastically, "has on the carton in very large letters—Cures Brights Disease—together with every other ill that the flesh is heir to."

Perhaps, he suggested, the *Star* didn't realize that his bureau chemists had found that the Swamp Root formula was mostly drinking alcohol and turpentine, flavored with a sprinkle of herbs and spices such as cinnamon, peppermint, and sassafras. But as the newspaper's advertisement guaranteed the tonic's cure-all potency, Wiley promised to send Ewing "a marked copy of the *Sunday Star* with this absolute guarantee and I shall expect soon to hear of his entire restoration to health." Ewing died of Bright's disease in October 1906 at age forty-seven.

To *Everybody's Magazine* in New York, Wiley fired off a series of questions: Could the magazine explain how Rubifoam made teeth look "just like pearls"? In what sense was Celes, the oxygen tooth powder, "chemically perfect"? And about that Kneipp Malt Coffee, which was made from roasted barley grains. How exactly did it manage to have "real coffee flavor? Is there anything that can have the 'real coffee flavor' except coffee?" How exactly did the magazine plan to stand behind these claims?

Needling the periodicals and their advertisers provided him with an amusing respite from the seemingly never-ending and increasingly bitter legislative fight. After the encouraging vote on Heyburn's bill in the Senate, after Wiley's acceptance of his role as the public face of the campaign, the opposition had escalated the frequency and the vitriol of their attacks on him, which were also becoming more personal in tone. "My attention is called to the fact that considerable agitation is going on here looking to your removal," wrote the director of Dudley & Co. Canned Goods in New York City to Wiley. *Grocery World*, a trade paper for wholesale grocers, had published two editorials in the previous two weeks demanding that Wiley be removed from office.

Critics described him as "the nation's janitor," busily sweeping up the kitchens and pantries of its citizens; the overzealous "policeman" of the American stomach; a would-be tyrant; a shoddy scientist; a man with mental issues and delusions of grandeur. The publicist for the borax industry sent letters to news editors under a fake name, calling the Poison Squad studies deeply flawed. The whiskey rectifiers and the wholesale grocers printed a pamphlet on Wiley's work on fake honey from the early 1880s, dating back to his years at Purdue.

Repeating the old charge, it was titled "Wiley's Honey Lie" and purported to be from still-angry honey producers. The American Honey Producers League denied any knowledge of the pamphlet but the damage was done. The whiskey rectifiers suggested that he was a bourbon-soaked alcoholic receiving packets of hard cash from Taylor and his friends. Wiley started receiving sympathy notes from members of Congress. "The attacks which are being made upon you by certain representatives of the liquor interests are contemptible," wrote a Wisconsin legislator to Wiley about one circular. In a good-humored reply, Wiley called the rectifiers' diatribe "[A]bout the best one that has been issued so far. I shall take pleasure in showing it to the Secretary of Agriculture." Wilson, despite his concerns, was still standing by Wiley and had recently renewed the chemist's contract.

In late February Wiley gave a pro-legislation speech to a national convention of the canning industry, held in Philadelphia. The president of the Midwest canners' group, A. C. Frasier of Wisconsin, had invited him. Frasier, who specialized in peas processed without preservatives, found Wiley's arguments compelling. But when the chief chemist arrived at the Philadelphia train station, he found his host pacing the platform in a state of alarm. He feared for Wiley's safety, Frasier said, should he attend the meeting. "What is the matter?" Wiley asked. "Well, they say you are trying to ruin their business," Frasier replied. "I can not help what they say," Wiley replied. "I am trying to save their business." He was not going to be a government employee who ran in fear from a roomful of American businessmen. That would send a terrible message to the canners. But he agreed that it made sense to have a backdoor exit ready, just in case.

The hall was packed with canners, food jobbers, and brokers, none of them smiling. An Iowa canner, William Ballinger, stood up to explain that he was opposed to allowing Wiley to become "dictator" of his industry. "I want to declare the job too big a one for Professor Wiley and his assistants," Ballinger said. "Furthermore it has been my observation, and I want Professor Wiley to know I do not mean anything personal, that a man who lives in an atmosphere of microbes and bacilli not only becomes a crank but absolutely monomaniacal on the subject upon which he is interested."

Wiley didn't deny that he could appear to be a crank. But he defended his record and that of the Chemistry Bureau in helping, rather than trying to control, the canning industry. "The canners of this country have a serious responsibility placed on them," he said. "Let me pay you the compliment of having progressed steadily in preserving the food you can, but there should never be a relaxation of efforts to move onward as there are some things that can be bettered."

He restated his belief that the canners' mushrooming use of dyes and preservatives, often to disguise poor-quality food, was driving consumers away from American products. "Honesty is what the American public demands and canned goods will have an ever-growing market as long as people are confident that the goods are free from anything injurious."

He could stand for both consumer protection and the American businessman, Wiley insisted, and he hoped those seated in the room could respect that. "You are honest businessmen," he continued. "Is there one man in this room that wants to take one dollar from an American citizen which, if that American citizen knew what he was selling him, he would not give?" To the surprise of both Frasier and himself, Wiley received a standing ovation. Some of the leading canners even promised to back the proposed pure-food legislation. Not all of them would do so, of course. Some of the canners had already allied themselves with the hostile National Food Manufacturers Association. But even among that contingent, there were attendees who agreed with Wiley that public perception of a chemically tainted and adulterated food supply was hurting their business.

Wiley told the story of his meeting with the canners at a congressional hearing about that canners' conference, stressing that he wanted to allay legislators' concerns about political retribution if they passed a pure-food law. There were plenty of processors who would welcome uniform safety standards, he told them. He offered the examples of Pittsburgh's H.J. Heinz and the Chicago-based Reid, Murdoch and Co. The latter had written to him in mid-February, "From the newspapers we notice that the attitude of the so-called National Food Manufacturer's Association is, in some instances, taken to represent the views of manufacturers generally. We desire to state that we have no connection whatsoever and we believe that none of the large manufacturing grocers of this country are identified with it. We are unreservedly for a National Pure Food Law."

Senate passage of Heyburn's bill had rallied supporters as well as opponents. "Your wonderful tenacity of purpose and persistence seems to have at last won out triumphantly," wrote a former state food commissioner from Ohio. Charles Reed of the AMA, who had successfully threatened Nelson Aldrich in the Senate, said he planned to put similar pressure on legislators in the House. "When the Pure Food Bill begins to draw to a focus in the House, let me know," he wrote to Wiley in early March. "It is my intention to do with the House what I did with the Senate, but in addition, I propose having telegrams pour into the members from all over the United States."

In early March Frank Doubleday received a visit from a lawyer representing meatpacking titan J. Ogden Armour. The Chicago meatpacking titan had organized the industry response to Sinclair's book, publicly declaring that the products were "without blemish," privately pressuring newspapers not to review the book and libraries not to carry it. The attorney invited the publisher to lunch with Armour, the meal to be served in a private car now awaiting his pleasure at Grand Central Station. The lawyer explained that Armour wanted to offer a generous advertising contract to the publishing firm, on the condition that Doubleday, Page curtail further publication plans for *The Jungle*, in particular any plan to publish the book abroad. As it happened, Doubleday had just received an offer from an English publisher, Alfred Harmsworth, Lord Northcliffe, seeking to buy both British and European rights to *The Jungle*. Harmsworth had founded two tabloid newspapers, the *Daily Mail* and the *Daily Mirror*, and he'd become famous—or notorious, depending on one's point of view—for his sensationalistic presentation of news stories. Doubleday had been personally and patriotically disinclined to accept the offer. He had only reluctantly followed Page's lead in agreeing to publish Sinclair's book at all. If he accepted Northcliffe's deal, he worried that he would be showing the world an unsavory side of American business, and he "did not care to wash our dirty linen in all the capitals of Europe."

But the lawyer drew out of his briefcase a can of corned beef and placed it, with a smile, on the publisher's desk, a gesture meant to symbolize a lucrative relationship. Doubleday, known for his quick temper, lost it.

"This chap made me so angry," he said. "I showed him [Northcliffe's] telegram and told him we would give permission to have the book reprinted in Europe." His visitor expressed bafflement, leading the still infuriated Doubleday to insult the attorney as a moral degenerate and throw him out of his office.

*The Jungle* was on its way to U.S. sales of more than 150,000 in its first year of publication, which would also see it translated into more than seventeen languages. In England the rising political star Winston Churchill recommended that all citizens read it; the playwright George Bernard Shaw called it an example of "what is going on all over the world under the top layer of prosperous plutocracy." Sinclair appreciated his sudden prosperity, but he did not enjoy every aspect of his newfound celebrity.

Meatpacking interests planted stories in friendly newspapers, claiming that the young author had spent more time in Chicago whorehouses than in the yards. The hostile *Chicago Tribune* had printed an editorial titled "Investigating a Novel," which described the book as "garbage fiction," Sinclair as a "pseudo-reformer," and Roosevelt as barely interested but concerned that "the American export trade in meat would be destroyed if foreigners were led to believe that the novel dealt with facts." Sinclair was in a resentful mood, discontented even with the public's response to his book. Despite incredible sales, no one was talking about the struggles of the workingman or socialist ideals. They were talking about filthy, germ-infested food and the possibility that their morning sausage contained scraps of rat and possibly human meat as well as the standard pork. "I aimed for the public's heart," he would later say, bitterly. "And by accident I hit it in the stomach."

Beginning the first week of publication in February, letters and telegrams of outrage arrived at the White House, demanding to know how Roosevelt planned to fix the problem of the country's disgusting food supply. The president had been one of the book's earliest readers and had also been appalled. The political humorist Finley Peter Dunne, in his syndicated newspaper column "Mr. Dooley," enjoyed imagining Roosevelt's reaction to the revelations in *The Jungle* while at the White House breakfast table. Veteran journalist Dunne wrote the popular column in the person of fictional Chicago barkeeper Martin J. Dooley, who spoke in a thick Irish brogue: "Tiddy was toying with a light breakfast an' idly turn'n over the pages iv th' new book with both hands. Suddenly he rose fr'm th' table, an cryin': 'I'm pizened', begun throwin' sausages out iv th' window." In Dunne's telling, a hurled sausage struck Senator Beveridge—who had played a part in Senate passage of the food and drug bill—right in the head "an' made him a blond" before whizzing on to injure a Secret Service agent and destroy a thicket of oak trees. Fearing for the president's life, the newly blond Beveridge rushed into the White House and "discovered Tiddy in hand to hand combat with a potted ham. . . . Since thin th' Prisidint, like th' rest iv us, has become a viggytarynan."

Doubleday, Page had also sent the president early proofs of the supporting articles scheduled to appear in *World's Work*, one of them a microbiologist's detailed discussion of dangerously prolific germ cultures in Chicago processing plants and the failure of government inspectors to address the problem. Dismayed, Roosevelt asked Secretary Wilson to explain what was going on with the Inspection Division of the Department of Agriculture. Its employees were supposed to make sure that diseased animals were not sent from the slaughterhouses into production of canned, dried, smoked, and chopped meat. In *The Jungle*, which Sinclair claimed was based on his own reporting directly from the yards, the packers simply paid the government inspectors either to look the other way or stay away.

The question threw Wilson on the defensive and he replied with an attack on Sinclair's "willful and deliberate" portrayal of corrupt inspectors. An irked Roosevelt warned Wilson that his department seemed to be more interested in hiding a problem than in solving it. The president then sought less self-protective points of view, including one from Chicago progressive activist Mary McDowell, a colleague and friend of Jane Addams, who had provided housing for Sinclair during his book research. McDowell had worked for years to help packinghouse laborers, earning her the nickname "Angel of the Stockyards." She told him that the novel was based in truth, allowing for some slight exaggeration. Like Doubleday, Roosevelt did not admire the book's socialist ideas, and he wrote to Sinclair directly to tell him so, but he also decided to invite the young author to the White House in early April to discuss the realities of the stockyards.

Roosevelt told Sinclair that he was bypassing the Agriculture Department and sending two independent investigators to Chicago: his commissioner of labor, Charles P. Neill, and the social reformer James B. Reynolds, a manager of settlement houses on the East Side of Manhattan. The president invited Sinclair to meet with them and perhaps suggest avenues of inquiry. Neill and Reynolds were leaving so soon that Sinclair managed only a brief discussion on the train platform. He returned home to find a letter from a friend in Chicago, saying that packers had been alerted to the new inquiry—purportedly by the White House itself—and were busily cleaning up the factories.

Sinclair had little trust in the president. In Roosevelt's speech that spring at the annual dinner of the Gridiron Club, he'd railed against investigative journalists as "muckrakers," filling the pages of periodicals and books with dirt while "ignoring at the same time the good in the world." The president's attack wasn't inspired by Sinclair or his friends at *McClure's* but by David Graham Phillips, author of a series titled "The Treason of the Senate," running in William Randolph Hearst's magazine *Cosmopolitan*. Phillips had characterized the Senate as an "agent of interests as powerful as any invading army could be, and vastly more dangerous." The opening article focused on corrupt Republicans and attacked New York senator Chauncey Depew, Roosevelt's friend and political ally. Roosevelt wanted to respond by excoriating Phillips personally, but advisers persuaded him to deliver a broader critique of overzealous, reform-seeking writers—a category that could be interpreted to include Sinclair, Lincoln Steffens, Ray Stannard Baker, Ida Tarbell, Henry Irving Dodge, and more. In defense of his profession, Steffens, long a cordial acquaintance of the president, visited the White House the day after the Gridiron speech to criticize the intemperate language. The resolute Roosevelt brushed off the scolding and reprised the speech in expanded form before the Senate itself. There he clarified that he would not abide corruption, but that overweening journalists could do more harm than good in their eagerness to expose wrongdoing: "The men with the muck rakes are often indispensable to the well being of society; but only if they know when to stop raking the muck."

The president's nuances were lost on Sinclair. He took the speeches personally, convinced that Roosevelt was a progressive only when it suited him. He'd learned that the meatpacking interests had quietly donated $200,000 toward Roosevelt's election campaign in 1904. He doubted that the president's investigators would or could confirm the truths that he'd depicted in *The Jungle*—at least not without help. He took the pragmatic step of persuading a longtime journalist friend to meet with Neill and Reynolds in Chicago and to arrange interviews for them with sources he had talked to for his book. At the same time, he took the undiplomatic step of writing to Roosevelt, expressing his fear that the government had no genuine interest in the truth. This was prompted, at least in part, by a report in the *Tribune* that the president planned to give another speech, this one attacking *The Jungle*. Roosevelt wrote back dismissively, counseling, "Really, Mr. Sinclair, you must keep your head." Roosevelt himself had read hundreds of lies about his own life, and all with "quite as little foundation" as the recent *Tribune* fabrication. To Doubleday, Roosevelt wrote with irritation, "Tell Sinclair to go home and let me run the country for a change."

Despite Sinclair's worries and despite the packers' efforts to polish things up before the investigators' visit, the Neill-Reynolds report deeply dismayed the president. The facts were as bad as or worse than the scenes in the novel. The findings read, in part: "Many inside rooms where food is prepared are without windows, deprived of sunlight, and without direct communication with the outside air. . . . Usually the workers toil without relief in the humid atmosphere heavy with the odors of rotten wood, decayed meats, stinking offal and entrails. The tables on which meat was handled, the tubs, and other receptacles were generally of wood, most of which were watersoaked and only half cleaned. The privies, as a rule, were sections of workrooms, enclosed by thin wooden partitions, ventilating into the workrooms. In a word, we saw meat shoveled from filthy wooden floors, piled on tables rarely washed, pushed from room to room in rotten box carts, in all of which processes it was in the way of gathering dirt, splinters, floor filth and expectoration of tuberculous and other diseased workers."

One dead hog had fallen out of a box cart and into a privy. Workers had simply dragged it out and sent it down the line with the other carcasses. "When comment was made to floor superintendents about these matters, it was always the reply that this meat would afterward be cooked, and this sterilization would prevent any danger from its use." But this, Neill and Reynolds noted, wasn't entirely true. A considerable amount of the meat went into sausages, uncooked and unsterilized. The leavings from the sausages were piled into a heap that also included floor sweepings of desiccated meat scraps, rope strands, and "other rubbish. Dismayed inquiry evoked a frank admission this garbage heap was to be ground up and used in making potted ham."

The factual report was, the president recognized, potentially even more explosive than *The Jungle*. The latter bore the label "fiction," after all, and had been penned by a self-avowed socialist. It could be dismissed. What Neill and Reynolds had found out could not. Roosevelt decided not to publish their report, holding it back as political leverage. But he showed some of the findings to a few trusted members of Congress, among them the reliable Albert Beveridge, asking him to draft an amendment to the Agricultural Appropriations Bill, which would impose new and more stringent federal inspections of meat on the industry. The Beveridge amendment passed the Senate on May 25 without a dissenting vote.

The appropriations bill then went to the House, where the meatpackers indeed had exceptionally good friends. The House Committee on Agriculture, chaired by a wealthy New York farmer and cattle dealer, James Wadsworth, held the necessary hearing on the Beveridge amendment. But Wadsworth filled the witness list with executives from the packinghouses and their friends. Most of the hearing was spent mocking both *The Jungle* and the Neill-Reynolds report. Congressman Charles Wharton, a Chicago Republican whose district included the yards, described the packinghouses as just as "clean and wholesome" as any home kitchen. The government inspectors, he continued, were simply not smart enough to understand how a reputable business operated.

"If a commission of men of average intelligence should investigate the meat producing businesses, they would find it conducted in a proper and sanitary manner," said Louis Swift, who had inherited Swift & Company from his father, Gustav. In turn, Neill replied that he was intelligent enough to avoid all products from the Chicago packinghouses. From the moment he had returned from the yards, he had insisted that no meat be served at his house unless it was fresh beef and mutton from local farms.

Upton Sinclair telegraphed the House committee members, asking permission to testify. They turned him down. In short order, the members voted to reject the Beveridge amendment. Wadsworth offered in its place an amendment that reduced inspections and penalties for the packing businesses and changed the funding plan for the inspection program. Beveridge's amendment had required the packers to pay into a fund that would support inspections. Wadsworth removed that burden on industry and returned it to the taxpayers. In doing so, he deliberately created a much smaller budget for inspections. Whatever Sinclair's suspicions about him, Roosevelt did recognize that the industry needed to be reformed. The message he sent to Wadsworth read, "I am sorry to have to say that this strikes me as an amendment which, no matter how intentionally, is framed so as to minimize the chance of rooting out the evil in the packing business."

Wadsworth replied that he considered the changes to be correct and appropriate. "I regret that you, the President of the United States, should feel justified, by innuendo, at least, in impugning the sincerity and the competency of a committee of the House of Representatives." He added that he had no intention of making further changes to the amendment. They conducted these exchanges in private. Publicly the legislation simply appeared stalled as usual. But by now Sinclair had had enough of political discretion. He'd become friendly with Neill and Reynolds and he knew their report was both solid and a confirmation of his own work.

In late May, Sinclair decided to leak what he knew about the Neill-Reynolds report to the *New York Times.* He stuffed a briefcase with notes, affidavits, letters, and everything he had on paper and marched off to a meeting at the newspaper. The *Times* editors recognized journalistic gold and ran the story on the front page on Monday, May 28, loaded with quotes from the government inspectors and from the novelist. "In Armour's own establishment I saw with my own eyes the doctoring of hams that were so putrefied that I could not force myself to remain near them," read a quote from Sinclair. The story quoted Neill recounting that "the pillars of the buildings were caked with flesh" and that "in these packing houses, the meat is dragged about on the floor, spat upon and walked upon." The *Times* even hunted down General Nelson Miles, who had brought the embalmed-beef complaint after the Spanish-American War. Miles's anger over the military food supply had not abated. "The disclosures about packing-house products now being exploited is no news to me," Miles declared. "I knew it seven years ago. Had the matter been taken up then, thousands of lives would have been saved."

In early June, exasperated with newspapers and with Upton Sinclair, but mostly with the members of Congress who had put him in this impossible position, Roosevelt released an eight-page summary of the Neill-Reynolds report. Newspapers printed the summary verbatim. Consumers were appalled—as were the meatpackers. The president, Armour declared, was no friend to businessmen and seemed to hold a particular dislike of those based in the heartland. "Roosevelt has a strong, personal animus against the packers of Chicago and is doing everything in his power to discredit them." Roosevelt responded by letting the packers and their friends in Congress know that he was out of patience. He wanted meat-inspection legislation on his desk in short order. If not, he would release the full report.

Within a week after Roosevelt released the Neill-Reynolds summary, even the *Chicago Tribune* was signaling the packers' defeat. On June 10 the paper ran a special report from a London correspondent headlined EUROPE THINKS U.S. LACKING IN HONOR. The sentiment on the Continent, the writer said, was in favor of sending the Chicago meatpackers to jail. By the end of the month, the British had stopped importing canned meat from the United States and both Germany and France were refusing American meat products in any form. American politicians recognized that they had to move to prevent further damage to the country's reputation and economy.

The battle-weary food and drug bill's advocates now realized the advantage of the moment. Finally circumstances were aligned in their favor. Once Roosevelt made up his mind, he honored his commitments. Heyburn, McCumber, and Beveridge in the Senate pressed the president again on broader food and drug legislation, as did Hepburn and his allies in the House. A new explosion of letters came flying from the women's clubs. The AMA's telegram campaign took off. Wiley hurried to meet with legislators and offer new findings from the Poison Squad studies, along with other research findings providing evidence of the need for change.

"The momentum of the Meat Inspection amendment carried with it the Pure Food Bill, which its enemies thought had been safely chloroformed in committee," wrote the investigative journalist Mark Sullivan. "In the end, the exposures of the packers by Roosevelt's commission, of the wholesale liquor dealers by themselves, of the patent medicines by *The Ladies' Home Journal* and *Collier's*, of food adulteration and food dyeing by Doctor Wiley and State and city food officials—the aggregate of all that worked into the strengthening of Roosevelt's hand, and was invincible."

There were still those who thought that Roosevelt and his

legislative allies compromised too much, among them the proud muckraking journalist David Graham Phillips. He'd already noted in his "Treason of the Senate" series that the New York congressman James Wadsworth had not entirely backed down from his defense of the meat industry. He'd successfully deleted the requirement that meat companies fund the inspection program. Further, Wadsworth had limited federal financing to $3 million a year when the "lowest estimate of the cost of adequate inspection" was twice that. The packers had also persuaded Wadsworth to remove a requirement that the inspections be marked with a date. The idea of that date was "so that the beef trust could not relabel three-and-four-and-five-year-old cans and furbish and 'freshen' decaying meat and work it off as good, new meat." Phillips deplored the fact that that requirement too had been deleted and warned that the planned legislation was far more corporate than consumer friendly. But in the rush to success, he doubted that he was being heard.

On June 30, 1906, Roosevelt triumphantly signed both the Meat Inspection Act and the Food and Drug Act. He presented Beveridge with the pen he'd used to sign the meat act. He did not acknowledge Sinclair's contribution, having decided, he told his friends, that the man was a crackpot. The president did not acknowledge Wiley either, not in the ceremony and not by any other gesture. Stung by the deafening silence, Wiley, after a modest interval, asked Beveridge if he would mind inquiring with the White House about whether he might also receive some token of the victory. Roosevelt's secretary replied: "Senator Beveridge spoke to me about presenting the Doctor with the pen with which the president signed the pure food bill, but on looking up the matter I found it had already been promised to Senator Heyburn, as author of the bill." Otherwise, the secretary politely continued, "it would have been a pleasure to have sent it to Dr. Wiley, to whom too much credit cannot be given for his long fight for pure food and against shams."

Roosevelt had a different view. As he would put it some years later: "The Pure Food and Drug bill became a law purely because of the active stand I took in trying to get it through Congress." Wiley and his allies had tried for years and failed, he said, because "some of them, although honest men, were so fantastically impractical that they played right into the hands of their foes." Newspapers might frequently reference the 1906 Pure Food and Drug Act as "Dr. Wiley's Law," but Roosevelt would never do so. And he worried that the doctor's uncompromising approach would only hamper, rather than help, the cause of safe food in the United States.

# PART II

*Nine*

# THE POISON TRUST

## 1906–1907

———◦———

*And you could not be certain, except for their shape,*
*That the eggs by a chicken were laid.*

"How does a general feel who wins a great battle and brings a final end to hostility?" Wiley would wonder, looking back on the passage of the food and drug law. "I presume I felt that way on the last day of June 1906." Bottles of champagne and Kentucky bourbon whiskey, fresh fruit and unadulterated candy, real honey and fine cheese had arrived in baskets and boxes at the Bureau of Chemistry, along with blizzards of celebratory telegrams and congratulatory letters, bearing wishes such as this one: "I have long contemplated writing you to express my admiration and encouragement in your contest for pure food, which I now express."

But Wiley, awash in that triumphant fizz of success, would later allow that he'd been too optimistic in believing that winning the legislative battle would end the hostilities. He'd gotten his hopes up, despite notes of caution mixed among the initial bravos. "I suppose you are pleased and I cannot refrain from writing my entire satisfaction in regard to the matter," wrote Wiley's old friend James Shepard, the South Dakota chemist who had publicized the preservative problem with his cautionary "daily meal plan." However, Shepard continued, "Perhaps it is not 'time to holler' yet for we may not be out of the woods." Shepard's assessment was accurate. The law had barely passed, Wiley later wrote, before manufacturers united to undo its proposed regulations "and then the real fight began."

On July 24 Wilson formally assigned his chief chemist to work with the three other departments—Treasury, Commerce, and Labor—to draft "for approval of the respective secretaries the rules and regulations necessary for the enforcement of the pure food act." They had some six months to do so; the law would not take effect until January 1907. The new law, as the government officials recognized, was big on ideas, minimal on specifics. The legislation, Wiley acknowledged in a letter to his friends at the American Medical Association, "is not as good as we would like it." It would take real work to render it effective. The best thing was that it had passed at all and that it had not—"when we consider the determined and able efforts which have been continually made by the opponents of this legislation"—been rendered completely toothless. Wiley's hope at this point, he continued, was to help strengthen it into a "more perfect structure in the future."

It did at least contain a definition of what constituted adulterated food, packed into one long sentence, one that became increasingly grim as it wound its way to the period. First, food would be considered adulterated if "anything" was mixed into it that reduced its quality or strength. Second, if one ingredient was surreptitiously substituted for another, as when manufacturers labeled cottonseed oil as high quality olive oil. Third, "if any valuable ingredient has been wholly or partially removed," as when vanilla extract contained no actual vanilla. Fourth, if the food was "mixed, colored, coated or stained" so as to conceal damage or fakery. The last items on the list were pure Harvey Wiley, the fifth declaring food adulterated if it contained "any poisonous or injurious ingredient" that might put health at risk, and the sixth barring acceptance of food that contained diseased animals, or consisted "in whole or part, of filthy, decomposed or putrid animals or vegetable substance."

But Wiley had wanted specific numbers, scientifically valid measurements to be part of the definition. As the bill was being drafted and revised, he had tried but failed to get such specific standards written into it. He knew enforcement would be hampered by vagueness. For instance, how was one to precisely measure what a reduction "in quality or strength" meant? As it now stood, the law lacked standards by which a material could be judged "injurious to health." It offered no definition of what constituted a poison; it qualified in no way why any part of an animal should be considered "unfit for food." It did not specify how ill or weak a steer or hog could become before it was officially judged "diseased."

Further, the new Agricultural Appropriation Act, which had also passed on June 30, hadn't authorized the Agriculture Department to set such standards. The original bill had done so, early drafts explicitly ordering the department to "establish standards of purity for food products and to determine what are regarded as adulterations therein." But the industry-backed National Food Manufacturers Association had successfully lobbied for removal of that language. Wiley had tried to have the authorization restored, but whiskey lobbyist Warwick Hough had successfully outflanked him.

When the bill was being drafted and revised, Wiley had warned legislators that a failure to set standards would make it easy for manufacturers to fight regulatory efforts by attacking them as arbitrary or political. "No set of authorities can equitably execute a food law without a set of standards of purity for their guide," he wrote to Congressman James R. Mann of Illinois. At the same time, Mann, a Republican, and other members of the House of Representatives were fielding intense pressure from business interests hostile to such standards. Journalist Phillips was right when he warned that the industry could weaken even the best-intentioned legislation. "For seventeen years the people had been trying to get a law that would check the operations of what is commonly known as 'the poison trust,'" Phillips wrote, using his favorite nickname for the American food manufacturing industry. He continued, "For seventeen years, the Senate had refused to permit the 'industry' to be molested." Phillips credited the passage of even minimal regulation mostly to the toxicity studies by Wiley's Chemistry Bureau and to the efforts of his energetic network of allies. He allowed some brief admiration for the pure-food exhibit at the St. Louis World's Fair, along with published articles, speeches, letters, telegraphs, and other determined advocacy. He judged that these combined had an even larger influence than Sinclair's famous book. "A campaign was coming on and the people were in an ugly mood." He credited Roosevelt for his political savvy in forcing consumer-protection measures and noted that Congress had been pushed into a corner where it had no alternative. The food and drug legislation, as proposed by Heyburn, had seemed a relatively honest attempt at regulation, Phillips added, modeled on successful laws already in place in Europe. But by the time Roosevelt had signed the bill, Phillips wrote, it had become perverted into what he now saw as a gift to the food processors and the chemical manufacturers.

Like Wiley, Phillips pointed out that the new law failed to set standards for "deleterious" ingredients, and, he complained, it didn't name a single toxic compound to be regulated. In his assessment, the final version also had been crafted to deliberately protect unscrupulous grocers and other food purveyors, notably including a clause declaring "No dealer shall be prosecuted" for selling adulterated products if the businessman could produce a written guarantee from a manufacturer, wholesaler, "or any other party residing in the United States" that the goods were pure. In other words, Phillips noted sarcastically, a note from the grocer's mother would serve to excuse him from selling fake or chemically risky products.

Further, he pointed out, the law was written so as to make the enforcement process nearly impossibly cumbersome. If a Bureau of Chemistry analysis found adulteration or misbranding, the secretary of agriculture was required to first notify the business in question. The business owner could then demand a hearing to defend the product. If the secretary sided with the manufacturer, the matter would be dropped. If the secretary sided with the bureau's findings, he was to "certify" the evidence as correct but still couldn't take direct enforcement action. Instead, he had to recommend legal prosecution to the appropriate district attorney, who could agree or not to take on the case.

Enforcement, if any was planned, would thus require a strong collaborative and cordial relationship between the Agriculture Department and the court system. And it would require an equally collaborative relationship between Wiley, as head of the Chemistry Bureau, and Wilson as head of the department. The two men had worked together with a fair degree of harmony in the past, but the need to function in a law-enforcement capacity would necessarily force them into a different and far more politically oriented partnership. "The new, the boasted pure food law adds nothing," Phillips wrote. "The pure food men did the shouting but the poison trust got the victory."

Despite that, Wiley found himself dealing almost daily with a corporate backlash that followed passage of the law. "Naturally when the battle array was formed, the first point of attack was on me," he wrote. Hough—who was by this time drawing a salary of $40,000 a year (almost $1 million today) as a liquor lobbyist—was among the first to attack. He had pelted Wilson with complaints about Wiley's interest in the whiskey question. "The word FOOD does not include drinks and beverage," Hough wrote to the secretary in late November. Therefore, the Agriculture Department had no standing to order—as Wiley had done—that liquor ingredients be put on labels. "The kind of actions taken by the Bureau of Chemistry," Hough continued, "would cause a renewal of trade disturbances, thanks to the kind of unwarranted statements of the Chief of the Bureau of Chemistry." In early December 1906, as implementation of the law loomed, Hough wrote again demanding the secretary's reassurance that his department would not permit Wiley to "discriminate against one class or grade of whiskey against another."

Wilson had been in office since shortly after McKinley's inauguration in 1897 and owed his continued employment in part to a diplomatic ability to distance himself from such quarrels. But Hough's hectoring tone pushed him to exasperation. He told the lobbyist that he had discussed the issue of labeling whiskey ingredients with the president, and that Roosevelt had promised that the White House would review the situation. In the meantime, Wilson advised that Hough stop criticizing the Bureau of Chemistry.

"Since you have objected to my writing about Dr. Wiley's efforts which only benefit the whiskey trust," Hough snapped back, he would temporarily halt his letter-writing campaign. In return, he expected the White House to support him, and he would send a message to the blenders and rectifiers, advising them that "no general onslaught is to be made by your department upon their business" when the law goes into effect in January. He had no doubt, he continued, that the secretary would comply with that very reasonable request. Wilson, still irritated, assured Wiley that he would continue to stand up to Hough, giving the chief chemist hope that he had the support to enforce the Food and Drug Act vigorously.

In a mid-December speech at the annual dinner of Chicago's Atlas Club, Wiley assured diners that the wide-reaching new law would change both food and country for the better. He added that the warnings he'd begun to lay out in his toxicity studies would help set enforcement standards that would continue to help protect the country's citizens: "This poison squad, gentlemen, is destined to play an important role in the future history of food regulation."

In 1907 the Bureau of Chemistry published the third of the hygienic table trial studies, this one focusing on the use of sulfurous acid in food processing. In a letter to Wilson, Wiley again credited his loyal staff members for doing the excellent work: F. C. Weber for overseeing the study, Willard Bigelow for doing the food and fecal analysis, B. J. Howard for the "microscopical examination of the blood and urine."

The letter also emphasized Wiley's intensifying belief that the bureau researchers—and the scientific community in general—were just beginning to understand the risks imposed by piling one preservative after another into the American food supply. "The relations of sulfurous acid to health are perhaps of greater importance than those of the preservatives already studied—namely boron compounds and the salicylic acids and its salts," he noted. He attributed this importance—and the need for well-thought-out regulation—to the fact that the compound was so widely used. Manufacturers were devoted to it, insisting that its use "approaches a necessity."

Sulfurous acid is related to the similarly named, better-known, and highly corrosive sulfuric acid. Chemically they differ by only a few oxygen atoms, but unlike sulfuric acid, sulfurous acid is relatively easy to handle. Manufacturers especially liked the fact that it could be converted into a solid form, such as sulfite of lime, by saturating lime (another name for calcium oxide) with sulfurous acid. This could be heated and its vapors used as a fumigant. In this form it was used to preserve a bright color in dried fruit while simultaneously preventing fermentation and fending off insects. Sulfurous acid was also used to treat syrup, molasses, smoked meats, and wine, as well as to disinfect wine-making equipment. Barrels used to age a vintage were typically given a good dose of acid fumes to sterilize the wood. Sulfur dioxide could also be directly bubbled into the fermenting liquid as a preservative and anti-oxidizer. Not surprisingly, the end result could be high levels of sulfites in wine. The Poison Squad study had thus focused on those compounds and on the chemists' suspicion that exposure could carry significant risks. To test that idea, the bureau used one of the better-known salts derived from sulfurous acid, sodium sulfite. This was, as in the earlier studies, placed into capsules of varying doses and dished up along with the daily meals.

To the surprise and dismay of the Agriculture Department scientists, only nine of the twelve squad members endured to the end of the sulfite study. At the highest dose (about four grams), two of the volunteers became so ill that the researchers halted the trial before anyone else was badly sickened. They were less sure about a third ailing squad member who was at the time suffering from a bad cold. But every single man had sickened to some degree after being dosed with sulfites, reporting loss of appetite, stomach pains, headaches, dizziness, and a shaky feeling of weakness.

Much more research was needed, but Wiley told the secretary that the government should move toward what he termed a "complete and somewhat speedy suppression" of manufacturing processes that put sulfites into food and drink. "It is evident that the prohibition of its use would necessitate a radical change in methods of manufacture," he wrote. But "assuming that in the manufacturing processes certain added bodies are used which are found on investigation to be injurious to health, the rational conclusions of such an investigation would be, not to excuse or overlook the presence of such bodies, but to institute investigations looking to their suppression." The compounds could never be wholly eliminated. Sulfites formed naturally in wine during the process of fermentation. But why add to those levels?

"The use of sulfurous acid and sulfites never adds anything to the flavor or quality of a food but renders it both less palatable and less healthful," Wiley wrote. "Every fact which has been brought out therefore in the investigation tends to accentuate the justness of the conclusion, namely, that the use of sulfurous acid in foods should be suppressed." A strong stand against these preservatives would, he predicted, encourage research into other, less toxic ways of preserving food and drink.

Wiley must have realized what a regulatory reach this was. To call for a ban of a widely used preservative, to anticipate industries quickly adapting newer, safer methods—these were beyond optimistic. But if he had momentarily forgotten the scale and intensity of the opposition to such ideas, he was soon to be reminded.

In January 1907, before Wiley and his colleagues had managed to put even basic enforcement guidelines into place, James A. Tawney, a congressman from Minnesota, moved to eliminate one of Wiley's favored aspects of the food and drug bill. The fifty-two-year-old Tawney—tall and stylish, sporting an imposing mustache—belonged to a faction of the Republican Party popularly known as the Stand-Patters. In contrast to reformers in general and the Roosevelt-led progressive Republicans, they resisted any move that reeked of change from what they saw as the more noble nineteenth-century approach to government. Tawney's move was to attach an amendment to the agricultural appropriations bill that blocked the use of any federal funds to support food safety work by scientists and officials working at the state level. It was potentially devastating. The Department of Agriculture depended heavily on cooperation with state officials; scientists like Edwin Ladd of North Dakota had shown how much of a difference collaboration could make. Opponents of the food and drug law had already capped its first-year enforcement funding at a mere $700,000, not even enough to cover a national food-inspection program. If the USDA lost its support from state regulators and researchers, there seemed little prospect of making the law work.

Once again Wiley contacted his allies in the pure-food movement; once again he asked them to help him fight back. Alice Lakey of the National Consumers League replied immediately, angrily describing Tawney's amendment as specifically designed to "impair the efficiency of the administration of the food and drugs act. . . . Our committee are doing all we can and please let us know if you have any instructions for us." *Club News*, the newsletter of the General

Federation of Women's Clubs, echoed her outrage. In a nationally circulated editorial, it pointed out that opponents of regulation had first campaigned against the law as a federal violation of states' rights, a claim that had helped array Southern Democrats against the food and drug bill. "The plot failed," the editorial continued. "It would now appear that the same thing is being attempted in a different way—that is, by practically prohibiting all plans for co-operation between the National and State Authorities."

Opposition to Tawney's amendment also came from a new source: the People's Lobby, an organization launched to fight government corruption. Its founders included two well-known muckraking journalists, Henry Beech Needham and Lincoln Steffens, along with crusading Kansas newspaper editor William Allen White; Kentucky food chemist Robert Allen, now secretary of the Interstate Pure Food Committee; James B. Reynolds, who had been part of the investigative team that Roosevelt sent to inspect the Chicago stockyards; and the widely admired and politically liberal novelist Mark Twain. "If anyone is naughty in Congress, he will have to reckon with a new force," Twain wrote in the *New York Times*. The People's Lobby, he said, should be considered an ally to good government, as it would "see, in a methodical manner, that Congress hides no secrets, no secret alliances." Like Steffens, Henry Needham had long been a supporter of Roosevelt's progressive policies, and he was optimistic that the president would favor the new organization. He and Roosevelt had a mostly friendly relationship, based on a shared interest in athletics. Needham was one of the nation's foremost baseball writers and an eloquent critic of excessive violence in football. He often wrote feelingly about his belief in fair play—in sports and in life. He had become so frustrated with American politics that he'd also helped organize the People's Lobby to take on government reform directly. The Tawney amendment became its first target.

Like Hough's presumptuous arrogance, the Tawney amendment

irked Secretary Wilson into abandoning his usual cautious approach to political issues. He too came out publicly against the measure. The combined opposition's strength, to the relief of many, caused Tawney's amendment to fail in committee. Wilson's public stance gave the impression that he was willing to back Wiley as strongly as ever, but those around them saw signs of strain between the two. Robert Allen wrote to Needham that the secretary was shutting his chief chemist out of key decisions regarding food regulation: "Secretary Wilson absolutely ignores Dr. Wiley."

Wiley and Wilson had, at least, earlier reached an agreement on a plan to expand their roster of food and drink inspectors; twenty-eight new men would be on board by year's end. Six new branch laboratories were being opened to handle regional demand for product analysis; the department had plans to add at least another ten facilities the following year. And Allen himself had successfully recommended a young lawyer from Kentucky, Walter G. Campbell, to head the Food Inspection Division: Working with public health officials in Louisville, Campbell had helped shut down numerous swill dairies there. Allen wrote to Wiley, "I unqualifiedly recommend him as one of the men that you will make no mistake in appointing and putting close to you." Campbell proved his worth rapidly, meticulously organizing the agency's inspection program and working tirelessly to improve the law and its enforcement. He would eventually direct the regulatory agency that, years later, would inherit the enforcement role of the Bureau of Chemistry, an agency that in 1930 would become the U.S. Food and Drug Administration.

Still, Allen's misgivings about Wilson grew. As he also wrote to Needham, "in thinking over Secretary Wilson's attitude toward the pure food work, there is nothing to show that he has ever been in sympathy with it." He recalled that during the embalmed-beef hearings, Wilson had been "unenthusiastic," leaving Wiley to be the public face of the issue. The secretary had even, during the hearings, told

Allen privately that he found Roosevelt's dramatic testimony "a pain in the side." Allen had an uneasy feeling that the People's Lobby would need to come to Wiley's aid "more than once in this fight."

The ever-festering conflict over whiskey was key among matters driving a wedge between Wiley and Wilson. Under the new law, the chief chemist had successfully pushed through one government seizure of rectified whiskey after another. The seizures included two barrels of Choice Old Monongahela Whiskey, which did not "contain enough whiskey to give it character"; fifteen barrels of Clark's Old Blend Rye Whiskey, which contained no rye; four and a half barrels of Old Kimroe Rye Whiskey Blend, which also lacked rye, and a barrel of Old Harmony Whiskey, which was simply a batch of dyed ethanol. In a single week the department had moved to seize more than fifty barrels of so-called whiskey with an eye toward prosecution.

And barely a month after the law went into effect, in February 1907, Wiley had reinforced Hough's fears about his Kentucky bourbon bias when the chief chemist gave some undeniably pro–straight whiskey testimony before the House Committee on Agriculture. House Speaker Joseph Cannon, the fiercely pro-business Republican from Illinois, seeking to protect the numerous bottling businesses in his home district, now wanted blended whiskeys exempted from labeling under the law. When asked before the committee to define "blended whiskey," Wiley gave in to exasperation and replied, "Crooked is the term you mean. If one is straight, the other is crooked. Crooked whisky is not whisky at all but is made of neutral spirits and flavored and colored. It is an imitation."

Politically his outburst did not serve him well. Hough fired off another angry broadside to Wilson. The secretary agreed that such statements could not be described as unbiased scientific commentary. The confrontation added to a sense by Wilson—and, perhaps more important at this point, by the Agriculture Department's powerful solicitor, George P. McCabe—that Wiley's long advocacy for regulation had turned him into more of a crusader than an unbiased researcher.

The argument between Wiley and Cannon had focused on one detail of the new law, a paragraph on misbranding. That section stated that all products that were compounds, imitations, or blends must be accurately labeled. A product could be called a blend only if it was a "mixture of like substances" under the law. This, by Wiley's reading, meant that blended whiskey must be a mixture of genuine whiskeys. If it was one of the rectified versions—whiskey mixed with neutral spirits, water and dye, or just dyed neutral spirits and water—then it should be labeled "imitation whiskey."

The rectifiers had developed a line of additives to mimic the taste of straight whiskey and even its tendency to bead or cling to a glass. These special flavorings and enhancers included bourbon extract, rye oil, rye extract, rye essence, Pittsburg rye essence, Monongahela essence, malt essence, Irish and Scotch essence, essence of gin (made from juniper berries), corn flavoring, aging oil, and bead oil. Hough argued that these coloring and flavoring agents were only trace additives and that all blended whiskeys—his organization was trying to do away with the term "rectified"—could be considered simply a mix of different types of alcohol. In a letter to Wilson he suggested that "everything mixed could be called a blend," rather than using the off-putting word "imitation." The idea—practical and business friendly—appealed to USDA solicitor McCabe. He wrote a recommendation that all alcohols be considered "like substances" in the future.

Wiley pushed back. He didn't buy the idea that synthetic ethanol, dyed with burned sugar and flavored with bourbon extract, was equivalent to aged bourbon. It was cheating the consumer to pretend so. Wilson this time took McCabe's part, rebuffing Wiley. The chief chemist refused to accept their decision and decided that the point was worth appealing over their heads. Requesting and receiving an appointment with President Roosevelt in late March, he took with him to the White House a miniature still and a briefcase loaded with samples of whiskey extracts and additives. For a "very fruitful hour," as Wiley described it, he explained and demonstrated to Roosevelt the differences between types of beverages labeled "whiskey." In a March 30 letter to Robert Allen, he described the president as agreeable to trying the different samples and overall "extremely courteous" and attentive. "At the end, he thanked me most cordially and said I had thrown new light upon the problem. . . . So I think, at least, I did not do any harm."

But in terms of in-house politics, he had also stirred up some trouble. Roosevelt called Wilson in for further discussion. He found the issue "very puzzling," he told the agriculture secretary, and he wasn't satisfied with the department's stand. Wilson, not pleased to find himself in this position, stood by McCabe and did his best to dismiss Wiley's arguments. He urged the president to adopt the single word "blended" for all the mixed whiskeys and alcohols, and Roosevelt agreed to consider it.

The president, though, had been impressed by Wiley's demonstrations and the science behind them. And he was suspicious that, as Henry Needham had recently warned him, the "imitation whisky alliance," having failed to prevent or further weaken the food and drug law, was now focusing its interests on "bulldozing" the Department of Agriculture. Needham pointed out to Roosevelt that if so early in the enforcement process a concession was made to one industry, it would set a precedent that others would easily pursue.

Judging that the department had grown too political within itself—on both sides of the argument—Roosevelt asked his attorney general, Charles J. Bonaparte, to review the evidence from all sides and to issue a formal ruling. Roosevelt considered the fifty-seven-year-old Bonaparte—a grandson of Jérôme Bonaparte, youngest brother of Napoleon I of France—to be thorough, tough, and unafraid of contentious issues.

After reviewing stacks of whiskey-related documents, including a voluminous report from the Bureau of Chemistry, Bonaparte found that he agreed with Wiley that not all whiskeys were created equal. Further, American consumers deserved detailed and accurate labels to help guide their purchases of such products. On April 10, 1907, Roosevelt notified Wilson that Bonaparte had so decided and that he, as president, accepted the ruling. He appended to that notice some instructions: "Straight whiskey will be labeled as such." The definition of a "blended whiskey" would be limited: Only "[a] mixture of two or more straight whiskies will be labeled as blended." If the blend was whiskey mixed with industrially produced ethyl alcohol, then things got more complicated: "Provided that there is a sufficient amount of straight whiskey to make it genuinely a 'mixture,' then the label would call it a 'compound whiskey.'" If there was no straight whiskey in the bottle, if it was simply colored and flavored neutral spirits, then it was a fake version of straight whiskey and needed to be so identified. In other words, "Imitation whisky will be labeled as such. Sincerely yours, Theodore Roosevelt."

Many in the pure-food movement saw the whiskey decision as a test of the government's willingness to address the labeling issue even when powerful business interests opposed it. It was to that end that Wiley had put himself—and his relationship with the secretary—on the line. His friends dared hope that the decision, carrying the clout of Roosevelt's approval, would restore the chief chemist's standing with his boss. "I write to congratulate you on your victory," wrote John Hurty, Indiana's public health officer, to his old friend about the whiskey ruling. "Your ideas in regard to 'blends' are exactly right and thus you see more than the President supporting you." The director of Kentucky's agricultural experiment station wrote, "Let me congratulate you for the victory won. Stick to it."

Wilson, however, saw the decision—especially the way it came about—as proof that his chief chemist could not be trusted. Making his own visit to the White House, he asked Roosevelt for permission to appoint another, more objective scientific expert to provide guidance on the pure-food law. He needed someone "level headed," he said, someone less eager for public attention, a scientist who could be "implicitly trusted in a confidential capacity." Roosevelt had sided with Wiley in the instance, but he valued his agriculture secretary and he was politically astute enough to recognize that the chief chemist had become difficult for Wilson to manage.

As if to underscore this difficulty, another labeling question had arisen. Wiley wanted the government to require the fully detailed listing of all ingredients in food and drink on labels, even those ingredients considered benign. He argued, for example, that sugar should be included on lists of ingredients. Wilson hated the idea. He wrote demanding that his chief chemist back down on the requirement: "It seems to me to be monstrous that we should require mention of salt or sugar or any of these things when we know them to be harmless. If we require mention of one of them we might as well require mention of all." Wiley countered that consumers deserved an all-inclusive listing of what was in their food and drink—he urged the secretary to side with them over industry.

But Wilson instead told the president that the law would place too many unnecessary burdens on manufacturers, and that they would resist it at every turn, stifling progress on the law. Roosevelt decided to give Wilson some additional departmental support and privately agreed to bring another chemist into the Department of Agriculture.

Seeking a scientist with the political savvy that he considered essential for the new job, Roosevelt personally chose Frederick L. Dunlap, a young assistant professor of chemistry from the University of Michigan, recommended by Roosevelt's friend James Burrill Angell, the university's president. Angell said that Dunlap could hold his own in Washington. He put forward a poised and polished presence— well groomed and impeccably dressed, with perfect manners that served his political ambitions. And most important for his new job, Dunlap knew how to keep a secret. Barely two weeks after the

Harvey Washington Wiley, age nineteen, when he was a freshman at Indiana's Hanover College in 1863.

Wiley (*third from right*) with his crew of chemists at the Department of Agriculture in 1883.

Look Before You Eat," from the cover of Britain's satiric *Puck* magazine, mocking the state of the food supply, in 1884.

Notes about poisonous candy from an investigator working for Wiley in 1890.

A state-of-the-art laboratory at the Bureau of Chemistry in the early twentieth century.

Jeremiah Rusk, secretary of agriculture from 1889 to 1893, affectionately nicknamed "Uncle Jerry" by his staff.

Julius Sterling Morton, secretary of agriculture from 1893 to 1897, was a ruthless cost-cutter.

James Wilson, secretary of agriculture from 1897 to 1913, started as a Wiley supporter and ended up as an enemy.

Ira Remsen, codiscoverer of saccharin, was tapped to head an industry-friendly board of scientists for the USDA.

William McKinley, twenty-fifth president of the United States, was assassinated in 1901, near the start of his second term.

Grenville Dodge, a former Union Army general, was named by McKinley to lead an investigation of shoddy meat given to soldiers in the Spanish-American War.

Theodore Roosevelt became the twenty-sixth president of the United States following McKinley's assassination.

President Roosevelt, shown here with his cabinet, signed the country's first food safety legislation in 1906.

Volunteers of the Poison Squad experiments in Wiley's dining room testing the safety of food additives.

Wiley and one of his chemists in a publicity shot taken during the Poison Squad experiments.

Cover of *The Jungle*, Upton Sinclair's 1906 novel, which exposed the horrors of U.S. meat production.

Novelist Upton Sinclair in 1906.

British postcards satirizing meat produced by the Chicago meatpackers circulated after *The Jungle's* publication.

The muckraking journalist Ray Stannard Baker, famed for his investigation of the railroad industry, advised Sinclair on his book.

Walter Hines Page, of the publishing firm Doubleday, Page & Company, authorized and supported publication of *The Jungle*.

J. Ogden Armour, president of Armour & Company in Chicago, tried to stop European publication of *The Jungle*.

Journalist David Graham Phillips infuriated President Roosevelt with his searing expose of corruption in the U.S. Senate.

The Heinz Company ran numerous ads promoting the purity of its products in the early twentieth century.

The American meat industry became a favorite target of *Puck* magazine as scandals emerged.

The American magazine *Collier's* took aim at congressional resistance to food safety legislation.

The Beef Trust," which became the nickname for the Chicago meatpackers, satirized in a 1906 *Puck* cover.

The 1906 Food and Drug law made "pure food" labels such as this one extremely popular.

During a lengthy battle to legally define "real" whiskey, distillers made a point of emphasizing the purity of their product.

Cartoon paying homage to Wiley's leadership in the fight for food safety legislation, despite bitter opposition.

One of the U.S. Department of Agriculture's newly authorized food inspection teams, Indiana, 1909.

William Howard Taft (*left*), twenty-seventh president of the United States, meeting with Elihu Root, secretary of state under Theodore Roosevelt.

A 1909 cartoon in the *Des Moines Register* commenting on President Taft's turn from Roosevelt progressives to congressional leaders who were closely allied with industry.

*NEW WINE IN OLD BOTTLES*
Cartoon by Darling in the *Des Moines Register and Leader*, reproduced in the *Literary Digest*, December 25, 1909.

The *Washington Star's* famed political cartoonist, Clifford Berryman, delighted Wiley with this drawing, mourning his retirement suggesting that his shoes would be impossible to fill.

Photo taken during a U.S. Department of Agriculture inspection of an early twentieth-century candy factory, emphasizing the need for regulation.

Anna Kelton Wiley, in 1920, with sons Harvey (*right*) and John (*left*).

The masthead for Wiley's regular 1920s column about food and nutrition.

A 1956 U.S. postage stamp honoring the fiftieth anniversary of the Pure Food and Drug Act and featuring a portrait of Harvey Washington Wiley.

Portrait of Harvey Washington Wiley in *World's Work* just before he left his government job.

whiskey confrontation, on April 24, 1907, Wilson formally appointed Dunlap as "associate chemist," skipping over the normal requirement of a civil service examination. As a demonstration of his own authority, the secretary neither consulted nor warned Wiley in advance.

As Wiley would later tell it, Wilson simply "walked into my office one morning in company with a young man whom I had never before seen, and introduced him as 'Professor F.L. Dunlap, your associate.' I said: 'Mr. Secretary, my what?' He said: 'Your associate. I have appointed an associate in the Bureau of Chemistry who will be entirely independent of the Chief [Wiley] and who will report directly to me. During the absence of the Chief he will be acting chief of the Bureau.' I was astounded and dumbfounded at this action."

After the secretary ordered him to make Dunlap welcome, Wiley gave the newcomer an unsmiling tour of the bureau offices, offering him the smallest and shabbiest quarters available. The bureau staff, intensely loyal to their longtime chief, barely spoke to their new colleague. Even the secretaries were unfriendly. Dunlap, perceiving that he was in hostile territory, decided to rely on McCabe's clerical staff instead. The new associate chemist recognized quickly that McCabe and Wilson would be his friends in the department. They had the real power anyway, so they were more worth cultivating.

Dunlap had no experience as a food chemist. Wiley took the appointment as a "direct insult" to him and to Bigelow, who had always served as acting director in his absence; he fumed that it was poor management to put a man "who knew nothing" of the bureau or its food-law activities in charge of the program. Making matters worse, Wilson at the same time announced the creation of a new entity, the Board of Food and Drug Inspection, within the USDA. There would be three members: Wiley, Dunlap, and George McCabe, the department's solicitor. Wiley would technically be the board's chief, but all decisions were to be made by a simple majority vote. The board would report directly to the secretary and, as Wilson wrote to Wiley, he expected the board to complete its work expeditiously, as "a matter of fairness to the manufacturers of foods and drugs."

To Wiley the new board clearly appeared designed "to take away from the bureau all its power and activities under the food law." Wilson made no effort to disabuse him of that idea.

On June 19, on Wilson's orders, Wiley embarked on a trip to Bordeaux, France, to join a panel of food judges at the International Maritime Exposition, a world's fair designed to celebrate the range of products carried around the world's oceans by the shipping industry. The U.S. government—which had proudly built a model of the White House to house its exhibits—planned to be well represented. But the State Department also saw in this exposition an opportunity for practical diplomacy. French food and wine exporters were eager to consult with the influential chief chemist on the new U.S. regulations and perhaps even get his help in modifying their own.

Wilson's initial response to France's invitation had reflected his growing dissatisfaction with Wiley. He tabled the request and didn't tell Wiley about it. But several weeks later, Wiley attended a party that also included the French ambassador to the United States, who said to him, "I do not think you are very polite in your country." The ambassador had been waiting three weeks for a response to the consul's invitation. When he heard that Wiley had never received it, the ambassador called the State Department—which insisted Wilson had been sent the invitation immediately—and then called Wilson directly. "In a short time, I received a summons to the Secretary's office and he gave me the invitation and said of course it must be accepted." At this moment, though, Wiley himself hesitated. He wasn't comfortable, he explained, leaving Dunlap as acting head of the Bureau of Chemistry in his absence. In the face of a flat refusal, the secretary agreed to name Bigelow as acting head for the duration of the trip—at least this time.

In addition to attending the exposition, Wiley did work diligently with the French government on updating its food laws. For his help—and for his dedication to the issue—he was elected a *chevalier* (knight) of the nation's Légion d'honneur. (As an officer of the American government, he was not allowed to take home the medal until after his retirement.)

During the visit, though, Wiley remained uneasy about his status at home. Before leaving Washington, he had given Bigelow very specific instructions to protect the bureau and the law. He asked that Bigelow keep him updated, especially if things started going wrong, which didn't take long. First Dunlap told Bigelow to hand over all correspondence relating to enforcement of the food and drug law. Bigelow replied angrily that the Chemistry Bureau by law had full authority to analyze food and drink and the authority to freely relay those results. Wilson agreed to put the matter on hold until Wiley returned, but Bigelow wrote to the chief chemist that the secretary appeared prepared to support Dunlap's power play. He warned his boss that the two men were meeting in confidence on food-law regulations and he doubted that boded well for the Chemistry Bureau.

It was while Wiley was away that the Agriculture Department issued a major package of rules on food safety. Known as Food Inspection Decision (FID) 76—and announced as a unanimous decision of Wiley, McCabe, and Dunlap—the rules were intended to provide overall guidance on chemical additives in foods. FID 76 reaffirmed that "no drug, chemical or harmful or deleterious dye or preservative" could be used in food. It stated that common salt, sugar, wood smoke, potable distilled liquors, vinegar, and condiments were considered reasonable additives. It barred dyes that were used to conceal damaged, inferior, or faked goods. Wiley had mostly supported those provisions. FID 76 also let it be known that the government would move slowly on additives still under study. Specifically, no prosecutions would be brought against two controversial additives—the greening agent copper sulfate and the preservative sodium benzoate—pending scientific investigation. Wiley had also somewhat reluctantly accepted these delays, but he had recommended a precautionary limit on copper sulfate. This was used mostly cosmetically to deepen the green of canned peas and beans but had a long history of known human health effects. When he'd left for Bordeaux, the ruling had included the precaution: a temporary safe limit for copper sulfate of 11 milligrams per 100 grams of the vegetable contents, an amount equivalent to about 110 parts per million. He considered this a compromise number, suspecting that further research would lead to a lower limit. And Wilson had agreed that it was a reasonable approach.

But in his absence, food manufacturers had put new pressure on the Agriculture Department, arguing the limit was just Wiley's backhanded way of forcing them to take copper out of their products. In response, Dunlap and McCabe had changed the decision's wording without notifying Wiley. The guidelines now merely banned an undefined "excessive" amount. Wiley wired a blistering memo to Dunlap, saying that FID 76 could no longer be considered a unanimous decision from the board. His signature should have been removed from the document if the board was going to make changes that he had not approved. Still steaming when he arrived back in Washington, he discovered his colleagues had quietly made other accommodations to satisfy business complaints.

The original FID 76 had also set a safety limit on sulfites. The department had agreed that Wiley's Poison Squad experiment raised troubling questions about those compounds but also believed that more research was needed. Pending further study, the board had agreed that the government would not act against manufacturers using sulfurous acid or sulfur dioxide in dried fruit, sugar, syrup, molasses, and wine if the produce did not exceed 35 milligrams per gram (about 350 parts per million) and provided the presence of sulfites was cited on the label. But that fairly modest proposal—including the idea of sharing sulfite information with the public—produced an exceptionally bitter outcry from wine and fruit producers in California.

"Telegrams began to come all around me, and it finally reached me that something was seriously the matter," Wilson said. He'd learned that the White House was reporting a similar deluge of complaints. The secretary met with fruit and wine industry representatives, a session that he would later describe as filled with "a very great commotion." The assembled group, as they reminded Wilson, represented a $15 million-a-year (nearly $400 million today) industry that might be damaged by the department's decision. Aside from the labeling requirement, which might scare off consumers, the California coalition said that limiting sulfur use posed potentially devastating problems. East Coast buyers were threatening to cancel contracts for fear that the goods would spoil without the preservative.

"After listening to these good people all day I said, 'I see the condition you are in, gentlemen. I do not think the American Congress in making this law intended to stop your business,'" Wilson related in a speech later that year. He assured them that the Agriculture Department did not want to harm American businessmen in the process of protecting food safety. He went on to reassure the concerned Californians: "I will tell you what to do. Just go on as you used to go on and I will not take any action to seize your goods or let them be seized or take any order into court until we know more about the milligrams to the kilo and all that."

Wiley again protested an action taken while he was away, without his consent, one that yet bore his signature. He reminded Wilson of his own findings and recommendations regarding sulfites. It was better, he insisted, to be overprotective of consumers in the absence of good information. Again he was overruled. The department, Wilson reminded him, had a duty to balance multiple interests, and consumer protection was only one of them. It was "not only that the provisions of the law should be fully executed, but also that there should be no unnecessary burden or annoyance placed on the trade."

Not surprisingly, then, Wilson was unhappy to learn, after the fact, of a speech that Wiley had given to the congregation of the Vermont Avenue Christian Church in Washington, DC, earlier that year. In short order, the chief chemist had managed to offend the flour industry, busy mixing wheat and rye flour and "selling the mixture as rye flour" with no mention of other ingredients. Also the syrup industry: "And when you put sirup on your buckwheat cakes, are you eating maple sirup? There is a nice picture of maple trees on the can and the word 'maple' is very prominent but that is all the maple there is about it." Then the dairy industry, with this appetizing description of ice cream: "I don't want it half gelatin, made of old hides and scrapings of beef, hides that are put down in South America, shipped to Europe and this country and so vile that they have to disinfect them before they will let them into the custom house." The secretary now informed the chief of the Bureau of Chemistry that the Agriculture Department was, in fact, dedicated to the support of agribusiness. From now on, he expected Wiley to do a better job of remembering that.

# Ten

# OF KETCHUP AND CORN SYRUP

## 1907–1908

———●———

*And the salad which bears such an innocent look*
*And whispers of fields that are green*

Ketchup (or catsup) was the most everyday of condiments. But its origin story was one of ancient mystery. A sauce made of fermented fish, it derived from China, where it was named *kentia*, according to one version. It was invented in Vietnam, according to another. British sailors first discovered it in Fiji during the 1500s, or possibly in the West Indies. A Chinese recipe, supposedly dating to 544 CE, instructed the sauce maker to "take the intestine, stomach, and bladder of the yellow fish, shark and mullet," wash them well, mix them with salt, seal into a jar, and let "sit in the sun" for up to one hundred days.

The version that made its way to English kitchens was a little tamer than that; the cookbooks of the late seventeenth century suggested methods to produce a golden, anchovy-based "paste of ketchup." During the next hundred years, "ketchup" became shorthand for an array of sauces made with mushrooms or oysters or even walnuts, the latter reportedly a favorite of British novelist Jane Austen. And by the early nineteenth century, James Mease, a Philadelphia physician and amateur horticulturalist, joined those proposing that "love apples"—the popular name for tomatoes at the time—also made "a fine catsup."

"Love apple" ketchup caught on slowly, partly due to an enduring belief that tomatoes could be poisonous. People had noted the painful deaths of tomato-loving aristocrats in Europe. Later investigations would suggest a cause for those fatalities: Acidic juices from tomatoes had caused toxic levels of lead to leach from pewter salad plates. It would take some decades of scientific research—and many healthy years of consumption—before people became fully comfortable with raw tomatoes.

Cooked products like ketchup were believed to be safer, and the earliest commercially bottled version was distributed in the United States in 1837. Such formulations posed challenges to the busy processor. The growing season was summer short, and it was difficult to preserve tomato pulp in containers for any length of time. Too often it provided a rich environment in which bacteria, spores, yeast, and mold thrived. In 1866 the French cookbook author Pierre Blot advised readers to stick to homemade ketchup. The varieties sold in the markets, he wrote, were "filthy, decomposed, and putrid."

Not that bottled ketchups were pure tomato—or pure anything. Food advocates complained that such sauces were too often made from assorted trimmings dumped into barrels after tomatoes were canned, then thickened with ground pumpkin rinds, apple pomace (the skin, pulp, seeds, and stems left after the fruit was pressed for juice), or cornstarch and dyed a deceptively fresh-looking red. Made in less-than-sterile conditions, they required a heavy dose of preservatives to keep microbes at bay. The protective compound of choice was sodium benzoate—in high enough doses to catch Wiley's attention. He added the compound to his list of proposed Poison Squad studies.

Sodium benzoate is a salt of a naturally occurring compound, benzoic acid, found in a wide variety of plants ranging from tobacco to cranberries. Its name refers to the benzoin tree, a plant native to Southeast Asia. Benzoin resin, scraped from tree bark, had been used for centuries in the making of both perfume and incense. And the isolation of benzoic acid was nearly as old; the compound was noted in the records of the French apothecary Nostradamus in 1556. But it had come into wide commercial use in the nineteenth century, following two scientific developments. In 1860 German chemists learned they could make a cheap, synthetic version of benzoic acid from the coal tar–derived solvent toluene. If the acid was neutralized with soda, this caused a salt to precipitate out of the mix. This was sodium benzoate. Some fifteen years later, researchers discovered that sodium benzoate had strong antifungal properties. It was tasteless, easy to make, and inexpensive. Not surprisingly, it became a favorite of the food-processing industry.

Recognizing its natural origins, Wiley's best assumption before he tested the preservative on his Poison Squad diners was that sodium benzoate wasn't especially dangerous. He worried more that the preservative was being used to disguise shoddy food production. Ketchup was a case in point. As noted in the bureau reports, his chemists had found that a sauce made with fresh tomatoes, heat-treated to kill microbes and placed into sterile containers, held up very well without chemical preservatives. It also tasted better.

Most food producers dismissed this recommendation, but there were exceptions. Indiana's Columbia Conserve Company proudly made a tomato ketchup that neither required nor contained any dyes or preservatives. It did so by adapting "housewife methods" to large-scale production, its president said. And Wiley's idea had caught the attention of one of the country's biggest food manufacturers, Henry J. Heinz, founder and president of the H.J. Heinz Company of Pittsburgh.

Heinz was the same age as Wiley—born in the same year and

month—and he had advocated in favor of clean and honest food-stuffs for even longer than the chief chemist had. Heinz had also built a remarkably successful company, one that processed and marketed scores of products. Although he had personally chosen a slogan to advertise "57 Varieties," by the early twentieth century, his canning and bottling plants produced nearly twice that number of foods and condiments. Unlike many of his peers in the food business, Heinz had lobbied in favor of the Pure Food and Drug Act of 1906. Company executive Sebastian Mueller had accompanied such activists as Robert Allen and Alice Lakey when they visited the White House to press the Roosevelt administration, and after its passage, Henry Heinz supported the law's enforcement. Some of his peers called him a traitor. More irked than worried by such remarks, he ordered his company's publicity department to disparage his critics in press releases.

Heinz, like other processors, had frequently used preservatives, following the industry standard. His original recipe for catsup (the spelling on the bottle) was based on his mother's, including a little finely ground willow bark, which added salicylic acid to the mix. The company had later shifted over to sodium benzoate. But Heinz had found himself impressed by the warnings raised in Wiley's Poison Squad studies and had decided to invest in developing an alternative approach. Mueller, in charge of food safety at the company, had at first balked, worrying that the move could prove too expensive. The H.J. Heinz Company had always offered a money-back guarantee, and Mueller feared a preservative-free ketchup would lead to costly returns due to spoilage.

But at his boss's insistence, Mueller ordered the creation of test batches made from recipes like those of homemade versions that were known to have longer shelf lives. His cooks searched for a correct acid balance in the formula, measuring out the right vinegar content to augment the acids that occur naturally in tomatoes. Discovering that he needed both high-quality tomatoes and high pulp content, Mueller developed a sauce that was thicker than the company's previous product, thicker than any on the market.

By 1906 Heinz was selling its new—and, yes, more expensive—ketchup (now spelled that way on the label). The company then launched an aggressive marketing campaign aimed at convincing consumers that it was worth spending a few cents more on a better and healthier condiment. The campaign, like so many run by Heinz, was so successful that in time Americans began to think of all good ketchup as thick and rich—eventually changing production standards industry-wide.

When the food and drug law went into effect, Heinz also proclaimed in newspaper and magazine advertisements that its preservative-free products were "recognized as the standard by Government pure food authorities." Heinz ketchup, as the ads also proclaimed, was not only free of sodium benzoate but was also the preferred choice of the famed Dr. Wiley himself.

Predictably, food processors still using sodium benzoate complained to both Wilson and Roosevelt that the chief chemist had become a shill for H.J. Heinz. Wiley planned to vindicate himself with the publication of his Poison Squad report on sodium benzoate, laying out the evidence that the preservative was clearly suspect in health problems. As 1908 approached, polishing up that report became a top priority, along with other potentially controversial investigations such as a study of the popular artificial sweetener saccharin.

Due to its low cost, saccharin was increasingly used as a sugar substitute in processed foods ranging from canned corn to ketchup itself—although that inclusion rarely appeared on labels. Leaders in the food-processing industry—aside from Heinz and a few others—braced for more bad publicity. The Poison Squad studies had yet to say anything good about food additives. Makers decided to try intervening before the sodium benzoate report was published, hoping to reach an agreement that would prevent its publication.

The National Food Manufacturers Association contacted Roosevelt, Wilson, and every legislator thought to be sympathetic, raising concerns about both the upcoming reports and Harvey Wiley. The chief chemist, the organization complained, was stuck in the old-fashioned past of preindustrial food production and biased against twentieth-century innovation. The association urged the president and the agriculture secretary to create a scientific review board, one that might be more balanced and more favorable toward modern food-production methods.

In January 1908 Roosevelt invited some of the most outspoken among the group's processors and grocers to visit the White House. They included representatives from Curtice Brothers of Rochester, New York, and Williams Brothers of Detroit, both in competition with H.J. Heinz. Also in attendance was Republican congressman James S. Sherman of New York, who was himself president of a New England canning company. Sherman's firm routinely, and surreptitiously, used saccharin instead of more expensive cane sugar to sweeten its canned corn. The Heinz company was not on the invitation list. Intrigued by the conversation, Roosevelt asked his guests to stay over and requested that Wilson, Wiley, McCabe, and Dunlap join them the next morning for a follow-up discussion.

They met in the Cabinet Room of Roosevelt's new office building on the west side of the White House, a precursor to the later West Wing. The meeting required the large chamber because the businessmen had brought along their attorneys. Roosevelt asked the previous day's visitors to repeat their concern that removing sodium benzoate from ketchup would destroy the entire industry. As Wiley would describe it: "There was no way in which this disaster could be diverted except to overrule the conclusions of the Bureau." Wiley was vilified from the outset of the meeting as "a radical, impervious to reason and determined to destroy legitimate business." These businessmen asserted that the Heinz company was an anomaly and its method of ketchup production unlikely to survive.

Roosevelt then turned to Wilson and asked him, "What is your opinion about the propriety and desirability of enforcing your Chief of Bureau?"

Wilson stood by his department's findings. He said to Roosevelt, "Dr. Wiley made extensive investigations in feeding benzoated goods to healthy young men and in every instance he found that their health was undermined." The president then asked McCabe, Dunlap, and Wiley for their individual opinions. Along with Wilson, McCabe and Dunlap had studied the Poison Squad results. In a rare moment of unity, they agreed that the table trial had raised legitimate concerns. The young volunteers in the study had exhibited, as the draft report noted, "unfavorable symptoms and disturbances of metabolism" including irritation, nausea, headache, vomiting, and weight loss. The chemists who had run the experiment were now urging that, "in the interests of health both benzoic acid and benzoate of soda should be excluded from food products."

"On hearing this opinion," Wiley wrote, "the President turned to the protestants, struck the table in front of him a stunning blow with his fist, and showing his teeth in the true Rooseveltian fashion said: 'Gentlemen, if this drug is injurious, you shall not put it into food.'" The battle, Wiley thought, was almost won. But Sherman, the New York congressman and canner, spoke out again. He also wanted to discuss the use of saccharin in canned goods. He strongly objected to Wiley's likely recommendation to restrict its use. "My firm saved $4,000 by sweetening canned corn with saccharin instead of sugar," he said, addressing Roosevelt directly. "We want a decision from you on this question." For decades after the meeting, Wiley would replay this moment and wish he had sat silently and waited for Roosevelt to respond.

By the early twentieth century, saccharin was well known to the public as a diet aid; although most didn't realize that canners like Sherman secretly used it as a cheap alternative to sugar in creating so-called sweet corn. Wiley considered the substitution a deceptive

practice and took a position against such use, at least until the sweetener could be proved benign. It was in his judgment an illegal adulterant under the law. Nor did he care for a move by chemical companies
to avoid the problem by simply rechristening saccharin as a sugar. He
was at that moment pursuing a court case against the Heyden Chemical Company's saccharin product, which was sold under the name
Heyden Sugar. In his cautious approach to the health effects, he differed with Dunlap and McCabe. While the two men agreed that the
sweetener ought to be listed on product labels, and even that it should
be properly described, they thought that until health risks were clearly
shown, the saccharin use should not be restricted.

Now Wiley jumped directly into the conversation: "Everyone who
ate that sweet corn was deceived. He thought he was eating sugar,
when in point of fact he was eating a coal tar product totally devoid
of food value and extremely injurious to health." The interjection was
political bad form. With Roosevelt, it would have been all right in
many cases to venture an opinion without having first been asked for
one. The president was known to tolerate interruptions if he thought
the point that the speaker made was worth being made. In this case,
however, Roosevelt thought the opposite. As he quickly made clear,
the president disagreed strongly with what Wiley had said.

Roosevelt was a regular consumer of saccharin. His personal
physician, Rear Admiral Presley Marion Rixey, had recommended
the sweetener as a healthy alternative to sugar. Roosevelt put a great
deal of faith in what Rixey said as the navy physician was also a
friend. The two of them, both accomplished equestrians, frequently
rode together. Despite regular exercise, the president showed a tendency toward corpulence, and Rixey—having observed the link between weight gain and long-term diseases like diabetes—had advised
Roosevelt to replace sugar with saccharin as a diet aid. "You tell me
that saccharin is injurious to health?" Roosevelt said to Wiley. "Yes,
Mr. President, I do tell you that," Wiley said firmly. No one had

clearly proved injury yet; the research was still going on. But Wiley believed it and he said so.

"Dr. Rixey gives it to me every day," the president said in rising anger. By this time Wiley had recognized his error and attempted to recover the moment: "Mr. President, he probably thinks you may be threatened with diabetes." Roosevelt would have none of it. "Anyone who says saccharin is injurious to health is an idiot," he snapped. Shortly later, he called the meeting to a close.

The following day, Roosevelt announced the appointment of a scientific review board—in fact, the very board that had been requested by the food-processing industry. It would reassess Wiley's research, starting with sodium benzoate and saccharin. Further, Roosevelt had decided on its alternative chief chemist. Ira Remsen of Johns Hopkins, the chemist who had in 1879 co-discovered saccharin along with Constantin Fahlberg, would lead the investigations.

Wiley protested to no avail. Remsen, he thought, had a clear conflict of interest. "According to the ordinary conception of a juror, Dr. Remsen would not have been entitled to sit on the subject of saccharin. Such little matters as those, however, were not dominating with the President of the United States." But although he was angry with Roosevelt, Wiley was angrier with himself for further alienating the president. Ever since the 1902 incident in which he had exasperated Roosevelt over the proposed import of Cuban sugar, he had tried to steer clear of disagreements with the chief executive—until this misstep. He knew that by giving Roosevelt a new reason to be annoyed with him, he had just made things more difficult for himself and his cause. And "I fear that I deserved it."

Not that he'd made an outright enemy. Roosevelt was quick to take offense, but his rational side often overruled his ire. The president would continue to back some of the chief chemist's positions, notably the regulation of whiskey. Wiley's chemists continued to demonstrate fraud in that industry. They had recently revealed that

University Club Whiskey contained no whiskey at all, merely industrial ethanol dyed brown, and that Sherwood Rye Whiskey contained not a trace of a rye product. Despite continued industry pressure to accept such products as simply the modern way, Roosevelt still stood by his attorney general's decision regarding whiskey, and he supported Wiley's determined insistence on accuracy in labeling.

Yet the president also found himself annoyed by other instances of Wiley's staunch unwillingness to compromise. The chief chemist continued to reject the term "corn syrup." Since his earliest food-analysis study, for the state of Indiana in 1881, Wiley had insisted that the word "glucose" was the only accurate way to describe this sugary liquid derived from corn. Within the corn industry, however, that name had long been disliked. It sounded unappetizing, manufacturers feared, and was likely to alienate consumers. A new firm called the Corn Products Refining Company, created by a merger in 1906, had recently petitioned the government to be allowed to call its new corn-derived sweetener a syrup. This appeal carried behind it the clout of company founder Edward Thomas Bedford, a longtime executive and current director of the Standard Oil Company.

E. T. Bedford, as he was known, sought to bottle and market a thick liquid product under the name "Karo Corn Syrup." He knew full well that "Karo Glucose" was never going to succeed in the market. He'd done his best to convince Wiley that the name was aptly descriptive and overall more accurate than the unappetizing word "glucose," which sounded too much like "glue."

Wiley was unmoved. The food and drug law's protective measures should not be "suspended or abandoned because it is hurtful to any interest or is displeasing to any men," he insisted. Bedford responded by appealing to Wilson instead, protesting the Agriculture Department's apparent indifference to what he called the "impossibility of popularizing our product under the name Glucose." He thought Wiley's refusal to reconsider was rooted in hostility toward industry in general and, he wrote to the secretary, such a stubborn refusal to listen "very clearly indicates the personal views of Dr. Wiley in a way that tends to cause us a lot of trouble."

Representatives of the corn industry had also petitioned Roosevelt. In a meeting attended by Wilson and Dunlap but not Wiley, the president had made it clear that he thought "glucose" was a ridiculous name for a syrupy material derived from corn. "You must make the manufacturers call a spade a spade," the president had said. "But don't make them call it a damn shovel." Wilson discussed the issue privately with McCabe and Dunlap. They had earlier sided with Wiley on the term but, at the secretary's request, now agreed to withdraw their support for Wiley's stance on the definition. A majority of the three-man Board of Food Inspection now favored the term that the industry wanted to use, and the department issued a formal endorsement of the term "corn syrup." Karo Corn Syrup was cleared for the grocery store market.

Such moves by Roosevelt and Wilson had established a precedent. Industry advocates now saw a way around Wiley and his insistence on strictly limiting chemical additives to food. This came to bear as French canning companies, which used toxic copper salts to make their peas and other vegetables look especially green, looked to bypass the new standards. Fearing that Americans would reject vegetables without the familiar bright green color, a delegation representing canners and importers took the issue not to the Department of Agriculture but to the Department of State. It proved an effective decision. Secretary of State Root pushed for an exemption to satisfy the French manufacturers. In response, Roosevelt suggested that Wilson refer the copper salts question to the newly created consulting panel—already better known as the "Remsen Board" after chairman Ira Remsen. Until the board reviewed the science—whenever that was—the French were free to continue greening up their canned vegetables as they chose.

Emboldened, makers and importers of other French food products started complaining directly to Roosevelt about Wiley's interference with the labeling of their wares. In May 1908 the issue came to a head regarding a so-called wine vinegar, which was, in truth, a synthetic acetic acid dyed to a golden tone. Manufactured by a company called Cessat of Bordeaux, it bore a cheerful label decorated with bunches of grapes and leaves meant to suggest a product fresh from the vineyard. At Wiley's insistence, Cessat had added the words "Distilled, colored with caramel" to the label. In addition, he wanted the company to remove all the vineyard imagery—grapes, leaves, and vines—which, he thought, erroneously gave the impression of a vineyard product. Cessat executives resisted. They would remove the grape clusters, they said, but leave the decorative vines.

But Wiley refused to compromise, believing that if he gave up on small details for one product he would be forced to give up on all. When the next shipment of Cessat of Bordeaux vinegar reached a U.S. harbor, he ordered that because it was deceptively labeled it could not be brought ashore. The company, encouraged by recent events, appealed directly to Roosevelt. The president promptly fired off an angry letter to Wilson, ordering that the shipment be released and demanding that the responsible officials (meaning Wiley) explain their "useless, illegal and improper interference with shipments of food from a friendly nation." In an impetuous, scrawled postscript to that letter, the president stressed that he did not mean to undercut the food and drug law. It was "one of the best laws on the statute book." He did, however, want it to be administered without "a nagging, vexatious, foolish or corrupt spirit toward honest business."

Meanwhile, Roosevelt worked with Wilson in appointing four other scientists, besides chairman Ira Remsen, to the board that was to review Wiley's work on chemical hazards in food. He wanted scientists with strong reputations. The final list included Russell Chittenden, John H. Young, Christian A. Herter, and Alonzo E. Taylor.

Chittenden, a Yale physiologist who specialized in food and

nutrition, was the best known. Chittenden had early on been cautious about food additives, but more recently his views, especially regarding preservatives, had stood in contrast to Wiley's. The chief chemist attributed that to industry influence; Chittenden, who had publicly endorsed the use of borax, received funding from the borax-mining industry. He also consulted with corn syrup producers. Bedford, the manufacturer of Karo, had cited him to both the president and Wilson as believing that "a strong solution of sugar made from a starch is entitled to be called a syrup."

Wiley was dismayed by the roles of Remsen and Chittenden but had no criticisms of the other board members. Young was a chemist specializing in pharmacology at Northwestern University. Herter, a Columbia University pathologist, was known for his work in diseases of the digestive tract. Taylor, a physiological chemist at the University of Pennsylvania, studied the role of grains in the human diet.

But overall Wiley's relationships with many of his more traditional scientific colleagues were beginning to deteriorate. The Society of Chemical Engineers—an industry-allied group—passed a public resolution criticizing his position on compounds such as sulfur dioxide. The leaders of the New York section of the American Chemical Society suggested that he was now more an advocate than a chemist. He refused to admit discouragement over such actions. "The men who led in such a ridiculous fight can only injure themselves," Wiley told a worried friend in a New York laboratory. "These little fellows do not bother me in the least. You can rest assured of that."

The Remsen Board, though, bothered him, and deeply. It seemed intended specifically to undercut and countermand the findings of the Bureau of Chemistry. He was dismayed that Remsen himself, the "alleged discoverer" of saccharin, as Wiley put it, was given authority to rule on the sweetener's safety. He was dismayed that Chittenden, so obviously pro-industry, was on the board at all. He saw both the creation of the board and its business-friendly composition, he told friends, as a betrayal not just of him but of the American consumer.

Wiley took the uncompromising position that "the creation of the Remsen Board of Consulting Scientific Experts was the cause of nearly all the woes that subsequently befell the Pure Food Law." Other voices agreed. "The Remsen Board," said a *New York Times* editorial, "was created on February 20, 1908 for the specific purpose of overruling the findings of Dr. Harvey Wiley of the Bureau of Chemistry with respect to the purity of food and drugs." The *Times*, along with Wiley's pure-food allies and a considerable swath of those Americans who followed the news from Washington, had come to realize that despite the successful passage of the 1906 law, there were forces within the Roosevelt administration, within the federal government at large, that were more than willing to adjust the law's requirements for the benefit of industry, and not necessarily with the public good in mind.

*Eleven*

# EXCUSES FOR EVERYTHING

## 1908–1909

———————●———————

*Is covered with germs, each armed with a hook*
*To grapple with liver and spleen.*

I
n April 1908, as his Poison Squad study of sodium benzoate and benzoic acid was being readied for publication, Wiley gave a somewhat defiant speech to a meeting of the venerable American Philosophical Society in Philadelphia, an organization that Benjamin Franklin had founded in 1743. He provided information about his preliminary results on sodium benzoate, pressed his case for strict enforcement of the pure-food law, and advocated for tighter limits on what processors could put into commercial foodstuffs.

"The use of chemical preservatives and artificial colors is of quite recent date," he told his audience. "I think I may say with safety that if one could go back thirty, or at most forty, years he would find a food supply practically free" of such additives. Rapid advances in chemistry had brought about the change, he continued, making it possible to "offer manufacturers chemical preservatives of high potency . . . at prices which make it entirely possible to use them freely in food products."

He emphasized that it was this ability to make a cheaper product—not safety, not quality—that drove the industry's embrace of industrial food chemistry. And it wasn't that much more expensive to do it right, he argued. A "conscientious manufacturer" of ketchup (clearly Heinz) had shown that it cost only an additional fifteen to twenty cents per case to make a preservative-free version of the product.

Previewing the impending official report, Wiley called sodium benzoate "highly objectionable." It "produced a very serious disturbance of the metabolic functions, attended with injury to digestion and health." This was a study, as he'd earlier told Congress, in which only three of the twelve volunteers had lasted until the end of the experiment. Wiley finished this speech by once again stressing that any compound proven dangerous or that was used only to support the "convenience, carelessness or indifference of the manufacturer" should be removed from the American food supply "entirely."

The sodium benzoate trials had deeply dismayed the chief chemist. He'd predicted minor or no ill effects in his Poison Squad volunteers and seen the opposite. As he'd told legislators, "The most pronounced symptoms were burning sensations in the throat and esophagus, pains in the stomach, some dizziness, bad taste, and when the limit of endurance was reached, the subject suddenly became nauseated and ill." Eleven of the twelve volunteers lost a measurable amount of weight during the trial and—except in two of the men—recovery was proving painfully slow. Following the other findings, this study cemented his conviction that industrially made preservatives posed a more serious health risk than he'd previously realized. "I was converted by my own investigation," he wrote.

But even as Wiley grew more alarmed about processed foods, and more anxious to police them, his boss was moving in the other direction. Secretary Wilson had grown tired of what he considered alarmist investigations. He'd also started blocking publication of what he considered industry-unfriendly findings. Over the course of 1907, he had forbidden the printing of a report on "Corn Sirup as a

Synonym for Glucose" and a Bigelow-authored paper on "Investigations of a Substitute (Weak Brine) for Sulfur Dioxide in Drying Fruits." Already, in 1908, he had prevented the release of a rather damning survey of "Sanitary Conditions of Canneries" at the urging of Congressman Sherman and his peers in that branch of the industry. Wilson had also squelched two other Poison Squad reports, one on the controversial issue of copper sulfate and the other on the old-time preservative potassium nitrate (saltpeter). Wiley had just returned from Philadelphia when Wilson sent for him to tell him that the sodium benzoate report, too, would not be published as scheduled. The secretary wanted it shelved, at least until after the Remsen Board had concluded its own study.

Colleagues around the department noticed and commented upon Wiley's obvious frustration. He didn't deny it. But his exasperation, he would insist, had not pushed him to secretly countermand Wilson's order halting publication of the sodium benzoate report. He swore that he hadn't done anything of the kind. When the Poison Squad report was unexpectedly published on July 20, 1908, Wiley protested that he was as shocked as anyone. He argued that it must have been the result of a misunderstanding at the Government Printing Office. And the people in the printing office backed him in that assertion; its administrators formally apologized for the inadvertent release of information. Wilson wasn't buying it. He knew that Wiley had good friends throughout not only the Agriculture Department but many government agencies, including the printing office. The secretary, already annoyed by the chief chemist's unbending nature, now saw signs of something worse: an instance of possible treachery by a willful and duplicitous subordinate.

In August 1908 the National Association of State Dairy and Food Departments held its annual conference at the elegant Grand Hotel on Michigan's Mackinac Island. The setting might have been beautiful and harmonious, the luxurious 1887 hostelry might serenely overlook a shining stretch of water, but the attendees—as journalists could plainly see—were spoiling for a fight.

"The convention will probably manifest the signs that are now being seen in various parts of the country," warned the *New York Times* on July 30. "Contrary to what was expected, the let down in food legislation has not been popular. . . . Consumer's leagues, clubs of different sorts and others are taking the subject up and making their ideas known to the authorities here." Among the discontents, the newspaper said, were officials of the Bureau of Chemistry and delegates from some of the western states, "where the pure food agitation is strong."

Edwin F. Ladd, the activist food chemist from North Dakota, was both president of the association and lead organizer of the protest movement. He opened the conference on August 4 with a tirade against secretary of agriculture James Wilson, noting the man's suppression of valuable food safety reports, his resistance to tough regulation, and his apparently cozy relationship with the food industry. Roosevelt, Ladd stated, was not much better, and the appointment of the Remsen Board—clearly an end run around the law—was evidence of both men's cold indifference to consumer protection. The actions by the federal government, he continued, were an insult to all who believed in allowing good science to help make good decisions.

The Mackinac conference included carefully selected representatives from the food-manufacturing industry, there to testify in favor of Wiley's views on food safety enforcement. A manager from the Columbia Conserve Company in Indianapolis noted that he'd been at first hostile to the new regulations. Columbia had been profitably selling a cheap "strawberry jelly" made of glucose, apple waste, and red food coloring and had strongly resisted calling it "imitation" for fear of losing customers. But the company had since discovered that it could make even more money by selling well-labeled, high-quality goods. Representatives of the Heinz company also appeared in starring roles. Following its success in removing preservatives from ketchup, the firm had developed a whole line of preservative-free products ranging from mustard to sweet pickles. Heinz's marketing director reported that a year of experience with these products, exposed to "the heat and cold of changing seasons, or wide distribution at home and abroad," had been one of "pronounced and unqualified success. Spoilage is less than one-fourth of one percent." Sebastian Mueller, now a vice president at Heinz, blasted competing manufacturers who insisted on preservative use. He stated firmly that sodium benzoate was being promoted by food manufacturers who found it profitable to use rot-prone waste and scraps in their "bulk" ketchups, sometimes at four times the proposed government standard of 0.10 percent.

Wiley added that food quality and safety represented not only good science but also moral decision-making. The wealthy, he pointed out, could easily afford fresh food and well-made condiments. The trade in cheap, chemically enhanced imitations catered to the poor. If the country could work to standardize good food, then it also would be promoting good health for all. "Whenever a food is debased in order to make it cheap, the laboring man pays more for any given nourishment than the rich man does who buys the pure food," he pointed out.

The attendees voted to adopt a series of resolutions, including a condemnation of the practice of bleaching flour—increasingly criticized for the resulting chemical by-products—and support for a contentious proposal that the weight of the contents should be listed on every food container, allowing consumers to know the actual quantity being purchased. Manufacturers and grocers stood fiercely opposed to such a "weight on the package" law, which suggested to the delegates that they were onto something. By a 42–15 vote, the food and dairy association also put itself clearly in the Wiley camp on the issue of preservatives and other food additives: "Resolved: That this association is convinced that all chemical preservatives are harmful

in foods and that all kinds of food products are and may be prepared
and distributed without them, and pledges its best efforts to use all
moral and legal means at its disposal to exclude chemical preservatives from food products." As another indication of their dissatisfaction with the federal government, the convention attendees agreed to
work on a uniform food-purity law that they proposed to pass at the
state level across the nation. Ladd appointed a committee to work on
drafting such a law, including himself, Robert Allen of Kentucky,
and Willard Bigelow of the Bureau of Chemistry.

Of all the actions taken at the conference, the most controversial
and potentially dangerous, especially for Harvey Wiley, was an organizational censure of Wilson, sparked by Ladd's opening tirade
against the secretary of agriculture. Wiley had warned his friend
Ladd in advance that a public attack might not be a good idea, that
further alienating Wilson might backfire and hurt their shared cause.
But Ladd, who clearly felt a deep sense of betrayal over the change of
direction by the federal department, refused to keep his peace. Wiley
and other bureau colleagues in attendance prudently abstained from
voting on any of the resolutions, let alone the one condemning their
department head. And when one particularly irate conventioneer
proposed charging Wilson with criminal negligence, they joined
other Agriculture Department employees in walking out of the room.

Wiley did not, however, publicly stand up to defend Wilson against
the attacks, and some in attendance felt the chief chemist neglected an
obvious duty to do so. "Those who watched events at Mackinac were
astonished at the course pursued by Dr. Wiley and the rest of the
Washington contingent, in absenting themselves from the meeting that
'roasted' Secretary Wilson," said one dismayed attendee, who felt that
the chief chemist might have defused the bitterness that accompanied
the confrontation. Wilson agreed completely with that assessment.
With some heat, he afterward told Wiley that he would never again
send anyone to a convention who refused to defend the secretary and

the department against unwarranted attacks. Yet as both Ladd and Wiley later noted, there were strong voices speaking up for the secretary, and they came from the food-processing industry. *American Food Journal*, a leading trade magazine, blamed Wiley for embarrassing the secretary and predicted that the chemistry chief would be fired over this "brazen attack." Corporations including Dow Chemical also jumped on the moment, urging that Wiley be replaced.

Shortly after the Mackinac meeting, an Agriculture Department inspector visited Dow's plant in Midlands, Michigan, and met with founder Herbert Dow, who complained of a drop in sales of sodium benzoate following both the passage of the food law and Wiley's pernicious attacks on the compound. Dow was "not sparing in his criticism of Dr. Wiley," whom he characterized as playing to the uneducated and temperamentally fearful public. The chemical industry, Dow asserted, was planning its own public education campaign to counter misinformation being spread by Wiley and his friends.

By now the rift between the agriculture secretary and the head of the Chemistry Bureau was public knowledge; their every action was suddenly scrutinized for political nuance. As newspapers including the *New York Times* pointed out with interest, even when Wilson backed Wiley on a point of food safety enforcement, his reasons often differed from those put forward by the chief chemist. A recent and clear example of that could be seen in departmental decisions regarding the controversial practice of bleaching wheat flour.

Snowy-white baked goods had become a measure of household status in the late nineteenth century. The traditional method of whitening flour was simply to expose it to direct sunlight or allow it to age in a well-ventilated room. But these methods took time—hours or even days. By the turn of the twentieth century, millers had turned to far more rapid techniques, mostly involving chemical oxidation of the flour with nitrogen peroxide or ozone. A review of industry practices after passage of the food and drug law found that chemical bleaching of flour had become nearly standard. The exception was usually small companies that could not afford to set up the oxidation process; they typically advertised in magazines with ads promoting the advantages of the old-fashioned ways: "no artificial pallor . . . no fictitious simulation of age."

Edwin Ladd, the North Dakota food commissioner, had the previous year begun investigating bleaching techniques at the request of the state's smaller millers; his friend and ally James Shepard, food commissioner of South Dakota, did the same. Ladd's investigation found that bleached flours, at least those processed with nitrogen oxides, were heavily tainted with nitrates, which are derivative nitrogen-oxygen based salts. These compounds, Ladd felt, should be considered a possible health risk and further studied in that regard. Pending the publication of his report, in 1907 Ladd issued a North Dakota state ruling prohibiting the sale of any bleached flour that contained nitrates.

Wiley's Bureau of Chemistry proceeded more cautiously, advocating at first only that flours be labeled clearly as bleached or not so that consumers could make a choice. But Wiley also authorized an investigation of bleached flour and any chemical fallout, such as nitrates, that might result from the process. The scientists in his laboratory proceeded to show a direct connection between bleaching and nitrates: The more nitrogen peroxide was used, the higher the nitrate residues in flour. Further, they discovered that most of these chemical residues survived even through the baking of bread. They found no evidence that levels of nitrates in either raw flour or baked products diminished over time. Further, according to a report from the department's Food and Drug Inspection Laboratory: "A summary of our results will tend to show that the bleaching of flour by nitrogen peroxide never improves the flour from the consumer's standpoint."

Wilson showed himself willing to at least consider the bleached flour issue. He followed the bureau report by convening a formal hearing on the subject in the fall of 1908. During that session, Ladd, Shepard, and Wiley formed a consensus on three main points: that daily consumption of nitrates could pose a health risk, that this question deserved further study, and that until such consumption was declared safe, the chemical bleaching of flour, which produced those compounds, should be disallowed.

Not surprisingly, the industry disagreed, as did a cadre of scientists whom milling firms hired to respond to the proposed ban. Seventy-five industry members attended the hearing and they had combined resources to employ a phalanx of experts, including well-known Chicago toxicologist Walter S. Haines, who had earlier defended the use of borax in foods. Haines testified that the nitrate amounts in bleached flour clearly were too small to do any real harm. That December, though, Wilson startled the millers by apparently agreeing with Wiley. He announced that the Agriculture Department would indeed declare bleached flour an adulterated product under the new law. That would mean, among other things, that it could no longer be transported across state lines. Ladd and Shepard hoped the decision was a sign of a healed rift between the secretary and his department's chief chemist. "Bleached flour is a dead duck," Wiley wrote happily in response to a query from the Indiana food commissioner, celebrating what appeared to be a rare instance in which he and the secretary of agriculture had worked in harmony.

The details of the decision revealed, however, that Wilson and Wiley had different motives for supporting a ban. Wiley opposed chemical bleaching of flour because of the health risk, but Wilson blocked publication of the Chemistry Bureau's toxicological findings on the subject. Wilson had ruled against bleached flour because he considered the practice a tool for deceptive marketing. With powerful bleaching techniques, millers could disguise cheap grades of flour and sell them for a much higher price. Newspaper coverage of the decision emphasized the political differences involved: "Secretary

Wilson and Dr. Wiley have disagreed again," reported the New York–based *Journal of Commerce*, and the chemist "has once again been turned down by his chief."

Wilson also remained responsive to flour-industry concerns. He allowed for a six-month grace period to review his decision and respond before initiating any prosecutions or product seizures. The secretary appeared so hesitant about enforcement, in fact, that millers decided to test his resolve by continuing to produce bleached flour and ship it as they chose.

Rumors began to circulate that Wiley had finally pushed his boss too hard and was in imminent danger of losing his job. Alarmed members of the National Association of State Food and Dairy Departments wrote directly to Roosevelt to defend their friend. In October, Ladd joined with two other state food commissioners, John G. Emery of Wisconsin and Arthur C. Bird of Michigan, in a letter that noted, "There is a persistent rumor that the Secretary of Agriculture will dismiss Dr. Wiley or ask him to resign," because of Wilson's assumption that the chief chemist was responsible for the confrontation in Mackinac. "His assumption is without foundation," the letter continued. Ladd took full credit, or blame, for organizing the protest. He and his cosigners hoped that Roosevelt would work to prevent any such unfair and harmful actions. But if things got worse, Bird wrote to Wiley, they were prepared to visit the White House in person.

Roosevelt, they acknowledged, would be in office only a few months longer. He had earlier announced that he would not seek another term (a decision he came to regret) and the upcoming November election pitted Roosevelt's chosen successor, William Howard Taft, against returning Democratic candidate William Jennings Bryan. If need be, the food chemists declared, they would take up defense of the food law—and of Wiley—with the next president as well. Even after Taft won the presidential election in November, new rumors flourished, suggesting that Roosevelt would dismiss Wiley before leaving office. Newspaper coverage made it clear that the nation's editors—and by proxy their readers—saw that idea as an industry-backed threat to American food safety.

The *New York World*, December 20, 1908: "Dr. Wiley says 'I have not been asked to resign but I have been fought at every turn of the road by adulterators of food and I am ready to go if the Government wants to take their recommendation. Otherwise, I will remain to defend the food law, no matter how thick the bullets fly.'"

The *Boston Evening Record*, December 29, 1908: "Pure Food Doc Wiley . . . has made hundreds of enemies but he has made them for the sake of the public. If the food tinkerers ever do actually get him removed, the consumer will pay the freight."

The *New York Evening Mail*, December 31, 1908: "It is earnestly hoped that Mr. Wiley will fight his enemies, open and secret, and that he will continue to denounce the modern system of mixing poison with food to increase the profit."

The chorus of public dismay became so loud that Roosevelt's executive secretary, William Loeb Jr., issued a statement declaring that he "knew of no friction" between the president and the popular chief chemist and had heard of no plans to replace Wiley. Roosevelt agreed that he had no plans to remove the chief chemist but he qualified that expression of support shortly later. He told a reporter that he had personally reviewed Wiley's opinions on the issues of corn syrup, accurate labeling of imported French vinegar, and the safety of saccharin, and he had disagreed with him every time. "Those instances gave me a great distrust of Wiley's good judgment." On the other hand, the president continued, "I have such confidence in his integrity and zeal that I am anxious to back him up to the limit of my power wherever I can be sure that doing so won't do damage instead of good."

If regulations became too rigid or petty, Roosevelt emphasized, then a backlash could lead to "upsetting of the whole pure food law." He hoped that reasonable men could agree that such a result would serve no one well.

That same December, the Bureau of Chemistry issued a summary report on formaldehyde as a food preservative. It was a straight-forward condemnation of the practice: Formaldehyde, still heavily used in milk, especially in summer, was a poisonous additive with an "insidious effect on the cells." The compound had sickened every single one of the Poison Squad members who had taken it with meals; they'd suffered sleeplessness, headaches, dizziness, vertigo, nausea, and vomiting. They'd lost weight. An analysis of their blood and urine had found that in every case calcium oxalate crystals were forming in the urine and white blood cell counts were dropping, suggesting immune system harm. The bureau concluded with a flat statement: The use of formaldehyde in food "is never justified." Despite the forceful language, this was one of Wiley's least controversial findings.

A review of findings in the *New York State Journal of Medicine* cited a litany of evidence that formaldehyde was a "violent poison." Examples ranged from the death of a teenager (who drank a 4 percent solution of formaldehyde and died twenty-nine hours later) to a study in which five kittens were given milk containing 1/50,000 formaldehyde. Three of the five died within hours. Despite their many differences, Wilson, McCabe, and Dunlap all concurred with Wiley that the federal government should bar formaldehyde as a food additive.

Wiley also could take comfort in the fact that he'd successfully argued against borax as a food additive and that his position had been upheld within the department. At Wilson's direction, the agency began seizing borax-laced products to get them off the market. After a seizure of a train carload of its cheese, the MacLaren Imperial Cheese Company (a Canadian manufacturer later purchased by the

J.L. Kraft & Brothers Company) asked Wilson to refer the borax question to the Remsen Board. Wilson refused to do so.

The secretary also had endorsed a November decision to seize fifty-two industrial-sized cans of eggs preserved in a 2 percent solution of boracic acid. The Hipolite Egg Company of St. Louis sold these huge cans—forty-two pounds each—to the baking industry at a price much lower than that of fresh eggs. Hipolite specialized in salvaging dirty, cracked, and even rotting eggs for use in breads and cakes. The company was particularly known for using "spots" (decomposing eggs); mixing their contents into a thick, homogenous mass; using boracic acid, a by-product of borax, to halt further decomposition; and then selling the eggy soup by the can. Wilson not only approved the seizure but also initiated a legal action against the company to halt its use of the preservative. As with the move to ban formaldehyde, this was a politically astute decision. Borax had fallen out of favor precipitously since Wiley's first Poison Squad report— and since the unscrupulous propaganda tactics of the Pacific Coast Borax Company had come to light.

For some years, magazines and newspapers across the country had been printing the anti-Wiley, pro-preservative opinions of H. H. Langdon, who identified himself as a public health advocate with a scientific background. Langdon's ideas usually appeared in letters to the editor but also in the occasional magazine essay. After Wiley had published in 1907 a book compiling the bureau's analyses under the title *Foods and Their Adulteration*, the apparently science-savvy Langdon had written a fiercely critical review of the work. But "Langdon" was a fictional creation of H. L. Harris, the chief publicist for the Pacific Coast Borax Company. Harris planted his Langdon letters in large publications and small. In a missive to a newspaper in eastern Ohio, the *Alliance Review*, he wrote, "A recent case of ptomaine poisoning in Alliance has caused the thought that it is certainly appalling to learn how rapidly ptomaine poisoning cases have increased since the passage of the pure food law."

To the *New York Times* the fictional Langdon described Wiley as an untrustworthy scientist of "radical views." In *Scientific American* he insisted that the health of the Poison Squad volunteers was improved by eating borax-laced food. His work even appeared in Paul Pierce's *What to Eat*, where he wrote that the Poison Squad experiments could not be trusted because the bureau's dining room was so shabby and dirty as to depress anyone's appetite. These entirely fictional statements were reprinted with enough effect that scientists hostile to Wiley—such as the German industrial chemist Oscar Liebreich, who had helped bring borax into favor—sometimes included them in their own testimony.

It was the adoption of the Harris/Langdon statements by high-profile pharmaceutical chemists like Liebreich that led the American Medical Association to investigate. AMA physicians reviewed the cases of ptomaine poisoning reported in the fake letters and discovered that many had never occurred; most of the illnesses ranged from indigestion to a few suicidal "self-administrations of arsenic." In other words, there had been no sudden increase in bacterial food poisoning due to the reduction in use of borax and other preservatives. In an article titled "Press Agents and Preservatives," the editors of the *Journal of the American Medical Association* (*JAMA*) faulted other periodicals for the tendency of the lazy editor to "calmly appropriate Harris's 'dope' as fact and print it as his own." They advised the group's physician members to report any Langdon letters to newspaper editors. In some cases, newspapers had started adding editors' notes to the Langdon opinions, a positive step that the AMA noted, "must cause chagrin and disgust at the headquarters of the Pacific Coast Borax Company."

But despite such evidence of skullduggery by the food industry, and despite his support for prohibiting additives such as borax and formaldehyde, Wilson remained deeply wary of Wiley and his activist tendencies. He again refused to consider restrictions on the use of sulfur compounds in food. He again said that he was waiting for the

Remsen Board's recommendation on sodium benzoate before he would make any decision. It surprised neither Wiley nor his allies when the board's report, issued on January 26, 1909, found no problem worth mentioning with sodium benzoate. "You will find it rich reading," Wiley wrote to a friend after reading the published report and noting that he had not been shown an advance copy. "Excuses for everything."

Three of the board members—Long, Herter, and Chittenden—had independently conducted their studies, loosely following Wiley's design, and failed to replicate the signs of serious illness seen in the Poison Squad study. They had tested the preservative on a group of young men, but they had added several additional months to the testing and they had experimented with a wider range of doses. All three of the Remsen Board researchers saw some signs of ill health in their subjects but dismissed them as "slight modifications in certain physiological processes, the exact significance of which modifications is not known." To a man, they suggested that the causes were anything from lack of sleep to the weather. Chittenden, for instance, blamed the nausea and diarrhea that he observed on a "hot, dry New England summer." The Remsen Board announced that it could reassure the government and the public that sodium benzoate—at an industry-standard dose of 0.01 percent—was perfectly safe.

Preservative makers declared the Remsen report a victory over an "arrogant official scientist." Once again, the food-manufacturing association called for Wiley's removal from office and predicted that the food additives he had criticized—from copper sulfate to saccharin—would be found innocuous. But such public celebration, as the *New York Times* reported, almost immediately backfired. Pure-food advocates immediately charged that the Remsen report was biased, beginning a new round in what the paper called "a first class fight."

The *Journal of the American Medical Association* wrote that the Remsen Board seemed determined to find no health implications.

"[T]his decision of the board leaves the question of the physiologic action of sodium benzoate on the community practically where it was before; that is, that while the substance is known to be a bacterial poison, its deleterious action on the human organs is, in the words of the Scotch verdict, 'not proven.'" A Scottish "not proven" verdict meant, in this context, that although the charge had not been established as true, the defendant had not been absolved of guilt, either. "It is to be hoped that Dr. Wiley will be in no way discouraged and will remain at his post and continue to hew to the line," the piece continued. "He is a government official of a type that happily is becoming more common—one of those men who appreciate that they represent the public and that they are expected to look after the interests of the public and not the interests of any class. . . . No wonder he is so cordially hated by those who heretofore fattened at the expense of public health and well-being."

Women's clubs, consumer leagues, newspaper editorial writers, even the Canners Association and the National Wholesale Grocers Association all came angrily to Wiley's defense. On the day that the Remsen report was published, Paul Pierce announced the formation of a new advocacy group, the American Association for the Promotion of Purity in Food Products, which included representatives from industry including the Shredded Wheat Company, the Franco-American Food Company, the Beechnut Packing Company, and the H.J. Heinz Company. Heinz paid for the association's press agent, who kept journalists supplied with pamphlets detailing both the risks of preservatives and the corporate corruption of the Agriculture Department. "If you could see the letters, telegrams and newspaper clippings pouring in upon me," Wiley wrote to Edwin Ladd, "you would think the Referee [Remsen] Board had not a single supporter in the country."

Wilson was unmoved by such political drama. He accepted the Remsen report without criticism, simply recommending that the preservative be allowed at a low enough level to be considered safe until proven otherwise by objective science. In March 1909, just before leaving office, President Roosevelt approved a regulation permitting the use of sodium benzoate in food at a level set at 0.01 percent. If he'd been less on the defensive, Wiley could have celebrated the fact that he'd at least gotten a limit put in place. But he, his allies, and the press took the decision as a resounding defeat for the chief chemist and his cause. The assessment was that the army of pure-food advocates had flexed their political muscle to an impressive extent, but they had lost.

Wiley thought again about quitting but rejected that idea. He'd come too far and he felt he owed his loyalty and allegiance to his many like-minded comrades in battle. As he wrote to a friend, it would be cowardly for "a general to resign his command because one part of his army was engulfed." He had flaws, he acknowledged, but he could say proudly that cowardice was not one of them.

# Twelve

# OF WHISKEY AND SODA

## 1909

—◉—

*The banquet how fine, don't begin it*

William Howard Taft won the presidency largely thanks to the support of Theodore Roosevelt, and he shared his patron's wariness of the Agriculture Department's crusading chief chemist: "I expect to give Dr. Wiley the reasonable and just support he is entitled to have," Taft wrote, shortly after taking office, to one of Wiley's anxious supporters. "But when I feel he has done an injustice I expect to differ with him even at the expense of having my motives questioned."

He expected, on the other hand, that his relationship with Roosevelt would stay cordial. But the sitting president and the former one grew apart over the next four years. A simple and widely cited explanation for the split is that the office brought out Taft's conservative tendencies even while Roosevelt, restless and unhappy at being out of power, grew more progressive. Their differences came to a head when a very public disagreement over wilderness protection prompted Taft in 1910 to fire the popular Gifford Pinchot from his position as U.S. Forest Service chief. The move alienated not just Roosevelt, who had appointed Pinchot to the position, but other progressive Republicans as well, creating a serious rift within the party.

Yet the alienation between the Taft and Roosevelt factions was rooted in more than one big dispute. From his earliest days in office, Taft showed a willingness to reconsider Roosevelt's rulings, including some controversial new positions on enforcement of the food law.

For example, the question of which alcoholic beverages could rightly be called "whiskey" arose yet again. Roosevelt and Attorney General Bonaparte considered that they had settled the matter. But bottling interests represented by that tireless lobbyist Warwick Hough never resigned themselves to the designations "compound whiskey" and "imitation whiskey." Roosevelt had quietly tried to appease the angry liquor wholesalers by appointing an informal "whiskey commission," supposedly to review the situation. It consisted of Wilson, Dunlap, and John G. Capers, head of the Department of Internal Revenue. The commission was so informal, and also apparently so secret, that Wilson and Dunlap at first denied it existed when reporters asked them about its rumored actions. This deceptiveness became a political embarrassment when Roosevelt and Capers acknowledged the panel's formation. Further, Hough acquired a copy of a pro-industry letter from the commission to the president and leaked it to newspapers in order to press his cause. The document, which infuriated Wiley and his purist allies, read in part: "[T]he term 'whiskey' should not be denied to neutral spirits diluted with water to a proper strength and colored with caramel."

Hough welcomed Taft's election—largely because he remembered that at the height of the whiskey deliberations, the then-secretary of war had spoken out in favor of the wholesalers' position. Not long after the 1909 inauguration, Hough brought members of the National Wholesale Liquor Dealers Association and his copy of the whiskey commission letter to a meeting with the new president. Afterward, with Taft's encouragement, the association filed a formal petition to once again revisit the question of how to define whiskey.

In response, Taft asked Solicitor General Lloyd W. Bowers for a formal review of Roosevelt's earlier decision and, at Bowers's recommendation, a new series of whiskey hearings began on April 8, 1909. It continued for almost a month. The resulting 1,200-page volume of testimony retraced the ground that had been covered in earlier hearings before congressional committees. Hough again represented the wholesale liquor dealers. As he had in the past, Edmund Haynes Taylor Jr.—now in his seventies but still an outspoken advocate for aged Kentucky bourbon—represented the straight-whiskey interests. And Wiley, yet again, was called as an expert witness on alcohol analysis and purity. The subject matter may have been somewhat dry, but the hearings were not. Participants repeatedly gathered around a table to taste the samples of whiskey—straight, blended, imitation—submitted in evidence. Henry Parker Willis, an economics professor at Washington & Lee University who served as an adviser on whiskey tax issues, noted a corresponding rise in noise and described the hearings as often "reminiscent of a German drinking club."

Typically impassioned, Wiley once again accused Hough and his association of dishonesty: "The evidence shows convincingly," he said, "that the protestants in this case did not come into court with clean hands; that they have been for half a century guilty of taking neutral spirits and from these neutral spirits making all forms of so-called whiskey." The use of dyes, he reminded the listeners, was purely to give products the false appearance of aged whiskey and to "make the article appear better than it really is, thus contravening the fundamental principles of the Food and Drug Act." After all, the act required many manufacturers to place the term "imitation" on their label—imitation vanilla extract, for instance—when they were made primarily of other ingredients. And he concluded: "There is no hardship, therefore, in imposing the word 'imitation' upon a beverage made in imitation of old genuine whiskey."

In late May, Bowers issued his opinion, agreeing with Wiley that neutral spirits—dyed, flavored, oiled—should not be called whiskey in an unqualified way. He ordered them to be labeled "imitation." But he also agreed with the rectifiers that a blend of alcohols, if it contained primarily straight whiskey, could fairly be called a "blended whiskey," even if it was dyed to a richer color. If this was "coloring matter of a harmless character," such as a vegetable dye, Bowers said he would not call the whiskey adulterated. After all, he noted, "Whisky is not a natural product. It is always a thing manufactured by man."

Wiley wearily accepted the verdict; he was, to the relief of his allies, ready to let the whiskey fight go. The ruling satisfied neither Hough nor Taylor, however, and on behalf of their respective groups both challenged Bowers's decision. Taft then announced he would make a presidential decision to end the argument, possibly later that year. Taylor was optimistic; he and his straight-whiskey colleagues had filed a detailed brief establishing the solid legal precedent for precise labeling of whiskey and its ingredients. In this they had the support of Senator McCumber, one of the powers behind the passage of the food law, who had written to the president that he considered it consumer fraud to allow cheap alcohol enhanced with "drugs and oils and colors . . . to be sold for a good brand of whiskey."

Less openly, Taft also reviewed another Roosevelt decision, the creation of the Remsen Board. Shortly after taking office, the new president had asked deputy attorney general James Fowler to affirm that the board had legal standing. Fowler responded with a memo, copied to Wilson, that dismayed both the secretary and the president. It warned that the board represented an illegal use of department funds: "I do not think the Secretary of Agriculture was authorized by law to employ scientific experts to be paid out of the fund named." Startled, Taft privately asked Attorney General George Wickersham to review Fowler's finding. Wickersham concurred. Indeed, the attorney general's office expressed concern over how much money Wilson was lavishing on these industry-friendly scientists—annual salaries of up to $60,000 and, from 1908 to 1909, an additional $40,000 for expenses. At Wilson's urging, however, Taft decided to keep the board in place. Both men agreed that the department needed a counterweight to Wiley's purist extremes. And both men agreed to keep the Justice Department ruling secret—another decision that would later prove a very public embarrassment.

At the Agriculture Department, Dunlap and McCabe now routinely joined hands against Wiley on every decision. McCabe had announced a "three-month rule," stating that if cases were reported to the board more than three months after samples were collected, they would not be prosecuted. Wiley protested, pointing out that the Chemistry Bureau was understaffed and not always able to turn analyses around so quickly. "I consider there is neither justice nor reason in the three months rule," he wrote. "I have never consented to it nor was I consulted in its adoption." McCabe responded by requiring him to attach justification to every delayed analysis. The attorney continued to think Wiley far too quick to prosecute violations and too resistant to work with companies on solving problems. There was some merit in slowing things down, he thought, even though some wrongdoers might slip by along the way.

In June 1909 Wiley recommended that eight barrels from Ohio labeled "Sweet Catawba Wine" be seized and the company reprimanded. Departmental inspectors had discovered that the barrels contained not wine but an alcoholic liquid made from fermented corn sugars sweetened with saccharin. McCabe and Dunlap took the position that rather than fraudulent, the wine was merely poorly labeled. They blocked the seizure and scheduled a hearing with the manufacturer to work out a compromise. At least, Wiley suggested, the department might keep the mislabeled—and again, he would argue, fake—product out of the market until the situation was resolved. McCabe wrote back with undisguised hostility that he considered that a "ludicrous recommendation."

Many of their disagreements centered on defining the risk of a poorly studied compound. In a typical argument with Dunlap that July, Wiley recommended barring the compound sodium acetate—a

salt of acetic acid used widely by the textile industry—from also being used as an additive in candy. He worried, he said, that sweets
were largely eaten by children, one of the groups that most needed
extra protection. A clause in the law forbade the addition of mineral
substances to confectionary. Admitting it was a stretch, he argued
that, as sodium was a mineral, the department could apply the law in
a protective sense until more was known. Dunlap countered that the
action would pose a troubling scientific precedent: "If sodium acetate is a mineral substance, so is cane sugar, for cane sugar is composed of over 40 percent carbon and no one could possibly deny the
fact that carbon is mineral." True, Wiley admitted, but wasn't it
worth risking interpretive overreach in the interest of protecting
the most vulnerable consumers? "I have not time to go into all
the reasons that would lead me to exclude sodium acetate from confectionary. The fact that confections are eaten especially by children
and others whose digestive systems are not the strongest is a good
and sufficient reason to me," wrote Wiley in a memo arguing his
case. Dunlap again replied that he found that unconvincing and would
not support enforcing the law in such an arbitrary way.

They also quarreled over whether the label "Norway Boneless
Cod Strips" could be applied to cod from New England that still
contained some of the smaller bones. "I do not know of but one
meaning of the word 'Norway' and that is probably the signification
of the word on this package," Wiley wrote. The three-man panel
eventually decided to order that "Norway" be removed from the
package but, in a two-to-one decision, allowed small bones to be
considered acceptable in a "boneless" product.

In another dispute they differed over whether a cookie could be
called an "arrowroot biscuit" when it contained only 15 percent arrowroot starch. Predictably, Wiley took the stance that a higher percentage was needed to justify the name; McCabe countered that if
they were so literal in applying the law, it would become a joke. This
kind of stance on arrowroot biscuits, he declared, "would lead to the

proposition that one product of the baker's art, now styled 'Lady Finger,' is misbranded unless actually the result of mayhem."

The battle over sodium benzoate, meanwhile, had not abated. Frustrated with federal government inaction, the state of Indiana had independently banned the product's use in foods. In 1908, fearing that Indiana's action would trigger similar moves by health officials in other states, two large food processors, Curtice Brothers of Rochester, New York, and Williams Brothers of Detroit, filed suit, petitioning the U.S. District Court in Indianapolis to block the state law, describing it as economically crippling. The court issued a temporary injunction and scheduled a full hearing on the issue for the spring of 1909.

In anticipation of the hearing, the manufacturers quietly asked James Wilson for two favors. They wanted representatives from the Remsen Board to testify in their favor and they wanted Wiley and his loyal chemistry staff kept out of the courtroom. Wilson agreed to both requests, arranging to fund members of the Remsen Board to testify in Indiana, preparing to block any opposite viewpoints. When James Bingham, attorney general of Indiana, asked to have Wiley and some of his bureau staff testify in support of the state's case, Wilson refused permission. When Bingham protested, Wilson sought Taft's approval for the refusal, emphasizing that representatives of the Department of Agriculture should not so publicly take opposite sides in a lawsuit over preservatives. The president readily agreed and the secretary prepared to block all access to the recalcitrant chemists in his bureau.

Bingham, however, cabled the department that he now would get on a train and come to them for the depositions. Harvey Wiley agreed to give his statement, despite knowing that it was against department policy and that he would once again anger his boss by doing so. But others in the Agriculture Department declined, telling the Indiana attorney general they feared Wilson's retribution. Now genuinely angry, Bingham filed suit in the Supreme Court of the District of Columbia (what is now called the U.S. District Court for the District of Columbia). Naming Wilson and the department, the suit sought to compel the department's full testimony in the Indiana case. The federal court agreed with Indiana's attorney general that the Agriculture Department could not suppress expert testimony. Bingham gathered all his requested depositions and put Wilson into a legal bind, forcing the secretary, against his will, to send Wiley to testify in the state case.

But the standoff between the federal government's quarreling experts doomed the state law. The court ruled that without a consensus it could not find the preservative to be a health problem: "Ingredients and processes may be prohibited as unwholesome or causing deception but not merely because they preserve." Further, the justices had been impressed by the manufacturers' arguments that they were wholly dependent on chemical additives to stay in business: "While it may regulate," they said, "the legislature may not destroy an industry."

Paul Pierce's magazine—its name now changed from *What to Eat* to the more serious-sounding *National Food Magazine*—responded with renewed attacks on sodium benzoate. The issue featured a strong warning from William Williams Keen—a Philadelphia physician acclaimed as the country's first brain surgeon—on the risks of repeated low doses of chemical agents in food: "It must be evident that any drug used as a food preservative, eaten constantly, must affect the general health deleteriously and hence is most undesirable. . . . I have warned my grocer that I shall not accept such food for use and, if furnished me, I shall simply change my grocer."

The issue also featured a full-page ad from H.J. Heinz. Titled "A Health Problem That Confronts the Nation," it read in part: "Are you sure that your own state of health justifies you taking, for an indefinite period, drugged foods into your system? Are you willing to drug your family according to the prescription of any food manufacturer?

"Benzoate of soda is not necessary in any food. Every food product sold in a preserved state can be and is put up without it. Reputable manufacturers (and there are many) who do not use waste products of canneries, evaporating plants and other refuse raw materials and who do not permit untidiness and unsanitary practices about their factories find it unnecessary and do not use it. . . .

"Heinz 57 varieties are prepared from fresh, sound, wholesome fruits and vegetables; by neat uniformed work people; in model kitchens that are open to the public every day and visited annually by thousands from all parts of the world.

"Our products do not—and regardless of any legislative action or Government ruling—they will never contain Benzoate of Soda or any drug or chemical." The ad concluded by suggesting that despite the new law, consumers still needed to protect themselves by reading food labels carefully.

Wilson knew that Ladd, Shepard, and many of the other critics who had so savaged his reputation the previous summer in Michigan would have another opportunity that August as the Association of State and National Food Dairy Departments was scheduled to convene in Denver. Just weeks earlier, the secretary had authorized Agriculture Department agents to start seizing bleached flour shipments and publicly proclaimed his vigilance against dishonest manufacturing practices. "I am utterly hostile to having the people's foods tampered with," he told the *American Food Journal*. "We want to know that what we eat is the pure product."

More privately, Wilson acknowledged that his decision had been urged as a test case by department solicitor George McCabe, who believed the bleaching issue offered a chance to sharpen up some vague wording in the law. The law, as McCabe correctly pointed out, did not provide clear definitions for what constituted an injurious additive or adulteration. On that point he agreed with Wiley, who had long complained about the vague standards. The solicitor thought judicial clarification was needed to improve the situation. "This can come only from the courts," he wrote, "and there is not a single serious administrator connected with the law who does not join in the opinion that further progress must depend very largely on judicial rulings. If the bleached flour people bring their case to trial, they will do a valuable public service whether they win or lose."

Despite agreeing to seizures for legal purposes, Wilson appeared increasingly hostile to his department's role in tackling public health issues. He moved to block a bureau report on the chemical risks inherent in bleaching flour. He had also, not surprisingly, refused a provocative request from Wiley in June to reprint the report on benzoic acid and benzoates. He'd also shut down a series of other planned publications: on the use of the sugar alcohol glycerin in processing meat, on preventing spoilage of tomato ketchup, on pathogenic bacteria growing in frozen and dried eggs, and even an assessment of the arsenic content of confectioner's shellac, the glaze used on chocolate candies. He'd further blocked the release of a troubling report from Lyman Kebler, chief of the bureau's Drug Division, on the growing problem of medicated soft drinks.

Wilson also tried to prevent Wiley from taking his case to popular publications. "I regret that I shall have to withdraw my offer to write you an article which would be truthful, readable and useful on the subject of 'The Campaign for Pure Food, up to Date,'" wrote Wiley to an editor at *Century* magazine. "As I told you, I submitted your request to the Secretary of Agriculture and he informed me that if I would write an article which he would approve I could publish it. The Secretary and I are so diametrically opposed in our view in regard to this matter that I am convinced it would be useless for me to try to secure his approval to any article which in my opinion would do anything like justice to the subject. . . . I reluctantly ask you to cancel the engagement."

When the Association of State and National Food Dairy Departments convened in Denver that summer, little of the previous year's bitterness from the Mackinac Island convention had faded. "James Wilson, secretary of agriculture, and Dr. H.W. Wiley, chief chemist of the department, have come to the parting of the ways on the subject of food," reported the *Chicago Tribune* in a story predicting a "battle royal" over preservatives, especially sodium benzoate. Wilson brought the entire Remsen Board with him to Denver, paying for their rooms at the city's Brown Palace Hotel, convention headquarters. Despite the luxurious setting, Ira Remsen would later describe the conference as "a bear pit." He found himself repeatedly defending the board against charges that it favored industry at the cost of public health and safety. The secretary had prepared an aggressive strategy. He demanded that a scheduled vote on the sodium benzoate question be decided on an open ballot. Then he privately assured attendees that the Department of Agriculture would withdraw funding to all those who voted against him.

Food commissioners from Pennsylvania and Michigan, both sodium benzoate critics, protested Wilson's heavy-handed approach by angrily walking out of the meeting. The walkout backfired, as the final tally—absent those votes and the influence of the two protesting officials—went narrowly in support of both the Remsen Board and its finding that sodium benzoate was a fully safe additive. An editorial in the *Los Angeles Herald* decried Wilson's tactic and its result: "As the inside facts concerning the Denver convention become more generally known it is revealed as one where the artifices of the politicians were considerably more in evidence than the sober thought of the expert charged with protecting the public health."

But Wilson was wholly satisfied. He wrote to President Taft that "we fully smashed the program, turned things end for end, fully endorsed the Referee Board and its findings." Wiley, Wilson added, was a troublesome "low class fellow" but he believed that the Denver vote had sent the chief chemist a warning to Wiley that his policy of defiance would not be tolerated much longer.

B etween his fight to maintain some level of toxicity research and his battles for enforcement and public awareness, Wiley's staff worried that their chief was beginning to sound exhausted. They were also angry over Wilson's dismissal of their own work and increasingly willing to push back. One of the most determined to do so was Lyman Kebler, still steaming over the suppression of his investigation of medicated soft drinks.

Kebler had left a lucrative job at Smith, Kline, French & Co. in Philadelphia for the Department of Agriculture, because he believed that it was critical to establish honest practices for pharmaceutical products. Now forty-three, he led the Chemistry Bureau's oversight of the drug industry and had earned a reputation as meticulous and, on occasion, ruthless. The *Bulletin of Pharmacy*, while not entirely an enthusiast, had described Kebler, with some respect, as the country's most eminent "foe to fakers."

Kebler, with Wiley's backing, decided to counter Wilson's suppression of his report with an even more in-depth investigation. To do so, he reviewed more than one hundred brands of medicated soft drinks and bottled waters on the market. The manufacturers ranged from small companies such as New Hampshire's Londonderry Lithia, which made a drink rich in the element lithium, to large ones, such as the Atlanta-based Coca-Cola Company, which had famously made its fortune through a nineteenth-century formula that had included the potent stimulant cocaine. By withholding his report, Kebler told Wiley, the department was hiding both knowledge and risk from American consumers. He knew Wiley was under constant attack; he knew that Wilson had very little patience with the bureau. He also knew that his planned publication had a very provocative title: "Habit-Forming Agents: Their Indiscriminate Sale and Use a Menace to Public Welfare." But, he added, that title realistically summed up a national problem.

The indiscriminate use of narcotics remained an enormous risk to public health, Kebler pointed out. Many "soothing syrups" for children were laced with morphine, heroin, and chloral hydrate, among other sedatives; cough syrups and asthma medications for adults could contain a mixture of several of these narcotics. Further,

Kebler considered the problem of medicated soft drinks particularly troubling because consumers often had no idea that the sodas contained stimulants and/or intoxicating agents. Doctors reported cases of soft-drink addiction, and insurance companies, he said, were trying to develop a plan to deal with "soft drink habituees [sic]." Wiley agreed to make the case to Wilson yet again. But, he told Kebler ruefully, he could make no promises that his argument would work.

The yet-to-be published "Habit-Forming Agents" offered a damning review of the unrestricted use of narcotics in over-the-counter remedies. It was equally unsparing on the subject of counter drinks: "During the last 20 years, a large number of soft drinks containing caffeine and smaller or greater amounts of coca leaf and kola nut products have been placed on the market. Preparations of this class, on account of insufficient information, were formerly looked upon as harmless, but they are now known to be an impending evil." Kebler had drawn up a list of the worst offenders, many of which were named to hint at their stimulant content: Mello-Nip, Dobe, Kola-Kok, Pillsbury's Koke, Kola-Ade, Kos Kola, Café-Coca, and Koke. As a further example, the department had ordered the seizure of two products from the American Beverage Corporation: Great American Coca Cream and Great American Pepsette. An analysis found that Coca Cream contained saccharin, benzoic acid, cocaine, and caffeine; and Pepsette, which advertised itself as a pepsin-based, fruit-flavored soft drink, contained no pepsin at all but plenty of cocaine.

It was one thing for the department to find fault with any of those companies—most of them serving limited regional markets—and even to take enforcement action against one or a few. It was quite another to take on Atlanta-based Coca-Cola. The *National Druggist* estimated that the company sold more than ten million gallons of Coca-Cola to American soda fountains alone, "representing 300,000,000 glasses" consumed annually. This combination of money and influence played a role in the careful approach of James

Wilson toward the company; he was especially wary of provoking the company's influential and combative president, Asa Candler.

The Georgia tycoon had publicly supported the 1906 food and drug law, emphasizing the "pure and wholesome" nature of Coca-Cola. And after the law passed, Candler's company also stopped secretly sweetening the beverage with cheap saccharin and returned to the old sugar formula. To Candler's unhappy surprise—expressed loudly to Wilson and others—those measures had not led to a perfectly harmonious relationship with government regulators.

The U.S. Army in 1907 dropped Coca-Cola from its list of approved beverages, responding to rumors that the drink contained a possibly intoxicating level of alcohol. Arguing its innocence, the company requested an analysis by the Bureau of Chemistry to prove such suspicions wrong. The results convinced the army to take Coca-Cola back: Wiley's chemists found only a trace amount of alcohol residue from the oils and extracts used in the soda, nothing even close to a level that could cause intoxication. The bureau analysis also confirmed that the soft drink was cocaine free. The only notable stimulant in Coca-Cola was caffeine. A glass of the soft drink, served at a soda fountain, contained slightly more than half the amount of caffeine in a cup of coffee and close to twice that in an average cup of tea. Candler assumed these findings were as reassuring to the Agriculture Department as to the Department of War. But as would gradually become clear, the tests raised other issues to trouble Wiley and Kebler.

Wiley, who, as his colleagues often complained, was given to literal-mindedness about labels, thought the word "coca" implied to consumers the existence of that ingredient; some of the labels even depicted the fruit of a coca plant. Kebler was more bothered by the caffeine levels. This was a drink marketed directly to children, without any disclosure of the stimulant involved, and he took that worry to the chief chemist and again asked his aid in raising the issue with the secretary of agriculture. "I am not a believer in the promiscuous use of caffeine," wrote Wiley to Wilson in a memo detailing his concerns about "so-called soft drinks." As always, the chief chemist had a list of other concerns, such as the artificial flavoring (industrial citric acid instead of real lemon juice, pepper dust instead of ginger), coal-tar dyes, and cheap saccharin as an unlabeled sugar substitute. These methods were "highly objectionable both on ethical grounds and because of their possible injury to health." But he'd come to agree with Kebler that the unlabeled caffeine issue should be addressed first.

They got support from an unexpected quarter. George McCabe thought Coca-Cola might offer a test case on the unlimited use of stimulants in products sold to children and urged Wilson to at least consider the idea. Meanwhile, Wiley continued to urge the secretary to act: "Coca-Cola is one of the most widely sold beverages in the country. Its use is to a certain extent habit-forming and great injury may come to health by the continued and excessive use of an alkaloid of this kind." In his memo to Wilson, Wiley emphasized that he wasn't deliberately singling out the soft-drink industry; it was a healthy alternative to alcohol for adult drinkers, and "there is much to be said good about it and little bad," he wrote. But publicly, the chief chemist was starting to take a harder stance.

In a spring 1909 speech at the Holy Cross Academy in Washington, DC, Wiley warned the students: "If you only knew what I know about these soft drinks you would abstain from them," he said. "It would surprise you that most of them have more caffeine in them than coffee—and a drug even more deadly." After newspaper accounts of the talk provoked angry complaints from the American Bottlers Association, he clarified that, emphasizing that caffeine was his major concern. "What I did say to the young girls at that academy is that parents often forbid their children to drink coffee or tea and yet they could get caffeine, the most injurious part of those drinks, at the soda fountain."

What he didn't mention was that, following the Coca-Cola

analysis, he'd sent Lyman Kebler down south to take a closer look at both the company and the culture surrounding soft-drink consumption. Kebler had combined a visit to the company headquarters and production facilities with some time spent lurking at Atlanta soda fountains. He was dismayed to observe children as young as four years old drinking glasses of stimulant-rich Coca-Cola. It was this report, in part, that had led Wiley to urge a legal test case, arguing that caffeine was an unlabeled additive that posed a genuine health risk to children.

Wilson, still annoyed, sent Wiley a memo ordering him to drop the subject—and again refused to publish Kebler's report. Wiley had no evidence that the Coca-Cola Company had helped influence the decision, but he thought it highly likely. "I was, of course, surprised and grieved at this action on the part of Mr. Wilson, but as usual I could see behind it the manipulation of powerful hands." He suspected that an action against Coca-Cola was never going to happen. And then a visit from a muckraking Atlanta journalist changed that prediction.

In October 1909 Wiley sat down for an unexpectedly hostile interview with Fred L. Seely, editor of the reform-minded newspaper the *Atlanta Georgian*. Seely was a longtime critic of the Coca-Cola Company's indifference to others and he saw the federal government as complicit in the company's bad behavior. He demanded to know why the Agriculture Department had never gone after Coca-Cola for the health issues linked to consumption of its product. Wiley responded defensively that he had in fact recommended that the company be prosecuted. His chemists had even done research suggesting that the soft drink might be both "habit-forming and nerve-racking." He then showed the journalist a handful of the memos he'd written to Wilson on the subject—all of which had been rebuffed.

There was, for instance, the memo telling the secretary that "this product contains an added ingredient [caffeine] which may render the product injurious to health." There was also one regarding false labeling, noting that "the name Coca-Cola would indicate that it contained the substances and active principals of the coca leaf and the kola nut, when as a matter of fact it contains only an extract derived from exhausted coca leaves, which is a refuse product obtained in the manufacture of cocaine." There was another memo urging that "an effort should be made to stop the traffic in a dangerous beverage."

In that last note, Wiley had written to his boss that Coca-Cola "contains an alkaloidal, habit-forming drug of a character which is forbidden to be used by hundreds of thousands of parents in this country who refuse to allow their children to drink either tea or coffee, which contain caffeine in its natural state and in a much less injurious form than this misbranded and adulterated beverage. Our duty is clearly in this case to protect the people of our country in every possible way."

Seely studied the memos that Wiley brandished at him. Then, newly outraged, he marched over to Wilson's office and demanded a meeting on the spot. When it was granted, he told Wilson that he planned to write a story about the department's refusal to protect consumers from a dangerous product. He would feature the secretary's order telling Wiley to leave Coca-Cola alone. He planned to make an example of Wilson as government corruption at its worst. The following day, Wilson called Wiley into his office and told him that it was time to make a formal seizure of Coca-Cola products. "It is remarkable," Wiley noted sarcastically, "what the fear of publicity will do!" The secretary also told Wiley that he would schedule Kebler's medicated-soft-drink report for the following spring.

On October 21, 1909, two weeks after Seely's visit, the U.S. government moved to seize a shipment of Coca-Cola syrup bound for the company's bottling plant in Chattanooga, Tennessee. The action meant that the government would need to schedule a formal court hearing into the company's famous and lucrative product. A date had not yet been set for the hearing, but the legal action was already gaining attention based on its title alone: *United States v. Forty Barrels and Twenty Kegs of Coca-Cola.*

T oward the end of 1909, rumors began circulating that Taft was preparing to announce his whiskey decision. The rumors also predicted which side the president would take. Newspapers began writing mockingly about the new "Taft Whisky," which would be "neutral spirits made from molasses and beet refuse."

On December 26 the president announced his decision, officially changing the Roosevelt rules and establishing final definitions. The president ruled that the term "whiskey" could and should be used for any and all liquors made from grain alcohol. The government would require some "subordinate" description—whether the product was blended and a list of ingredients, such as coloring agents or neutral spirits. But there would be no requirement to label a quick-stilled and well-dyed product as imitation and there would be no describing barrel-aged whiskeys as the only real thing. Taft said that he agreed with the wholesale group that all alcohols were basically "like" substances. Or as economics professor Henry Parker Willis put it, "Whiskey appears to be virtually anything that will serve to intoxicate."

Lloyd Bowers, the solicitor general who had issued the more nuanced decision earlier in the year, called Wiley the next morning. As Wiley described the conversation, Bowers, who was an old friend of the president, said that he was about to depart on a much-needed vacation. But before he left he wondered, "What do you think of Mr. Taft's decision?" Wiley replied ruefully that he felt as if he'd been spanked. "He laughed and said so do I."

Not everyone took Taft's decision with such grace. In January 1910 Arthur Stanley, head of the Louisville-based Glenmore Distillery, wrote to Wiley that he thought the president was mostly a very good friend to Joe Cannon and his Peoria rectifiers: "What I fear is that wine distillers of Illinois will be allowed to brand their output as whisky, it will then be shipped to the rectifiers and mixed with real whisky and then called a 'Whisky Blend.'" It was a terrible precedent for those who cared about honest labeling, Stanley said bitterly, and had the potential of "virtually nullifying the Pure Food Law."

Alice Lakey felt the same. Her organization, the National Consumers League, issued a formal resolution to that effect: President Taft's statement "that neutral spirits, which the most eminent food chemists have declared an unlike substance to whisky, may be added to whisky and the whole product colored with burnt sugar or caramel without stating the latter fact on the label, etc. is destined to open the door for the return of all the evils of adulterated foods, drugs, liquors and medicines that have for a time been held in check by the operation of the pure food law. . . . We the executive board protest against this action and urge state officials to stand up."

Lakey also wrote to magazines and newspapers: "We believe that Mr. Taft's decision is the most serious blow to the pure food legislation this country has had. We believe that it is class legislation. We believe it permits special rulings for one product coming under the pure food law which was designed to make uniform regulations specific. . . . If this decision holds, it opens the door for every other product to demand the same 'immunity bath.' . . . If we follow this reasoning when, then, should blackberry brandy contain any blackberry juice? . . . This decision robs the consumer and the honest manufacturer of the protection designed by the pure food law."

To Wiley she wrote privately that she doubted the decision could be changed: "It is a very strong illustration of how clever the rectifiers are." But Wiley, increasingly besieged at the Department of Agriculture, put most of the blame on Wilson, who he suspected had quietly moved to undermine the law. In a letter to Lakey, he wrote, "There is but little we can do as long as the present Secretary of Agriculture is in the saddle."

*Thirteen*

# THE LOVE MICROBE

## 1910–1911

―――――⟨○⟩―――――

*Till you think of the past and the future and sigh*

Wiley wasn't prepared to give up. As Wilson knew all too well, his chief chemist never was. With the idea of pressing his beleaguered cause outside the department, by the start of 1910, Wiley had lined up months' worth of public talks.

In January he had promised to talk to the Men's Club of Newark, New Jersey, on the "morality of business"; to testify about aluminum levels in baking powder at a state trial in Harrisburg, Pennsylvania; to talk about food additives to the Montgomery County Medical Society and the Medical Society of New York. In February, the Harvard Club in Philadelphia; in March, the New York State Department of Health; in May, the Historical and Art Society; in July, the United States Pharmaceutical Convention in Washington, DC, and the National Dental Association in Denver. He'd also tentatively accepted engagements in Oklahoma City; Des Moines; Lawrence, Massachusetts; and Brooklyn, Newburgh, and Buffalo, New York.

In March, at Lakey's urging, Wiley agreed to add a trip to Cincinnati for a presentation at the national convention of the General

Federation of Women's Clubs. More than ever he recognized how important politically motivated women were to the pure-food cause. The same month, he accepted an invitation to speak to a women's suffrage club in Washington, DC. Although that decision was perhaps less political. The invitation came from Anna Kelton.

Kelton, now thirty-two years old, was still single and living at home, still working as a clerk at the Library of Congress. Still elegant, intelligent, well read, still a deep supporter of progressive change, she was also, these days, a passionate advocate for equality. She'd joined the National American Woman Suffrage Association (NAWSA) to help in the drawn-out, frustrating fight for women's right to vote. The association worked closely with other women's organizations, from the WCTU, which now had a ratification committee, to the General Federated Women's Clubs. And like them, the suffragettes had begun to take on consumer issues such as the struggling food and drug law. That interest encouraged Anna Kelton—Nan to her friends—to draw on an old relationship and invite Wiley to speak to her group about the importance of the national food law. He was happy to say yes—and just as happy that she still embodied the kind of crusading zeal that had always appealed to him.

In May 1910 Wilson issued a formal directive (General Order 140) giving George McCabe full authority over the regulation of food and drugs, including the ability to revoke earlier decisions by the Bureau of Chemistry.

Wiley, now perpetually on edge, told his friends that he feared that with this new power McCabe would enact further rollbacks on the regulation of preservatives. But the attorney surprised him by tackling a different contentious issue. Responding to industry complaints, McCabe moved to loosen restrictions on food dyes, one of the more successful enforcement actions taken after the passage of the 1906 law.

Before the law, even food manufacturers had become alarmed about the toxic nature of industrial coloring agents. Some still used the old-time vegetable-based dyes, such as saffron or annatto for yellow. But those dyes were both comparatively expensive and muted in tone. They did not offer the eye-popping yellows, reds, and greens that could be achieved by using metallic elements such as arsenic, mercury, lead, and copper. Yet thanks to a combination of toxicology studies and occasional poisoning episodes, such metallic additives were increasingly regarded as more trouble than they were worth. The National Confectioners Association had recommended back in 1899 that to avoid injuring customers, members voluntarily avoid almost two dozen coloring agents in their candy and other sweets.

New options arose with synthetic dyes made from coal tars—dense, chemically complex residues left over from the processing of coal. These compounds dated back to work by the English chemist Sir William Henry Perkin, a student of August Wilhelm von Hofmann, who pioneered analysis of coal tars and whose lectures Wiley had attended on his 1878 sabbatical in Germany.

Some decades earlier, in 1856, Perkin had used the coal-tar derivative benzene to create a purple dye that he called "mauvine" (a name later shortened to "mauve"). Benzene, a neatly linked ring of carbon and hydrogen atoms, also proved a handy base for other synthetic dyes, offering up a vivid chemical rainbow. The new dyes were durable, cheap, and potent—and rapidly adopted by industrial processors of everything from fabric to food. Chemists called them "aniline" dyes but they were widely known by a more direct description as coal-tar dyes. By the time the food and drug law passed, more than eighty such coloring agents were being used in American food and drink, without any safety review or restriction.

After passage of the 1906 law, the USDA had quickly banned food dyes based on lead, mercury, arsenic, and other toxic metals. And Wiley had hired an outside expert, a respected German food dye chemist named Bernhard Hesse, to evaluate the safety of the coal-tar dyes. Hesse's research led him to conclude that only seven of eighty such dyes on the market could fully be considered safe. A resulting 1907 Food Inspection Decision approved only those seven—three red, one orange, one yellow, one green, and one blue—as "certified colors." Predictably, makers of colorful foodstuffs sought to lengthen that list. But Hesse had stockpiled an arsenal of evidence showing that many of these other dyes could be directly linked to health problems. Wiley had firmly kept the list short, moving to block any coloring agents that weren't clearly identified as safe.

Newly employed by James Wilson in 1910 to guide the law's enforcement, McCabe decided to review Wiley's consumer-friendly decision. Deliberately splitting legal hairs, he wrote that "certification" was not a strictly approved process under the food and drug law. The legislation provided a framework for banning food products and additives considered injurious, but not for official sanction of others as safe.

Wiley pointed out in return that prior certification was less punitive to manufacturers than after-the-fact seizure and prosecution—something that he thought McCabe should find appealing. Further, the process had removed some very risky products from the food supply. He warned that weakening the certification provisions would allow unsafe dyes back onto the market. McCabe, unmoved, joined with Dunlap on the three-member Food Inspection Board to remove the certification requirement from the rules governing dyes. Wiley refused to sign the paperwork. The department issued the decision without his signature but the chief chemist decided to fight that move. He asked Hesse to prepare for Secretary Wilson a full report on the safety of coal-tar dyes. Perhaps the actual evidence would prove persuasive.

W hile Hesse worked on the new report, McCabe moved ahead with his legal test of bleached flour. He had a major enforcement question that needed clarifying. The nitrates that occurred as a result of bleaching were but by-products of processing. Did the government have the authority to regulate by-products as well as additives? It was an issue that needed a quick resolution. The Agriculture Department had that spring seized 625 sacks of bleached flour en route from the Lexington Mills and Elevator Company of Lexington, Nebraska, to a large grocery company in Missouri. The National Millers Association—also seeking a test case—decided to fight the seizure in the U.S. District Court in Missouri.

In court, the millers' group argued that bleaching did not degrade flour; rather it enhanced it. Thus the practice rose above the standard of adulteration under the law. The manufacturers further asserted that residual nitrates and nitrogen peroxide were not unsafe or injurious industrial additives but products of nature, created by a whitening process that used such harmless methods as electricity and naturally occurring gases, "a blast of God's own pure fresh air." Bruce Elliott, the attorney representing the millers, pointed out in court that nitrates occurred in nature, including in the human body. Even if they carried some hazard, he continued, the average American undoubtedly had a natural tolerance for them.

The Agriculture Department's experts countered with evidence that bleached baked goods contained an unnaturally high nitrate level. In a courtroom demonstration, a bureau chemist brought in two batches of biscuits, one made with unbleached flour and the other with some of the seized bleached flour. Both had been treated with a compound that turned red when exposed to nitrates. He offered to the jury a choice between a plate of golden brown biscuits and a plate of bright pink ones.

The defense did not deny that the bleached-flour biscuits

contained nitrates, enough to produce a rosy color in the chemical test. But, changing tactics, the millers' attorneys argued that even if nitrates were indeed injurious to health no safe level had been established scientifically. Therefore, it was impossible to argue how much was too much. The government's insistence on a low and "harmless" level of the compounds could then not be based on solid evidence and ought not to be admitted. The Missouri judge found that final assertion completely reasonable.

As he told the jury, "The fact that poisonous substances are to be found in the bodies of human beings, in the air, in potable water . . . does not justify the addition of the same or other poisonous substances to articles of food, such as flour, because the statute condemns the adding of poisonous substances." But it was the character of the additive, not the amount, that should guide the rules, the judge said, and if nitrates had no clearly defined toxicity levels, then they did not meet the law's definition of a poisonous substance. The jury, composed of bread-eating citizens clearly unhappy about the addition of nitrates to their daily meals, did not embrace such over-legal reasoning. As their verdict made clear, they wanted their food to be safe before all. The jurors found for the government, rejecting the judge's advice, firmly declaring that the bleached flour was both adulterated and misbranded and had been seized legally.

On behalf of his shocked clients, Elliott responded— embarrassingly for the White House—by complaining to newspaper reporters that he'd been promised better results. In fact, he had personally met with President Taft and been assured of a fair trial, which he took to mean a decision in his favor. He added that he had also met with Wilson and been assured that the flour studies would be taken away from Wiley and turned over to the far more sympathetic Remsen Board. In his opinion, the case was evidence of the unreliable nature of administration officials, not to mention government failure to support good American businessmen. He made it clear that he and his clients would appeal the decision and were prepared to fight for years if necessary. This government overreach would never stand, Elliott declared, and he predicted that the U.S. Supreme Court would agree.

B ernhard Hesse's eighty-page report, *Coal-Tar Colors Used in Food*, described experiments in which he had supplied colored food and water to test subjects—dogs and rabbits—over periods of not less than thirty days. The dosage of the dyes was calculated to be comparable to a possible high end of human exposure in a daily diet. The resulting health effects on the animals included weakness, nausea, vomiting, irritation of the intestinal tract, damage to the mucous membranes, fatty degeneration of the liver, swelling and discoloration of the kidneys, and, on occasion, evidence of dyes in the brain or the lining of the lungs.

The most common effect seemed to be a lingering stupor, sometimes followed by a gradual slide into a coma and on rare occasions the death of the test animal. He also noted minor side effects such as mild diarrhea and low levels of albuminuria, or protein in the urine, a symptom of kidney disease.

"It must be remembered," Hesse noted, "that smaller amounts of drugs, and therefore coal-tar colors, affect children as a rule than are effective upon adults." He suggested that a three-year-old child's dose should be about one-fifth that of an adult's—a twelve-year-old should receive no more than half. "All of this should be taken into account in drawing conclusions as to the harmfulness of coal-tar dyes on humans." As a large variety of dyed foods—candies, decorated cakes and pastries, soft drinks—were marketed largely to children, he worried that animal research–based "deductions" about the risks to adults might well underestimate the problem. To the surprise of some in the department, Hesse's thorough job, impassive and scientific, won over Secretary Wilson. The certification program, he announced, would remain in place—a decision that allowed Wiley a moment to savor an increasingly rare victory.

By 1910 Wiley had been at the USDA for twenty-seven years. There'd been tumult and struggle at the department, but he had prospered personally. He had good friends in Washington and across the country. After twenty years rooming with a Washington family, he had acquired his own house, a three-story brownstone, just a short walk from Dupont Circle in northwest Washington. He turned sixty-six that year and had confided in letters and in his daily journal that he had considered retiring—especially after recent professional setbacks—and he'd bought himself a modest country place in anticipation, a farm in Loudoun County, Virginia, in the eastern lee of the Blue Ridge Mountains. Admiring its rolling meadows, he'd named it Grasslands. He'd even purchased a newfangled steam-powered automobile, among the first in Washington, with the idea of driving himself out to his country property. The car, however, had been almost immediately damaged in a collision with a horse-drawn wagon, an incident that Wiley would describe, with some amusement, as a collision between past and future.

The accident would also return him, while repairs were under way, to traveling by public transportation. In late October 1910, Wiley was waiting for a streetcar when he found himself standing near Nan Kelton. She appeared genuinely glad to see him again. Before they parted, he impulsively asked her if he could come call, perhaps take her to a show or out to dinner. To his surprise and happiness—confided to his journal—she said yes. Over the next month, he embarked on a renewed courtship. They quickly rekindled their relationship, and in the first week of December Wiley again proposed. This time she accepted without reservation. The engagement announcement was received with pleasure—and amusement—by the nation's newspapers.

DR. WILEY WILL TAKE A BRIDE, began a headline in the *Chicago Tribune*. PURE FOOD EXPERT TO DESERT CAFES FOR HOME COOKED MEALS. The paper added a cheerful subhead: "Fiancée Not Terrified." As the story that followed put it: "Dr. Harvey Washington Wiley, pure food expert and rampant foe of the near-lamb chop and almost-chocolate drop, conserver of the national digestion and chief exponent of the we-must-have-pure-food-to-be-happy cult, is getting married."

The *Los Angeles Examiner* headlined its story GREATEST ENEMY OF FOOD GERMS FALLS VICTIM OF LOVE MICROBE. The writer speculated that the wedding cake "will have no old eggs, no alum, no clay-clad eggs or near-butter. Nothing but the purest of flour and baking powder and dairy out put [*sic*] will be used." The *Denver Post* printed a cartoon showing a fainting Kelton being carried away as her relentless husband searched the kitchen for chicory in coffee and preservatives in jam.

Kelton, swamped by interview requests, took the attention in stride. She used the opportunity to advocate for women's right to vote. A newspaper in Bangor, Maine, headlined its resulting story WILEY TO WED SUFFRAGETTE. She cheerfully told the *Boston Journal* that she didn't know how to cook. "I have been in the Congressional Library almost since I left college so I have had little time for domestic science." Fortunately, she added, her husband-to-be happened to be an excellent chef. That made Wiley laugh. He appreciated the story, which described her as a woman who "admires and takes pride in her fiancé and doesn't hesitate to say so."

At work he was so visibly happy that Wilson permitted himself to hope that his obsessive chief chemist would finally have another interest besides pure food. "There is a shade of hope for Wiley's future," the secretary wrote to Ira Remsen. "He is going to marry a suffragette, I believe, which may result in a change for the better; at least in these Christmas holidays, let us hope so."

After the passage of the 1906 law and his savage evaluation of its shortcomings, David Graham Phillips, the journalist whose work had so enraged President Roosevelt, had been undaunted by presidential insults. He saw nothing wrong with being described as a "muckraker." Phillips had continued to expose backroom deals between federal lawmakers, state legislatures, and the corporate interests—including food processors and their ilk—to whom so many officeholders were in deep financial debt. His articles detailing those well-financed connections would eventually help spur passage of the Seventeenth Amendment to the U.S. Constitution. That amendment threw out the old and increasingly corrupt system in which state legislators chose the U.S. senators to represent their re-spective states, and put in place public elections. The reform would not happen, though, until 1913, and Phillips would not live to see it.

After completing the last of his exposés of senatorial corruption, Phillips decided to take a break from muckraking and return to the relative tranquility of writing fiction. The choice, ironically, proved more dangerous than investigative journalism. Fitzhugh Coyle Golds-borough, a well-born member of a Baltimore family, who apparently suffered from mental illness, arrived at the deluded notion that a character in Phillips's novel *The Fashionable Adventures of Joshua Craig* was based on Goldsborough's sister. He confronted the author in front of the Princeton Club in New York, shot him multiple times, and then fatally shot himself. Taken to Bellevue Hospital, Phillips, just forty-four years old, died the next day, January 24, 1911. It marked an unhappy start to a year that would become one of the most stressful in Wiley's career.

Barely two months later, in Tennessee, the matter of *United States v. Forty Barrels and Twenty Kegs of Coca-Cola* at last went to trial. Wiley, McCabe, Wilson, and the whole Bureau of Chemistry had been conferring for months on how to approach the lawsuit. The government's case rested on three main points. First, it objected to what it described as the company's shoddy manufacturing processes. Second, on Wiley's recommendation, it challenged the very name "Coca-Cola" as false advertising because it implied that the drink contained both cocaine and kola (or bissy) nut extracts in its formula. This had been true in the nineteenth century but was no longer so; the Chemistry Bureau's latest analysis of the drink showed that its primary ingredients were water, sugar, phosphoric acid, caffeine, caramel, glycerin, and lime juice.

The government's third point—and this would become the primary focus of the trial—was that the drink did, however, contain another potent stimulant, namely caffeine. This charge immediately caught the attention of a dedicated nation of coffee drinkers as well as soft-drink imbibers. The Coca-Cola trial was going to put caffeine—and early-twentieth-century scientific understanding of its effects—at center stage. Not surprisingly, reporters flocked to Chattanooga for the show.

Newspaper coverage was constant and varied widely according to the editors' perspectives. EIGHT COCA-COLAS CONTAIN ENOUGH CAFFEINE TO KILL, the *Atlanta Georgian* announced based on testimony in the trial's first week, continuing its ongoing crusade against Asa Candler and his company. COCA-COLA DRINKERS SAY IT IS NOT BAD, the *Chattanooga News* countered. Wiley hadn't wanted the trial to be held in that southern city, where a large Coca-Cola bottling plant was one of the city's main employers. He had urged McCabe to get a change of venue to Washington, DC. But McCabe refused, fueling conspiracy theories among Wiley's allies that the solicitor—and the agriculture secretary—wanted the case to fail as a means of further crippling the influence of the chief chemist.

McCabe began the prosecution by calling J. L. Lynch, an Agriculture Department food and drug inspector. Lynch promptly provided a detailed and alarming portrait of Coca-Cola production methods. Describing the way the syrup soft-drink base was made, he said: "The Negro cook engaged in dumping the ingredients in the kettle was scantily attired in a dirty undershirt, old dirty trousers and broken shoes. His bare feet were protruding from his shoes in places and he was perspiring freely. He was chewing tobacco and spitting from time to time, the expectorate falling on the floor and on the platform from which he was dumping the sugar." Excess sugar also fell onto the platform, and the cook would shove it into the kettle with either a board or his feet, Lynch said. The caramel coloring was added on another floor of the building, he continued, and that level was so slimy with tobacco spit and other substances—"it had apparently never been scrubbed"—that the inspector declared that he'd been afraid of slipping and falling.

After Lynch came two scientists—H. C. Fuller, a pharmaceutical industry chemist, and W. O. Emory of the Bureau of Chemistry—who had independently analyzed the syrup. Both verified it no longer contained either coca leaf or kola nut extracts—although pictures of the plant leaves still decorated Coca-Cola barrels. Both verified that the primary stimulant now found in the drink was caffeine. They also noted some other unexpected ingredients—such as dirt, straw, and insect parts.

The government's main expert on caffeine was Henry Hurd Rusby, professor of botany and *materia medica* at Columbia University's College of Pharmacy and a longtime editor for *U.S. Pharmacopeia*, the publication that set uniform standards for pharmaceutical compounds. Rusby—fifty-six, slight, fair haired, brisk of manner—was a former physician who had developed a passionate interest in medicinal botany. Among other research projects, he'd spent more than a year in South America researching the plant sources of cocaine and caffeine. He was relieved to find the former missing from Coca-Cola but testified that caffeine was "apt to be deleterious to human health."

Given the quantity of caffeine in the soft drink, as described by Fuller and Emory, Rusby testified, if the "product known as Coca-Cola were taken into the system in repeated doses it would be injurious." Some twenty other government witnesses supporting Rusby's claim were also part of McCabe's expert list, a roster that showed he intended to win, despite rumors to the contrary. Expert after expert spoke of the risks involved in continually consuming the alkaloid, some telling the jurors about animal studies with alarming outcomes.

USDA chemist F. P. Morgan had found that a regular dose of Coca-Cola appeared to cause inflammation and lesions in the stomachs of rabbits. Boston-based toxicologist William Boos of Massachusetts General Hospital had looked at caffeine's effect on frogs, finding that it interfered with heart rate and affected the nervous system and caused "reflex irritability." The jurors also heard about unsettling effects on humans. "I consider caffeine a habit-forming drug," said Dr. John Musser of the University of Pennsylvania. His patients who drank caffeinated beverages rarely consumed a single glass or cup: "Once taken, there is a desire or craving of the system to repeat the dose." Dr. Oliver Osborne of Yale Medical School testified that several glasses of Coca-Cola a day registered above the recommended dose for caffeine set by *U.S. Pharmacopeia*. Dr. Maurice Tyrode of Harvard University testified that eight glasses of Coca-Cola contained so much caffeine that their rapid consumption was potentially fatal.

The court also heard from "Coca-Cola addicts." A patient from Philadelphia reported that he had found the soft drink a helpful stimulant—at first. "When I felt tired or fagged a glass or two of Coca-Cola would revive me. As the habit increased, I consumed about a dozen drinks a day." He sought treatment after developing insomnia and a state of constant jitters: "After I quit using Coca-Cola my general health improved and has continued to improve."

Lyman Kebler represented the Bureau of Chemistry position. "I have traveled extensively in the United States and have observed that Coca-Cola is sold indiscriminately to all comers at soda fountains, without distinction as to youth or old age, nervous or robust persons. I have seen children as young as four years old drinking Coca-Cola at fountains," Kebler said. Both as a scientist and a family man, he found this irresponsible and dangerous. He'd accompanied Fuller on the tour of the Coca-Cola plant, where he'd also been appalled by the filthy conditions; he'd been particularly struck by the spiderwebs' dangling over the vats and the workers dripping sweat all over the floors and spitting tobacco juice everywhere: "I saw no cuspidors." But Kebler had also noticed the two-hundred-pound containers of caffeine, in crystalline form, sitting alongside the cooking vats.

Like everything else in the plant, Kebler testified, the caffeine had appeared somewhat grimy. It was "not as white as the ordinary article." There was a reason, Kebler continued, that Coca-Cola had two popular nicknames. One was "dope" and the other was "Coke," and both referred, he said, to its well-known stimulant effects. That had been true when it contained cocaine and it was true now. "Caffeine is a drug having poisonous tendency," Kebler said.

Coca-Cola was angrily prepared to counter these accusations. Its defense began with testimony from two members of the company's founding family. First, John S. Candler, who had partnered with his brother, Asa, and other investors in forming the soft-drink company in 1892, declared that he consumed at least one glass of Coca-Cola a day—and sometimes six or more—but did not consider that evidence of addiction. He just liked it. "I have never experienced any inordinate craving for it or observed any tendency to form a habit." In other words, he stated, "My health is good."

Asa Candler's oldest son, Charles Howard Candler, who was vice president and general manager of the company, directly contradicted the government's accusations of cheapjack production standards. "About eight men, three white and five colored, are employed in making the Coca-Cola syrup," he said. "The sugar is dumped into the kettle by a Negro who has been employed since 1906. He does not chew tobacco." And that cook wore good protective gear while working on a well-cleaned factory platform, Candler added. The company called the cook, James Gaston. He said that he wore coveralls and heavy shoes while working in the factory—and for good reason. It would be dangerous to wear shoes with holes in them, he said, because "the stuff splashes out of the kettle and would scald my feet."

Candler suggested that the government was untrustworthy. Certainly he doubted the veracity of its finding of dirt and insect parts in the soft-drink syrup. And he dismissed Kebler's reference to the beverage's drug-linked nicknames as unfair. The street terms were unauthorized and unwanted by the makers of Coca-Cola. "The company has never advertised or sold Coca-Cola under the names 'Dope' or 'Coke.'" (This was true at the time; the company wouldn't trademark the name "Coke" until 1945.) Further, the company disputed the idea that it was selling just another version of a stimulant—or a toxic substance—because its formula happened to include caffeine.

It also offered a lineup of expert witnesses. Rudolph Witthaus, a New York toxicologist known for his testimony in high-profile murder trials, promised, "I know of no case of caffeine in any quantity causing death." John Marshall, of the University of Pennsylvania, one of the founders of American toxicological analysis, said that he'd tested caffeine's effect on protein metabolism and found no measurable impact. Charles F. Chandler of Columbia University, an industry-allied sixty-five-year-old chemist who had testified for the meatpackers in the oleomargarine hearings before the U.S. Senate in the 1880s, declared, "I am familiar with caffeine. It is not a toxic or poisonous substance."

Victor Vaughan, a chemist from the University of Michigan, who had earlier disputed Wiley's contention that sodium benzoate might pose a health risk, also came forward as a soft-drink company witness. In his testimony Vaughan said he'd based his analysis on the

possibility of imbibing an ounce of Coca-Cola syrup, mixed with a
cup of carbonated water, six or seven times a day. "I have no doubt
it would be stimulating to the brain and muscles, and to some extent,
possibly the kidneys, slightly, but such stimulation would be normal." Vaughan had fed guinea pigs Coca-Cola for almost four
months and, he said, seen no ill effects worth mentioning.

Coca-Cola had also hired Columbia University psychologist
Harry L. Hollingworth to run tests on caffeine's effect on human
mental processes and physical reactions. Later hailed as doing the
most impressive research presented during the trial, Hollingworth's
study involved sixteen subjects, ten men and six women, between the
ages of nineteen and thirty-nine. All had swallowed capsules daily
during a four-week period. The capsules contained either no caffeine
or caffeine in a range of different doses.

It was a classic double-blind study; neither the participants nor
Hollingworth knew who received what capsule. At regular intervals,
every subject was tested to evaluate motor skills and cognitive function. Each was also required to keep a journal recording sleep patterns and noting periods of either alertness or fatigue. By the end of
the study, Hollingworth had accumulated 64,000 data points that he
presented to the slightly stunned jury through a series of complex
charts.

The psychologist found that caffeine did speed up motor reactions briefly. Its influence on cognitive processes was more gradual
and more persistent. He described caffeine as a mild stimulant that,
overall, seemed to enhance general performance across the spectrum
of given tasks, without measurable harm that he could identify. The
journalists covering the trial, many of them regular coffee drinkers,
reported these results in great detail.

John F. Queeny, founder of the Monsanto Chemical Company in
St. Louis, followed Hollingworth. The company was, as it was proud
to say, the maker of both saccharin and the crystalline caffeine used
by the soft-drink company. Queeny testified that Coca-Cola's

caffeine contents remained modest compared with other beverages such as coffee and tea. His company's chemical analyses suggested that a strong cup of tea, for instance, could contain almost three times the caffeine in a glass of Coca-Cola.

The company then focused on consumers. A group of Atlanta doctors testified that none of the children they treated ever drank Coca-Cola—a counter to Kebler's assertions. Witnesses also included ten carefully selected adult Atlanta residents—ranging in age from twenty-four to fifty-seven. These upright citizens, Coca-Cola's attorneys said, had been consuming their product for an average of seven years, some drinking fifteen or more glasses a day. None of them had reported ill effects. The physicians hired by Coca-Cola were also confident that the adults who did imbibe Coca-Cola handled it without side effects. One doctor told of a traveling salesman who regularly knocked back nearly two dozen drinks a day. Or as the *Chattanooga Daily Times* put it—to the undoubted annoyance of the Candler family—the salesman had consumed "20 dopes daily" but remained in "perfect health."

Before McCabe could assemble his rebuttal witnesses, Coca-Cola's lawyers made a surprise appeal to Judge Edward T. Sanford to dismiss the case. They did not argue that Coca-Cola had proved that caffeine was harmless or that heavy soft-drink consumption was without risk; clearly that remained a matter of scientific debate. Rather the company now made an entirely new argument: The scientific debate was irrelevant because the company had made a new reading of the law. Coca-Cola now argued that caffeine was not an "added ingredient" but a basic part of the soft-drink formula. The law addressed additives and adulterants. If caffeine was not an additive, as Coca-Cola now argued, then the Agriculture Department had no standing to prosecute.

It was something of a legal gamble at this stage of a three-week trial. But to the surprise—not to say shock—of those on both sides, Judge Sanford readily accepted the company's position. He agreed that the inclusion of caffeine in a soft-drink formula—regardless of whether the compound posed a health risk—was legally different from, say, adding formaldehyde to milk or copper sulfate to canned peas. On Friday, April 7, the day after Coca-Cola presented the new argument, Sanford dismissed the jury and closed the case: "I am constrained to conclude that the use of the word 'added,' when applied to poisonous and deleterious ingredients . . . cannot be considered meaningless."

COCA COLA IS THE WINNER, announced the *Chattanooga Daily Times* headline, adding with some partisan pleasure, "Case is practically thrown out of court." The paper speculated that the judge had taken sides, to protect not only the soft-drink company but also American business in general. The *Daily Times* claimed to have discovered that "if the government proved successful in the Coca-Cola case, it was the first of 2,500 prosecutions planned." That number was a journalistic exaggeration, but it was true that the Agriculture Department had hoped for a clear legal precedent that would support better enforcement of the law and smooth the way for other cases.

For once, George McCabe and Harvey Wiley were united in dismay; on the same day that Sanford announced his decision, McCabe announced the government's decision to appeal the Coca-Cola verdict.

The defeated delegation from the Agriculture Department had barely returned from Chattanooga to their jobs in Washington when the increasingly contentious saccharin question reemerged—and this time in ways that did not please Monsanto and its allies. A just-completed report by the Remsen Board, based on a review initiated at industry request, had found that the sweetener did indeed present a potential health risk if consumed in large enough doses.

And those large doses were made the more likely because of the common practice among food processors of substituting cheaper saccharin for more expensive sugar without informing the consumer, leading to a cumulative exposure. This was what Wiley had been warning about since before his unfortunate confrontation with the previous president. It underscored not just the chief chemist's belief that saccharin could damage health but also his near obsession with truth in labeling. The finding, from the supposedly industry-friendly Remsen Board, headed by saccharin codiscoverer Ira Remsen himself, was a shocker to McCabe and Wilson—and one that infuriated Monsanto's head, John Queeny.

It had come about in part because Remsen had prudently recused himself from the investigation. The lead investigator had been board member Christian Herter, a physician on the faculty of Columbia University and cofounder of the *Journal of Biological Chemistry*. In December 1910 Herter had unexpectedly died, at age forty-five, of what his doctors called a neurological wasting disease. His friend and colleague Otto Folin, a professor of biological chemistry and molecular pharmacology at Harvard University, had then completed the research.

Swedish-born Folin had used a Poison Squad–style method of adding capsules containing saccharin to the meals of healthy male volunteers. A tally of the results after four weeks found that tiny amounts of saccharin (less than 0.3 grams) taken daily did not produce any signs of obvious injury. In trace amounts, Folin reported, it appeared to be safe.

But in subjects given higher doses, both Herter in the early stages of the study and Folin in his follow-up work had recorded signs of digestive upset, ranging from nausea to stomach pain. Further, such higher doses were a real possibility for average American consumers, the report reminded the authorities, given that unlabeled saccharin was now found in products including canned fruits and vegetables, jams, jellies, wines, and other spirits. The Remsen Board also, again to industry dismay, concurred with Wiley that saccharin lacked any of the nutritive (caloric) value of natural sugar and therefore lessened the quality of food.

McCabe had long believed, along with Theodore Roosevelt and

Secretary Wilson, that saccharin was relatively harmless, too benign to merit Agriculture Department regulation. That belief had become a de facto federal policy, reflected in the way that the U.S. War Department now included saccharin tablets in its military rations. But department policy was also to consider the Remsen Board findings the final word. In late April, just three weeks after the Coca-Cola trial ended, the Agriculture Department announced that starting in July 1911, all foods containing saccharin would be considered adulterated and therefore subject to prosecution.

Queeny, energized by the Coca-Cola trial, hurried to Washington to mount an immediate counterattack. He summoned Monsanto's new attorney, Warwick Hough, the same Hough who had so ably represented the liquor wholesalers on the whiskey question. Together they gathered a cadre of chemical and food industry representatives, secured a meeting with Wilson, and asked the secretary to rethink the decision. First they contended that the government had moved too fast. They recognized that Wilson was a supporter of the Remsen Board. But the manufacturers, Hough now said, had a right to read and respond to the Remsen report before a rule was issued. Second he asserted that if the rule was to be issued, it should be amended to allow industry time to adapt, particularly time to gradually sell and reduce existing saccharin inventories.

Following the Coca-Cola debacle, Wilson was reluctant to rush into another industry showdown. He accepted both points. Following the meeting, and without consulting either Wiley or Ira Remsen, the secretary announced that the saccharin ban would be delayed until January 1912. He also reassured the business leaders that the Remsen Board had not been co-opted by the overly purist Wiley faction. "I want to say frankly to you gentlemen," Wilson told the assembled group of saccharin industry representatives "that the referee board was organized and put into action for the very purpose of conserving the interests of manufacturers." He then took a sly swipe at Wiley. The board, he added, was there to give industry a "sane hearing."

The conversation was meant to be private, and Wilson would deeply regret both that it didn't stay that way and, even more so, the reason it became national news. The exchange would soon be reported during a Senate investigation of a scandal at the Agriculture Department, one that would eventually involve not only the secretary and his underlings but also the president, drawing unwanted comparisons to the political storm over Taft's 1910 firing of forestry chief Gifford Pinchot.

This new mess—and it would be publicly revealed to be one of many in the Agriculture Department—grew out of a plot hatched by Dunlap, backed by McCabe and Wilson, with the goal of removing Wiley and his allies from the department. The ill-managed conspiracy was rooted in the Coca-Cola trial and particularly focused on the government's prominent expert witness, Henry Rusby, the prosecution's prized critic of caffeine.

At first Rusby had refused to testify because of a reduction in federal pay for scientific consultants. The rate for such work had been $20 a day under Roosevelt. Taft's thrift-minded attorney general, George W. Wickersham, however, had cut it to a mere $9 a day. With reluctance, Rusby had accepted the lower pay for his drug-analysis work for the government. He thought it too important to give up, he explained. But he said he couldn't afford to accept so little for testifying in the Coca-Cola case. At that rate, by the time he had paid for unreimbursed travel from New York to Tennessee, not to mention hiring a substitute to teach his classes, it would be a money-losing endeavor.

Wiley pointed out to McCabe that Wickersham's ruling allowed for some independence; several federal departments, also confronting witness reluctance, were still paying $20 a day for trial testimony. But McCabe refused to consider any additional money for chemistry experts. So, quietly, Wiley's lieutenant Willard Bigelow devised a work-around arrangement. The bureau would hire Rusby for an annual fee of $1,600 a year. This would cover any expert testimony and all analytic work that might be required over the next year.

The Agriculture Department's respected pharmaceutical expert, Lyman Kebler, wrote to Rusby, urging him to take the offer and pointing out that the flat fee would guarantee a regular monthly stipend no matter what the workload. "Personally, I am of the opinion that your new option is much better than the old." Rusby accepted the deal and Wiley approved it, making a point of sending it to the department secretary. Wilson signed off as well, although, once the scandal blew up, he would hastily deny responsibility, saying that he had not been fully informed about the details.

The correspondence and records regarding the Rusby arrangement were filed in Wiley's office before he left for Tennessee. There, Frederick Dunlap "discovered" them while searching through the chief chemist's documents when he was gone. Dunlap was serving as acting bureau chief while Wiley attended the Coca-Cola trial, and he had requested and received access to Wiley's office. After pulling the Rusby file and studying the arrangement, Dunlap—knowing of Wilson's discontent with the chief chemist—realized that he could use Rusby's hiring arrangement as the basis for charges that the chief chemist and his allies had defrauded the government.

In May 1911, he prepared a memo accusing Wiley, Kebler, and Bigelow of illegal misuse of government money, carefully keeping his action secret. Dunlap had his memo typed outside the department so that none of the secretaries or clerks—whom he had found to be distressingly loyal to Wiley—knew anything about it. He then took the memo to Wilson. The agriculture secretary did indeed see Dunlap's memo as a political gift, an opportunity to remove a perpetual thorn in his side.

Not surprisingly, Wilson also decided to keep the memo secret from Wiley and his staff, referring it directly to the department personnel committee chaired by McCabe. The solicitor, also weary of Wiley's endless arguments, instructed the committee to find that

Wiley, Kebler, and Bigelow had acted "in defiance" of Wickersham's ruling on pay. McCabe recommended that Rusby's contract be declared invalid, that Kebler be demoted, and that Wiley and Bigelow be offered the opportunity to resign. Wilson then reported the affair to Wickersham and asked him, as the country's attorney general, to move the recommendations forward.

It was a politically fraught recommendation, as all would recognize belatedly. Wickersham carried the scars of the embarrassing Pinchot affair, in which he had favored the controversial firing, but his critics would complain that he appeared not to have learned from the experience. Major Archie Butt, an aide to Taft, described the attorney general as having the "political judgment of an ox." Despite that earlier fiasco, in mid-May Wickersham wrote to Taft supporting McCabe's decision.

It was the president himself who hesitated. He had warned Wilson earlier about having "too great of a disposition to charge people with bad faith and too great encouragement to newspaper controversy." Taft remembered well the catastrophic fallout of the Pinchot decision and, recognizing that Wiley too was immensely popular in the country, saw a real risk of repeating it. He didn't need another political struggle, especially within his own party, with an election year approaching. Also, Taft was himself a legal scholar. The president worried that Wilson's procedure in this case had violated due process. None of the accused employees had been shown any of the charges against them or allowed to respond to them. Further, some of Taft's most trusted confidants, such as U.S. senator W. Murray Crane of Massachusetts, had recently warned him that legislators were beginning to consider the Agriculture Department something of a snake pit.

Taft took some weeks to consider the recommendation. Finally he decided to proceed—but with caution, and with an eye to due process. On Monday, July 11, 1911, the president ordered Wilson to inform his subordinates of the accusations and proposed actions. No decisions would be made until the accused scientists had a chance to respond. Even so, Taft expected some blowback, maybe some bad press. But, as with the earlier Pinchot decision, he underestimated the popularity of the civil servant involved and the extent of public anger that would greet the news. Although not, perhaps, as much as James Wilson had done.

# Fourteen

# THE ADULTERATION SNAKE

## 1911–1912

———•———

*How I wonder . . .*

After he received the president's instructions, Wilson had no choice but to inform the bureau chemists of the impending charges. He decided to have McCabe handle the problem. The attorney waited until week's end, hoping to deliver the news and then escape for the weekend. Wiley was not at the department on the afternoon of Friday, July 15. He had left with Anna for a few days at Grasslands, their Virginia farm. As a shocked Kebler and Bigelow absorbed McCabe's news, the solicitor indicated that he had no wish to confront Wiley in any case. Perhaps one of his subordinates might want to relay the details to their boss.

The next day Bigelow drove unhappily to Grasslands. As he would recall it, he was shocked once again by Wiley's reaction. The chief chemist sat silently, carefully reading through the written charges. Then, to Bigelow's surprise, he leaped up, waving the papers above his head, shouting, "Victory, victory!"

Walking the farm's sunny fields with Bigelow, Wiley explained: For years there'd been rumors of political plots against Wiley and his work. Now he had clear documentation of an actual plot, one that included Dunlap rummaging through his desk, secret meetings, and trumped-up charges. If he handled it right—and he'd been in federal service long enough to think he could—his enemies had just put a weapon in his hands. Back at his desk on Monday, he was even more confident. He was also touched to find himself surrounded by secretaries, clerks, other bureau scientists, and officials from other sections within the department, all of them offering to help prepare a defense. To the bureau's chief clerk, Fred Linton, who offered his services, Wiley simply smiled his thanks. "We need no defense," he said. "I am planning an attack."

That Wednesday, July 20, the *New York Times* broke the carefully leaked story. "After having failed in many vigorous attempts to separate Dr. Harvey W. Wiley, the pure food expert, from his place at the head of the Bureau of Chemistry, his opponents seem in a fair place to at last achieve their desire," it said, describing the plot in detail. If his opponents succeeded, Wiley's resignation "will be hailed with delight by the food and drug adulterers and misbranders from all over the country." The story quoted Rusby, who defended the pay arrangement, and Wiley, who emphasized that Wilson had approved the compensation. The secretary, the paper reported, refused to answer any questions at all.

Newspapers nationwide picked up the story and expanded on it, painting a portrait of corruption not by the dedicated food chemists but by Wilson, McCabe, and Dunlap. The *Evening Star* of Washington, DC, reported that other cabinet secretaries in the Taft administration had begun ducking for cover. "They . . . showed a tendency to sharply criticize Secretary Wilson for not having settled the whole thing without letting it get outside of his department." The *Evening Star* article also trumpeted the fact that the federal Agriculture Department had spent more than $175,000 (more than $4 million in today's dollars) on the Wilson-backed Remsen Board. Ira Remsen alone had received an $11,631 annual salary (more than twice

Wiley's) and been given $4,000 in expenses. Board members Russell Chittenden and John Long had both received more than $13,000 in salary and a combined $15,000 in expenses. The remaining board members had received almost $10,000 each in salary and an average $4,000 each in expenses. The *Evening Star* also revealed, with some glee, that the members' expense accounts covered—in addition to monkeys, dogs, ice cream, Belgium peas, and electric griddles—chiffoniers (mirrored chests of drawers) and horoscopes.

Embarrassed and angry, Ira Remsen called reporters into his office at Johns Hopkins to decry what he saw as an unwarranted, gratuitous attack. He received a chilly hearing from the DC newspapers. In fact, *Evening Star* wasn't finished digging up dirt. It next reported on the existence of the attorney general's memo that Wilson and Taft had tried to keep secret, the one warning that the Remsen Board payment system was illegal. An *Evening Star* correspondent who had attended Wilson's early meeting with the saccharin makers now revealed just how industry-friendly the arrangement was, quoting the Secretary telling the businessmen that "the Remsen referee board was organized for the purpose of conserving the interests of manufacturers." When some Wilson supporters expressed doubt about the accuracy of the statement, the Agriculture Department stenographer who had been in the meeting confirmed that the secretary had said exactly that.

Such revelations further stoked public outrage. Wiley received encouragement and offers of support from fellow chemists, from state food commissioners, from the director of publicity at the Shredded Wheat Company—"You have had a hard struggle against the manufacturers of impure foods and drugs and we don't propose to desert you at this critical moment"—from women's groups, from the head of Old Dutch Mill Coffee Roasters—"I shall do all I possibly can to aid the work"—from medical societies and insurance executives—"I am prompted to write you personally about the disgraceful and detrimental exposition now being conducted at the nation's capital."

President Taft was also inundated with messages of support for

Wiley. The telegrams received at the White House that week didn't deviate from that point. From the board of trustees of the American Medical Association: "to express the hope that Dr. Wiley, Chief of the Bureau of Chemistry, will be continued in office as the chief exponent in the execution of the pure food law. The manufacturers of impure foods and drugs would rejoice in his dismissal." From the American Association for the Advancement of Science's committee on national health: "The services of Dr. Wiley and Dr. Rusby are of such value we earnestly hope that no action be taken against them. We respectfully urge that a technicality ought not to be employed to afford a reason for dismissing two such honorable and loyal servants." From the president of the Florida Board of Pharmacy: "I wish to assure you of my full confidence in Dr. Wiley. I feel that after due personal investigation by yourself you will find the charges groundless." From the pastor of the Methodist Episcopal Church in south Baltimore: "Dr. Wiley is worth more to the people of this country than the whole aggregation of his traducers combined." From a chemical engineer in New York City: "I most respectfully and earnestly request that your Excellency see that Dr. Wiley not be hampered in the prosecution of the splendid work he has been doing for more than a quarter century to protect the food and drug supply of this country." From Ballard and Ballard Company, a flour mill in Louisville, Kentucky: "We think it would be a public calamity for Dr. Wiley to be allowed to leave the service." Not unexpectedly, Alice Lakey also telegraphed the president that Wiley's removal would cause "manufacturers who wish to deprive the law of its efficiency" to rejoice.

The same scenario played out in Congress. A consulting engineer in Pottsville, Pennsylvania, wrote to his congressman, Robert Difenderfer, that the charges against Wiley were so childish and overwrought that he thought the accusers should instead be dismissed. Difenderfer replied, "The case against Dr. Wiley, to which you refer, is only another evidence of the infamies that are so evident and have grown to such mammoth proportions in the last few years that it seems appalling that such a system could be propagated in a country such as ours. . . . It seems to me the minute a man has the courage to attack dishonesty, he becomes a mark."

Congressman William Hughes of New Jersey wrote to Wiley: "Just a line to let you know that I am in hearty sympathy with you and the work you have been doing. If there is anything I can do to help you defeat the 'Poison Brigade' let me know." Congressman Burton Harrison of New York wrote, "I observe your enemies are trying to put a crimp in you. You have a lot of friends in the House and perhaps we can turn the crimping process on the other fellows." And Congressman Ralph W. Moss of Indiana, chairman of the House Committee on Expenditures in the Department of Agriculture, scheduled a hearing in which he promised a thorough investigation of internal politics at what appeared to be a very troubled agency. The *Wall Street Journal* suggested that for the good of the service, James Wilson should resign. And "if Mr. McCabe is a sample of the growths fostered by the Department of Agriculture, some weeding out might be in order."

Appalled, George Wickersham wrote to President Taft, apologizing for pitching the administration into "all the worriment of another Pinchot affair." But although Taft was annoyed with his attorney general, he was angrier with Wilson. Taft wrote bitterly to his wife, Nellie, who was at their "summer White House" in Massachusetts, that Wilson was "as weak as water and shows how poor a secretary he is. He has very little grasp of his department. I ought to get rid of him but I don't know how I can do so now."

The Moss committee hearings on "expenditures in the Department of Agriculture" now became front-page news, filled with daily dramatic detail. In a story rather unfortunately headlined HAD GIRL ON GRILL, the *Evening Star* reported testimony by USDA stenographers who said McCabe had taken them into his office, locked the door, and grilled them about any possible secret doings of Wiley,

Kebler, and Bigelow. Other employees testified about McCabe's "third degree methods," including bringing in a fake Secret Service agent to threaten them and hiring private detectives to spy on them. Kebler testified that McCabe had told him that sharing information with any member of Congress or any U.S. attorney was a fireable offense. He was "arrogant and domineering," Kebler said, and deliberately intimidating.

The *Washington Star* wrote, "Lawyer McCabe has been bossing the whole department," and the *New York Times* said, "By the clever framing and manipulation of departmental rules, he [McCabe] became the sole judge of whether cases against manufacturers of food and drugs should be prosecuted."

McCabe admitted that he had refused to prosecute more than five hundred cases recommended by the chief chemist, but he pointed out that hundreds of other recommendations had been either prosecuted or worked out in arbitration or more informal discussions. He also admitted that he had blocked Wiley from appearing in court hearings regarding preservatives, notably sodium benzoate, because he didn't want him contradicting Remsen Board findings. But he absolutely denied that he had "the real power" in the department. That belonged to Wilson. Secretary Wilson, who was called next, admitted to the committee that he'd suppressed the publication of almost twenty reports from the Bureau of Chemistry. He'd also suppressed information internally, blocking Wiley and his men from knowing much about the Remsen Board or its findings. But like McCabe, he blamed those decisions on Wiley. The chief chemist had become too stringent, too rigid, and too prone to become angry over such matters, he said. Wilson explained that he was a man who preferred to operate in a more peaceful atmosphere than Wiley allowed.

The committee also called Frederick Dunlap, who admitted that he'd drafted the accusatory memo, the main subject of the hearings, in secret and delivered it to Wilson on a day when he knew that Wiley would be out of town. He also acknowledged that when he and

Wiley disagreed on a matter of food safety, he routinely deferred to McCabe in making the final decision on any regulatory issue. "And Mr. McCabe is not a chemist, is he?" asked one committee member pointedly. "Not that I ever heard of," Dunlap replied. Legislators from both sides of the aisle, the newspapers reported, were unanimous in finding that the Agriculture Department was a personal and political mess.

Taft, who had joined his wife for the summer in Massachusetts, followed the daily newspaper reports as well as consulted with his staff as he tried to decide how best to handle the situation. In mid-September 1911, just before returning to Washington, he announced his decision on the charges related to the Rusby affair. Considering the tenor of the Moss hearings, his findings surprised no one. WILEY UPHELD BY PRESIDENT IN RUSBY CASE read the *New York Times* headline.

In a letter to Wilson that he made available to the public, the president declared that he'd found no evidence of conspiracy to defraud the government in the payment arrangements to Henry Rusby. In fact, Taft wrote, the payment of the Remsen Board was among many precedents that showed that Rusby's contract was justified by ordinary government procedure.

By presidential order, Rusby and Wiley both were cleared of all charges. In a diplomatic concession to Wilson, Taft recommended that Kebler and Bigelow be reprimanded for overzealousness in recruiting the New York expert, although he also praised their effort to pay an expert witness fairly. The president stopped short of ordering a reorganization of the department or punishing McCabe or Dunlap. But he signaled his dissatisfaction. "The broader issues raised by the investigation, which have a much weightier relation than this one on the efficiency of the department, may require much more radical action than the question I have considered and decided," Taft wrote.

In response, Wiley issued a statement to the Associated Press, thanking the president for his sense of justice, the American press for "the practically unanimous support which it has given me during this ordeal," and especially the many people who had written to encourage him. Neither James Wilson nor George McCabe responded to requests for comment, which the newspapers made a point of emphasizing in their coverage of Taft's decision.

"My heartiest congratulations," wrote the muckraking journalist Samuel Hopkins Adams, whose exposé of patent medicine, "The Great American Fraud," had been central to some of the regulations written into the food and drug law. "I didn't think Taft had the nerve to come out flat-footed. The slap against Kebler (and the same for Bigelow) was unfair, I thought, and rather cowardly. But everyone who knows Taft will read between the lines and know it for what it is worth. A slight sop to the forces of the enemy."

In the public view, Wiley had triumphed against his oppressors. Certainly he'd kept his job. But privately he was keenly aware that he hadn't really shifted the balance of power regarding food regulation. The "adulteration snake," he told one reporter, still coiled through the department. Again he wondered how long he could persevere. Along with the letters of encouragement and congratulation, he began receiving job offers—most of them from businesses in the food and drink industry. The R.B. Davis Company (makers of phosphate food products, baking powder, and starch) of Hoboken, New Jersey, for example, proposed to create a position for him and match his $5,000-a-year government salary, if he wanted to "leave the pressures of federal service." He firmly declined them all, replying to R.B. Davis that "I am still in my present job and I intend to hold onto it until I am forcibly ejected." But at home, talking to Anna, he was thinking very seriously about whether he had outlasted his usefulness.

In January 1912 the Moss committee issued its report, reinforcing the president's decision and approving Taft's dismissal of the Rusby charges. The committee dismissed any suggestion that the bureau chemists had conspired to defraud the government. It emphasized the importance of Rusby's testimony in the Coca-Cola case, praising the bureau's strategy to accommodate him as part of an essential effort to build a strong regulatory system for food and drink: "One cannot withhold one's sympathy with an earnest effort on the part of Dr. Wiley to pay proper compensation and secure expert assistance in the enforcement of so important a statute, certainly in the beginning, when questions arising under it are of capital importance to the public."

The committee reprimanded McCabe and Dunlap for their heavy-handed tactics. It joined the president in criticizing Wilson for the secretive support lent to industry by the Remsen Board and for his direction of that body, which, said the report, often paralyzed reasonable enforcement of the law. It characterized the department as poorly managed, which was yet another embarrassing blow to Wilson, but it did not find that the USDA was, as Wiley suggested, entirely in thrall to industry. Wilson, McCabe, and Dunlap might not believe in Wiley's consumer-before-all approach, but they had prosecuted businesses, worked to build a regulatory structure, proved willing to fight questionable practices such as the bleaching of flour all the way to the Supreme Court. A willingness to work with manufacturers, the committee noted, was not always the evidence of corruption that Wiley and his allies believed. Sometimes it was merely evidence of practicality.

Publicly Wiley declared the double whammy of Taft's decision and the committee report a "sweeping victory" for his side. To his friends he was a little more cautious, writing to one of them that "while the verdict was not as sweeping as I had hoped it is nevertheless a good one."

Following the Moss report, Wilson made visible efforts to repair the damage. He removed McCabe from the Food and Drug Inspection Board and appointed an ally of Wiley's, Roscoe Doolittle, director of the department's New York–based food laboratory, as its chairman. But he kept Dunlap on the board in order to maintain some of that practicality. And Wilson, who had served under three presidents, remained as agriculture secretary. (He'd privately asked to finish out the current term, his fourth, and Taft had consented.) He calmly assured the president and Congress that the situation in the department was much improved. But the calm was deceptive; he was furious about having his reputation so tarnished. Within a few weeks following Taft's decision, Wiley was increasingly aware of that, noting that Wilson had become "alertly antagonistic."

"I found that my recommendations to the secretary were being returned unapproved," he said. It was obvious that "I would have continually to fight my own associates on the Board of Food and Drug Inspection in carrying out my orders and policies." The scandal, the Moss hearings, the fact that little had changed at the Agriculture Department—all had made it clear to both Wiley's allies and his enemies that though he had survived the attack, though he had undaunted public support, he lacked vital internal support for his strict approach to food regulation.

"Be sure of your ground for the conspirators will not cease to lay pitfalls for you," warned J. G. Emery, Wisconsin food and dairy commissioner. The food industry was now neatly sidestepping Wiley on a regular basis, taking complaints directly to Wilson. The chief chemist had just recently tried to regulate mold and dirt in grain shipped across state lines, and Wilson, responding to pressure from the industry, had directly overruled him again.

Wiley had declared that he would stay as long as the department would have him, but he had begun to see the futility of remaining in such a hostile environment. He wasn't interested in going to work for a baking soda company, but he thought there might be somewhere else that he could make a difference. If he could find a place that would allow him to fight as he chose, he wondered if he should now explore such opportunities. And there were also welcome family reasons for considering a job that might pay better. To their surprise and delight, he and Nan were expecting their first child in the spring.

The women's magazine *Good Housekeeping*, known for its crusading tendencies, had offered him $10,000 a year—double his current salary—to become director of a new department of "food, health and sanitation." It would include his own state-of-the-art laboratory, based in Washington, DC, that would test products on the market, offer advice to readers on their safety and merits, and perhaps even award them a *Good Housekeeping* "seal of approval" where deserved. He could also write a column in the magazine on both food safety and nutrition.

The Redpath Lyceum Bureau, an agency that booked lecturers and performers into halls across the country, also contacted Wiley to offer him a lucrative speaking contract. The agency, founded as the Boston Lyceum Bureau in 1868, had represented such luminaries as Mark Twain, Julia Ward Howe, Susan B. Anthony, and Frederick Douglass. Wiley was honored by the opportunity to join that list. It was a pleasant reminder that, due to both his public successes and his public failures, he had become an influential celebrity.

Anna Wiley was also becoming a well-known reform advocate. She was president of the Elizabeth Cady Stanton Suffrage Club in Washington, DC, lobbying not just for women's right to vote but also for bank reform. In December 1911 she'd also been elected to the Congressional Committee of the American Women's Suffrage Association. "As I read the papers and I diagnose the signs, I find you are slowly but surely becoming known as the husband of Anna Wiley," wrote Nathaniel Fowler to his friend Wiley. Fowler, a Boston-based journalist and author, joked that Wiley would soon find himself featured in a new *Ladies' Home Journal* series titled "Unknown Husbands of Great Women."

By March 1912, rumors had begun circulating again that Wiley might finally leave the department. Wilson, who might have welcomed such news, was slow to believe it. He told his friends that Wiley himself had planted such rumors, probably to angle for further concessions. When a reporter for the *New York Times* asked the secretary about the possibility of the chief chemist resigning, Wilson snapped, "That story isn't ripe yet." But on the morning of March 15, Wiley sent a notice to his favorite newspaper reporters, telling them that he had an important message to share. He also prepared a simple resignation letter for Wilson, extending not even a day's notice to his employer: "I hereby tender my resignation as chief of the bureau of chemistry at a salary of $5,000 per annum in the Department of Agriculture, to take effect at the termination of the 15th day of March 1912."

He asked for a meeting with Wilson to deliver the letter. The two men talked for almost an hour. Wiley said, as he had before, that he would gladly stay if Wilson would clear the department of opponents of honest regulation, particularly Dunlap—whom he described as a sneak and a liar—and the equally devious George McCabe. Wilson replied, as he had before, that he would not consider it, that he did "not see his way clear" to dismissing the people in question. At the end of the discussion, the secretary scrawled, "Your resignation is accepted," on Wiley's note and handed it back to him.

Later that day—mostly for the benefit of the press—Wiley released a "supplementary statement" of resignation, emphasizing his long dedication to the civil service and adding, "It is also a matter of extreme gratification to me that in the twenty-nine years which I have been chief of this bureau, there has not been a cent, to my knowledge, wrongfully expended." He reminded reporters that he was quitting the government, but not the cause. "I propose to devote the remainder of my life with such ability as I may have at my command and with such opportunities as may arise, to the promotion of the principles of civic righteousness and industrial integrity, which underlie the Food and Drugs Act."

Wiley also made a point of thanking Wilson for "the personal kindness and regard which he has shown me during his long connection with the department." He was grateful that one of his most trusted lieutenants, Willard Bigelow, had been appointed acting chief of the Bureau of Chemistry in his absence. But, he added, the situation in the department had become intolerable for him, and he saw no other "self-respecting" course but to leave.

To members of the press who gathered for an afternoon news conference at the department, Wilson praised Wiley's long and valuable service but said that he had chosen to respect his chief chemist's decision. He had told Wiley, he said, "that I should not for a moment stand in his way" if he felt that he could better himself by resigning. "I could only acquiesce and wish him Godspeed." The listening reporters maintained their skepticism; a number of the resulting stories described the secretary as looking relieved. The *Druggist Circular* described Wilson's response to the resignation with that ironic American saying "Here's your hat, what's your hurry?"

Like Wilson, President Taft was moderate in his public statement. He praised the outgoing chief chemist, commenting, "I would be very glad if he could continue in the service of the government. I feel that I shall have difficulty finding a man to fill his place." But he then added that he was already moving to consult with university presidents in search of an appropriate replacement.

But elsewhere in the Department of Agriculture, the news brought an almost universal outpouring of grief. As McCabe and Dunlap had often noticed with irritation, Wiley had many more loyal friends on staff than they, or Secretary Wilson, could ever hope for, especially among the many women who served in clerical positions, the clerks whom he'd always made a point of treating with kindness and respect. Employees from throughout the building rushed to Wiley's office to wish him well.

WOMEN WEEP AS WATCH DOG OF THE KITCHEN QUITS AFTER

TWENTY-NINE YEARS, read the headline in the *Buffalo Courier*: "With tears streaming down their cheeks, hundreds of women clerks, many of them employed in other sections of the Department of Agriculture, filed in to say goodbye. So crowded were the elevators leading to Dr. Wiley's office that numerous women walked up four long flights of stairs." It was, the *New York Times* wrote, a remarkably affecting scene: "Some of the employees had worked with him for more than a quarter-century and they left crying like children."

Wiley's allies and supporters were both surprised and deeply disappointed by his decision. Paul Pierce wrote in *National Food Magazine* that he feared his friend had been secretly threatened or pressured out of the job. "Dr. Wiley is known to be a man of indefatigable will and courage; it is not reasonable to believe that he would thus quit under fire. . . . It is hard, therefore, to account for his strange action unless there be a cause back of it all which has not yet come to light." Alice Lakey interpreted the resignation as a triumph for Wiley's enemies, blaming the agriculture department for putting Wiley in an impossible situation: "his hands have been tied so far as possible to hinder the strict enforcement of the pure food law." Secretary Wilson and his alliance of corporate friends had worked toward this end, she said, so that the Agriculture Department, instead of enforcing the law, could "make everything easy for the food adulterer."

The *Journal of Commerce* pointedly headlined its story THE SACRIFICE OF DR. WILEY. The editor of a consumer-advocacy publication called the *Oil, Paint and Drug Reporter* began his lament by quoting from *Macbeth*: "So clear in his great office that his virtue will plead like angels, trumpet tongued, against the deep damnation of his taking off." Ralph Moss, the congressman who had chaired the investigative hearings into the Rusby case, sounded a similar note. "I regard the passing of Dr. Wiley from public service as the greatest loss that the American people have sustained in a generation," wrote Moss, who was also from Indiana. Like Lakey, though, he acknowledged that it might have been an unavoidable choice. "I have known that the conditions of administration in the Department were such that he could not remain in his place. . . . He has done more, in my judgment, than any other man in the country for mankind in general."

Wiley saved the testimonials and newspaper clippings for years, but his favorite of all the tributes was a cartoon in the *Washington Star*. It pictured his office, containing tables cluttered with test tubes and beakers. A pair of battered shoes was sitting on the floor. Next to the desk stood Uncle Sam, looking sadly down at those shoes. They were labeled as belonging to Harvey Wiley. The shoes were unmistakably oversized, unmistakably far too large for anyone else to fill.

*Fifteen*

# THE HISTORY OF A CRIME

## 1912–1938

———◉———

*. . . I wonder, what's in it.*

Theodore Roosevelt's unhappiness with Taft as president, combined with his absolute belief that he himself would do a far better job, had drawn him back into national politics. During the same spring, of 1912, he campaigned to be the Republican nominee for the fall election. His odds looked promising; he'd started sweeping presidential primaries, including in Taft's home state of Ohio.

The embattled Taft realized that just one more controversy would end his chance of staying in office. With outrage over Wiley's resignation still simmering, he put off naming a replacement to the position of chief chemist. Quietly he and Wilson replaced Bigelow as temporary acting chief, but with another ally of Wiley's—Roscoe Doolittle, who had recently taken McCabe's place on the Food Inspection Board.

In a report to Wilson that May, Doolittle reported that fakery and adulteration continued apace. Products most frequently at fault, he wrote, included "cordials containing artificial color without declaration . . . figs unfit for consumption because of worms and excreta . . . flour bleached to conceal inferiority, eggs decomposed and unfit for food, arsenic in baking powders [also in gelatin and the shellac used to give chocolate a shine], so-called egg noodles containing artificial color but little or no eggs . . . black pepper containing added pepper shells, maple products adulterated with cane products, confectionary products containing talc and unpermitted colors, misbranded mixtures of olive oil and cotton seed oil," and more.

Doolittle wasn't the only one noticing that manufacturers seemed newly emboldened. A *New York Globe* series that spring bore the headline SODA WATER SOLD TO CITY CHILDREN IS FULL OF POISONS. For the *Globe*, writer Alfred W. McCann hired chemical analysts who found that many of the "fruit syrups" used to mix fizzy drinks contained anything but fruit. Both "raspberry" and "wild cherry" extracts were mostly alcohol, glycerin, acetic acid, succinic acid, benzoic acid, alcohol, and coal-tar dyes. The drinks were heavily sweetened with unlabeled saccharin; of the more expensive sugar there was barely a trace. As McCann made a point of concluding: "There wasn't a single sign hanging at any soda fountain in New York City advertising the artificial and chemical character of the drinks."

At the Republican National Convention that June in Chicago, Roosevelt failed to unseat Taft as the nominee. Despite the fact that he'd won the popular vote in the primaries, the GOP's conservative leaders blocked Roosevelt's return to the ballot. Believing that party bosses had stolen the nomination from him, he marched out of the convention. And shortly later, declaring himself "fit as a bull moose" going into the contest, he mounted a third-party bid for president under the Progressive banner. Predictably, the GOP vote in November split between Taft and Roosevelt, allowing Democrat Woodrow Wilson to win the presidency with only 41.8 percent of the popular vote.

With James Wilson surely on his way out at Agriculture, Wiley partisans pushed for the former chief chemist to become the next secretary. Wiley's longtime foes—such as the National Association of Food Manufacturers—united instantly in opposition. The *Chemical Trade Journal* editorialized in near panic, "We cannot conceive of Mr. [Woodrow] Wilson inviting to his cabinet a secretary to create turmoil, commotion, confusion, tumult, disturbance, disquiet, annoyance, vexation, uneasiness, agitation, affliction, calamity, misfortune, anxiety, sorrow and misery. If Mr. Wilson wants that, Dr. Wiley is well-equipped."

"I have no cabinet aspirations," Wiley wrote in December of 1912, to a physician in Oregon who urged him to apply for the position. ". . . I shall hope to continue on the lecture platform and with my pen to speak a forceful word for pure food and the public health along many lines." Since taking the magazine job, he had been offered several much more lucrative industry positions—one from his longtime fan the Kentucky distiller Edmund Haynes Taylor Jr.—now past eighty but still a force in politics. But Wiley turned them all down; for the first time in many years, he said, he was enjoying his work again.

On December 11 Wiley's secretary at *Good Housekeeping* wrote to J. G. Emery, the food commissioner of Wisconsin, that Wiley was traveling but had left instructions for how to respond to any call for his return to government service. "The doctor doesn't expect that the secretaryship will be offered to him and is not a candidate in any way; in fact, he is discouraging his friends from making any efforts in that direction and his enemies are very busy in the opposition direction. The National Retail Druggists Association has passed resolutions to the effect that the doctor's appointment to the cabinet would be a national disaster."

The retail druggists' group was especially opposed to Wiley because of his longtime advocacy of honest and detailed labeling of food and drug products. Cure-all manufacturers had been fighting that requirement ever since the passage of the Food and Drug Act. In

1911 lawyers for the over-the-counter industry had convinced the U.S. Supreme Court that the 1906 law did not explicitly forbid "false therapeutic claims" but only misleading statements about individual ingredients. The decision sparked such public outrage that in 1912 Congress amended the act (a change known as the Sherley Amendment) to specify that "false therapeutic claims intended to defraud the consumer" were in violation of the law. Yet the industry successfully pushed back on that law too, repeatedly tying up enforcement attempts in the courts. Many Wiley advocates had urged him to return to the Agriculture Department, if not as secretary then to his old job, specifically to deal with the drug-labeling problems that continued to put so many at risk. He considered it but worried that such a move would involve a deep pay cut. As his secretary also wrote, in a message passed along from Wiley, "I do not think he would consider at all going back to the Bureau of Chemistry as it would be a great sacrifice financially."

In late December 1912, James Wilson picked Dr. Carl L. Alsberg as the new chief of the Bureau of Chemistry. Taft, in the last month of his presidency, promptly approved the appointment. Alsberg, a biochemist, had been working in the USDA's Bureau of Plant Industry and was known as a careful scientist and a far-less-flamboyant personality than his predecessor. But Alsberg surprised those expecting him to quickly drop the agenda set by the former chief chemist. He began determinedly pursuing some of the key cases that had arisen during Wiley's tenure—returning to the issues of caffeine content in Coca-Cola and the regulation of saccharin as a food additive. More than Wiley had, he would put an emphasis on the investigation and regulation of pharmaceutical products—and even Wiley's longtime supporters would come to admire the way he could do so without being hampered by political baggage. Or, as it turned out, by Wiley's long-standing opponents. Secretary Wilson, as expected, stepped down just a few days into Woodrow Wilson's term (now having served under four presidents). Frederick Dunlap also left the department later that year. George McCabe left government service in January 1913 for a position with an Oregon law firm.

President Wilson chose David Houston, chancellor of Washington University in St. Louis, to be the next secretary of agriculture. Houston kept Alsberg on as chief of the Bureau of Chemistry and—to the surprise and dismay of the food industry—the new secretary proved far less willing than Wilson to change the rules at corporate demand. This change was highlighted after a new federal policy on saccharin—banning it from foods as a nonnutritive additive with pharmaceutical properties—was formally instituted in April 1912.

Once again Warwick Hough, representing Monsanto, prepared for battle. He contacted Houston directly, pushing him to reverse that policy, which, he complained, was rooted in outdated research done during the Wiley days. Hough again cited the company position: The artificial sweetener was harmless, possibly helped preserve food, and had "value from an economic standpoint." Houston merely referred him to the new chief chemist, who dismissed such points as lacking any real merit. Alsberg countered by pointing out that the soft-drink industry was now generally using such high levels of saccharin that a consumer's daily intake, when other artificially sweetened foods were considered, could easily exceed the safe levels identified by even the Remsen Board. Following yet another hearing on the subject in June 1913, Houston further backed his chief chemist. He refused to lift the ban on saccharin and—in the face of warnings from Hough that Monsanto would fight this in court—merely encouraged Alsberg to continue building his case against it.

Meanwhile, as promised, the organization of millers that had lost the bleached-flour trial in Missouri had appealed their case all the way to the U.S. Supreme Court. In February 1914 the court issued a business friendly decision. The justices agreed that—as Wiley had always argued—vulnerable populations should be considered in drafting regulations. Flour offered a perfect example of why the most vulnerable must be considered, because the product "may be used in many ways, in bread, cake, gravy, broth, etc. . . . It is intended that if any flour, because of any added poisonous or other deleterious ingredient, may possibly injure the health of any of these, it shall come within the ban of the statute." But the court also said that just because a product contained a compound considered toxic didn't mean that said compound was harming the bread and gravy consumers. Toxic effects had to be demonstrated for the law to apply, and the burden of proof was on the government. Thus nitrates, though poisonous in large quantities, could not be considered poisonous as residues in bleached flour unless the government could prove that they were directly harming consumers. The high court concluded that in the Lexington Mill case, the government had failed to prove such harm. The ruling, though, ignored the fact that the government did not have the resources to safety-test all products and that the law did not require businesses to do so at all. It thus threatened to cripple the existing regulatory process. The justices had not only found in favor of the millers—they had set a formidably high standard, especially given the state of toxicology in the early twentieth century, for the banning of any additive as "injurious."

Appalled, Wiley sent a furious statement to the wire services, complaining that the Supreme Court seemed set on delivering "knockout blows" to the food and drug law. "To permit the unrestricted addition of poisons into foods unless such can be proved specifically injurious paralyzes that section of the law relating to harmful adulterations," he warned. "Under the present decision, a man may add traces of arsenic or strychnine to a food with impunity." Further, the court decision left the responsibility for product safety entirely in the hands of regulatory agencies. Without a legal requirement—explicit or implied—for companies to safety-test their products in advance of selling them to the public, the consumer safety net would only continue to fray.

Over the following several years, the millers and the Agriculture

Department would wrestle with how the court decision should be applied specifically to flour. They would finally agree on three main points: (1) bleached flour had to be labeled as such; (2) the government would withdraw the charge that such flour contained "deleterious" compounds; and (3) the millers would accept the original charge of misbranding their flours. Recognizing that the federal government had basically lifted all restrictions on bleaching flour, some states tried tackling the issue on their own, but to little effect. Only a few unbleached-flour cranks—Harvey Wiley being the most notable—continued to argue in favor of "natural flour." In *The Pure Food Cookbook*, published in 1914 by *Good Housekeeping*, he explained with uncharacteristic diplomacy, "I am not an enemy of white flour but I am a friend of whole wheat flour."

*Good Housekeeping* was now his public platform—and it was an effective one. At the magazine, a Hearst publication with some 400,000 subscribers, he had the title of director of the bureau of foods, sanitation and health, and he was free to write what he chose in a monthly column. Not surprisingly, he wrote in support of state food safety regulations and better federal protections. He also reported on scientific developments in food and nutrition. An essay on everything wrong with poultry was typical, beginning, "There is perhaps a greater quantity of unfit poultry offered on the American markets than any other kind of food," before exploring the causes of food poisoning and the need for sanitary practices at both farms and processing plants.

He produced a detailed series on the significance of vitamins, a new and exciting area of nutritional science. When his editors complained that housewives were unlikely to appreciate so much technical chemistry, he brushed off the criticism. Women should be treated as intelligent human beings, not as children, he stated. His contract with the magazine specified that no advertisements of food, drugs, or cosmetics would be run without his approval. He sent samples of all advertised products to a commercial laboratory for analysis. Based on the results, advertisements received a star (approved by Wiley) or not (a noncommittal rating). If he found the products deceptive or risky, he had the power to censor the ad—and he did so. He enjoyed the ability to say what he thought so freely. "I had no longer to restrict myself on account of official propriety. What I thought would be good for the people at large and for the readers of *Good Housekeeping*, in particular, I was at liberty to express in my own way."

In 1915 the members of the Remsen Board, ruthlessly ignored by the new secretary of agriculture, resigned from federal service. Carl Alsberg had ignored them too. He was less publicly combative than Wiley but he shared his predecessor's zeal for investigating business practices, which made him almost as disliked by the food-processing industry. In 1916 Alsberg authorized an undercover sting operation aimed at McCormick & Company's pepper production. The bureau's inspectors had discovered that McCormick was importing large amounts of pepper shells in addition to the pepper itself. The company refused to explain why; tests of McCormick's "Pure Black Ground Pepper" suggested impurities but at levels too low to identify. The chief chemist of the New York station, which had been tracking the imports, suggested that the Agriculture Department intercept the shells as they came into port and secretly spray them with an identifying agent. The department sprayed almost two hundred bags of pepper shells with the drug quinine and then followed their delivery to the McCormick plant in Baltimore. In May 1916 the government seized six barrels of black pepper, heavily contaminated with quinine, and charged the company with misbranding.

Embarrassed and angry, the company fought the accusation in court. And lost. The judge in the case ordered McCormick to label its adulterated product accurately as "ground black pepper containing from 10 percent to 28 percent added pepper shells." The company also was required to offer that product at a public sale to be conducted by U.S. Marshals, to pay all legal costs, and to pay a fine of $750.

The same year, Alsberg again took on the issue of deceptive use of saccharin. That spring the chief chemist ordered the seizure of a one-pound can of saccharin sent from the St. Louis Monsanto plant to a Chicago soft-drink supply house. He formally charged Monsanto with misbranding, citing the company's dishonest statements on the label, ones that described the artificial sweetener as "positively harmless" and "healthful." Alsberg's action set the stage for a legal fight over the sweetener, and there, he would later admit, he was perhaps too optimistic.

But he, Wiley, and just about everyone involved in consumer protection had been buoyed by a U.S. Supreme Court decision, also in 1916, regarding the Coca-Cola case. In a decision written by Chief Justice Charles Evans Hughes, the court overturned the lower court's finding that the soft-drink company's use of caffeine was merely part of a brand-name formula and therefore could not be classed as an adulterant.

The ruling had created a dangerous loophole, Evans wrote, in which any compounded product could be deemed out of reach of federal regulation. Coca-Cola, "like any formulaic product," was subject to the law's primary intent, "which was to protect the public from poisonous and deleterious substances which might pose a danger to public health." Further, Evans declared, "Coca-Cola" was not the distinctive generic name of a substance, like coffee, but the brand-name hyphenation of two common words. Caffeine, therefore, should be considered not integral to the product but an added ingredient; the Supreme Court ordered the case back for retrial.

Hoping to avoid another deluge of bad press coverage and uncertain that this time it would prevail, the soft-drink company moved to settle the case. Alsberg rebuffed the offer and instead authorized new research into the risks of caffeine. The company's lawyers, noting that the new chief chemist was known primarily as a thorough and careful researcher, again warned the Candler family that they might well lose this round. Secretly the company began experimenting with

reducing caffeine levels in the soft drink. In late 1917, surprising the
Agriculture Department, the company entered a no-contest plea to
the original charges of adulteration. And by providing proof that it
had now reduced the amount of caffeine in the drink by half, it
negotiated a final settlement to the court case.

This time the Coca-Cola machinations received little public notice. World affairs had by that time taken over the nation's newspaper headlines. In April 1917 the United States had made a belated
entry into the Great War (later known as World War I). As Alsberg
wrote to Secretary Houston, "the urgent demands of the various war
agencies" meant that most of his scientists had been reassigned to
military duty, the regulatory teams were for the most part disbanded,
and projects that had "no immediate bearing on the prosecution of
war" had been closed down. He assured his boss that enforcement of
the food law continued, however. The bureau had managed that year
to prosecute an impressive eight hundred cases of adulterated or misbranded products.

Even in the shadow of war, the Wiley family managed to annoy
a U.S. president. Anna Kelton Wiley, now the mother of two young
sons—Harvey Washington Jr. and John Preston—went to jail for
picketing the White House on behalf of women's right to vote. After
a 1917 demonstration in which she and fellow activists in the suffrage movement demanded that President Wilson stop stalling and
put his support behind equal voting rights for all, the president impa-
tiently requested an end to "women howlers" and recommended a
more dignified approach from equal-rights supporters. Wilson, who
had been reelected in 1916, had deeply disappointed voting rights
activists. He'd flatly rebuffed calls for federal action on suffrage, insisting that voting rights should be decided on a state-by-state basis.

In protest of such an unrealistic position, the militant National
Women's Political Union mounted another demonstration, one that
Anna Kelton Wiley proudly joined. Dressed in a gray carriage dress
and her best hat, she marched carrying a sign reading: MR.

PRESIDENT: HOW LONG MUST WOMEN WAIT FOR LIBERTY? On November 10 she and other protest leaders were arrested and she was sentenced to fifteen days in the city jail. On appeal, she accepted a five-day sentence. Harvey Wiley at first encouraged her to ask for a pardon and stay out of jail. But when she refused, he supported the decision. He was proud of her suffragette activities; shortly after starting at *Good Housekeeping* he'd prompted the magazine to do a feature story on her right-to-vote work: "She believes the ballot to be a necessary tool for the advancement of women." To his friends who wondered how he could let his wife and the mother of his children serve jail time, Wiley answered that "he had fought all his life for a principle and hardly could deny her the same privilege."

The U.S. entry into the Great War had helped speed its end, although not before more than fifty thousand U.S. troops had died in combat. American losses were a mere fraction of the total, however; military deaths from the more than two dozen countries involved in the war topped eleven million, and civilian deaths exceeded those. The war concluded, on notes of both relief and grief, with the Treaty of Versailles in November 1918. The following January, Theodore Roosevelt died in his sleep during a stay in his Oyster Bay, New York, home at the age of sixty. Many attributed his decline into illness to the death of a favored son during the war. NATION SHOCKED, PAYS TRIBUTE TO FORMER PRESIDENT read the *New York Times* headline. "Our flag on all seas and in all lands at half-mast."

But Harvey Wiley spared no mourning for Roosevelt, who remained central to his grievances over the fate of the food and drug law. "Even if . . . the President favored the food bill, it is perfectly clear that he took the most active part in preventing the Bureau of Chemistry from enforcing it," he would write bitterly some years after Roosevelt's death. He had been further disillusioned by Woodrow Wilson's complete indifference to issues of food safety—although being ignored by the president had tended to reduce interference and work in the Chemistry Bureau's favor. Still, when Wilson had run for reelection in 1916, Wiley had campaigned for Republican challenger Charles Evans Hughes.

Wiley, by contrast, came to appreciate Wilson's presidency, at least regarding her leading cause. In 1918, after a series of meetings with suffrage leaders, the president changed course and backed a constitutional amendment favoring women's right to vote, publicly urging Congress to draft language that would enable that action. On June 4, 1919, after much argument and presidential pressure, both houses passed an amendment granting women's right to vote, and it was sent out for ratification as the Nineteenth Amendment to the U.S. Constitution. In just over a year, the required thirty-six states ratified it—the last being Tennessee, by a single vote from a young legislator whose mother ordered him to cast it or be forever barred from the house—and it became national law on August 18, 1920.

The case against saccharin had been halted during the war, due in part to its use as a substitute sugar in military supplies, a use that Alsberg publicly criticized. He remained committed to regulating the controversial sweetener. In December 1919, his case against saccharin as a food additive at last went to court in St. Louis, home of Monsanto. Government attorneys began the trial by demonstrating how widespread the unlabeled use of saccharin was in the food supply: in sodas and ice cream, candies, cakes, pies, breads, canned fruits and vegetables, sweet wines. American consumers, often without their knowledge, now consumed the artificial sweetener with almost every meal. "Unrestricted consumption" of saccharin had been shown to be dangerous, the Agriculture Department insisted, and it had plenty of evidence in that regard.

The government's leading expert during this round was Anton Carlson, professor of physiology at the University of Chicago. Born in Sweden and with a PhD from Stanford University, Carlson was known for his evidence-based approach to toxicology. He liked to sarcastically describe scientists who theorized without studies to support their ideas as "chicks who chirp but don't scratch."

Carlson pointed out that the saccharin (an easily identifiable compound that meshed the well-known elements sodium, carbon, nitrogen, hydrogen, and oxygen) "gets into every place in the body and appears in every secretion in the body; it appears in the saliva; it may appear in the tears; it appears in the bile; just the same as it appears in the urine." If fed to goats, it appeared in their milk. In every place, in every cell, he said, it had a physiological effect. His own studies on the digestive tract found saccharin caused an increase in stomach acids and a decrease in protein absorption. He absolutely would not describe it as "positively harmless," the phrase used by the chemical industry. Monsanto's lawyers didn't attempt to rebut his studies but instead used a defense strategy inspired by the Supreme Court's bleached-flour decision. Yes, saccharin might pose some risks, they argued, but the government had failed to positively show that putting it in the U.S. food supply caused active harm. Therefore, the Agriculture Department could not restrict it.

The jury failed to reach a verdict, splitting with seven in favor of the government's case to five against. Against Monsanto's urging, the judge agreed to a new trial, and Alsberg again directed his staff to begin building a case.

For many involved in the pure-food cause, these battles had become seemingly unending, largely because of the inadequacy of the 1906 food law itself. For example, the "Wiley law," as everyone still called it, required ingredient labels but did nothing to address the problems of deceptive containers, designed to mislead consumers as to the amount of product they contained. Nor did it require manufacturers to reveal the number of ounces within those containers. Echoing the battles over the 1906 law, a "slack-fill" bill, introduced in 1919 and meant to improve regulation of such chicanery, was firmly opposed by the food industry and had failed in both houses of

Congress that year. It then failed again the following year for the same reason.

In 1921, just before Republican Warren G. Harding took office as president, Carl Alsberg, himself battle weary, resigned as chief chemist. He took a position at Stanford as founding director of its new Food Research Institute. His replacement as chief of the Bureau of Chemistry was Walter G. Campbell, the Kentucky attorney whom Wiley had selected to direct the food-inspection programs created by the 1906 law. Wiley was pleased, although the two would not always agree on how to address the limitations of the old food and drug law. Campbell, for instance, would come to believe that an updated law was needed to address the deficiencies. Wiley fiercely defended his signature legislation, insisting that it simply needed better enforcement.

In the summer of 1923, President Harding suddenly died—doctors thought probably from a cerebral hemorrhage—during a visit to San Francisco. His vice president, Calvin Coolidge, succeeded him and won 1924's election to continue in the office. Coolidge, a small-government conservative and former Massachusetts governor, had earned a well-deserved reputation as a friend to business and staunch opponent of regulation.

That same year the government's prosecution of Monsanto and saccharin again ended in a mistrial, again on a 7–5 split in the government's favor. Despite the president's reputation for siding with industry, Coolidge's secretary of agriculture, Henry Wallace, wrote to Monsanto's Queeny, saying that the department was not giving up. This was echoed by a statement from the Bureau of Chemistry that "it would be a serious mistake to accept any form of compromise which would in any way, even partially, sanction the use of saccharin in food." But the judge in St. Louis told the government attorneys that he was done with the case. He was prepared to strike it from the docket rather than revisit the issue. Further, if the government pursued it, he warned, then he was prepared to simply declare for the defendant. Angry Agriculture Department officials suspected that Monsanto, a major employer in the judge's hometown, had finally applied enough pressure to end the case in the company's favor. But they were stymied as to how to go forward.

The following year the government dropped its effort to regulate the artificial sweetener but issued a formal statement reiterating its lack of enthusiasm for the product: "The Government has much scientific evidence to show that saccharin is harmful to health and believes that it should not be used except as a drug under direction of a physician. It is sometimes prescribed for patients suffering with diabetes who demand some sweetening agent but who are prohibited the use of sugar. As a drug, saccharin has its uses. In our opinion, it has no legitimate use as food and is harmful to health." The department used its authority to formally require that saccharin be listed as an ingredient on product labels, a measure that proved surprisingly effective in limiting its use. Many food companies, rather than reveal that they were surreptitiously using saccharin, removed it from their products. Others, inspired by the government's preference for its health-related uses, began marketing saccharin and saccharin-sweetened products to diabetics and others who either needed or wanted to limit their sugar intake.

Wiley fumed over the decision to drop the case. He was increasingly disenchanted with everything about the federal approach to consumer protection. Upon Coolidge's election, he'd written him an open letter, published in *Good Housekeeping*, urging newly aggressive enforcement and a reversal of decisions that allowed nitrates, sulfites, preservatives like sodium benzoate, and additives like saccharin and caffeine in the food supply. The letter closed: "It is the crowning ambition of my career before I die to see these illegal restrictions, which now make a prisoner of the Food Law, removed and the Law restored to the functional activity which Congress prescribed for its enforcement at the time of its enactment."

Coolidge did not reply. Instead Wiley received a letter from assistant secretary of agriculture Renick W. Dunlap (no relation to Frederick Dunlap). In diplomatic language, it emphasized the department's essential support on protection issues and agreed that the compounds listed by Wiley were "for the most part undesirable from the broad general standpoint of human health and nutrition" and that to eliminate them was "an object greatly to be desired." But Dunlap also emphasized a growing consensus that the 1906 law was inadequate. Its primary enforcement mechanism—seizure of goods followed by prosecution—had turned out to be a cumbersome tool. More important was its failure to define key terms, such as "injurious," or to provide a mechanism for doing so. Due to that failure, the court decisions, notably the bleached-flour ruling, had ended up hobbling enforcement. "To bring cases and fail," Dunlap pointed out, "invited an increased employment of these [harmful] substances."

Wiley had known since before the food and drug law passed that it was flawed. He'd argued in 1906 that it should include exactly the kinds of specifics that Renick Dunlap now cited as lacking, but away from the bureau, he had grown increasingly protective of "his" law. It was a position that would alienate him from some of his longtime friends at the agency, but not one that he could bring himself to change.

Still, in 1926, at age eighty-one, he joined former colleagues in a campaign to protect the law against a new push from an old enemy. The Corn Products Company, the corporation that had persuaded Roosevelt to allow the term "corn syrup" instead of "glucose," had now persuaded a friendly Iowa senator to introduce an amendment to the food law that would have stripped away any power to regulate corn sweeteners in the food supply. The new language had been slipped in as part of an agricultural relief bill, and it specifically exempted dextrose—another name for sugar made from cornstarch, especially in its dry form—from being indicated on any label. Under the proposed amendment, dextrose would just be called sugar.

The proposal had gone through the Senate's committee process without a single dissenting vote when Wiley, Campbell, and the alarmed regulators at the Agriculture Department learned of it. They also learned that Monsanto was providing lobbying money in support of the amendment; the company hoped that this exemption would pave the way for others to follow. Walter Campbell immediately organized an Agriculture Department pushback against the amendment, warning publicly that this move was designed to mislead consumers into believing they were purchasing a cane sugar– or beet sugar–sweetened product.

Wiley, back in warrior mode, canceled plans for a Florida vacation with his family. He sounded the alarm in newspapers, giving a widely printed interview to United Press in which he said: "I had hoped to do my small share in protecting the country from the wicked actions of food adulterers but I am afraid the battle is going against us." Congress, he warned, was moving to allow food manufacturers to deliberately cheat American consumers, "mak[ing] legal the grossest kind of food adulteration in this case," opening the door for countless other cheats and basically nullifying the good done by the 1906 law.

He said the same in his *Good Housekeeping* column, he personally wrote to all senators and congressmen, and he requested a private meeting with Coolidge to urge a veto if the law did pass. He did not gain the president's help but he attracted the attention and support of Senator Matthew M. Neely of West Virginia, who took up the cause and, when the bill reached the floor of the Senate, conducted a filibuster. Throughout it Neely held a copy of *Good Housekeeping* in one hand, and he interspersed his speech with paragraphs read aloud from Wiley's column, including the plea "Why should legislation be used to deceive the public?" The proposed amendment failed shortly later. The following day, Wiley wrote a glowing note to Neely: "The country owes you a vote of thanks for your heroic and successful endeavor yesterday to block the approval of the so-called 'Corn-Sugar Bill.'"

In a 1927 efficiency move, the Agriculture Department split the old Bureau of Chemistry in two. It created a Food, Drug and Insecticide Administration to handle consumer protection duties, with Campbell as its head. The other division was the Bureau of Chemistry and Soils, with a focus on more basic agricultural research. The former chief hated the change, which he felt dismantled the agency that he had nurtured and shaped. He feared, as he wrote in his column, that the government had split and weakened the unit and would next simply set pure-food issues aside. Despite the positive signs— three years later Campbell's agency was renamed the Food and Drug Administration, a clear sign of sharpened focus—he saw nothing but his own work being undermined and dismissed. He was now eighty-two years old and he was weary of the war. He stepped down from his full-time job at *Good Housekeeping* and decided to channel his remaining energy into detailing his grievances.

Wiley poured his anger and disappointment into a self-published book, *The History of a Crime Against the Food Law*. It appeared in 1929, bearing the unwieldy subtitle *The Amazing Story of the National Food and Drugs Law Intended to Protect the Health of the People, Perverted to Protect Adulteration of Food and Drugs*. A four-hundred-plus-page tirade, it detailed the many often-vicious attacks on Wiley and derided his attackers. It revisited in detail the early corruption of the law's enforcement and leapfrogged into the enforcement failures of the 1920s.

The government had gotten it wrong, he wrote, on everything from toxic food dyes to imitation whiskeys, preservatives, labeling, corn syrup and soft drinks, and, most recently, saccharin. He decried "the ignominy and disgrace of great scientific men bending their efforts to defeat the purpose of one of the greatest laws ever enacted for protection of the public welfare." If successive administrations had not bent to industry pressure, he asserted, the government would have avoided "outraged public opinion," the American people would have become stronger and healthier, and "this History of a Crime would never have been written."

The book's bitter tone dismayed Wiley's old colleagues, but they could recognize that his weariness and anger came partly from his declining health. Suffering from heart disease, he kept mostly to his home. But he too felt that his angry screed should not be his last word. Wiley began working with freelance writer Orland "O.K." Armstrong on another book, an autobiography to be published by the Bobbs-Merrill Company of Indianapolis.

It may have been the influence of Armstrong, a social activist and reform-minded journalist (and later a member of Congress from Missouri), but the resulting work reflected a personality much closer to that of the younger Wiley—the Indiana-born chemist and occasional versifier with a lively sense of humor. It reflected his old passion to do good and his abiding belief in the power of science to benefit society. "The freedom of science should be kept inviolate," he urged in its conclusion, and he returned to his old call for moral standards in research—that science should live up to its ultimate calling, which was "to search for truth and thereby to elevate and improve mankind."

*Harvey Washington Wiley: An Autobiography* was published in late 1930, but Wiley never had a chance to hold that last book or learn how it was received. He died on June 30 of that year exactly twenty-four years to the day after Theodore Roosevelt had signed into law the Pure Food and Drug Act. He was buried in Arlington National Cemetery with a full military service, and his tombstone, on Anna Wiley's orders, bore the legend FATHER OF THE PURE FOOD LAW. She'd also asked the minister to base his final tribute in a sermon on St. Paul's words in the second Gospel of Timothy: "I have fought a good fight, I have finished my course, I have kept the faith."

Walter Campbell was at the graveside to pay his respects. Despite Wiley's late-life doubts about him, Campbell would continue to lead the fight for stronger food and drug regulation. In this he would be joined by activist groups formed in the 1930s, such as the Consumers' Union, as well as longtime Wiley allies such as the American Medical Association and the still-powerful women's organizations. New adulteration abuses would also come to light, ones that again highlighted the weaknesses of the old law. In a scathing book on the country's health policies, *100,000,000 Guinea Pigs*, the founders of the Consumers' Union stated flatly, "Pure food laws do not protect you" and provided instances of everything from fake antiseptics to mascaras thick with lead to apples tainted by arsenic-rich pesticides. The consumer group directly blamed the pro-business U.S. government for the "squeezing out of Dr. Wiley and his policies," a program that daily put American citizens at risk.

Consumer advocates renewed those charges to real effect when, horrifically, more than one hundred people—many of them children—died in late 1937, poisoned by cough syrup sweetened with the solvent diethylene glycol (often found in antifreeze). The Tennessee company that made the lethal concoction had, of course, not been required to safety-test it under the 1906 regulation. In fact, the only charge possible under the law was mislabeling; the syrup had been labeled an "elixir" despite the fact that it did not contain alcohol.

Campbell's FDA had mounted an investigation of the event and now put it to political use. He'd been pushing the administration of Franklin D. Roosevelt on this issue for years, with limited success. Now, with everyone from pediatricians to parents expressing deep anger at government inaction, the cough syrup tragedy spiraled into a national scandal, one that soon sparked passage of that better law, the Food, Drug, and Cosmetic Act of 1938. The legislation replaced and greatly expanded on the 1906 legislation, correcting many of its deficiencies and enlarging the authority of the U.S. Food and Drug

Administration. And although he did not live to see it, the new law, signed by President Roosevelt on June 25, 1938, marked the moment that Harvey Wiley's once-tiny, six-man Division of Chemistry achieved one of his long-held dreams. The newly empowered FDA would become an independent agency with the real authority to protect American citizens against risky drugs and tainted food.

Wiley might have seen, at last, in the new agency that "more perfect" regulatory structure he'd hoped would arise from the 1906 law. He would have also undoubtedly continued to harangue the FDA to pursue even more perfect protection of his fellow citizens. "I believe," he said while lobbying year after year for the first food and drug law, "in the chemistry of inward and spiritual grace. And I believe in its application to the welfare of humanity," and nothing less would do.

# EPILOGUE

The story of consumer protection in the United States is often the story of a country playing defense, an account of government regulators waking up, time and time again, to yet another public health crisis.

The 1906 food and drug law, which established federal food regulation, was propelled into being largely by a series of scandals over food processing, including the gruesomely spectacular case of the Chicago meatpackers. The 1938 law, which created the modern U.S. Food and Drug Administration, was passed following the deaths of dozens of children who were poisoned by a cough syrup legally sweetened with the antifreeze ingredient diethylene glycol. A 1956 decision by the FDA to ban some of the old coal-tar dyes arose from the sickening of children by Halloween candy that contained unsafe levels of orange and red coloring agents. A 1976 law authorizing the agency to regulate medical devices was passed after some 200,000 women reported injuries from an intrauterine birth control device called the Dalkon Shield.

More recently, the Food Safety Modernization Act (FSMA), a sweeping update to the FDA's protective authority, was signed into law after one of the most severe food-poisoning outbreaks in American history, one that continued for months—from late 2008 to early 2009—and derived from one of the country's most trusted and ordinary food staples.

The cause was a line of peanut butters made by the Virginia-based Peanut Corporation of America. The company used factories that were deliberately unregistered to avoid government attention. Many of the jars and containers of peanut butter, produced in notably unsanitary conditions, contained the pathogenic bacteria salmonella. People in forty-six states were sickened; the U.S. Centers for Disease Control and Prevention linked the products to an estimated nine deaths and up to 22,000 illnesses. To the dismay of consumers and legislators alike, the source of the contamination was identified not by the federal government but by state laboratories in Minnesota, Georgia, and Connecticut, harking back to nineteenth-century failures in enforcing nationwide consumer protection.

Two years later, in 2011, President Barack Obama signed the FSMA into law. The act once again enhanced the FDA's ability to prevent food safety problems. It included new requirements that food growers, food importers, and food processors adhere to specific, agency-determined safety practices and keep records of compliance. The first stricter rules for crop management began to go into effect in the summer of 2017, prompting some farmers—in language eerily reminiscent of early-twentieth-century complaints—to protest that the government now expected their fields to be as sterile as hospitals. Agricultural business groups have asked that the federal government tone down the regulations and expressed optimism that the current administration, under President Donald J. Trump, will do so.

During his successful 2016 campaign for the White House, Trump promised to have his cabinet "submit a list of every wasteful and unnecessary regulation which kills jobs, and which does not improve public safety, and eliminate them." His FDA commissioner, Scott Gottlieb, followed that promise by saying that while he recognizes the importance of food safety legislation he wants to "strike the right balance" in its implementation. Consumer groups now anticipate delayed and reduced protections from agencies facing deep budget cuts. The Earthjustice Institute has warned of the "Trump administration's willingness to accommodate even unfounded and partial industry opposition to the detriment of the health and welfare of people and families across the country."

Such a warning, with its mix of theatrical anger and genuine dismay, could have been written, almost word for word, by Harvey Washington Wiley more than a century ago. This sense of déjà vu, echoing down the years, should remind us of the ways that food safety practices have dramatically changed in this country—and of the ways they have changed hardly at all.

Thanks to the work of people like Wiley and his colleagues at the turn of the twentieth century, thanks to generations of consumer advocates, scientists, attorneys, journalists, and, yes, dedicated public servants, we've come a long way from the unregulated and unsafe food and drink that imperiled American citizens in the past. Today we are buffered by rules and institutions created over the past century to protect American citizens from deceit and danger in the food supply.

If we pay attention, we see signs of those protections every day, in large ways and small. Food labels, for instance, contain a wealth of information about ingredients and nutrition—not as much as some of us might want, but more than many of us will ever take the time to read. New products are safety-tested. Food-poisoning outbreaks are monitored and traced; tainted products are subject to recall; food and drug manufacturers who cause harm can be criminally prosecuted. In 2015 the chief executive of the Peanut Corporation of America was sentenced to twenty-eight years in prison for fraud, conspiracy, and the introduction of adulterated food into interstate commerce.

And these same principles, also built on lessons learned from crises, have been applied to other protective measures— environmental regulations being an outstanding example of that. About a half century after Wiley's crusade for food and drug protections, Americans became increasingly alarmed over evidence of industrial and agricultural pollution. In her influential 1962 book *Silent Spring*, Rachel Carson drew a vivid portrait of the destructive nature of untested pesticides. In 1969 Congress passed the National Environmental Policy Act, and the following year President Richard Nixon established the U.S. Environmental Protection Agency. The EPA has, over the years, been a central force in cleaning up our land, air, and water, but again new fears have risen about the agency's increasingly corporate-friendly policies. The agency administrator, Scott Pruitt, appointed by President Trump, is known as a longtime friend to the oil and gas industry. Pruitt has ordered all reference to the well-documented links between the use of such carbon-rich fuels and climate change removed from the agency website. He began his tenure by, among other actions, shutting down a program that collected information on gas emissions from industrial sites. "The number of environmental rollbacks in this time frame is staggering," said Harvard University environmental law professor Richard Lazarus after Pruitt had been in office for just six months.

We have succeeded in creating a protective system that at its best protects all of us impartially. But it's our responsibility to value and maintain that system. We still need those who will fight on the public's behalf; we still need our own twenty-first-century version of Harvey Washington Wiley—or rather a cadre of them—to fight for those protections if we are to remain safe.

And that, in part, is why stories like his remain so important today. If we are to continue moving in a direction that preserves what's best in this country, we need not romanticize the past but we must learn from what it tells us about our earlier mistakes. The people who fought to correct those long-ago errors still have lessons to share. The story of Harvey Washington Wiley, at his fierce and fearless best, should remind us that such crusaders are necessary in the fight. That the fight for consumer protection may never end. But if it does, if that long-awaited final victory is achieved, it will be because we, like Wiley, refused to give up.

# *Gratitudes*

When I finish a book, one of my first thoughts—after those of cartwheeling around the room—is to thank everyone I know for putting up with me. A book of this nature is an obsessive and often antisocial project. So as I return from this sojourn into the nineteenth and early twentieth centuries, I'd like to thank all for their patience with the time traveler.

At the top of that long list is my editor, Ann Godoff, not only for her patience but also for her deep interest and often brilliant counsel during the book-writing process; my terrific agent, Suzanne Gluck, who is ever both encouraging and wise; my husband, Peter Haugen, for his generosity and invaluable help in pulling a very messy story into a coherent one; my sons, Marcus and Lucas Haugen, for their savvy twenty-something perspective on fake food and for their help in prioritizing my enormous stack of early-twentieth-century publications with a special thanks to Lucas for his smart analysis of *What to Eat*; my former graduate student Kate Prengaman for her tireless investigations of the history of food safety, including a visit to the Library of Congress that involved days of sorting through a daunting stack of boxes from the Wiley papers; and the truly wonderful librarians in the Science Reading Room and the Manuscript Division of the Library of Congress, who collect and watch over some of our country's most important history. As always, thanks to my friends Kim Fowler, Denise Allen, and Pam Ruegg for their interest and encouragement throughout this book and others.

And a special thanks to my mother, Ann Blum, who never failed to listen to my food horror stories with grace and humor and who frequently kept me on track with the question about the book's progress, beginning, "My friends are wondering when . . ."

Finally, that there is a "when" at all owes more than I can say to the many dedicated professionals at Penguin Press. Special thanks to Casey Denis, Will Heyward, Hilary Roberts, Eric Wechter, Sarah Hutson, and Matt Boyd. They are the often unsung heroes of every book you pick up and it is a pleasure to thank them here.

# *Notes*

Harvey Washington Wiley was married to an outspoken and widely admired Washington, DC, suffragette—Anna Kelton Wiley—who had also worked for years at the Library of Congress. Not surprisingly, she donated his carefully kept and voluminous (70,000 items spanning almost 250 file containers) papers to the library. They are kept in the manuscript division there, and the online finder's guide can be found at http://findingaids.loc.gov.

In the course of researching this book, I made several visits to study these papers; many of the details in this book are drawn from letters, memos, telegrams, invitations, programs, diaries, newspaper and magazine articles, and other resources in the archive. For those interested in food, history, and public health, I also spent time at the remarkable Cookery, Nutrition and Food Technology collection at the Library of Congress, where I found everything from magazines like *What to Eat* to a collection of cookbooks that are in themselves a history of the United States: www.loc.gov/acq/devpol/cookery.pdf.

All other resources—books, papers, documents, and other publications—are described below with, on occasion, some additional context and explanation.

*Introduction*

1   **Milk offers a stunning:** Many of these outrages are cited in *The Milk Trade in New York and Vicinity*, by John Mullaly (New York: Fowler and Wells, 1853). The *New York Times* also published a series of exposés on the subject in the 1850s that reflected Mullaly's outrage in stories such as "How We Poison Our Children" (May 13, 1858). The many problems with nineteenth- and early-twentieth-century milk are noted in numerous other publications, both contemporary, such as Thurman B. Rice, "The Milk Problem," in *The Hoosier Health Officer: The History of the Indiana State Board of Health to 1925* (Indianapolis: Indiana State Board of Health, 1946), pp. 161–68, and more recently, in food safety histories such as James Harvey Young, "Mercury, Meat and Milk," in *Pure Food* (Princeton, NJ: Princeton University Press, 1989), pp. 18–39.

2   **Fakery and adulteration:** These fakeries were studied by Harvey Wiley and his chemistry group for years. He summarized many of the findings in Harvey Washington Wiley, *Foods and Their Adulteration* (Philadelphia: P. Blackiston's Sons, 1907), and in Harvey W. Wiley and Anne Lewis Pierce, *1001 Tests of Foods, Beverages and Toilet Accessories, Good and Otherwise* (New York: Hearst's International Library Company, 1914).

3   **"Ingenuity, striking hands":** La Follette's speech can be found in *Congressional Record*, 49th Cong., 1st sess., vol. 17, appendix, pp. 223–26, and is noted in Young's book *Pure Food*, which also focuses on the pure-food crusade that gained power in the late nineteenth century, notably in chapter 6, titled "Initiative for a Law Resumed," pp. 125–46.

4   **This especially galled:** The comparison of unregulated U.S. alcoholic beverages with those in Europe can be found in Charles Albert Crampton, U.S. Department of Agriculture, "Fermented Alcohol Beverages, Malt Liquors, Wine and Cider," part 3 of U.S. Department of Agriculture, bulletin 13, *Foods and Food Adulterants* (Washington, DC: Government Printing Office, 1887). Between 1887 and 1893, the Bulletin 13 series, established by Wiley, investigated dairy products, spices and condiments, alcoholic beverages, lard, baking powders, sweetening agents, tea, coffee and cocoa, and canned vegetables. These are summarized in Oscar E. Anderson Jr., *The Health of a Nation: Harvey W. Wiley and the Fight for Pure Food* (Chicago: University of Chicago Press, 1958), pp. 73–74.

4   **"this great country":** This is a quote from Frank Hume, chair of the Local Call Committee of the National Pure Food and Drug Congress of 1898. The quote is highlighted in *Pure Food,* p. 125, and the full presentation can be found in the *Journal of Proceedings of the National Pure Food and Drug Congress Held in Columbia University Hall* (Washington, DC, March 2, 3, 4–5, 1898). Further description can be found in Suzanne Rebecca White, "Chemistry and Controversy: Regulating the Use of Chemicals in Foods, 1883–1959" (PhD diss., Emory University, 1994).

6   **great food safety chemist:** Anderson, *Health of a Nation*, p. 148.


*Chapter One: A Chemical Wilderness*

11   **"I am not possessed":** This quote can be found on page 20 of Harvey Washington Wiley, *An Autobiography* (Indianapolis: Bobbs-Merrill, 1930), which served as one of the primary sources for this section. For the biographical material in this chapter, I also drew upon the letters and diaries archived at the Library of Congress and voluminous biographical material, including that found in Oscar E. Anderson Jr., *The Health of a Nation: Harvey W. Wiley and the Fight for Pure Food* (Chicago: University of Chicago Press, 1958); James Harvey Young, *Pure Food* (Princeton, NJ: Princeton University Press, 1989); and Laurine Swainston Goodwin, *The Pure Food, Drink and Drug Crusaders, 1879–1914* (Jefferson, NC: McFarland, 1999), among many other sources.

12   **"can not climb to Heaven":** Anderson, *Health of a Nation*, pp. 10–11.

14   **In 1820 a pioneering book:** Accum's *A Treatise on Adulterations of Food, and Culinary Poisons* is cited by many food safety historians as one of the most influential nineteenth-century publications. It can be found (along with its wonderful cover featuring a skull peering out of a cooking pot) as a public-domain publication on the Internet Archive: https://archive.org/stream/treatiseonadulte00a ccurich#page/n5/mode/2up. The British physician Arthur Hill Hassall built on Accum's work, publishing many accounts of toxic foods, such as candies, in the *Lancet* and summarizing those reports in *Food and Its Adulterations* (London: Longman, Brown, Greene and Longmans, 1855).

14   **"millions of children are thus":** This quote is from another book on arsenic: John Parascandola, *King of Poisons: A History of Arsenic* (Lincoln, NE: Potomac Books, 2012), p. 128. A remarkable overview can also be found in environmental historian James C. Whorton's book *The Arsenic Century: How Victorian Britain Was Poisoned at Home, Work and Play* (New York: Oxford University Press, 2010), in a chapter titled "Sugared Death," pp. 139–68.

15  "They poison and cheat": Angell's push to protect the food supply is described in Young, *Pure Food*, pp. 45–48.

16  "Not only are substances": Young, *Pure Food*, p. 51.

16  In 1881 the Indiana: Wiley's investigation of fraud in sweetening agents was titled "Glucose and Grape Sugar" and was published in *Popular Science Monthly* 19 (June 1881). The article can be found online at https://en.wikisource.org/wiki/Popular_Science_Monthly/Volume_19/June_1881/Glucose_and_Grape-Sugar. His comment about entering the fray over "Wiley's Lie" can be found on p. 151 of Wiley, *An Autobiography*.

19  "The dangers of adulteration": Anderson, *Health of a Nation*, p. 22.

21  "These were the first": Wiley. *An Autobiography*, p. 165.

21  In 1883, the Agriculture: Wiley's decision to leave Purdue, his battle with Peter Collier, including the quotes about "public attacks," his impressions of the Division of Chemistry, the political background of his start in federal service, and his decision to ban smoking can be found in Wiley, *An Autobiography*, pp. 159–75. Wiley was early in his belief that tobacco smoking was harmful to health; in 1927 he even warned that it might contribute to cancer, a fact noted in his official FDA biography: www.fda.gov/aboutfda/whatwedo/history/centennialoffda/harveyw.wiley/default.htm.

23  "I have every year": John Mullaly, *The Milk Trade in New York and Vicinity* (New York: Fowler and Wells, 1853). Further investigation of "swill dairies," which used cheap waste products from breweries as the food source for milk cattle, can be found in "Swill Milk: History of the Agitation of the Subject: The Recent Report of the Committee of the New York Academy of Medicine," *New York Times*, January 27, 1860, p. 1. The issue is also explored in Bee Wilson, *Swindled: The Dark History of Food Fraud, from Poisoned Candy to Counterfeit Coffee* (Princeton, NJ: Princeton University Press, 2008). Wilson offers in particular a vivid description of swill dairies (pp. 159–62).

23  "so numerous a proportion": Albert Leeds, "The Composition of Swill Milk," *Journal of the American Chemical Society* 42 (1890): pp. 451–52.

23  "sticks, hairs, insects": Thurman B. Rice, *The Hoosier Health Officer* (Indianapolis: Indiana Department of Health, 1946), pp. 162–63.

23  It revealed, as expected: "Dairy Products," part 1 of U.S. Department of Agriculture, *Foods and Food Adulterants*, bulletin no. 13 (Washington, DC: Government Printing Office, 1887).

24  The ability of producers: The history of oleomargarine is detailed in Ethan Trex, "The Surprisingly Interesting History of Margarine," *Mental Floss*, August 1, 2010; and Rebecca Rupp, "Butter Wars: The Margarine Was Pink," *The Plate*, August 13, 2014, http://theplate.nationalgeographic.com/2014/08/13/the-butter-wars-when-margarine-was-pink/; among others. The battle over the first margarine law is described in those articles, in Young, *Pure Food*, pp. 71–94, and in detail in Geoffrey P. Miller, "Public Choice at the Dawn of the Special Interest State: The Story of Butter and Margarine," *California Law Review* 77, no. 1 (January 1989): 81–131.

25  "We face a new situation": Young, *Pure Food*, p. 66. The other comments from legislators—such as Grout on "bastard butter," are from the same source at pp. 71–80. The congressional debate over oleomargarine, including many of the same quotes, can also be found in chapter 10 of Douglass Campbell M.D., *The Raw Truth About Milk* (Rogers, AR: Douglass Family Publishing, 2007).

27  "It is undoubtedly true": "Dairy Products," p. 10.

27  "nearly the same chemical": "Dairy Products," p. 73.

27  "the use of mineral coloring": "Dairy Products," p. 107.

27  That same year: Jesse P. Battershall, *Food Adulteration and Its Detection* (New York and London: E. & F. N. Spon, 1887) can be found online at https://books.google.com/books?id=i-AMAAAAYAAJ&pg=PP11&lpg=PP11&dq=battershall,+food+and+detection&source=bl&ots=EB3hZWz-BN&sig=9qeRqV_92ipt89D1dY27qthifHM&hl=en&sa=X&ved=0ahUKEwjm27um3q7WAhUHySYKHeFxAtEQ6AEINDAC#v=onepage&q=battershall%2C%20food%20and%20detection&f=false.

28  "Could only a portion": Clifford Richardson, "Spices and Condiments," part 2 of U.S. Department of Agriculture, *Foods and Food Adulterants*, Bulletin 13 (Washington, DC: Government Printing Office, 1887).

### Chapter Two: Cheated, Fooled, and Bamboozled

29  Yet Battershall's 1887 book: Jesse P. Battershall, *Food Adulteration and Its Detection* (New York and London: E. & F. N. Spon, 1887).

30  **Richardson, writing in the bulletin:** Clifford Richardson, "Spices and Condiments," part 2 of U.S. Department of Agriculture, Bulletin 13, *Foods and Food Adulterants* (Washington, DC: Government Printing Office, 1887).

32  **The third and final:** C. A. Crampton, "Fermented Alcoholic Beverages, Malt Liquors, Wine, and Cider," part 3 of U. S. Department of Agriculture, Bulletin 13, *Foods and Food Adulterants* (Washington, DC: Government Printing Office, 1887).

32  **Found in plants:** The backstory of salicylic acid is widely published, in places ranging from Daniel R. Goldberg, "Aspirin: Turn-of-the-Century Miracle Drug," *Distillations,* summer 2009, www .chemheritage.org/distillations/magazine/aspirin-turn-of-the-century-miracle-drug, to T. Hebner and B. Everts, "The Early History of Salicylates in Rheumatology and Pain," *Clinical Rheumatology* 17, no. 1 (1998): 17–25.

33  **"In this country but little":** Crampton, "Fermented Alcoholic Beverages," p. 35.

34  **"This report closes":** Crampton, "Fermented Alcoholic Beverages," pp. 142–44.

34  **"a healthy stomach can":** Harvey Wiley, "Introduction," in Crampton, "Fermented Alcoholic Beverages," p. 4.

35  **Like Wiley, Rusk had:** Wiley describes Rusk's tenure in Harvey Washington Wiley, *An Autobiography* (Indianapolis: Bobbs-Merrill, 1930), pp. 181–83, as "the golden epoch in my service in the Department of Agriculture."

35  **The lard study again:** H. W. Wiley, "Lard and Lard Adulterations," part 4 of U.S. Department of Agriculture, Bulletin 13, *Food and Food Adulterants* (Washington, DC: Government Printing Office, 1891).

36  **Increasingly frustrated that:** Harvey Young, *Pure Food* (Princeton, NJ: Princeton University Press, 1989), p. 106.

36  **"utter recklessness and hard-heartedness":** Alexander Wedderburn, U.S. Department of Agriculture, "A Popular Treatise on the Extent and Character of Food and Drug Adulteration" (Washington, DC: Government Printing Office, 1890).

36  **The division's 1892 investigation:** Guilford L. Spencer and Ervin Edgar Ewell, "Tea, Coffee and Cocoa Preparations," part 7 of U.S. Department of Agriculture, Bulletin 13, *Food and Food Adulterants* (Washington, DC: Government Printing Office, 1892).

36  **"This substance, as its name":** Spencer and Ewell, "Tea, Coffee and Cocoa Preparations," p. 886.

36  **"there is probably":** Spencer and Ewell, "Tea, Coffee and Cocoa Preparations," pp. 933–45.

37  **"Dear Sir," began one:** Spencer and Ewell, "Tea, Coffee and Cocoa Preparations," p. 915.

38  **Lawmakers had taken:** Oscar E. Anderson Jr., *The Health of a Nation: Harvey W. Wiley and the Fight for Pure Food* (Chicago: University of Chicago Press, 1958), pp. 77–79; Young, *Pure Food,* pp. 95–100; Suzanne Rebecca White, "Chemistry and Controversy: Regulating the Use of Chemicals in Foods, 1883–1959" (PhD diss., Emory University, 1994), pp. 1–15.

38  **"The devil has got hold":** Young, *Pure Food,* p. 95.

38  **"as nearly nonpartisan":** Young, *Pure Food,* p. 99.

39  **"To be cheated, fooled":** Harvey W. Wiley, "The Adulteration of Food," *Journal of the Franklin Institute* 137 (1894): p. 266.

39  **"Angry waves of popular":** Young, *Pure Food,* p. 99.

39  **The new secretary was:** Background on Morton can be found at https://en.wikipedia.org/wiki /Julius_Sterling_Morton, which includes links to his biography and his stature as a founder of Arbor Day. His contentious time at the Agriculture Department is detailed in Wiley's autobiography, in *Health of a Nation* at pp. 86–94, and in the internal correspondence of the Agriculture Department archived at the Library of Congress.

40  **"well on the way":** Anderson, *Health of a Nation,* p. 87.

40  **"Is there any necessity":** Morton's increasingly exasperated exchanges with Wiley, regarding both Wedderburn and the budget of the Chemistry Division, can be found in the Harvey Washington Wiley Papers, Library of Congress, Manuscript Division, box 29, folders 1892–93. The work of Wedderburn is further described in Steven L. Piott, *American Reformers 1870–1920: Progressives in Word and Deed* (Lanham, MD: Rowman and Littlefield, 2006), pp. 168–70, and in Courtney I. P. Thomas, *In Food We Trust: The Politics of Purity in American Food Regulation* (Lincoln: University of Nebraska Press, 2014).

41  **The secretary also ordered:** Anderson, *Health of a Nation,* pp. 86–94; Wiley, *An Autobiography,* pp. 183–84. Further budget-cutting measures and exchanges over test tubes, typewriter ribbons, and other reductions, as well as notes from members of Congress regarding the Agriculture budget, can be found in the Wiley Papers, box 29, folder 1894.

42  "The sentiment and truths": Alexander Wedderburn, U.S. Department of Agriculture, *Report on the Extent and Character of Food and Drug Adulteration* (Washington, DC: Government Printing Office, 1894).

42  "President of all": Wiley, *An Autobiography*, p. 186.

43  Wiley wasn't happy: Wiley Papers, box 29. The chemistry exhibits at the 1893 World's Columbian Exposition, including Wiley's speech, are described in "The American Chemical Society at the World's Fair 1893 and 1933," *Chemical & Engineering News* 11, no. 12 (June 20, 1933): pp. 185–86.

44  In the last week: Helen Louise Johnson to Harvey Wiley, October 31, 1893, Wiley Papers, box 29.

45  "I was the manager of": W. L. Parkinson to C. F. Drake, July 28, 1895, Wiley Papers, box 33.


*Chapter Three: The Beef Court*

47  "I was plunged at once": Harvey Washington Wiley, *An Autobiography* (Indianapolis: Bobbs-Merrill, 1930), p. 180.

48  the nickname "Tama Jim": Wiley described his early days with James Wilson in less than glowing terms. "He had the greatest capacity of any person I ever knew to take the wrong side of public questions, especially those relating to health through diet." Wiley, *An Autobiography*, pp. 190–91. But there are a host of more objective Wilson biographies online, including this one from Iowa State University: www.public.iastate.edu/~isu150/history/wilson.html.

48  Perhaps it was under: Wiley, *An Autobiography*, pp. 194–97.

49  The term dated to: The battles over how to define "real" whiskey and how to define "good" whiskey began in the late 1890s and continued throughout the rest of Wiley's time in office. For an outstanding overview of magazine length, I recommend H. Parker Willis, "What Whiskey Is," *McClure's*, April 1910, pp. 687–99. At book length, the issues are covered in depth in Gerald Carson, *The Social History of Bourbon* (Lexington: University Press of Kentucky, repr. ed. 2010), including the political maneuverings of Kentucky's Edmund Taylor. Regarding the Bottled-in-Bond Act, the Web site Bourbon & Banter offers "A Brief History": www.bourbonbanter.com/banter /bottled-in-bond-a-brief-history/#.WcEGbJOGM0Q.

49  "carelessly made whiskeys": Reid Mitenbuler, *Bourbon Empire: The Past and Future of America's Whiskey* (New York: Penguin Books, 2016), p. 163.

50  Although they could not: The blended whiskey makers, including the Hiram Walker Company, saw Wiley as hostile to their interests. Walker's efforts to protect its brand, as well as its political stance and actions over defining whiskey, are outlined in Clayton Coppin and Jack High, *The Politics of Purity: Harvey Washington Wiley and the Origins of Federal Food Policy* (Ann Arbor: University of Michigan Press, 1999). They get an even more detailed focus in Clayton Coppin and Jack High, "Wiley and the Whiskey Industry: Strategic Behavior in the Passage of the Pure Food and Drug Act," *Business History Review* 62, no. 2 (Summer 1988): 286–309, and in James Files, "Hiram Walker and Sons and the Pure Food and Drug Act" (master's thesis, University of Windsor, 1986). The subtitle of Files's thesis, "A Regulatory Decision Gone Awry," will tell you that he is not a fan of Wiley's position, and Coppin and High are similarly hostile to Wiley's regulatory approach.

51  To the president's dismay: Many of the issues regarding army mismanagement are summarized in Burtin W. Folsom, "Russell Alger and the Spanish American War," Mackinac Center for Public Policy, December 7, 1998, www.mackinac.org/V1998-39. Russell A. Alger was secretary of war during the conflict.

52  The "embalmed beef" scandal: This was news in newspapers across the country, starting in 1898, when the first stories began to appear, and continuing into 1899. As Chicago was home to the meatpacking industry, the *Chicago Tribune* was one of the first to report on the charges by General Miles and to repeat the term "embalmed beef." A December 22, 1898, story, at the top of page 7, was headlined simply "Miles Tells of Embalmed Beef." The scandal was covered by many other newspapers. Coverage in the *New York Times*, for instance, included "The Army Meat Scandal," February 21, 1899, p. 1; "Chemists to Inspect Beef," March 10, 1899, p. 1; "Roosevelt on Army Beef," March 26, 1899, p. 2; "The Army Beef Inquiry," April 14, 1899, p. 8; and "Army Beef Report Is Made Public," May 8, 1899, p. 1.

    The scandal is neatly summarized in Andrew Amelinckx, "Old Time Farm Crime: The Embalmed Beef Scandal of 1898," *Modern Farmer*, November 8, 2013, https://modernfarmer. com/2013/11/old-time-farm-crime-embalmed-beef-scandal-1898/, and gets a more academic treatment in Edward F. Keuchel, "Chemicals and Meat: The Embalmed Beef Scandal of the Spanish American War," *Bulletin of Medical History* 48, no. 2 (Summer 1974): pp. 249–64.

52 **"had to retire to a distance":** "Inspector Fears Embalmed Beef Men," *Chicago Tribune*, October 29, 1899, p. 3. This story also detailed the threats made by the meatpackers against investigators.

52 **"apparently preserved by injected":** Miles's remarks are cited in "Eagan and Embalmed Beef," *New York Times*, February 2, 1899, p. 6.

53 **"He lies in his throat":** "Charles P. Eagan," Wikipedia, https://en.wikipedia.org/wiki/Charles_P._Eagan.

53 **The Dodge hearings satisfied:** "Army Beef Report Is Made Public," *New York Times*, May 8, 1899, p. 1; Harvey Young, "Trichinous Pork and Embalmed Beef," *Pure Food* (Princeton, NJ: Princeton University Press, 1989), pp. 135–40.

54 **In anticipation, the president:** Correspondence concerning the hearings and details of the specific findings can be found in the Harvey Washington Wiley Papers, Library of Congress, Manuscript Division, box 41, folder 1899.

54 **"fill all the interstices":** Memo, Harvey Wiley to James Wilson, January 18, 1899, Wiley Papers, box 41. In addition, Wiley's testimony and his results are in the *Report of the Commission Appointed by the President to Investigate the Conduct of the War Department During the War with Spain* (Washington, DC: Government Printing Office, 1899), pp. 854–62.

54 **"Packingtown," as the locals:** A portrait of the old Chicago stockyards can be found in Ron Grossman, "'Hog Butcher to the World,'" *Chicago Tribune*, February 19, 2012: http://articles.chicago tribune.com/2012-02-19/site/ct-per-flash-stockyards-0219-2-20120219_1_union-stock-yard-butcher-shop-packingtown. Another retrospective look is Anne Bramley, "How Chicago's Slaughterhouse Spectacles Paved the Way for Big Meat," NPR, *The Salt*, December 3, 2015, www.npr.org/sections/thesalt/2015/12/03/458314767/how-chicago-s-slaughterhouse-spectacles-paved-the-way-for-big-meat. And there's a fine overview also at Wikipedia: https://en.wikipedia.org/wiki/Union_Stock_Yards.

55 **The average housewife:** Food prices are taken from "Prices from the 1899 Sears, Roebuck Grocery Lists," Choosing Voluntary Simplicity, no date, www.choosingvoluntarysimplicity.com/prices-from-the-1899-sears-roebuck-grocery-lists/.

55 **The Beef Court convened:** Testimony and later comments, such as from Carl Sandburg, are covered in Young, *Pure Food*, pp. 135–39, and in Edward F. Keuchel, "Chemicals and Meat: The Embalmed Beef Scandal of the Spanish American War," *Bulletin of Medical History* 48, no. 2 (Summer 1974): 253–56. Miles's testimony and grievances are reviewed in Louise Carroll Wade, "Hell Hath No Fury Like a General Scorned: Nelson A. Miles, the Pullman Strike, and the Beef Scandal of 1898," *Illinois Historical Journal* 79 (1986): 162–84.

56 **"It was a disgrace":** "The Army Meat Scandal," *New York Times*, February 21, 1899, p. 1.

59 **The army also sought:** Coverage of the soldier's death can be found in "Poisoned by Army Ration," David B. McGowan, *New York Times*, May 27, 1898, p. 2.

59 **Metal poisoning from canned:** K. P. McElroy and Willard D. Bigelow, "Canned Vegetables," part 8 of U.S. Department of Agriculture, Bulletin 13, *Foods and Food Adulterants* (Washington, DC: Government Printing Office, 1893).

60 **In a *Munsey's* article:** Frank Munsey to Harvey Wiley, July 14, 1899, with a copy of Wiley's article attached, Wiley Papers, box 41.

61 **"embalmed milk" causing:** "Embalmed Milk in Omaha: Many Infant Deaths Believed to Be Due to a Preservative Fluid," *New York Times*, May 30, 1899, p. 1; *Sanitarian* (publication of the Medico-Legal Society of New York) 42 (1899): p. 372; "Sale of Embalmed Milk Less Frequent," Preliminary Report of the Dairy and Food Commissioner for the Year 1907, bulletin 16, Commonwealth of Pennsylvania, p. 25; A. G. Young, "Formaldehyde as a Milk Preservative," Report to the Maine Board of Public Health, 1899, www.ncbi.nlm.nih.gov/pmc/articles/PMC2329554/pdf/pubhealthpap00032-0152.pdf; "The Use of Borax and Formaldehyde as Preservatives of Food," *British Medical Journal*, July 7, 1900, pp. 2062–63.

61 **"an epidemic of stomach trouble":** "Embalmed Beef Troubles in Cincinnati," *New York Times*, June 16, 1899, p. 4.

62 **"It is noticeable":** "Embalmed Milk in Omaha: Many Infant Deaths Believed to Be Due to a Preservative Fluid," *New York Times*, May 30, 1899, p. 1.

62 **"Two drops of a":** Thurman B. Rice, *The Hoosier Health Officer: The History of the Indiana State Board of Health to 1925* (Indianapolis, Indiana State Board of Health, 1946), p. 162.

63 **"Well, it's embalming":** Rice, *Hoosier Health Officer*, p. 165.

63 **"state confidently that":** Rice, *Hoosier Health Officer*, p. 163.

*Chapter Four: What's in It?*

65  **In 1899 U.S. senator:** Mason and his role in the hearings are profiled in "Senator Mason, the Champion of Liberty," *San Francisco Call*, January 10, 1899, p. 1. Hearing overviews can be found in Harvey Young, "The Mason Hearings," in *Pure Food* (Princeton, NJ: Princeton University Press, 1989), pp. 140–45; Oscar E. Anderson Jr., *The Health of a Nation: Harvey W. Wiley and the Fight for Pure Food* (Chicago: University of Chicago Press, 1958), pp. 127–32; and Michael Lesy and Lisa Stoffer, *Repast. Dining Out at the Dawn of the New American Century 1900–1904* (New York: W.W. Norton, 2013), which on pages 29–31 includes some of Wiley's most pointed testimony to the committee. A complete summary of the hearings can be found in *Hearings Before the Committee of Interstate and Commerce of the U.S. House of Representatives, on Food Bills Prohibiting the Adulteration Misbranding and Imitation of Foods, Candies, Drugs and Condiments in the District of Columbia and the Territories, and for Regulating Interstate Traffic Therein and for Other Purposes* (Washington, DC: Government Printing Office, 1902).

69  **sodium borate, or borax:** A basic chemical profile of borax can be found on the Azo Materials Web site, www.azom.com/article.aspx?ArticleID=2588. The history of Pacific Coast Borax Company can be found at the Santa Clarita Valley history Web site, https://scvhistory.com/scvhistory/borax -20muleteam.htm; and at Wikipedia, https://en.wikipedia.org/wiki/Pacific_Coast_Borax_Com pany; and an interactive time line of its most positive moments can be found on the company's own Web site, https://www.20muleteamlaundry.com/about.

69  **During the Mason hearings:** *Hearings Before the Committee.*

70  **In the early spring:** William E. Mason, *Adulteration of Food Products: Report to Accompany S. Res. 447, Fifty-fifth Congress* (Washington, DC: U.S. Government Printing Office, 1900), https:// catalog.hathitrust.org/Record/011713494.

70  **"This is the only civilized":** https://books.google.com/books?id=XelP2FtgWxkC&pg=PA17 &lpg=PA17&dq=Senator+Mason,+1900,+adulteration,+speech,+Senate&source=bl&ots=j51z dLIgP8&sig=NU1WBa_7ePzHO6g7spTpiRpgNv8&hl=en&sa=X&ved=0ahUKEwiDvfmrwqzX AhXB7yYKHaygAfsQ6AEINDAC#v=onepage&q=Senator%20Mason%2C%201900%2C %20adulteration%2C%20speech%2C%20Senate&f=false.

71  **"before the public eye":** Marriott Brosius to Harvey Wiley, November 23, 1899, Harvey Washington Wiley Papers, Library of Congress, Manuscript Division, box 41.

71  **applauded the action:** Anderson, *Health of a Nation*, p. 127.

72  **That same spring:** Anna Kelton to Harvey Wiley, May 22 and 25, 1900, Harvey Washington Wiley Papers, Library of Congress, box 43; Harvey Wiley to Anna Kelton, May 19, 1900, Wiley Papers, box 43.

72  **"When I left for Paris":** Harvey Wiley to William Frear, July 29, 1900, Wiley Papers, box 43.

73  **"You say, 'Why don't'":** Harvey Wiley to Anna Kelton, May 24, 1900, Wiley Papers, box 43.

73  **Secretary Wilson wrote:** James Wilson to Harvey Wiley, August 7, 1900, Wiley Papers, box 43.

74  **In 1901, shortly after:** Anheuser-Busch to Harvey Wiley, June 4, 1900, Wiley Papers, box 45.

74  **The Woman's Christian Temperance:** The Woman's Christian Temperance Union provides a history on its Web site at www.wctu.org/history.html, and there's another from the Frances Willard House museum: https://franceswillardhouse.org/frances-willard/history-of-wctu/. The organization's role in the pure-food fight is covered in detail in Laurine Swainston Goodwin, *The Pure Food, Drink and Drug Crusaders, 1879–1914* (Jefferson, NC: McFarland, 1999). Frances Willard's vision for the organization is outlined on pp. 31–35 and the WCTU's work on a state-by-state basis is noted throughout.

75  **Wisconsin-based Pabst:** Pabst to Harvey Wiley, July 13, 1901, Wiley Papers, box 45.

75  **"This is our secret":** Anheuser-Busch to Harvey Wiley, June 4, 1900, Wiley Papers, box 45.

75  **In May 1901 the Pan-American:** The adulterated food exhibit is described in E. E. Ewell, W. D. Bigelow, and Logan Waller Page, *Exhibit of the Bureau of Chemistry at the Pan-American Exhibition, Buffalo, New York, 1901*, Bulletin 63, U.S. Department of Agriculture, Bureau of Chemistry. It can be found in full at https://archive.org/stream/exhibitofbureauo63ewel/exhibi tofbureauo63ewel_djvu.txt.

77  **Reporter John D. Wells:** John D. Wells, "The Story of an Eye-Witness to the Shooting of the President," *Collier's Weekly*, September 21, 1901; Lewis L. Gould, *The Presidency of William McKinley* (Lawrence: University Press of Kansas, 1981); William Seale, *The President's House: A History* (Washington, DC: White House Historical Association, 1986); "The Assassination of President William McKinley, 1901," EyeWitness to History, 2010, www.eyewitnesstohistory.com/mckinley.htm.

77   **"I told William McKinley":** "1904: Alton Parker vs. Theodore Roosevelt," The Times Looks Back: Presidential Elections 1896–1996, *New York Times*, 2000, http://events.nytimes.com/learning/general/specials/elections/1904/index.html.

78   **"In this hour of":** James Ford Rhodes, *The McKinley and Roosevelt Administrations 1897–1909* (New York: Macmillan, 1922), p. 218.

78   **Wiley feared that if:** Anderson, *Health of a Nation*, pp. 100–102.

79   **"'If I go up there'":** This quote, as well as the excerpt of Wiley's testimony and exchange in Congress on the sugar policy, Roosevelt's response, and Wiley's rueful acknowledgment of the long-lasting effect of this episode, can be found in Harvey Washington Wiley, *An Autobiography* (Indianapolis: Bobbs-Merrill, 1930), pp. 221–23. Wiley also recounts this episode in a self-published and angry book reviewing the fate of food safety legislation: Harvey W. Wiley, *The History of a Crime Against the Food Law* (Washington, DC, 1929), pp. 270–74.

79   **"I consider it a very unwise":** Wiley, *An Autobiography*, pp. 220–21.

79   **"I will let you off":** Wiley, *An Autobiography*, pp. 220–21.

*Chapter Five: Only the Brave*

80   **By 1901 the Bureau:** Suzanne Rebecca White, "Chemistry and Controversy: Regulating the Use of Chemicals in Foods, 1883–1959" (PhD diss., Emory University, 1994), pp. 8–10.

80   **The American chemical industry:** White, "Chemistry and Controversy," pp. 20–27. Additional information on the well-known Herbert Dow can be found at www.encyclopedia.com/history/encyclopedias-almanacs-transcripts-and-maps/dow-herbert-h and on the less well-known Jacob Baur, of the Liquid Carbonic Company, at http://forgottenchicago.com/articles/the-last-days-of-washburne/.

82   **combative Edwin Ladd:** State Historical Society of North Dakota, "Edwin F. Ladd and the Pure Food Movement," no date, http://ndstudies.gov/gr8/content/unit-iii-waves-development-1861-1920/lesson-4-alliances-and-conflicts/topic-6-progressive-movements/section-4-edwin-f-ladd-and-pure-food-movement.

83   **"By God, no Eastern":** Culver S. Ladd, *Pure Food Crusader: Edwin Fremont Ladd* (Pittsburgh: Dorrance Publishing, 2009).

83   **To showcase the problem:** Shepard's menu appears in Mark Sullivan, *Our Times*, vol. 2 (1927; repr. New York: Charles Scribner and Sons, 1971), pp. 506–7.

84   **"According to this menu":** Sullivan, *Our Times*, p. 507. See also James Shepard, "Like Substances," Association of National Food and Dairy Departments, Eleventh Annual Convention (1907), pp. 165–74.

85   **Wiley had long worried:** Wiley's hygienic table trials, renamed the "Poison Squad" by newspaper reporters, grew out of his concerns about the lack of good—or often any—science behind chemical additives in the food supplies. He summarizes some of this backstory in Harvey W. Wiley, "The Influence of Preservatives and Other Substances Added to Foods upon Health and Metabolism," *Proceedings of the American Philosophical Society* 47, no. 189 (May–August 1908): pp. 302–28. His subsequent investigations on compounds ranging from borax to formaldehyde to salicylic acid cite in the introductory sections the previous research or lack of it. The Poison Squad studies themselves have been widely covered, both by newspapers and magazines of the time and by more recent food safety historians. For simplicity's sake, I'll provide here some of the most comprehensive summaries: White, "Chemistry and Controversy," pp. 46–91; Laurine Swainston Goodwin, *The Pure Food, Drink and Drug Crusaders, 1879–1914* (Jefferson, NC: McFarland, 1999), pp. 219–24; Harvey Young, *Pure Food* (Princeton, NJ: Princeton University Press, 1989), pp. 151–57; Oscar E. Anderson Jr., *The Health of a Nation: Harvey W. Wiley and the Fight for Pure Food* (Chicago: University of Chicago Press, 1958), pp. 149–52; Michael Lesy and Lisa Stoffer, *Repast: Dining Out at the Dawn of the New American Century 1900–1904* (New York: W.W. Norton, 2013), pp. 31–34; Bruce Watson, "The Poison Squad: An Incredible History," *Esquire*, June 27, 2013; Natalie Zarelli, "Food Testing in 1902 Featured a Bow Tie–Clad 'Poison Squad' Eating Plates of Acid," *Atlas Obscura,* August, 30, 2016, www.atlasobscura.com/articles/food-testing-in-1902-featured-a-tuxedoclad-poison-squad-eating-plates-of-acid.

85   **"young, robust fellows":** Harvey Washington Wiley, U.S. Department of Agriculture, *Influence of Food Preservatives and Artificial Colors on Digestion and Health: Boric Acid and Borax* (Washington, DC: Government Printing Office, 1904), p. 10.

85   **"whether such preservatives":** Wiley, *Influence of Food Preservatives*, p. 23.

86   **"enable the Secretary":** Wiley, *Influence of Food Preservatives*, p. 8.

86 "Cheerful surroundings, good company": Wiley, *Influence of Food Preservatives*, pp. 13–14.

87 "open, for the first time": Carol Lewis, "The 'Poison Squad' and the Advent of Food and Drug Regulation," *U.S. Food and Drug Administration Consumer Magazine*, November–December 2002, http://esq.h-cdn.co/assets/cm/15/06/54d3fdf754244_-_21_PoisonSquadFDA.pdf.

87 "They are clerks": Lewis, "The 'Poison Squad.'"

87 "Dear Sir," wrote one: Bruce Watson, "The Poison Squad: An Incredible History," *Esquire*, June 26, 2013, http://www.esquire.com/food-drink/food/a23169/poison-squad/.

87 "You will begin": Harvey Wiley to H. E. Blackburn, August 15, 1901, Wiley Papers, box 45.

88 "so they came to us": Wiley, *Influence of Food Preservatives*, p. 10.

88 "Did you explain": *The Borax Investigation: Hearings Before the Committee of Interstate and Foreign Commerce*, U.S. House of Representatives (Washington, DC: Government Printing Office, February 1906).

88 As the details of the project: Newspaper coverage of Wiley's toxicity studies is discussed in wonderful detail in Kevin C. Murphy, "Pure Food, the Press, and the Poison Squad: Evaluating Coverage of Harvey W. Wiley's Hygienic Table," 2001, www.kevincmurphy.com/harveywiley2.html.

89 "Should they become hungry": Murphy, "Pure Food, the Press, and the Poison Squad."

89 "pursue their ordinary": Wiley, *Influence of Food Preservatives*.

90 One of them involved: John C. Thresh and Arthur Porter, *Preservatives in Food and Food Examination* (London: J & A Churchill, 1906), pp. 16–52.

90 Unlike Wiley, who: F. W. Tunnicliffe and Otto Rosenheim, "On the Influence of Boric Acid and Borax upon the General Metabolism of Children," *Journal of Hygiene* 1, no. 2 (April 1901): 168–201.

91 Wiley knew his study: H. W. Wiley, "Results of Experiments on the Effect of Borax Administered with Food," *Analyst*, January 1, 1904, pp. 357–70.

91 "It is pointed out": Wiley, "Results of Experiments on the Effect of Borax."

92 "Those who thought": Wiley, "Results of Experiments on the Effect of Borax."

92 his experiment had attracted: Brown's approach to covering the Poison Squad is described in Murphy, "Pure Food, the Press, and the Poison Squad." Among his stories published in the *Washington Post*: "Dr. Wiley and His Boarders," November 21, 1902, p. 2; "Borax Ration Scant: Official Chef Falls in Disfavor with Guests," December 23, 1902, p. 2; "Dr. Wiley in Despair: One Boarder Becomes Too Fat and Another Too Lean," December 16, p. 2; and "Borax Begins to Tell—at Least the Six Eaters Are All Losing Flesh," December 26, 1902, p. 2.

92 "I can't say anything": "Borax Begins to Tell."

93 "The authorities are apprehensive": Murphy, "Pure Food, the Press, and the Poison Squad."

93 "braving the perils": "Dr. Wiley and His Boarders."

94 Christmas dinner menu: Murphy, "Pure Food, the Press, and the Poison Squad," p. 3.

94 That December he'd been: American Association for the Advancement of Science to Harvey Wiley, November 22, 1902, Harvey Washington Wiley Papers, Library of Congress, Manuscript Division, box 48. Harvey Wiley, "Poison Dinner Invitation," 1902, Wiley Papers, box 48.

95 Molineux was one of: Deborah Blum, *The Poisoner's Handbook: Murder and the Birth of Forensic Medicine in Jazz Age New York* (New York: Penguin Books, 2010), pp. 61–63.

95 "F.B. Linton, who weighs": "Borax Begins to Tell."

96 "Dr. Wiley is in despair": This and the other comedic lines from Brown's reporting are in Murphy, "Pure Food, the Press, and the Poison Squad."

96 "The change in the complexion": "The Chemical Food Eaters," *Summary* (Elmira, NY), April 18, 1903, available at https://books.google.com/books?id=OgFLAAAAYAAJ&pg=PR116&lpg=PR116&dq=borax+turns+boarders+pink,+wiley&source=bl&ots=wCg8DwtqXr&sig=U1hq-ozDBsBsC2rQaX5IcnkNgew&hl=en&sa=X&ved=0ahUKEwiy97LB2azXAhWE7iYKHeD2B0OQ6AEISDAI#v=onepage&q=borax%20turns%20boarders%20pink%2C%20wiley&f=false.

96 By that time, the once sedate: Dockstader's song is reprinted in Murphy, "Pure Food, the Press, and the Poison Squad," p. 4, and in most accounts of the studies.

97 the paper's editors had to: Scott C. Bone (editor of the *Washington Post*) to Harvey Wiley, December 24, 1902, Wiley Papers, box 48.

*Chapter Six: Lessons in Food Poisoning*

98 In 1903 Fannie Farmer: A basic biography can be found here: www.notablebiographies.com/Du-Fi/Farmer-Fannie.html.

98 **"Food," the book began:** Fannie Merritt Farmer, "Food," in *The Boston Cooking-School Cookbook* (1896; repr. Boston: Little, Brown, 1911), full text available at https://archive.org/stream/bostoncookingsch00farmrich#page/n21/mode/2up.

100 **Farmer may have been:** Fanny Farmer, *Food and Cookery for the Sick and Convalescent* (Boston: Little, Brown, 1904), full text available through the Historic American Cookbook Project: http://digital.lib.msu.edu/projects/cookbooks/html/books/book_56.cfm.

100 **"unappetizing and unhealthful":** Farmer, *Food and Cookery for the Sick and Convalescent*, pp. 50–58.

100 **"The pathogenic germs":** Farmer, *Food and Cookery for the Sick and Convalescent*, pp. 50–58.

100 **"borax, boracic acid, salicylic acid":** Farmer, *Food and Cookery for the Sick and Convalescent*, pp. 50–58.

100 **Earlier cookbook authors:** To give a couple of examples: Mary Johnson Bailey Lincoln, *Mrs. Lincoln's Boston Cookbook* (Boston: Roberts Brothers, 1884), discusses adulteration of cream of tartar and baking powder (pp. 49–55) and chemicals used to disguise bad chicken (p. 251); and Sarah Tyson Rorer, *Mrs. Rorer's New Cookbook* (Philadelphia: Arnold, 1902), http://digital.lib.msu.edu/projects/cookbooks/html/books/book_54.cfm, cites adulterated arrowroot powder, flour, coffee, mustard powder, and vanilla.

100 **"eating poisons under":** "Borax Preservatives Found Injurious," *New York Times*, June 23, 1904, p. 9.

101 **But the *Times* anticipated:** "Borax Preservatives Found Injurious," *New York Times*, June 23, 1904, p. 9; Wiley, *Influence of Food Preservatives and Artificial Colors on Digestion and Health*, vol. 1, *Boric Acid and Borax* (Washington, DC: Government Printing Office, 1904).

101 **In June the Department:** Wiley, *Influence of Food Preservatives.*

103 **Congress once again weighed:** Hepburn, McCumber, and their push for food and drug legislation are reviewed in Harvey Young, *Pure Food* (Princeton, NJ: Princeton University Press, 1989), pp. 164–82; Oscar E. Anderson Jr., *The Health of a Nation: Harvey W. Wiley and the Fight for Pure Food* (Chicago: University of Chicago Press, 1958), pp. 158–82; and Mark Sullivan, *Our Times*, vol. 2 (1927; repr. New York: Charles Scribner's Sons, 1971), pp. 268–70.

104 **As Warwick Hough, the chief:** Young, *Pure Food*, pp. 165–68; James Files, "Hiram Walker and Sons and the Pure Food and Drug Act" (master's thesis, University of Windsor, 1986).

105 **"will seriously impair":** Warwick Hough to Harvey Wiley, quoted in Files, "Hiram Walker and Sons," p. 120.

105 **The issue of drug fakery:** In Harvey Washington Wiley, *An Autobiography* (Indianapolis: Bobbs-Merrill, 1930), pp. 203–9, Wiley discusses his concerns about the issue. The hiring of Lyman Kebler, signifying that he was prepared to put more emphasis on the issue, is discussed in Anderson, *Health of a Nation*, p. 103; and Young, *Pure Food*, pp. 118–19. Kebler's meticulous research and reputation for undaunted investigation are profiled in D. B. Worthen, "Lyman B. Kebler: Foe to Fakers," *Journal of the American Pharmaceutical Association* 50, no. 10 (May–June 2010): pp. 429–32.

106 **The Proprietary Association:** James Harvey Young, *The Toadstool Millionaires: A Social History of Patent Medicines Before Federal Regulation* (Princeton, NJ: Princeton University Press, 2015), pp. 227–35.

106 **"If the Federal Government":** Young, *Toadstool Millionaires*, p. 229.

106 **"It will take more":** Sullivan, *Our Times*, p. 270.

107 **He also began courting:** The importance of women and women's organizations in the battle for regulation is a main focus of Laurine Swainston Goodwin, *The Pure Food, Drink and Drug Crusaders, 1879–1914* (Jefferson, NC: McFarland, 1999); "Women Join the Pure Food War," *What to Eat* 18, no. 10 (October 1905): pp. 158–59; and "Women's Clubs Name Special Food Committee," *What to Eat* 18, no. 12 (December 1905): pp. 191–92.

107 **In his Hanover College days:** Wiley, *An Autobiography*, pp. 55–65. See also speech to USDA researchers, 1904, Harvey Washington Wiley Papers, Library of Congress, box 189 ("we regard women as human beings").

108 **"Man's highest ambition":** Harvey Wiley, speech to USDA researchers, 1904, transcript in Harvey Washington Wiley Papers, Library of Congress, Manuscript Division, box 189.

108 **"I know she is not intended":** H. M. Wiley in "Men's Views of Women's Clubs: A Symposium by Men Who Are Recognized Leaders in the Philanthropic and Reform Movements in America," *Annals of the American Academy of Political and Social Science* 28 (July–December 1906): p. 291.

108 **Born in 1856, Lakey:** Nina Redman and Michele Morrone, *Food Safety: A Reference Handbook*, 3rd ed. (Santa Barbara, CA: ABC-Clio, 2017), pp. 130–65; Sullivan, *Our Times*, pp. 521–22.

109 **Addams to begin to speak:** Goodwin, *Pure Food, Drink and Drug Crusaders*, pp. 258–75.

109 **"I think women's":** Wiley in "Men's Views of Women's Clubs."

110 **Lakey urged Wiley:** Alice Lakey, "Adulterations We Have to Eat," *What to Eat* 18, no. 6 (June 1905): pp. 9–10.

110 **"For the purpose of":** Thomas H. Hoskins, M.D., *What We Eat: An Account of the Most Common Adulterations of Food and Drink* (Boston: T.O.H.P. Burnham, 1861), p. iv, text available at https://archive.org/details/whatweeatanacco00hoskgoog.

111 **"flour is present":** John Peterson, "How to Detect Food Adulterations," *What to Eat* 16, no. 2 (February 1903): pp. 11–12.

111 *Some Forms of Food Adulteration:* Willard D. Bigelow and Burton James Howard, U.S. Department of Agriculture, *Some Forms of Food Adulteration and Simple Methods for Their Detection* (Washington, DC: Government Printing Office, 1906), text available at https://archive.org/details/someformsoffooda10big.

111 **"Sir," wrote Wiley:** Bigelow and Howard, *Some Forms of Food Adulteration*, p. 1.

111 **"It is not in their":** Bigelow and Howard, *Some Forms of Food Adulteration*, p. 34.

113 **On April 30, 1904:** The pure food exhibit at the St. Louis World's Fair is described in "Novel Exhibit of Food Adulteration," *What to Eat* 17, no. 4 (April 1904): pp. 131–32; and Mark Bennett, "Lessons in Food Poisoning," *What to Eat* 17, no. 7 (July 1904): pp. 161–62; Sullivan, *Our Times*, pp. 522–25; Goodwin, *Pure Food, Drink and Drug Crusaders*, pp. 229–32; and Marsha E. Ackermann, "Promoting Pure Food at the 1904 St. Louis World's Fair," *Repast, Quarterly Newsletter of the Culinary Historians of Ann Arbor* 20, no. 3 (Summer 2004): pp. 1–3. The food served at the fair is described in Kate Godfrey-Demay, "The Fair's Fare," *Sauce*, April 9, 2004, pp. 1–4.

114 **"Now let the food adulterer":** Paul Pierce, "Our Allies in the Pure Food," *What to Eat* 16, no. 5 (May 1903): p. 1.

115 **"increase public interest":** Robert Allen to Harvey Wiley, January 24, 1902, Wiley Papers, box 48.

115 **"While potted chicken":** E. F. Ladd, "Some Food Products and Food Adulteration," bulletin 57, North Dakota Agricultural College, Fargo, ND, 1903.

115 **"If you want to":** Bennett, "Lessons in Food Poisoning."

116 **"one of the most":** Sullivan, *Our Times*, p. 522.

117 **"It is true that":** Harvey Wiley, speech given at City College of New York, November 7, 1904, Wiley Papers, box 197.

117 **"There are times in life":** *Journal of Proceedings of the Eighth Annual Convention of the National Association of State Dairy and Food Departments*, September 26–October 1, 1904, St. Louis, Missouri, p. 64.

118 **Hough was also in attendance:** Warwick M. Hough, "The Pure Food Bill and Bottled in Bond Whiskey," *What to Eat* 18, no. 2 (February 1905): pp. 74–75; Anderson, *Health of a Nation*, pp. 159–62.

118 **"I agree with you":** Warwick Hough to Harvey Wiley, quoted in Anderson, *Health of a Nation*, pp. 159–62.

*Chapter Seven: The Yellow Chemist*

119 **In early November 1904:** The background here for Upton Sinclair's research on the Chicago stockyards and the creation of *The Jungle*, first as a series for *Appeal to Research* and then for book publication, is based on numerous sources. The story is woven through this chapter, and sources for those sections include Anthony Arthur, *Radical Innocent: Upton Sinclair* (New York: Random House, 2006), pp. 43–85; Doris Kearns Goodwin, *The Bully Pulpit: Theodore Roosevelt, William Howard Taft and the Golden Age of Journalism* (New York: Simon & Schuster, 2013), pp. 459–55; Michael Lesy and Lisa Stoffer, *Repast: Dining Out at the Dawn of the New American Century 1900–1904* (New York: W.W. Norton, 2013), pp. 37–61; Mark Sullivan, *Our Times*, vol. 2 (1927; repr. New York: Charles Scribner and Sons, 1971), pp. 471–80; Harvey Young, *Pure Food* (Princeton, NJ: Princeton University Press, 1989), pp. 221–40; and "Upton Sinclair, Whose Muckraking Changed the Meat Industry," *New York Times*, June 30, 2016, www.nytimes.com/interactive/projects/cp/obituaries/archives.

120 **The novel's main character:** Upton Sinclair, *The Jungle* (1906), full text available at www.online-literature.com/upton_sinclair/jungle/.

121 **And a new senator:** Sullivan, *Our Times*, pp. 525–27. A biographical sketch of Heyburn plus a guide to his papers at the University of Idaho can be found at www.lib.uidaho.edu/special-collections/Manuscripts/mg006.htm.

121  **"I am in favor":** Lorine Swainston Goodwin, *The Pure Food, Drink and Drug Crusaders 1879–1914* (Jefferson, NC: McFarland, 1999), p. 227.

121  **The confrontational Heyburn:** Oscar E. Anderson Jr., *The Health of a Nation: Harvey W. Wiley and the Fight for Pure Food* (Chicago: University of Chicago Press, 1958), pp. 173–78.

122  **Meanwhile, the blended-whiskey:** Clayton Coppin and Jack High, "Wiley and the Whiskey Industry: Strategic Behavior in the Passage of the Pure Food and Drug Act," *Business History Review* 62, no. 2 (Summer 1988): pp. 297–300.

122  **"suffer to an extent":** "Labeling Ruinous to Liquor Trade," *New York Journal of Commerce* 131, no. 30 (December 1, 1904): p. 3.

123  **"There is a bill":** Goodwin, *Pure Food, Drink and Drug Crusaders*, p. 242.

123  **"Who is that":** Gerald Carson, *The Social History of Bourbon* (Lexington: University Press of Kentucky, repr. ed. 2010), p. 164.

123  **"What now?" wrote:** Goodwin, *Pure Food, Drink and Drug Crusaders*, p. 243.

123  **"Let somebody muzzle":** "Chemistry on the Rampage," *California Fruit Grower* 15, no. 2 (February 1905): p. 3.

123  **"The greater part of":** "Grocers Stand Against Food Bill Excesses," *Grocery World* 39, no. 12 (March 5, 1905): p. 41.

124  **"I believe in chemistry":** Harvey Wiley, "Food Adulteration and Its Effects" (lecture, Sanitary Science class, Cornell University, 1905).

124  **"On the platform":** Sullivan, *Our Times*, p. 520.

124  **It was a "great battle":** Harvey Washington Wiley, *An Autobiography* (Indianapolis: Bobbs-Merrill, 1930), p. 231.

126  **"it is useless to tell":** Carl Jensen, *Stories That Changed America: Muckrackers of the Early Twentieth Century* (New York: Seven Stories Press, 2002), p. 55.

126  **"I had to tell":** Jensen, *Stories That Changed America*, p. 57.

127  **Meanwhile, other writers:** Charles Edward Russell, *The Greatest Trust in the World* (New York: Ridgeway-Thayer, 1905), full text available at https://archive.org/details/greatesttrustin01russ goog; Henry Irving Dodge, "The Truth About Food Adulterations," *Woman's Home Companion* 48 (March 1905): pp. 6–7; Henry Irving Dodge, "How the Baby Pays the Tax," *Woman's Home Companion* 49 (April 1905): pp. 5–8.

128  **"The Senate does not indulge":** Henry Irving Dodge, "How the Baby Pays the Tax," *Woman's Home Companion* 49 (April 1905): p. 8.

129  **Also in 1905, Pierce's magazine:** The series, "The Slaughter of Americans," appeared in five issues of *What to Eat*: *What to Eat* 18, no. 2 (February 1905): pp. 1–4; *What to Eat* 18, no. 3 (March 1905): pp. 1–3; *What to Eat* 18, no. 4 (April 1905): pp. 1–5; *What to Eat* 18, no. 5 (May 1905): pp. 1–3; and *What to Eat* 18, no. 6 (June 1905): pp. 1–5.

132  **"I recommend that a law":** Theodore Roosevelt, "Fifth Annual Message," December 5, 1905, transcript available at www.presidency.ucsb.edu/ws/index.php?pid=29546.

132  **"Are we to take up":** Horace Samuel Merrill and Marion Galbraith Merrill, *The Republican Command 1897–1913* (Lexington: University Press of Kentucky, 2015), p. 27.

132  **"On the contrary":** Young, *Pure Food*, pp. 182–83.

133  **"Heyburn said he could":** Sullivan, *Our Times*, pp. 533–34.

134  **Back at the Bureau:** Carol Lewis, "The 'Poison Squad' and the Advent of Food Regulation," *U.S. Food and Drug Administration Consumer Magazine*, November–December 2002, pp. 1–15, http://esq.h-cdn.co/assets/cm/15/06/54d3fdf754244_-_21_PoisonSquadFDA.pdf.

134  **"It is hardly necessary":** Harvey W. Wiley, *Influence of Food Preservatives and Artificial Colors on Digestion and Health*, vol. 2, *Salicylic Acid and Salicylates* (Washington, DC: Government Printing Office, 1906), p. 5, text available at https://archive.org/details/influenceoffoodp84wile_0.

135  **"exerts a depressing":** Wiley, *Influence of Food Preservatives*, p. 8. A critical rebuttal of Wiley's conclusions was published in the industry magazine *American Food Journal* under the title "Salicylic Acid and Health," November 1906, pp. 6–15.

*Chapter Eight: The Jungle*

137  **To the *Washington* (DC) *Star*:** Harvey Wiley to the *Washington Star*, January 30, 1906, Harvey Washington Wiley Papers, Library of Congress, box 60.

138  **To *Everybody's Magazine*:** Harvey Wiley to *Everybody's Magazine*, February 12, 1906, Wiley Papers, box 60.

138  "My attention is called": Arthur H. Bailey to Harvey Wiley, February 26, 1906, Wiley Papers, box 60.

139  "The attacks which are": H. C. Adams (27th district, Wisconsin) to Harvey Wiley, February 5, 1906, Wiley Papers, box 60; Harvey Wiley to H. C. Adams, February 12, 1906, Wiley Papers, box 60.

139  In late February Wiley gave: Harvey Washington Wiley, *An Autobiography* (Indianapolis: Bobbs-Merrill, 1930), pp. 212–15.

141  "From the newspapers we notice": F. H. Madden (director, Reid, Murdoch & Co., Chicago) to Harvey Wiley, February 12, 1906, Wiley Papers, box 60.

141  "Your wonderful tenacity": J. E. Blackburn (National Bond and Securities Company) to Harvey Wiley, March 5, 1906, Wiley Papers, box 60.

141  Charles Reed of the AMA: Charles Reed to Harvey Wiley, March 6, 1906, Wiley Papers, box 60.

141  In early March: Anthony Arthur, *Radical Innocent: Upton Sinclair* (New York: Random House, 2006), pp. 43–85.

142  "did not care to": Arthur, *Radical Innocent*, p. 71.

143  "what is going on": George Bernard Shaw, *John Bull's Other Island* (New York: Brentano's, 1910), p. 179.

143  The hostile *Chicago Tribune*: Arthur, *Radical Innocent*, p. 57.

143  "I aimed for the public's": Eric Schlosser, *Chicago Tribune*, "'I Aimed for the Public's Heart, and . . . Hit It in the Stomach,'" May 21, 2006, http://articles.chicagotribune.com/2006-05-21/features/0605210414_1_upton-sinclair-trust-free.

143  "Tiddy was toying": Mark Sullivan, *Our Times*, vol. 2 (1927; repr. New York: Charles Scribner and Sons, 1971), p. 535.

144  The question threw Wilson: Sullivan, *Our Times*, p. 547. The conflict is covered in his book on pages 536–51. Accounts can also be found in Doris Kearns Goodwin, *The Bully Pulpit: Theodore Roosevelt, William Howard Taft and the Golden Age of Journalism* (New York: Simon & Schuster, 2013), pp. 459–65; and Michael Lesy and Lisa Stoffer, *Repast: Dining Out at the Dawn of the New American Century 1900–1904* (New York: W.W. Norton, 2013), pp. 37–61.

145  "ignoring at the same": Theodore Roosevelt, "The Man with the Muck-rake," speech delivered April 14, 1906, transcript available at www.americanrhetoric.com/speeches/teddyrooseveltmuck rake.htm.

145  The president's attack: David Graham Phillips, *The Treason of the Senate*, ed. George E. Mowry and Judson A. Grenier (Chicago: Quadrangle Books, 1964), pp. 9–46.

146  "The men with the muck rakes": Roosevelt, "Man with the Muck-rake."

146  "Really, Mr. Sinclair": Maureen Ogle, *In Meat We Trust: An Unexpected History of Carnivore America* (Boston: Houghton Mifflin, 2013), p. 78.

146  "Tell Sinclair to go": Gary Younge, "Blood, Sweat and Fears," *Guardian*, August 4, 2006, www .theguardian.com/books/2005/aug/05/featuresreviews.guardianreview24.

146  "Many inside rooms": "Conditions in Stockyard Described in the Neill-Reynolds Report," *Chicago Tribune*, June 5, 1906, p. 1.

148  "clean and wholesome": "Conditions in Stockyard Described."

148  "If a commission of men": "Discuss New Meat Bill," *Chicago Tribune*, June 4, 1906, p. 4.

148  "I am sorry to have": Sullivan, *Our Times*, p. 548.

149  "In Armour's own establishment": Lesy and Stoffer, *Repast*, p. 54.

149  In early June, exasperated: David Moss and Marc Campasano, "*The Jungle* and the Debate over Federal Meat Inspection in 1906," Harvard Business School case no. N9-716-045, February 10, 2016, https://advancedleadership.harvard.edu/files/ali/files/the_jungle_and_the_debate_over_fed eral_meat_inspection_in_1906_716045.pdf.

149  "Roosevelt has a strong": Lesy and Stoffer, *Repast*, p. 57.

150  "The momentum of the": Sullivan, *Our Times*, p. 552.

150  There were still those: Phillips, *Treason of the Senate*, pp. 204–7.

151  Roosevelt's secretary replied: William Loeb Jr. to Thomas Ship (clerk, Committee on Territories, U.S. Senate), July 12, 1906, Wiley Papers, box 60.

151  Roosevelt had a different: Daniel Ruddy, ed., *Theodore Roosevelt's History of the United States (in His Own Words)* (New York: Smithsonian Books, 2010), pp. 211–12; Oscar E. Anderson Jr., *The Health of a Nation: Harvey W. Wiley and the Fight for Pure Food* (Chicago: University of Chicago Press, 1958), p. 190.

## Chapter Nine: The Poison Trust

155 "How does a general feel": Harvey Washington Wiley, *An Autobiography* (Indianapolis: Bobbs-Merrill, 1930), p. 231.

155 "I have long contemplated": L. D. Waterman, MD, to Harvey Wiley, March 15, 1906, Harvey Washington Wiley Papers, Library of Congress, Manuscript Division, box 60.

155 "I suppose you are pleased": James Shepard to Harvey Wiley, April 27, 1906, Wiley Papers, box 60.

156 On July 24 Wilson: Memo, James Wilson to Harvey Wiley, July 24, 1906, Wiley Papers, box 60.

156 "is not as good": Oscar E. Anderson Jr., *The Health of a Nation: Harvey W. Wiley and the Fight for Pure Food* (Chicago: University of Chicago Press, 1958), p. 228.

156 It did at least contain: Federal Food and Drugs Act of 1906 (noted on the U.S. Food and Drug Administration Web site as the "Wiley Act"), Pub. L. No. 59-384, 34 Stat. 786 (1906), www.fda .gov/regulatoryinformation/lawsenforcedbyfda/ucm148690.htm; and Robert McD. Allen, "Pure Food Legislation," *Popular Science Monthly* 29 (July 1906): pp. 1–14.

157 "establish standards of purity": Robert McD. Allen, "Pure Food Legislation," *Popular Science Monthly* 29 (July 1906): pp. 1–14.

157 "No set of authorities": Anderson, *Health of a Nation*, p. 198.

158 "For seventeen years": David Graham Phillips, *The Treason of the Senate*, eds. George E. Mowry and Judson A. Grenier (Chicago: Quadrangle Books, 1964), pp. 204–6.

159 "Naturally when the battle": Wiley, *An Autobiography*, p. 223.

159 "The word FOOD does not": Warwick Hough to James Wilson, November 26, 1906, Wiley Papers, box 60.

160 "discriminate against one class": Warwick Hough to James Wilson, December 3, 1906, Wiley Papers, box 60.

160 He told the lobbyist: James Wilson to Warwick Hough, December 22, 1906, Wiley Papers, box 60.

160 "Since you have objected": Warwick Hough to James Wilson, December 23, 1906, Wiley Papers, box 60.

160 In a mid-December speech: Harvey Wiley, lecture at the Atlas Club, Chicago, December 14, 1906, Wiley Papers, box 60.

160 In 1907 the Bureau: Harvey W. Wiley, *Influence of Food Preservatives and Artificial Colors on Digestion and Health*, vol. 3, *Sulphurous Acid and Sulphites* (Washington, DC: Government Printing Office, 1907), https://archive.org/details/preservafood00wilerich.

161 "microscopical examination of": Wiley, *Influence of Food Preservatives*, p. iii.

161 "The relations of sulfurous": Wiley, *Influence of Food Preservatives*, pp. 761–66.

162 "complete and somewhat": Wiley, *Influence of Food Preservatives*, pp. 761–66.

162 "The use of sulfurous": Wiley, *Influence of Food Preservatives*, pp. 761–66.

163 In January 1907: James Tawney's maneuvers to limit food regulations and pure food advocate responses are described in Anderson, *Health of a Nation*, pp. 200–218; and Laurine Swainston Goodwin, *The Pure Food, Drink and Drug Crusaders, 1879–1914* (Jefferson, NC: McFarland, 1999), pp. 275–77.

163 "impair the efficiency of": Alice Lakey to Harvey Wiley, February 14, 1907, Wiley Papers, box 63.

164 "The plot failed": Goodwin, *Pure Food, Drink and Drug Crusaders*, p. 276.

164 Opposition to Tawney's amendment: Samuel Merwin, "The People's Lobby," *Success Magazine* 10 (January 1907): pp. 17–18; People's Lobby to Harvey Wiley, December 13, 1906, Wiley Papers, box 60.

164 "If anyone is naughty": "A People's Lobby to Watch," *New York Times*, September 18, 1906, p. 6.

165 "Secretary Wilson absolutely": Robert Allen to Henry Needham, March 3, 1907. Wiley Papers box 63.

165 And Allen himself had: Anderson, *Health of a Nation*, pp. 211–12.

165 "I unqualifiedly recommend him": Robert Allen to Harvey Wiley, May 14, 1907, Wiley Papers, box 63.

165 Still, Allen's misgivings: Robert Allen to Henry Needham, April 20, 1907, Wiley Papers, box 63.

166 The ever-festering conflict: Harvey Washington Wiley, "1908 Report of the Bureau of Chemistry (from June 1907 to June 1908)," Bureau of Chemistry, U.S. Department of Agriculture, September 14, 1908, Washington, DC.

166 And barely a month after: Harvey Young, *Pure Food* (Princeton, NJ: Princeton University Press, 1989), pp. 206–18.

166 "Crooked is the term": Anderson, *Health of a Nation*, p. 202.

167 In a letter to Wilson: Warwick Hough to James Wilson, October 4, 1906, Wiley Papers, box 60.

168 In a March 30 letter: Harvey Wiley to Robert Allen, March 30, 1907, Wiley Papers, box 63; Wiley, *An Autobiography*, pp. 257–59.

168 But in terms of in-house: Young, *Pure Food*, pp. 206–18; H. Parker Willis, "What Whiskey Is," *McClure's*, April 1910, pp. 687–99; Mark Sullivan, *Our Times*, vol. 2 (1927; repr. New York: Charles Scribner and Sons, 1971), pp. 509–10.

168 After reviewing stacks of: William Wheeler Thomas, *The Law of Pure Food and Drugs* (Cincinnati: W. H. Anderson, 1912) pp. 450–455; Clayton Coppin and Jack High, *The Politics of Purity: Harvey Washington Wiley and the Origins of Federal Food Policy* (Ann Arbor: University of Michigan Press, 1999), pp. 100–110.

169 On April 10, 1907: Theodore Roosevelt to James Wilson, April 10, 1907, Wiley Papers, box 63.

169 "I write to congratulate you": James Hurty to Harvey Wiley, April 18, 1907, Wiley Papers, box 63.

169 "Let me congratulate you": M. A. Scovell to Harvey Wiley, April 20, 1907, Wiley Papers, box 63.

170 "level headed," he said: Anderson, *Health of a Nation*, p. 204.

170 As if to underscore: James Wilson to George McCabe, March 23, 1907, Wiley Papers, box 63.

170 "It seems to me": Wilson to McCabe, March 23, 1907.

170 But Wilson instead told: Wiley, *An Autobiography*, pp. 237–39; memo, James Wilson to Harvey Wiley, April 24, 1907, Wiley Papers, box 63.

171 "walked into my office": Wiley, *An Autobiography*, p. 238.

172 "a matter of fairness": James Wilson to Harvey Wiley, memo, April 24, 1907, Wiley Papers, box 63.

172 "to take away from the": Wiley, *An Autobiography*, p. 239.

172 On June 19, on Wilson's: Department of State to James Wilson, June 8, 1907, Wiley Papers, box 63.

172 "In a short time": Wiley, *An Autobiography*, p. 319.

173 During the visit, though: A week after Wiley left, Dunlap moved to take over his duties. Willard Bigelow, who was acting chief of the Bureau of Chemistry, tried strenuously to prevent this, eventually insisting on meeting with Secretary Wilson. Bigelow also found himself battling George McCabe on the solicitor's efforts to undermine food safety enforcement. "I am sorry to trouble you," he wrote to Wiley on July 26, 1907, while the chief chemist was still in France, and warned him that the department was moving to a probusiness stance. These actions are contained in a memo from Dunlap to Bigelow on June 27, 1907, demanding that he be given authority over all bureau correspondence; a reply from Bigelow, on the same day, flatly refusing to do so; a letter of warning from Bigelow to Wiley on June 29, 1907; a memo of reassurance from Wilson to Bigelow on July 1, 1907; and the letter of dismay from Bigelow to Wiley, cited above, on July 26, 1907, all contained in the Wiley Papers, box 63.

173 Known as Food Inspection Decision(FID) 76: Anderson, *Health of a Nation*, pp. 206–7.

175 "Telegrams began to come": "Question of Sulfur in Dried Fruit at Rest for the Present," letter from James Wilson, *California Fruit Grower*, March 21, 1908, p. 1.

175 "After listening to these": *Pacific Rural Press*, August 17, 1907, p. 1; Suzanne Rebecca White, "Chemistry and Controversy: Regulating the Use of Chemicals in Foods" (PhD diss., Emory University, 1994), p. 57.

175 The department, Wilson reminded: Memo, James Wilson to Harvey Wiley, August 24, 1907, Wiley Papers, box 63.

176 Not surprisingly, then: Harvey Wiley, "What Pure Food Laws Are Doing for Our People," speech at Vernon Avenue Christian Church, Washington, DC, September 5, 1907, transcript in Wiley Papers, box 63.

Chapter Ten: Of Ketchup and Corn Syrup

177 Ketchup (or catsup) was: Jasmine Wiggins, "How Was Ketchup Invented?" *The Plate* (blog), *National Geographic*, April 21, 2014, http://theplate.nationalgeographic.com/2014/04/21/how-was -ketchup-invented/; Dan Jurafsky, "The Cosmopolitan Condiment," *Slate*, May 30, 2012, www .slate.com/articles/life/food/2012/05/ketchup_s_chinese_origins_how_it_evolved_from_fish _sauce_to_today_s_tomato_condiment.html.

177 "take the intestine": John Brownlee, "How 500 Years of Weird Condiment History Designed the Heinz Ketchup Bottle," *Co.Design*, December 21, 2013, www.fastcodesign.com/1673352 /how-500-years-of-weird-condiment-history-designed-the-heinz-ketchup-bottle.

179 Sodium benzoate is: James Harvey Young, "The Science and Morals of Metabolism: Catsup and Benzoate of Soda," *Journal of the History of Medicine and Allied Sciences* 23, no. 1 (January

1968): pp. 86–104; Floyd Robinson, "Antiseptics in Tomato Catsup," *American Food Journal*, August 1907, pp. 39–41.

179   **Indiana's Columbia Conserve:** Harvey Washington Wiley, *An Autobiography* (Indianapolis: Bobbs-Merrill, 1930), pp. 234–36.

179   **Heinz was the same age:** Anna Slivka, "H.J. Heinz: Concerned Citizen or Clever Capitalist?" no date, The Ellis School, www.theellisschool.org/page/default?pk=29093.

181   **When the food and drug law:** Heinz Co. Food Products to Harvey Wiley, May 7, 1907, Harvey Washington Wiley Papers, Library of Congress, Manuscript Division, box 63.

181   **Due to its low cost:** "Saccharin from Coal Tar," *New York Times*, February 16, 1897, p. 3; Jesse Hicks, "The Pursuit of Sweet," *Distillations*, Spring 2010, www.chemheritage.org/distillations /magazine/the-pursuit-of-sweet.

182   **The National Food Manufacturers:** The anger of industry is outlined in the food manufacturers' publication, "Benzoate of Soda in Food Products," *American Food Journal*, January 15, 1908, pp. 7–9, in which Wiley is described as a man with "total lack of consideration for the financial interests involved." The meeting with Roosevelt has been widely covered, including in Young, "Science and Morals of Metabolism," pp. 89–92, and in Harvey Washington Wiley, *The History of a Crime Against the Food Law* (Washington, DC: self-published, 1929), pp. 160–68.

182   **"There was no way":** Wiley describes his meeting with the president in rueful detail in *An Autobiography*, pp. 239–41.

183   **"in the interests of":** Harvey W. Wiley, *Influence of Food Preservatives and Artificial Colors on Digestion and Health: Benzoic Acids and Benzoates* (Washington, DC: Government Printing Office, 1908).

183   **"On hearing this opinion":** Wiley, *An Autobiography*, pp. 239–41.

183   **"My firm saved $4,000":** Wiley, *An Autobiography*, pp. 239–41.

184   **"Everyone who ate":** This quote and the discussion that followed are found in Wiley, *An Autobiography*, pp. 240–43.

185   **The following day, Roosevelt:** Wiley, *An Autobiography*, pp. 242–43; James C. Whorton, *Before Silent Spring: Pesticides and Public Health in Pre-DDT America* (Princeton, NJ: Princeton University Press, 1974), pp. 105–10.

185   **"According to the ordinary":** Wiley, *History of a Crime Against the Food Law*, pp. 160–65.

185   **Wiley's chemists continued:** Harvey Wiley to Charles Bonaparte, October 3, 1907, Wiley Papers, box 63; Harvey Wiley to James Wilson, October 7, 1907, Wiley Papers, box 63; Charles Bonaparte to Warwick Hough, October 21, 1907, Wiley Papers, box 63; summary of Wilson's memo to Bonaparte, October 25, 1907, Wiley Papers, box 63.

186   **Yet the president:** "Effect of the Food Law on the Glucose Interests," *American Food Journal*, December 1906, p. 10; Anthony Gaughan and Peter Barton Hutt, "Harvey Wiley, Theodore Roosevelt, and the Federal Regulation of Food and Drugs" (third-year paper, Harvard Law School, Winter 2004), https://dash.harvard.edu/bitstream/handle/1/8852144/Gaughan.html?sequence=2.

186   **E. T. Bedford, as he was:** E. T. Bedford to James Wilson, December 16, 1907, Wiley Papers, box 63; memo, James Wilson to Harvey Wiley, December 20, 1907, Wiley Papers, box 63; Harvey Wiley to William Frear, December 27, 1907, Wiley Papers, box 63.

186   **the unappetizing word:** E. T. Bedford to Frederick Dunlap, January 9, 1908, Wiley Papers, box 65.

187   **"You must make the manufacturers":** Oscar E. Anderson Jr., *The Health of a Nation: Harvey W. Wiley and the Fight for Pure Food* (Chicago: University of Chicago Press, 1958), pp. 205–6.

187   **This came to bear as:** Anderson, *Health of a Nation*, pp. 207–8.

187   **In response, Roosevelt suggested:** Whorton, *Before Silent Spring*, pp. 107–9.

188   **"The president promptly fired":** Theodore Roosevelt to Harvey Wilson, July 30, 1908, Wiley Papers, box 64.

188   **Meanwhile, Roosevelt worked:** Charity Dye, *Some Torch Bearers in Indiana* (Indianapolis: Hellenbeck Press, 1917), pp. 210–15, quotes Wiley as saying, "This board was created by President Roosevelt in direct violation of the food and drug act"; Samuel F. Hopkins, "What Has Become of Our Pure Food Law?" *Hampton's Magazine* 24, no. 1 (January 1910): pp. 232–42; "The Referee Board," Expenditures in the U.S. Department of Agriculture, Report No. 249 (Moss Hearings), 62nd Cong., Government Printing Office, Washington, DC, January 22, 1912, pp. 2–17; "The United States Referee Board: How It Came to Be Appointed," *American Food Journal* 6, no. 9 (September 15, 1911): pp. 48–50.

189   **"a strong solution of":** E. T. Bedford to James Wilson, December 19, 1907, Wiley Papers, box 63.

189   But overall Wiley's relationships: *Proceedings of the American Chemical Society*, Easton, Pennsylvania, 1907, p. 83.

189   "The men who led": Harvey Wiley to C. A. Brown, New York Sugar Trade Laboratory, November 20, 1907, Wiley Papers, box 63.

190   "the creation of the": Wiley, *History of a Crime Against the Food Law*, p. 160.

190   "The Remsen Board": "Getting Results in the Fight for Pure Food," *New York Times*, May 10, 1908, p. 33.

190   The *Times*, along with Wiley's: An example is this letter to Roosevelt from Thomas McElhenie, a pharmacist in Brooklyn, on January 25, 1908: "The makers of food products are besieging you to appoint for their benefit a commission of chemists to be the superiors in Dr. Wiley's office. . . . I hope they will not prevail. In shotgun practice other birds are bound to be hit. Let them flutter. . . . The Food Law is a right law and should therefore stand."

*Chapter Eleven: Excuses for Everything*

191   "The use of chemical": Harvey Wiley, "Influence of Preservatives and Other Substances Added to Foods upon Health and Metabolism" (lecture, Annual Meeting of the American Philosophical Society, Philadelphia, April 25, 1908), Harvey Washington Wiley Papers, Library of Congress, Manuscript Division, box 190.

192   The sodium benzoate trials: Harvey W. Wiley, *Influence of Food Preservatives and Artificial Colors on Digestion and Health; Benzoic Acids and Benzoates* (Washington, DC: Government Printing Office, 1908). The Remsen Board's report, "The Influence of Sodium Benzoate on the Nutrition and Health of Man," was released in preliminary form in the summer of 1908 and formally published in January 1909 by the U.S. Department of Agriculture through the Government Printing Office in Washington, DC. To no one's surprise, where Wiley found health problems, the Referee Board found none.

192   Over the course of 1907: The publications suppressed by Wilson are listed by Wiley in a section titled "Data Refused Publication" in his self-published book *The History of a Crime Against the Food Law* (Washington, DC, 1929), pp. 62–64.

193   In August 1908 the: "Report of the Proceedings of the Twelfth Annual Convention of the Association of State and National Food and Dairy Departments," *American Food Journal* 3, no. 8 (August 15, 1908): pp. 1–12; Ronak Desai, "James Wilson, Harvey Wiley, and the Bureau of Chemistry: Examining the 'Political' Dimensions of the Administration and Enforcement of the Pure Food and Drugs Act 1906–1912" (student paper, Harvard Law School, May 2011), https://dash.harvard.edu/handle/1.8592146.

194   "The convention will probably": "Food and Drug Disagreements Become Public," *New York Times*, August 5, 1908, p. 7.

195   "the heat and cold": "Report of the Proceedings of the Twelfth Annual Convention," p. 8.

195   "Whenever a food": "Report of the Proceedings of the Twelfth Annual Convention," p. 10.

195   "Resolved: That this association": "Report of the Proceedings of the Twelfth Annual Convention," pp. 11–12.

196   "Those who watched events": Desai, "James Wilson, Harvey Wiley, and the Bureau of Chemistry."

197   this "brazen attack": Clayton Coppin and Jack High, *The Politics of Purity: Harvey Washington Wiley and the Origins of Federal Food Policy* (Ann Arbor: University of Michigan Press, 1999), pp. 123–26.

197   "not sparing in his": Suzanne Rebecca White, "Chemistry and Controversy: Regulating the Use of Chemicals in Foods, 1883–1959" (PhD diss., Emory University, 1994), pp. 108–10.

197   Snowy-white baked goods: White, "Chemistry and Controversy," pp. 112–34.

198   Edwin Ladd, the North Dakota: E. F. Ladd and R. E. Stallings, *Bleaching of Flour*, bulletin 72 (Fargo, ND: Government Agricultural Experiment Station of North Dakota, November 1906), pp. 219–35; James Shepard, "Nitrous Acid as an Antiseptic," *Monthly Bulletin of the Pennsylvania Department of Agriculture* 10 (November 1919): pp. 4–12. Shepard describes nitrous acid as a "vicious" additive in this article.

198   Wiley's Bureau of Chemistry: Aaron Bobrow-Strain, *White Bread: A Social History of the Store-Bought Loaf* (Boston: Beacon Press, 2012), pp. 51–72.

198   "A summary of our": *Annual Reports of the Department of Agriculture, Bureau of Chemistry* (Washington, DC: Government Printing Office, 1908), pp. 402–408.

198  **Wilson showed himself willing:** "Hearings of the Food and Drug Inspection Board," Preliminary Hearing #155, September 1908, National Archives, U.S. Food and Drug Administration, boxes 3 and 4.

199  **"Bleached flour is a":** Harvey Wiley to H. E. Barnard (Indiana food and drug commissioner), May 5, 1909, Wiley Papers, box 71.

199  **The details of the decision:** White, "Chemistry and Controversy," pp. 125–27.

199–200  **"Secretary Wilson and Dr. Wiley":** "Food Inspection Decision 100: Bleached Flour," *American Food Journal* 4, no. 1 (January 15, 1909): p. 26.

200  **Rumors began to circulate:** Michigan Dairy and Food Department to Theodore Roosevelt, October 22, 1908, Wiley Papers, box 65. The convention lived up to the promised drama, and both the events and their fallout appear in Clayton Coppin and Jack High, *The Politics of Purity: Harvey Washington Wiley and the Origins of Federal Food Policy* (University of Michigan Press, 1999), pp. 125–27; Andrew E. Smith, *Pure Ketchup: A History of America's National Condiment* (University of South Carolina Press, 2011), pp. 77–118, in a stunningly good chapter titled "The Benzoate Wars," which covers not only the convention but also Wiley, the Remsen Board, and the battles between Heinz and other manufacturers in the most fascinating way; Ronak Desai, "James Wilson, Harvey Wiley, and the Bureau of Chemistry: Examining the 'Political' Dimensions of the Administration and Enforcement of the Pure Food and Drugs Act, 1906–1912" (student paper, Harvard Law School, May 2011), https://dash.harvard.edu/bitstream/handle/1/8592146/Desai%2C%20Ronak.pdf?sequence=1; and Oscar E. Anderson Jr., *The Health of a Nation: Harvey W. Wiley and the Fight for Pure Food* (Chicago: University of Chicago Press, 1958), pp. 230–31.

201  **Newspaper coverage made it clear:** All newspapers quoted are from a clippings file, Wiley Papers, box 229, folder 1908.

201  **The chorus of public dismay:** James Harvey Young, "Two Hoosiers and the Food Laws of 1906," *Indiana Magazine of History* 88, no. 4 (1992): 303–19.

202  **That same December:** Harvey W. Wiley, *The Influence of Preservatives and Artificial Colors on Digestion and Health*, vol. 5, *Formaldehyde* (Washington, DC: Government Printing Office, 1908), https://archive.org/details/influenceoffoodp84wile_3.

202  **a "violent poison":** Wiley, *Influence of Preservatives and Artificial Colors*, p. 30.

202  **Wiley also could take:** Anderson, *Health of a Nation*, pp. 234–35.

203  **For some years, magazines:** "Booming the Borax Business," *Journal of the American Medical Association* 49, no. 14 (October 5, 1907): 1191–92; "Preservatives and Press Agents," *Journal of the American Medical Association* 303, no. 1 (January 6, 2010): p. 81 (reprint of January 1, 1910, article).

205  **It surprised neither:** James C. Whorton, *Before Silent Spring: Pesticides and Public Health in Pre-DDT America* (Princeton, NJ: Princeton University Press, 1974), pp. 106–8.

205  **"You will find it":** James Harvey Young, "The Science and Morals of Metabolism," *Journal of the History of Medicine and Allied Sciences* 23, no. 1 (January 1968): p. 97.

205  **"slight modifications in":** U.S. Department of Agriculture, Referee Board of Consulting Experts, *The Influence of Sodium Benzoate on the Nutrition and Health of Man* (Washington, DC: Government Printing Office, 1909), pp. 9–13.

205  **"hot, dry New England":** U.S. Department of Agriculture, *Influence of Sodium Benzoate*, pp. 88–90.

205  **Preservative makers declared:** Smith, *Pure Ketchup*, pp. 97–103.

205  **"a first class fight":** Young, "Science and Morals of Metabolism," p. 100.

206  **"[T]his decision of":** E. E. Smith, MD, "Benzoate of Soda in Foods," *Journal of the American Medical Association* 52 , no. 11 (March 13, 1909): p. 905.

206  **"If you could see":** Anderson, *Health of a Nation*, p. 218.

206  **Wilson was unmoved:** *Literary Digest* 38 (March 20, 1909): pp. 463–64; J. F. Snell, "Chemistry in Its Relation to Food," *Journal of the Chemical Industry* 28 (January 30, 1909): pp. 52–53.

207  **Wiley thought again:** Harvey Washington Wiley, *An Autobiography* (Indianapolis: Bobbs-Merrill, 1930), pp. 241–43.

*Chapter Twelve: Of Whiskey and Soda*

208  **"I expect to give Dr. Wiley":** Oscar E. Anderson Jr., *The Health of a Nation: Harvey W. Wiley and the Fight for Pure Food* (Chicago: University of Chicago Press, 1958), p. 224.

208 But the sitting president: Nicholas Lemann, "Progress's Pilgrims: Doris Kearns Goodwin on T.R. and Taft," *New Yorker*, November 18, 2013, www.newyorker.com/magazine/2013/11/18 /progresss-pilgrims; Doris Kearns Goodwin, *The Bully Pulpit: Theodore Roosevelt, William Howard Taft and the Golden Age of Journalism* (New York: Simon & Schuster, 2013), pp. 605–21.

209 Roosevelt had quietly tried: H. Parker Willis, "What Whiskey Is," *McClure's*, April 1910, pp. 687–99.

209 "[T]he term 'whiskey'": Willis, "What Whiskey Is," p. 696.

210 In response, Taft asked: James Files, "Hiram Walker and Sons and the Pure Food and Drug Act" (master's thesis, University of Windsor, 1986), pp. 84–89.

210 "reminiscent of a German": Willis, "What Whiskey Is," p. 697.

210 "The evidence shows": Willis, "What Whiskey Is," pp. 693–95.

210 In late May, Bowers: Harvey Washington Wiley, *An Autobiography* (Indianapolis: Bobbs-Merrill, 1930), pp. 257–59; memo, Harvey Wiley to Frederick Dunlap, October 2, 1909, Harvey Washington Wiley Papers, Library of Congress, Manuscript Division, box 71 ("My opinion of the letter of Mr. Hough, addressed to the commissioner of the IRS, is that Mr. Hough will use every effort in his power to protect the adulterers and debasers of distilled spirits from receiving the penalty they should under the law.").

211 "drugs and oils and colors": Willis, "What Whiskey Is," p. 698.

211 Less openly, Taft also: The background on Taft's inquiry about the legality of the Remsen Board and the suppression of the findings comes from congressional testimony during hearings held by U.S. senator Ralph Moss of Indiana in August 1911. Full coverage of the hearing can be found in a report from the U.S. Senate, "The Referee Board," Expenditures in the U.S. Department of Agriculture, Report No. 249 (Moss Hearings), 62nd Cong., Government Printing Office, Washington, DC, January 22, 1912.

211 "I do not think": "The Remsen Board's Opinion," *New York Times*, August 6, 1911, p. 8.

212 "I consider there is": Harvey Wiley to George McCabe and Frederick Dunlap, memo, July 2, 1909, Wiley Papers, box 71.

212 a "ludicrous recommendation": George McCabe to Harvey Wiley and Frederick Dunlap, memo, July 6, 1909, Wiley Papers, box 71.

212 Many of their disagreements: By the fall of 1909, the departmental warfare among Wiley, Dunlap, and McCabe was ceaseless, at least judging by the memos archived at the Library of Congress. And Wiley's tone was shifting from outrage to resignation. Two examples: On October 30, 1909, Dunlap rejects Wiley's concern about phosphoric acid as a health issue and demands evidence. On November 9, 1909, Wiley's response begins, "I have no time to hunt up information to convince you that articles are injurious to health. It is too much of a task." On December 21, 1909, Wiley writes to Dunlap, "I regret that I have no time to expound all the reasons which lead me to believe that the addition of a substance to foods which is not a food and which takes no part in nutrition need not be proved absolutely harmful before it can be excluded under the law." Wiley Papers, box 71.

213 "If sodium acetate is": Frederick Dunlap to Harvey Wiley, memo, July 15, 1909, Wiley Papers, box 71.

213 "I have not time": Harvey Wiley to Frederick Dunlap, memo, August 2, 1909, Wiley Papers, box 71.

213 In another dispute: C. D. Regier, "The Struggle for Federal Food and Drug Regulation," *Law and Contemporary Problems* 1 (1933): pp. 11–12.

214 The battle over sodium: Andrew E. Smith, *Pure Ketchup: A History of America's National Condiment* (Columbia: University of South Carolina Press, 2011), pp. 105–13; Samuel F. Hopkins, "What Has Become of Our Pure Food Law?" *Hampton's Magazine* 24, no. 1 (January 1910): 232–42.

214 In anticipation of: Anderson, *Health of a Nation*, pp. 228–32.

215 But the standoff between: "Injunction Granted in Favor of Benzoate of Soda," *American Food Journal* 4, no. 4 (April 15, 1909): pp. 15–16; the decision is outlined in the legal record of the ruling, *Curtice Brothers v. Harry E. Barnard et al.*, United States Circuit Court of Appeals, 4:2987–3043, National Archives Great Lakes Region, Chicago.

215 "It must be evident": William Williams Keen, "The New Pure Food Catsup," *National Food Magazine* 28, no. 1 (July 1910): pp. 108–9.

216 Wilson knew that Ladd: Smith, *Pure Ketchup*, pp. 105–13; Clayton Coppin and Jack High, *The Politics of Purity: Harvey Washington Wiley and the Origins of Federal Food Policy* (Ann Arbor: University of Michigan Press, 1999), pp. 128–32.

218 **Just weeks earlier:** Suzanne Rebecca White, "Chemistry and Controversy: Regulating the Use of Chemicals in Foods, 1883–1959" (PhD diss., Emory University, 1994), pp. 127–34.

216 **"I am utterly hostile":** "Bleached Flour Men Try to Get Wilson Reversed," *American Food Journal* 4, no. 3 (March 15, 1909): p. 25.

216 **"This can come only":** Anderson, *Health of a Nation*, pp. 220–22.

217 **Despite agreeing to seizures:** Anderson, *Health of a Nation*, pp. 220–22.

217 **He moved to block:** Suppressed documents are listed in Harvey W. Wiley, *The History of a Crime Against the Food Law* (Washington, DC: self-published, 1929), pp. 62–64.

217 **"I regret that I shall":** Harvey Wiley to R. U. Johnson, September 13, 1909, Wiley Papers, box 71.

217 **"James Wilson, secretary":** "Pure Food Feud Nearing a Climax," *Chicago Tribune*, August 26, 1909, p. 4.

218 **"a bear pit":** Anderson, *Health of a Nation*, p. 230.

218 **"As the inside facts":** "Politics Reign at the Agriculture Department," *Los Angeles Herald*, September 3, 1909, p. 3.

218 **"We fully smashed the":** Ronak Desai, "James Wilson, Harvey Wiley and the Bureau of Chemistry: Examining the 'Political' Dimensions of the Administration and Enforcement of the Pure Food and Drugs Act 1906–1912" (student paper, Harvard Law School, May 2011), p. 29, https://dash.harvard.edu/handle/1/8592146.

218 **"low class fellow":** Desai, "James Wilson, Harvey Wiley and the Bureau of Chemistry."

219 **"foe to fakers":** Dennis B. Worthen, "Lyman Frederick Kebler (1863–1955): Foe to Fakers," *Journal of the American Pharmacists Association* 50, no. 3 (May–June 2010): pp. 429–32, www.japha.org/article/S1544-3191(15)30834-7/abstract.

219 **The indiscriminate use of:** Lyman F. Kebler, U.S. Department of Agriculture, *Habit-Forming Agents: Their Indiscriminate Sale and Use a Menace to Public Welfare* (Washington, DC: Government Printing Office, 1910), https://archive.org/details/CAT87202997; "Medicated Soft Drinks," 1910 Report of the Bureau of Chemistry, U.S. Department of Agriculture, p. 156; and backgrounder on "so-called soft drinks" by Harvey W. Wiley for James Wilson, Wiley Papers, box 208. The issue had also been gaining some public health attention, as seen in "Drugged 'Soft' Drinks: The Food Law Has Partly Revealed Their Character," *New York Times*, July 7, 1909, p. 8.

220 **"representing 300,000,000 glasses":** "All Doubts About Coca-Cola Settled," *National Druggist*, August 1908, p. 274.

221 **he was especially wary:** Coca-Cola Company, "The Chronicle of Coca-Cola: The Candler Era," January 1, 2012, www.coca-colacompany.com/stories/the-chronicle-of-coca-cola-the-candler-era; Mark Pendergrast, *For God, Country & Coca-Cola* (New York: Basic Books, 2013), pp. 45–66.

221 **The U.S. Army in 1907:** Stephen B. Karch, *A Brief History of Cocaine* (Boca Raton, FL: CRC Press, 2005), p. 126.

221 **Wiley, who, as his colleagues:** White, "Chemistry and Controversy," pp. 134–39.

221 **"I am not a believer":** Harvey Wiley to James Wilson, October 28, 1909, Wiley Papers, box 71.

222 **"highly objectionable both":** Harvey Wiley to George McCabe, November 2, 1909, Wiley Papers, box 71. (The memo also argues that "an effort should be made to stop traffic in this dangerous beverage.")

222 **They got support from:** White, "Chemistry and Controversy," p. 139.

222 **"Coca-Cola is one of":** Harvey Wiley to James Wilson, November 13, 1909, Wiley Papers, box 71.

222 **"there is much":** Wiley to Wilson, November 13, 1909.

222 **"What I did say":** "Dr. Wiley Throws a Stone at Our Industry and Then Runs," *American Bottler*, December 1909, p. 182.

222 **What he didn't mention:** Pendergrast, *For God, Country & Coca-Cola*, pp. 107–9.

223 **"I was, of course":** Wiley, *An Autobiography*, pp. 261–63.

224 **"contains an alkaloidal":** Pendergrast, *For God, Country & Coca-Cola*, pp. 109–10.

224 **"It is remarkable":** Wiley, *An Autobiography*, pp. 261–63.

224 **On October 21, 1909:** *United States v. Forty Barrels and Twenty Kegs of Coca-Cola*, 241 U.S. 265 (1916), http://caselaw.findlaw.com/us-supreme-court/241/265.html.

225 **"Taft Whisky," which would:** Bob Eidson, "The Taft Decision," *Bourbon Review*, February 17, 2014, www.gobourbon.com/the-taft-decision/.

225 **On December 26 the president:** Wiley, *An Autobiography*, pp. 257–59; Michael Veach, "20th Century Distilling Papers at the Filson," *Filson Newsmagazine* 7, no. 4 (no date), www.filsonhistorical.org/archive/news_v7n4_distilling.html.

225  "**Whiskey appears to be**": H. Parker Willis, "What Whiskey Is," *McClure's*, April 1910, pp. 698–99.

225  "**What do you think**": Wiley. *An Autobiography*, p. 258.

225  "**What I fear is**": A. O. Stanley (Glenmore Distilleries) to Harvey Wiley, January 14, 1910, Wiley Papers, box 81.

226  "**that neutral spirits, which**": Alice Lakey to Harvey Wiley, January 12, 1910, Wiley Papers, box 81. Wiley too was deeply unhappy. He prepared a rebuttal, should the occasion occur again, arguing strongly for the old classifications of whiskey: whiskey folder, 1908–1910, Wiley Papers, box 209.

226  "**We believe that**": from Alice Lakey to *Detroit News*, January 12, 1910, Wiley Papers, box 81. This letter is also cited in "Pure Food Progress," *Collier's*, March 12, 1912, p. 3.

226  "**It is a very**": Alice Lakey to Harvey Wiley, January 12, 1910, Wiley Papers, box 81.

226  "**There is but little**": Harvey Wiley to Alice Lakey, January 22, 1910, Wiley Papers, box 81.

*Chapter Thirteen: The Love Microbe*

227  **In January he had promised**: Wiley's schedule, Harvey Washington Wiley Papers, Library of Congress, Manuscript Division, box 81.

228  **That interest encouraged**: Oscar E. Anderson Jr., *The Health of a Nation: Harvey W. Wiley and the Fight for Pure Food* (Chicago: University of Chicago Press, 1958), p. 242.

229  **Before the law, even**: Adam Burrows, "A Palette of Our Palates: A Brief History of Food Coloring and Its Regulation" (paper submitted as a Food and Drug Law course requirement, Harvard Law School, May 2006); H. T. McKone, "The Unadulterated History of Food Dyes," *ChemMatters*, December 1999, pp. 6–7.

230  **A resulting 1907 Food**: Dale Blumenthal, "Red Dye No. 3 and Other Colorful Controversies," *FDA Consumer* 24 (May 1990): pp. 18–21.

230  **McCabe decided to review**: Daniel Marmion, *Handbook of U.S. Colorants* (New York: John Wiley and Sons, 1991), pp. 11–12.

231  **While Hesse worked**: The Lexington Mill case and the first stages of litigation are described in Suzanne Rebecca White, "Chemistry and Controversy: Regulating the Use of Chemicals in Foods, 1883–1959" (PhD diss., Emory University, 1994), pp. 127–33; and William G. Panschar, *Baking in America: Economic Development*, vol. 1 (Evanston, IL: Northwestern University Press, 1956), pp. 235–39. The first public victory was celebrated in newspaper stories such as "Bleached Flour Is Adulterated: Government Wins Important Test Case," *Sacramento Union*, July 7, 1910, p. 2; and deplored in great detail in "Government Wins Bleached Flour Case," *American Food Journal* 5, no. 7 (July 15, 1910): pp. 1–11.

231  "**a blast of God's**": and "Flour Bleachers to Be Prosecuted Pending Appeal," *American Food Journal* 5, no. 8 (August 15, 1910): pp. 8–12.

233  **Bernhard Hesse's eighty-page**: Bernhard C. Hesse, U.S. Department of Agriculture, Bureau of Chemistry, *Coal-Tar Colors Used in Food Products*, (Washington, DC: Government Printing Office, 1912), https://archive.org/details/coaltarcolorsuse14hess. (The report was first circulated in 1910.)

234  **he'd named it Grasslands**: Elesley Mour, "Dr. Wiley and His Farm," *Country Life in America* 28, no. 4 (August 1915): pp. 19–21.

234  **he'd even purchased a**: Harvey Washington Wiley, *An Autobiography* (Indianapolis: Bobbs-Merrill, 1930), pp. 279–80.

234  **In late October of 1910**: Anderson, *Health of a Nation*, p. 242.

235  DR. WILEY WILL TAKE A BRIDE: THE *Tribune* story and other newspaper clippings regarding the engagement can be found in Anna Wiley's scrapbook, Wiley Papers, box 227; Wiley, *An Autobiography*, pp. 281–83.

235  "**There is a shade**": James Wilson to Ira Remsen, December 11, 1910, Wiley Papers, box 189.

236  **After the passage of the**: Peter Duffy, "The Deadliest Book Review," *New York Times*, January 14, 2011, www.nytimes.com/2011/01/16/books/review/Duffy-t.html.

236  **Barely two months later**: The Coca-Cola trial appears in Mark Pendergrast, *For God, Country & Coca-Cola* (New York: Basic Books, 2013), pp. 110–15; White, "Chemistry and Controversy," pp. 139–47; and countless newspaper stories, including the one cited in the next note and others which can be found in the Coca-Cola clippings file, Wiley Papers, box 200. The *American Food Journal*'s coverage of the trial, "Coca-Cola Litigation Ends with Defeat for the Government," April 15, 1911, pp. 10–17, provides an invaluable witness-by-witness review of the case.

237 **McCabe began the prosecution:** "Candler Cursed Me, Says the Inspector," *Atlanta Georgian*, March 4, 1911, p. 1.

242 **Coca-Cola had also hired:** Ludy T. Benjamin, "Pop Psychology: The Man Who Saved Coca-Cola," *Monitor on Psychology* 40, no. 2 (2009): p. 18, www.apa.org/monitor/2009/02/coca-cola.aspx. For more about Hollingworth and the trial, it's worth checking out Anne M. Rogers and Angela Rosenbaum, "Coca-Cola, Caffeine, and Mental Deficiency: Harry Hollingworth and the Chattanooga Trial of 1911," *Journal of the History of the Behavioral Sciences* 27 (1991): pp. 42–55, www.researchgate.net/publication/229960591_Coca-Cola_caffeine_and_mental_deficiency _Harry_Hollingworth_and_the_Chattanooga_Trial_of_1911.

243 **"20 dopes daily":** "Coca-Cola Drinkers Suffer No Harm," *Chattanooga Daily Times*, March 16, 1911, archived in Wiley Papers, Coca-Cola files, box 200.

244 **"if the government proved":** "Coca-Cola Trial Was Only the Start," *Chattanooga Daily Times*, April 30, 1911, archived in Wiley Papers, Coca-Cola files, box 200.

244 **The defeated delegation:** Referee Board of Consulting Scientific Experts, U.S. Department of Agriculture, *Influence of Saccharine on the Nutrition and Health of Man*, report 94 (Washington, DC: Government Printing Office, 1911).

245 **It had come about:** James Harvey Young, "Saccharin: A Bitter Regulatory Decision," in *Research in the Administration of Public Policy*, ed. Frank B. Evans and Harold T. Pinkett (Washington, DC: Howard University Press, 1974), pp. 40–50.

245 **McCabe had long believed:** Board of Food and Drug Inspection, U.S. Department of Agriculture, Food Inspection Decision (FID) 35, April 29, 1911.

246 **Queeny, energized by:** "Saccharin Makers at Washington," *Oil, Paint, and Drug Reporter* 79, no. 22 (May 1911): p. 28.

246 **"I want to say frankly":** Testimony before the U.S. Senate, hearings held in August 1911 by Senator Ralph Moss of Indiana, recorded in "The Referee Board," Expenditures in the U.S. Department of Agriculture, Report No. 249 (Moss Hearings), 62nd Cong., Government Printing Office, Washington, DC, January 22, 1912. The statement is also cited in "The Remsen Board's Opinion," *New York Times*, August 6, 1911, p. 8.

247 **This new mess:** Anderson, *Health of a Nation*, pp. 244–45; Harvey W. Wiley, *The History of a Crime Against the Food Law* (Washington, DC, self-published, 1929), pp. 174–82.

248 **"Personally, I am of":** Anderson, *Health of a Nation*, p. 244.

249 **"political judgment of an ox":** L. F. Abbott, ed., *Taft and Roosevelt: The Intimate Letters of Archie Butt*, vol. 2 (New York: Doubleday, Doran, 1930), p. 696.

249 **"too great of a disposition":** Ronak Desai, "James Wilson, Harvey Wiley, and the Bureau of Chemistry: Examining the 'Political' Dimensions of the Administration and Enforcement of the Pure Food and Drugs Act 1906–1912" (student paper, Harvard Law School, May 2011), https:// dash.harvard.edu/handle/1/8592146, p. 29.

*Chapter Fourteen: The Adulteration Snake*

251 **Then, to Bigelow's surprise:** Oscar E. Anderson Jr., The *Health of a Nation: Harvey W. Wiley and the Fight for Pure Food* (Chicago: University of Chicago Press, 1958), p. 246.

252 **"We need no defense":** Anderson, *Health of a Nation*.

252 **"After having failed":** Harvey W. Wiley, *The History of a Crime Against the Food Law* (Washington, DC: self-published, 1929), p. 258.

252 **"They . . . showed a tendency":** "Row over Wilson," *Evening Star* (Washington, DC), August 1, 1911, p. 1.

253 **"The Remsen referee board":** "Row over Wilson."

253 **Such revelations further stoked:** Telegrams and letters regarding the Rusby affair, July 13–August 18, 1911, Harvey Washington Wiley Papers, Library of Congress, Manuscript Division, box 88. I do not cite them all here, but the file contains dozens. One of my favorite uncited ones was dated August 18, 1911, to Wiley from J. H. Hunt of the canning company Hunt Brothers. It concludes, "Give 'em H—l Doctor!"

255 **Appalled, George Wickersham wrote:** Anderson, *Health of a Nation*, p. 247.

255 **"as weak as water":** Anderson, *Health of a Nation*, p. 247.

255 **The Moss committee hearings:** My description is based on numerous sources, including "The Referee Board," Expenditures in the U.S. Department of Agriculture, Report No. 249 (Moss Hearings), 62nd Cong., Government Printing Office, Washington, DC, January 22, 1912; and Wiley, *History of a Crime Against the Food Law*, pp. 88–210 (citing directly from the report). See

also the *Herald*'s highly critical coverage, Wiley Papers, box 221, 1911 clippings folder. The *Evening Star* clippings can also be found in this folder.

256 **"Lawyer McCabe has been"**: "McCabe Ruled Hard, Scientists Assert," *Evening Star* (Washington, DC), August 11, 1911, p. 3.

256 **"By the clever framing"**: "Big Fees Were Paid by Remsen Board, Dispersing Officer Admits," *New York Times*, August 2, 1911, p. 2.

257 **"The broader issues raised"**: Anderson, *Health of a Nation*, pp. 247–48.

258 **"My heartiest congratulations"**: Samuel Hopkins Adams to Harvey Wiley, September 17, 1911, Wiley Papers, box 88. Among dozens of notes of congratulations, "I believe there is rejoicing all over the country," wrote Arthur Bailey of Bailey's Extract of Clams, Boston, on September 16.

258 **The R.B. Davis Company:** R.B. Davis Company to Harvey Wiley, July 14, 1911, Wiley Papers, box 88; Harvey Wiley to R.B. Davis Company, July 21, 1911, Wiley Papers, box 88.

258 **In January 1912 the Moss:** "The Referee Board"; Wiley, *History of a Crime Against the Food Law*, pp. 88–210 (citing directly from the report).

259 **"while the verdict was"**: Harvey Wiley to Frank McCullough (Green River Distillery, Kentucky), January 29, 1912, Wiley Papers, box 88.

260 **Within a few weeks following:** Harvey Washington Wiley, *An Autobiography* (Indianapolis: Bobbs-Merrill, 1930), pp. 288–89.

261 **"As I read the papers"**: Nathaniel Fowler to Harvey Wiley, January 15, 1912, Wiley Papers, box 88.

261 **By March 1912:** Wiley, *An Autobiography*, pp. 288–89; Wiley, *History of a Crime Against the Food Law* (coverage of the conversation with Wilson at pp. 55–56; copy of the resignation letter at p. 92).

262 **"That story isn't"**: "Dr. Wiley Resigns," *Druggists Circular*, April 1912, p. 211.

262 **"I hereby tender my"**: Harvey Wiley to James Wilson, March 15, 1912, Wiley Papers, box 88.

262 **"It is also a matter"**: Wiley, *History of a Crime Against the Food Law*, pp. 92–94.

263 **"that I should not"**: Wiley, *History of a Crime Against the Food Law*, pp. 92–94.

263 **"Here's your hat"**: "Dr. Wiley Resigns," *Druggists Circular*, April 1812, p. 211.

263 **Like Wilson, President Taft was:** Anderson, *Health of a Nation*, pp. 252–53.

263 **But elsewhere in the Department:** Wiley, *An Autobiography*, pp. 290–91.

264 **"With tears streaming down"**: Wiley, *An Autobiography*, p. 292.

264 **"Some of the employees"**: "Dr. Wiley Is Out, Attacking Enemies," *New York Times*, March 16, 1912, p. 1.

264 **"Dr. Wiley is known"**: "Dr. Wiley Resigns," *National Food Magazine* 30, no. 4 (April 1912): p. 2.

264 **"his hands have been"**: "Dr. Wiley Resigns," *Druggists Circular*.

264 **"So clear in his great"**: "Dr. Wiley Resigns," *Druggists Circular*.

264 **"I regard the passing"**: Wiley, *An Autobiography*, p. 292.


*Chapter Fifteen: The History of a Crime*

266 **In a report to Wilson:** Roscoe Doolittle, Acting Chief, U.S. Department of Agriculture, *1911 Report of the Bureau of Chemistry* (Washington, DC: Government Printing Office, July 30, 1912).

267 **"There wasn't a single"**: Alfred W. McCann, "Food Frauds as Revealed at the National Magazines Exposition," *National Food Magazine* 31, no. 9 (September 1912): pp. 505–6.

268 **"We cannot conceive"**: "A New Head for the U.S. Department of Agriculture," *Chemical Trade Journal*, November 17, 1912, archived in Harvey Washington Wiley Papers, Library of Congress, Manuscript Division, clippings file, box 199.

268 **"I have no cabinet aspirations"**: Harvey Wiley to R. W. Ward (Oregon physician), December 4, 1912, Wiley Papers, box 88.

268 **"The doctor doesn't expect"**: Harvey Wiley to J. G. Emery, December 11, 1912, Wiley Papers, box 88.

268 **The retail druggists' group:** "United States Supreme Court; The Sherley Amendment to the Pure Food and Drugs Act Is Constitutional; A Misbranded 'Patent Medicine' Condemned; *Seven Cases Eckman's Alterative v. United States, U.S.* (Jan. 10, 1916)," *Public Health Reports (1896–1970)* 31, no. 3 (January 21, 1916): pp. 137–40; Nicola Davis, "FDA Focus: The Sherley Amendment," *Pharmaletter*, October 11, 2014, www.thepharmaletter.com/article/fda-focus-the-sherley-amendment.

269 **"I do not think"**: Wiley to Emery, December 11, 1912.

269 **Alsberg, a biochemist:** U.S. Food and Drug Administration, "Carl L. Alsberg, M.D.," March 15, 2017, www.fda.gov/AboutFDA/WhatWeDo/History/Leaders/Commissioners/ucm093764.htm.

270 **This change was highlighted:** "Clearing the Atmosphere in the Saccharin Controversy," *American Food Journal* 7, no. 1 (January 15, 1912): 16–17; "An Opinion on the Saccharin Decisions," *American Food Journal* 7, no. 9 (September 15, 1912): p. 7.

270 **Following yet another:** Suzanne Rebecca White, "Chemistry and Controversy: Regulating the Use of Chemicals in Foods, 1883–1959" (PhD diss., Emory University, 1994), pp. 154–60; James Harvey Young, "Saccharin: A Bitter Regulatory Decision," in *Research in the Administration of Public Policy*, ed. Frank B. Evans and Harold T. Pinkett (Washington, DC: Howard University Press, 1974), pp. 40–50; Deborah Jean Warner, *Sweet Stuff: An American History of Sweeteners from Sugar to Sucralose* (Lanham, MD: Rowman and Littlefield, 2011), pp. 185–94.

270 **Meanwhile, as promised:** White, "Chemistry and Controversy," pp. 131–33; *United States v. Lexington Mill & Elevator Co.*, 232 U.S. 399 (1914), www.law.cornell.edu/supremecourt/text/232/399.

270 **Appalled, Wiley sent:** Harvey W. Wiley, *The History of a Crime Against the Food Law* (Washington, DC: self-published, 1929), pp. 381–82.

272 **"I am not an enemy":** Harvey Washington Wiley and Mildred Maddocks, *The Pure Food Cookbook* (New York: Hearst's International Library, 1914), p. 71.

270 ***Good Housekeeping* was now:** Harvey Washington Wiley, *An Autobiography* (Indianapolis: Bobbs-Merrill, 1930), pp. 302–6; "The Original Man of the House," *Good Housekeeping*, April 10, 2010: www.goodhousekeeping.com/institute/about-the-institute/a18828/about-harvey-wiley/.

272 **"There is perhaps":** Wiley and Maddocks, *Pure Food Cookbook*, p. 171.

273 **"I had no longer":** Wiley, *An Autobiography*, p. 304.

273 **In 1916 Alsberg authorized:** Carl Alsberg, U.S. Department of Agriculture, *1916 Report of the Bureau of Chemistry* (Washington, DC: Government Printing Office, July 30, 1917).

274 **But he, Wiley, and just about:** Mark Pendergrast, *For God, Country and Coca-Cola* (New York: Basic Books, 2013), pp. 114–15; White, "Chemistry and Controversy," pp. 149–50; *United States v. Forty Barrels and Twenty Kegs of Coca-Cola*, 241 U.S. 265 (1916), http://caselaw.findlaw.com/us-supreme-court/241/265.html.

275 **As Alsberg wrote:** Carl Alsberg, U.S. Department of Agriculture, *1917 Report of the Bureau of Chemistry* (Washington, DC: Government Printing Office, July 30, 1918).

275 **Even in the shadow:** Roxie Olmstead, "Anna Kelton Wiley: Suffragist," History's Women, no date, www.historyswomen.com/socialreformer/annkeltonwiley.html.

276 **"She believes the ballot":** Katherine Graves Busbey, "Mrs. Harvey W. Wiley," *Good Housekeeping*, January 1912, pp. 544–46.

276 **To his friends who wondered:** Oscar E. Anderson Jr., *The Health of a Nation: Harvey W. Wiley and the Fight for Pure Food* (Chicago: University of Chicago Press, 1958), p. 264.

276 **"Our flag on all seas":** "Theodore Roosevelt Dies Suddenly at Oyster Bay Home; Nation Shocked, Pays Tribute to Former President, Our Flag on All Seas and in All Lands at Half Mast," *New York Times*, January 6, 1919, p. 1.

276 **But Harvey Wiley spared no:** Wiley wrote an entire bitter chapter about Roosevelt's hostility toward him and his perceived undermining of food regulations: "Attitude of Roosevelt," in *The History of a Crime Against the Food Law*, pp. 263–75.

277 **The case against saccharin:** White, "Chemistry and Controversy," pp. 155–66.

277 **The government's leading expert:** R.M. Cunningham and Williams Greer, "The Man Who Understands Your Stomach," *Saturday Evening Post* (September 13, 1947): pp. 173–75; A. J. Carlson, "Some Physiological Actions of Saccharin and Their Bearing on the Use of Saccharin in Foods," in *Report of the National Academy of Sciences for the Year 1917* (Washington, DC: Government Printing Office, 1918).

278 **"slack-fill" bill:** *Food and Drug Law* (Washington, DC: Food and Drug Institute, 1991), p. 46.

279 **"it would be a serious":** Suzanne Rebecca White, "Chemistry and Controversy: Regulating the Use of Chemicals in Foods, 1883–1959" (PhD diss., Emory University, 1994), pp. 160–62.

280 **"The Government has much":** "Chronology of Food Additive Regulations in the United States," Environment, Health and Safety Online, no date, www.ehso.com/ehshome/FoodAdd/foodadditivecron.htm.

280 **Upon Coolidge's election:** Harvey W. Wiley, "Enforcement of the Food Law," *Good Housekeeping*, September 1925, www.seleneriverpress.com/historical/enforcement-of-the-food-law/?.

281 **"for the most part undesirable":** Wiley's letter to Coolidge and Dunlap's reply to Wiley can be found in this digital text version maintained by the Library of Congress: https://memory.loc.gov /mss/amrlm/lmk/mk01/mk01.sgm.

282 **"I had hoped to do":** UPC News Services, "'Food Poisoning General,' Says Wiley; Expert Charges Pure Food Law Is Being Ignored, Attacks Proposed Starch Sugar Law as Fraud," July 26, 1926.

282 **"Why should legislation be":** Anderson, *Health of a Nation*, p. 275.

282 **"The country owes you":** Anderson, *Health of a Nation*, p. 275.

284 **"The freedom of science":** Wiley, *An Autobiography*, p. 325.

285 **In a scathing book:** Arthur Kallet and F. J. Schlink, *100,000,000 Guinea Pigs* (New York: Grosset and Dunlap, 1933), p. 196.

285 **Consumer advocates renewed:** Barbara J. Martin MD, *Elixir: The American Tragedy of a Deadly Drug* (Lancaster, PA: Barkberry Press, 2014).

285 **Food, Drug, and Cosmetic Act of 1938:** The full text of the act can be found at www.fda.gov/regu latoryinformation/lawsenforcedbyfda/federalfooddrugandcosmeticactfdcact/default.htm.

286 **"I believe," he said:** Harvey Wiley, "Food Adulteration and Its Effects" (lecture before the sanitary science class at Cornell University, 1905), Wiley Papers, box 198.

### Epilogue

287 **A 1956 decision by:** Deborah Blum, "A Colorful Little Tale of Halloween Poison," *Speakeasy Science* (blog), PLoS, October 31, 2011, http://blogs.plos.org/speakeasyscience/2011/10/31/ a-colorful-little-tale-of-halloween-poison/.

287 **A 1976 law authorizing:** Gina Kolata, "The Sad Legacy of the Dalkon Shield," *New York Times Sunday Magazine*, December 6, 1987, www.nytimes.com/1987/12/06/magazine/the-sad-legacy-of-the-dalkon-shield.html.

288 **More recently, the Food Safety:** The full text of the act and additional information on it can be found at www.fda.gov/food/guidanceregulation/fsma/.

288 **The cause was a line of peanut butters:** A history of the issue can be traced through multiple articles at *Food Safety News*: www.foodsafetynews.com/tag/peanut-corporation-of-america/# .WcfMUZOGM0Q.

288 **as sterile as hospitals:** Donita Taylor, "R.I. Farmers Push Back on New Federal Food Safety Rules," *Providence Journal*, July 25, 2017, www.providencejournal.com/news/20170625/ri-farmers-push-back-on-new-federal-food-safety-rules.

289 **During his successful:** Scott Cohn, "Food Safety Measures Face Cuts in Trump Budget," CNBC .com, July 1, 2017, www.cnbc.com/2017/06/30/american-greed-report-food-safety-measures-face-cuts-in-trump-budget.html.

289 **The Earthjustice Institute:** "Food Watchdog Groups Sue FDA over Menu Labeling Day," *Quality Assurance and Safety*, June 8, 2017, www.qualityassurancemag.com/article/food-watchdog-groups-sue-fda-over-menu-labeling-delay/.

290 **In her influential 1962 book:** Rachel Carson, *Silent Spring* (Boston: Houghton Mifflin, 1962).

290 **"The number of environmental":** Coral Davenport, "Counseled by Industry, Not Staff, EPA Administrator Is Off to a Blazing Start," *New York Times*, July 1, 2017, p. 1, www.nytimes.com/ 2017/07/01/us/politics/trump-epa-chief-pruitt-regulations-climate-change.html.

# Photo credits